W9-BSC-570

Foreign and Female

IMMIGRANT WOMEN IN AMERICA, 1840–1930

REVISED AND EXPANDED EDITION

Doris Weatherford

Facts On File, Inc.

AN INFOBASE HOLDINGS COMPANY

Foreign and Female: Immigrant Women in America, 1840–1930, Revised and Expanded Edition

Copyright © 1995 by Doris Weatherford

All rights reserved. No part of this book may be reproduced or utilized in any form or by any means, electronic or mechanical, including photocopying, recording, or by any information storage or retrieval systems, without permission in writing from the publisher. For information contact:

Facts On File, Inc.
11 Penn Plaza
New York, NY 10001

Library of Congress Cataloging-in-Publication Data

Weatherford, Doris.
   Foreign and female : immigrant women in America / Doris Weatherford.
      p. cm.
   Includes bibliographical references and index.
   ISBN 0-8160-3100-2 (hardcover)
   ISBN 0-8160-3446-X (paperback)
   1. Women immigrants—United States—Social conditions.   2. Women immigrants—United States—History—19th century. 3. Women immigrants—United States—History—20th century.   I. Title.
   HQ1410.W43   1995
   305.48′8—dc20   95-6685

Facts On File books are available at special discounts when purchased in bulk quantities for businesses, associations, institutions or sales promotions. Please call our Special Sales Department in New York at 212/967-8800 or 800/322-8755.

Text and jacket design by Catherine Rincon Hyman

VB FOF 10 9 8 7 6 5 4 3 2 1

This book is printed on acid-free paper.

Printed in the United States of America

To my darling daughter

Margaret Marie Weatherford

who grew up with this book.

It was conceived when she was,
and she slept on my lap as the first chapters were written
and gave me roses when it was finally published
while she was in junior high school.

And now, as it is reissued, she will graduate from Harvard.

With pride and joy, this book is dedicated to Meg.

CONTENTS

WHO, WHERE, AND WHEN:

AN INTRODUCTORY OVERVIEW

Ports of Entry, Paths of Settlement

Early in 1994, southeastern Ireland's town of Cobn opened a museum commemorating its "Harbor of Tears." The most prominent sculpture was a life-sized portrayal of Annie Moore, a teenager who sailed away from Queenstown—as Cobn was called from 1849 to 1922—on the SS *Nevada* late in December 1891. The ship, "gayly decorated with bunting" in New York's harbor, disembarked its 148 passengers on New Year's Day, 1892, and Annie Moore "tripped across" the gangplank to be honored with a $10 gold piece as the first of what would eventually be over 17 million immigrants processed through Ellis Island.[1]

Annie Moore was fifteen years old—and she brought two younger brothers to America. They came to join their parents, who had settled in New York while their teenage daughter supervised her brothers in Ireland. On the train side of the new facilities of Ellis Island, the first railroad ticket "was purchased by Ellen King, on her way from Waterford, Ireland, to a small town in Minnesota."[2] Despite stereotypes to the contrary, Annie Moore and Ellen King were not unusual.

Women were a majority of those escaping impoverished Ireland at the turn of the century: between 1899 and 1910, 52% of Irish emigrants were female. About 89% of them "were single at the time of their departure, and most were under the age of twenty-four." Indeed, the rarity became a women who emigrated *with* a husband: during 1901–8, for example, of the females between fifteen and thirty-five who left Connaught, an astonishing 98% were single.[3]

Large numbers of women of other ethnicities also emigrated, often traveling alone. Even married women frequently made the move without their husbands; because men commonly preceded women to America, it was the women who closed up the family property in Europe and shepherded the children halfway around the world. By 1910, women accounted for more than four of every ten Jewish immigrants, while Scandinavian and British women came to America at nearly similar rates.[4] In some years at the end of the nineteenth century, women were an absolute majority of those leaving Swedish ports, and "as early as 1886, women constituted a majority among the emigrants from towns."[5]

Another noteworthy exception to the rule of male leadership in immigration occurred in the 1870s, when skilled female cigar makers emigrated from Bohemia, leaving their husbands and children behind. After these women had earned enough money to bring their families, they taught the men—formerly farmers—the less skilled portion of cigar work, while they continued to be the chief source of family income. Similar occasional cases occur with all ethnicities: even among the culturally conservative Mediterranean groups, there were Greek and Italian women who emigrated and put their skills to work—especially in textile mills, garment manufacturing, or domestic service—and then brought their loved ones.

Like Annie Moore, most entered via New York. Long before Ellis Island, the docks of the city received most of America's newcomers; over the years, approximately 70% of all immigrants arrived in its harbor. The state of New York formalized the process of entry in 1855 through Castle Garden, a former opera house near the Battery, and through a subsidiary in Wards Island in the East River. Almost eight million used these facilities before they were declared inadequate, and the federal government assumed responsibility for immigration with the opening of Ellis Island.

But there were other ports of entry, too, especially in the early era before the nation created admission standards. New Orleans was the second most popular port in the pre–Civil War era because, before extensive railroads, the mighty Mississippi was the best highway to the interior. "Over 350,000 immigrants jammed the docks" of New Orleans in the decade between 1847 and 1857. Many of the 19,752 Germans[*] living in the city when the 1850 census was taken were professionals; they built Protestant, Catholic, and Jewish congregations, as well as secular societies. Though New Orleans—ever the party town—already had a St. Patrick's Day celebration in 1809, the Irish were few until the potato famine of the late 1840s; they grew to 24,398 by 1860. Despite New Orleans's Catholicism, the Irish—too poor to move on—were not welcome, and the city saw appreciable xenophobic violence.[6]

Most of the Germans who landed at New Orleans, however, headed up the river. Many stopped permanently at St. Louis, which had an emigrant aid society as early as 1818. There they founded significant Lutheran and Catholic institutions, but St. Louis was like New Orleans in that it also functioned as a distribution center. Travelers in the late 1830s spoke of "a veritable German highway" out of St. Louis.[7] Some of these early settlers were part of planned colonies to which congregations and villages

---

[*] Since Germany did not exist as a unified state until 1871, they were identified by their language rather than by any political entity. Americans used various names for them, especially "Dutch." This confusion goes a long way to explain why these immigrants, in fact, developed a cultural identity as Germans before Germans in Germany did.

sent emigrants together to the New World. Jette Bruns, who will weave in and out of this book, was part of such a community. Her Missouri town of Westphalia had more than 600 Catholic Saxon families by 1840, when the land was still a wilderness with wild bears.[8]

Just as St. Louis was the spiritual home of many Catholic and Lutheran Germans, so was Boston institutionalized in the 1840s as the perennial Irish town. Boston was the closest American city to Europe, and "from 1847 to 1854, no fewer than twenty thousand immigrants arrived annually," most of them Irish. Because the city was chosen as the terminus for the first transatlantic steamship line and because its "rates were subsidized by the British government, even the poor could cross."[9] Another Irish migration pattern was to sail to New Brunswick or Nova Scotia, which are even closer to Ireland, and then go south—often on foot—to Boston. Few Irish had the capital to go into American-style farming in the way that Germans and Scandinavians did; instead they built an urban haven that attracted the Irish—especially self-supporting women—for eight decades. Toward the end of the nineteenth century, Italians and Jews joined the Irish in Boston, and the area's textile mills also became the destination of relatively large numbers of Portuguese, Greeks, Syrians, and Armenians.

New York, New Orleans, and Boston all made more sense as a port of entry than Philadelphia did: its "harbor" is up the Delaware River, which freezes, and it is farther from Europe than either Boston or New York—and yet, over "1.3 million immigrants entered America through Philadelphia" before immigration restrictions took effect in the 1920s. The city was the nation's second largest through most of the nineteenth century, and more than one in every four of its residents in the 1870s had been born abroad. As usual, many of these urbanites were working women: one 1875 occupational census of the foreign born, for example, showed 1,650 male "laborers," compared with 851 female domestic servants. Like the pattern elsewhere, these British, German, and Scandinavian immigrants were joined in the 1880s by Jews escaping Russia's pogroms and by others from eastern and southern Europe; in 1914, for instance, as many as 19,000 Italians arrived directly in Philadelphia.[10] Moreover, just as Boston was the receiving station for immigrants drifting down from Canada, so did Philadelphia and its New Jersey environs receive those who went south from New York.

Finally, some arrived still south of Philadelphia: by the Civil War, 25% of Baltimore's population was foreign born. It was about one-third Irish and two-thirds German, with the majority of Germans being Catholics, but there also were Lutherans and some 7,000 German Jews. These immigrants landed at Locust Point, which remains a "gritty," solidly German waterfront area today: "Until recently, residents say, it was almost unheard of for houses to be advertised for sale. When the old generation died, the houses were quickly purchased by younger members of the same family." One descendant of these Germans, Mary Koch, demonstrated their working-class attitudes when she said in 1989, "We've always had heavy industry and welcomed it. To us, it meant good jobs."[11]

The majority of those who landed at these ports, however, moved on to the interior, where women as well as men provided labor in such industrial centers as

Pittsburgh, Cleveland, and Chicago. Even in metropolitan areas that avoided the smokestack image of these great cities, there were nevertheless large numbers of immigrants in small factory towns. The 1900 census, for instance, showed that Connecticut had 908,420 residents, of whom 238,210 were born abroad. New Jersey had 1,883,669, with 431,884 foreign born; some towns were solidly immigrant, such as Passaic, with 48% born abroad. With their American-born children, foreign-language speakers constituted a huge proportion of the state's population.[12]

Similar concentrations occurred in the Midwest. Whether they came up the Mississippi or overland by wagon and canal boat and train, immigrants spread out from Cincinnati and St. Louis to Milwaukee and Minneapolis—and to tens of thousands of farming towns that became the heart of the immigrant Midwest. The greatest numbers came from the various German states; in modern Nebraska, for instance, nearly one in every two persons is of German ancestry.[13] They generally came as families, with about 40% of German immigrants being female.[14] Along with large numbers of Scandinavian women and the occasional Hollander, Finn, Ukrainian, Bohemian, or Belgian, they populated America's breadbasket from the plains of Kansas to the woods of northern Michigan. These were the women and men who found their way into American literature through *My Àntonia* and *Giants in the Earth*.

While most ended up either in the great metropolitan areas of the industrial Northeast or on the farms of the upper Midwest, there were in fact immigrant communities all over the nation. Those isolated from the mainstream were often the result of specific colonization schemes: the leadership of Lutherans, Catholics, Mennonites, and other sects set up many plans to transplant their faithful far from both European heresies and the temptations of American cities. Religion, too, was the motivation of those who traveled in companies bound for the Mormon theocracy in Utah; often these were not families, however, but single young women recruited by missionaries, especially from Britain, Denmark, and Switzerland.

Agents of American industry also provided motivation for migration. Women were the target of New England textile mill recruiters who searched for skilled weavers, especially in Scotland and England. Other women ended up at remote locations in America when recruiting agents arranged the transportation of families to coal and copper mines in such places as Colorado and Arizona. Though the slave-and-sharecropper economy of the South meant that it was seldom an immigrant destination, Tampa's population doubled in five years at the end of the century when immigrants—many of them female—were recruited for newly-built cigar factories.

Texas was another southern exception, with a number of centers for European immigrants. Elise Waerenskjold left dozens of letters telling of her Norwegian community there, and it was the object of early planned emigration for Germans. Some 400 came to Austin County in 1844, and the following year, "3084 immigrants arrived at Galveston in 21 ships." By the end of the 1840s, there were probably 17,000 Germans living in south central Texas.[15] Other ethnicities found their way there, too, and in 1970, there were more Czech-Americans in Texas than in any other state.[16]

Isolated colonies of foreigners carved out similar niches for themselves all over the country. Both Finns in New Hampshire and Czechs (called Bohemians) in Virginia specialized in rebuilding farms abandoned by Americans who had moved farther west. Hungarians raised onions in New Jersey, and German-Russians from Ukraine grew peppermint in Michigan. While the mass of Polish immigration centered itself in Chicago, Detroit, and Pittsburgh, there were isolated Polish colonies who worked the cranberry bogs of Wisconsin and shucked oysters in Baltimore. All over America, there were such anomalous groups, outsiders to everyone nearby.

Arkansas may serve as a detailed example of how widespread immigrants were. German Lutherans settled towns such as Lutherville and Augsburg in the Ozark foothills, while on the other bank of the Arkansas River, German and Swiss Catholics built the wine-producing town of Altus. Tontitown was born in 1898 with a band of Italians: Some 500 families had been brought over from Romagna, via New Orleans, to work as sharecroppers near the Mississippi River, but when their patron died and a fatal epidemic broke out, they wrote home for help. A priest arranged their move to the Ozarks, where they specialized in grape growing and wine making.

Finally, the Ouachita Mountains, in the southwestern part of the state, feature towns named Vandervoort, Mena, and Dierks, and even in the unlikely delta of South Arkansas—where the topography supported a plantation economy—there is Stuttgart, where Germans began building large farms in 1878 and where their descendants support several Lutheran churches through rice farming today. The state's northeastern quadrant includes the towns of Denmark, Auvergne, Tyronza, and Sitka. Thus, even in a place that was far from a common immigrant destination, there are a number of communities that reflect a substantial foreign heritage more than a century later.

Causes and Effects

From the American Revolution until the 1840s, only about 850,000 immigrants are estimated to have come to America—but almost 1.4 million arrived in the tumultuous decade of the 1840s alone.[17] The immigrant era is usually defined as beginning then, when a European potato blight resulted in famine. That starvation stalked Ireland is clear in the numbers. Its population in 1845 is estimated to have been 8.5 million—and six years later, in 1851, it was 6.5 million. A million or more people may have died of hunger and resulting disease, while another million streamed out of the country. Some of those who managed to leave were in such weakened condition that in 1847 alone, perhaps 17,000 died on the journey and another 20,000 soon after arrival. Most deaths were in Canada—the closest point to Ireland—with one 200-bed quarantine station near Quebec City seeing 3,228 deaths in the summer and fall of that year.[18]

The famine devastated Ireland, but other areas were also affected. By 1847, food prices in some German provinces had risen by as much as 450%, and "hunger riots were widespread."[19] Political revolution throughout the area in 1848 added to the flight. These Germans, joined by British and Scandinavian emigrants, dominated the

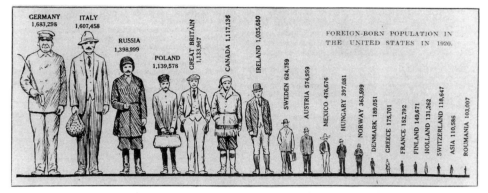

This chart indicates the relative size of foreign-born groups as the immigrant era drew to an end.

The various provinces of Germany sent the largest numbers of people from the 1840s on. In contrast, the second-largest group, Italians, came almost entirely at the turn of the century. The third group, from Russia, was actually mostly Jewish by ethnicity, not Russian.

Note also that the stereotypically dressed figures are exclusively male. A truly representative chart would have about four of every ten figures dressed as women. The Irish figure certainly should be female, for the majority of immigrants from Ireland in this era were women. (LIBRARY OF CONGRESS, CITING THE *LITERARY DIGEST* OF MAY 7, 1921)

migration before and immediately after America's Civil War. Nearly 2.6 million Europeans came in the decade just before the war; the stream swelled again when the guns quieted, so that the decade of the 1860s ended with a total of just over 2 million immigrants. The 1870s saw the flow return to nearly as high as it was in the 1850s, and it more than doubled in the 1880s, with over 4.7 million arrivals.

Steamships had replaced sailing ships, making the trip easier and cheaper, and agents for railroad and ship lines roamed Europe, spreading the good news about America and easing the traveler's way. For the first time, more than a million immigrants in the 1880s were from central—as opposed to northern—Europe, and the numbers of eastern and southern Europeans would continue to rise throughout the rest of the era. Irish Annie Moore was thus something of a poor choice for the Ellis Island image, for it was the "new immigration" of Italians, Jews, and various Slavic peoples that better fit the more bureaucratically complex process that Ellis Island entailed. Indeed, it would be the very "foreignness" of these newcomers—and their huge numbers—that brought about legislation in the 1920s strictly limiting immigration.

A serious depression in 1893 caused a drop in that decade to 3.6 million, but the following decade saw the peak of immigration: over 8 million arrived between 1901 and 1910. The outbreak of World War I almost halved the numbers to 4.4 million. When the war ended, however, there were still so many eager to come that Congress began to enact quotas. In 1921–30, the newcomers numbered less than half of those in the preceding decade, thus ending what is called the immigrant era. During the 1930s, there was virtually no immigration, and the numbers dropped back to less than they had been a century earlier in the 1830s. The Great Depression added to the effect of the quota laws, and there were actually more people who left America that decade than entered. Toward the end of the thirties, as fascism rose in Europe, immigration again increased, but American isolationism was such that many refugees were refused entry. There were slight increases in the forties and fifties as war brides and a small portion of the millions of displaced persons from wartime Europe were allowed in, but these were almost entirely professionals—not the "huddled masses" of earlier immigration. New legislation in the 1960s defined even further the priority for immigrants with assets clearly beneficial to the nation.

But the poor people of the earlier immigration formed the backbone of farms and factories. They transformed America—and even Europe, through their absence. In making the translatlantic move, they not only brought the great benefit of their prodigious labor to the pioneering nation, but they also did something less often recognized: they relieved Europe of the surplus population that created poverty and famine. Except for extreme conditions caused by war, Dickensian scenes of poverty have largely disappeared from twentieth-century western Europe. Indeed, the sad irony is that America at the end of the millennium features more of the great inequalities of wealth that immigrants sought to escape than does their Old World now.

Norway is an excellent example. No other country except Ireland sent as large a portion of its people—almost 100% of its 1820 population would depart for America during the next century. And yet, when the Immigration Quota Act of 1924 went into effect, many non-Europeans found their national quotas filled soon after midnight on the first of each month—but Norway would never fill a quota during the forty-one-year life of that legislation.[20] It simply had become a much more desirable place to live than it had been, for Scandinavia's days of "rotten potatoes served out in small amounts" were over.[21] While much of the improvement there and elsewhere in Europe is due to the policies of democratic socialist governments that replaced nineteenth-century monarchs, their task was made more manageable by the simple fact that some 35 million poor peasants and indigent industrial laborers were no longer there. About one-third of these were women, who left home to bear the next generation in America.

A Personal Note

The impetus for this book came in the summer of 1969, when I took a graduate course in immigration at Harvard. One day the professor made the statement that men adjusted faster to America, that women were more apt to get homesick, remain unassimilated, and want to return. Young, unsophisticated, and impolitic as I was, I challenged him: What about women like my Norwegian and German grandmothers, who got jobs in American homes? Wouldn't they learn from the inside what Americans ate and wore and how they lived? Wouldn't they learn the new language and customs faster than, say, Slavs working in the steel mills with other Slavs or Irishmen building railroads with other Irishmen?

He looked at me (or at least, I felt as though he looked at me) as though he thought I was crazy. After class, I went over to Widener Library to check out a book on immigrant women but could not find what I had in mind. Except for the Library of Congress, Harvard's is the biggest library in the world, and it had numerous books on some aspects of immigrant women in some places or times, but there was no inclusive, general book that simply spelled out the story of immigrant women. When the first edition of this book was finally published, I wrote: "On the shelves of almost any library are several volumes on the Italians in America, the Germans in America, and so on. One can read hundreds of pages in these books to glean a handful of references to women; if one did not know that it was biologically impossible, one could be led to believe that men populated the country by themselves. Similarly, standard works on the history of women make only slight reference to immigrants. This book attempts to partially fill that lack."

The growth of feminism, of course, has resulted in much more attention to these and other women as important topics for historical research. The revised edition of this book, however, has the same aim as the first: to reach a general audience and to provide the average reader with some details of the transatlantic transition of the women of her family. Although it is addressed to lay readers, scholars too can find new information here, some of it from previously unpublished archival sources. Again, I am aware that any chapter easily could be expanded into a volume. And once again, there are chapters on other topics—among them, education, politics, and language—that were excluded for lack of space. My goal once more is to provide a glimpse into the lives of these women and to encourage the asking of new questions.

This book thus concerns those women who came to America during the traditional immigrant era of 1840–1930—the women who were the grandmothers and great-grandmothers of most of today's adults. Only European women are covered, since those from Asia, Latin America, and Africa have backgrounds and problems that are vastly different. Finally, this study is of ordinary women, excluding the famous and those whose lives were too far from the mainstream. They are truly our mothers' mothers.

Too often their lives have been quickly glossed over in flowery praise; too seldom has there been serious acknowledgment of their frequently hard fate. For many, biology was destiny, and nothing defined their lives as much as the babies they bore. At the same time, millions were also wage earners and often even the chief source of family income—long before "the era of the working woman." They contributed vastly to a national economy that largely ignored their existence.

Though often illiterate and superstitious, they nevertheless dealt with the business and legal complexities of moving half a world away. They endured the emotional pain of separating from their mothers, sisters, and other loved ones whom they could never expect to see again on this earth, and then they suffered the ingratitude and scorn of Americanized children ashamed of their mothers' Old World ways. The honest details of their lives have been too long neglected. They deserve to be remembered.

PART I

THE BODY
AND THE
SOUL

1

FATALISTIC CONCEPTIONS

Fertile Foreigners: Birthrates

An annual pregnancy was a fact of life for a great many immigrant women. More than any other factor, this situation determined a woman's life, defined its value, and proscribed its horizons.

The word that most fittingly describes the immigrant woman's attitude toward her body, her life, and her world was fatalism. It was a European attitude, developed from long centuries of a class structure that wiped out the peasant who showed any signs of assertion. It was a woman's attitude, formed by eons of submission to the men who controlled her life—and her body.

Among peasants who had close ties to the world of agriculture, the springtime births of lambs and calves set a precedent for human beings. In many European cultures, fear of the supernatural was strong, and among those fears was a belief that infertility in women could signal infertility in plants and animals. The Irish were not alone in believing that "an annual birth was the expected contribution of a wife to general well being."[1]

The direct result was a fecundity among immigrant women far greater than that of the average American woman. A New York social worker in the early twentieth century recorded that among her cases were "one with 14 living children, the product of 29 pregnancies, and another with 17 remaining from 26 live births. The mother of

15 children in a third family is humorously labeled by her . . . neighbors, Mrs. Birth Control Rocca."[2]

Although these numbers are exceptions, large families were certainly the rule. While American women were generally ignorant of contraception, too, the following figures reveal the more numerous pregnancies of immigrant women:[3]

NUMBER OF CHILDREN PER 1,000 BIRTHS WHO ARE THE TENTH CHILD IN THEIR FAMILY, BY NATIONAL ORIGIN OF THE MOTHER, 1920

German	30	Scandinavian	16
Italian	27	British	12
Polish	22	Irish	11
Austrian	21	Russian	11
Hungarian	21	U.S.	10*

*The relatively low birthrate of the Irish, who were virtually all Catholic, is explained by the fact that they married less often and later. Note also that women from Russia are highly likely to be Jewish.

In other words, the child of a German immigrant was three times more likely than an American baby to be the tenth in his family.[4] Given that Germans, back in the 1840s, were the first large group of non-English speakers to leave Europe, these figures from 1920—after almost a century of immigration—are very striking.

A half century earlier, the 1870 Baltimore census showed that women from Saxony were particularly likely to have a string of children listed under their name; almost every page of the census for the immigrant 9th Ward included such cases.[5] The same was true in New York's Kleindeutschland, or "Little Germany," where "in each census after 1850, the average number of children . . . was greater than the United States average, and considerably greater than the average for families in the Northeast."[6]

At the very beginning of the immigrant era—and long before Germany existed as a nation—Jette Bruns personified these German immigrant mothers. When, after months of travel, she arrived in the Missouri wilderness in November 1836, Jette had an infant and was in the advanced stages of pregnancy—though, like many other letter writers and diary keepers, she made no allusion to pregnancy until the baby arrived. A chronology of her reproductive life—pieced together by the birth dates of her children and ignoring the miscarriages that in all probability took place—looks like this:

Hermann, born October 1833, when she was age nineteen
Max, born February 1837
Johanna, born March 1839
Rudolph, born February 1841
Heinrich, born September 1842
Euphemia (Effie), born May 1844

Albert, born December 1845
Adolph, born August 1847
Ludwig (Louis), born July 1848
Ottilie (Tillie), born April 1852
Wilhelm, born November 1853, when she was forty

Jette Bruns bore eleven children over a twenty-year period, or more than a child every other year. In fact, the pregnancies came even closer than that average appears, because of the relatively long time between her first and second—during which her husband was in America, while she remained in Germany. For all of her young adult life, from eighteen through forty, Jette Bruns was either pregnant or lactating or

This 1905 mother of eight was not unusual in immigrant communities. Most women, however, made the transatlantic voyage when they were younger, and their families grew after arrival.

These "Russian Germans" from Ukraine were headed to the farms of North Dakota, where the boys' labor would be valuable—but the mother doubtless was glad that her oldest child was a girl, who surely performed the role that social workers called "little mother." Note also the destination tag pinned to the man. (NATIONAL PARK SERVICE, STATUE OF LIBERTY MONUMENT) both—and she was married to a well-educated physician, who had greater ability to control these births than others.[7]

Other foreigners were similarly fertile. Though Irish women married less often and later than other immigrant groups, when they did marry in this era, they had more children than either natives or other immigrants. In New York and Massachusetts—states that attracted a large number of immigrants, especially the Irish—foreign-born women in 1895 had birthrates of 43 and 52 per 1,000 population, while the native rate for both states was a mere 17.[8]

By the early twentieth century, German and Irish women had reached the respectable status of "old immigrants." Instead, it was the women of the "new immigration" from southern and eastern Europe that shocked Americans with their fertility patterns. A study done in the era of peak immigration estimated these rates:[9]

COMPARATIVE BIRTH RATES OF WOMEN IN NEW YORK STATE, 1910–1915

Nationality of Mother	Births per 1,000
Italian	91.6
Austro-Hungarians, including Austrian Poles	89.6
Russian, including Russian Poland and Finland	88.6
Other Foreign Born	30.8
Native white	17.2

A nurse who worked on the Lower East Side confirmed the first-place birthrate of Italians, citing cases from her experience:

> One of my mothers has been the victim of fifteen pregnancies. She now has five living children . . . I have another broken-down little woman who married at sixteen—and when twenty-six years old had . . . twelve children. Of these only six lived . . . Another woman has five living children out of eleven pregnancies . . . Mary S . . . has been married five years; has four living children.[10]

The physically debilitating effect of repeated pregnancies was noted by public health authorities, but their interest often focused more on the quality of newborns produced by such worn-out women rather than on the women themselves. In a 1908 report, for example, an Italian-American physician spoke of women as merely parenthetical to their babies:

> The birth rate, which is very high among the Italians of the first generation . . . explain[s] their high infant morbidity and morality. The percentage of rickets* is

---

* A bone deformity disease that is caused by lack of calcium and vitamin D, which are obtained primarily through dairy products and sunshine. Its presence in infants was a clear indication of the malnourishment of mothers and their confinement to indoor work.

exceedingly high (75 to 80 percent) . . . The defective composition of the mother's milk [is] in my opinion, the principal factor of the prevalence of disease, which in turn . . . diminishes the stamina of the mothers.[11]

Social workers, journalists, and others echoed interminable cases of women whose lives were diminished by repeated childbirth—often using language that indicates nothing at all of the father's presence. The situation of a Polish woman in the immigrant town of Passaic, New Jersey, during a 1926 strike of its silk mills is wholly typical:

> Mrs. P . . . lives in a miserable tenement on 2nd street [and] has seven children. She lives in three dark rooms, two of which are windowless . . . The oldest child is fifteen and expects to go to work soon; the youngest is two months old. Mrs. P, although twenty years in this country, speaks little English. All these years she has worked in the mills, slaving in them as her babies came, and as soon after they were born as possible. Her rooms are squalid and cluttered, unlike most Polish homes, which are usually spotless. But Mrs. P. is too wearied and ill to clean house. All in a heap she sat, one baby on her knees, and two others clinging to her skirts. One white faced girl of nine, her eyes red from malnutrition, interpreted for her mother. With an apathy like hers, the child repeated the story of low wages, insufficient food, an increasing family, and the necessity of the mother's working at night. Nothing perhaps is more tragic than . . . these long starved children. Even the babies of two and three reflect the dreariness and misery that has surrounded them ever since they came so unwelcomed into the world.[12]

The harsh immigrant economy demanded that some poor children were put to work at an unconscionably early age. One Italian mother with four preschoolers harshly summarized their plight, "We must all work if we want to earn anything."[13] Like others of her ethnicity and poverty, she expected these toddlers to assist in the home manufacture of artificial flowers. Another with four children complained of her small labor pool: "Making flowers at home is poor work, especially if you have only a few children to help you."[14]

A large family was a liability in urban areas, not an asset, but it took a while for former peasants to absorb that economic lesson. Instead, this era of simpler commerce and agricultural predominance saw child labor as essential in both factory and field. This was especially true on farms, and farm women continued to have large families after their immigrant sisters in the cities began to limit their pregnancies.

Gro Svendsen, an educated Norwegian on the Iowa frontier at midcentury, for example, had no complaints in her lengthy, intimate letters about bearing five sons in seven years. However, on the sixth pregnancy she wrote, "It took quite a while to get my strength back." The seventh child proved to be the long-awaited girl, but "she is still very small, because she has frequently been ill." More pregnancies brought more sickness, and by the ninth one, she was fearful enough to need the comfort of sharing her dread: "Next month, if God wills it, I shall have another child . . . It is difficult these last days because I am always quite weak, but God, who has always been my help and comforter during my confinements, will surely help me this time, too . . . If I live and recover, I shall indeed write."[15] She lived, but she never really recovered. The tenth pregnancy was the last, taking the life of this exceptional woman. Her first child was born in 1864, and she died in 1878 at age thirty-seven. Gro Svendsen had borne ten children in fourteen years.

Her husband mourned her sincerely—he was well aware of what a fine woman she was, and they loved each other deeply—and his grief must have been increased by the knowledge that his loving her had, in a sense, killed her. The Svendsens may well have practiced birth control if they had that option; Gro wrote, for example, "When I think of our sacred duties as parents and the heavy responsibilities laid on us, I often become sad and discouraged, for I am not able to do what I would."[16]

But they lived among farmers who saw more children as an axiomatic good, much like having more cows or pigs. Children could pick corn and feed chickens and perform any number of income-producing tasks, and thus the daughters of rural immigrants continued to have large numbers of children. Polish women—who were largely urban dwellers—had 23% fewer children in the second generation, but Norwegians—who were more likely to farm—dropped their birthrate only 5%.[17]

City social workers also noted that daughters of immigrants had fewer children than their mothers. One who was familiar with Italian families in New York explained:

> Children do not appear so frequently in Italian families as they did abroad or among first generation immigrants. The number of offspring now varies from 1 to 4 or 6 . . . Women of the first generation, however, become pregnant every year or so. They are frequently able to limit their brood to 11 or 12 only through abortions . . .
>
> Many young couples make a real effort to restrict the size of their families. They ordinarily use the simplest and cheapest method known, called "sleeping the American way." This always means separate beds, or more often the separate rooms, for the father and mother, with the additional safeguard of having the girls in the mother's bed and the boys in the father's.[18]

Ambivalence and Attempts to Limit Pregnancy

The feelings of women on the subject of children form a pattern of ambivalence, but many of these pregnancies were far from wanted. Newspapers in Lawrence, Massachusetts—a city of immigrants—at midcentury had repeated reports of infanticide and abortion. Babies were found thrown in the river; a case in 1866 of the discovery of one such child's maggot-covered body was termed "not unusual."[19]

Even among the more comfortable middle-class Germans living in New York's Kleindeutschland in the same era, "infanticide was not unknown."[20] One such case was that of "Frau Weidenmeyer of 74 Mulberry Street. After being widowed early in pregnancy, she was arrested early in 1848 for strangling her newborn baby and claiming that it had been stillborn."[21] A modern scholar, commenting on Irish life in the late nineteenth century, said that "although abortion was rare, infanticide and the abandonment of illegitimate children were more common."[22]

Most women, of course, did not kill or neglect their children, but nevertheless the annual additions were less than welcome. "All the mothers," a social worker said succinctly of her 1905 clients, "complain that they have to bear too many children."[23] Similarly, when a nurse visiting a maternity ward used by New York City Italians asked a "very white and tired" woman "if she would like to go to the country for a rest and convalescent care, her answer was, 'I don't want the country . . . I want rest from having babies.'"[24] Little could be done about that fact of life, however, and most immigrant women lived and died without fundamental knowledge of their anatomy, let alone an understanding of how to control their reproduction.

A half century after Gro Svendsen died—presumably because she was unable to stop the pregnancies that she feared—a considerably more urbane setting brought no change in knowledge of birth control. Elizabeth Stern was a Jewish college graduate who grew up in America, yet she seemed to think that all that was necessary to prevent pregnancy was to wish it so. Later, as an older and wiser woman, she wrote:

> At that time birth control was a word not spoken. There was a sin called preventing the conception of children, but Margaret Sanger had not yet appeared. Girls became pregnant and had abortions. But married women had as many children as fate chose. If they were much advanced they might live only at certain times with their husbands, and have protection against pregnancy so. That was mentioned, in an awed whisper, by prurient minded, but kindly, married women to young brides. One spoke of it to me, and made me feel as if she had torn the door open on our love by even mentioning my husband and me in this way.[25]

No one "spoke of it" to most women, however, but the possibility of preventing pregnancy seemed reasonable to thoughtful observers. As a woman of German origin who also grew up in America said, it was strange that "rich folks has so few and us poor ones so many." The only solution that she could see was celibacy, and her conclusion was that "it is much better not to marry and to have so many children."[26] Like her, the Italian Lola Anguini believed family limitation ought to be possible, but she searched in vain for an answer to the mystery:

> There was always the fear of pregnancy that I had to live with . . . If you asked a priest for advice, he told you any contraception was a sin, babies were a gift of God. If you could summon the courage to ask a doctor, he would either avoid the question or tell you there was nothing to do but avoid intercourse. Trying to avoid relations with flimsy excuses would create arguments . . . But there again, all of the women had this problem, and no one would ever talk about it.[27]

There were important variations between ethnic groups on sexual mores, but information on the scientific area of birth control was lacking for almost all. Again, some exceptionally thoughtful women read between the lines of newspaper ads that offered relief for "female complaints," but as the medical profession became better organized and more influential with legislatures, such information (always of questionable value) became even more unavailable. Postal authorities beefed up their censorship in the early part of the century, and even foreign-language newspapers had to cut anything related to contraception.

When, for example, a paper of the more sexually liberated Poles ran a 1911 ad for a book on what "girls and married women should know," the Chicago Vice Commission declared it "indecent and vulgar language. Among other things the advertiser describes a rubber instrument which is to be used to prevent contraception. The translation . . . is full of vile and abhorrent information. It cannot be printed."[28]

But it was not only lack of information that contributed to large foreign families—it was also a matter of values. It had more to do with the lower status of foreign women and the dominance of males who believed that children were proof of virility as well as potential earners. As length of residence in the United States increased and those values changed, family size decreased, but men of the first generation were apt to have strong feelings on the subject.

An Italian fisherman, speaking of a couple who had been married ten years and had two children, commented tersely, "That man should feel shame to himself." A common view was stated by a mother of twelve when she said, "If you do anything to stop it, the man he get ill. He get the bad blood. God, he means it to be this way. The woman must do it to keep the peace."[29] Another quickly summarized the impossibility of celibacy: "I get pregnant every two or three months, and in a few weeks miscarry . . . It is killing me—soon I'll be gone and then who will see to my little children . . . It is one thing for certain my husband won't give up his right as a husband for I've plead[ed] for it."[30]

Many immigrants saw continence as bad for women as well as men. The belief was common that if a woman of child-bearing age did not become pregnant regularly, she would develop tumors. Continence also was thought to cause mental illness. Nervousness in adolescent girls was seen as the result of chastity, and the prescription was prompt marriage. The advocates of puritanical self-restraint were almost always natives; immigrants generally took a more earthy approach that saw sex—and the babies inherent to that—as natural and essential.

If celibacy was unacceptable, another method of birth control was a lengthy lactating period. Though they nursed their children for other good reasons, many immigrant women apparently understood that it afforded at least some protection against pregnancy. One woman of German background gave as her reason for nursing a long time "so as to keep them from coming so fast."[31] A public health worker among Italians on the Lower East Side also testified that—despite "the great number of children who are afflicted" with evidence of lack of "proper bone-making materials"—mothers continued breast-feeding for a year or two or even more because "the women hope in this way to escape pregnancy."[32]

If attempts at celibacy, prolonged lactation, or coitus interruptus failed, another method of birth control was abortion. At least until the public mind-set began to change late in the immigrant era, many immigrant women seemed to see little difference between contraception and abortion. In their view, what was important was the philosophical decision to overcome the fatalism to which they had been trained and make the conscious choice to control their bodies. To many, the distinction between preventing pregnancy or "bringing on a late period" (and thus ending pregnancy) was a too-fine line. The difference between the two techniques did not matter nearly as much as finding the assertiveness to interfere at all with what was seen as "God's will" for women.

Americans of that era, too, saw contraception and abortion as much more analogous than is the case today. By the World War I era, for example, at least some therapeutic abortions were routinely performed in urban centers—while advice on birth control was still withheld:

> In cases of tuberculosis the danger of pregnancy is recognized as especially grave. Yet several clinics for tubercular women in New York City replied, on inquiry, that they were not giving their patients any information as to how to prevent conception. After a woman has become pregnant, however, the clinic physician may send her to the hospital, where she is operated upon—to save her life. This is a stupid way of begging the question—a barbarous way.[33]

For most immigrant women, the idea of a hospital-sanctioned therapeutic abortion was a total impossibility. Instead, they ended their own pregnancies. "Abortions are common," said a 1914 writer of the working mothers she studied, "and unsuccessful attempts are even commoner . . . A practice which the women know to be so common they can scarcely regard as immoral, and in any case, they feel it is justified by their necessities."[34]

A nurse among Italians in the Lower East Side said that one of her patients had three abortions among her eleven pregnancies. The mother of five living children, she "barely escaped death after the last abortion. Another sad case (and it is only one of many) is that of a woman who lost her life from an abortion, leaving six little children . . . I could go on and on telling of various cases."[35] It is possible that in fact abortion was part of a commonly accepted, though undiscussed, European background. A rare survey on the subject, conducted around 1910 by a Berlin doctor, "illustrates the extent of abortion. Among one hundred women interviewed, twenty-four had aborted themselves at least once."[36]

Even at the end of the immigrant era, when all state legislatures had responded to organized medicine and outlawed abortion, a detailed analysis of maternity in New York concluded that although "there are no figures available on the extent of the practice of abortion," the investigating physician believed "it is extremely widespread, being practiced by practically everyone."[37] During World War I, another study "conservatively estimated that fully 250,000 abortions are performed in the United States each year, with a death rate of 50,000—one out of each five cases."[38]

Usually these furtive attempts to end pregnancy were conducted by the frantic woman alone, but midwives often also practiced as abortionists. A German midwife uncovered by the Chicago Vice Commission was perhaps typical; her rooms were described as dirty, but she showed concern for her patients in that she required a return visit and her fee was a moderate $10—unlike American abortionists whose fees were up to five times higher.[39]

Surgical abortions, whether done by professionals or by desperate amateurs, probably were less common than attempts to bring about a "miscarriage" by using drugs. Both English and foreign-language newspapers carried advertising for medications that the sponsors understood would be used in attempts to end unwanted pregnancies. A modern scholar of New York City Germans in the mid-nineteenth century, for example, says that "abortifacients were widely advertised in the German press under the guise of pills to 'regulate the monthly cycle.'"[40] Douches also were sold with couched language that could be interpreted as pregnancy-ending, while patent medicines aimed at women were so frequently sold in this way that some customers wrote complaining letters when the tonics they bought failed to bring the expected result.[41]

Whether or not they suffered any moral pangs, women seeking abortions almost certainly endured physical pain and risked death. The blundering way they attempted to end pregnancies is illustrated by a Syrian woman who said: "I was not happy about my last baby. My youngest daughter was 12 . . . and I did not want to start raising children all over again. I did not have an abortion, but I took pills hoping they would help me to lose my baby. Nothing happened and my last child was born when I was about 35."[42]

A Wisconsin woman was more successful in her similarly frenzied approach. The mother of three children in three years, she wrote that when she discovered she was pregnant again, she "was compelled to get rid of it by taking all kinds of medicine." This risk was preferable to what she saw as the larger risk of another pregnancy, for she concluded, "I am a very weak woman, and this is endangering my health."[43]

Only despair could drive a mother of little children to the point of recklessly "taking all kinds of medicine," and most yielded instead to the passivity of fatalistic acceptance. Though some practiced abortion and what they knew of birth control, most immigrant women apparently did not. They accepted their fate and agreed with the mother who stated simply, "It is God's will and not man's that the child comes to us."[44]

The Search for Information

Even for educated women, fatalism was dictated by religion. Linka Preus, the Norwegian wife of a Lutheran minister on the Wisconsin frontier in the 1850s, mused in her diary, "In a couple of months, I shall again become a mother. It is indeed, painful and hard, but God's will be done! Hexa [her sister], thy death was the result of bearing a child; Mother's death also; I cannot know what God may have ordained for me; but His will be done; may we all, as Death calls, be prepared."[45]

Plainly Linka's moral convictions did not allow her to avoid it, and she became pregnant again and again with increasingly deleterious effects to her health. Her diary shows a sad metamorphosis as a bright, cheerful young woman turned into a sick and fearful creature, her life shortened and pained by unwanted pregnancies.

Though women may have wished to control the situation, the only proven method of birth control—celibacy—was likely to lead to just the opposite of the desired result, for studies of desertion noted that a man was most apt to leave when his wife was pregnant. The way to keep your husband, then, was to avoid pregnancy, and the way to avoid pregnancy was to avoid your husband—which was also likely to drive him out.

Social workers whose ostensible aim was to build happy families sometimes had the knowledge that could have given couples a satisfactory sex life without impairing their health and financial resources. The diaphragm had been successfully developed in the Netherlands by the World War I era, but the few crusading Americans who tried to import these devices found themselves in serious legal trouble. The average social worker could not be expected to defy the law and the era's moral code and thus was unable to give the family the one tool that was most important for saving it.

Hundreds of poignant pleas for such information found their way to the Voluntary Parenthood League.* Probably most with "ethnic names" were second-generation women, for writing such a letter in English would have been an insurmountable task for most of their mothers—but both the names and locations of some letter writers clearly indicate that they were not far removed from an immigrant origin. Women with the Scandinavian and German names of Fjeld, Vik, Hunget, Schneider, and Busch managed to find the league's Long Island address, mustered up courage to write a stranger about intimate problems, and, from small post offices in farm and mining towns, mailed off these cries for help:

From Mayville, North Dakota:

My husband and I are happy and proud parents of a son . . . The advice [that I want] is that we want to bring our child up in right way and in order to do this, we

---

* Formed in 1918 by Mary Ware Dennett, the league was a successor to Margaret Sanger's National Birth Control League, which had begun in 1914. Dennett's leadership developed while Sanger was in Europe avoiding prosecution for violation of federal law that prohibited the distribution of "obscene" material through the mail—and anything related to contraception was deemed inherently obscene.

For more information on Dennett, Sanger, and birth control, see those entries and other cross-references in Doris Weatherford, *American Women's History: An A to Z of People, Organizations, Issues, and Events* (Prentice-Hall, 1994).

don't want to have another to come for about two or 3 years till I get real well and fit to bear another, also that we can afford.

I want to know if it could be done, how could it be done without causing abortion and illegal preventing conception which I am so against on account of ruining woman's health, also I am against having many children and not being brought up right, it is just as bad as abortion itself. I believe in less babies and better babies.[46]

From Indianola, Iowa:

I find your name in my book on "Sex Hygiene" and felt like you would be the one to help me, for no, my Dr. will not. I have six children all within nine years and now this last month I have failed to mensurate [sic] and of course I am worried. Is there some safe thing I could use to make me do so. and is the catheter tube a sure remedy and how do you use it?[47]

From Hibbing, Minnesota:

We have been married nine years now and have four children and I'm sure I'm two months on the way again . . . We just move from one place to another and all we have to live from is what Mr. can earn around on odd jobs. We haven't even a home of our own . . .

It [is] quite an ordeal for me each time of pregnancy because I have such a lot of trouble with my heart. I'll be thankful to you the rest of my life for telling me. It don't make any difference if we have to pay some to find out because things simple [sic] can't keep on this way much longer. My life might go like a wink on one of those ordeals and all these little ones would be motherless. [S]uch things happen quite often.[48]*

From Akron, Ohio:

We have four children, the oldest six years old . . . There are times when we are driven almost to things that are horrible to think about. We are almost sure that anymore children at this time and we might go insane.

. . . Enclosed is a 2¢ stamp. If any more cost send C.O.D. or advise by letter.[49]

One of the few urban women with a southern European name was motivated by her precarious health:

* The homeless state of this letter writer was clear in that her return address was in care of another Norwegian family, which is indicative of a support network based on ethnicity.

> I am a mother and I have a very weak heart. I asked my family doctor and several others what to do [to] prevent conception. I could not get any satisfaction and know that the laws are such that you could not help me by mail, but is there not some society, on Birth Control in Detroit? or is there some doctor in this city you know could help me?[50]

Nor was it solely women who needed information, for many letters make it clear that husbands did not know any more about sexuality than did their wives. Even in cases in which the person was knowledgeable, however, the law and circumstances conspired to hinder contraception. A fifty-four-year-old Polish pharmacist in Burlington, Iowa, poured out his heart on the difficulties of dealing with these sad situations:

> I have been in business here since 1907.
> I am writing to inquire if you have . . . a booklet, dealing with the subject of "Prevention of Conception," written in such a way that it can be understood by the laity . . . I have calls from my customers for such information . . . It takes too long to explain these facts and often it is quite impossible to do so in privacy . . .
> There is one thing above all, it seems to me, and this is that a child shall and ought to have a right kind of start in life and that means that it ought only to be born when and where it is wanted . . . They try to do that much for other domestic animals.
> . . . It may be, I do not know, that you wish to write me a frank letter on this subject and if so it could not be mailed, but you could send it by Express. Therefore, I am enclosing 35¢ in stamps . . . Many thanks in advance.[51]

The league's Mary Ware Dennett explained that "it is not only a crime to send birth control information, but equally so by express; there is a specific statute on the subject"—but her reply to this professional man was less guarded than responses to imploring women. While reminding him that "Iowa has very drastic laws," she went on to promise "that before long some literature will come to you. You will not know from whom it comes. There is and has long been a useful kind of co-operation."[52]

Such legalistic evasion, however, was hardly an option for immigrants, especially those of the "new immigration" from southern and eastern Europe. They came from countries where contraception was unknown and repeated pregnancies virtually mandatory, regardless of the deleterious effect on women. It was no coincidence that the vast majority of information-seeking letter writers with non-English names were from the "old immigrant" groups of Scandinavia and northern continental Europe, for, as a turn-of-the-century international study shows, women in those places were adopting a mind-set that resulted in fewer pregnancies.[53]

RATES OF BIRTH AND INFANT DEATH
PER 1,000 IN VARIOUS COUNTRIES, 1920

	Birthrate	Baby Death Rate
Russia	48	265
Bulgaria	40	190
Roumania	39	190
Hungary	37	210
Germany	35	221
Spain	35	190
Italy	33	180
Denmark	28	116
England	27	128
New Zealand	27	60
Australia	26	81
Holland	26	87
Norway	26	75
Sweden	25	76
France	20	135

Though the likely correlation between high numbers of pregnancies and high rates of infant death may seem axiomatic today, many physicians of that era argued that there was no connection. Holland, Norway, and Sweden, along with the immigrant nations of New Zealand and Australia, provided clear evidence not only of this correlation but also of the efficacy of programs these countries were beginning for public education on birth control.

The best infant mortality rates in the world were in New Zealand, where "information has been taken as a matter of course, like any other item of personal hygiene, and has been available though the natural medical channels."[54] After beginning public birth control clinics in 1881, Holland lowered its birthrate from 37.7 per 1,000 to 25.3 two decades later; meanwhile, deaths of children under one year of age fell even more dramatically—from 209 to 70.[55]

Though change came slowly, eventually the United States would adopt the models of these more progressive nations. Both World War I, with its large numbers of recruits who were rejected as physically unfit, and the later poverty of the Great Depression made the case for quality over quantity in reproduction. When the needs of the state finally coincided with the needs of individual women, the cause of contraception began its climb to respectability.

By 1931, the affluent natives of the American Birth Control League, with a committee "composed of young society women," began aiming contraceptive information at immigrants. One of their brochures was illustrated with a healthy child who contrasted to one with bone deformities; the captions read, "There is enough

Food for this Baby" and "There is not enough Food for this last little Baby." The text inquired:

Do You Know that

1. You must be healthy to have healthy children.
2. You must have enough time between the births of your children to recover your strength.
3. You should not have more children than you can feed.
4. You can be shown a safe simple way not to have children when you should not have them.
5. It is not an operation.
6. It is not an abortion.
7. To obtain this information go to a Mothers' Health Bureau in a settlement house where the Doctor in charge will give you a careful examination and the proper instruction.[56]

But such educational effort did not begin until the end of the immigrant era. During virtually all of that time, birth control was viewed by most as both sinful and illegal, and women were shamed into acceptance of whatever reproductive rate befell them. Most emulated Linka Preus, who prepared for "Death's call" while stoically accepting that female fate was "indeed painful and hard."

Meanwhile, countless Americans, mostly male, preached against the "race suicide" that they saw in the high rates of immigrant reproduction, while their own wives and daughters had fewer children. Almost no one drew the analogy between the immigrants and the foremothers of the complaining Americans: few remembered that colonial families were equally large—often so large that several mothers and numerous children not uncommonly surround one patriarch in New England cemeteries. But the real natives of that time, the American Indians, apparently did not indulge in excessively large families. As the Anglo-Saxons became "natives" in the New World, their family size, too, decreased; they then wrote books and mounted platforms to warn against the growing numbers of "inferior" foreigners. They forgot that children are a source of security to people who are trying to make a home of a strange land and that the immigrants of the nineteenth and twentieth centuries were following the pattern laid down by the colonists of the seventeenth and eighteenth.

Security for the group, though, is not necessarily security for the individual. For individual unhappy women the perennial pregnancy was but a step in a swift and tiring march to an early grave.

2

THOSE
UNCONTROLLED BIRTHS

Childbirth Customs

If birth control was taboo, pregnancy itself was hedged about with superstitions. To avoid the evil eye, for example, a prospective Sicilian mother had to hide her condition as long as possible and stay indoors, exercising only in the dark. She had to be careful not to let her eyes glance upon any ugliness, lest her child resemble such. Her cravings were warnings that the child's skin could be marked with the desired item; so strong was this belief that Italian couples during the Great Depression tried desperately—and unsuccessfully—to convince welfare agencies that craved luxury foods were legitimate needs. And to Sicilians belongs the most bizarre custom of all: intercourse at the onset of labor! Doubtless this practice, which apparently reaffirmed fatherhood, was responsible for a great deal of infection and at least in part may explain the higher death rate of that group.[1]

But Italians were not the only immigrants with peculiar ideas on childbirth. A study of the "older" immigrants—English, Irish, and Germans—found plenty. In addition to familiar notions about cravings and birthmarks caused by emotional upset, some believed that mothers should abstain from meat, as the baby would be unable to digest it. Among the more unfounded ideas were that an infant born with teeth would become a murderer and that rubbing a baby's gums when teething would cause him to have a sharp temper.[2]

[handwritten margin notes: PAN OF WATER UNDER BED / BLOWING INTO BOTTLE / S...]

Jewish women told sociologists that "a pan of water set under the bed of a woman in confinement will keep away poisons and bedsores."[3] They avoided looking at a dead person while pregnant, lest the child's skin be unnaturally white. The belief that blowing into a bottle encouraged quicker delivery of the placenta may have been based on successful experience akin to Lamaze techniques today. Similar muscular exertion may have been the object behind the Polish belief that floor scrubbing was particularly beneficial during pregnancy. "As soon as a Polish woman is pregnant," said one, "she gets a scrubbing job . . . A countess will scrub when she knows a baby is coming."[4]

Indeed, a sensible rationale can be found in many seemingly strange beliefs if the context is thought through. The refusal of some women to bathe during pregnancy, for example, was based in the reality of bathing in cold streams in Europe; when social workers explained that a warm tub bath would not cause a miscarriage, most were willing to try the American way. In doing so, they overcame fears and asserted new courage—but their fears were genuine, and achieving this personal growth was not necessarily without trauma.

One Italian couple, for example, debated for weeks about whether or not the man should work on St. Aniello's Day, because to violate that taboo was to risk the health of their unborn baby. Finally he decided that since his American boss would never understand and since it was also a sin to lie and feign illness, he would go to work. Horrified to see the expectant father at work on that day, an Italian co-worker predicted trouble—and when baby was born with a disfiguring birthmark on his face, the taboo-breaking father was blamed.[5]

Even after a healthy baby arrived, women continued to be on guard for other dangers. Nursing Italian mothers burned their meal scraps, for if a cat ate them, the mother's milk could be stolen for kittens; if such a disaster took place, she could rectify it by sharing a bowl of bread and milk with the cat. Pregnant or menstruating Sicilian women could harm a baby by kissing it on the face, so all women opted instead to kiss its feet.[6] Polish babies, after initial cleanup at birth, were not bathed for a week, for it was thought that if water touched a baby during its first week, it would die in its first year.[7]

Belief in the evil eye was extremely strong in Mediterranean cultures—and, though not so candidly acknowledged, similar prohibitions on "tempting fate" also were buried in the psyches of more sophisticated societies farther north. For people from southern Europe, however, the evil eye was a factor in every aspect of life. Future fates could be ruined by one thoughtless misstep, so the daily lives of young women were a constant battle against unseen powers that threatened their young.

Women from the Near East kept babies partially clothed during diaper changing, for example, because nakedness left one especially vulnerable, and "if the evil eye falls on him, bad luck is soon on the way."[8] Some women refused to use prenatal clinics for fear that the evil eye would discover their pregnancy, and it was even more likely that mothers would not give permission for children to be weighed, lest the evil eye notice its progress. Taking a baby's photograph posed the same danger of supernatural jealousy.

Salt was believed to have magical powers to divert the evil eye, and even in the Great Depression, there were unassimilated immigrants who used it copiously. In one exceptionally graphic case, an Italian man requested that his family's cash relief payment be changed to a grocery order because, he said, his wife was spending half of their money on salt. An investigator found it to be true; the door and window areas of the home were covered in salt, which the woman hoped would end the "bewitch-ment" that caused her son's cholera.[9]

Religion and superstition combined when salt was placed in a baby's baptismal water, and christening itself occasioned other superstitions. Catholics of several nationalities believed that an early christening was essential not only for salvation but also because an unbaptized baby would die much more easily. Some thought giving a child a name prior to baptism was unlucky and that a baby who did not cry during baptism was apt to die. Borrowing a christening dress tempted fate, while carrying the baby to church on a "straight line" helped ensure that it would not lose its way in life. Of all these ideas, by far the most important was early baptism, which was believed to have earthy, as well as heavenly, effects: many would have agreed with the Irish mother who regretted the fifteen-day delay to which she attributed her child's small size. "If he had been christened sooner," she insisted, "he would have grown more."[10]

Failure to follow all of the prescribed rules was a serious matter when dealing with vulnerable young life. Fear could grip even young people with years of experience in America, as was the case when this leisurely scene of affluent Italian women turned to horror:

> A group of women meeting at a friend's house to pass the afternoon noticed with misgivings that a childless woman, said to have the Evil Eye, was present . . . It is considered dangerous to antagonize such a person . . . A young mother who had brought her 6 month old baby was especially uneasy and planned to leave as soon as she could without attracting attention. Everyone said something complimentary about the child, carefully adding, "God bless it" afterwards. The childless woman did not say this . . . A few weeks later the baby died, and its death was attributed to the woman with the Evil Eye . . .
>
> When the baby first began to ail, a doctor had been called in and had said that its diet needed changing, but the mother and her friends knew better. After what had happened, no diet would help. She followed the physician's advice only halfheartedly and depended more on the counsels and practices of every maga she could find. Lemons were stuck full of pins, and the heads cut off; strings were knotted; sacred cakes were baked and placed at the feet of the patron saint. All to no end. It was too late.[11]

Given the high possibility that an infant would in fact die, it seems likely that a major psychological purpose of complex taboos was that they would serve as insurance in case the worst happened. Sickness, death, and ill fortune of all sorts plagued immigrants, but if their lives were insulated with manifold taboos, one could be sure of having some kind of "explanation" for every evil.

"Make a Miracle": Delivery Experiences

Rosa Cavalleri, an Italian from northern Italy who lived in Missouri and then Chicago, based her life on a compendium of such beliefs. Hers was a happy fatalism, for she had a fundamental faith that the Madonna would "make a miracle" to solve whatever troubles resulted from her failure to plan.

Her first child had been born in Italy when she was still a teenager and was such a traumatic delivery that even though she had two doctors, she almost died. When in America her second was due, she was seriously frightened. In the lonely coal camp where she lived, there was no midwife and her drunken husband was undepend-able—but Rosa made no plans for delivery. Amazingly, even though this was her second child, she still did not know where children came from!

> Domiana said that the husband planted a seed in his wife and it was from that seed that babies grew. I never knew before where babies come from, but it sounded probably true. But even a seed couldn't grow into something alive unless God and the Madonna made it.[12]

Her first pregnancy, not surprisingly, had been a complete mystery to her:

> I kept getting bigger and bigger. And then one day I felt kicking inside of me and I knew it was a baby. How that baby got in there I couldn't understand. But the thing that worried me most was how it was going to get out! . . . I didn't want to ask Mama Lena, but what was I going to do? That baby was kicking to get out . . .
>
> "Well," said Mama Lena, "You'll have to pray the Madonna . . . Maybe the Madonna will make a miracle for you and let the baby come out without the doctor cutting . . .
>
> And so I prayed . . . and every night I gave myself more Ave Marias to say, so that when I woke up in the morning I would find the baby there in bed beside me. But it never was. It was still inside and kicking.
>
> At last there came a day when I had to leave work and go home. After that I didn't know what happened. I was three days without my senses.[13]

Incredible though the thought may be, it is possible that Mama Lena could not tell Rosa more than she did because she did not know herself; Rosa was adopted and Mama Lena never bore a baby. It could be that she did not understand the mechanisms of reproduction, for during this near-fatal delivery, the doctors chastised Mama Lena for forcing Rosa into early marriage: "How can a girl make new bones when her own bones aren't finished growing?"[14] On the other hand, she was married and presumably had sex but also failed to tell Rosa what to expect on her wedding night.

At any rate, perhaps because Rosa was older, the second child was born normally. All alone, she tied and cut the umbilical cord herself—something she had learned shortly before when she helped a friend give birth, and the patient had instructed the "midwife." After cutting the cord, Rosa passed out, and a German neighbor found her and the baby on the floor. She put Rosa to bed and returned home. When Rosa awoke:

> I knew the men would be coming to eat and there was nothing prepared . . . I tried, but I couldn't get up. Santino [her husband] came in first . . . I knew he was angry because there was nothing prepared . . . I was hungry and so thirsty. Maybe if I had something to eat I could get up . . . so I asked Santino if he will bring me a bowl of warm water . . . with bread and butter in it. He didn't answer me at first. Then he started swearing and told me if I wanted something to eat to get up and get it myself.[15]

Just as Rosa had continued to work in the silk mills of northern Italy until labor pains drove her home, immigrant women in the silk mills of Passaic, New Jersey, also worked through their pregnancies. Maternity leave was an unknown concept; instead, some of these women took on double duty by working there at night while continuing their household work in the daytime. As one investigator reported:

> The coming of a child is always a source of acute financial anxiety among Passaic workers, and it is only natural that night work among mothers should increase at such times. The practice is common also of women working as near the birth of their babies as possible, the foremen apparently making no objection to women far advanced in pregnancy standing all night . . . or running up and down with a spinning mule. Three women told of witnessing births of children in the mills, and several confessed to having worked up to the day or night before their own babies arrived. Several women ascribed the death or weakness of their children to the strain of heavy work during pregnancy, but asked with the cynical shrug so common among them, "What can do? . . . Pay not enough."[16]

Though bearing a baby in the mills would seem to be evidence of a fatalistic failure to plan, these hardworking women were doing the best they could. Among more affluent women, however, there were many who were akin to Rosa Cavalleri in an apparent reluctance to acknowledge their pregnancies. A number of immigrant diaries and letters are alike in surprising the reader with the birth of a baby when nothing has been said of the anticipation of one.

The most striking case may be that of Elisabeth Koren, a young Norwegian capable of reading three languages, who kept a detailed diary of her adjustment to Iowa during 1853–55. Though the published diary is 350 pages long and is filled with a great deal of trivia, she mentioned neither her own pregnancy nor that of the couple with whom she and her husband shared a two-room cabin. The diary ends abruptly, without any comment at all on this most important personal experience. Only the editor's note reveals the childbirth that began her transformation from diarist to busy mother.[17]

Similar reticence on pregnancy and even birth was exhibited by both men and women. Gottlieb Klinger, who was more literate and sensitive than most German men, wrote a long 1862 letter to his father, adding only toward the end: "I must also mention that my son Heinrich also died on December 7th at the age of 2 1/2 years and has now been replaced by a daughter."[18] Neither the daughter's name nor her birth date is mentioned, and he went on to inquire about money recently sent. Other letters in this family collection are similarly cursory when telling the German parents about the births of their grandchildren. Interestingly, the child who received by far the most loving attention was illegitimate.

Like Norwegian Elisabeth Koren, German Jette Bruns made no mention of pregnancies, though her letters home were lengthy and intimate. She probably did not know that she was pregnant when, with her husband and infant, she left Germany in July 1836; they arrived in frontier Missouri in November, and her second child was born the following February—with no mention of the additional problems pregnancy entailed when traveling and moving into a primitive home.

Indeed, some of the seasickness that women experienced may well have been complicated by pregnancy, for immigrants who intended to farm on undeveloped frontiers had to depart Europe in the spring so that crops could be planted early enough to have food for the following winter. To delay for an anticipated birth was to delay for a whole year—when a woman might again be pregnant—and therefore many young families emigrated despite pregnancy. Jette was in the early months of expectancy, but at least one other woman on her ship sailed in the late stages, for Jette's physician husband delivered a baby at sea.

Her pattern of reporting almost-annual additions was set with letter entries such as this, when her third baby was born: "For seven weeks now a Johanna has been resting in my arms."[19] Allowing seven weeks or more to pass after a birth seemed to be the norm, with a fatalistically implicit assumption that there was no point in reporting a birth until it could be said that there was no death. Jette's health clearly suffered, though, for soon after this birth, when she was still only twenty-five, she wrote in the humorous vein that she used when making light of a problem: "My Johanna still does not have teeth. But her mother will soon be toothless. At the present time she has a swollen cheek again after the disturber of the peace was yanked out."[20] Thus she casually revealed not only the presumable calcium loss that was going into her babies but also the inevitable digestive problems she would endure as she continued to be annually pregnant or nursing without teeth to chew her food.

At the fourth delivery, she finally expressed fear. She began her 1841 letter, "First let me report for myself that I once again, in spite of all the fear that I would lose my life, have a stout boy on my lap, who drinks mightily, screams, sleeps . . . My health is returning gradually."[21] It was not until her fifth pregnancy that she told her family ahead of the fact; Jette wrote her brother that it would be his "turn to become a godfather . . . in the near future."[22]

It may have been the deaths of other children that made her reluctant to tempt fate by rejoicing when the sixth was born, for she not only took from early May to late September to inform her family, she did not even mention the name of the new baby. When the seventh arrived, she wrote a long portion of the letter—primarily on the mental illness of her brother and another male relative—before she got around to mentioning the new baby, whom she described in three sentences before returning to the economy and other subjects. The attention to her new baby was so slight that her brother in Germany overlooked the event, and almost a year later, she had to clarify: "When I read your letter over again I almost had to assume that you did not understand who Albert is . . . Therefore, the seventh child of the Bruns couple saw the light of the world . . ."[23]

Her eighth child was born and died within eight days in August of 1847, when her sister-in-law also died. Not surprisingly, this child received no attention at all in the letters that have been preserved. The pattern of confused and late reporting to Germany on childbirth was repeated with the ninth pregnancy, when her husband neglected to mention their new baby. Writing on Christmas Day, 1848, Jette said, "Bruns recently wrote you, and when I inquired I learned that he had forgotten the most important thing while discussing other matters. Namely, that little Ludwig was born . . ."[24]

Jette mentioned at age thirty-nine that she was in fact toothless, but the comment was parenthetical, and she seemed to enjoy her tenth and eleventh babies even more than the earlier ones. She wrote, for example, in 1849, "You should see Albert. Such a smart, funny fellow. And Louis [is] so beautiful! We are so proud when people say that I have had no child that looked as healthy."[25] Her final comment on an infant came when she was forty-one: "Little Willaemken was quite good and quiet during the first year of his life. Now that he can walk, he is becoming spirited."[26]

The fact that her husband was a physician brought Jette great comfort—though she mentioned this only in the context of children's illnesses, not her pregnancies. Her family, however, did have her maternal health in mind when they allowed her to marry Dr. Bruns: Jette's mother had died in childbirth, and the family blamed this early death on an early marriage. Their permission for her to wed at eighteen was clearly based on the medical abilities of the thirty-one-year-old groom.

Like Jette, Emilie Lohmann Koenig of Hannover had lost her mother at age four when a younger sibling was born—and since Emilie was the fifth of eight children, it is clear that her mother was almost constantly pregnant during these years. Despite this personal history, however, Emilie exhibited a largely optimistic attitude about her own pregnancy; unlike many immigrant women, she shared the news with those back home. She wrote from Lafayette, Indiana, in April of 1854:

> We will soon have even greater joy when He blesses us with a baby. Please thank
> God now already for this blessing and ask Him in your prayers to be with us . . .

How much I would like to have you here with me, dear Berta! But it is not God's will that you be here, and I know He will hold his protecting hands over me. So I am content and cheerful, for I know His strength is great in our weakness. I will again experience His blessing . . . through my ordeal. Oh, how happy we will be then![27]

By July, however, she was more anxious, and the heavy period of pregnancy was complicated by her lack of acclimation to the heat of American summers. "I have been happy during the past few weeks to get even two hours sleep," she wrote. "At times I become very panicky . . . [and] fearful that my loved one will not get back in time when I will have so great need of him."[28]

He did get back in time, but that was Emilie Koenig's last letter. On August 10, her husband wrote:

The birth was an easy one, and Emilie began feeling quite well . . . On the sixth day Emilie began feeling worse, showing great nervousness. She had been extremely nervous during her entire pregnancy, and this agitation became worse after the birth . . . No one was aware of the danger. On Sunday evening the doctor said that she had a high fever, but had hopes for her recovery . . .

Her illness became worse, in spite of the utmost care, careful nursing, and the doctor's efficient medical care. Nothing was neglected. We watched over her day and night. The doctor came several times daily to watch her progress and prescribe further medication. Nothing was left undone. I am comforted by this knowledge. The fever kept getting worse, the doctor called it *nervenfieber* [typhoid fever].

At ten o'clock . . . when the doctor came, he said she had recovered somewhat, and gave us renewed hope. But it was only a short reprieve . . . Her breathing became weaker and weaker, and finally at quarter past eleven . . . she sank into Jesus' arms and fell asleep.[29]

Though the physician called it typhoid, the symptoms of Emilie Koenig's disease more nearly resemble puerperal fever. Typhoid is a communicable disease that likely would afflict others in the community even more than Emilie, since its cause is poor sanitation, and Rev. Koenig doubtless would mention other cases in his lengthy explanation to his in-laws. Puerperal fever, in contrast, is a direct consequence of childbirth, and in that era prior to germ theory, it was often spread by the attending physician. The ironic result was that in both Europe and America, more affluent women, who had physicians at childbirth, were more likely to die from this cause.

Norwegian Linka Preus fit into this affluent category, and like Germans Emilie Koenig and Jette Bruns, she also lost her mother to the birth of a younger sibling. That, plus an uncommonly strong streak of independent thought, was the basis of Linka's youthful comment: "Children I shall never want; that is certain."[30]

But children came, and she openly expressed her fears in a three-page prayer prior to her first delivery. It was more than two months later when she made another diary entry, which revealed not only postpartum illness but also the possibility of an overzealous doctor—she noted cryptically that "the opening in my right breast is not yet healed."[31]

Her sister died in childbirth between Linka's first and second pregnancies, which naturally increased her fears. While pregnant with her third in 1856, she was injured, and her health (and diary) never recovered. Busily baking *fattigmandsbakkelse* and *julekage* for Christmas, she wrote, "My maid is about to go down into the cellar and warns me that now she is going, but I am so preoccupied with my baking that I completely forget . . . and suddenly tumble down through the trap door."[32] Her baby arrived dead the following month.

After that, she was often both physically and emotionally ill, as this typical entry from 1858 reveals: "In my weakness it became clear that I did fear death; I was always anxious and seemed unable to explain this in any other way than that the joy of living and the fear of losing life was the cause of my anxiety."[33] Despite her fears, however, the pregnancies continued, and she wrote in 1860, "[F]ollowing a summer during which I suffered from a rather serious weakness, Thou O God, didst give us . . . a sweet little girl."[34] The next year brought her fifth, and in 1864, she endured another birth and death. As though to unburden herself, Linka wrote extensively about this, and it became her last diary entry: "How I prayed to Thee, O God, that I live . . . I prayed as I perhaps never have prayed before. I seemed so reluctant to leave the dear little ones . . . Yet it was Thou who took me from them, if I were called away."[35]

She lived through this difficult delivery, though the baby did not, but Linka never fully recovered. Eight years later she had a stroke, and four years after that she departed the life she had loved so much. Throughout it all, there was not anyone who seemed to understand or truly care; at the last delivery when she nearly died, her husband was again traveling on church-related business.

Like Linka Preus's probable experience with an overzealous doctor at her initial childbirth, English Rebecca Butterworth's first delivery was unnecessarily complicated by a man who claimed to have studied medicine. Less stoic than most, she also was unusual among immigrant women in viewing her pregnancy as an illness, not a natural event, and allowed far too much medical intervention. She wrote from the "Backwoods of America," Outland Grove, Arkansas, in 1846:

My Very Dear and Tender Father,

. . . I was taken sick a month since today. I commenced with bilious intermittent fever which nobody thought I would get over. Thomas was with me nearly all the time. He did not expect me getting over it. I was almost covered with mustard plasters, had a large blister on my back and I cannot tell you what kind of medicine . . . I had nearly 60 grains of calomel [mercury] steamed bricks put to me. I had a burning head, my extremities getting quite cold . . . Well, the result was the mercury had a happy effect. I had one of my cheeks cut halfway through. Indeed it would have scared you to look in my mouth.

On Sunday the 14th of June labour came on. I had a many come to see me
expecting it almost the last time. I was insensible at times . . . about 3 o'clock on
Monday morning my dear baby was born . . . our little Wm Barton was born and
crying like a baby at full term. Thos did not like to help me as he had not studied
midwifery much. I had to remain in that situation for two hours before the doctor
could be got, the little dear boy crying all the time and alarmed at what would be
the result. Doctor Howard come [sic] when he took the little darling and gave it to
sister. In about ten minutes after he took his flight to heaven.[36]

Rebecca Butterworth's experience was early in the immigrant era; near its end, during
World War I, more than 15,000 women died annually in the United States while
delivering life—statistics that, if amassed year by year, would add to totals much
higher than the death rates of professional soldiers. In 1913, "more women between
the ages of 15 and 44 died in childbirth than from any other cause except tuberculosis"[37]—and doubtless many of the deaths attributed to tuberculosis were complicated
and hastened because of being pregnant while chronically ill.

In fact, it is likely that childbearing was indeed the chief cause of death among
women of that age, for the connection between pregnancy and the ostensible cause
of death probably was seriously understated. A careful study of death certificates
found that maternal mortality was frequently obscured: "For example, lobar pneumonia on the death certificate [should] be changed to puerperal asepsis, it being a known
fact . . . that pneumonia commonly sets in . . . as a result of [infection during] delivery."[38] A Lower East Side nurse agreed, giving the emphatic example of "Mollie K.,
[who] was brought to the hospital three weeks after the birth of her twelfth child . . .
The doctors called her illness Septicemia—but ought to have added 'death due to
exhaustion from having too many children.'"[39]

That immigrant women had a considerably greater chance of dying in childbirth
than their American counterparts is shown by the following table.[40]

COMPARATIVE DEATHS RELATED TO PREGNANCY, 1900

Mothers Born in:

Italy	121.7	Canada	45.6
Russia	66.2	Ireland	45.1
Poland	54.7	United States	34.7
Germany	52.7	Scotland	33.7
Hungary	52.6	Bohemia	30.6
England	50.7	France	22.5
Scandinavia	45.7		

Note: Although women from three countries had better rates than native Americans, this did not amount
to many actual women because immigration from those nations was very small compared with others.

Deaths are among women 15 to 45, per 100,000 female population.

Many factors contributed to the generally higher rates of immigrant maternal death: frequent pregnancies, inadequate prenatal care, overwork and undernourishment, unsanitary conditions during childbirth, and more deliveries at both the younger and older range of maternal age. The multiplicity of negative factors was sufficiently daunting that some considered the wonder to be that so many women did survive, continue to work hard, and bear more children. As one expert wrote,

> The peasant women of the first generation amaze our women by their endurance. One of their own mid-wives told me that they have as hard confinements as Americans, but that they recover more quickly. In Allegheny [Pennsylvania] a settlement friend went to see a neighbor and found her at 9:00 barefoot in the yard hanging out clothes. She had borne a child at midnight, after which she had arisen and got breakfast for the men of her family and then done the washing.[41]

Similarly, when asked if his wife had a doctor or a midwife for her delivery, a Hungarian man replied, "Oh, she had her baby while I was at work—only the children here. She sat up in bed and cared for herself."[42] Her case was not unusual; a government investigator reported that more than 30% of the births among Serbo-Croatian women in Pennsylvania occurred without any trained assistance and that cases without even a husband or neighbor present were not uncommon.[43] The writer gave this cryptic account of a Polish woman's "confinement":

> At five o'clock Monday evening went to sister's to return washboard, having just finished day's washing. Baby born while there; sister too young to assist in any way, so she cut cord herself; washed baby at sister's home, walked home, cooked supper for boarders . . . Got up and ironed next day and day following; it tired her, so she then stayed in bed two days.[44]

Other studies found other similar cases of women who worked until the day of delivery and returned to work soon afterward.[45] But these "amazing" women did not have superwoman abilities: they aged sooner; their children were more sickly and died more often; and they themselves rolled up appalling death statistics. They did not return to work because they felt healthy enough to do so but because they had no choice.

Perhaps it was true, as many observers noted, that the first generation of immigrants was hale and hearty. Many peasants—though not all—came with a reserve of health built up by outdoor work in fields and vineyards. Life in America instead often meant crowded tenements and polluted air, which caused tuberculosis and other respiratory diseases that were especially dangerous when a baby pressed on the lungs. Instead of eating farm-fresh foods, women had to produce milk from a diet of adulterated canned goods, and they often grew anemic from inadequate nutrition. Working longer hours in factories instead of the weather-regulated schedule of agricultural work, they exhausted themselves—and delivering a healthy baby became harder.

If physical health suffered from inadequacies, mental health care was nonexistent. In some immigrant cultures, women were criticized if a baby was born sick or dead; an Irish man, for example, "reproached" his wife, saying, "A dead child is worse than none." She, in turn, blamed on the German midwife because "the baby's head stayed in too long."[46]

A mother could be emotionally torn, too, when the baby turned out to be a girl, for many immigrants had a candid preference for male offspring. Italian women in labor were not told the baby's sex until the placenta was delivered, lest disappointment at having a girl delay this process.[47] Among the Irish, "males were preferred and cherished" to such a great extent that one scholar avers that "well into the [twentieth] century . . . boys in their teens were dressed in petticoats and long frocks . . . to mislead the thieving fairies."[48] If a girl was stolen by supernatural forces, it was understood, the loss would be much less.

The emotional distress of one Mrs. Pagano,* an Italian who lived in Colorado and Utah at the turn of the century, increased with her childbearing years. Her early pregnancies had gone well, even though she delivered her first baby alone when she was only sixteen. But by the time the sixth child was on its way, she had developed symptoms of mental illness:

> She had nightmare after nightmare in which she dreamed that the child would be born dead or deformed. If she had been able, by sheer force of desire, to counteract the fact of her pregnancy, she would have done so . . . After a prolonged and difficult confinement, my brother Carl was born. When they brought him to my mother (he was the only one of the children for whom she had to have a doctor), she burst into tears. Tiny and shrunken . . . he could not have weighed more than five pounds.[49]

Her daughter adopted this distress as her model for pregnancy. Though the immigrant mother bore her first child thousands of miles from her family entirely without assistance in a lonely Colorado mining camp, it was now catastrophic that the pregnant daughter was in California and the mother in Utah:

> Nearly every day a letter . . . arrived, and my mother lost no time answering. "Now be sure you get plenty to eat," she would say. "There's two of you to feed now!" Or: "be careful not to get frightened of anything. Remember Annie Masto I told you about in Denver? She was frightened by a cat while she was carrying her first baby, and when he was born he had a red mark just like a cat on his forehead." And in return Rose wrote such things as "I can't hold anything on my stomach but peanuts

---

* The real name of this woman is not clear, for although the author's name is Pagano, his references in the book use another surname for his family; he gives his mother no first name.

and apples. What should I do?" . . . "Povero me!" my father sighed on more than one occasion. "You'd think this was the first time a baby had been born in the world."[50]

The daughter seemed to feel that as an American woman she had a right to insist on not only long-distance daily attention from her mother but also a level of indulgence and subservience from her husband that no Italian woman of the first generation would have imagined. Her husband's role change was, indeed, greater than her own, for first-generation men did not dote on their pregnant wives.

Even after Rosa Cavalleri left the cruel Santino and married her gentle Giovanni, she had no expectations that he would be particularly supportive of her pregnancies—nor did experience at maternity mean that Rosa herself planned any better than she had in the past. She was in Chicago when her last was born, while her husband "went away because he was sick—he went by a doctor in St. Louis to get cured. That doctor said he must stay away from his family one year." Though she knew she would be alone and though the baby was overdue, she made few preparations. When labor finally started, she sent the children to a neighbor:

> I was on my bed all alone by myself . . . Just when the baby was born, I saw Sant' Antoni right there! . . . Then the door opened and the midwife came in to take care of the baby! . . . She washed the baby and put him by me, but then she ran away. She didn't light the fire or nothing. Oh, that night it was so cold! And me in my little wooden house in the alley with the walls all frosting—thick, white frosting. I was crying and praying, "How am I going to live?"
>
> . . . My Visella was bringing up the wood and the coal and trying to make that room warm. But she was only a little girl, she didn't know, and . . . the ceiling caught fire. I had to jump up from the bed and throw pails of water . . . Then God sent me help again. He sent that Miss Mildred from the settlement house. She didn't know about me and my Leo born; she was looking for some other lady and she came to my door . . .
>
> Then she ran away and brought back all those little things the babies in America have . . . Oh, that Miss Mildred and Miss May, they were angels to come and help me like that! Four nights Miss May stayed there and kept the fire going. They were high-up educated girls—they were used to sleeping in the warm house with the plumbing—and there they came and slept in my wooden house in the alley and for a toilet they had to go down to that shed under the sidewalk. They were really, really friends![51]

Midwives and Medicos

Most women were better prepared and put their faith not in the appearance of angels but in midwives—and most midwives were more responsible than the one who disappeared from Rosa's room. The bad reputation that midwives have held for most of the twentieth century is only now being rectified, as the advantages of using empathetic paraprofessionals for routine maternity care becomes reestablished.

Midwives had a long tradition in America prior to the immigrant era, and they continued to be honored in foreign-born communities after natives began abandoning them for physicians. The Baltimore City Directory for 1879, for instance, listed forty-six women and one man under "Nurses and Midwives," with the names about evenly divided between English and German,* with one Irish name.[52] After the turn-of-the-century waves of immigration, the newcomers' predilection for midwives was even more pronounced; a 1916 report showed that women born abroad were far more likely than Americans to employ a midwife instead of a physician:[53]

USE OF MIDWIVES BY WOMEN IN NEW YORK STATE, 1910–1915

Mother Born in:	Percentage Using Midwives:
Poland	66
Austria-Hungary	54
Italy	41
Russia	32
Germany	28
United States	4

In 1915 in New York City—where more sophisticated medicine was practiced than in most of the country—about 30% of births took place in hospitals. The remaining two-thirds that took place at home were evenly divided between physicians and midwives as attendants.[54] But among unassimilated immigrant groups there, midwives were far more likely: one study reported that 92% of the city's Italian women were attended by midwives.[55]

Italians, with their rigid rules of gender separation, were particularly likely to want a woman, instead of a man, in the bedroom at this intimate time, but women from other cultures also made it clear that they thought male attendants were inherently less empathetic. A Minnesota woman wrote to the Voluntary Birth Control League, for example, of her frustration with a doctor who "said it was best I had no more children, but that is all he say, and I don't like to go to a man for such information, even he be [sic] a doctor. He says it is because I am strong and healthy that I have such large children and hard times at child birth."[56]

While some immigrants may have hired a midwife because of modesty or because she charged less, there were other sound reasons for preferring them to physicians. A midwife was more likely to speak the native language, which is important in the anguish of childbirth; a midwife not only charged less but also accepted installment payments; most midwives were willing to perform household services such as cooking and looking after older children. It was simply a better

---

* The German names seem to be disproportionately German-Jewish.

bargain: in Detroit, for example, midwives charged $7 to $10 in 1917 and visited daily for five days or more. Doctors came only once and charged $10 to $30.[57]

The doctors argued that their services were sufficiently superior to justify the higher fee, and most twentieth-century Americans agreed. Katharine Anthony, who was Susan Anthony's niece and the author of a study of working mothers, shared this critical view:

> The midwives of the West Side are nearly all German women. As a class they are not more intelligent than their neighbors; their only superiority is that which results from a few months training and such knowledge as comes from practical experience . . . The poor woman who has only five or seven dollars to pay for care during confinement is liable to fall into the hands of a clumsy learner or an ignorant bungler. Two of the women who were visited for this investigation, and died while it was in progress, were the victims of peritonitis due to neglect on the part of the attending midwife.[58]

Upton Sinclair popularized this view with vivid pictures of *The Jungle*'s murderous midwife. His plot was based in part on a Polish doctor in the Chicago stockyards area who told him, "I have been practicing for thirteen years in this district, and during that time never a week has passed that I have not been called in to two or three cases of women who have been mangled and mutilated by midwives."[59]

Yet there was a great deal of evidence to support the opposite view. Those who looked objectively saw that some European countries offered specialized training to midwives that was at least equal to the education a physician received on this aspect of his general practice. One supervisory nurse praised the immigrant midwives with whom she worked as "well-educated, thoroughly trained" and "scientific women," adding that "in Italy none but a well-educated woman can qualify for the training, which covers from two to four years."[60]

Several studies of the subject that were more rigorous than Sinclair's "realism" found public health departments and medical leaders who agreed that prejudice against foreign midwives was unjustified. In a variety of settings, objective observers concluded:

> If the midwife is the cause of much infant mortality we should have a high infant mortality rate, for . . . 88% of all foreign-born mothers are attended by midwives. The maternal mortality in our city among midwife cases is no higher than in the city as a whole.

> Of the forty-one cases of complications from pregnancy, it developed that in only ten had a midwife been in attendance at any time, and in no instance did the doctor claim that the midwife was in any way responsible for the result.

> Last year 10 percent of physicians' reports were late and only 1 percent of the midwives . . . In Providence, in 1917, the infant mortality rate of midwives' babies was 77, while of all others it was 117.[61]

The immigrant city of Newark demonstrated the same: while seventy-one women died with a midwife in attendance, eighty died with a doctor in the home and ninety-one died in hospitals.[62] Interviews with medical school professors also found "that the majority of teachers . . . consider that general practitioners lose as many and possibly more women from puerperal infection than do midwives."[63] Their explanation was that, in this less sanitary age, physicians spread infections from diseased patients to the previously healthy internal organs of women at delivery, whereas midwives specialized in patients who were not disease carriers.

Finally, no less a personage than the president of the American Medical Association had strong language on the subject, critical, not of midwives as might be expected, but of doctors: "Of 116 cases of ophthalmia neonatorum . . . 22 occurred in the practice of physicians and 11 in that of midwives. Of the 11 midwives, 3 had used nitrate of silver; of the 22 doctors, only 1. According to these reports, . . . the doctors should be replaced by midwives."[64]

Nonetheless, as the immigrant era drew to a close, the use of midwives began dropping even in the immigrant stronghold of New York City. A 1927–28 report showed that of 3,104 cases followed by the Manhattan Maternity Center Association, 1,234 were delivered by "Dr. in Home," 945 by "Dr. in Hospital," and 875 by "midwife."[65] At the same time, a study sponsored by the New York Academy of Medicine and the city's Department of Health found that midwives still gave "the best" care. After detailed analysis of 675 cases of maternal death, the report concluded "that the pregnant woman is safer at home than in a hospital even when crowding and dirty conditions may exist."[66] The investigators wrote candidly:

> The figures . . . indicate the rank and file of physicians as more culpable than abortionists or midwives . . . The best results have been obtained by the midwife where the woman was attended at home. This is true in spite of the fact that . . . if the patient is attended by a doctor as well as a midwife and dies, the public records credit the midwife with the death; if she lives, the doctor is credited with the case.[67]

But these facts were not known by most Americans, who generally supported the physicians' efforts to eliminate midwifery through government regulation. By the 1930s, when both state laws and restrictive immigration quotas made the entrance of foreign-trained midwives more difficult, immigrants would be increasingly constrained to accept the doctors, who would charge more and give less in terms of time and service.

The change was not necessarily welcomed by all, as one Jewish mother summarized: she preferred the unhurried midwife who encouraged a natural delivery to doctors who hastened births with forceps, saying, "The doctor, even the professor doctor, he comes to your house to get your baby. He hurries you up; he hurries you up, and that is not so good."[68]

Prenatal Precautions versus Fatalistic Acceptance

For most of the immigrant era, prenatal care was an unknown concept. As late as 1915, "comparatively few pregnant women were receiving prenatal supervision"—even in New York City and despite a decade of national publicity on "the appalling loss of life occurring in maternity and infancy."[69] The simultaneous loss of life occurring in World War I drew attention to the era's childbirth casualties. Though American involvement in the war lasted less than two years, the rhetoric on babies was cast in the long term:

> Is YOUR city playing its part in the country-wide campaign to save 100,000 babies during the second year of America's participation in the war so the citizenry of the nation can be assured for the future? How far does the black line of death extend alongside your city in the chart below? Get behind the Government and shorten it.[70]

Without spelling out the correlation, the chart's "black line of death" nonetheless demonstrated the connection between infant mortality and immigration: cities that had rates three times higher than tolerable included the textile mill towns of Manchester, New Hampshire, and Fall River and New Bedford in Massachusetts; the factory centers of Reading, Norristown, and Erie in Pennsylvania, and New Jersey's Hoboken and Trenton. In the Midwest, high rates were to be found in the industrial areas around the Great Lakes that attracted immigrant labor: Duluth, Peoria, and Green Bay, Wisconsin, all had extraordinary numbers of infants who died.*

Dramatically headed with "ARE YOU IN THE BABY SAVING DRIVE?" the document ended, "Give the baby a square deal and you give your country a square deal. The nation that has the babies has the future!" It was sponsored by the New York Milk Committee, an organization that understood the efficacy of such programs: New York City's infant mortality rate of 88.8 was appreciably better than that of the next-largest cities, Chicago (106.4) and Philadelphia (110.0).[71]

This wartime attention to childbirth casualties was the catalyst for the Maternity Center Association of Manhattan, which opened three centers in 1917–18 and quickly expanded to "thirty centers operat[ing] throughout the year." The association conducted prenatal classes and clinics and, by 1921, did a study of 8,743 case histories. Even the sponsors seemed surprised by the good results, which "showed a reduction in maternal and neonatal deaths and stillbirths compared with the . . . country as a whole. This reduction was the result of prenatal care alone, as the Association has had no responsibility for the care of patients during delivery and the post partum period."[72]

---

* Other high rates were found in southern cities, which is indicative of the poor health care available to the black population that concentrated there in this era.

This 1923 New York City child-care class was subsidized by Rockefeller funds aimed at reducing infant mortality. The blackboard emphasizes milk; bottled cow's milk was unfamiliar to many immigrants, and American women educated immigrant women on its use. (ROCKEFELLER ARCHIVES CENTER)

Another study demonstrated a correlation between prenatal care and stillbirths: women who had care for three months or more accounted for only 20 of 107 stillbirths—or, in other words, more than 80% of the women whose babies arrived dead had received no health care during more than two-thirds of their pregnancies.[73] A third report detailed pregnancy complications, finding that the most common was albumin in the urine, followed by influenza and—tellingly—alcoholism.

The efficacy of acknowledging pregnancy and planning for it was demonstrated by other organizations. The language of these educational campaigns, however, emphasized *infant* mortality rates—even when reductions in maternal deaths were much more impressive. The New York Milk Committee provides an excellent example: "Since 1912," it reported, when it "commenced experiments . . . by providing medical and nursing care for expectant mothers, gratifying results have been attained. Within this period stillbirths have been reduced 22% . . . and maternal deaths by 69%." But the dramatic 69% rate of progress among women was parenthetical—hidden at the bottom of three pages of elaborate charts on infant deaths.[74]

It was almost as though the committee did not want the public to notice that its program for babies necessarily entailed lifesaving results among adult women.

The same was true of officials who carried out the programs of the Sheppard-Towner Act. This pioneering federal legislation was passed in 1921 as a result of the national attention to infant mortality during World War I.[75] It offered states matching funds for the establishment of clinics, but—like the private volunteer groups—the language of Sheppard-Towner officials made it clear that infants were their primary concern, and a good result for their mothers was merely a biological imperative. Margaret Sanger was critical of these clinics, saying that they "taught a poor woman how to have her seventh child, when what she wants to know is how to avoid . . . her eighth."[76]

In any case, many states failed to take advantage of the funds, and by 1929, when conservative administrations dovetailed with congressional attention to the declining economy, the act was repealed. Thus, although such programs could demonstrate their efficacy, they did not make much of a national impact before the immigrant era ended. Even in New York City, even after years of attention to the problem, and even among the 30% of women whose babies were born in hospitals in 1927, there still was not "adequate prenatal supervision." Fatalistic procrastination continued: "Patients might make arrangements at about the seventh month of pregnancy to go to [a] hospital for delivery. Practically no care or supervision was given between that time and delivery."[77]

These statistics would grow worse in the next few years as the Great Depression made it even more unlikely that women would spend money on what they saw as the luxury of protecting their health while pregnant. To truly change the situation, it was necessary to change the mind-set of women: The crucial time for building a strong child was before a baby was born, but this meant important changes in parental thought. Their fatalism was so strong that many immigrants saw little point in investing in a child who had a good chance of dying—and by the time the child survived to what they saw as an age worthy of investment, the damage often was so severe, as in the case of bones deformed by rickets, that it was more difficult to correct.

Changing attitudes on prenatal health also necessarily involved encouraging a certain degree of maternal selfishness, of urging the pregnant woman to indulge herself with protein-rich meat and milk and vitamin-laden fruit and vegetables. These were things that families often could not afford, and when they could, it was axiomatic that the mother served herself last, not first. Even health educators found it difficult to recommend openly that a woman feed herself first, for such behavior was too immodest and unfeminine, even for individualistic Americans. The mother was indeed parenthetical to the child—and the woman that she might be outside of motherhood was beyond conception.

3

IN SICKNESS
AND IN HEALTH

Between Hope and Fear: Views of Medicine

"Italian women," said one sociologist, "approach their confinement, particularly their first, with wonderful hand-woven sheets, embroidered pillowcases, and beautiful satin coverlets, often made by the mother herself during girlhood."[1] A new baby called for festivity, with friends and family visiting, the house decorated, and special drinks served. It was another reason for preferring a midwife who understood the Old World ways, for these treasured traditions did not fit with the rules laid down by austere American physicians.

If women were reluctant to have a doctor in their homes for deliveries, one can imagine their abhorrence of hospitals. There visitors were restricted, and no drinks or festive foods could be served. The baby was isolated in a nursery; how, then, could Italian babies have pinned on them the charms that friends gave in the wish for a good life?

Suspicion of hospitals, however, ran far deeper than this. "It was not an easy thing for my people to send me to the hospital," Rose Cohen wrote of her teenage experience with chronic anemia:

> The very word filled us with fear . . . It was quite understood that in the hospital patients were practiced upon by hardened medical students and then neglected. Whenever we saw anyone miserable, dirty, neglected, we would say, "He looks like

a 'hegdish' (hospital). And so we saw our neighbors all about us borrow and pawn but keep their sick at home. And when once in a while we saw a person taken to the hospital we looked after him mournfully as if he were already carried to the burial grounds. It was also an open acknowledgement of the direst poverty.[2]

She was Jewish, but these views were shared by immigrants of all ethnic groups. Their negative view of hospitals was based on an assumption that hospitals were charities, run by municipalities or churches for those too poor to pay the private-duty nurses and house-call physicians for the in-home care that was the era's middle-class standard. Some Europeans held an even lower view of hospitals: "an old Neapolitan curse" translated as, "May you end your days in the hospital."[3] The sense of "ospedale" was different, for it implied an asylum for the destitute, but how were immigrants to understand that American ones offered decent treatment? In Sicily, the word signified a mental institution, and a person who had been hospitalized was thereafter branded insane.

Social workers, acknowledging the fear of hospitals, saw outpatient clinics as an alternative and urged their clients to use them, but this was not easy either. Unable to read signs and ask directions, how was a woman to find her way to the clinic and back in the big city? Worse, how could she leave her children and lose wages at work and spend carfare on the chance that this clinic would prevent some vague problem she couldn't even define?

Then, too, acknowledging sickness also meant risking quarantine. One family, suspecting their child had smallpox, refused to call a doctor because they had heard of the American system of quarantine. They continued to operate the clothing sweatshop in their home and called a doctor only when it was too late. The child died, and perhaps hundreds of people were exposed to smallpox through the clothes that went out of their shop.[4]

Earlier in the era, when smallpox broke out in the immigrant town of Holyoke, Massachusetts, public health officials were frustrated at every turn in their efforts to stem the epidemic. Quarantine signs were torn down, free vaccinations were refused, and the sick were hidden from officers who would have placed them in isolation.[5] In Lawrence, "old" immigrant Germans vociferously protested vaccinations as an "invasion of privacy and a scheme to make doctors and druggists rich."[6]

Like quarantines, surgery was another frightening thing to most. Rosa Cavalleri, never reluctant to express her views, raged on about this Americanism:

The American doctors they ruin the people. I say, "People don't go to the doctors!" You get a pain in your stomach, and they say, "Take off the tonsils." They tell you to take off those things and they won't cure you till you do. In Italia we don't take off nothing—we keep everything and we are not sick. God gives us all those little things; what for the doctors take them off? The American people ruin themselves by running all the time to those crazy doctors.[7]

A nurse on the Lower East Side spoke to the fear that her patients had of surgery by citing the example of a woman who had lost ten of her fifteen babies—and four of the five survivors had serious health problems. Two had bone deformities from rickets, one was deaf, and "another has had a foul discharge from the ear for nearly two years. Only an operation can cure this." Despite the deafness of their other child, "the parents refuse to have it done."[8] Another of her cases was a twenty-six-year-old woman who had borne twelve children, only half of whom lived—and four of those six had "bow legs" caused by rickets.

Rickets, incidentally, was almost always discussed by public health authorities in terms of children. Undoubtedly, however, many adult women suffered from

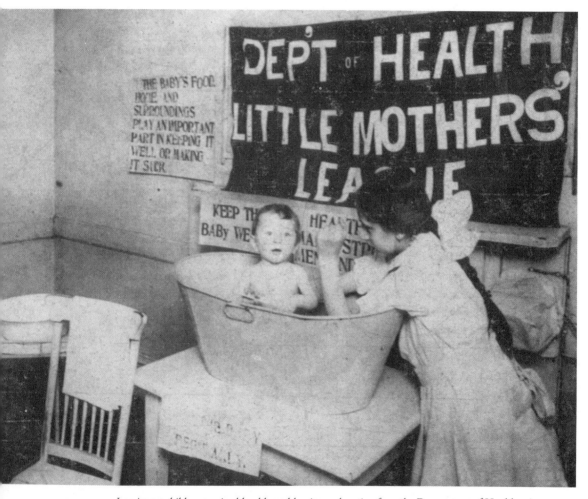

Immigrant children received health and hygiene education from the Department of Health prior to World War I. The advantage of teaching this schoolgirl how to bathe a baby was twofold: her mother probably spoke no English, and she herself was a future mother. (NEW YORK PUBLIC LIBRARY, IMMIGRANT LIFE COLLECTION)

it—but the telling evidence of curved legs was hidden by their floor-length skirts. Rickets probably was a greater problem for women than for men, too, because women lost bone density as a result of pregnancy and menopause; in addition, childbirth can be more painful and dangerous when pelvic bones are misshaped. Yet women—even pregnant and nursing women—were rarely mentioned in health campaigns, which concentrated on children.

Prevention efforts took years to produce results, however, and the notion of deliberately breaking a child's legs to reset them straightly was absolutely foreign to immigrants. Their fatalistic response to surgery—especially preventative surgery—was simply to avoid doctors who would suggest such treatment. A Slavic woman wrote that when there was illness among her people, a witching woman was called first, and if she could not produce a cure, a pharmacist was the second choice, but physicians were seen as a last resort.[9] A writer among the New York Irish observed that doctors were frequently referred to as "charmers," a term indicative of the blending of magic and medicine in their minds. Some rated magic above American science and expressed the view that New York doctors were much less effective than Ireland's charmers.[10]

Late in the twentieth century, Athena Theokas, who emigrated from Greece in 1902 to the textile mill town of Lowell, near Boston, spoke at length about her cultural convictions on the superiority of magic to medicine. She firmly believed that "of course" illness was caused by the evil eye: it was the *mateor mate* that caused one to "take very fever and throwing up and sick believe it or not. My brother died twenty-three years old from evil eye because they never believed that time." Effecting a cure was complicated, but both witching women and the church were important:

> When I go to Church the woman's know how to read things. Read some kind of letters and put oil in a glass. They show if you have it or not. If you have evil eyes . . . the oil . . . disappear. But if you don't have nothing the oil—they drop the oil in the water they stay there. That's the way to find out if you have that evil eye . . . You go to Church the priest got to say that word "the evil eye" two or three times, course they change the clothes . . . Incense, you put that and you put the clothes outside and . . . don't leave them in the house.[11]

She also sent to Greece for *phylachto*, a talisman or charm that was made by a priest and blessed in the church. With this protection, she could walk safely through life: "Take them to the church leave them there for a couple days, put it on. After that . . .no have evil eyes no more." She added that priests in Greece kept such amulets at the altar and that they were given to people to "put them in even letters, even cloth and sew them together [so that] nobody know what's inside . . . A lot, lot of people had that. Evil eyes is the worst thing you can have because the doctor can't do nothing about that, he don't know about that."[12]

Nor was it only immigrant ghetto dwellers who looked to medicine women as their first choice when dealing with illness; rural immigrants also consulted local female experts, especially for healing herbal preparations. Despite the scornful attitude of the male writer who told of "a midwife from Norway" who "began practice as a medical doctor" in Wisconsin, it is clear that many thought her an effective practitioner, for he wrote: "The influx of people was immense, and many had to wait for days before they could get an opportunity to speak to her."[13]

The connections between mental attitude and physical illness were clearly a strong factor in consultations with practitioners of one's own ethnicity, but nevertheless, almost all immigrants refused to have anything to do with modern psychology. An Italian woman who finally agreed to see a psychiatrist at the insistence of her social worker, for example, took with her a large bag from which she would not be parted. After the interview, she disclosed its contents—all the amulets she could find in her neighborhood. "'The doctor,' she triumphantly asserted, 'he no hurt me.'"[14]

The witching woman and druggist were a known part of the neighborhood, but if a doctor was called, he was often chosen because of advertising in foreign-language newspapers. It was common in Europe for reputable doctors to advertise, and many American quacks took advantage of this. They placed large, eye-catching ads, complete with false testimonials and dire warnings of death, in these papers that went unread by their American colleagues.

Immigrants were doubly confused, for not only did respectable European physicians advertise, but also newspapers in many countries were so strictly regulated by the government that anything advertised was taken to have official approval. Here immigrants innocently assumed that the doctors who *did not* advertise were the quacks, for it seemed obvious that these nonadvertisers could not get permission.

Another factor in choosing a doctor was his fee—and not, as one might expect, necessarily the lowest. While of course many poor immigrants had to accept what they could afford, most tended to think that a doctor who charged more was better. They were suspicious of health care provided by American charities; a Polish woman expressed the typical attitude when a representative of the Visiting Nurse Association came to her door: "I do not know who sent that woman to my house. She must be one of the educated people and she must have done something wrong or she would not be going around this way instead of living with her own class and taking life as they do."[15]

Such suspicion, of course, did not extend to the services of doctors and nurses provided by the mutual aid societies that were organized by immigrants in many cities, for, even when there was no fee, these were dues-paying insurance programs, not charity. It was the concept of philanthropy that was foreign to them, for most had seen little of it the despotic era of Europe when they lived. The belief that "you can't get something for nothing" fit with their fatalistic cynicism—while their devotion to the family often meant that they spent more than they could afford in the hope that additional money would increase the chances of a cure.

This correlation between money spent and illness cured also meant that they were apt to call in additional doctors if the first one did not bring a quick cure. There are numerous recorded cases of immigrants who waited only a few hours and if there

seriousness of their daughter's condition, to provide her with milk and eggs, to allow her to sleep alone with windows open, to lessen her heavy household tasks, and to take her regularly for reexamination to her doctor.[28]

The girl's recovery was slower than it would have been in the mountain air of sanitariums, where tuberculosis was treated with rest and fresh food, but Mediterranean mores simply would not allow an unmarried daughter to depart that far from family supervision. Such refusal of treatment is a bald example of the factors that caused women to suffer poorer health and die more frequently than men: A 1908 study of Italians in New York found that women died at a rate from 2% to 5% greater than men.[29] Girls also died at a higher rate than boys of the same age, which was attributed to the cultural mores that kept girls indoors, where they were more likely to contract the respiratory diseases that were the greatest killers. It is also possible that families spent more freely on medical care for boys, and other studies suggest that boys got better nutrition. In Ireland, for example, there is evidence that girls were given less to eat than boys during famines.[30]

Other frequent problems for the women in the 1908 study were (1) chronic anemia, caused by inadequate food and lack of gynecological care; (2) amenorrhea and dysmenorrhea ("the average Italian girl in New York menstruates after the fourteenth and sometimes in the fifteenth year of age, while in Sicily the average period is at eleven or twelve"); and (3) muscular atony, which led to displacement of abdominal organs, "with which 85 per cent of the Italian women that present themselves for examination at gynecological clinics are afflicted."[31] The last was a severe consequence of a culturally imposed lack of recreation, which gave women such poor muscles that it literally affected the lives of their unborn babies.

But it was tuberculosis that was the chief statistical culprit. That women died from it at a higher rate than men was not only due to the complications of pregnancy but also because they were more apt to contract it in their housebound lives. According to the investigating physician, its devastating effect for women was due to "their early marriages, frequent pregnancies, and long periods of lactation." But, because these factors "prevail also in their native land, . . . their rapid deterioration and high mortality in New York must be charged against urban congestion."[32]

Though tuberculosis was known as an urban disease, it also frequently occurred in rural areas. Again, the nature of women's housebound lives encouraged it, for cabins on even isolated prairies were crowded and dense with the smoke of wood or coal fires—even in summer, cooking had to be done with fire. The name of the era's most deadly disease—"consumption"—was an ironically perfect fit for fatalists. There was no cure, and it literally "consumed" a body until the patient was a coughing skeleton. Jette Bruns, ever the empathetic nurse, never mentioned that she was pregnant with her eighth child when she dealt with her sister-in-law's case:

Trute, Franz's wife, had a little boy last January. She is suffering from consumption and is very low . . . [She] has to be fed, has to lie on her stomach because her back is sore, and she is emaciated to a skeleton. This is really some disease. I feel very sorry for Franz; he is quite patient and usually cares for her himself . . . The poor, sick woman still has a good appetite, but Bruns tells me that some people with consumption eat to the very end . . .

It is always a hard thing for me to go over there, and this has been going on for three months. It makes me feel so sad. And she likes it so much when I am there. The soup I cook is the best, and I have to bake this and that for her . . . On her name-day I gave her a little Madonna as a present. She was as pleased as a child, she shouted with joy, she told everybody and showed it to everybody who came. And what will happen later? Four little children! I don't know, and I also fear so much for myself. [33]

Besides fresh air, the era's prescription for consumption was rest, but how could a woman with four little children rest? It was, indeed, the bearing of children that made tuberculosis into the statistical killer of women that it was.

Ancient Magic and Modern Snake Oil

Jette knew that her homemade soup was a solace, not a solution, but home remedies for illness were ubiquitous among immigrants. Some were helpful, but others were useless and even harmful. Elisabeth Stern, writing of her adolescent years at the turn of the century, said that her aunt, a kindly Lithuanian Jew, "used to fret over me. She fed me goose fat on bread, made me eat warm dough, and one day put glass cups on my skinny young arms to bleed me, to 'get the thinness out' of me."[34]

Athena Theokas, who emigrated in 1902, maintained a home pharmacopoeia of Greek herbs in the late twentieth century:

I take care of it years and years and they not spoil like they have in the drug store. Sure I boil that [and] I give it to the kids. That's the best—all the medicine come from the ground . . . But American people don't know nothing about these things, never believe it. But the doctor I used to have, the Syrian doctor . . . he believed because his mother, his mother bring the grass—the different things from Syria . . . I says, "How you know that, doctor?" He says, "My mother used to teach me." I believe, still I believe the old stuff to boil on the stove to put honey and drink it. I . . . boil it and give to the kids. I never give them medication—pills, never.[35]

Because Theokas imported familiar herbs, she had the benefit of centuries of experience that other women had put into their local botanical store of knowledge. When immigrants tried to substitute American products for unobtainable items, however, the result could be seriously damaging. In the silk mill town of Passaic, New Jersey, for example,

A child [was] suffering from exema on the back of its head and ears; the ointment prescribed at the dispensary did not seem to effect a cure after two days use, so when a neighbour suggested that in her country ink was used for skin disease, a child was promptly dispatched to purchase five cents worth of the log-wood and acid which does service as ink here and a copious dose was applied to the baby's raw scalp. Erysipilis* set in at once and within twenty four hours the child died in convulsions.[36]

When investigating Americans explored the reasoning behind the use of ink on a child's head, they found that ink in Hungary was made of sloe berries, which have healing properties.

Curious home remedies also existed in rural areas and among "old" immigrants. Some Irish placed "holy bones" on crippled children to cure their orthopedic problems. In the Midwest, some Norwegians thought sheep dung effective against tuberculosis when worn as a poultice, and they gave bits of brass to patients with broken bones on the theory that this would serve as solder to hold the bones together.[37]

In an area of Minnesota where many immigrants settled, a recommended diphtheria cure was to "put one teaspoonful of flour of sulphur into a wine-glass of water," and if the patient's throat was too swollen to swallow, the mixture should be blown "through a quill into the throat."[38] This was a treatment preferable to what a sociologist reported she had been told was a sure cure for "dipthery" in Ireland: tying a frog to a string, which was pulled up and down the patient's throat until the frog "took out the lump."[39]

One of the most dangerously erroneous ideas of Italians was that "contact with a virgin was . . . an unfailing cure for gonorrhea."[40] A cure for women afflicted with chronic disease (but not for men) was door-to-door begging for money to pay a priest for a mass. Whether or not a woman needed the money was beside the point; the benefit was in the self-abasement.

Among the assorted misinformation North Italian Rosa Cavalleri believed was that it was possible to biologically inherit environmental events: "It's a wonder I didn't get the heart trouble . . . from all those scares . . . I didn't get it, but I guess my blood caught it and I passed it on to my Visella, because she got the heart trouble and died young. Probably she got it from me—from all those scares I had when I was a little girl."[41]

Innocent of basic biology and predisposed to accept almost anything said by an authoritative voice, such immigrants made easy prey for the era's patent medicine purveyors. These salesmen operated among natives, too, but immigrants were particularly gullible; the respect they had for American dress and manners made them targets for exploitation, while their inexperience with the language encouraged deception. Halloway's Salve or Pills was only one of hundreds of products that used extravagant language to promise effectiveness with multiple problems: "malaria,

---

* Erysipilis is a streptococcal skin infection accompanied by fever; logwood is a West Indian tree from which dye is extracted.

headache, all kinds of fever, epilepsy, rheumatism, colic, venereal disease, jaundice, liver complaint, constipation, indigestion, gravel, female diseases, dropsy and so forth." The salve was "a sure remedy in cases of sore feet, burns, swollen glands, backache, skin disease, sores, boils, cancer, mosquito bites, sore throat, scurvy and rheumatism."[42]

Advertising that equated cancer with mosquito bites was not unusual. A Wisconsin store offered a similarly wide range of goods, but its advertisement is especially revealing in its condescending attitude toward the Norwegians who settled there at midcentury—and especially toward the immigrant woman:

> Yes Nels—How do you do—It is true that I have lots of fine coffee for sale, and besides I have all sorts of things, . . . mercury, magnesia, cream of tartar, red pepper, black pepper . . . percussion caps, powder, shots, Poor Man's Plaster for sore back . . . Wineas' Vermifuge, which never fails to cure children for worms, violin strings, salve for cattle . . . and many other things which I could tell you about, if you did not have to leave Ola waiting outside. You must tell your wife to call and see Morgan in Waterford.[43]

The money that some families spent for cure-all products was a sadly substantial portion of their incomes. A Philadelphia widow named Gallardo, for example, had a daughter hospitalized the day after her husband died, a baby who died while she was at work, and a son who "did not look well"—but she "brought out an apronful of medicine bottles, 'all emptied by her children,' as she explained with evident pride."[44] It is entirely possible that, prior to the Pure Food and Drug Act, this loving mother was spending her hard-earned wages to slowly poison her children.

While they poured money into cures, spending for prevention was too hopeful a concept to be part of the fatalist's intellectual baggage. Indeed, many seemed to feel the idea of prevention was suspect, that it was wrong to interfere too much with the natural course of disease. Certain illnesses were inevitable, they thought, and, since prevention was impossible, the sooner a child got it, the better. In fact, even though they objected to the mysterious vaccination needle, some immigrant women understood the concept of immunity sufficiently that—in a hopeful blend of rationality and fear—they tried to create it by exposing their children to contagious diseases, with their fingers crossed in the wish for a mild case. So firmly did Sicilians believe in the inevitability of epidemics, for example, that there was an old adage to the effect that no girl could be called beautiful until it was seen what smallpox would do to her face.[45]

That the first smallpox vaccinations were administered in the 1700s was not part of their ken. Though they lived in the twentieth century, many immigrant women were essentially medievalists in believing that evil was inexorable; disease was part of God's will and one must simply accept it. To try to change fate was to contradict divine edicts, and modern medicine that claimed to prevent illness could well be the work of the devil. Instead, they believed, what will be, will be.

Superior Old World Ways

Studies of working women often included Americans as well as foreigners, and there are abundant examples of native women every bit as ignorant as the immigrants they often scorned. The most egregious example of many may be the American woman who "chased the Board of Health away" because she believed vaccinations killed; she also thought it bad luck to wash a baby's hair and had never cleaned the scalp of her fifteen-month-old son.[46]

Poor health practices were much more a matter of class than of nationality, for educated Europeans in America carried out good health practices, while uneducated persons who grew up in this country often refused to follow them. It is far from true that American health was clearly superior, for in almost any index of health, some other group outranked natives.*

Although the Irish-born, for example, had a scandalously high tuberculosis death rate in 1900—340 per hundred thousand compared with 113 for natives—the Jewish foreign-born had only 72.[47] Jews probably had acquired greater immunity because they were more likely to have lived in urban settings in Europe, but Jewish women also deserve some of the credit for this and other good health statistics, for they developed exceptional homemaking skills with their traditions of culturally imposed cleanliness and careful cookery.**

Americans are also outranked in many health indices by Scandinavians, who often saw their Old World health care as superior. They had learned to enforce quarantines there, for example; while urban immigrants hid their sick, Scandinavians in the Midwest took the opposite approach—even though most lived apart from others on farms. In Chippewa County, Minnesota, where many immigrants settled, a red card was placed on "any building in which Scarlet Fever exists," and when smallpox struck, even more severe measures were adopted: "the sick person and the entire family were removed . . . to an isolated pesthouse."[48]

They also protested the lack of stringent licensing for doctors in America and missed their own government-regulated system. Scandinavians were appalled that in America, "doctors are not appointed to any one district but settle where they see the best chances."[49] Elise Waerenskjold, who almost always praised her new home of Texas, nonetheless had a low opinion of its physicians: "Thorvald suffers daily from toothache as a result of all the calomel the doctors gave him when he was feverish," she wrote of her son. "How many times I have wished that we had as good doctors here as we had in Norway!" She felt, too, that such medical aid as was available was distributed in a discriminatory way:

---

* See, for example, page 26 of Chapter 2.

** The Irish, on the other hand, remained at or near the top of tuberculosis statistics throughout the whole of their long immigrant era. Much medical speculation centered on this, with the most frequently offered explanations being poor dietary habits and excessive use of alcohol.

Wilhelm got the fever and since there was no quinine in the store or anywhere else . . . Anne, the maid, had to do part of his work, so she got it, too, and then when I was left alone, Otto and I got it also. After a few days passed, however, we were lucky enough to get some quinine. It is wonderful how quickly and surely one can break the fever with quinine. In the shops it was soon sold out to doctors, and so the Norwegians got little. The result was that nine people died, most of whom surely would have been saved if they had had this remedy.[50]

Many decades prior to the American woman who "chased the Board of Health away," Jette Bruns wrote of vaccination as routine in her Westphalia, Missouri, community of settlers from Saxony. "This winter smallpox was around," she wrote in 1857, "and so there was a good deal of inoculation to be done."[51] Despite her husband's medical ability and supplies, however, their colony did not escape the epidemics that regularly swept the American South.

St. Louis, Memphis, Tampa, and other southern cities were repeatedly over-whelmed by yellow fever, typhus, and other disease caused by mosquitoes, fleas, and water pollution during torrid summers. When urbanites fled to the country, they carried disease to rural communities such as Westphalia. New Orleans, which is barely above swamp level, was especially vulnerable—and because it was also a port of entry for immigrants headed up the Mississippi to the Midwest, immigrants were often blamed as the cause of the epidemic. Instead, these northern Europeans were especially vulnerable, and even as far north as Minnesota, adjustment sickness was to be expected in the first summers. Jette wrote routinely in 1845 of those who "arrived during the heat of the summer":

The water had risen in all the rivers and brooks and tainted many [wells]. Twice people arrived here. The first ones were doing fairly well; the later ones, however, Heavens only knows why, became ill, and most of them have died. A few orphans have been taken care of nearby. The illness wiped out whole families. The sea voyage seemed to have weakened them considerably. It was horrible![52]

Four years later there was a cholera epidemic in St. Louis, where her son attended Catholic school:

We urged him to be careful . . . Suddenly at the beginning of July he appeared in our room. It seems the professors were satisfied to be rid of their worries. Nobody got sick at the college . . . , [but] it is believed that approximately ten thousand people died. Half of the inhabitants fled into the country . . . In this manner, it also came here, and the residents of our town were neighborly and did not pay attention to admonitions until it was too late. Thirteen people died; this was approximately one-third of the inhabitants.[53]

She worried over her husband, a hardworking physician who put in long days despite illness of his own severe enough that "for about two months he could not eat anything except soup." The community was fortunate to have the Bruns family, for most European physicians saw little reason to emigrate. That was the case in northern Iowa, where Gro Svendsen wrote in 1864 to her home in Norway: "Can you, Father, tell me how I can get my little boy vaccinated? I haven't heard of their doing it here, to say nothing of having seen it done . . . Is it impossible to send the vaccine in a letter? What do you think?"[54D]

Gro's father carefully packaged three bottles of vaccine, which arrived safely a month later. In North Dakota twenty years later, Norwegian Mrs. Realf Ottesen Brandt* wrote after her Lutheran-minister husband conducted a funeral for a smallpox victim: "With people living in crowded conditions . . . far from town and doctors, and having only limited means, the possibility of an epidemic was a serious menace. My husband had a talk with the doctor at Esteline and brought back a supply of vaccine points. Many people, old and young, came to the parsonage for free vaccination."[55]

Mrs. Assur Groth also spoke of a pastor in the 1850s who doubled as doctor—"Rev. Clausen helped those who were sick, as far as he was able"—but it was primarily women who were the health care providers in her community:

> Thirteen children were born to us, all of whom are still living . . . We never had a doctor in the house. At first there were no doctors and no medicines . . . Mrs. Mikkel Tollefson Rust served as midwife, and Sonnova Knutson, a trained midwife from Norway, served as midwife and also as doctor, practicing both cupping and bloodletting. There was no cholera in the new settlement, and no fever except ague, which troubled us some. The people were well, and very few died during the early years.[56]

Though Sonnova Knutson joined her male colleagues in the era's practice of bloodletting, undoubtedly she and other female medical practitioners rendered valuable service to their people: among them were Mrs. Johan Nordbes, Gunhild Grovum, Anne Sprigen, and Alberta Ulfers Hanssen, a nurse who, with her surgeon husband, served in the Civil War. Elisabeth Koren also practiced medicine, though she viewed it as something of an imposition and not an honor; because she was botanically knowledgeable, sick neighbors expected her attention as part of her role as the pastor's wife. Her diary often spoke of looking up diagnoses and prescriptions in medical books, while she also doubled as an unpaid pharmacist, making plasters, powders, and similar remedies.

German Jette Bruns also treated the patients of her absent husband. Even Americans consulted the couple, as she wrote in her playful third-person style: "If he was not at home, then Mrs. Bruns always had to have some 'fever medicine' ready and could advise the Americans on the time they were to take the medicine, the

* First names are not available for either Mrs. Brandt or Mrs. Assur Groth below, as both used only their husbands' names.

avoidance of sour milk, melons,* etc., in a most learned manner.[57] The respect that others had for her is clear in that she was addressed as "Doctoress Bruns."

Knowledgeable or not, every woman was assumed to be a nurse when illness struck her family. A Norwegian who wrote in 1850 of nursing her husband for four months was akin to millions of other women: "That sickness I can never forget. Think, in one terrible day and night, my husband lost eight pints of blood. That was the night before he was near death, and I was alone with him and my children . . . For seven weeks, I was not out of my clothes."[58]

Jette Bruns, too, frequently wrote of nursing not only her own eleven children but also an extended family of relatives and employees. She nursed to the point of exhaustion in the summers of the first years. In October of 1838 she wrote,

> The fever has been quite at home with us this summer; six times it reappeared. The last time was the worst. Perhaps my sensitivity contributed to that because of the constant illnesses I have had and the work that was left undone; now my strength does not want to come right back; the last few days I went to bed occasionally. My feet do not want to carry me up the hill again after I have gone down into the garden.[59]

What she did not say—except for the allusion to "sensitivity"—was that she was pregnant; we only discover that in a letter the following spring, after her third child was born. There would be many other instances of nursing others while she was sick herself. Often she was also alone, for most educated men in those days did a good deal of traveling: physicians and ministers rode a circuit of delivery to patients and parishes, while businessmen had to travel to suppliers and customers. Prior to telephones and good roads, men were inevitably gone much of the time, and many immigrant women on the frontier spent much of their young lives alone with their children.

Frontier isolation also increased the probability of serious accidents, for life there was inherently dangerous. Poisonous snakes and wild animals were a constant threat, while other risks were imposed by the daily use of fire, guns, axes. Death from accidents could be excruciating when there were no pain relievers to help the injured person cope with the trauma. Such was the case for a Minnesota woman, whose first name was not noted in the newspaper account of her horrifying death:

> On Monday afternoon a terrible accident occurred on the farm of Ingelbrecht Grinden, in Mandt township, in which Mrs. Grinden lost her life. It seems a team . . . became frightened and started to run away. Mrs. Grinden, seeing that one of her children was playing right in the path of the runaway . . . rushed out in front of the horses . . . to save the child but she was struck just below the pit of the stomach

---

* The reference to melons is not explained. After she had been in America several more years, she wrote, "Almost every day now we eat melons, a delicious fruit, better than the sun pears from the garden of the Spliethof."

by the end of the wagon tongue, which entered the abdominal cavity, completely disemboweling her . . . She lived twelve hours in this mutilated condition . . . She leaves a husband and four children, . . . the youngest of whom is only two months old.[60]*

Jette Bruns wrote of a similarly tragic case:

Today young Mrs. Huber was buried. It has been almost two weeks since she rushed into the arms of her husband already dying and enveloped in flames. She suffered tremendously. Her face, arms, and shoulders had been burned. Still affected by giving birth and by the death of her second son, she must have been overcome by dizziness, for she could give no other reason for the outbreak of the fire . . . The wounds began to heal, she could see with both eyes, but the fever became stronger . . . and she died last Monday . . . She was not yet twenty years old.[61]

Every Woman a Nurse: Health Education

As the decades passed, deaths of young people would increasingly be caused by accidents rather than illness—not because of an increase in accidents but rather because of a decline in disease. This happened when cures were discovered, of course, but to a surprising extent, disease reduction was due to health education.

Infectious diseases declined because of progress in sanitation—and while the hygiene of immigrant women received much of the blame for such illness, the truth is that most deaths were from diseases that were due to systems over which women had no control. It was poor sewage, water, and drainage systems that accounted for typhoid, typhus, dysentery, and other diseases, while the respiratory killers were worsened by chronic air pollution. These conditions changed when educational efforts brought changed behavior.

Attitudes on health issues also changed because health experts eventually educated themselves in immigrant mores and then adjusted their programs accordingly. By the end of the era, some authorities had become so empathetic that immigrants quarantined in the 1918 worldwide influenza epidemic were served by translators in even esoteric languages. The Akron YWCA, for instance, had "4 workers representing some 14 languages." All were "busy interpreting in hospitals and homes where foreign people were sick . . . [and] distributing the many language bulletins on Spanish influenza."[62]

---

* The author's Norwegian great-grandfather also was killed by a runaway team of colts. When he fell from the buggy, they dragged his head along the roadway for nearly a mile. He was in severe pain for over twenty-four hours before dying.

It was these cooperative attitudes on the part of both immigrants and public health officials that eradicated many of the nineteenth century's deadly diseases. Tuberculosis was especially susceptible to educational programs, for its cure, at the time, was largely in the prevention. Much of the language used in these efforts appealed to the usual immigrant desire to be "modern" and "American" in behavior. "DID YOU SEE THAT MAN SNEEZE!" read one poster, and went on to explain, "He covered it with a handkerchief. He is helping to PREVENT TUBERCULOSIS." Another spoke directly to gender differences: "MEN! IT'S UP TO US! Let's quit the unnecessary disease spreading habit of SPITTING. Women don't spit."[63]

The decline of tuberculosis was truly a triumph of public education, for cases fell dramatically long before there was effective medication. It was the decades-long accumulation of conversations between social workers and mothers that caused its decline, more than any medical care provided by physicians. It was education, too, that changed immigrant attitudes on clinics and hospitals. By 1934, a study of Italians in New York City could measure the success of such preventative medicine: there was an appreciable difference between those Italians who lived in the traditional Mulberry Street ghetto and those who had moved uptown, where a new public health clinic was well patronized.[64]

But to a large extent, the money that was spent in eradicating tuberculosis was spent because it is contagious. No precedent was set for similar preventative medicine in cases that were not personally threatening to the more affluent. The most apt example may be dental care, which still receives little attention among poor people. Virtually nothing was done in the immigrant era; aching teeth were simply pulled, usually at home and by a family member. A rare dental program was briefly funded by the all-male board of the New York Association for Improving the Condition of the Poor in the early 1920s—but only by cutting funding for prenatal care.[65]

Philanthropic archives are full of similar preventative programs that disappear without explanation. There are also numerous detailed proposals for surveys of needs, often by ethnicity, that would be very revealing if we knew the answers to the survey's questions—but there are no results, because the questions were never asked. In refusing to explore these needs, the erstwhile philanthropists displayed an attitude akin to that of the fatalistic immigrant, for how can illness or any other problem be solved if it is not even acknowledged?

4

The Immigrant Way of Death

Soon Angels: Infant and Child Mortality

Lawrence, Massachusetts, was a cotton mill town whose looms demanded a constantly fresh supply of labor. At the time of the Irish influx in 1850, life expectancy in Lawrence was a mere fifteen years. By 1880 it had climbed to twenty five, but epidemics swept through the sections of town crowded with new immigrants, and in the next decades, life expectancy dropped to twenty and then again to fifteen. After fifty years of "progress," as the twentieth century began, this important vital statistic was at the same level it had been before the Civil War.[1]

A life expectancy of fifteen years seems absurd on the face of it. Obviously the figure is misleading when applied to adults, and just as obviously it reflects a huge rate of infant mortality.

Lawrence, with infants accounting for 44% of all deaths in 1900,[2] was not alone. In an 1890 New York City tenement, of 138 children born in a three-year period, 61 had died.[3] A 1914 study of 370 working mothers showed that they had borne 1,758 children, of whom 437 had died.[4] Nor were cities the only places to have such shocking deaths of babies. The church records of a Wisconsin settlement of Norwegians at midcentury showed that of 194 deaths, 94 had been children under five.[5] Chippewa County, Minnesota, in the 1880s was even worse: 85% of recorded deaths were those of children.[6] There was additional cruelty for mothers in the easy trivialization of many of these deaths, for most were from seemingly "minor" childhood diseases.

For some women, it was more common to have children die than to have them live. One woman married nineteen years had fifteen pregnancies but only five living children; two others married twelve and thirteen years respectively each had ten pregnancies with only two living children; still another had six pregnancies in nine years with just two children. A woman widowed during the last of her eight pregnancies began working in her fourth month to support her two remaining children: she scrubbed floors until the day of delivery.[7] Babies born of such exhausted mothers were not good candidates for survival. Moreover, there was a clear correlation between the number of children a woman bore and the likelihood of infant death, as a survey in the Hull House area of Chicago revealed:[8]

CORRELATION BETWEEN THE NUMBER OF CHILDREN PER FAMILY
AND CHILD MORTALITY PER 1,000 BIRTHS, 1910

Number in Family	Child Mortality Rate
4 children and less	118
6 children and less	267
7 children and less	280
8 children and less	291
9 children and less	303

Despite these appalling statistics, a surprisingly large number of physicians argued that no correlation existed—or if it did, it was the mother's fault. Instead of acknowledging the debilitating effects to a woman's body from repeated pregnancies and even the obvious fact that she would have less time to give to each child, they argued that maternal skill was the overriding factor in infant mortality. Because they chose to believe that infant death was almost always related to poor care, they then had to argue that the more experienced a mother was, the more likely it would be that her babies would survive—despite the contradictory facts.[9]

The babies of immigrant mothers suffered disproportionately. A detailed study in New York State came down to this concise summary: "Whereas three children died to every ten native mothers, six died to every ten foreign mothers"—in other words, immigrant mothers experienced death twice as often.[10] The point was also clear by community: Passaic, New Jersey, and Holyoke, Massachusetts, for example, were both textile mill towns that attracted many immigrants; their infant mortality rates were two and three times those of similar-sized but nonimmigrant towns such as Jacksonville, Florida, and St. Joseph, Missouri. A baby in Perth Amboy, New Jersey, was almost seven times more likely to die before its first birthday than one born in Colorado Springs.[11]

Even in the same geographical area, however, infant mortality rates also varied by ethnicity. In New York in 1905–6, Italian children under five in different neighborhoods died at rates of 92 and 87 per 1,000, while blocks in the same area that had more Jewish residents dropped down to 52 and 50.[12] A decade later, another study showed Italian infant death rates to be five times higher than those of native whites and almost twice as high as immigrants in general.[13]

Clearly, the repeated pregnancy rates of Italian women played a significant role, but physicians also had a point in their argument that health at delivery was just one factor in infant mortality. Women could give birth to well babies, but if they could not care for them adequately, the baby would sicken. The single most important factor in whether a baby grows well is the food it receives, and there seems to have been considerable variation between ethnic groups on proper nutrition for infants. A detailed investigation of the subject showed that Italian, Polish, and French Canadian mothers were slow to begin solid foods, while Jewish and Irish women were more likely to balance diets. Portuguese women in this study exhibited particularly exotic ideas on infant nutrition, many of them beginning solids in the first week.[14]

But even if a woman understood what constituted an adequate infant diet, it was a herculean task to provide it. Foods sold before the Pure Food and Drug Act often were adulterated; pushcart merchandise was exposed to flies; refrigeration was unavailable; there were no blenders to puree meat or vegetables. The result was that children existed on crackers, cookies, and pudding—or the milk of a malnourished mother. In more than half of the cases where breast-feeding ceased, it was because the woman no longer could produce milk.[15] The baby would ail and the mother would mourn and no one would ask why except to say it was God's will.

Acceptance of death is a constant theme. One social worker reported that they started this mental self-protection from the very beginning of motherhood, believing that "the first one has to go."[16] Another confirmed this, saying of the mothers she studied: "They are strangely apathetic toward the loss of their children by death. Almost as soon as the first pang of sorrow is past, the bereaved mother is ready to say that the little one is 'better off' and to speak of death as a merciful release from a life of hardship."[17] Nevertheless she added, "The same mother who resents the coming of children and resigns them so apathetically to death, will toil fourteen hours a day and seven days a week to keep up a house for the young lives in her charge."[18] German Angela Heck was one of those "strangely apathetic" women. In a long letter in the fall of 1862, she detailed the Civil War and wrote extensively of family finances before dealing with the death of her son in three short sentences: "I lost a five-year-old boy to dropsy. Now it's about a year ago, when my husband left. His whole regiment helped bury him. My daughter is 7 years old . . ."[19] She made no expression of grief, not even mentioning the child's name.

But Angela Heck also "toiled fourteen hours a day," sewing for a living not only when her husband was gone to war but from the very day they docked in New York. Such toil was a way of life for a Bohemian woman who worked as a maid while her mother cared for her children. Elizabeth Stern, just beginning social work around 1900, wrote that in a dilapidated tenement

was an old woman . . . with a baby in her arms, a little child at her knee . . . and a
little body of a boy twenty hours dead . . . on the table. Her daughter was working
in a flat in the Bronx and would not be home until the following day . . . I lifted the
old woman to the bed, put the dead little boy on two chairs and covered the tiny
face, so still and frozen and thin, wrapped the two other children and then ran out
to buy milk and crackers and meat at the corner delicatessen. I cleaned up the house,
washed the boy and girl and then sat and waited for the mother . . . [She] came into
the room [and] saw me. Her parcels dropped. She came over and pulled back the
cover . . . I helped place the little figure in the coffin. I watched the mother bid it
good-by. In those days servants were not ladies of importance; a good job was
precious. She could not even go to see her child buried . . . I went with the old
grandmother and heard her anguished cry.[20]

The mother's grief took second place to the needs of the present, and she went
to work rather than to her child's funeral. Elisabeth Koren, writing in Iowa in the
1850s, was shocked by the seemingly easy acceptance her Norwegian neighbors
showed in the death of their son; to her there was an excess of stoicism. "They must
feel or bear their sorrows in a different way from what I could," she wrote. "As I
listened to their way of talking of it, I was not able to say a word . . . It seemed as if
the main thing they were thinking of was that the father would not now have his son
to help with the work."[21]

Linka Preus, like Elisabeth Koren, was educated and married to a Lutheran
minister. When her four-year-old boy became critically ill, she tried to be stoic but
only compounded her grief with guilt. She wrote in the long-running conversation
with God that was her diary:

Some eight to fourteen days ago, I thought Thou wouldst take my little Christian
Keyser unto Thyself. Never did I believe that taking leave of such a little one would
be so grievous. We all said good-bye to him; then God let him fall into a deep sleep;
for a day and a half he lay in a death-like coma, breathing heavily. Finally came a
change and to our great joy he improved steadily . . .

For Jesus sake Thou wilt forgive me; but it seems, now that Thou hast permitted
me to keep Christian, that my love for Thee is greater than it was before. Alas, my
Father, forgive me; a very great sinner am I.[22]

Another educated Norwegian, Elise Waerenskjold, who lived in Texas at midcentury, offered no explanation for the sudden death of her son except as an example
of God's enigmatic will. She wrote of the Sunday afternoon Death's Angel called,
while her family was out visiting:

I wanted to go home to bring in the sheep . . . Thorvald wanted to go with Mama
and on the way chatted quite cheerfully with me. We had gone just about 10 steps
after he last spoke when, without complaint, without a sound, he sank down at my

side; he spoke no more until Wednesday morning when he regained consciousness and could speak a few words and gave Mama the last kiss. I was so happy then, for I believed he would recover, but that was not to be. At 4:00 he died.[23]

Elise found comfort in the fact that the day before Thorvald had asked several questions about death and resurrection. Even though she was a thoughtful and independent woman, she never looked for a medical explanation of this mysterious death.

A study of English, Irish, and German women in New York found a similar lack of scientific curiosity into the causes of their babies' deaths. A German mother whose four-year-old child died in 1894 was reported thus: "Mother does not know cause of death; died in hospital; mother never thought of asking nurse."[24] Death was simply inexplicable. The mind-set against exploration of cause was so strong that many immigrants refused to allow autopsies; the wholeness of the body in the afterlife was more important to them than medical reasoning.[25]

This fatalistic acceptance of death could be the cause of more death, for some did not learn from their mistakes. There was, for example, the Irish woman who had borne eight children; four infants died in four years and two others as teenagers. Of her eight children, only two were alive, but she seemed to count herself lucky, for her sister-in-law in Ireland had borne twenty with only four reaching adulthood.[26] Her life was such that, like other women, she had to believe her children were better off not to have lived.

"One son," reminisced an old Irish mother, "would be fifty-two if he had lived through his first year. Another son was born in 1853. In 1855 Katie was born. She died in 1868. Then there was Mike and Stephen and Pat, God knows I don't remember thim [sic] all, but they is blessed for they died young." Similar fatalism was shown by a German American who, though she had grown up in New York, nevertheless seemed to have so little comprehension of the possibility of positive intervention that, by her own statement, she did not "know enough" to take her baby to a doctor, though he was sick for the entire twenty months of his life.[27]

In fact, the death of little babies perhaps was sometimes a secret relief to overwrought mothers. Kate Bond, an Englishwoman in Kansas, typifies this; incredible as it may be, her letter seems to say that she will mourn her baby later when she has more time: "We had a little boy born the 23rd of December," she wrote. "He lived to be eight weeks old. As soon as harvest is over and things straight I will not forget him."[28]

But when a grown daughter died, she was distraught. This daughter, unlike the baby, was a personality and provided companionship for her mother on the isolated frontier. Her letter read:

I suppose you have heard of Maggie's death. I miss her so much . . . It is so lonely without her. But I suppose we should have parted if she had lived and perhaps it is better as it is, for I know where she is now and wants for nothing . . . She was ready and willing to go and missed a troublesome world.[29]

It was as if such women were afraid to be resentful of death, afraid to express a justifiable complaint of their hard lot, lest worse befall. Always there is the rationalization that the child probably would have had an unhappy life. Kate Bond and women like her must have found this reasoning solacing, for they never failed to offer it. When a friend back in England was bereaved, Mrs. Bond comforted her with written beauty seldom seen among farmwives, an articulateness motivated by strong feeling:

> We was sorry to hear of you loss. For I know it is a loss that none but a mother can feel. But, Ellen, when the first pain is over you will thanck [sic] God in your heart that it has pleased Him to take him out of this world of sin and sorrow . . . It seems as though there is extray strength given us for our trials. The other children will miss him, I know, but you must try not to fret too much for their sakes. Peter is in Heaven and at rest and it is those that are here that need our care now. If it had not been for my younger ones I thinck they would have laid me beside [Maggie] before now. So thinck of yours now and it will help you in your trouble.[30]

Gro Svendsen waited until her seventh child for the daughter she longed for, and then the eighth was a girl, too. Her joy, however, was soon taken away, for the second daughter died at twenty months. "I enclose a picture of my little Sigri," she wrote. "It was taken eight days before she died. We realized that death would soon be coming, and we did want to have some memory of her. She was then very weak and thin, but the picture is all we have."[31] When Gro's next baby was another girl, she exclaimed, "We were happy beyond words to get this child for we feel that she is a special gift from God . . . , resembling very much the one we lost."[32]

They named her Sigri Christine, a combination of memorialization and cautious distinction, but Gro could not fully put her mind at ease. Much like the women of southern Europe who were candid about their belief in the evil eye, this Norwegian Lutheran feared for her child: "I have a feeling, a foreboding, that this little one, who is so very dear to all of us, will not be with us long. I feel that the good Lord has given her to us for just a short while."[33] Wary of seeming to tempt fate, she protected her mental health by anticipating the worst. Whether because of magic, religion, or a realistic assessment of infant mortality facts, many mothers were like Gro in fearing to love their children unabashedly, lest they be taken away.

Few women, however, experienced the trauma that befell Jette Bruns. She wrote her brother in Germany on October 17, 1841:

Dear Heinrich!

We all had dysentery. Hermann [age 8] was the first to become sick. On the 8th of September Max [age 4] and Johanna [age 2] were afflicted by it. The latter was indescribably sick and died on the 13th of September at 2:30 in the morning. "Mother, mother!" she cried loudly. I still believe I can hear her. On Tuesday Rudolph [eight months] became sick, then I on Thursday, then Bernhard [brother] and Bruns [husband]. On Sunday the 19th, at 1:30 during the night, Max died. It was the third night that I had feared his end almost any hour. He quietly fell asleep and passed away. It was God's will to also take Rudolph from me. He died on Sunday, the 2nd of October, at 7:30 in the morning. He was buried at 5 o'clock on Sunday. All three of them rest side by side now.[34]

A month later, writing on November 15, her mournfulness is clear:

Now all wishes, all striving have been quieted! I even no longer wish to go back to you, to Germany! . . . How I wish I could have said farewell to the world six weeks ago . . . It really hit me too hard that I also had to lose little Rudolph. It had been twelve days since his dysentery had been over. I had already tried again to breast-feed him . . . Johanna always played so nicely with him. She was the pride of her father, an angel on earth . . . She had a little doll (a rarity here), which everybody had to admire, and at night she held her in her arms . . . Max, who was more serious and deliberate, became happier and more confident through her . . . They were always marching one after the other, Max in front, Hanna a few steps behind . . . You see, dear Heinrich, that I do not tire of talking about the little ones.[35]

Openly and frankly grieving, Jette was unlike most others in exhibiting some anger about her fate and even a bit of doubt on eternal reward. She qualified heaven as "probably" beautiful, and when her tenth anniversary occurred on Johanna's name day, the loss of her daughter overwhelmed any pleasure in remembrance of her wedding. "I loved all these children so much," she said, "but the girl should not have been taken with them—it was not right."[36]

Death continued to stalk her, despite the skills of her physician husband. "In August, 1847, we had a boy," she recorded, "a very delicate, early plant. We wanted to name him Adolf. I was sick, and he died in spite of the anxious care which I devoted to him for over eight days."[37] In 1853, she curtly clarified confusion caused by missing mail: "My letter was a repetition of an earlier one . . . I had informed you of Albert's death and don't like to write about it again."[38] Decades later, she spoke again of his death, an unusual one only slightly better explained than that of Elise Waerenskjold's Thorvald. Little Albert, aged five, Jette said, was lost to "a sunstroke on the 24th of August 1851 . . . He had forgotten to put on his hat."[39]

Mothers' and Other Adult Death

Mothers weren't the only ones to mourn, nor infants the only ones to die. When Gro Svendsen died in the delivery of her tenth baby, her husband's grief was deep, as his love had been. He found it very hard to inform her parents. "I must arouse myself and try to write you . . . It is not so easy to write." Though his letters tried to be manly, his unhappiness cannot be hidden:

> I also want to send you a lock of my dear Gro's hair . . . How much I miss her cannot be told . . . You, too, will feel the loneliness for her who is gone . . . I want to tell you about Gro's grave. It has a white marble stone, on which are engraved the date and place of her birth, the date and place of her death, and the names of those she left behind. Last of all, a verse from David's Psalms: "In Thee, O Lord, do I put my trust; let me never be put to confusion." . . . I myself planted a tree on her grave to keep the weeds away. Her friends planted flowers. The grave is enclosed by a pretty (white) picket fence.[40]

Gro's husband must have found the reminders of her around the Iowa farm where they had lived too sorrowful to bear, for soon this widower with nine small children packed up and moved to a Dakota homestead. He cared for them alone, not remarrying as was the custom of the day, and his life was hard with frequent visitations from death. Only four of the ten children Gro brought into the world would live to adulthood.

Some women seemed to grow so tired, so achingly weary of their frustrated lives that they only wanted to lay their burdens down. Barbro Ramseth's sister-in-law Marit seemed to will herself to death; Barbro tried "everything to get her to talk, but no. Once she said she would rather die, but that is all I could get out of her." The depression was profound, and two years later, Barbro wrote her family in Norway, "God be praised that Marit has passed away, and has been allowed to lay down her wanderer's staff."[41]

Such was the case also of an Englishwoman, whose father cried out with loneliness after his daughter resigned herself to death: "Isabella never was well after her baby was born. She knew she was dieing and made all her arrangements, talked about it as calmly as if she were going on a journey," he wrote sadly. "I had all the advise I could get for her but it was no use. Death was there and we could do her no good."[42]

Though she did not wish to escape from life in the way that some women did, Elise Waerenskjold exhibited a similarly abstract attitude in speaking of her own possible death. "The baby arrived well and happy," she wrote at age forty-four:

> I cannot express to you how glad I was that everything went well because, after all, I am no longer young, and therefore, I was worried for fear I might have to leave my beloved children. Neither Wilhelm nor I have a single relative in this country, so it isn't easy to say what Wilhelm would have done with the children if I had died, because it is absolutely against the custom in this country for a white girl to keep house for a widower—and as to a stepmother, well, they are seldom good.[43]

Like other women, Elise's concern was first of all for her family, as though she is embarrassed to mention any thought—much less fear—for herself. She followed the pattern exhibited by most immigrant women in not telling her family of danger until it was over—but when the news was bad, this policy only increased the shock for those in Europe. Wilhelmina Krumme, who emigrated as a single woman and married another German in America, was healthy when her first child was born in 1839. She did not mention illness to her family—but, on the other hand, she did not tell them of either her wedding or her pregnancy until after the fact. In 1842, her husband sent this traumatic letter to her family:

> The reason I must write you a sad letter, which I cannot conceal from you, is that my dear and your dear Willemina* fell sick on February 14th. And the Lord God who called her into this life and gave her to me took her away on April 21st at midnight when she passed away in my arms, and she died of consumption and dropsy . . At first I sometimes wished that if it were God's will then all three of us should lie in one coffin, but it was not God's will, but I still miss her all the time. For I can tell you that it was almost 6 years ago since we swore our love to one another and since that time it never grew cold . . . Even if I can no longer see her with my eyes, my thoughts are always with her, and I will never forget her, since we never had any quarrels, instead we lived in peace and harmony.[44]

The fatal dangers for women were childbirth and disease, while they were more likely to be widowed by accidents. "Horse and wagon accidents were common" among men, and men were also more likely to die from exposure. The blizzard of 1873 was an especially severe one: 61 Minnesota people were "frozen to death and bodies found," while bodies were never recovered in other cases. Total casualties were put at 101, and the state appropriated $50 to "each widow whose husband perished."[45]

Deaths from gunshots, drowning, and suicide were also common causes of adult death on the frontier. Drowning was less likely to be related to recreation than to transportation: It was "venturing out on thin ice" that was the most frequent cause. Suicides of both men and women "were common on the prairie," but those most apt to take their own lives were "elderly male immigrant farmers," who, oddly enough, were likely to kill themselves in the spring months. Newspapers were quite candid about reporting suicides as such, though they often added an explanation of "temporary insanity."[46] The "Latin Farmers," educated Europeans who attempted to set up utopian communities on frontier land, were particularly prone to suicide.[47]

In the cities, disease was more likely to be the cause of adult death, especially among women. The following table shows that there was considerable disparity in the likelihood of death, depending on where a woman was born:[48]

---

* The name is spelled this way here, though elsewhere it appears as Wilhelmina.

WOMEN'S DEATH RATE FROM ALL CAUSES BY
NATIONAL ORIGIN, NEW YORK CITY, 1906

Italy	36	Bohemia	17
Ireland	24	Scotland	15
Austria/Hungary	23	United States	14
France	22	England	13
Switzerland	19	Germany	12
Russia/Poland	18	Sweden	11

The Italian mortality rate, high though it was, arguably was still worse than the statistics reflected, for, as an Italian physician said, "All adult Italians once affected by a serious disease go back to Italy to die among the vines and orange groves." To get proper statistics, he suggested, health officials "should count the wan-faced women that crowd the steerage of departing ships, or we should search the Bureaus of Vital Statistics of the little towns in Calabria or Sicily, where they swell the local death rate, and import from America tuberculosis where first it was unknown."[49] Though they seldom went home to cold, damp Ireland, the second-ranked Irish also were likely to die of tuberculosis, with a rate of 473 compared with the United States' 157. The Irish also died from heart disease at a significantly higher rate than other groups.[50]

In addition to these chronic diseases, America regularly hosted epidemics that struck immigrants with particular certainty, and when newcomers died soon after arrival, their survivors might find only cold comfort for their grief. Doubtless thousands of women buried their loved ones in lonely bottomlands, a half world away from the sympathy they would find at home. To leave one's husband in a New Orleans cemetery and continue up the Big Muddy alone took tremendous courage, and probably there were women who instead took the next ship back to Europe. Often there would be no money for that, however, and a woman would simply have to make her way in a world where death was a frequent visitor.

Though emotionally devastated by the loss of her three little children, Jette Bruns seemed to feel her brother's death just as deeply, for he was her only sibling in America and, as she said, "had been with me since he was born." She wrote in November 1858:

> Franz was ill. We nursed him, but now our Good Lord has called him. He died yesterday afternoon, on the 28th, at 4 o'clock.
>
> It is still so new to me, and my head is still so upset. Yet I shall report to you. Approximately two months ago he experienced pain in his abdomen . . . He was visibly getting weaker . . . and we called for a priest. He answered only when asked, did not make any comments, showed no concern, no hope. Only once I told him, "Soon you will be well." And then he looked at me with such a serious and profound look that both of us were satisfied. This was his farewell.[51]

His wife, also a German, had died of tuberculosis when their children were little, and they were teenagers when Jette assumed their care. "The children are hit hard," she wrote, adding that Franz was doing well financially and "probably never, as long as he had been here, was so satisfied and full of hope. And just now, as he had the best prospects for himself and for his children, he had to leave them."[52]

More grief was to come. Only four years later, one of these orphaned teenagers died from wounds in the Civil War. Jette delayed writing to Germany about this because "I wanted to spare our uncle. For I do not doubt that the death of his godchild and his last namesake will hit him harder." The young man had been shot in Tennessee and suffered further from frostbite in a field hospital. "We found his name on the list of the wounded," she explained, and Jette's husband went to bring him home:

Widow Kari Froslan, who emigrated from Norway to Minnesota in 1871, with her teenage children and the casket of her husband Hans, who was killed by a runaway horse in 1897. Note that Kari wears a shawl even on this formal occasion, while her American daughters wear hats. (PHOTOGRAPH BY J. T. RICHARDSON, ST. JAMES, MINNESOTA; COURTESY OF ELSIE SCHULTZ)

We all hoped for the best. . . . He was conscious, he prayed with the priests till the evening, and at times his thoughts wandered away . . . As it went on he became fearful, and he shouted, "Mother, Mother, I am so afraid!" I said then, "Casper, in Heaven it will be better!" "Yes, I believe that," he answered, and his voice was as firm and deep as that of his grandfather and his father. Then he mostly dozed, the phlegm rose higher, there was some twitching, and it was all over . . . He was a good boy. We would have liked to have kept him.[53]

A little more than a year later, she lost her son, a twenty-year-old Union captain: "Our Heinrich is gone," Jette wrote. "The handsome, good boy, the pride of his father, the quiet worry and joy of his mother. He fell in battle at Iuka, Mississippi, shot through the chest . . . It seems impossible . . . It hit us so unexpectedly, like a thunderbolt. It is too hard! . . . The whole war, and the whole miserable world—one gets so tired of it!"[54]

Finally, her husband might also be considered a casualty, for overwork and anxiety probably were contributing factors in the death of a physician in his sixties who was busy with both Civil War politics and with its medical effects. She wrote with anxiety of his illness, reporting treatment by a doctor who was also a member of the legislature and by "a very well-known regimental surgeon." Neither could stay the course of "fever, pain, deliriousness," and she wrote, "we believed he could not stand it any longer. He admitted this and made all kinds of arrangements . . . This constant vacillation between fear and hope numbs me."[55] Yet almost another month would pass before she wrote:

On Friday, 1 April, my beloved husband died. He suffered much, and yet it hit me suddenly . . . I was sitting with Ottilie in the room and writing . . . Then I went downstairs and outside to the two boys. After about two minutes I was back upstairs again, and his life had escaped. Ottilie had not noticed anything. I was terribly upset, and I could not get over it at first that I had spent day and night for these past twelve weeks with him and had failed him just during his last moment . . .

I have still not quite come to my sense yet. He was buried on Saturday beside brother Franz with the two boys in front of them . . . I do not yet know how I can continue living . . . Such a deadly lonesomeness takes hold of me.[56]

They would have celebrated their thirty-second anniversary the following month. In widowhood, she continued to endure the deaths of younger people. Her son-in-law, of whom she was very fond, died in 1871, leaving Jette's daughter with two small boys—two weeks prior to the birth of a third. In 1875, when she was sixty-one and the news came that her brother's child had died soon after birth, she wrote: "Since it was my destiny to lose seven children, big and small, I perhaps know more how to sympathize than others. But even now in the death of relatives, it grieves me most when they are children. I never completely get over it."[57]

Jette would live on for most of three decades, enduring more pain but also much pleasure, as she embraced life fully and tended to flowers even after she was blind. She lived in America for more than sixty years, and most of her family in Germany died before she did. Young Emilie Koenig, in contrast, left a family shocked by her death. They had been wary about her emigration, and less than a year later, she was dead. Twelve days after the birth of a daughter, she was perilously ill. "She prayed along with me," her husband wrote:

> After that her face became transfigured, and she said joyfully and softly, "Now farewell, world." As she saw me standing there so sorrowful, she said, "Why do you sorrow so much? Do not be sorrowful, I am going to everlasting joy." . . . On her face lay a saintly expression of rest and peace, so that I could not tear myself away from her.[58]

Such acceptance of death was typical. Rosa Cavalleri, too, not only looked with fatalism on her possible death, but even described it with macabre humor. Her physician had announced there was little hope and a settlement house worker sobbed at her bedside, while Rosa, in a curious role reversal, comforted her nurse: "Don't cry like that, Miss Taylor. I go to heaven and I'll pray God for you and for Chicago Commons." But Rosa lived, to the chagrin of her son-in-law, and laughed about her brush with death. "That new husband Visella got, he was mad at me that I didn't die . . . He was running around to get all the money I had. And there I fooled them—I didn't die. They were so mad."[59]

Saying Farewell: Immigrant Funerals

Money did indeed matter all too much, and often death demanded a resigned attitude because there was no place for emotion in lives so overwhelmed by the practical. Frequently the mourning for a loved one was cut short by the pressures of the immediate: where was the money for the burial? "Many a mother," said one charity doctor, "has told me at her child's death bed, 'I cannot afford to lose it. It costs too much to bury it.'"[60]

In immigrant cities extended families and networks of lifelong friends created a strong social obligation for an elaborate funeral, no matter how poor the bereaved family was. Funerals among almost every Christian immigrant group that was well established in urban areas, especially the Italian and the Irish, were an occasion. Wakes lasted for days, with food and drink provided; the bereaved was expected to provide an ornate hearse, flowers, expenses for a priest and mortician and burial plot, and new clothes and countless other details. Tradition—and the fear of the neighbor's gossip—prevailed against the practical admonitions of the social workers, and the debts were made. "Funerals of children," reported a New York case worker in 1907, cost from $10 to $90, and for adults $100 to $200 . . . The ostentatious display in flowers and number of carriages is much to be regretted. One family, which was dependent most of the time, insisted on having two carriages for the funeral of their son, with no one to ride in the second one, but, as the mother said, "Sure, it's all I can do for him." They were burdening themselves with a debt which it would take years to pay. In one case the funeral of a child four years old cost $84, and there was no insurance. The mother has been years trying to pay for it.[61]

A 1913 study of widows showed that approximately two-thirds of the resources available to most widows—insurance, savings, and everything else—were used immediately for the husband's funeral. Of the 237 widows who gave information on the cost of their husbands' funerals, all but 86 had spent over $100 to have their mate laid to rest in style.[62] At the average wage most widows could expect to earn, a $100 funeral could be the equivalent of a third of her annual income. Nor were Catholics the only group to indulge in expensive funerals. A German Lutheran woman who had not been on good terms with her husband nonetheless gave him "a fine layout," and explained to her charity case worker that she "was anxious to give her husband 'a big funeral' in spite of the fact that she did not think he deserved it . . . as the neighbors would talk if she didn't."[63]

The worst thing that could possibly happen was burial by the state. Fear of Potter's Field filled an immigrant heart, and in many homes, the insurance money came before food, before rent, even before the medical aid that would bring life, not death. Death was the greater fear, and with its frequency, perhaps the greater reality. Their experience was summed up by an Italian woman whose child died: "I had to pay $95 for the funeral; with drinks it came to $115 . . . I thought it was bad enough to lose the child without having to do without insurance money, so since then I have had insurance."[64]

Sociologists examining family budgets sometimes failed to understand these realities of immigrant culture: One said, for example, "for some unaccountable reason more of the low-income families carried life insurance than did those with the higher incomes."[65] But this was not at all "unaccountable" from their point of view, for it was not so much life insurance as death insurance—its purpose was not to ensure income for a family after its breadwinner died but rather to pay for funerals. Policies were carried on children as well as on adults, not because the children's earning capacity was worth insuring, but because there was even greater likelihood that a child would need a funeral.

The city, with its established businesses interested in promoting funerals, encouraged excess in memorialization, but on the frontier there was little opportunity—or pressure—to bankrupt oneself on behalf of the dead. Among the Scandinavians and Germans who largely settled the Midwest, long wakes with heavy drinking at a time of sorrow were scandalous. Yet the simplicity of such funerals was a step down from what some were accustomed to in Europe, especially in the early days.

Wilhelm Krumme, for example, described his wife's 1842 funeral in the mountains near Pittsburgh: "I also want to tell you the circumstances of the burial, that here in this country many people are buried like animals, but I had the preacher to the house . . . the text you can find in Job 19, verses 25 to 27."[66] A half century later, Barbro Ramseth still viewed Wisconsin funerals as rather austere compared with those at home: "We meet at the house and everyone goes to the church together where the pastor preaches a sermon, with no refreshments. There have been many funerals here this summer, young people have been dying of tuberculosis."[67]

The funeral of Emilie Koenig, also, may have been too stark to comfort the family she had left in Germany only a year before. Her husband described it in two sentences: "On the 29th I gave her a Christian burial on God's acre. The whole congregation was present." She had died just the day before, but quick burials were necessary in the heat of summer, and her husband, as the only available minister, had no choice but to preach the sermon. It was another practicality of life, and his letter went on to others: "I will keep Emilie's things for the baby, if that is all right with you. I am told, however, that the linens will not keep so well because of the sea voyage . . . so will sell them." At the same time, he asked his in-laws for a picture of his dead wife, for he had none and "would like that very much. Please send it soon. I now am . . . even more lonely."[68]

Harshly simple funerals that took place the day after death spared the bereaved from expense, but frontier funerals may well have been too bleak. Aaste Wilson told of burials in her Norwegian community.

> There were always two meals, one before they went to the graveyard and the other after they came back. Simple black homemade coffins were used, with nails driven halfway into the covers. The service opened with a hymn: "Who Knows How Near Me is My Death." . . . Father, a layman, usually had charge of the services. He would give a talk in remembrance of the departed one and give thanks for him. Thereupon the people walked past the coffin for a last look, and immediately afterward we heard the sad sound of the hammering of the nails on the coffin lid . . . The coffin was put in a wagon, driven to the graveyard, and the mourners walked behind it. Men took turns in digging the grave. When it was ready they placed their spades crosswise on it and sang, "Now the Grave is a Comfort to Me, for Thy Hand Shall Cover Me." Then all said the Lord's Prayer, and that was the end. It was simple but dignified and there was a Christian spirit and a deep sincerity in it all . . . They did it as well as they could.[69]

5

RELIGION
HERE AND HEREAFTER

New World, New Ideas

On Rose Cohen's first Saturday in America, her father took her for a walk. He had preceded her here and no doubt was happily anticipating the little treat he planned for her—Rose's first taste of watermelon.

> I felt proud of him that he had credit at so beautiful a fruitstand. As I received the melon in my fingers I saw father take his hand out of his pocket and hold out a coin. I stood staring at him for a moment. Then I dropped the melon on the pavement and ran . . . My father had touched coin on the Sabbath! Oh, the sin! . . . Then I remembered Yanna, who, on hearing that father was in America, and feeling that perhaps we were too happy over it, came one day to torment grandmother. "The first thing men do in America," she said, "is to cut their beards and the first thing women do is to leave off their wigs. And you . . . you who will not break a thread on the Sabbath now, will eat swine in America."[1]

Her father had indeed cut his hair, and now she saw that he violated the Sabbath, too. The poor girl felt that his soul, and probably hers, were doomed. Yet in a few years Rose's father would be admonishing her to remember the old ways as she edged dangerously away from Judaism.

For some immigrants, the strangeness of America made even more necessary the security to be found in clinging to the old faith. For others, part of the freedom of the New World was the liberty to break away from the religion in which they had been born. For most, of course, the process was an evolutionary one, and the immigrant herself was generally not aware that she was changing her religious views. Others never did change.

To midwestern Scandinavians, the Lutheran church brought the serene remembrance of home, and they turned out in great numbers for services. Even the largest available house empty of furniture would not permit everyone to crowd in, as Elisabeth Koren wrote: "I did not have such a bad seat . . . until the communicants had to come forward. But then, with many others, I had to give up my place . . . There were many more outside than in; they crowded about the windows and doors in order to hear.[2]

Naturally the burden of rearranging furniture and cleaning for the crowd fell on the congregation's women. Gro Svendsen complained that though funds had been collected for a church building, "a great deal more is needed in order to build. In America money was said to be so plentiful, and it may be. But it's hard to get any of it when it's to be used for the common good, for such as teachers' salaries, ministers' salaries, and other expenses connected with the church."[3]

Like a number of other women of her background, Gro frankly missed Norway's state church and deplored the religious freedom of Americans. The lack of Sunday restrictions also bothered her: "Coming into town . . . we saw the Americans working just as on any other day . . . It was disturbing, accustomed as we are to the quiet and peace of the Sabbath."[4] So irreverent did she find her rural Iowa community that at one point—perhaps in a state of mental depression—Gro wrote that she knew "only one person, an old woman from Flo, who, I think, is sincerely religious."[5]

Undoubtedly, many people did come to church to see others as much as from pure piety. Elise Isely, a Swiss woman in frontier Kansas, candidly admitted that the social functions of the church were as important as the spiritual:

> City people surfeited with close daily contact with others . . . can hardly understand the hunger for church that pioneer families had . . . Out of our desire for company as well as out of our need for spiritual development, we dressed our children in their best clothing and journeyed to Fairview . . . If we could avoid it, none of our family ever missed attendance; if it rained we put up an umbrella; if it snowed we wrapped up in blankets . . . We were happy in being there. We no more thought of missing church than of missing our meals.[6]

Others made even stronger efforts to get to church: Elisabeth Koren wrote of a "grown-up girl" who had walked twelve miles under the mistaken impression that church services were to be held that day. She was then "at a loss for a place to stay, being a total stranger."[7] This was the case of many during the settlement decades, for the clergy could not easily serve their far-flung laity. When the preacher appeared, farm families dropped their weekday work to worship, and the minister caught up with the community's backlog of baptisms and weddings.

The relative infrequency of religious services increased their appeal, and the camp meetings of revivalist American sects therefore were especially attractive. Not only were these glorious social events for isolated women, but the evangelistic congregations were fascinating to immigrants accustomed to the stolid state churches of Europe. Ann Whittaker, an Englishwoman in Illinois during the 1840s and 1850s, was smitten by the Baptist religion; its blessings became the lengthy theme of her letters:

> We have had a great revival of religion in our neighborhood . . . There has been a great many of the wickest [sic] characters brought to a knowledge of the truth . . . I can truly say I feel more satisfied the [sic] I ever did since we came into the country . . . I find for my own part that there is nothing like living to God . . . My dear Brother, if you have not begun to serve the Lord it is high time to be up and doing.[8]

Both Norwegian Elise Waerenskjold and German Jette Bruns, on the other hand, were contemptuous of their friends who deviated from the traditional ways and attended these obstreperous revivals. Nevertheless, both were curious enough to visit one. Jette went soon after her arrival in Missouri and reported to her family in 1837: "Some women became enrapted, others moaned mightily (this is a special sign of reverence), others wept . . . Americans who do not believe in anything nevertheless ride there, shake their heads, and smoke, talk, chew, etc., which does not particularly please the preachers, who often have to ask them to quiet down."[9] Elise, too, investigated a camp meeting in Texas and was shocked by what she saw: "One after another they begin to sing and clap their hands, crying out 'Glory! Glory!' as loudly as they can. They begin pounding on the ones nearest to them, throwing themselves on their knees or on their backs, laughing and crying—in short, conducting themselves like perfectly insane people."[10]

These practices of southern fundamentalists were less likely to appear in Indiana, where Emilie Koenig lived in 1853, but she nevertheless found American churches scandalously different. "I heard things about so-called Christian pastors that one would absolutely not believe in Germany," she wrote. "Here in the neighborhood is a so-called temperance sect that actually celebrates Holy Communion by using buttermilk instead of wine . . . Methodists also cause disturbances."[11]

She could not believe that Germans would be interested in these churches, and down in Texas, Elise Waerenskjold shared her feelings. She was saddened to report that what was so repulsive to her was attractive to some of her friends: "Several of the Norwegians have abandoned their Lutheran faith. Andreas and Mads Vincentz have . . . gone over to the Carmelites, Marie Grogaard to the Episcopalians, Mother Staack to the Methodists, and her brother to the Baptists. I wish very much," she lamented, "we could get a good Lutheran minister."[12] It was an oft repeated sentiment in isolated settlements such as hers, for many went years and decades without spiritual leadership from their native church. When a group of German Catholics, for example, settled in Arkansas in 1880, the first mass was not said for more than five years. Though they named their settlement Engelberg—Angel Town—it was almost a decade before they had a church.[13]

In these southern states, Catholicism and Lutheranism were Old World oddities more quickly abandoned in favor of religions popular with Americans. Catholics who cared deeply about regular mass stayed in the cities, while Lutherans who wished to maintain their traditional faith remained amid their neighbors in the upper Midwest—where both German and Scandinavian Lutheranism grew increasingly conservative. (The large Lutheran synod founded by St. Louis Germans, for example, did not allow its women to form an organization by and for themselves until 1942.)[14] Eventually, almost every European denomination that was transplanted to America became more conservative than its counterpart abroad.

Those who wanted more freedom moved west. When midwestern churches were crowded with the faithful, pews in the Pacific Northwest went empty: Portland, Oregon, was home to approximately 6,500 Norwegians and Danes in 1882, but only 25 joined the church. In the 1860s when San Francisco's secular Scandinavian Society was large enough to expend over $27,000 on concerts, lectures, and parties, the church membership never exceeded 30.[15] A pastor there acknowledged that many of the Scandinavians who should have been in his flock instead were taking "tramcars to the parks, breweries and all kinds of pleasure spots"; they had "fallen into free thought and led a gay life." The greatest cause, to his mind, was that "many seem to be ashamed of their homeland and prefer to be—Yankees."[16]

But it was not merely the distractions of San Francisco that caused these people to abandon their religion; it was instead a deliberate rejection of something that symbolized to them the Old World. The Rev. Mr. Hvistendal had to admit that "parents cannot feel strongly drawn to a church to which they cannot take their children." Their English-speaking offspring, he said, felt "more at home among Americans, to whose Sunday schools they go. Many are even ashamed of their nationality and regard a Scandinavian church as an absurdity."[17]

Mothers who sent their children to American Sunday schools were not neglecting religious education—they were instead rejecting the old church and the old language. They correctly saw the churches that used English as more relevant and as a part of upward mobility. Conservative clergy could not accept the reasonable solution of services in English and insisted that religion be tied to nationalism, and so these women removed their children from the traditional faith.

In other denominations, too, Old World clergy lost their transplanted flock when they refused to accept new ways. A number of Catholic women made it clear that their priests offered little that was relevant to their lives. The assessment of a Slovenian woman was typical: she preferred "to attend an American church . . . She looks to the church for inspiration, which she does not get from the community priest, who preaches a poor sermon and seems not nearly as well qualified as priests in the American church."[18] A young Hungarian agreed, saying that because "the priest was unkind to her and a group of girls," she "would very much like to attend any other" church besides the Hungarian Catholic.[19]

The dissatisfaction of these women had a rational basis, for many clergymen ministering to immigrant churches felt little obligation to the laity—and virtually none to young females. Moreover, this lack of communication was a long-term problem, which was exacerbated for Catholics by the fact that Vatican assignments were slow to follow waves of ethnic migration. Throughout the era, immigrants dealt with priests who not only made little effort to relate to them but also often did not speak their language. The Irish who came at the beginning of the immigrant era were served by French priests from colonial days; later, it was primarily Irish priests who greeted the massive numbers of Italians, Slavs, and other Catholics from eastern and southern Europe.

It was a problem from the beginning. Jette Bruns repeatedly made negative comments about the priests sent to her frontier Catholic community—often none were present, and when they were, she found them disappointing. Moreover, because school and church were closely linked in such communities, it meant not only a lack of preaching but also of teaching. "Hermann should really go to school," Jette wrote five years after their arrival, "but we have none. Things are not going well with our pastor."[20] More than a decade after her settlement began, the bishop, an Irishman, finally visited. They requested "a permanent clergyman," and he "promised to send one as soon as one could be had who knows how to speak German. He said they had written to Germany without success . . . Now, as always," Jette sighed, "we live in hope."[21]

Women like her worried endlessly about this problem, for they were the ones most concerned with children's education and other church-sanctioned milestones of life. It meant deep emotional pain for women with infants likely to die—getting them baptized, conducting last rites in time, having a priest at the burial—an inability to perform such religious obligations could be a terrible mental burden to women whose babies died. The shortage of clergy was also a practical problem for couples wishing (or needing) to marry; cases were not unheard of in which they simply moved in together until a wedding could be conducted.

All of these were arguments against leaving Europe, and indeed, countless European clergy preached against emigration. They correctly viewed America as dangerous to faith, not only because of its new temptations but also because its democratic attitudes encouraged the laity to question the clergy. It is understandable that those who emigrated often would be the most irreligious, and that in America, they would drift still further away from the faith of their fathers.

Minority Views: Jews and Mormons

The vast majority who came during the immigrant era were motivated by economics, but one significant group came because of religion: the Jews. Millions of them escaped the pogroms of Russia and Eastern Europe for the freedom of New York. It was a great irony for them to discover that even in America they were not entirely free.

Disturbed by her father's cutting of his beard, Rose Cohen finally spoke to him about it. His explanation was grimly realistic: "They do not like Jews on Cherry Street. And one with a long beard has to take his life into his own hands." She asked why they had to live on that street, and again his answer was fiercely practical: "I save here at least two dollars a month . . . This is not like home. There the house was our own. There, too, we were among friends and relatives. While here, if we haven't rent for one month we are thrown out on the street."[22]

It was not like home economically, but it was entirely too much like home religiously. Though the persecution was not official as it sometimes was in Europe, it was nonetheless real. Once again, Jews had to choose between their conscience and their physical safety. Rose's eyes were opened to the reality instead of the hope, and she wrote:

> I had seen from the first that Jews were treated roughly . . . I had often seen . . . them attack a Jewish peddlar, dump his push cart of apples into the gutter, fill their pockets and walk away laughing . . . And yet as soon as I was safe in the house I scarcely gave the matter a second thought. Perhaps it was because to see a Jew maltreated was nothing new for me. Here where there were so many new and strange things for me to see and understand this was the one familiar thing.[23]

It bothered her more as time went on. The violence grew worse, and she had nightmares about her father being murdered and herself left alone. Her fears, though, were for her father, for, as a girl, she was exempt from this particular prejudice. That circumstance could be a godsend for the males, as Rose revealed:

> I was returning about five o'clock through Clinton Street when I saw him watching me as I came up. When I was near he asked, "Are you Jewish?" I nodded my head and stopped . . . "You can do me a favour," he said in a pleading tone. "You see this handful of fish? This is all my profit. If I could get over to that group of Jewish houses on Cherry Street," he pointed to our tenements, "I could sell it though it is late. But I dare not pass those loafers hanging around the saloons . . . They have great respect for a lady in America . . . If you will just walk beside me while I am passing the loafers, they won't touch me." I remember now often having seen Jewish men escorted past dangerous places. And the women would as often be Irish.[24]

In addition to the Jews, there was another, smaller group whose immigration was motivated by religion: Mormons from northern Europe came by the shipload. They were not driven as the Jews were, but came to find Zion in Utah, pioneering the American desert before the Americans. Between 1850 and 1904, when the church changed its assisted emigration policies, almost 27,000 Mormons journeyed from Scandinavia alone. The majority were Danes, with lesser numbers of Norwegians and Swedes; more significantly, "there was an amazing preponderance of women."[25] Many single women chose to make this pilgrimage.

Fanny Stenhouse converted to Mormonism in 1849 as a young woman in England, before the doctrine of polygamy was instituted. The self-sacrificing attitudes of its converts impressed her, and doubtless the missionary did, too, for she married him a few months later. It was a conversion that she was to regret bitterly. The church's demands were so great that she and her children nearly starved while accompanying her husband on missions to France and Switzerland. By the time they emigrated in 1852, she already felt "the greatest horror of going out to Salt Lake."[26] Other women, she said, felt similarly trapped: "What living contradictions we were!— singing the songs of Zion night and morning in a circle, and listening to prayers of thankfulness for being permitted to gather out of Babylon; and during the day, as we trudged along over the plains, in twos and threes, we were expressing to each other the bitterness of our thoughts."[27]

She sorrowfully gave the husband whom she still loved in marriage to another. Finally, after twenty years in Utah, he tired of the financial burdens, quarreled with the leadership, and left the church. "I am a free woman," she wrote ecstatically in 1872. "I feel the pleasure of the captive who shakes himself free from his chains."[28]

Many other women, however, continued to emigrate to the colony both before and after polygamy was outlawed. Some Mormon women promoted the lifestyle to the era's feminists as more independent, for women maintained their own farms and lived much of the time without a man present. These women resisted the end of polygamy, fearing that it would raise questions on the legitimacy of their children and that they would lose property and civil rights, including easily obtained divorces. The intellectual leaders of Mormon women, however, were natives, not immigrants. For immigrants, the Stenhouse story was more apt to ring true, for they lived in the most alien of cultures, truly outside the mainstream of both European and American life.

Money and Morality

While many immigrants clung to the faith in which they had been born, others abandoned it for reasons that had little to do with spirituality. One Americanized German woman, for example, said that she left the Lutheran Church for a nondenominational one because it was "foolish to have German services, and you get more Christmas presents there besides."[29] Her reasoning was echoed by a Catholic whose husband did not attend church, but she went occasionally—because "the Sisters are good to us then at Christmastime." According to a student of the Irish, German, and English families of New York's West Side, it was not uncommon for women to attend a particular church for this baldly materialistic reason.[30]

Those expressing such views had been in America long enough to realize the differences between churches and to respond to the incentives that some offered. Studies of family budgets confirmed a correlation between length of residence and the size of church contributions. As many as 90% of the Catholic Poles and Lithuanians in the Chicago stockyards area reported small but regular church donations,[31] while another study showed "foreign families gave twice as much" as natives. The second generation, however, adopted American ways and was not as devout as the first; "the direct influence of the Christian churches," the report concluded, "seems to . . . be regrettably unimportant.[32]

Emilie Koenig made similar observations of her German Indiana community a half century earlier. In her view, the most pious were those who were least Americanized and poorest, while the fact that pastors lived on charity, rather than on state-subsidized salary, was another significant difference. As Christmas approached, she wrote:

> I noticed several richly dressed people in church, strangers who do not belong to the congregation. Usually only the poor, the lowly, and those despised by the world belong and go to church. The rich Germans are caught in the bonds of their own riches and scorn God's Word, or at least never show any interest in the church . . .
>
> I suppose you wonder that we here accept so much generosity from other people . . . But here it is quite different from what it is in Germany. Everyone knows that the pastors are very poor. Even those people who do not go to church . . . feel they must do something to support the pastor in the neighborhood . . . We humbly accept everything as coming from the Lord.[33]

Immigrants gave the same excuses as Americans for not attending church—that they were too busy or too tired or perhaps lacked suitable clothes—but some gave an interesting reason unique to the immigrant experience: "Nobody cares now if we go or not."[34] In Old World villages there was pressure to attend church, but immigrants in American cities were free of this obligation, and having no innate desire to attend, these women stayed away. Their husbands were even more likely to ignore the church, and "husband and wife rarely attend church together."[35] A social worker among New York Italians added: "Church contributions did not play a large part in the family expenditures. Though all were Roman Catholic . . . The older generation seldom went to services. The attendance of the girls seemed to compensate for the shortcomings in this direction of the remainder of the family."[36]

As these Italian girls took care of the religious obligations of their families, so Jewish men sometimes relieved their wives in this area. One Jewish girl stated:

> In Poland I and my father and mother used to go to the synagogue on the Sabbath, but here the women don't go to the synagogue much, though the men do. They are shut up working hard all week long and when the Sabbath comes they like to sleep long in bed and afterwards they must go out where they can breathe the air. The rabbis are not so strict as in the old country.[37]

Economic reality in fact took a significant toll on religious observance, as the era's merciless capitalism—and its ties to Christianity—caused some to question their faith.

A poverty-stricken Italian woman expressed the view succinctly: "Bread is bread, and candles are candles. When you have eaten, your stomach is full; when the candle is burned, you are still empty."[38] When a missionary visited a needy Scottish home during the Depression of 1893, the woman responded: "God keep them that's starving us all by bits, if there is a God, but I'm doubting it, else why don't things get better, an' not always worse and worse?"[39]

The economic inequality of the late nineteenth century was a factor in the growing expression of open atheism by nationally known figures, including women.[*] Even immigrant communities in the religiously conservative Midwest were affected. Barbro Ramseth wrote from rural Wisconsin in 1899 that her Norwegian Lutheran church was losing membership: "They have been reading some books that have heretical teachings in them," she deplored, "so they are opposed to the pastor and everything churchly. They practice Rational Christianity."[40]

Bohemians deserted their official faith en masse. Subjected to governmental suppression of religious freedom in their homeland, they dropped the facade of faith that had been forced on them as soon as America made that possible. According to government figures back home, fewer than 1% of Bohemians (Czechs) were "without confession," but Thomas Capek, an apologist who was anxious to impress others with his people, acknowledged, "It is within the truth to say that 50 percent of the Cechs[**] in America have seceded from their old country faith."[41] Many put the figure even higher.

Other immigrant women appeared to be faithful and fulfilled their religious obligations but nonetheless quietly accumulated grievances. When Jette Bruns's daughter—who had been educated by St. Louis nuns—married a Protestant in a civil ceremony because the priest refused to wed them, Jette seemed almost to sigh with relief at the impending end of her dealings with the church: "My Wilhelm will soon go and take his first communion and then the church education of the children will be finished. Our priests here are not like those back home."[42]

For other immigrants, too, the church lost importance, and in some instances the significance that remained had a negative effect. During the Great Depression, for example, some Italian couples felt they could not afford a church wedding and were married in civil ceremonies. Problems resulted when the bride became pregnant. Then they had to go to a priest and confess their sin of omission and be married by him—otherwise the baby could not be baptized when it was born. Sometimes young wives, desperate to save money, went from priest to priest to see who would marry them most cheaply.[43] Religion had become an empty shell where the forms remained but the substance was gone.

---

[*] See, for example, Matilda Joselyn Gage, *Woman, Church, and State* (1893) and Elizabeth Cady Stanton, *The Woman's Bible*, published in two volumes in 1895 and 1898.

[**] The word that Americans spelled *Czech* was spelled *Cech* by natives of that place. Most Americans referred to them as *Bohemians*, ignoring the distinction between their Germanic (Bohemian) or Slavic (Czech) ethnicities.

Freedom versus Security: Variants of Faith

For many Yankees the hordes of immigrants were anathema; and not least among their faults was that they insisted on keeping un-American religions. It was the goal of a good many natives to convert the Jews and Catholics to Protestantism. Their methods were at best insensitive and sometimes cruel.

The Depression of 1893 brought destitution to Rose Cohen's newly arrived family, and they lived on the edge of starvation. Christians controlled the city's public schools, and they provided bread and honey for the hungry pupils—but only for those who would bow their heads and repeat a Christian prayer. Famished Jewish children had to watch others eat. In the Cohen family, finally one day:

"Jews Taking Home Free Matzoths" is the title of this April 1908 photograph taken in New York City. The Passover necessity was apparently given by a grocer sympathetic to the poor, but no food source can be seen in the photo. Instead, the signs advertise "Room to Let"—a feature of the boarding immigrant community—and the nicely ironic "Practical Furriers." Note also that the older women wear shawls and aprons, while the girl has a fashionably styled coat.   (LIBRARY OF CONGRESS, BAIN COLLECTION)

as the children were leaving for school Mother asked them without looking at them whether bread and honey was still given to the children at school. "Yes," sister said, "to those who bow their heads and pray." The boy was already out of the room when mother called after them. "You can bow your heads and pray." Then she went into her dark bedroom.[44]

Nor was it enough to use such methods to convert Jews to Christianity—many Americans also felt that only Protestants were truly Christian, and they employed similar pressures on Catholics. Early in the era, a Massachusetts case became a *cause célèbre* on this issue: Bridget Hogan had emigrated with her mother and two sisters in the late 1840s; her mother soon died, and Bridget was taken in by a wealthy Protestant family. Her sisters tried without success to take her to mass, and then went to court for custody. The Massachusetts courts still considered the battle against popery to be a valid one and awarded Bridget to the Protestants. At the announcement of the decision, Catholics rioted in the streets.[45]

Though neither Jews nor Catholics converted in any significant numbers, Protestant missionaries had an occasional success. Bessie Pehotsky was a Slavic woman who saw conversion to Protestantism as an essential part of the change from the Old World to the New, and she was untiring in her efforts to bring similar enlightenment to other Slavs. She and her American friends were absolutely undaunted, though she admitted that they visited foreign women on a monthly basis for years before they could persuade them to come to one of their meetings. Judging by her slow success, Bessie Pehotsky's Slavic sisters preferred either to remain faithful to the Catholic Church or to attend none at all; they had little interest in Protestantism.[46]

In time, Americans became more tolerant of the new religions. Some Protestant organizations modified their approach and even worked with newcomers to preserve their ethnic religiosity. Even as it continued to be known as the Young Women's Christian Association, for example, the YWCA developed programs for young women of any faith. One example was a mission committee in Minnesota's iron ore ranges that served immigrant families without regard to their differing sects. In the years just before World War I, with the population booming along the shores of Lake Superior, the area's Protestant churches included twelve Swedish, eight Finnish, three Norwegian, and one German; the Catholic congregations were made up of three Slovenian, two Italian, and one Polish; and there were even two Jewish synagogues and a Greek Orthodox church with a membership of Serbs.[47] The supportive American response to this microcosm of religious diversity demonstrated a profound change from the hysterical response that greeted Irish Catholics less than a century earlier.

Even the same ethnic group could quickly develop remarkable religious variety in the open American atmosphere. South Dakota, for example, became home to thousands of "German-Russian" immigrants who colonized as a group around 1870. By 1920, about 40% belonged to Lutheran and Reformed churches, while the rest were "divided among . . . the Roman Catholics, the Mennonites and Huterisch . . .

German Baptist and the Evangelical churches."[48] Again, the YWCA ministered to young women from all these sects—with the particular concentration that year being the study of botany.

That an ostensibly religious organization would send an employee to teach a purely secular subject is not coincidental. For the leadership of the YWCA—and for most educated people in both America and Europe—religiosity was inextricably bound up with notions of "culture." Jette Bruns, Elise Waerenskjold, Elisabeth Koren, and numerous other immigrant women made it clear in their writing that they thought of "Christianity" and "civilization" as virtually synonymous terms. To them, to be "heathen" was to be ignorant—and it was the educational, social, and aesthetic functions of the church that mattered more than the theological. They cared deeply about buildings suitable for traditional functions; they wanted to hear music from a decent organ and to receive material in their own language from denominational publishing houses.

A similar view of the church as primarily an educational and aesthetic organization was expressed by Ukrainian Mary Ann Bodner:

> I had often heard of the Riverside Church and seen its spires from a distance. I would have liked to go in before, but dared not. But now I had been asked to go, so I found myself before the massive doors of the church. Hesitantly I entered and gazed in awe . . . I felt completely out of place, lost, and was about to retreat when the sight of a Russian girl . . . braced me up and we both wandered around becoming acquainted with the place. We heard the organ playing. Oh! It was *beautiful*! . . . Way up front we went, so we could hear and see everything.[49]

Many women expressed similar sentiments. Jette Bruns was thrilled with the Baltimore cathedral she attended on her first Sunday in America; while her husband stood at the back with their infant son, a tired and pregnant Jette restored herself by drinking in the beauty of this building. Much later, a St. Louis visit failed to impress her—except "one thing touched me tremendously: the music mass in the College Church on Easter morning. Was it the music I had not heard in such a long time, was it the view of a big church?" The answer was clear in her next sentence, for she added, "[H]owever, the Mass and the sermon lasted too long; in the end it was embarrassing enduring it."[50]

The aesthetic accoutrements of religion that mattered to her—organ music, stained glass, cathedral spires—were paid for with tax dollars in the state churches of Europe. The realization that people in America had to dig into their own pockets to pay for these things was a disincentive to religious practice. And when they clashed with clergy who literally did not understand them, the natural response of many was to develop an individual spiritual life outside the church.

Again, Jette provides insight into the internal thought of a woman who outwardly appeared a conformist Catholic: listening to a visiting priest whose thought she found "repulsive," she said, "In my innermost soul there was a voice that whispered, 'You have not been cast out even if your service to God is of a different kind.' And the Mother of God looked down on me so quietly and so peaceably as if she agreed with me and did not approve of all this commotion."[51]

Judging from their privately written words, it was not unusual for immigrant women to develop similar individualistic religious views. Even Linka Preus, who was married to a minister, kept a diary that is a long-running argument with herself over theology that she struggled to believe more fully than she truly did. Sometimes her attitude was light, as when she smiled at the argumentation of pastors at a conference. Other times it was darkly brooding.

Some struggled to continue to believe the old doctrines, others became lax in the expression of faith, and still others abandoned their native denominations for American ones, but most immigrant women nevertheless held to traditional ideas on fundamental issues. Most were careful to use the church in time of need—for baptisms, weddings, funerals, and confirmation for their children. Many continued to hold pre-Christian ideas on the evil eye and other beliefs that limited their lives while also providing a comforting rationale for the tragedies that befell them. Over and over again, they expressed strong ideas about "God's will" and "tempting fate." They fatalistically accepted whatever happened in this life, considered it at least somewhat sinful to try to change the status quo that God had decreed, and hoped for a better life beyond.

Faith was an individual thing; religion was a group thing. Religion was often determined through what group one had been born into or the place where one settled. There were, in fact, striking differences between various ethnic groups and between urban and rural immigrants in the importance attached to the church. For Scandinavians and Germans in the rural Midwest, it was an extremely vital part of their social life. To not belong to the church was unthinkable, for it labeled one a community pariah. In the city it was different. One might or might not attend. There was far less pressure to do so, and there were many other sources of companionship and diversion.

The urban-rural distinction in church attendance was true for natives as well, but an additional factor for the immigrant woman was her remembrance of the church back home. Where the church had been an arm of an oppressive government—as for the Bohemians—they were quick to abandon it. Where the church had been the people's ally against the government—as for the Irish—they held to it with fierce loyalty. And for those whose religion had been a source of deep personal comfort at home—as for the Scandinavian and Italian women—the remembrance of that religion was more necessary than ever, a source of security in a strange new world.

PART II

AMBIVALENCE
IN
MORALITY

6

COURTING CUSTOMS

A Family Matter: Chaperons, Matchmakers, and the Old World Ways

Whether considering courting customs or any other aspect of morality, a woman's religion did not seem to matter as much as her national mores. The Italians, for instance, were extremely conservative in sexual matters; the Irish were more liberal but still very far from liberated; the Poles generally were willing to tolerate deviation from the accepted moral code; and the French established a notorious reputation for illicit sex as a national pastime—yet all of these groups ostensibly believed in the same Roman Catholic Church.

Ethnicity was clearly more important than formal religion in defining values. Where one was born was the key to what sort of life one would lead, and this was especially true for women, whose options were always more limited. Of those limited options, none was more important than those related to courtship and marriage. A woman's whole life revolved around her courtship, for no decision she would ever make would be as crucial as whether or not to accept a proposal. It could well be the only significant decision she would ever be allowed to make, a transfer of subordination from father to husband.

Further, these vital decisions were made early in her life, sometimes before she was out of childhood. Indeed, courtship and marriage were so immutably the focus of female life that little girls often began their hope chests as soon as they could do needlework. In Croatia, for example, custom demanded that a woman provide not only a trousseau for both herself and her husband but also enough stockings to last both of them a lifetime.[1] Girls competed in this attempt to buy husbands with clothing, demeaning themselves and diminishing the joy of youth in their race to wedlock.

From birth, a woman learned that her value was defined by whom she married. For her family, the decision was also momentous because marriage was not merely a joining of bodies and lives but a property exchange involving dowries, land, and inheritance. Courtship, therefore, was closely supervised. "My parents belonged to the Tuscon Club in Providence," remembered an Italian woman of her courtship in the 1920s, "and every other month they would have a social."

> Families took their teenage children . . . This particular night a stranger came in with a group of gentlemen. He stood out because he was blond and blue-eyed and everyone else in this group was dark with olive skin . . . I was relieved to hear an Italian accent, though, because I knew that if he were not of our race I couldn't be friends with him . . . We danced and between dances sat with the family. He bought refreshments for my brothers and sisters.[2]

Having thus paid homage to the family, the young man asked through a note to be allowed to call the next Sunday. "This started a ruckus at home. My father wanted to know who was this stranger? Where did he come from? Who were his people? Where did he work? What did he make? And I didn't even know." He called, was thoroughly interrogated and found suitable: "We got permission to go to an afternoon movie in his car but I had to take my sixteen year old sister along, and be home before dark. This was the pattern for all of our dates."[3]

More than other ethnic groups, those that bordered the Mediterranean—Greeks, Spanish, and especially the large numbers of Italians—insisted that their young women live by rigid rules segregating the sexes. "The seclusion that Italians regard as incumbent on their girls," wrote a sociologist in 1910, "makes it impossible for Italian girls to attend any evening classes . . . (as all other nationalities freely do), or in general to move about unchaperoned."[4] Another reported that in Sicily, a woman doing outdoor tasks would not speak even to male relatives, lest she be seen talking to a man. A Sicilian man who once spoke impulsively to a woman—a stranger to him—received a three-month jail sentence for the offense.[5]

Such practices would modify in America, but formality in courting and arranged marriages continued to be the rule during at least the first generation. Katherine Speronis, for example, who was born in Laconia, Greece, in 1899, was unusual in that she came with her mother and three sisters to the textile mills of Lowell, Massachusetts—leaving her father and brothers behind. This unconventional assertiveness did not mean, however, that Katherine was liberated; instead, the bonds of gender were simply replaced by those of age.

The women planned to "get rich" and return to Greece in three years, but World War I intervened. Katherine was an attractive teenager, and her mother was presented with several offers from Greek men, including one from the man she eventually married. His brother attempted to broker with her mother about a match, but the mother refused:

> My mother say no. Because of war time . . . Other men asked the same story, you
> know, want to marry me. But mother is a very smart woman, she says no, it's war
> time and I don't marry my daughter. She rather be single than be widow.
> . . . But after the war, he talk about again . . . He came into the house with the
> family and say hello . . . For three months engaged and marry after.[6]

Most of her friends, she said, had similarly negotiated marriages. Though life in America slowly changed these customs—especially for women whose families were sufficiently poor that they had to allow their daughters to work at jobs away from home—parental control of courtship remained powerful well into the twentieth century. Guided by the object of keeping their daughters pure for the marriage market, some parents viewed every action with suspicion. A social worker summarized,

> One girl told me that her mother made a note of the exact time at which she returned
> every day from work, and that she had to account for every minute of deviation . . .
> Seldom are Italian girls permitted to join clubs or evening classes . . . When they are
> allowed this privilege, they are invariably escorted to and from the gathering by a
> parent or older brother, who must be assured that no mingling of the sexes has been
> allowed.[7]

Parents also intended that daughters be innocent in knowledge as well as in experience. According to one Italian woman who grew up in the America of the flapper age:

> I found out about menstruation when it happened . . . What little we knew was put
> together from girlfriends, most of it on the scary side . . . A girl you married you
> didn't touch or kiss,* you must respect her like a queen. During the ten months we
> dated we were never left alone except in the parlor when I played the piano.[8]

Though young Jewish women had much more freedom of movement, they shared with Italians the custom of parentally arranged marriages. Rose Cohen's first date was managed by her mother and a neighbor. She was sent to buy sugar at an unfamiliar store and said a few words to the clerk there. Two days later her mother said, "Well, what do you think of that young man?" A confused Rose asked, "What young man?" "The young man from the grocery store," her mother replied, explaining that he was a potential suitor and that a date had been arranged for them next

---

* Indeed, no kisses were permitted before marriage, and some said that little was done afterward. "Kissing," according to one Italian woman, "is an American custom."

Saturday. "I was bewildered," Rose wrote. "I was grown up, a young man was coming to see me! I would be married perhaps! . . . It seemed incredible."[9]

At the "date," her father, mother, a cousin, younger siblings, and the suitor's uncle were all present and quickly began to bargain about marriage. When Rose and the young man went for a walk, his conversation was almost entirely devoted to showing that he could support her, and after this short meeting his family proposed an "alliance." Rose's father was delighted, for she had no dowry and was sickly, so he thought it incredibly lucky that anyone should want her.

As for Rose, "I could not understand why father was so happy . . . Somehow I had never quite realized that this question would really be put to me." Though she had earned a substantial portion of the family's income for years, she "had never been allowed to decide the smallest thing before—the shape of my shoes, the length of my dress." Nor did they give her long to decide: "'Well,' father said in an easy tone . . . 'there is plenty of time. Think it over. Take until tomorrow night to decide.'"[10]

She bowed to the family pressure and said yes. On her second date, Rose and "the young man"—for that is how she thought of him—went to a jeweler to buy a ring. The third weekend, their families held an engagement party. Rose felt so little concern for her bridegroom's feelings, let alone love for him, that she danced with everyone else and left him sitting alone and neglected.

The next time they were together was in his store, and he asked her to add some figures. Rose had never gone to school, and this was close to traumatic for her—and, perhaps, for him; in a freer form of courtship, a man might have determined what sort of education a woman had before asking her to be his lifetime business partner. After their fifth date, during which they had absolutely nothing to say to each other, he asked for a kiss, and Rose realized that she could never marry him. Though disappointed, her parents did not try to force her, and the engagement was broken. It was a cruel method of courtship for all involved.

Indeed, despite their added years of experience, there was no assurance that marriages arranged by parents would be satisfactory. Rosa Cavalleri's foster mother could not have done a worse job of choosing Rosa's mate, for example. She had always maintained that Rosa needed a lot of discipline and refused proposals for the beautiful teenager from a number of men, including wealthy ones, saying that they would let Rosa "have her own way."[11]

When Rosa fell in love with a nice young man named Remo, Mamma Lena gave a reluctant promise to consider marriage for them—but then she discovered that Rosa and Remo once had gone to a dance without her permission. She announced that Rosa was going to be married to Santino, an older man whom Rosa hated. She objected, but Mamma Lena refused to listen, and that night Rosa ran away to Remo's family. Her mother dragged her back and starved and beat her into submission.

The marriage was a tragic mistake, and even Mamma Lena was forced to admit after only a few months that her judgment was wrong:

The other nights when Santino was drunk and beating me Mamma Lena had sat up in bed and watched, but she had said nothing. This night—I guess she could see it that he wanted to kill me for sure—she jumped up and came over and stopped him. She pulled him away so he couldn't reach to kick me . . . In the end she put him out the door and he went rolling down the steps. "And don't ever come back to this house!" she yelled after him.[12]

Santino then headed for America, and the two women hoped to be rid of him. Eventually, however, he sent for Rosa: "Those men in the iron mines . . . need women to do the cooking and washing."[13] Mamma Lena decided that despite Rosa's fears, she must go; he was her husband and it was her duty. Once again, Rosa had no voice in the decision; her life had been arranged for her.

On Their Own:
Practical Courtships by Immigrant Couples

Women from nothern Europe had more freedom, but formality between unmarried men and women remained the rule there also. Hanna Sagabiel explained:

> As there had been no co-education in Germany, a deep distinction between girls and boys had always been maintained, and the relationship was rather formal and unnatural. Because nobody knew enough about the other's life, because a strict line was drawn which could not be overcome, the interest in the other sex often misled and was stronger than it would have been under healthier circumstances.[14]

Despite these barriers, young women from nothern Europe were far more likely to act for themselves in marital matters because parental authority was less powerful than in Mediterranean cultures. Arranged marriages instead took a different form—they were likely to be created by the couples themselves, when strangers arranged by letter to marry.

Thousands of couples in Europe and America put intimate thoughts on paper, proposing and planning by mail. Sometimes they knew their intended, often they did not. Occasionally, the relationship had been so long ago that it had faded from memory. In 1907, for example, a Swedish man in America sent a letter via the pastor of the parish where he had lived almost a quarter of a century earlier; enclosed was a dollar to pay for the trouble of locating his intended, to whom he addressed this surprisingly question:

> Dear Anna,
>
> I wonder how you have it and if you are living. I have it very good here. It is a long time since we saw each other. Are you married or unmarried? If you are unmarried,

you can have a good home with me. I have my own house and I make over ten *kronor* a day. My wife died last year . . . and I want another wife. I only have one girl, eleven years old. If you can come to me I will send you a ticket and travel money . . . It is around twenty-four years since we saw each other. You must wonder who I am. My name is Einar, who worked over at Vensta for Adolf Johanson when you were at Anderson's, and you were my first girlfriend.[15]

His recollection of his first love clearly had a romantic cast, but he assumed that it was his bank account and house that would be most appealing to her. Such combinations of emotion and economics were common, with men frequently using more sentimental expressions than women. Martin Weitz, who wrote to his parents in Germany in 1858, provides a good example of the links between parents and children, money and love, in these matters:

You agree that I should send my sweetheart the money for the passage so I got together 35 dollars right away . . . and will send it to my beloved, so I can grant the wish of my future parents-in-law too and they can see and be really convinced that I don't just want to lure my dear beloved over here and then maybe leave her in the lurch. Heaven forbid that, I'd sooner die . . . But . . . I don't blame my sweetheart's parents that they want to see if I really have a decent living here, that their daughter isn't being taken for a ride, I can support a wife here better than in Germany . . . Dear family, when I read in your letter that my bride came to visit you the tears came to my eyes.[16]

But language could be extravagant and letters could be deceptive, sometimes appallingly so. Swiss Jules Sandoz imported three women from Europe to frontier Nebraska to marry him: the first went mad living with this violent man who refused to work; the second soon left him; the third stayed to live an unhappy life. The courtships of these women were marked by fear and irresolution on their part and by an unaccustomed decency on the part of Jules, which dissipated with the wedding vows. At the arrival of the second:

Once more Jules, hunched down on the wagon seat, brought home a bride. He had tried to keep Emelia's coming a secret—with a fresh shave, a moustache trim, a haircut, and a new suit. Every loafer in town followed him to the depot to see what got off.

A pale, slender, rather pretty girl in a well-tailored blue suit with fashionably large sleeves hesitated on the car-step . . .

"Mlle. Parcel?" a hopeful voice asked at her elbow.

"Oui—but who are you?" the girl asked in French, drawing her arm away.

"I am Jules," he said proudly, glad to have them all see this fine young lady.

At first the girl could only drop her veil over her confusion. Then at last she whispered, "No, no—you are not the Jules—"

But it was he . . . An old man. Gray under the greasy cap, limping despite all he could do . . . Then she noticed the hands: long, fine fingers, smooth almost white . . . Perhaps it was with him as he said.

Besides, what could she do?[17]

Occasionally, a woman made a more thorough investigation of a prospective husband. A young German woman who had been living in America without relatives for five years had substantial savings; she did not want to risk marrying a wastrel and went to the Immigrants' Protective League in Chicago "to ask advice regarding a man she wanted to marry. The man lives in West Virginia. She would like the League to find out if he is a good man."[18] But such cases were rare, for few women had the inclination or the means to conduct such investigations. More commonly they took the love letters at face value, especially if they were in Europe and the man was in America. They wanted to believe, and most were convinced that anything America offered would be better than their current options.

Experts in Polish immigration, for instance, stated that women viewed Americanized husbands as so much more desirable than those at home that they were eager to emigrate to a stranger: "They risk going alone to America while they are often afraid to go alone to the nearest town in their own country."[19] A Croatian writer agreed that the practice of emigrating to wed a stranger was common: "When she comes to America—generally she does not know her suitor—she is married. If she is unwilling, not finding him to her liking, she must pay back the money, but it very often happens that another lad pays it for her and takes her for his wife instead."[20]

Just as America made men more considerate, it also made women more assertive. While foreign women almost always preferred to marry Americanized men, immigrant men frequently sent back to Europe for a wife—often candidly looking for an "unspoiled" girl. Men who wanted an old-fashioned wife routinely wrote home for one, expecting that, whenever they indicated their willingness to wed, their families would take care of finding a good prospect. German Matthias Dorgathen was wholly typical when he wrote from Pennsylvania in 1881, "Give my best to all relatives and friends and all the girls, send me one soon, because I want to get married, since then you can live much better than when you're single, but she should be nice and pretty."[21]

Often couples knew each other in Europe, and the idea of marriage took hold in the male mind after he found himself lonely in America. German Emilie Lohmann's mail contained one such missive in 1852: "I received a letter from America from Friedrich Koenig . . . He asked me . . . to share his life there on the other side of the ocean."[22]

Emilie described him as a "good friend of the family" and confessed that she was interested in him. Yet she was ambivalent about taking the plunge into marriage and emigration. She came from a happy and affluent home and was not looking for an escape, as was the case with so many immigrant women. Instead, she felt some dread: "What a journey! What a separation!"[23]

Even after she said yes, letters continued to be exchanged for months, while they waited for permission from both her father and his father and while the details of the voyage were arranged. Her father found several "ladies" to chaperon twenty four-year-old Emilie on the voyage and another to greet her in New York. There she discovered that she was part of a pattern of emigration: "It was interesting to hear . . . how many brides had been taken care of by the Brohms . . . All arrived safely and most of them traveled alone."[24]

At her final destination of Indianapolis, there were more courtship rituals, for even in America, class structure meant that the pastor's bride would be treated differently from that of the ordinary Lutheran immigrant woman. A greater protectionism was extended to upper-class women and the rules of etiquette applied more strongly, with confining results that Emilie resented: "We have so much to tell each other and have need of this exchange and of talking and being alone," she wrote while she was housed at one home and he was at another. "So far I have seen him alone only twice, and then only for ten minutes."[25]

Such inability to communicate was common—and greatly multiplied for those couples from cultures that more rigidly separated men and women and for those who were illiterate or inarticulate in letters. In addition, the longer that a betrothed couple spent apart, the greater was the likelihood of changed personalities. Often he deliberately looked for a European wife who fit the traditional model of docility—and then found when she arrived that he, without realizing it, had become so Americanized that he was embarrassed by her unstylish appearance and ideas.

Sometimes it was the female half of an engaged couple who emigrated first, especially from those eastern European countries that required men to serve in the military before they could emigrate. It was not unusual then, for the woman to exhibit second thoughts about marrying a man who appeared a stranger in the new surroundings. A Jewish girl who had been proud of her fiancé in Poland found that in America, "When I introduced him to my friends, they looked at him with disappointment. 'This greenhorn is your fiancé?' they asked."[26]

If her embarrassment proved too much and the greenhorn found his engagement canceled, the chances nevertheless were very great that these young people would pursue courtships with other people who had similar backgrounds, for almost all immigrants courted and married within their ethnic group. Reams of statistics show that it was extremely rare for a foreigner to marry a native American who did not share the same ethnic heritage. In those relatively few cases when immigrants did court and marry outside the group, it was almost always a closely related group, as, for example, a Norwegian marrying a Swede.[27]

Even at the end of the 1930s—after immigration had all but ceased due to restrictions passed in the early 1920s—these patterns continued, and women who grew up in America exhibited reluctance to consider marriage to a man outside their ethnicity. The Cleveland YWCA conducted interviews in 1939, speaking with women who were usually over twenty, mostly Slavs from four eastern European countries, with lesser numbers from Italy and Greece. The majority planned to marry within their nationality, and some even indicated willingness to accept a less than desirable husband if that was necessary: they "would marry in their own nationality to please their parents even if their prospective mates would be old."[28]

For some of the women, this was a strictly practical matter, for they "said in effect that they had no opportunities to meet men outside of their nationality." Despite growing up in America, these women exhibited a high degree of fatalism; about one-quarter of them said apathetically that "marriage was not too important and they would marry anyone."[29] Only a couple of them indicated a strong assertion on deciding this vital question for herself. One, a Hungarian, said, "My boy friend, whom I hope to marry, is a Slovene. Of course mother was not so crazy about the idea . . . I don't know why it is that almost all my girl friends are Hungarians, but with the Hungarian boys, I just can't get along. For one thing, I think they are too bossy."[30] The other had no prospective husband in mind but resented her parents' expectations: "I am told that I mustn't let a boy give me anything or pay my way into anything . . . He must be Hungarian. They want me to keep steady company with only one boy and then marry him." Though this eighteen-year-old faithfully attended a Hungarian Catholic church, she vowed to marry outside her nationality "just because of her parents' pressure."[31]

A few more years of maturity, however, may have brought a different result, and she could well have joined the prevalent pattern with a wedding in the local Hungarian Catholic church. The chances of that were great, while the probability that she would marry *someone* was so nearly true that it was virtually a predictable fact. Despite their considerable fatalism on the subject of marriage, despite indecision and even dread, few thought there was any alternative to the assumption that young women should court and courtship should end in marriage.

A German governess typified their attitudes; she was enjoying her youth and saw marriage as an end to freedom—but seemed to believe that it was nonetheless imperative:

> I don't want to get married yet, because when a girl marries she can't have so much fun . . . A good-looking girl can have a fine time when she is single, but if she stays single too long she loses her good looks, and then no one will marry her. Of course I am young yet, but still, as my mother used to say, "It's better to be sure than sorry," and I think I won't wait any longer. Some married women enjoy life almost as much as the young girls.[32]

She was not in love and viewed marriage as oppressive but still assumed she must get married. With the possible exception of the Irish,* this assumption prevailed. Couples entered into the blessed state because they deemed it time to get married, without waiting for the romantic attraction considered important by Americans.

---

* See references to Irish women in the Introduction and in Chapters 15 and 20.

Their European heritage taught them that property exchanges and parental approval were the essentials of a marriage contract, not notions of love.

Practicality and property were similarly of utmost importance to Wilhemina Stille. She emigrated with a group of Westphalians in 1837, including her brother and her intended groom, a man who was less well off than she. When she married him about a year later, she justified this to her parents in economic terms:

> I have to tell you that Krumme* left his first boss in April, and went to Adolp Oberhelman, he gave him 15 talers a month . . . So Oberhelman told him to get married, for he wouldn't lose anything on it. 2 talers would easily do for food for the two of us. And also because his work clothes were all torn and the Americans don't want to mend the old clothes of the Germans, so we got married on August 10th.[33]

Though she described herself as a financial burden, in fact the opposite seems to have been the case, for they immediately bought eighty acres of land, and she asked her parents to "send me the rest of my money." The egalitarianism of their arrangement is clear in the rest of her letter. "The new start cost us a lot, we had to buy feathers for the beds . . . and we bought a cow . . . I have a happy marriage and live in peace."[34]

Happiness rated only parenthetical mention at the end of a letter filled with financial detail. Moreover, although the bride clearly was more affluent than the groom, she assumed the traditional view that women were an inherent liability. Because women were seen as a lifelong drain on their husbands' wallets, women were expected to bring money or property to a marriage—and there was open disappointment when a couple married without monetary incentives.

Even kind, generous Jette Bruns took note of the fact that her new sister-in-law, recently arrived from Germany, "did not bring anything along." The young woman violated the norm in failing to present her husband with compensation for the marriage, and Jette thought it necessary to explain, "Franz knew this and has already asked me to take care of some things that otherwise make the beginning of a trousseau."[35]

Especially for southern Europeans, a bridal dowry remained important for a decade or two after emigration. A number of working women told labor investigators that they were employed because they needed to earn a dowry. Indeed, so ingrained was the idea that a woman needed to bring money into the marriage contract that some late-nineteenth-century labor unions even experimented with offering dowries in their benefits, hoping—without much success—to attract women into the union.[36]

The increased status of women in America contributed to the demise of the dowry, but another factor may well have been the initial financial loss that almost every immigrant experienced. Making the move was expensive, the cost of living in

---

* Note that she referred to his surname even after marriage.

America was high, and rising expectations for food, housing, and other aspects of American life made saving for a dowry seem less important. Just as the dowry came into being through economic considerations, its demise was caused in part by other monetary practicalities.

New World Weddings

Indeed, during the first years of immigration, less was spent on any romantic or celebratory activity than had been the case in Europe. While weddings there often featured two or three days of dancing and feasting, here young couples—who usually emigrated without supportive parents—frequently could manage only the plainest of weddings.

Emilie Lohmann and Rev. Friedrich Koenig, for example, could afford a better-than-average wedding, but it was still a somewhat disappointing affair, especially by European standards:

> It was a strange and peculiar wedding day, believe me, because up to the last minute we did not know whether Pastor Fricke would get here. Friedrich told me to be ready by twelve o'clock . . .
>
> So I sat all alone at the given time with Mrs. Apkens, fully dressed except for the veil and the wreath. Mr. Apkens had gone to town to get my suitcase. I made a wreath of rose leaves in the event the other one in my suitcase would not be fit to wear anymore . . . I thought of all of you and was inclined to weep because I was so all alone . . .
>
> When I opened my bag I found that the wreath had become quite black. So I had to wear the one I had made myself. Everyone was so sorry about the wreath, for they could see with what loving hands it had been braided. In the church we met the two elders who were going to be our witnesses. We sang the hymn "Lord, as Thou wilt, deal Thou with me in life and death," which I had selected myself . . . We had a very nice intimate dinner and afternoon with our friends.[37]

In calling the dinner "intimate" rather than "small," she adopted the attitude of many immigrant women, for most were inclined to put the best possible construction on anything that might otherwise give Europeans reason to think that they regretted their decision. Brides like Emilie would not dwell on the contrast of what their weddings could have been like in Europe; they omitted mention of such accoutrements as organ music and ornate decor that would have enhanced a wedding there. Instead, they emphasized solemnity and spoke of the meaning of psalms and hymns.

A civil ceremony without this religious context was a new thing to many. When Jette Bruns's daughter married outside the Catholic faith, Jette explained to her family in Germany: "In the morning she went to church to attend to her devotions. At 10:00 o'clock, at their mutual request, Judge Krekel tied the knot . . . As I have said, I would have preferred a Catholic wedding, and the bridal pair had agreed to this. To you this civil act will appear more strange. Here it is quite common."[38]

More often, civil ceremonies occurred because the young couple—far from home and virtually friendless—had no contact with a church and no reason to go to the expense of a church wedding. Indeed, the weddings of young immigrants were sometimes so pragmatic that there was little or no mention of the ceremony. A young Chicago woman, for example, wrote her social worker in 1913 of the economic need that motivated her stark marriage:

> Honorable Lady, you are asking me what kind of work I have now. Since I stopped working in that shop, I had no work . . . I talked to my man about it, and he told me . . . that we rather get married, so I thought it would be better for me to get married . . . I am only married this week and had many worries over this week. I looked for a rent and it was very hard to find a clean rent. In meantime I live only in a simple rent, pay $6, but the name of the street I do not know . . . It would give me a great pleasure if you would come to see my household; later I write you a correct address.[39]

She typified the newly arrived who could afford virtually no wedding, but as immigrants lived longer in America and became more prosperous, their children enjoyed much more elaborate events. (Still, a distinction remained between the weddings of immigrants from southern and northern Europe.) In the early days of Norwegian migration, for example, nuptials were described as "sometimes sedate, even severe, affairs, unattended by special celebrations."[40] They became more festive as time passed, but the weddings of northern Europeans remained relatively somber in comparison with those held for second-generation brides with family roots in southern and eastern Europe. Elise Waerenskjold, for example, had been in Texas many decades by the time her son married, but his wedding was still simple in comparison with those in Norway:

> The wedding was held at the house of the bride's parents, of course, and was followed by a party in the evening. The following day we had a dinner at my house and in the evening there was a dance for which 130 persons had been invited . . . It does not cost as much to give a party as it does in Norway, since people here usually do not use any other beverages than coffee, milk, and water. We do not have as many different courses here either.[41]

Even the Irish, whose fondness for alcohol was legendary (and statistically verifiable), established their reputation for drinking primarily at wakes, not weddings. Indeed, the elaborateness of a wedding, including the amount of alcohol consumed, seems to be in inverse proportion to the status of women. In those northern European cultures where women had a relatively high legal and economic position, weddings were less showy, but those cultures in which a woman's only goal and identity came with her marriage, the celebration of that event was boundless—whether or not the bride was included in the decision making. When the Paganos married in a Colorado mining town, for example, the bride was a waif who had been virtually bought by the groom:

> It was, for the coal camps, a magnificent wedding . . . The priest arrived from Rockton in a horse and wagon, and they were married in the Grazzioto home, which had been extravagantly decorated . . . Huge bowls of spaghetti and gallon after gallon of wine were consumed . . . [The groom], by his own admission, got more drunk than he had even been in his life . . . [The bride] dressed in the stiff silk which he had bought her . . . sat rigidly in a corner, darting terrified glances around the room.[42]

Eastern Europeans often enjoyed similarly riotous celebrations, although American job obligations often shortened them from the two- or three-day weddings they had known at home. A sociologist sympathetic to these groups nonetheless wrote that "such occasions too often turn into debauches, and too often they end . . . in brawls. This does more to injure the reputation of Slavs in this country than everything else put together."[43]

Not surprisingly, "debauches" as a nuptial aspect declined with time in America. By the time that their daughter was married, the Paganos were affluent, and the second-generation wedding was more Americanized in regard to drinking. The emphasis instead was on food, clothing, and decor, as the guests, "dressed in their Sunday best . . . sat stiffly on the edges of their chairs and sipped their liqueurs and made halting attempts at conversation." After the ceremony, they enjoyed the high point—a wedding feast of "Italian hams, cheese, sausages, and jars of olives and pickled peppers . . . Besides the chickens, there were veal and beef roasts, spaghetti, salads, Italian fried pastries . . ."[44]

Eastern Europeans also spent lavishly on weddings once they could afford that. A study of spending among those in the Chicago stockyards area, for example, included the outlays of two Polish families for their daughters' weddings: both spent around $200, at a time when the average annual income of Polish families was $870—or nearly one-fourth of their available money.[45] But a wedding was for life, and these expenses would not be repeated. Moreover, immigrants felt obliged to demonstrate to their compatriots that they were doing well in America, and a wedding provided the perfect opportunity.

These expenses broke down nearly equally between the bride's trousseau—with the largest cost being linen for her hope chest—and the huge wedding dinner. Guests reciprocated with practical gifts: in the Slavic area of Homestead, Pennsylvania, men endowed the bride by dancing with her and paying—usually a dollar—for the privilege.[46] In a New York Italian community, brides were literally showered, for presents were hung on lines falling from the ceiling. In addition to standard household items, shower gifts could also include baby clothes; this was no slur on the bride's morality but simply reflected the assumption that marriage meant children.[47]

So strong was their supposition that a baby was the inevitable result of a wedding that April was the favored month: if all went properly, a child would arrive in January—and babies born in that month had a natural immunity to the evil eye. At the same time, an April ceremony could not occur before Easter, since weddings during Lent were taboo. In fact, Sicilians had only a small window of opportunity in the spring, for weddings were banned during May—the Virgin's month—as well as during numerous saints' days throughout the liturgical year.[48] Such bans served as still another warning to couples tempted to experiment with premarital sex, for a wedding could not be quickly arranged when pregnancy was discovered.

"Wasting Your Chances": Pressure to Marry

Edna Vidravich Balkus typified the first-generation immigrant whose wedding was simple and who did not consider herself to be in love—even though she met her husband in the seemingly romantic setting of a dance. Virtually all ethnic groups sponsored dances that were designed to encourage courtship, and many marriages developed out of that device. "I met him in a dance," she recalled. "We go . . . every Saturday . . . [It was] full of people, all Lithuanian, nobody else . . . They make party, all people go, spend the evening, you know, it's nice."[49]

She married her intended after knowing him only two months. He seemed to view their relationship as romantic— "when I met him he wants to married"—but for her, it was a practical arrangement. Orphaned in Lithuania, she had joined a sister in America; her sister's husband was abusive, and she wished to escape from that situation. The example of her brother-in-law made her skeptical of marriage, however, and she resolved that if her husband "is bad to me or hits me I will leave him in three months."[50]

Indeed, many immigrant women—possibly even a majority—married to escape from something. Whether it was an unhappy home situation or the poverty of their working lives, countless women were clearly motivated by the assurance of financial security that they assumed marriage provided, for that was the way it was supposed to be according to both the American dream and the heritage of most Europeans. So attuned were women to the necessity of marriage and so eager were some to escape from the present that they took desperate chances, contracting to marry strangers and dealing with disreputable matchmakers.

A young Lithuanian Jew did both: she agreed by letter to marry an older man and then found that he was terminally ill when she arrived. Soon after widowhood, she turned to a matchmaker, who claimed to have "many suitors 'in stock.'" "I spilled out all my heartaches to her. First she talked me out of marrying a work-worn [man] . . . What I lived through afterward is impossible for me to describe. The woman handed me over to bandits, and when I wanted to run away from them they . . . beat me savagely."[51]

Her view of marriage as necessary, and the resultant dependency on the match-maker, made her a prime target for sex exploiters. Most women, of course, did not allow themselves to fall into such traps, but the common opinion that marriage was inevitably desirable made the gullible apt to accept dangerous proposals. There were other ways, too, in which immigrant women were particularly vulnerable. Rose Cohen, for instance, while still in her early teens, became the object of attention from a messenger boy who demonstrated his interest by pushing her on the sidewalk and pulling her hair; she, thinking that his uniform represented governmental authority, was afraid to resist. One day he stepped on her new shoes and broke the toe; she was so angered that she seized his cap, jumped on it until it was ruined, and ran home. "I locked the door and sat all morning . . . listening for a policeman's heavy footsteps in the hall. I felt sure that a policeman would come and drag me to prison."[52]

After she had lived longer in America, of course, Rose came to understand the proper role of police. Similarly, as she—like millions of other women—spent years in the workforce, she would become more independent and assertive. Immigrant families were so often desperately in need of income that they were forced to allow their daughters to work, and this eventually brought greater freedom. When women were capable of making an independent living, a lessened role in courtship for families and matchmakers was the natural result.

Instead of arranged meetings that were also burdensome to families— "We had to make great preparations to receive a stranger," Rose Cohen wrote, since her family of seven lived in "really only the one room"—young women began to meet eligible young men outside the family context. They became acquainted with men in the workplace, where relationships developed more easily and pleasantly. Cornelia Parker wrote that a favorite socializing opportunity occurred as young people traveled to and from work:

> Where did working girls get a chance to meet men, anyhow? . . . About the only place was the dance hall, and goodness knows what kind of men you did meet at a dance hall . . . But the subway! Now there you were likely to pick up the dependable kind. Every girl at the table knew one or several married couples whose romance had begun on the subway, and "everyone of 'em turned out happy."[53]

On the subway and in the factory, the formality of arranged contact between marital prospects eventually relaxed into American-style dating; yet such change takes time, and the ambivalence between the old and the new ways continued for a generation or two.

Moreover, family pressure to wed lingered long after the fading of arranged marriages. Rose Cohen would predate the sighs of many when she complained, "Wherever I went to visit now I was sure to find a young man, and the relative or friend acting as matchmaker . . . What are you waiting for? You are wasting your best years. You are losing your chances."[54]

Men, too, were pressured to marry, for most immigrants viewed the single state as unnatural for both sexes. This was particularly true in farm country, where the standard division of labor insisted that every farmer take a wife. Missourian Jette Bruns worried endlessly about her brother's Bernhard's failure to marry. She wrote six years after their emigration,

> To tell him again to "take a wife" does not work, either. He is deliberate in this matter since he sees by observing Franz that everything is not always fine, that a wife also has certain claims at times, for which one cannot blame her. A completely unedu-cated woman would not suit him either, and to choose according to his own liking isn't possible here. Earlier we thought that he would do best to go back to Germany and get himself a wife, but there the costs are too high and one could not count on her dowry.[55]

A few months later she added, "He is still with us . . . He spoke seriously again of marrying, without knowing whom . . . I told him recently he should look around among the daughters of the land. He has been out sometimes, but . . . it is quite difficult because he has little skill in courting."[56]

Even in urban areas, where there was less economic value in marriage, the pressure remained strong, especially among more newly arrived groups. Italians who did not marry were viewed with great prejudice by others in their communities, who generally thought it unhealthy for anyone except priests and nuns to be unwed. A woman who remained single became a virtual family pariah; in one example, a spinster who lost her job was destitute, but her affluent brother refused to help. "She should have got married," he insisted. "She had chances enough."[57] Similarly, a Polish girl found that her aunt back in Europe admired her independence in emigrating and yet could not allow her to remain independent maritally:

> It is true that you have been courageous in going so far . . . I really cannot imagine that you are there at the other end of the world; I should not muster courage enough to do it . . . I advise you also to marry, not to wait and not to select, for this is the worst . . . I shall wait soon for news about your marriage. It is to be hoped that such a girl as you are should not waste her time.[58]

To be sure, few parents wanted marriage for their daughters so badly that they would approve courtship with a man of another religion or background, but within the group, the pressure to wed remained strong. Courtship then was not dating of today; the purpose was not to have fun, but to make a match. Time and money were too precious to be spent simply enjoying a pleasant evening; a man who had no more than that in mind was not to be trusted. The sole purpose of courtship was marriage.

7

MARRIAGE, DIVORCE, AND DESERTION

Special Stresses of Immigrant Marriage

Marital stress in immigrant families was compounded by many factors that did not affect natives. Because Old World marriages often were not based on love, but on property, there was frequently a substantial difference in the ages of the couple. By the time a man accumulated enough property to bid for a wife, he had aged—and yet he was likely to want a young bride.

Older husbands tended to be tyrannical, treating their wives like children. A woman, in retaliation, might use her only weapon and withhold sex, which to the male European mind was an incumbent "wifely duty" and grounds for withholding household money. According to social workers, some immigrant men were irrationally insistent on "wifely duty," even when a woman was pregnant or sick, and this was a frequent source of violence and family disruption.

The years of separation that many European marriages endured also weakened them. Men often came alone to America, leaving their wives in Europe, and couples grew to be strangers. Women realized their independent capabilities and were no longer submissive when they reunited; men sometimes found other women here. The attractiveness of fashionable Americanized women was tempting to a man, who often remembered his wife "as a plain, hard-working, slow-thinking drudge."[1]

Most important was the lack of the restraint that had been provided in Europe by a respected peer group. The families that arranged marriages had an interest in maintaining them, to protect both their social status and their property. A husband who was excessively abusive would find his wife's brothers dealing with him. A woman who neglected her household duties could expect reproof from her own family, as well as from her in-laws. Nor did the villages of Poland and Russia provide the opportunities for "misbehavior" that tempted the Poles in Chicago or the Jews in New York.

Finally, external pressures of life in America had their effect. Financial stress had been more easily borne when one had a garden, a cow, and family to fall back on. The pride of males was assaulted when they could not prevent unemployment and want. When their women could find work, fragile egos sometimes broke. Alcoholism and violence increased, desertion rates soared, divorce became thinkable.

As a result, women who had been reared unquestioningly to accept marriage as the great female goal in life began slowly to reject this presumption. A woman of Irish background stated flatly, "[A]ll married women are unhappy . . . The children keep coming faster than you can get them shoes."[2] That marriage inevitably meant motherhood gave pause to many; especially those who had grown up in America and improved their lives were hesitant to surrender their gains. One who had become a teacher in Minnesota explained, "I have an opportunity for marriage, but like most girls, I dislike the possibility of having to settle down."[3]

Such suspicion of marriage was certainly common, but it is, of course, important to remember that the records of social workers inherently emphasized those families in which marital ties were most likely to be eroded and that good marriages naturally existed among immigrants as well as among natives. In fact, the immigrant experience and the isolation of America was likely to promote egalitarianism, commonality, and true friendship between husband and wife. Gro Svendsen and Jette Bruns provide just two of many possible examples of such happy marital relationships, and no one could have been more lovingly supportive of a wife than Gionin was of Rosa Cavalleri. Indeed, much of the criticism that immigrant women offered on the subject speaks more directly to the *institution* of marriage than to individual husbands—many of whom were viewed as wonderful exceptions to the rule of disappointment.

Nevertheless, the interminable complaints about marriage from women of all nationalities are striking. One social worker who interviewed mothers of mainly German and Irish origin on the subject summarized: "'If I had it to do over, I'd never marry,' was the almost universal remark."[4] This was not a whimsical thought, but a deeply held conviction: "More than one woman candidly confessed that her husband's death had been a relief. Mrs. Brunig, a sincerely religious woman, said to me, 'You may think we have been having a hard time. But I don't mind it. It's nothing compared to what it was when Brunig was alive. I never had a happy day then.'"[5]

Hattie Reid, an Englishwoman who with her husband ran a grocery store in Brooklyn in the 1880's had borne eight children and wrote, "My life has been one long series of misfortunes ever since I have been a wife." She too advised her daughters not to rush into marriage: "It spoils all their enjoyment and makes old women of them before their time."[6] Cornelia Parker, a sociologist who worked incognito in several different settings, reported, "The subject of matrimony, as ever, came up. Not a soul at the table but was agin it. Why should a woman get married when she can support herself? All she'd get out of it was . . . work that never ended."[7] Other employed women agreed, having observed too many co-workers who "have come back to the factory after a few years of married life, all their gayety and high spirits gone."[8]

Not surprisingly, most widows were wary of remarriage. An Irish woman illustrates the pragmatic approach they took to this question:

> My first husband . . . never drank, but he beat me. Even before I married him . . . I was always dreading it . . . I would have left him after Henry was born, but he was sickly and I knew he wouldn't live long. I took care of him till he died, but it's God's truth, I was glad when I saw him in his coffin . . .
>
> I had had enough of married life . . . But one day I come home and there was Samuel standing before the door. He told me he was married thirty-two years to his first wife and she never did a day's work outside her house all that time. I left him waiting three months and then I married him in the fall . . . I didn't mind working in the summer, but when winter came I wished I had a husband so's I wouldn't have to go out.[9]

Blatant financial need seems to be the overwhelming reason for marriage, for most women seemed to expect little from matrimony except monetary support. Study after study testified that husbands and wives in most immigrant homes did not assume that there would be mental companionship or shared experiences. Even in the cases of exceptionally fine marriages such as of that Jette Bruns, romantic gestures were so infrequent that she wrote, for example, in 1842, "On the 24th of May, Bruns congratulated me on our tenth wedding day; it came as a surprise because I had not thought of it."[10]

Like many other women of her era, Jette consistently referred to her husband by their surname; it was still another indication of the formality that existed between husband and wife. This was especially true in cases such as hers where there was great disparity in age: Jette had been eighteen at marriage, and while her groom's exact age is not clear, it was somewhere between thirty one and thirty three—or nearly twice her age. In the isolation of their frontier home, they grew close, but this was not likely for urban immigrants, who usually followed European habits of men and women spending what leisure they had separately. Men went to the pub in Europe and the saloon in America; they played cards and talked politics, activities that were forbidden to women. The common situation was:

> After the evening meal the husband frequently goes to . . . the saloon or club. He does not seek the companionship of his wife, even if he stays at home. She keeps house for him and bears his children. He does not ill-treat her, unless he is a brute

or habitual drunkard, but there is little spiritual companionship. He does not help his wife in the duty of child rearing. He does not heed her physical weariness . . . There is little respect. They refer to each other as "Him" or "Her" or "my man." They do not hide their feelings when speaking of each other, not even before the children. The women speak of marriage as a necessary evil, and yet most of them marry at eighteen.[11]

One can also find the "necessary evil" view of marriage even in some that were externally happy. A young Italian woman confided to a sociologist that her husband was so in love with her when they got married that they actually took a honeymoon. She had not loved him when they were wed, but now she did, for he was very good to her. Yet, despite these idyllic circumstances, when she discovered the sociologist's single status, she urged her not to get married. "Wish I wasn't married," she said. "Oh gee! Wish I wasn't married. I'm crazy of my husband, but I wish I wasn't married. See—once you are married—pisht—there you are."[12]

Women who were more educated and articulate also held reservations about marriage, again even in cases when no marital problems were apparent. Linka Preus's lifestyle was such that none of her contemporaries would have reason to suspect that she had any reservations about her proper wifely role, yet she had considerable misgivings. She mused in her diary the night before her wedding:

> There must indeed, be something attractive about being a wife since I have decided to become one; but what is it?
> "Te ll me, my cousin Independence, do I enjoy thee more as a wife or as a maiden?"
> "Indeed, as wife you become nothing but a slave."
> "Dear me, then I dare not marry—"
> "Indeed, that is what you ought to do. Very likely you will never feel the slavery of wifehood; rather you will be giving thought to a woman's calling in life."[13]

But Linka expressed her doubts to her diary; she never wrote of speaking to anyone about them, and she, like so many others, did what society intended. Likewise, most of the factory girls who were advised by older women to avoid marriage chose to disregard that advice—and the same women who spoke against marriage as an institution nonetheless usually saw that *their* daughters were properly courted and married.

The societal view was as ambivalent as that of an Irish woman who averred, "Not so many girls would get married if they knew what they were gettin' into," and then went right on to state that the alternative was not acceptable, either: "It is awful to be an old maid or widow. I'd rather take worriment than that." She managed to blend her contradictory views by leaving it all to destiny, as so many fatalistic immigrants were prone to do. "You meet your fate and if you are to be happy, you will be happy."[14] Such fatalism, such ambivalence was key to their thought. Marriage was a necessary evil.

Ambivalence and fatalism were part of the intellectual baggage of most immigrants, and more than a few resorted to witchcraft and magic in their marital relationships. Some couples from southern Europe wore amulets to ensure harmony, and refusal to wear them was taken as insensitivity to one's spouse. When one Italian bride felt her husband's attention wavering, she had her mother perform rituals over ribbons she found in his pocket; afterward, all involved believed that the groom was freed of bewitchment by another woman.[15]

Immigrant newspapers ran many advertisements for magical methods of entrapping lovers and potions to improve sex lives. A Polish man spent $12—probably a week's wages—for a love potion that he intended to slip into his wife's tea; it arrived while he was at work and the angry woman threw it out. He persevered, however, sending off another $12 for the happy results the newspaper promised.[16]

But in far too many immigrant homes husbands did not use such gentle methods to achieve their aims. The files of social agencies are replete with examples of drunken, violent men who were both rapists and sadists to their wives, as in this one case of many:

> Lena Ziejewski complained . . . that her husband beat her with unusual cruelty, particularly when he was drunk or in the morning when he had not slept well . . . They . . . had been married only 3 months before their first child was born. He taunts her because she had relations with him before marriage. About 2 weeks after the child was born he tied her hands and feet and bound her mouth. When she was almost suffocated, he released her. His family opposed the marriage and continued to incite him against her . . . When she put too much salt in his food, he beat her and once because she spilled some lard on the stove he struck her in the face, cutting it, and knocked her down. The neighbors often saw her with dress torn and eyes blackened.[17]

Wife beating had been sufficiently a part of life in much of Europe that neighbors frequently closed their eyes to it, considering it none of their affair. As long as a husband was not too severe, both the victim and her family were willing to consider it unfortunate but nevertheless a male prerogative.

Occasionally, however, a woman was driven to violence when her helplessness at last turned to rage. Mrs. Gaszynski was one of many women whose husband interpreted American liberty as license. In Poland he had treated her well, but no longer restrained by family or village reputation, he "began to run around with other women" and finally deserted. Mrs. Gaszynski supported their children alone and heard nothing of him for two years, when she discovered that he was living with another woman. She first attempted reconciliation, but he refused to see her, and finally she went to court for child support. He did not pay, and at last a desperate Mrs. Gaszynski "planned to kill her husband, Mrs. Dujek [the mistress] and herself, but she had only 10 cents left. With this she bought some vitriol. She went to the home of the other woman, called her to the door, and threw the vitriol in her face."[18] The woman would lure no more husbands, for she was disfigured for life, but Mrs. Gaszynski and her husband would both go to prison, she for this assault and he for nonsupport.

The Unthinkable: Divorce

The obvious end for such broken marriages would seem to be divorce, but most immigrant women were highly reluctant to take that step. Religious prohibitions, fear of dealing with American courts, the expense, and the likelihood that she could lose custody of her child in an era when courts gave automatic preference to men—all of these combined to make divorce an impossible idea. Immigrants were generally more conservative than Americans in all aspects of relations between the sexes, and a slower divorce rate is one aspect of that conservatism.

In a study of Philadelphia working women in the World War I era, for instance, 6% of the natives and 2% of second-generation women were divorced, while the number of foreign-born divorced women was too small to be measured.[19] A 1910 study of northern and southern textile mills provides an even greater contrast: in the New England mills where immigrants predominated, only 13 of some 4,700 women were divorced, deserted, or separated, while in the southern mills that employed almost exclusively native white women, 146 of 4,300 fell into that category.[20] Census figures from 1890 through 1920 show increasingly large numbers of divorces, but the pattern of a slower rate for immigrants continued to hold.[21]

While divorce through the courts was rare among immigrants, in practice, many marriages were over in all but legality. Not infrequently, people simply set up a second partnership with another spouse without dissolving their first union. Social workers bemoaned the foreigners' tendency to ignore marital formalities, especially in cases where they had through great effort obtained a divorce for some abused woman who then received her ex-husband back into the house.

The proceedings of the American legal system were so foreign to them that, for instance, one woman was shocked to find that she had not been legally married at all; she and her fiancé had obtained the marriage license and thought this action alone constituted marriage.[22] Revealing similar ignorance, Martha Gutowski went to a legal aid society and "wished to know whether she was divorced or married."[23] Another Polish woman ignored her summons until the court granted custody of her children to her husband, based on her lack of a defense; after they reconciled and she became pregnant, her husband informed her that the divorce in fact had been finalized. He announced that he would not support the unborn child if it was a girl, though he chivalrously offered to legitimize a boy.[24]

Nor were such cases limited to recent arrivals from countries with low educational standards. German Anna Maria Klinger, who emigrated in 1847, fatalistically refused to think about her legal entanglements over almost two decades. Twice widowed, in the post-Civil War era she married a man who apparently deserted her. Her brother Gottlieb wrote in 1868, "Marie's . . . husband is . . . still in the army, she's better off on her own than when that lazy fellow is with her."[25] Nothing more was said of him and she was referred to in family letters as "still a widow" until 1883, when she wrote this surprising letter:

> Dear sister-in-law, I have a request, if you would please be so kind as to ask around in Korb about the old wheelwright Schwartz family, that is old Schwartz married a second time, her name was Mrs. Rappold, she brought a son into the marriage, his name was Karl Rappold. Dear sister-in-law, I imagine you remember that I married this Karl Rappold, it was about 16 years ago, we didn't get along and so we separated, but not legally, up to now I haven't tried to find out anything about him, but now I'd like to ask you to please find out from the family or friends, and if you can't find out anything then please go to the mayor's office and ask . . . If he is dead I would like to have the death certificate. I'll pay for all the costs.[26]

Though in America for almost four decades, she still expected her international network to know more about her erstwhile husband's activities than was known in America. The mayor's office of her village was still a more important authority on this most intimate aspect of her life than was the American judicial system, despite the fact that the marriage took place in New York.

American courts were similarly irrelevant to many Jewish women, whose religion made the subject of divorce particularly problematic. While Jewish law required that the wife consent to the divorce—although the husband was the only partner who could issue it—a wife might fear that rabbi and husband would combine to force her to accept a divorce she did not truly want. The terror that some women had of such arbitrary divorce is shown in this pathetic letter to the *Jewish Daily Forward* in 1912:

> I am a twenty-eight year old woman, married for six years, and my only trouble is that I have no children . . . My husband eats my heart out with a few words, like rust eats iron. He keeps saying it's "nearer than farther" to the ten-year limit when, according to Jewish law, I will have to give him a divorce if I don't have a baby by that time . . . A short time ago I was quite sick and he spent a lot of money to cure me. When I got well my husband said to me, "You'll have to earn your own living, so I want you to be healthy."
>
> Dear Editor, I am all alone here, and I ask you to advise me what to do. Can my husband get a divorce after ten years through the court, too? I know he can get it through a rabbi . . . How shall I act?[27]

The editor told the distraught woman that U.S. law did not recognize rabbinical law and that her husband could not get a legal divorce. The fear that she had, though, was realistic, for many men obtained divorces without their wives' consent or even their knowledge. A fairly frequent device of men who wished to end their marriage but had no legal ground was to file in a state where divorce "by publication" was allowed. Nevada and other western states were most likely, although Arkansas also long ran a thriving industry for lawyers who used this technique.

A notice was listed in local newspapers that the faraway spouse naturally would not see, and one day she would discover herself to be a divorced woman. The Jewish National Desertion Bureau had local representatives throughout the country who took note of such ads that involved people with Jewish names. They followed through with legal advice and travel expenses for the wronged woman, enabling her to contest the divorce.[28]

The judicial system that allowed such divorce suits took advantage of immigrant women in other ways: some lawyers took fees from both husband and wife, and many judges unquestioningly gave custody of children to the parent with the higher income—almost invariably the man. Nor was there proper protection of assets; a Polish woman, for example, agreed to an amicable divorce so that her husband could marry the young woman he had impregnated, and then was shocked when he ordered her out of the business they had built together for twenty-three years.[29]

Legal obstacles were not the only problem of women seeking divorce, for certainly religious prohibitions played an important role, too. Rosa Cavalleri, who was married against her will to man she despised, nevertheless put up with his cruelty. Her fear of physical abuse was so real that she was grateful when he began spending most of his time in a brothel. The breaking point of the marriage did not come until Santino spent his savings to buy a bordello and insisted that Rosa manage it because he could not read or do arithmetic. Up until then Rosa believed it was God's will that she obey her husband, but now that there was a clear difference between God's will and Santino's, she refused. Santino threatened her with a razor, and Rosa fled. Taking her two children, she went to Chicago to the friend of a friend. Santino followed, trying to get the police to arrest his runaway wife, and she in fact was brought to court:

> There I was, a young Italian girl with a shawl over my head, and I couldn't understand nothing. When we went by the judge, there was Santino from Missouri! He was telling the judge that I was the worst kind of woman . . . He wanted the judge to punish me and put me to jail.
>
> I can't tell you very much what happened, because the judge was talking English to all those friends of Gionin and Toni [Rosa's protectors]. When he asked me the questions Toni told me what it was and I answered the truth, that's all. In the end the judge told Santino to get out of town. He said if he was not gone by 6:00 the same day he would put *him* to jail instead of me. Then he said, "And don't you ever come back, either."[30]

And so at last Rosa was free of Santino, but she still did not seek the divorce; Santino got it. Rosa's second husband was kind, but the cloud of divorce hung over their innocent hearts. Though Rosa had been forced into the unhappy marriage; though she did not say her vows at the ceremony (the nearly deaf priest failed to notice); though she had not been the seeker of her divorce—still her religion made her suffer for the broken marriage. When she wanted to marry Gionin, "The priest said he couldn't marry us in the church because I had the first husband living . . . Me, I was crying . . . and praying to God, 'Oh, God, why do you make it a sin for me to live with this good man Gionin?'"[31]

They were married in a civil ceremony, but the problem continued to plague the marriage:

> After Gionin and me were married together about ten years and have already three children, a missionary from Italy came in our church. He preached so strong against divorce—what a sin it is against God, and the punishment God is going to give those people and all and all—that Gionin he left me alone to take care for all those [five] children . . . So then one day he went to confession . . . and Father Alberto told him it's a sin to leave me alone like that with those children. Oh, Gionin was glad to hear that, so he could come back! He said he only left me because he didn't want to go to hell.[32]

Desertion: "The Poor Man's Vacation"

Amicable divorce was almost incomprehensible.* Much more frequent was divorce after long endurance of abuse and nonsupport. More frequent than that were marriages that did not end legally at all but simply faded away. Desertion was a far easier way of simply evading a decision; one study of deserters found that most of them did not consider their action to be final: "desertion, instead of being a poor man's divorce, comes nearer to being a poor man's** vacation."[33]

Desertion was harder on a woman than either divorce or widowhood because of its uncertainty. Moreover, this generally was a new problem for immigrant women to face, for several commentators noted that desertion was not an Old World phenomenon. A German authority said he was "dumfounded" by the desertion rate here because at home men just did not abandon their families.[34] Europe, with its passports and workbooks and military service registration, made it much more

---

* One rare exception was Elise Waerenskjold, who divorced her husband in 1842, prior to leaving Norway. It was extremely unusual to divorce for even the most valid of reasons in this era, but they "agreed to a friendly separation . . . due to incompatibility." Fifty years later, she said there was "absolutely nothing else" except his expectation that she "iron shirts and darn socks." She emigrated without him and did not formalize the divorce until several years later, after she had married a second man. When she was a poor widow in 1887, her ex-husband sent her $400, and she wrote gratefully, "There is not . . . one man in a million who would have done so much for a divorced wife." (Waerenskjold, *Lady with the Pen*, p. 11, and Blegen, *Land of Their Choice*, p. 349).

** The vast majorities of deserters were in fact men. Another study of 591 deserters in 25 cities found only 17 cases where the wife had left (Lilian Brandt, p. 9).

difficult for men to disappear, whereas the lone male adventurer was part of the American tradition. A second vital factor was that many immigrant men had separated consentually when they emigrated without their families. Once gone, they saw that their wives could manage without them, and, having tasted the joys of renewed bachelorhood, they were sometimes reluctant to resume the burdens of a family.

The size of the family did not seem to be a factor. Studies showed that fathers of large families—who had the biggest obligations—were not the most likely candidates for desertion. Seventy percent of the deserted families in one report had fewer than four children. (On the other hand, only 3% deserted a wife without children.)[35] Nor did men leave during economic depressions. Apparently instead of leaving because financial pressures were overwhelming, they valued the security of a family in hard times and left when conditions improved.[36]

Sociologists agreed that most desertions were to be blamed mostly on the husband. While acknowledging that fault is difficult to assign, one student concluded that in about two-thirds of the cases, men were largely responsible for the marital breakdown, with women being at fault in 12% of the cases.[37] A common element, said one male sociologist, "is an excessive lack of responsibility . . . He wants to be free to come back when it suits him, and he would be the last to welcome a divorce court."[38]

There was, however, a slight difference in the way male and female sociologists would have solved the problem. Males generally wanted strong laws and jail sentences to discipline the men; females, while not disagreeing with the above, put their emphasis instead on making the family independent. In general, male social workers aimed at laws that would force the potential deserter to return, while women sought to compel him to stay away.

Indeed, making a woman economically independent was likely to be a more realistic goal than reforming a man's basic character. Of 574 deserting husbands, for instance, 255 were reported as "not working regularly" prior to leaving.[39] The desertion brought no economic change and, in fact, could well be a good thing, since the wife then had control of the income and it would not be spent on the vices that afflicted many of these men.

Financial pressures on the women were nonetheless great, especially in view of the fact—according to still another study—that more than two-thirds of the husbands who abandoned their families did so before they were thirty five; "it is obvious that their families must have been composed of young children. They deserted the family when its need was greatest."[40] Because little children prevented her from working, a woman sometimes had no choice except to search for her man and try to get him back.

She didn't receive much societal help with these problems. Social agencies in their early days feared that they would encourage men to desert if they were very solicitous toward the family, so if they aided the family at all, "relief was given . . . in smaller amounts than to a widow or the wife of a man in the hospital."[41] Immigrants particularly were hurt by the residence requirements of some agencies. One distraught Jewish woman poured out her bitterness against these charities in a letter to the editor:

My husband . . . deserted me and our three small children . . . The local Jewish
Welfare Agencies are allowing me and my children to die of hunger and this is
because my "faithful" husband brought me over from Canada just four months ago
and therefore I do not yet deserve to eat their bread.

It breaks my heart but I have come to the conclusion that in order to save my
innocent children from hunger and cold I have to give them away . . . I will sell them,
not for money, but for bread, for a secure home . . . Those who are willing and able
to give my children a good home can apply to me.[42]

If social agencies were indifferent to the plight of the deserted, the judiciary was
of even less help. Social workers often insisted that deserting husbands be taken to
court. The women's reluctance to follow this advice was due to ingrained timidity
that made them afraid of both judges and angry husbands, but another important
factor was that these women understood the realities of the system.

A man would simply ignore the court order and then the only recourse would
be to put him in jail, where he could not earn anything. Moreover, immigrants had
to be wary of making such complaints; the favorite solution of one Chicago Domestic
Relations Court judge for husbands who were cruel or negligent was deportation—a
method that couldn't help but make things much worse for the family.[43]

But before a man could be brought to justice, he must be found. If the police did
not take this responsibility seriously, some social agencies did. The National Desertion Bureau was a Jewish organization that was superbly efficient at tracking down
deserting fathers. Their chief technique was the publication of a "Gallery of Missing
Husbands" in the leading Jewish newspapers. Many persons reputedly bought newspapers for the sole purpose of studying these pictures, and the agency received "tips"
on their fugitives from all over the country. The deterrent value was doubtless strong,
for a man who left his family knew that he must cut himself off from the life of all
Jews everywhere.

Despite the difficulties of detective work, it was still easier than social work: the
National Desertion Bureau located three-quarters of the men for whom they searched,
but of 2,405 deserters they found in their first three years, reconciliations were
obtained in only 780 cases.[44] Even when the location of the father was known, he
seldom could be relied upon for support. Only 29% of the deserters in one study ever
contributed anything, whether from conscience or from police pressure, and those
contributions were sparse and irregular.[45]

Women simply had to make their own way, but little in their backgrounds had
prepared them for this. Another Jewish woman's letter to the editor, intended to reach
her husband's eye, shows the fatalism and dependency that made women beg a father
for his children's bread:

Max! The children and I now say farewell to you. You left us in such a terrible state
. . . For six years I loved you faithfully, took care of you like a loyal servant . . . Max,
where is your conscience? . . . I bore you four children. And then you left me. Who

will bring them up? . . . My tears choke me and I cannot write any more. Be advised that . . . I am leaving with my two living orphans[*] for Russia. We say farewell to you and beg you to take pity on us and send us enough to live on.[46]

In going back to Europe, this woman probably made their separation permanent, but for many who remained here, desertion was anything but a clearly defined status. Husbands would return, upset the household, and perhaps take along a child or two when they disappeared again. The case of Polish Mrs. Kulas, whose employer sent her to Legal Aid to get a divorce, exemplifies the problem. Though her husband earned fair wages, she always paid the household expenses from her cleaning job. Finally he deserted, reappeared, and deserted again. "She was afraid he would get drunk, break into her house and either force her to have sexual relations with him or kill her. He had often threatened to kill her."[47]

Social workers' records, of course, are likely to emphasize the wife's side of the story because wronged men seldom went to a charity agency to complain. Occasionally, there were cases where the wife was the direct cause of the desertion. Henry Slokowski had put up with a woman who was a slovenly housekeeper, poor mother, and impossible nag for ten years; "possibly Henry would have gone on to the end in this humble, hen-pecked existence had not Martin Pribiloff appeared on the scene. He had come into the home as a boarder; he remained as Anna's lover. Obviously Henry was in the way; so as meekly as he had been a husband, he became a deserter. The charities know where he is and know that he would go back willingly if she would give up the lover."[48]

A group of men jailed for nonsupport complained that they too were wronged, that they had been jailed for "the merest nonsense," and that "even in the worst times of the Russian reaction people didn't suffer as the men suffer here in America because of their wives."[49] The women probably were more assertive than they had ever been in Europe, but the evidence does not support the men's claim to innocence. Even the male sociologist who told the tale of meek Henry Slokowski agreed that Henry was a rare exception and that in most desertion cases husbands were at fault; they were, he said, guilty of "a superlative selfishness."[50]

Although desertion in America was much more common than it had been abroad, immigration specialists noted one exception. Several researchers reported that some Europeans had long traditions of desertion during a wife's pregnancy. "The institution of 'pregnancy desertion,'" said one expert, "is one of undoubted antiquity. Its prevalence among certain European immigrants would almost point to its being a racial tradition."[51]

Not surprisingly, the tradition of pregnancy desertion continued in America. One study found that almost one-third of deserters had "left a short time before, or just after, the birth of a child."[52] Another sociologist wrote that "some pregnancy deserters

---

[*] In this era, the word *orphan* was frequently used when a child was missing just one of two parents.

take the step in the hope that their wives will bring about an abortion; but this is a modern and sophisticated development."[53]

For newcomers in a strange land, where there was often no extended family, this meant that when a woman most needed support, she was most likely to be alone. "Regularly before the birth of each child," one social worker wrote of a client, "Mr. Brady has deserted, and as regularly, when the family crisis was past and Mrs. Brady once more supplied with a paying job, has he returned."[54] In a second case, the father "had deserted before the birth of each" of his seven children, "as well as at other times when there was sickness."[55] The most egregious case was that of a social worker who reported knowing a woman who had given birth to nine children—seven of whom had died—and the father had deserted before the births of all nine.[56]

Pregnant women became wrecks from the strain, like the Italian woman who worked at three jobs until just a few days before her delivery.[57] The Mrs. Brady mentioned above worked in a laundry from seven in the morning until six at night.

> When her baby was born she left off work only a week beforehand and returned when it was two weeks old. She tells the following story of that time to show her employer's good heart:
>
> I went to Mr. Mack in the office . . . on Saturday night. I'd rather died than do it, but I was afraid not to give notice or maybe he wouldn't let me back. "I've got to take a holiday," says I. "Have ye?" says he. Then he says, "Come with me," and he took me downstairs and gave me two sets of clean sheets and pillowcases.[58]

Such charity was exceptional, and of course the idea that she ought to have a right to maternity leave occurred to no woman in this era. But Mrs. Brady would stay at her job, her babies "most grown up in St. Joseph's nursery," and Mr. Brady would eventually show up to impregnate her and leave again.

Obviously many women accepted pregnancy desertion as unfortunate but unexceptional and unavoidable, for some allowed their mates to return and repeat the pattern over and over again. If even disinterested observers noted that "desertion and pregnancy occur together in a great many cases,"[59] the women themselves doubtless were sufficiently aware of the problem that they dreaded pregnancy and wished to prevent it, but such seemed impossible.

As the purpose of courtship was marriage, the reason for marriage was procreation. But time and the American example would slowly bring a woman to question the old ways, to make her ambivalent about what her mother had believed, and gradually the institution of marriage would change to accommodate a female partner who had become more free and equal.

8

ILLICIT SEX

Premarital Pregnancy

Seventeen-year-old Anastasia Bazanoff from Russia was not even two months pregnant when she passed through Ellis Island. Morning sickness must have revealed her secret to the sharp-eyed arbiters of American morality, for she was detained on suspicion of pregnancy. Her denials were in vain, her condition became obvious, and in April of 1915, her baby was born. What she could not achieve by protestations was achieved by the war that had begun in August; deportation would be difficult, and Anastasia and her little daughter were allowed to enter.[1]

No questions were asked about the father of Anastasia's child. Even when officials knew a man was an unwed father, they apparently felt that, in cases of heterosexuality, the "moral turpitude" clauses of immigration law* applied only to women. Margaret Heckert found herself detained while the father of her child, Leopold Koenig, was admitted. Leopold had honorable intentions, but the law of his native land insisted he live up to his obligations to the state before he could fulfill his obligations to a woman: until a young man had served his three years in the military he was not free to marry, and so, with Margaret's pregnancy and the threat of war in 1914, the young couple fled to America.

---

* The first federal regulation of immigration began with an 1875 law forbidding the "importation" of prostitutes and convicts. Stronger legislation in 1882 and 1891 excluded polygamists and persons with "a loathsome disease." A 1907 revision placed additional emphasis on the personal character of potential citizens.

But America, while unconcerned at that time with male duty to the state, was concerned with female morality, and Margaret and her unborn child were threatened with exile. Leopold appealed to the Immigrants Protective League, whose agent wrote to immigration authorities: "I cannot protest too strongly against a policy which excludes a helpless and friendless girl and admits a man who is responsible for her condition and for bringing her to this country."[2]

Authorities seldom fretted over morality in the early days of immigration, but by the early twentieth century, even the wholly innocent could be ensnared in horrible legalisms both in America and abroad. A Norwegian man who lived in the Pacific Northwest for seven years serves as a good example: he was doing well until his wife died, when he went back home to find a mother for his three little children. A woman agreed, but Norway refused a marriage license because he had no proof of his first wife's death, so they emigrated with the intention of marrying at his home. At Ellis Island, however, their premarital experimentation was discovered, and immigration officials—oblivious to the evidence that professional prostitutes were rarely hampered by pregnancy—refused them entry. Even the fact that he had bought her ticket was used as "proof" that she was being imported for immoral purposes. They finally resorted to telegrams from respected citizens on the West Coast, who appealed that they be allowed to come to the children.

Statistically, officials had little basis for their suspicions, for census figures showed that immigrants were considerably less likely than Americans to give birth out of wedlock:[3]

ILLEGITIMATE BIRTHS PER 1,000 BIRTHS IN THE UNITED STATES, 1920

U.S. natives	16.7	Austrians	5.3
Canadians	15.0	Hungarians	5.0
English, Scots, Welsh	10.6	Poles	4.0
Irish	10.1	Russians	2.5
Scandinavians	8.4	Italians	2.5
Germans	6.6		

Occupationally, domestic workers were the most likely to find themselves pregnant and unmarried. Second ranked were girls who had never worked, while the number of women in factories and commerce who became pregnant illegitimately was very small by comparison. Domestics accounted for well over half the admittances at homes for unwed mothers.[4] The work exposed a woman to a higher risk because the male members of the employing family were in a position to take advantage of her, and she lacked the safety of numbers that existed in business. Moreover, the loneliness of domestic work made a young woman long for excitement, while work in a group was less boring.

Yet domestic work was constantly recommended to immigrant women by moralists who felt that the home was inherently the right place for women. Even more curious is the fact that when managers of homes for unwed mothers were asked what occupations they felt were most dangerous, they invariably replied that stores and factories were. On further questioning they admitted that they seldom got girls from those places and had no way to account for their contradiction.

In Ireland, where sexual mores were as conservative as anywhere in northern Europe, the illegitimacy that did occur was closely linked to domestic service. The prefamine rate was believed to be around 6%;[5] a half century later, another study ranked Ireland, with about 25 illegitimate births per 1,000, the lowest of fifteen European countries.[6] Those few babies that were born outside marriage, however, were likely to be fathered by the mother's employer: "Unwed mothers were not unusual among servants living in their employers' household," according to a modern expert, and "the 'gentleman's miss' was a fairly common figure." When these women found themselves pregnant, they usually had no choice except to carry the baby to term, for "abortion was rare"—but infanticide and abandonment were "common."[7]

The home in fact was an excellent site for exploitation, even for women who were not employed there. Then as now, sexual harassment and incest occurred within families, but patriarchy was so much stronger then that the public seldom heard of such cases. A rare exception was a young Jew who had been brought to America by her uncle, who had been in America long enough to become a prominent businessman and synagogue leader. After he seduced her and she became pregnant, he proposed an abortion:

> I didn't want to undergo such a criminal operation and told him I would tell everyone the truth. He said, "Fool, who would believe you!" Soon he came up with another suggestion: he would say I was seduced by my tutor. Naturally, I could not agree to the vile proposal, to smear the good name of such a decent and innocent person. My uncle ignored me, however, and carried out his evil plan.[8]

Going to homes for unwed mothers and giving away their babies were common solutions to unwanted pregnancies—even legitimate mothers in this era sometimes put up children for adoption when they could not afford to maintain them. Jacob Riis, writing in 1890, said the Foundling Asylum of the Sisters of Charity alone had taken in nearly 21,000 infant New Yorkers:

> Years ago the crib that now stands just inside the street door . . . was placed outside at night; but it filled up too rapidly. The babies took to coming in little squads instead of in single file, and in self-defense the sisters were forced to take the cradle in. Now the mother must bring the child inside and put it in the crib where she is seen by the sister on guard. No effort is made to question her, or discover the baby's antecedents, but she is asked to stay and nurse her own and another baby. If she refuses, she is allowed to depart unhindered.[9]

Premarital pregnancy was looked upon with tolerance among some northern European groups; the assumption was that the wedding date simply would be moved up, since courtship presupposed marriage. "In certain more northern countries," wrote one expert, "intercourse between young people before marriage has always been a common custom. If a child were born as a result, the wedding ceremony was celebrated as soon as a dwelling house for the new family could be obtained."[10] Thus, their rate of illegitimacy remained low, for families saw that men carried out their obligation to marry. The unusually empathetic conclusion of a government report on this subject was:

> Among certain classes abroad, premarital relations seem to be common, and not to be looked upon as objectionable, provided the expected marriage follows. . . . [An immigrant woman] may consider that such relations constitute a pledge of marriage, a view which the man, brought up in other traditions, may not share. If, then, he fails to carry out his side of the implied agreement . . . the girl is left to bear . . . the weight of disapproval of a social standard to which she has never subscribed and of which she has very little comprehension.[11]

Speaking of the English lower classes, one writer said that prostitutes were not commonly patronized—but not so much because of strict morality but rather because free sex was so widely available. "Pre-marital relations are very common, perhaps even usual," said one expert. "It is noted by the clergy who marry them, how often both the addresses given are from the same house."[12]

The Klinger family, siblings who emigrated from Germany at midcentury, provide an excellent example of the frequency of premarital sex among people who considered themselves morally upright. Two of the family's six children who emigrated had babies out of wedlock—following the example set by their parents, who had four children when they married in 1824. This was not any indication that Barbara Durst and Eberhard Klinger were immoral—indeed, the opposite was strongly the case, for they stayed together despite any legal requirement that they do so. Instead, their failure to marry was caused by local authorities who refused them the right to wed because, until he was forty-one, Eberhard Klinger could not demonstrate that he had acquired sufficient property to support the family that he had already begun.

Their son Daniel and his common-law wife, Rikke Kaiser, had the same problem. They were devoted to each other but were not allowed to marry in the kingdom of Württemberg, where an 1852 law required "a minimum of 150 guilders as a prerequisite for legal matrimony."[13] The result was illegitimacy for almost one in every five babies. Rikke Kaiser and Daniel Klinger had two children and she was pregnant with a third when his sisters in America provided him with the funds to emigrate in 1857.

Rikke, however, encountered considerable difficulty in joining him. She asked the authorities of the village of Kleinheppach to appropriate forty-five guilders for passage for herself and the two children, which eventually was done because otherwise they "would shortly become public charges." Then she had to write again from

LeHavre, asking for more money for food during the trip. The town's officials voted to "sacrifice from the treasury another 25 guilders, as well as 14 kreuzers for postage, for the loose creature."[14] In America, however, she showed her true nature: she and Daniel not only remained together, but prospered, and when she died in 1910 at age eighty-one, Rikke Klinger was a successful Albany homeowner and grandmother.

The second Klinger child to have a baby out of wedlock was Barbara (Babett), who arrived in 1851 to join her sister and brother-in-law, Marie and Franz Schano. In 1853, they wrote to the parents in Germany:

> After a lengthy delay we are compelled to . . . explain . . . Babett made an acquaintance, which we could see from the start would not be to her advantage, and we tried everything to dissuade her, but to no use, and now what we foresaw has come true, she now has a baby son . . . When we noticed that she was expecting, we urged him to marry her but then he said he had never promised to marry her . . . and anyway he was Jewish and wouldn't abandon his faith and didn't want to hurt his family . . . He asked that a *Contrakt* be drawn up that he'll take care of her . . . One week after the birth he told us he had decided to pay her off completely, because he said she would cause him difficulties later on, and so we demanded one hundred dollars . . .[15]

Her family was uncommonly supportive, giving Babett money and eventually keeping the child while she went west, where she soon had two offers of marriage. It took her a while to save enough money to return from Indiana and fetch her son, but she ended her life on a prosperous farm, the mother of seven.

Likewise, Norwegian Berta Serina Kingestad* overcame the trauma of unwed motherhood. She was pregnant when she came to northern Illinois in 1886 but did not confess this to her family until the following year, when—after several paragraphs on the weather, crops, and other matters—she wrote:

> I see from your letter that there is a good deal of gossip at home, which unfortunately I can witness to the truth of. I had . . . a little smiling blue-eyed boy on the seventh of February, so he is already nearly four months old now . . . I want to implore all of you, my dear ones, that you must not despise me or be angry with me as I rightly deserve . . .
>
> You can imagine how my heart was beating fast when I went to Tom last October . . . His face turned white as a sheet and I saw how he fought to control his anger, but then his brotherly love won, as he said to me in a voice choked with tears, "You should try and go down to Aunt, and if you need anything there I will send you money."

---

* Surnames were not standardized in Norway until the twentieth century. She used "Kingestad" on this letter, but others were signed "Bjoravag," "Svendsen," and "Svendsdatter," with variant spellings on all.

The subject of surnames is further discussed in Chapter 21 of this volume, "Woman's Place in the New World."

. . . I had to travel by all alone by train, forty miles among only Yankees, and
when I finally arrived, there was the question of how Aunt would receive me, who
had come over in this condition . . . They accepted me in a friendly way, these two
old folks, and they have been as kind to me as though they were my own parents. . . .
People here are far different than in Norway. People that I had never seen came and
looked after me.[16]

She made her way in the New World alone, protecting the identity of her baby's
father. The only hint on him was in 1888, when she added in a postscript, "Listen
here, Anna, I am very curious to hear something or the other about Christian . . . He
is probably married now, but tell me who he is married to. I don't think I either could
or would want to get anything from him, but I would like to hear."[17] Instead of
pleading for help from the child's father, she did domestic work and barnyard chores
for farm families in the Norwegian community.

Her first years were hard, as few wanted to hire a woman with a child. But she
never considered returning to Europe or even burdening her family in America with
her needs. Finally, Berta Serina found a wonderful employer: an elderly Englishman
who did not "count the crumbs I give to my little boy." In time, they grew so close
that she wrote, for example, "the old man is sleeping in his rocking chair with
Svennemann in his lap, also fast asleep."[18]

When her son was about five, she married. Little was revealed about her husband
or the circumstances of the marriage, for the news was announced in a playful note
supposedly from the child. The wedding date remained unspecific—but when her
second baby was born on December 22, 1892, Berta Serina was well on her way to
establishing a life that marked her as no different from any other respectable farmwife.

Adultery and Unfit Motherhood

Unwed mothers of the first generation appeared only infrequently in social workers'
records, while more space seems to have been devoted to problems resulting from
extramarital sex. Some cases were so entangled that the truth is hard to discover.
Consider, for example:

Charles Zielinski reported to the Legal Aid Society in December, 1912, that when
he went to Canada to find work his wife went to live with another man . . . Mrs.
Zielinski's story was that . . . he often drank and abused her and before going to
Canada slipped off to Kenosha and tried to marry another woman, but his previous
marriage was discovered. She said he had committed adultery with the wife of the
man who was living with her, and whom she claimed was only a boarder. This wife
arrested her husband and Mrs. Zielinski on a charge of adultery.[19]

Nativists threw up their hands at such moral disorder, so deviant from Victorian codes of behavior. Moreover, the standards of one ethnic group differed widely from those of another. Married Catholic women who were Irish or Italian might find their lives ruined by the merest whisper of adultery, but Slavic women from eastern Europe—who officially practiced the same religion—nonetheless exhibited great sexual freedom. One sociologist, for example, wrote that she was "impressed by instances of the tolerance of the Polish husband and the independence and self-will in establishing sex relations for herself, of the Polish wife."[20]

Indeed, so liberated were some Slavic boardinghouse mistresses that, with the knowledge of their husbands, they included sex as part of the deal. The practice was sufficiently common "to bring into use a special term to describe it—full board."[21] While most observers did not so candidly acknowledge this female sexual liberation, virtually all native writers on immigrants expressed concern that the common practice of strangers boarding together encouraged illicit relationships. This was especially likely, they thought, because the men in such lodgings greatly outnumbered the women—often there was only one woman, the boardinghouse mistress. Even if she was a respectably married, hardworking woman, moralists felt that the situation offered temptations, especially when the husband worked the night shift while other men slept in the woman's home.

Occasionally their fears came true. A Jewish man, for instance, said that he had lived "in peace and security" with his wife for thirteen years, until a friend of his brother's began boarding with them:

> Neighbors began to whisper that my wife was carrying on an affair with this boarder, but . . . I didn't believe them . . . It was all true. My brother took it badly, because he had brought trouble into my home, and in remorse and shame, shot himself . . . For the children's sake we remained together. I promised never to mention the tragic story and she promised to be a loyal wife . . . But my wife couldn't restrain herself and betrayed me again.[22]

Social workers cited other examples like Polish Mrs. Zielek, who had a child by one of her boarders. She nonetheless was "almost a model mother, clean, neat and attractive," and social workers helped her obtain a divorce from her husband so that she could marry the father of her child. But she operated from a morality different from theirs, and they soon heard that "she was living with the god-father of her last child without being married to him." They were further confounded by the appearance of the ex-husband, who was "unusually decent, neat, and clean," and were taken aback at his claim that "he did not know how or why he had been divorced" but that "his former wife was not a fit person."[23]

But even if Slavic women enjoyed greater sexual freedom than either native women or most immigrants, the American judiciary took no cognizance of such community norms—and for most of the immigrant era, the courts favored men in guardianship cases. Several cases exist of children being awarded to fathers even when they were guilty of behavior that the era deemed "immoral," while the mothers were circumspect—simply because the man could support the children more easily than the woman. Immigrant women who were accustomed to freer sexuality soon found that any illicit activity by females in America was sufficient to label them an "unfit mother," even if the male behavior was much worse. For example, a Polish woman who had lost the custody of her child called on the Chicago Legal Aid Society, saying, "with tears in her eyes, that the child meant everything in the world to her":

> In preparation for the final hearing the Legal Aid Society called on the girl for whom Michalski had left his wife. She did not resent the suggestion that she come to court to tell of her relations with Michalski. She "felt sorry for poor Minnie and would be glad to help her out," but it was a most inauspicious moment, as she was suing her own husband for a divorce and she did not wish to be placed in the situation of telling the same Judge in Minnie's case that she was an immoral woman and in her own case that she was an irreproachable wife seeking separation from an undeserving husband.[24]

Nor was extramarital activity limited to urban areas or eastern Europeans or the twentieth century. Even so pious a woman as Gro Svendsen did not consider it necessary to condemn moral lapses in her Iowa community of Norwegians. She wrote noncommittally in 1862 of a friend, "his wife has left him. She is living with another man in a place some 200 miles to the west." In another revealing remark she wrote: "Will you tell Margit Arnegaard that I have made inquiries about her daughter? She is living in comfort. She married the man she left with."[25]

Referring to immigrants in general, one sociologist wrote:

> Marriage is to his mind the normal avenue of gratification . . . but if a man has to remain single too long, or . . . if a woman is widowed, he or she is not blamed overmuch for finding satisfaction . . . in some unobtrusive way. In the peasant communities of some countries sex relations before marriage . . . are not infrequent, and are not severely blamed . . . Often the husband will accept with his bride her child by the man she did not marry.[26]

Of course, not all ethnic groups subscribed to such ideas. An Italian man whose wife or daughter engaged in sex outside marriage would be horrified and would consider himself duty bound to seek bloody revenge, while the woman involved would find herself forever a pariah. Jewish families likewise closely guarded themselves against such shame. The men of these groups might surreptitiously visit brothels, but the women had no latitude in matters of sex.

Within any ethnic group the closer to middle-class Americanization a family was, the more circumspect was their sexual behavior. Indeed, much modification of immigrant morality was based on an awareness of American standards. Barbro Ramseth's ambivalence about her Wisconsin neighbors, for instance, clearly was more concerned with what outsiders would think than with any innate standard of right and wrong; writing in 1903 of "Rationalists" in her Wisconsin community, she said: "Embret Nilsen also never goes to church. He is . . . still not married. It is strange and shameful for both Norwegians and people from Tynset, for you can be sure that other nationalities notice such things. Living together without being married. It may be that they live right, but the example is poor."[27]

Yet common-law arrangements often were taken very seriously by couples who viewed themselves as "living right," who saw their commitment to each other as more important than statist legalisms. In some cases, women candidly preferred this freedom to the binding ties of marriage. A Lithuanian woman in Chicago was typical; abandoned by her drunkard husband, she moved in with another man because, she frankly said, she had no money and needed support. They saw no reason to deal with the difficulties of divorce and remarriage. Having a marriage license had not made a difference in her first marriage, and she saw no point in obtaining one a second time.[28]

Women who "lived in sin" nonetheless could hold firm moral beliefs. An Irish woman, for example, who lived with a man and had two children by him did not get married until her brother insisted. But despite her lack of conventionality, she refused to allow her sister-in-law to live with them on the grounds that this woman, who had separated from her husband and placed her children in an orphanage, was immoral.[29]

Especially if one's first marriage had been unhappy, some women were wary of being legally bound again and preferred a common-law arrangement. In the words of one Pole, "That began all the trouble, getting married. A man feels sure of you as soon as you marry him. I'll never marry another man if I get free of this one."[30] Indeed, social workers who nagged unwed couples to marry and took men to court on adultery charges may have unintentionally hurt women as much as helped them.

They took the American view that marriage conferred benefits on a woman, for it was assumed that law and custom then protected her. Immigrant women, however, often seemed to consider marriage as much of a risk as a protection. Not only did a woman give up a hard-saved dowry, but also it was difficult for her to get a divorce, both in the law and in the church. To some, it seemed more practical to avoid the legalisms. Realizing American standards, a common-law wife was willing to make a pretense of being married—as in using her mate's name and allowing priests to assume marriage when children were christened—as long as she knew, and more important, her mate knew, that she was free.

Deadly Scandal—Venereal Disease in the Victorian Age

In 1914, an anti-vice group in New York City complained about "the Friendly Inn, a 50-cent Italian disorderly house on Hester and Mott Streets."[31] The owner had operated this and similar places since 1905 but had been fined only once; clearly, American officials closed their eyes to the activities of this Italian man. Though he had operated for nearly a decade before pressure arose, 1914 was a logical year for such complaints. As World War I intensified, campaigns began to clean up illicit sex—not from any new interest in female welfare but because of danger to the troops. In addition to the war, attention focused on the subject because the newly invented Wassermann test for syphilis had just begun to reveal what a grave problem it was.

"Syphilis is a very widespread disease," said a Johns Hopkins expert in 1914. "We had no idea until the introduction of the Wassermann reaction furnished us with reliable data . . . At the present time it cannot be positively stated what proportion of the entire population has this disease, but I believe it to be fully 10%."[32] Clearly, if one man in every ten was afflicted with syphilis, then literally millions of women were also exposed. So serious was the rate of female infection that one authority reported "frequent estimates place half of all gynecological operations as the result of this disease."[33] Another expert called syphilis "one of the most important causes" of miscarriages.[34]

Despite the great damage done to women by men who thoughtlessly transmitted their diseases, it took decades for physicians to begin speaking candidly to their female patients on this subject. Women were treated for venereal disease far less frequently than men, with one study showing an approximate ratio of about one female patient for every four males. Worse, the women's cases were more likely to be serious than those of men; about 10% more women than men in this study had "chronic" conditions.[35] Similarly, a 1929–30 report on a Boston dispensary showed 1,180 men sought help, while only 213 female patients were seen.[36]

At the end of the immigrant era, the New York State Health Commission used scathing language on the slow pace of reform; it reported in 1931 that physicians not only failed to acknowledge venereal disease in women but also failed—for forty years—to follow procedures that prevented blindness in newborns whose mothers were infected:

> In 1890 a law was passed requiring silver nitrate to be placed in the eyes of all new-born infants . . . There is no excuse whatever for the number of cases which now occur, and state and local health authorities should inquire searchingly into every case with a view to eliminating the occurrence of the preventable tragedy of gonorrheal blindness. The almost universal acceptance . . . of this [test] . . . should serve to reassure those physicians who hesitate to make routine Wassermann tests on pregnant women.[37]

They "hesitated to make routine tests" because physicians were not comfortable in talking with women about sex, and that lack of communication doubtless was even greater in the immigrant community, where both language difficulty and cultural reticence limited the flow of information. Midwives, many of whom were foreign born, were more likely to speak candidly with their patients. Moreover, they also had an excellent record in treating newborns to undo the effects of parental gonor-rhea[38]—but during the economic competition of the Great Depression, physicians were increasingly successful in limiting the practices of midwives.

That male physicians seemed to address this subject in almost exclusively male terms may have been motivated by their personal situations: one referred to his colleagues as literally "lousy docs" because of "the high rate of venereal disease prevailing among them."[39] Even the American Social Hygiene Association, which developed such thoughtful programs as targeting the high disease rate of railroad men, failed to serve women. Though "prenatal treatment of infected mothers" was considered "very important," their report reluctantly acknowledged that "this is an item that does not appear on the present program."[40]

Such reticence affected all women, but it was especially damaging for immigrant women, who were privy to less information on all subjects. This was especially true for the large numbers of Italian women, for no European culture placed more barriers in the way of women on sexual matters than theirs. It was particularly ironic, therefore, that many Italians believed that "contact with a virgin . . . was an unfailing cure for gonorrhea."[41] Such a dangerously erroneous idea was an excellent rationale for the strict control that Italians made of their daughter's movements, and that control was in fact so strict that one Italian doctor reported he knew of only two cases of women being used for this purpose, both involving mentally retarded girls. On the other hand, however, other women may have hidden this shameful disease even from physicians, especially since there was little hope of a cure. Moreover, much infection in married women may have been the result of bridegrooms who hoped a virginal bride would cause a medical miracle. The woman, in all probability, would not recognize the symptoms of her contagion; she could even give birth to blind babies and die of the disease without understanding the crime that had been done to her.

A 1934 study in fact found the death rates from syphilitic disease to be "significantly higher" among Italian men than among other white men, while Jewish men had a distinctly lower rate. "The figures for deaths of females," the report concluded, "are too small to be significant."[42] But while "the figures" indeed may have been small, the probability is that actual cases were much higher than the report reflected, for both physicians and women were likely to attribute female deaths to other, less scandalous causes. The 1908 report of an Italian physician was far more thoughtful than most such studies:

> Venereal diseases . . . are spreading with alarming rapidity among our immigrant population . . . The death rate . . . was higher for the Italians than for any other element of the white population . . .
>
> Gonorrhea and syphilis insontium, the scourges of the innocent, are more prevalent than people suppose . . . When people live huddled together at the rate of five and six in a room, it is impossible not to come in touch with . . . the disease, and in this way harmless children and honest women contract the virus without their knowledge . . . I [know] of hundreds of silent tragedies enacted in some poor honest Italian family, where the presence of a chance boarder or a lodger brought the poison . . . And what about the thousands of innocent Italian women who have had

their vital organs sacrificed and their health forever wrecked, after joining their long-departed husbands.[43]

Few physicians of the Victorian Age exhibited such understanding of their female patients, however, and many opposed both sex education and scientific study of sexuality issues. Too frequently any such study was greeted as in Baltimore, where a 1916 report "caused a storm of protest" and "a good deal of personal abuse" for health authorities. The contradictory attitudes of public opinion were clear in the *Baltimore News*, which "carried eight columns of the Report," while "an editorial of the same issue said the Report was too filthy to print."[44]

Prostitution, Formal and Freelance

Sometimes illicit sex was unwilling, engaged in only because a woman felt that she had no viable alternative. Women's wages were so inadequate and job security so lacking that sometimes one felt she had no choice except to make "concessions" to her boss. From there she might drift into the sale of the only commodity she had that the world seemed to value. Such cases, noted a Pittsburgh sociologist, were "scarcely typical, but far from uncommon."[45]

New York City authorities were sufficiently aware of the economic incentive that they made "the penalty for prostitution in tenement houses severe." Though they might overlook it in other parts of the city, in the tenement homes where the mass of immigrants lived, the city fathers aimed to prevent "the contrast between well-dressed ladies who seem to do nothing, and the shabby, hard-working women, [which] is a disturbing influence on the minds of impressionable girls."[46]

Sexual crime did pay: in 1906 when the average wage of newly arrived women was $5.58 a week, a Boston "hurdy-gurdy girl" earned $20 to $24.[47] Full-fledged prostitutes, operating in a Chicago house, could earn up to $400 a week—though of course they didn't keep it all—while street walkers could expect a minimum of $25 weekly.[48]

Yet while the wages of sin were attractive, on the whole not as many foreigners as Americans accepted them. From the advent of the immigrant era to its end, "scarcely typical, but far from uncommon" seems an appropriate summation—though many nativists were convinced that decadent Europeans brought prostitution along with their baggage.

Often the crime had to be broadly defined to ensnare a measurable number of foreign women: In New York City's Kleindeutschland of the 1850s, for instance, attention centered on "basements with friendly service." These were beer halls that "catered to the rougher elements and to single men looking for easy girls—or outright prostitutes."[49] About 2,000 women worked in "friendly basements," where their primary purpose was to encourage consumption of alcohol, for "they were paid by the drink." These women indeed may have "frequently supplemented their income by prostitution"—but, because "the German term for serving girls, *Dirne*, means both 'girl' and 'prostitute,'"[50] it is difficult to say with certainty that they were in fact practicing the illicit trade.

Estimating the numbers in prostitution, especially in New York, remained an attractive subject for studies throughout the immigrant era. In the decade before it began, an 1835 analysis of the city's House of Refuge showed just four foreign women—all from the British Isles—compared with twenty-six Americans.[51] At midcentury, the city's prostitutes were estimated at 6,000, and a study of inmates at Blackwell Island found that the one-eighth who were German "were greatly outnumbered by their Irish and American sisters."[52] Moreover, most of these German prostitutes did not fit the stereotype, for they "worked in small-scale and relatively respectable brothels. Three or four young women would pay half their earnings to a couple who ran the establishment, the man tending bar in front and the wife doing the cooking and cleaning."[53]

An 1858 census described such a place in almost appealing terms: "The room is very clean . . . There is a small table with some German newspapers upon it [and] a piano . . . Two or three girls are in different parts of the room engaged in knitting or sewing." Behind or above this pleasant living room were "bedrooms where the women took customers who wanted more than a drink and conversation."[54] Other immigrant brothels adopted a similar pose, operating under the guise of boarding-houses in respectable neighborhoods. An 1882 male observer was "struck by the number of handsome young widows who are to be found in these establishments. Sometimes they do not assume the character of a widow, but claim to be the wives of men . . . in Europe . . . Their object is simply to make money."[55]

Yet the number of foreign women involved in such activity was statistically insignificant, and as immigration moved to the more conservative cultures of southern Europe toward the end of the nineteenth century, there was even less likelihood that large numbers of immigrants would be involved in prostitution. Nonetheless, they remained a constant priority of investigators. The 1911 report of the Vice Commission of Chicago, for instance, shows immigrants were not sufficiently prevalent in the trade to excite the attention that they nonetheless got. Though the report was done in a time of great immigration and in a great immigrant city, the examples of foreign-born prostitutes among the dozens of case histories literally can be counted on the fingers of one hand.

In New York—the nation's haven for both immigrants and iniquity—another writer reached the same conclusion after studying the inhabitants of brothels: "Nearly all the women in those dens," he wrote in 1906, "were native Americans, or came from what we call the better immigrant stock . . . Most of the Slavs who come here do not know anything about the business of prostitution . . . and until a few years ago this was true of the Jews also."[56] Similarly, throughout the long decades of immigration from Ireland, even those writers who were prejudiced against the Irish testified to the chastity of their women. As late as 1914—after there had been a steady stream of Irish immigrants for seventy years—one male observer wrote that "rape, pandering, and the white-slave traffic are almost unknown among them."[57]

Nonetheless, authorities continued to study prostitution and to issue reports reluctantly acknowledging that their statistics could not justify the thesis that most preferred to believe. In 1933, for example, a Chicago commission reported:

> Only 6 of the 63 girls studied were reported as immigrants . . . None of these was a "just-arrived" immigrant. Most of the 6 had been in this country over 5 years . . .
>
> Contrary to general opinion, it is clear that the highest concentration and rates of vice resorts both in 1920 and 1930 were not located in the tracts with the highest percentages of immigrants but rather in those with the lowest.[58]

But the mind-set of most authorities remained distrustful of the foreign born. Though he had no arrests to show for his efforts, a New York police lieutenant in 1914 wrote a three-page letter to the mayor in which he detailed more than twenty visits that his detectives had made to various "suspicious" addresses:

> A three-story brick building occupied by one Bertha Hirsh, in the basement of which she conducts a restaurant . . . Although they kept this place under surveillance . . . they were unable to discover anything which would indicate that the premises were being used for immoral purposes . . . They visited the "Little Bohemia" [and] they . . . saw a number of men and women seated in the rear room, but did not see anything indicating that those women were prostitutes.[59]

The assumption that women in public places were inherently suspicious is most blatant in this portion of the officer's letter: "They visited the New Hotel . . . This hotel is conducted for men only; they did not observe any women enter or leave the hotel."[60] In such male minds, a woman had no legitimate business in a hotel. Moreover, because a hotel owner who rented to a woman took the risk of being considered a pimp, these places were often closed to her. The implications for immigrant women at the traveling stage of settlement are enormous; any woman who stepped outside a family group to travel alone could expect to have her morality questioned and her journey complicated.

Decades later, another New York investigation operated on the same suspicions. This was a massive study that included an incredible number of interviews with "go-betweens": 1,168 taxi drivers/chauffeurs, 732 white and 461 "Negro bellboys and elevator operators," plus 2,205 "casuals" (casual conversations with other white men). The actual prostitutes interviewed, on the other hand, numbered 22. This figure was carefully broken down into three women in "parlor houses," twelve in "apartments," and seven "without addresses." To track down the twelve "in apartments," they had visited 86 "separate addresses . . . in search of alleged prostitutes." Between January and October of 1932, these diligent workers also took 439 "street reports"—which resulted in 13 "prostitutes who solicited investigators."[61]

While again the majority were natives, a few immigrant women turned up in this investigation, which was done in the worst of the Great Depression and after decades of immigration. One who was born near Hamburg, Germany, told the incognito investigator who solicited her that her two little children had died and she could not find work: "I'd take any kind of job. But I can't seem to get hold of one, so I go out and maybe I meet a man. Then I take him back to my apartment with me, and he gives me a few dollars." Her inexperience and discomfort with prostitution was clear from her inability to set a price: "Finally, she reluctantly said, 'It's up to you . . . whatever you give me . . . I'll not argue about it nor ask you for more.'"[62]

Though the majority of prostitutes were natives, there was one significant exception to the statistical rule: French women were greatly involved in the trade in comparison with their numbers in the population. Immigration from France was very small throughout the entire era, but French women came in first in prostitution—at least in the eyes of immigration officials who denied them admission:[63]

ALIENS DEPORTED AS PROSTITUTES AT TIME OF ENTRY, 1908–1909

French	42	Slavic	3
English	38	Irish	3
German	12	Scandinavian	2
Italian	7	Polish	2
Hebrew	7	Dutch	1
Scottish	5		

In Chicago, where the relative frequency of arrests for "offenses against chastity" was 11.6 for French women, the comparable rate for the Slavic groups—who made up the vast majority of Chicago immigrants—fell below 3.0.[64] A study of New York arrests in this era agreed that the influence of the French in prostitution was disproportionate. Moreover, it concluded, "It seems probable that the percentage of French women who practiced prostitution before arrival is decidedly larger."[65] Most other immigrant women were seduced into the business after their arrival, this report argued, and national experts agreed:

> The investigation of the United States Immigration Commission into the relation of the immigrant woman to the social evil showed that very few prostitutes are brought into the United States. The great majority of young immigrant women who were found in resorts were virtuous when they came here, and were ruined because there was not adequate protection and assistance given them after they reached the United States.[66]

This "protection," however, hampered the free movement of guileless women while it did little to bother those who were more sophisticated about sex. Women in steerage were carefully checked for any appearance of immorality, while the experienced importers of prostitutes sent them second class, where female passengers were not subject to such insulting inquiry. In addition, unsuccessful suitors sometimes vindicated their hurt pride by maliciously reporting their former girlfriends to immigration authorities as immoral. Immigration officials took such reports quite seriously, seemed inclined to believe the worst, and assumed the woman was guilty until she proved herself innocent.

After the League of Nations was organized near the end of the immigrant era, it too undertook prostitution control—but the effort was almost entirely conducted by men, many of whom combined a limited understanding of women's lives with a penchant for additional bureaucracy. The summary of a 1932 meeting complained that "practically no country has a specialized staff for this work" and that important "countries are not yet parties to the Convention." Among their "suggested remedies" was this tentative proposal: "It might be a good plan to attach one or two women police agents to the central authority."[67] Ironically, France was praised for its "well organized central authority" and for refusing "passports to French women and girls suspected of going abroad to engage in prostitution." The more relevant notation instead may have been: "No women police in France."[68]

French pimps also appeared frequently in reports. According to a study done in the World War I era, Italians and Jews also ranked high[69]—something that is not surprising among men who came from traditions of arranged marriages and other culturally condoned practices that resulted in an image of women as sexual objects. Foreign-born pimps were sufficiently numerous that 5,895 aliens were deported or denied entry "because of their connection with the business of prostitution" during the heavy immigrant period between 1892 and 1918.[70]

In a loose international network, these procurers exchanged letters on likely prospects and warned each other of government crackdowns. The language used in these letters makes the era's term of "white slavery" an apt one, for they speak of buying and selling women as chattel, often at high prices:

> [S]tatements were made by a certain keeper of a house of prostitution in Chicago that for a certain French girl named Marcelle he had paid the sum of $1,000; that for a certain French girl named Mascotta . . . he had paid $500 . . . Lillie, also a French girl, was sent from Chicago to Omaha and sold to a keeper of a house of prostitution in that city for the sum of $1,400 . . . $500 is the ordinary price for a French prostitute when delivered in America.[71]

Indeed, while it was not as common as Americans feared, occasionally there were naive young women who were deceived into becoming friendly with pimps or madams and finally, if they did not join the trade willingly, were brutalized. A common method of madams was to hire European girls as maids, bring them to the United States, and then, when it was difficult for them to escape, break them into the work. Consider the case of this innocent German girl:

> On my way to Bremerhoffen in the train Marie G.——— happened to be in the same compartment. Marie G.——— asked . . . all about myself and my family . . . She told

me that she was a respectable married woman and owned a house in Los Angeles . . . I thought it quite natural to ask her if she could assist me in obtaining a position . . . After arrival she told me, "Well, now we go to my house." . . . I saw girls half-dressed, and Marie turned on me right away and said I should not bother about what I saw, and look around so much . . . I did not know where to go; I had no money; . . . She would not allow me to speak to anyone . . . I asked Marie G.——— for some paper. I wanted to write home . . . she . . . never would give it to me . . . I was crying and she said she had done so much for me already that I was really ungrateful. I told her I was going to get a policeman, and Marie G.——— said if I got a policeman I would get arrested, and not her.[72]

A Lithuanian Jew was also betrayed by a woman who posed as a matchmaker and obtained her trust. When she realized what was about to happen to her, she tried to escape, but was imprisoned and beaten.

Time passed and I got used to the horrible life. Later I even had an opportunity to escape, because they used to send me out on the streets, but life had become meaningless for me anyway, and nothing mattered anymore. I lived this way for six months, degraded and dejected, until I got sick and they drove me out of that house.

I appealed for admission into several hospitals, but they didn't want to take me in . . . I had decided to throw myself into the river, but wandering around on the streets, I met a richly dressed man who was quite drunk. I took over six hundred dollars from him and spent the money on doctors, who cured me.[73]

She then got a job as a domestic and the family liked her. Later the mistress of the house died and the man wanted to marry her, but she was unsure because of her past. She wrote to a Jewish newspaper for advice and the editor advised her to tell the truth, and if the man loved her sufficiently, he would understand. The paper, however, showed little sympathy for these unfortunate women, adding, "Such letters from victims of 'white slavery' come to our attention quite often, but we do not publish them. We are disgusted by this plague on society, and dislike bringing it to the attention of our readers."[74]

Not only did the community generally refuse to aid fallen women, but the women themselves usually felt so degraded that they did not consider their lives redeemable. Moreover, the rehabilitative efforts that did exist usually were run by native Protestants and were aimed at native women, while the faiths to which many immigrants adhered participated less often in this work. Two exceptions were projects run by nuns who were themselves immigrants: Sister Blandina Segale, an Italian-born nun, in a five-year period at the end of the nineteenth century "had restored 157 women to normal living" in Cincinnati.[75] The Irish Magdalens also specialized in this work, and while it is not clear how many of the women that they helped were immigrants, their effort was large: in New York from 1857 to 1907, they "received 13,108 girls, of whom 8,581 were committed by the courts."[76] They also

RESCUE FROM WHITE SLAVERY

ran similar projects in St. Louis, Boston, Philadelphia, Chicago, Baltimore, and other cities.

More commonly, however, government and social agencies aimed at prevention of prostitution, for most believed there was little hope of cure for those already fallen. It was unusual both for society to forgive and for women to think themselves worthy of forgiveness. Their self-abasement, their fatalism, kept them in the life. "In one of the recent raids," said a 1911 report, "a big Irish girl was taken and held as a witness. She was old enough, strong enough, and wise enough . . . to have overcome almost any kind of opposition." Asked why she did not leave, her reply was:

> Get out! I can't. They make us buy the cheapest rags, and they are charged against us at fabulous prices; they make us change outfits at intervals of two or three weeks, until we are so deeply in debt that there is no hope of ever getting out from under. Then, to make matters worse, we seldom get an accounting . . . and when we do . . . it is always to find ourselves deeper in debt than before. We've simply got to stick, and that's all there is to it.[77]

It was a strange system of morality that convinced a woman the property rights of one's exploiter were more to be reckoned with as a moral obligation than her own human rights—but this emphasis on property values as opposed to human values appeared to them to be one of the strongest of American characteristics. It seemed to be the basic premise of the industrial system that immigrants knew so well, and therefore, it is not surprising that daughters of immigrants were statistically more likely to become prostitutes than their foreign-born mothers had been.

Perhaps the language barrier and lack of knowledge of American techniques had some small inhibiting effect on the foreign born, but more important was a well-defined moral code that enabled resistance. Children of immigrants were more ambivalent in their beliefs, for the conflict between the values of their parents and those of the surrounding American society often left them with no strong standards. Caught up in the syndrome of rising expectations, to many of the second generation the best thing to do was what made the most money in the easiest way. A government study had to admit that "the foreign born are not so likely to become prostitution offenders as their children are."[78] America had taken away the validity of their mothers' mores and left these women with none of their own.

PART III

DOMESTICITY:
THE OLD
AND THE NEW

9

THE FRUIT OF THE LAND

Every Letter a Grocery List: Adjustment amid Abundance

Change was the only constant in the life of an immigrant woman. The one thing she could feel sure of was that the future would be different from the past. If she had felt sure of the solidity of her wedding vows in Europe, in America she saw devastating things happen to marriages. If she had been positive that what the priest or rabbi spoke in Europe was truth, in America she saw that even these sacred areas were open to question. Everywhere there was change, and with the change, ambivalence.

Whether the subject was as significant as religion and morality or as mundane as the way she dressed and what she ate, always there was ambivalence about the new ways versus the old. Often the changes that mattered most to her were the ones that were not the most important in societal terms. It is of these personal, seemingly trivial, things that letters were filled.

Food was one of those things. The change in diet was of tremendous importance to immigrant women, and many a letter reads like a menu. They gloated over the abundance of food in America and considered this the best of justifications for emigration. Listen to Jannicke Saehle, a young Norwegian who came alone in 1847 to seek her fortune in Madison, Wisconsin:

> I have food and drink in abundance. A breakfast here consists of chicken, mutton, beef or pork, warm or cold wheat bread, butter, white cheese, eggs, or small

pancakes, the best coffee, tea, cream and sugar. For dinner the best courses are served. Supper is eaten at six o'clock, with warm biscuits, and several kinds of cold wheat bread, cold meats, bacon, cakes, preserved apples, plums, berries, which are eaten with cream, tea and coffee—and my greatest regret here is to see the superabundance of food, much of which has to be thrown to the chickens and the swine, when I think of my dear ones in Bergen, who like so many others must at this time lack the necessities of life.[1]

Likewise, German Emilie Lohmann was tremendously impressed with the New York open-air markets she saw upon her arrival in August of 1853. "I had no idea it would be something so grand," she said of the Washington Market.

It is a huge place, all under one roof. Long rows of tables contain all kinds of foodstuffs. Each variety of food took several rows of tables . . . We walked through first the fish department . . . next the meat department, with huge slabs of beef lying in rows on the table, a large variety of sausages, all kinds of fowl, live rabbits in hutches—anything one can think of. Then the fruits, a variety of berries, apples, pears, pineapples, vegetables, herb markets and flowers . . . To think that daily this much food is sold and consumed! . . . There were smaller tables where they sold bread, *kuchen,*[*] pies (as they are called here), and drinks. On the corners little girls have lemonade stands where they sell glass after glass to hot, thirsty customers. One can think of nothing edible that could not be bought here.[2]

Nor did it take a great deal to satisfy the newcomers at first. Praise of the American white, soft bread especially runs like a theme through letters; it alone made a meal luxurious. Rosa Cavalleri's first supper in Missouri was unexceptional by American standards but a banquet by hers. "Bread! white bread! Enough for a whole village! And butter to go on it! I ate until I no longer had any pains in my stomach!" The next morning she reported, "For breakfast there was white bread again and butter and coffee and sugar and sausages and eggs besides! Mama mia! Did all the poor people in America eat like kings?"[3]

She soon became accustomed to this diet and accepted it as the only adequate fare. When she returned to Italy for a visit sometime later, she was appalled at the meager menus that she had eaten all of her earlier life: "I was no longer content with sour-tasting black bread, or thin onion-and-water soup, or a little polenta. I wanted to make thick soup with rice in it every day or cook the rice the way I had learned to cook it in America. 'Whoever heard of such extravagance!' Mamma Lena would scold. 'The people in America make pigs of themselves.'"[4]

By American standards, Rosa's cooking plans were far from extravagant. Nor was it only southern Europeans who thought of commonplace American menus as

---

[*] *Kuchen* is the German word for coffee cake.

gourmet treats; this Norwegian woman, writing from Wisconsin in 1850, plainly thinks that she is inordinately blessed:

> Our daily food consists of rye and wheat bread, bacon, butter, eggs, molasses, sugar, coffee and beer. The corn that grows on large cobs is rarely eaten by people ... but is used as fodder for the animals ... This year we have produced so much foodstuff that we have been able to sell instead of having to buy, and we all have cattle, driving oxen, and wagons. We also have children in abundance.[5]

The children doubtless were abundant—yet if the food list is carefully analyzed, it has only the items of an unexceptional breakfast of bacon, eggs, and toast. The "daily fare" included nothing else for other meals, for there was no variety of meat, no vegetables or fruit, not even any dairy products. Instead, it was largely staples that Americans, even of that time, would not think worth mentioning.

When immigrants found that they could afford in America foods that had been beyond their reach in Europe, some went wild. Social workers cited examples of children being fed doughnuts, pies, and cookies for all of their meals. Italian women went from being one of the world's lowest sugar consumers to one of its highest,[6] and many seemed to believe that their children were akin to animals in instinctively choosing the food that was best for them. When mothers realized that visiting nurses had other nutritional theories, they simply didn't tell them the truth rather than "make that nurse too sad."[7]

Of course they wanted to do what was best for their children, but in this new environment, it was difficult to decide what was best. First it was hard to obtain the accustomed foodstuffs, even if one had sufficient money, which was often not the case. Cooking utensils were unfamiliar, with appliances still stranger. Women were puzzled by the "stoves with no fires in them and no place for the wood, just holes in irons, and if you turn a handle and apply a lighted match, fire comes."[8] Learning the necessary techniques and adjusting the family's preferences to the available ingredients and doing this in a way that promoted good nutrition was an adjustment that took years.

It would seem to be the mothers' inability to obtain nourishing foodstuffs that, for example, was the best explanation for underweight children in a 1919 program. In a section of New York City that was 91% Italian, children were identified who were "decidedly underweight for height and anemic in appearance." Visiting nurses weighed them weekly, while also working with their mothers on nutritional education, and the results were wonderfully significant. During eighteen weeks, the fifty-four children had an "average gain of 68% above that of the normal gain for a child of that age and height."[9]

Peasant women, though untutored in nutritional theory, generally had evolved moderately well-balanced diets for their families in Europe. The disruption of life that emigration wrought could seriously disturb these habits. In one revealing case, for example, a sick baby was brought to a public health clinic and the mother questioned in regard to its diet:

> "What do you give the baby?" asked the nurse through an interpreter.
>
> "What we have ourselves," was the reply.
>
> "But why should you do that to a little baby?" chided the nurse.
>
> "I always did that in our own country with my other children before we came here."
>
> "But what did you give your children in the old country that you had yourselves?"
>
> "Soup and buttermilk," answered the mother, smiling, apparently at the pleasant recollection of those days.
>
> "What do you give your child now that you have yourselves?"
>
> "Beer and coffee."[10]

Inadequacy of milk was frequent. When milk had been readily available on European farms, women used it, but in the big cities of America, it was unreasonably expensive. As one tubercular woman said when she refused to drink the milk her doctor had prescribed: "The milk comes in a bottle; in my country, I get it from the goat . . . I do not know what else is in the bottle; there must be something besides milk, to make it cost so much."[11]

That something else was in the bottle was entirely possible—but not beneficial. Prior the Pure Food and Drug Act of 1906, a good deal of milk was thinned with water and even adulterated with chalk and other substances to increase the quantity while disguising the poor quality. In addition, there was serious risk of contamination because milk was sold in open buckets, and prior to pasteurization and refrigeration, it quickly spoiled in the summer months.

In large cities, some charities provided "milk stations"—ice-laden wagons that kept milk cool and clean, but even then, they found that some of their would-be clientele was unwillingly to use it. Milk, especially cow's milk drunk as a beverage, was not part of the standard diet of Mediterranean cultures, and a number of taboos were associated with it.

In Italy, for example, it was given to little children and the sick, but when Rosa Cavalleri wanted milk with her breakfast, she was told that she was too old and given wine instead. Others believed that milk caused worms and that it would make the person look like the goat or cow from which it was obtained. The level of distrust was clear when a woman was unable to nurse a newborn: a wet nurse was secured at all costs to avoid the risk of animal milk.

An important part of the regular diet of these groups was cheese, from which they obtained their calcium. But when the familiar cheeses—feta, romano, parmesan, and so forth—were not to be had in nineteenth-century America, a dearth of calcium resulted. This calcium deficiency caused rickets, which appeared so frequently, especially among Italians, that it was not unusual to have several children in a family who were so severely bowlegged that their legs had to be broken and straightened to undo the damage.

Milk was a basic element of the Scandinavian diet, where cool summers caused no refrigeration problems and no taboos evolved. Nonetheless, for Scandinavians too there were dietary disruptions in America because summers were much more severe and women were at a loss in dealing with dairy products. Gro Svendsen wrote home from northern Iowa:

> I remember I used to wonder when I heard that it would be impossible to keep the milk as we did at home. Now I have learned that it is indeed impossible because of the heat here in the summertime. One can't make cheese out of milk because of flies, bugs and other insects . . . If one were to make cheese here in the summertime, the cheese itself would be alive with bugs. Toward late autumn it should be possible to keep the milk.[12]

A skeptical immigrant girl is greeted by a Red Cross volunteer who is pouring her a drink of milk. Note also that it is the women who skillfully carry the luggage of this group on their heads.   (LIBRARY OF CONGRESS, AMERICAN RED CROSS COLLECTION)

Perhaps the greatest Americanization of eating habits was in the staff of life, bread. So quickly did immigrants change from brown bread made with rye or oats to white bread made with wheat that it could have been a law. It was doing what the natives did that motivated Emilie Koenig, for—like a number of others—she did not seem particularly happy about this change. "Twice a week I bake bread," she said, "not the substantial, solid, leavened rye bread we were used to in Germany, but white bread."[13] She got her initial yeast from a German brewery and kept it alive in the basement for this semiweekly baking.

In the South, of course, cornbread was fundamental to the diet, and Elise Waerenskjold baked it instead of bread made from the familar rye and oats "because the Americans use these grains only as feed for cattle."[14] In the cities where commercial bakeries were established, bread baking of any sort soon disappeared, even among nonworking women. Some Italian women mixed their dough at home and took the loaves to a bakery to be baked, paying ten cents a week for this service,[15] but most budgets of immigrant households included purchases of bread.

Indeed, it is seldom that one reads of urban immigrants baking anything. Some city homes had no ovens, and even when they did, a metal oven fueled by dangerous gas was very different from the brick one heated with wood that Old World women understood. It also was hard to obtain ingredients for familiar recipes, and in summer, baking made tenement homes impossibly hot. Probably also women (and especially their children) were attracted by the novelty of baked goods available in stores. Cookies were on the shelves in grocery stores, and buying them was part of being a good American.

Nor was it necessarily the adjustment to new ingredients and methods that explains the absence of baking, for some immigrant women may not have acquired these skills in the Old World either, especially those who came from cities. Rosa Cavalleri lived in a village near Milan, but she worked in a silk mill and had no homemaking experience. Because she was a woman, however, she was imported to a Missouri coal camp to cook—though she did not even know how to make coffee. "It's easy," an Italian man explained to her. "Just make the water boil and grind the coffee and put it in like this. And always we have plenty of sugar and cream to go in. The German women on the farms taught me that."[16] And thus, immigrant to immigrant, and occasionally even man to woman, an understanding of how to cook in America developed.

Missing from the Menu: Nostalgia and Shortage

Praise of American food was likely to come early in an immigrant's personal history; the longer they wrote, the more likely women were to speak of missing Old World favorites. In 1887, forty years after Elise Waerenskjold had emigrated to Texas, she wrote nostalgically of home-country cooking, wishing she could have "some of the good food you know so well how to prepare . . . I have not eaten fish cakes since we lay in Drobak, waiting for a favorable wind."[17] Though extremely fond of Texas, there were things she missed from the beginning, for she had written earlier:

> We have many good things in Norway that are lacking here . . . Such a simple thing as ale I haven't been able to get up till now because of a lack of yeast; but since the last emigrants brought yeast with them, almost all of us have now brewed ale for Christmas . . . I haven't tasted a glass of wine in four years. If I could get fruit, I would certainly have wine and juice, too. A person certainly misses refreshing drink.[18]

Eventually, she would get the fruit trees necessary for juice and wine, but it took time for plants to mature and even more time for import systems to develop that would allow immigrants to purchase their familiar foodstuffs. Indeed, the knowledge that they could not obtain their customary foods elsewhere was a strong reason for the existence of immigrant ghettos.

European-style delicatessens—with their traditional cheeses, sausages, olive oil, pastas, wines—flourished only in cities, and many women preferred to stay in a "Little Italy" or "Little Poland" expressly because their shopping needs were met and their language understood. For Jewish women, the demand for kosher foods was crucial in limiting them to urban lives—but if the import business was well established there, they could go on cooking and eating much as always.

This was not the case for women who settled outside cities, especially while the frontier was new and food supplies depended on what one had preserved from the previous summer. Writing in late winter, Elisabeth Koren said:

> We cannot say that we live so exceptionally well here. The dishes vary from boiled pork to fried pork, rare to well done, with coffee in addition (milk when we can get it), good bread and butter. To this are added now and then potatoes, which are now all gone; fried onions once in a while, and above all, the glass jar of pickles. That is our meal, morning, noon, and evening.[19]

Another Norwegian woman echoed her complaint about the monotonous diet of pork: "Alive, the pigs invaded both church and cabin, and slaughtered, they appeared on the poineer's table three times a day."[20] Because they complained of such tiresome menus and missed their traditional food, it seems very odd to find that immigrant women rarely mention eating fish. In Elise Waerenskjold's Texas it was more difficult to obtain, but in the upper Midwest, where most other Scandinavians lived, fish were certainly plentiful. In fact, one of Elisabeth Koren's friends told her that he lived "next to a river so full of fish, mostly carp and pike, that at times one cannot see the bottom. One evening he himself caught a large mess of fish with his hands."[21] Whether or not this is a "fish story," it is true that fish were abundant in the virgin days of the Midwest. Yet neither she nor other immigrant women speak of frequently using fish, even though it was a mainstay of the northern European native diet. Perhaps it was again a simple case of doing what the Americans did.

If their daily diet accommodated itself to American reality, women did try to serve native food for special occasions. Norwegians might not regularly eat much fish, for example, but *lutefisk** was a special treat for weddings and Christmas. Similarly, while Elisabeth Koren's cook served interminable pork and pickles, other enterprising women hoarded their goodies for the pastor's visits; when Rev. Koren returned from his parish rounds, "he wounds Helene's heart by telling her about the *flodegrod,*** apple charlotte, roast chicken, and I know not how many other glorious things he has had."[22]

Obtaining special foodstuffs often presented real problems, of course, for not only was it difficult to find suppliers, but greater prices were sure to be charged for what was now an exotic item. Some Italian families ate meager meals for weeks before a festival in order to assure having the proper foods then—but even in families that were charity cases, the special items often appeared, with the budget carefully reworked to hide this necessary extravagance from the social worker's scrutiny.

Sometimes the problem was not merely adjustment from familiar to new foods but one of eating to stay alive. Although many immigrants were enthusiastic about the plentiful food America, at other times and places, the situation was the opposite—even for the same person. Rosa Cavalleri, for example, was thrilled by the abundance of food when she arrived, but when the Depression of 1893 struck, it was a totally different story. She was facing near-starvation when one night a kindly neighbor, an organ grinder, shared with Rosa and her children the fifteen cents he had earned: "We ran out and for 3¢ we got the bag of cornmeal; then we got some liver. The liver was cheap in that time—they were throwing it to the cats and dogs . . . So I cooked the cornmeal with the liver in it and made a nice polenta. My children, when they got that good supper—oh, I wish you had seen it! They thought it was the king's wedding."[23]

That depression meant serious malnourishment for many immigrant families. Rose Cohen's mother and siblings arrived shortly before it struck and had no memories of better days to make it easier to bear. "Among strangers in a strange country," her mother was anguished at being unable to give her children even the food they had known in Russia. She "began counting the potatoes she put into the pot and would ask the children over and over again when they wanted more bread, "Are you sure you want it?"[2][4]

Jette Bruns had been in America for a half century by then and was comfortably affluent, but she not only empathized with those less well off, she also understood the long-term change that this depression signaled in the destruction of the egalitarian America she had loved. "The bad times continue," she wrote from Missouri to her family in Germany. "Daily hungry people pass, and they always receive something here. You do not know such things. In all the bigger cities here, organizations have been created to give the fathers of families work and bread."[25]

---

* *Lutefisk* is codfish preserved in a lye of potash. It is now commonly imported for holidays in the Midwest, and its distinctive taste has become the source of entire books of jokes.
** *Flodegrod* is a molded cream pudding.

Even during better times, the threat of hunger remained real for some, especially for newly arrived working women without families, who were often so seriously underpaid that their diets were meager. Bread and tea were their mainstays, bread to quiet the stomach and tea to soothe the spirit. In Senate testimony on female factory workers that took place just prior to World War I—an era of prosperity—there were cases such as that of "Rebecca C., a Russian Jewess," who said "she had lived many an entire day on a penny's worth of bread, and the landlady added that she had known the girl to go without even that much sustenance."[26] A clergyman in Lawrence, Massachusetts, averred that he knew a laid-off woman who had subsisted on just two crackers a day.[27]

Indeed, many of these women were so accustomed to meager fare that they felt eating decently was a luxury that required explanation: when a group of Italian women in industry were questioned about their diet, most had only bread and coffee for breakfast; "if eggs appeared on the menu, the girl usually explained that it was because she was anemic or otherwise run down."[28]

It was largely limited incomes that caused these limited diets, but for some young working women, a lack of culinary and nutritional knowledge also may have been a factor. This was especially true for the millions of young women who emigrated alone in their teens, before they absorbed the homemaking skills that mothers traditionally taught through example. A Swiss woman who had worked as a servant in a wealthy home understood this; age and a drunken husband had lowered her to earning just $2 a week by sewing in the 1880s, but she prided herself on eating more healthfully than her better-paid tenement neighbors:

> I try sometimes to teach. I give some of my soup, and they eat it and say it is good, but they cannot stop to do much dat is fuss. All this in the saucepan is seven cents—three cents for bones and some bits the kind butcher trow in, and the rest vegetables and barley. But it make me two days. I have lentils, too . . . Never tea, oh no! Tea is so vicket. It make hand shake and head fly all round. Good soup is best, and more vegetables and many salad, and when I make more dollar I buy some egg.[29]

The subsistence meals of working women of course did not fully satiate: Anzia Yezierska* was one such, and her pay was never enough to satisfy the demands of her still-growing body. "I used to be more hungry after a meal than before," she wrote retrospectively:

> Years ago, the food I could afford to buy only whetted my appetite for more food. Sometimes after I had paid down my last precious pennies for a meal . . . I'd get so mad with hunger I'd want to . . . cry out like a lunatic . . . "I want real food. I want

---

* For a longer profile of Yezierska, see Doris Weatherford, *American Women's History: An A–Z of People, Organizations, Issues, and Events* (New York: Prentice-Hall, 1994).

to bite into huge chunks of meat. I want butter and quarts of milk and eggs—dozens of eggs. I want to fill up for once in my life."[30]

Perhaps it was because they knew that the small meals they could afford would "only whet the appetite for more" that so many women avoided eating much beyond their daily bread and tea. If the stomach could be kept slightly numb and not tempted with protein-based treats, the mind might fall quiet and the appetite stop its teasing.

That wouldn't happen with children. There were sickening pictures of hungry children amid the alleged abundance of America. Holyoke, Massachusetts, during post–Civil War northern affluence, was nevertheless a town filled with poor Irish. Its newspaper editorialized on the lengths to which some were driven by their stomachs:

> There is one pitiful and miserable sight which we have seen night after night in front of the fruit and vegetable stands . . . It is a drove of poverty-stricken children, often girls, clad only in one or two ragged garments, down on their hands and knees in the gutters, greedily picking out of the mud and dirt and eating the bits of spoiled and decaying fruit which have been thrown out as worthless.[31]

It is possible, however, that the Irish did not see the behavior of these girls as necessarily degrading, for they certainly had experienced hunger at home, too. Indeed, even in the prefamine era, Irish peasants were accustomed to restricted diets in early summer before the potato crop was ready. At that time and during blights, some "entire meals consisted of meadow greens or seaweed gathered by the wife."[32]

Living on the land was no assurance against hunger in Europe or America, especially in late winter when the previous year's produce was gone. This was particularly the case among urbanites who tried to farm in America. Rebecca Butterworth, an Englishwoman in Arkansas in the 1840s, was typical of those who expected a manna-from-heaven experience, and her letter asking for money to return shows the lack of horticultural skills that made her group destitute: "What little corn we had the cattle as [sic] jumped the fence and eaten it . . . We have not bread to last above a week and meat, very little coffee, about 1/2 lb. of sugar. John can milk one cow which makes us a little butter but the other wont let him."[33]

Almost a century later, in a more sophisticated setting and a more prosperous era, hunger remained in immigrant communities. A journalist noted these effects of a 1926 New Jersey strike against night work by mothers:

> Mrs. L. has seven children . . . The strike, she said, had given her a little chance at night sleep, but always she was "like a dead person for tired." Two or three of the younger children stood dully about, their eyes staring with hunger. Another child was stealthily eating from the frying pan on the stove. She would watch her mother furtively, and then, like a starved animal, filch a bit of food. Her peculiarly sharpened features, [and] dead white cheeks . . . looked like the famine pictures from China.[34]

In the Great Depression of the next decade, hunger stalked both natives and immigrants. During those long years of unemployment (and niggardly wages when work was found), even the women fortunate enough to be chosen for the remarkable Bryn Mawr Summer School for Women Workers were acquainted with hunger. In the 1932 class, for example, 80 of the 110 women "were found by the medical examiner to be suffering from undernourishment."[35] Yet if depression relief efforts refused to accommodate cultural differences of newcomers, some immigrants found that, despite stomach pains, their palates still rejected food that was alien. Many Italians simply could not eat the canned meat and processed cereals given them in government programs. They traded with Americans if they could, secretly sold them at a reduced price, or guiltily threw them away—but they could not force themselves to eat the unfamiliar food.[36]

To the Last Ounce of Rice: Food Buying

The waste inherent in this reflects the attitude of even charity-based bureaucrats that women, and especially immigrant women, could not be trusted to budget their family food needs wisely. Despite the would-be philanthropists' suspicions, however, the evidence is that women generally managed their grocery money quite well.

More data is available on this than on most subjects relating to immigrant women, for sociologists were concerned that they be able to show the public—especially legislators and philanthropists—exactly how immigrant families spent their money. Such quantitative research appealed to the fledgling field of sociology, and there are reams of data showing grocery lists down to the last ounce of rice.

Unfortunately, most sociologists missed this opportunity to ask more important questions: Everyone wanted to know how much money a woman earned by the week and by the year and how much was spent on meat and rent and fuel. Few asked how she felt about America or if she was glad she had emigrated or any questions relating to her personality and opinions.

While it is regrettable that so few investigators were imaginative with their questions, nevertheless we are left with a valuable body of data on the income and outgo of immigrant households. One point that is clear from this mass of data is that most immigrant women were delighted at the food available in this country, and when their family income was steady, good food was the chief spending priority.

Analysis of the grocery lists of typical Croatian women in a Michigan mining town around 1910, for example, shows that family food costs for the month were $43, of incomes that averaged $58 or $60—meaning that the family spent 75% of its income on food![37] The remaining 25% would have to cover the rent, clothes, and any incidentals or savings. They would live in a hovel where the rent was low and dress in rags, but they would eat well.

And eating well in their minds meant eating meat. A butcher in this mining town reported that a working Croatian male ate two or three pounds of meat a day, and other studies showed similar patterns. Lithuanians and Poles near the Chicago stockyards spent over 50% of their budgets for food, with meat taking the largest portion. For Lithuanians especially a good steak must have been a glory; they spent nearly one-fifth of their annual income on meat, while spending only 8% for clothes. The next largest grocery expense was baked goods, taking 10% of the annual income. By comparison, milk and alcohol took about 4% each, with slightly more spent on alcohol.[38]

The same patterns hold in an analysis of letters written by seventeen German women in response to a query on household budgets by *New Yorker Volks-Zeitung* in 1882. The average family spent "about half of its income on food," with the "thriftest" woman of those who provided detailed accounts spending more than 60% on this one cost.[39] Most budgets included "a pint of beer a day and over one pound of coffee a week." Again, these women served more protein and fats than was the typical case back home: "workers in Germany only ate a third to a fifth as much meat as most of their German counterparts . . . Butter, a regular item on German-American tables, was a rarity for German working-class families."[40]

Massachusetts, where immigrants settled in industrial towns from Fall River in the southeast to Holyoke in the northwest, confirmed that its "workers also spent about half of their income on food."[41] Three decades later, the same priority for food appeared among the relative newcomers from Italy: "The general impression gained from a study of the weekly food purchases in these families is that they are more generous in providing food for themselves than for any other need of life."[42]

Contrary to the era's stereotype that Italians ate nothing but macaroni, actual analysis showed they ate a good deal of meat and fish in addition to pasta, and numerous writers noted that they were wiser than Americans in using large quantities of fresh vegetables and fruit. Even city-dwelling Italian families often kept a garden, especially for herbs, and they patronized pushcart sellers of fresh produce far more than others. Where possible, they also raised their own chickens, rabbits, and goats; a social worker among Sicilians said that "not one will buy ready-ground hamburg steak or slaughtered poultry."[43] Another observer agreed that Italian women were reluctant to buy anything they had not processed themselves, and their markets routinely included live chickens.[44]

English and Irish accounts, on the other hand, were apt to have much greater expenditures for pastries and sweets—including, for example, one Irish woman whose account featured such small purchases as one carrot and two eggs, along with a half pound of sugar per day.[45] Indeed, this detailed study and others repeatedly noted that Irish women seemed to be unimaginative cooks who served a monotonous diet.

Yet the era's racism was such that good cooks from the "new" immigration seldom got credit for their skills. Without bothering to gather data on the "old" groups, for example, a Senate report assumed their superiority:

> The Italians, Polish and Portuguese . . . have a lower standard of living . . . To prepare a meal, set the table in an attractive manner, and sit down to it, as is done in the homes of the English, Irish and French-Canadian, is practically unheard of . . . It

was possible to obtain menus for a few meals from them . . . Menus could not be obtained from the English, Irish and French-Canadian families.[46]

While the assumption of northern European superiority is not justified, it is possible to conclude that the food spending priorities of almost all immigrant groups emphasized meat and bread, while they were short on milk and—except for Italians—on fruit and vegetables.

A Fall River Polish family is typical: they purchased over 120 grocery items in a nineteen-day period, but the only vegetables were potatoes and cabbage. Another Polish family bought milk only once during the period, despite their four young children. Portuguese accounts also showed a complete dearth of green and yellow vegetables; beans, onions, and garlic were the only vegetables in their grocery lists.[47]*

Many immigrant women also were plagued by the perennial problem of the poor: having to buy small quantities and pay a premium price. While it could be argued that urban immigrants who shopped daily were preserving European marketing customs and shopping for freshness, the evidence seems to be at least equally strong that this was done because of a lack of money and storage facilities.

Women who lived on American farms, of course, could not market daily, despite European habits. It was in fact a fundamental change—in Europe, most farm families lived in small villages and went out in daily groups to work the fields, but in America, people lived in isolation on their land. For women especially, the change meant far less sociability in their lives. Particularly when they were confined by pregnancy and nursing and during severe winters, women could go for weeks without seeing another woman. But American tradition also meant that men did most of the marketing—even in towns. Emilie Koenig, who lived in a mid-sized Indiana town, was stating the facts when she succinctly observed, "Here the men usually do the buying."[48]

Men typically went to town, while their wives stayed home with the children. Farmers took produce to sell, picked up whatever supplies the family needed, and then usually spent a few hours in the saloon or gossiping at the livery station. Toward the end of the nineteenth century, businesses in some farming towns began to encourage female shoppers by providing facilities for them to nurse their babies, change diapers, and attend to other needs. It was not until well after the invention of the automobile, however, that most women began to shop independently of men.

The fact was that there were many fewer things to be bought, for farm women were expected to grow most of their menus. Meat, poultry, eggs, fruit, vegetables, dairy products—all of these and more came from her own farm yard. Only staples such as coffee and sugar were purchased, and these required little shopping skill. One amusing little anecdote, however, testifies to the authority of women in placing such orders via their men: Norwegian Mrs. Brandt sent her husband to town for three pounds of sago, a starch used as a thickener for both cooking and laundry. Her writing

---

* The study was done in May, which is too early for garden produce in Massachusetts.

was careless, but neither her husband nor the grocer questioned it—and he dutifully returned with three pounds of sage. Nearly thirty years later, Mrs. Brandt still had some of that sage.

The Cook as Gardener, Gatherer, and Hostess

Sociologists seldom studied the dietary habits of farming women, but we have information from their own pens. Because of the virgin soil, a skilled gardener could grow produce that would have been a dream in the Old World. An Englishwoman wrote that she had raised about 200 bushels of potatoes and was blessed with other bounty, too:

> We had a good crop of turnips and an excellent garden. We had beets in our garden that weighed from 8 to 11 pounds. I weighted them through curiosity . . . Also last year we had a great deal of fruit. It was supposed we had 4 hundred bushels of peaches in our orchard and cherrys and apples. The trees were propped. They could not bear their weight of fruit.[49]

This orchard was established, but immigrant women in new areas often wrote of problems in obtaining familiar seed and young fruit trees. Elise Waerenskjold wrote that while grapes, plums, and cherries grew wild near her Texas home, peaches were the only cultivated fruit available. She told potential emigrants to "bring along all sorts of seeds," explaining that "to the best of my knowledge, seed cannot be either bought or raised here," especially for items familiar to Europeans but not to Americans. Among the seeds she could not locate were "May turnips, any kind of cabbage or cauliflower, kohlrabi, Swedish turnips or French turnips."[50]

On the other hand, she was much impressed by some new foods America had to offer. She liked pumpkins and proclaimed sweet potatoes "delicious," explaining that they "are not boiled in water but are baked in the oven." She praised the variety of game that could be obtained free; once, she claimed, her husband had killed thirty quail with one shot: "they come by the millions, they look like a dark cloud."[51]

Of the new foods, the biggest hit was watermelon. Many immigrants wrote home of this exciting discovery, for even though unhybridized melons were only "as big as a child's head," they were dearly loved. Gro Svendsen was among those thrilled by the new fruit:

> I must tell you something about a fruit called "watermelon." We have an enormous quantity of them; I can't compare them to anything I ever saw in Norway . . . They are eaten just as they are taken from the field . . . I have cooked molasses from them, and I have also brewed juice several times . . . We sometimes sell watermelons to wayfarers passing by. We usually get ten cents apiece for them. However, most of

the melons we shared with our friends and neighbors, many of whom had walked several miles in order to get a chance to taste our watermelons.[52]

Jette Bruns, too, had high praise in 1840: "Almost every day now we eat melons, a delicious fruit.[53] Even Elisabeth Koren, who was not easily impressed, was delighted: "Do you know the watermelon? It is extremely juicy and refreshing . . . You should see how people here eat one big melon after another."[54] She also called muskmelons superior to anything available in Norway and was especially enthusiastic about the wild bounty available in frontier Iowa. Taking long walks in the unsettled country, she found honey, raspberries, strawberries, and even asparagus. "I gather seed," she wrote, "wherever I go."[55] Jette Bruns, too, was excited about the free food available in frontier Missouri: "But now something else! Now and then, when it occurs to us, we partake of the bag of nuts. They grow here in tremendous amounts. In an hour, in a space as big as our living room, I picked a whole big bag. Then one throws it on one's horse and trots casually home."[56]

That food could be obtained with so little effort was a very good thing, for otherwise the budgets of many settlers would have been stretched to the breaking point with obligatory hospitality to new arrivals. In the first summer after Jette Bruns arrived, for example, she fed three meals a day to at least twelve people. Because she had borne a baby in the spring, "We could plant only a very few vegetables . . . The few things on the stiff upper land did not succeed very well. Now we have many people and little to eat. A great worry for the housewife!"[57]

Every spring brought boatloads of immigrants to the port cities, and they often were fed and housed by compatriots as they moved inland. A Norwegian Quaker wrote without complaint of this annual influx: "Twelve Norwegians came here today, and are now eating their supper. About two weeks ago there arrived from ninety to one hundred people. They stayed at our house and my brother's house for about a week, and we furnished meals for nearly all of them."[58]

With true hospitality, she made no mention of the work involved in feeding this horde, nor of the expense. Even if they paid for their meals—and nothing in her letter indicates that they did—there were bound to be costs that would not be repaid. Fredricka Bremer, a well-known Swedish novelist, also noted the generous hospitality with which she was greeted by Swedes in America. Even on the Wisconsin frontier, there was "incomparably excellent coffee and tea; good venison, fruit, tarts, and many good things, all as nicely and deliciously set out as if on a prince's table." Even more unexpected was the fact that "the young sons of the house waited upon us. At home in Sweden, it would have been the daughters."[59]

Constant visitors appeared at Elisabeth Koren's home, too, especially when her husband returned from his pastoral circuit. Some days her life consisted of nothing but serving meals to guests: "Evenson happened to be here, his two sisters had not yet gone home . . . For breakfast I also had Magnus, Erik, John, and Per." Making hot chocolate for this meal was "quite a quandary" because "it goes twice as far as what I was accustomed to at home and consequently became so thick I had to thin it with all the milk in the house." She had "scarcely gotten them out before Brandt's sisters came. After much discussion it was decided . . . we would have dinner . . . , but I poor creature, was not prepared for so many guests. The chickens . . . would not go round. So I had to bring up a piece of pork from the barrel, salty as it was."[60]

Women such as this, some of whom fed as many as a hundred people three meals a day out of tiny, ill-equipped kitchens on the badly supplied frontier, had to be wonders of good management. They had to have good hearts, too, and an active concern for the welfare of their people.

City immigrants had less obligation, but there was still some family pressure to put up newly arrived relatives, often for weeks, without recompense. They were also invariably hospitable to American visitors. "If a family does not offer refreshment," said an observant social worker, "one may be sure that the process of Americanization has advanced rapidly."[61]

For southern Europeans especially, eating and drinking was a significant part of any social or business contact. Refusing the offer of, for example, a cup of espresso, was taken as an insult to the host. Nor was this a one-way relationship, for newcomers also often went out of their way to accommodate their American guests:

> The Italian woman has such a keen sense of fitness that the food she offers an American is usually of an American type. She sets out store pies or cake for the guest and politely nibbles at it herself, but she much prefers her own kind of scantily sweetened cake. At a lunch to which a social worker was invited, the family went so far as to provide butter, but forgot to offer it to the guest because it was not naturally a part of their own diet. The pound of butter remained in the middle of the table untouched through the meal.[62]

Social workers also applauded the ability of city Italians to grow their own fennel, oregano, and other seasonings essential to their cookery on tiny bits of land. Students of Slavic peoples also commented on how they maximized the space outside their tenement homes with stakes that grew upright tomatoes, cucumbers, squash, and other produce. One family, with "deft pruning and cultivation, coaxed from a bit of ground not more than a foot square" a vine that covered their third-floor porch. Having the familiar, fresh food was sufficiently important that they made herculean efforts.

In time, it was easier. Though her first garden in America "did not succeed very well," by the 1880s, Jette Bruns was happily growing plants for enjoyment as well as food. "We grew all kinds of things on an experimental basis," she wrote. "Fine silver onions, sage, horseradish . . . popcorn, and . . . sweet potatoes, which grew so well that one was as big as a child's head . . . Then I unselfishly set a few hundred plants of tobacco for Wilhelm." She experimented with mulberry trees and silkworms, despite the fact that "all advised against it." Such activity kept her mentally alert as she aged, and on a visit to Germany, she noted that she was "more agile" than her younger sisters. Even in her eighties, when she was too blind to see the plants, she gardened by touch, and her daughter wrote in 1896, "Mother is still occupied with her flowers every day."[63]

Gardening was no longer an imperative for survival, as it had been when she was a young woman on a wild frontier that demanded she weed and hoe despite her continual pregnancies and the children at her feet. Her situation is a paradigm for the immigrant experience: hard work and great difficulties, even for the educated and relatively affluent, during the first decades—and with luck, the reward of comfortable prosperity to pass on to one's children.

Within a generation or two, immigrant women adopted each other's cuisine as well as that of the New World, and so America developed a diet that is more varied and interesting than anywhere else on earth. The chief dietary problem today, in fact, has become restraining ourselves from eating all that is available. Mrs. Pagano knew this particular ambivalence before most immigrant women did; though Americanized and affluent, she still grew "basilica, finnocchio, leaf-chicory," and other herbs with which to flavor the Old World dishes: "On the stove bubbled aromatically the spaghetti sauce, while from the oven came a tantalizing fragrance of roasting stuffed chickens. Inside in the great iron pot [she used] as far back as the coal camps, lay the slowly browning chickens, stuffed with spinach, cheese, and pine nuts."[64]

But the creator of this goodness, who had lived on the verge of starvation in Italy, could not enjoy it. The land had blessed her so richly that, as for many modern Americans, a weakened heart demanded that she cease partaking of the bounty. "Eh!" she lamented, "When I was a little girl, back in the old country, I couldn't get enough to eat; and now that I can have all I want, I still can't get enough to eat!"[65]

10

HOVELS, HOMES, AND HOPE

Teeming Tenements

Wearing the layers of heavy clothes the era demanded, immigrant women worked in kitchens that seemed hellishly hot, for summers in the Old Country were never so warm as August in America. Gone was the cool dimness of her European home with its foot-thick walls and outdoor oven; now she must cook with a wood fire added to the ninety-degree day—nor would the night offer much relief, for virtually every kitchen served as a bedroom, as well as a dining and sitting room. Rose Cohen remembered:

> There were five of us, the two boys in one cot and we three girls in the other, in the one room filled with the odour of cooking, of kerosene oil, the smell of grimy clothes, of stale perspiration, the heat of the body . . . As I lay with my two sisters in the sagging cot, with an unconscious limb of one or the other thrown over me, I wept. Then I thought, "Why, need it be so? Why?"[1]

Her home, perhaps more than anything else, caused a woman to wonder if she had made a mistake in emigrating, for often it left a great deal to be desired. This was almost invariably true for those who settled on the raw American frontier, but it was also the case for a multitude of city dwellers. Indeed, "many immigrants," said an expert on the industrial towns that surrounded New York City, "are living at a lower standard here than they did in their own country."[2]

The kitchen was usually the literal center of these homes, for even in those privileged cases of five-room apartments, the kitchen was in the middle, surrounded by the "front" and "back" rooms. Floor plans were done this way because the kitchen contained the cookstove that was intended to heat the rooms to the front and rear of it. In a 1912 study, only four of eighty immigrant homes reported any source of heat other than the kitchen stove.[3]

Consequently, the kitchen was the most inadequately lighted and ventilated room, which condemned a woman to rebreathing the smells of burning wood while taxing her eyes to see by the light of kerosene lamps that burned in windowless rooms even in the daytime. Nor was it uncommon for other rooms to be equally bad, for a study done in 1905 found that one-third of New York tenement rooms were without windows—"pitch dark and unventilated."[4] Figures in Chicago were similar, and they got worse as the immigrant flow increased.[5]

Some who constructed these buildings were woefully indifferent to those who had to live in them. At a national conference in 1919, a speaker related experience with architects who were to design affordable housing: "In the plans of houses they [were] required to show the position of the bed in the bedroom, and the size of the bed. It was found that many architects did not know that size and had to learn it. In this way space was always allowed for the opening of doors."[6]

Other housing was not laid out in this "modern" tenement style, but that did not mean it was better. Immigrants often lived in the once-elegant homes of the rich, which had been subdivided into dark cubicles to house dozens of poor people. Remnants of the past made for crazy contrasts—such as cookstoves jammed into beautiful marble fireplaces—but the space seldom was arranged so that there was enough light or air. Often their floors were dangerously rotten; it was not unusual for landlords to post signs cautioning residents about structural dangers they did not bother to repair.

In summer, these unventilated rooms were impossible to cool, and the Boston Board of Health recommended mothers take their babies up to rooftops for night air. According to one New York source, summer was here in earnest when police dispatches began to "record the killing of men and women by rolling off roofs and window sills while asleep." While the city's affluent residents fled to their country homes, New York saw "sleepless mothers who walk the streets in the gray of early dawn, trying to stir a cooling breeze to fan the brow of the sick baby . . . Fresh air excursions run daily . . . but despite all efforts the grave diggers in Calvary work over-time, and little coffins are stacked mountains high on the deck of the Charity Commissioner's boat."[7]

As it was impossible to cool ghetto homes in the summer, so it was hopeless to heat them decently in cold weather. Studies of budgets often noted that expenditures for fuel were too low for comfort. Some women violated the law by sending their children to walk the railroad tracks, gathering coal that fell from trains. They themselves hunted any burnable wood or trash they could find; the sight of women carrying "enormous bundles" of scavenged firewood on their heads was not uncommon.[8] Despite such efforts, a number of immigrant women reported that they went to work even when sick because it was warm at work and freezing at home. Even after wood and coal stoves were replaced by gas, in shabby tenement housing, the gas lines sometimes froze.

The shivering woman could be warmed by huddling close to someone else, for it was virtually certain that her home overflowed with other people. A tiny minority of immigrant women lived alone or with just one roommate, but it was vastly more likely that she lived in a household as either wife or daughter or lodger. The era's moral code was skeptical about women who lived outside the family unit, and in more practical terms, it was a rare woman who could support her own home, even if that home was only a room. Almost every immigrant household included friends, relatives, or strangers who slept on cots and kitchen tables, in closets or under the stairs.

To say that they were overcrowded does not begin to show the situation. Cases that were in fact appalling lose their impact because they were also so common: One Philadelphia tenement held thirty families in thirty-four rooms, an average of four people per room.[9] A Lithuanian woman lived with her husband and five children in a tiny closet of a home that contained only slightly more air space than the law required for one adult.[10] A woman and her child actually suffocated to death sleeping in a minuscule room that contained two other occupants.[11] New York City police, enforcing health department orders, found many rooms similar to one that was less than thirteen feet square and slept twelve men and women, most of them on the floor. In one of the worst cases, they found twenty people from five families of all ages and sexes who lived in just one twelve by twelve room.[12]

Yet if these reports strain credulity, it is probable that the statistics err in minimizing the overcrowding. Immigrants soon learned that they were in violation of the era's new housing codes. They certainly understood—if the law did not—that an overcrowded home was preferable to eviction, and they became adept at hiding cots and inventing cover stories to dupe the investigators. The experience of this social worker among Slavs was typical:

> I recall one case where a Polish couple who at first insisted that only they and their two children occupied their two-room apartment acknowledged, after unusual insistence on my part, that two women boarders used one of the rooms; and finally, when further pressed, threw open the door of a little closet under the stairs—a cubbyhole scarcely three feet wide and sloping to the floor—and showed a cot on which a male boarder slept. This is not an extreme example of overcrowding.[13]

Not only were the rooms incredibly crowded, but the buildings themselves were jammed together so that the population of many an immigrant city block was equal to that of an entire town. Even outside the cities, immigrant houses also were packed close together in the small mill towns. All greenery around the housing was eradicated so the landlord could maximize his investment. While these tenements had windows, they admitted little light or air, since they virtually abutted the windows next door. In fact, women increased their wall space by reaching out the window and hanging things on the outside of the house next door, and rental agents saved themselves the walk up three flights by reaching their hands across from one apartment to that next door. Houses were so close together that a woman could even carry on a conversation with her neighbor while each was in her own kitchen.

But if her neighbor was someone she did not like, the situation could be most unpleasant, for privacy was unobtainable. A woman had no life of her own, no chance for solitude. Her every sound could be heard by neighbors, her every action noted by gossips. Such overcrowding had an adverse effect on mental health, but its physical effects were of more obvious concern.

Fire was a constant threat. Most tenements were wooden and had only one exit. The fact that each apartment had its own stove multiplied the danger, especially when the fires were tended by children left alone while parents worked. Fire escapes were almost nonexistent early in the tenement era—a 1904 study found fewer than one in every twenty-five buildings.[14] When they were required, the space-starved immigrant family extended itself into this available area. Periodic raids by the fire department could not permanently remove the impediments to escape, for worried parents placed boards "intertwined with heavy wire or rope, rendering the fire escapes useless as such in a fire, but helping to make it a safer playing space . . . Fire escapes are further obstructed with bedding, . . . the gaily colored family wash, chairs, food, swill, ashes, growing plants, and anything else moveable."[15]

Once a fire started, the proximity of houses made it a death trap for hundreds of people jammed into the same area. Many of the victims of the great Chicago fire of 1871 were immigrants. Their poor wooden shacks made ideal fuel, and some people could not even outrun the fire: "on an area not more than forty acres, there were found the bodies of forty-five poor creatures, none of which were recognizable, but which were undoubtedly the German and Scandinavian people inhabiting that quarter."[16] These were generally one-story houses, and fire danger would be even greater as higher tenement-style homes replaced them.

A second danger was epidemics, which spread as rapidly as fire. In New York's Gotham Court in the 1880s, a cholera epidemic that barely touched the rest of the city killed there at a rate of 195 per 1,000 residents.[17] It was a rare person who was *not* exposed to tuberculosis in these unventilated rooms: One national health authority said of the housing where women lived day in and day out, "If we had invented machines to create tuberculosis we could not have succeeded better."[18]

But the aspect of overpopulation that worried investigators most was the moral danger of such close proximity between the sexes, and commentary on crowding almost always includes sexual innuendos. Even the report of an Italian physician accepted this American tenet; he wrote in a 1908 report of Manhattan Italians: "The mixing of sexes in sleeping rooms, though not common, was discovered in a number of cases," including one case in which "five men and seven women were found sleeping in three rooms."[19]

Outhouses in the backyard of a Jersey Street section of New York where Italians lived in 1888. Women who had to use these facilities not only endured unsanitary conditions but also were subject to the leers of onlookers. (LIBRARY OF CONGRESS, PHOTOGRAPH BY JACOB RIIS)

In Chicago, too, sociologists worried about cases like a "Russian-Polish" home where a thirteen-year-old girl slept in the same bed as her father and brother, and that of a newly arrived young Polish woman who lived with a male relative and a dozen young men who boarded with him.[20] Certainly, it was difficult to protect modesty and privacy under such conditions, but while the prudish worried over the orgies they believed must naturally result from so many bodies so close together, the actual result of overcrowding probably was directly the opposite. Where privacy was so unobtainable, a free and healthy sex life was unlikely.

Rats lived in these overcrowded buildings along with the people. Women hung food from ceilings in the hope that rats wouldn't be able to reach it, and they watched their babies carefully. Even the social workers who made their home in the Chicago Commons could not keep the rats from their abode in this neighborhood that teemed with them. Rosa Cavalleri, who was a cleaning woman there, said it was all full of rats—three pounds, five pounds, I don't know how many pounds to make those rats, but they were big! The residents used to wait in line by the bathroom door, and when somebody didn't come out, they'd push the door and there it was the rats playing tag with themselves. And when the residents were all sitting down eating dinner, those rats chased between their legs.[21]

The rats were there because filth was there—or was, at least, nearby. Indoor toilets were rare, and when available, were located in dark halls and shared by many tenants. Since no one was responsible for their cleanliness, their usual state was one of filth. New flush toilets sometimes proved worse than the old outhouses, for the cold of the halls caused pipes to freeze. With sewage lines backed up sometimes for weeks, the stench could be overpowering. The usual arrangement prior to the twentieth century had been privies in the backyard; later, flush toilets were installed there, where they were almost certain to freeze.

These outdoor locations were greatly inconvenient, and women suffered most from this. Women had the frequent bladder demands caused by pregnancy, and they were responsible for nursing the sick and for taking young children to the toilet, but these personal hardships seldom occurred to investigators, who were concerned only with cleanliness. Even when a janitor was in charge of communal toilets, she often gave up the task as an impossibility. One such woman took an inspector out to a yard closet, "confident of our approval because she had scrubbed it an hour before. She was embarrassed to find a thick, filthy pool upon the seat."[22]

City slums were bad enough, but probably worse were the hundreds of company-dominated mill and mining towns. Rarely did they take any responsibility for public sanitation; raw sewage usually drained directly into rivers, and when the water was high, it backed up into cellars—which were often immigrant homes. "Slops from the sinks . . . are allowed to run wherever they can make their way. Portions of yards are covered with filth and green slime."[23]

Even remote areas were ruined by the era's callous industrialism. Hancock, Michigan, for example, sits surrounded by Great Lake waters on a spit of land at the uppermost end of the state, but its natural beauty was destroyed by copper mining. Emma Huhtasaari, a northern Swede whose native tongue was Finnish, wrote plaintively from there in 1905: "There is never a birdsong in America . . . There is only coal smoke and dusty streets. Coal smoke from many factories so that the air gets heavy. It feels so bad when you have grown up in Norrland's fresh air."[24]

Crowded Country Cabins

Such towns were in the country, yet of the city, in that people were powerless, dependent upon a governing class that did not care about their needs. Those who lived on farming frontiers had more control over their lives. Yet sanitation there too often left a great deal to be desired. Germ theory was not known in the early immigrant era, and people did not grasp the correlation between sanitation and disease. They built their outhouses and wells conveniently close to the house, and dangerously close to each other.

In the early days, privies were often not even constructed: "No one thought of building a log house for so simple a purpose. The discharges of both the sick and well were deposited in the open, where they were accessible to hogs and chickens, as well as to the myriads of flies which always infested the homes, for no window screens were used."[25]

The result was fevers, which, since they arrived with summer, the new arrivals blamed on the climate. Mosquitoes abounded, and foreigners quickly developed diseases to which Americans had built up immunities. Elise Waerenskjold wrote of a group of Norwegians who disregarded advice and settled in bottom lands conveniently close to a river: "Almost everyone became ill . . . Consequently many were discontented, and some had died. The group had consisted of eight families crowded into two small rooms."[26]

Eight *families* in two small rooms! Indeed, though they were surrounded by miles and miles of empty land, farmhouses often were as crowded as city counterparts. Usually the motivation of the city housewife who accepted boarders was extra income, but the country woman was obligated to live among others because there was nowhere else to go. Often hotels or public lodging places were simply nonexistent, and newcomers had to move into whatever home would accept them until they could build their own. Elisabeth Koren, as the wife of the only clergyman for a hundred miles or more, was invited to stay at the best available place, yet it was only a one-room cabin, partitioned off with curtains for a little privacy. She stayed with another couple and their two toddlers, and her husband made a sixth person in the one room when he was not circuit riding. Personalities clashed, and after several months of forced companionship in the snowbound Iowa house, she was asked to leave. Spring came and construction began on her own home, while she lived more fretful weeks in another crowded household. When finally she moved into her own home, she was as ecstatic over a rough three-room abode as she would have been over a castle back in Norway: "How pleasant it is to have a bedroom, and in the morning to go into a tidy room to a breakfast table all set, instead of first having to clear away the toilet articles . . . We really learned to prize all such little things, . . . which at home it never occurred to us to think about."[27]

Emilie Lohmann Koenig also found the lack of privacy a difficult adjustment. "Amazed at the small houses with their limited space," she initially shared a bedroom with her hostess, "the girls, and the two children . . . I can never be alone. This was particularly difficult for me at first . . . but one gets used to everything."[28] This experience reinforced her low expectations of Indiana and made her absolutely thrilled with moving into her own home, which she called "too comfortable and too lovely."

There are four rooms, two downstairs and two upstairs . . . There is a carpet in the living room. We have wooden chairs . . . Sofas are not known over here. Instead, no room is without its rocking chair . . . Mrs. Ulrich presented me with some embroidered curtains . . . They must cost over one dollar a yard, and there are at least ten yards. I was struck dumb.[29]

Because her husband had preceded her and other German women helped prepare the parsonage, Emilie Koenig did not have to wait long for a house like many others did. Months or even years of sharing a house with other families while waiting for one's own was a common experience for frontier settlers. Though Jette Bruns was the soul of optimism, even she grew frustrated with the delay. "We arrived here at eleven in the morning on All Souls Day," 1836, she recorded.

> The log cabin was locked up, but Bruns broke the lock. It consists of one room . . . with one window; in it there were a table, four chairs, and two bedsteads. So this was to be our home for the winter! . . .
>   I nevertheless felt good to have reached a safe asylum . . . The sun shone warmly and kindly through the leafless trees; soon a bright fire was burning . . . Our belongings could only be transported very slowly, and thus in the first week we lacked all kinds of things; however, I still am happy.[30]

Less than a year later, the settlement's most prestigious family, the Hesses, returned to Germany because Mrs. Hesse was extremely unhappy in Missouri. One aspect of their departure, however, was thrilling to Jette:

> A very beautiful piece of furniture, which outshines all other items, a piano found its way into our log cabin . . . How could I have imagined that just such an instrument as I had denied myself would be made available to me in America! Until a few days before the departure of the Hesses we had not thought of it; then the Hesses offered it. German price, German work, without the cost of transportation![31]

Still, she had no decent home for the piano, for her house seemed to be endlessly under construction. She wrote of "many annoying hours have I spent because of procrastinations . . . We are now firmly resolved that . . . we will make a few mud walls and move in anyway. We just cannot go on as we are now!"[32] Her frustration was increased because of the size of her household, which, in addition to children, also included relatives and employees.

Linka Preus lived with just her husband when she arrived, and though accustomed to a large house with a staff of servants, she accepted her crowded Wisconsin home cheerfully. It was one room, twelve by twelve, in which were squeezed together one and a half beds; a "sofa" that was actually two chests covered with pillows; two bureaus, one "with a cupboard for a hat"; two easy chairs ("my treasures"); and a storage chest under the bed. The room, she wrote, was "well-filled, . . . two persons can barely pass."[33] Later a table was added, a truly unique furnishing that filled Linka with marvel:

My kitchen table consists of a box we brought from Norway . . . This we inverted and provided with four legs, beautifully trimmed and polished by nature herself, from a poplar tree growing in the woods just outside our door. To be sure they were frozen and raw, but what of it? . . . To my great delight, I discover that the legs have been sprouting lovely green side branches, covered with green leaves. Behold, thus our kind God causes summer to flourish in our home while winter still prevails outside.[34]

Few prairie homes were as crowded as Linka's, for most could not afford to transport or buy much furniture. Some homes had virtually none. Elisabeth Koren wrote that the house chosen for church services in her Iowa community was selected because "furniture is scarce at Vesle Rognald's—no chairs, and only a large chest to serve as a table."[35] The problem of furnishings was another case for ambivalent debate among those planning to emigrate. There were few clear imperatives, but Elise Waerenskjold warned her friends of the differences to expect: "Bring your own bedclothes . . . A featherbed would run into some $20 . . . Good furniture is expensive and hard to get, but I imagine the cost of transportation would be too high if you were to bring your own from Norway. Yet I would bring at least a chest of drawers or a chiffonnier."[36]

Regardless of their content, most homes were not well built; the usual situation was that they had been hurriedly erected by husbands who were not professional carpenters. Floors sagged, doors and windows—the few that they had—hung crazily, and roofs leaked. The home that Elisabeth Koren had been so happy to have soon proved how poorly built it was when she lamented after a thunderstorm:

> The floor was a pond, so I had to tiptoe about with great caution, holding up my dress . . . The rain streamed in through the curtains and across the table, soaking them thoroughly. We had to pull the bookcases and bed away from the walls and cover them with towels, for the rain came through the walls . . . and soaked the bedclothes and other clothing.[37]

Cold, like rain, poured in the countless cracks. Many women slept in beds that were fully occupied all night and yet awakened to find frost on pillows and sheets frozen stiff. Mrs. Brandt wrote that she had enough snow on her bed to "fill a washtub" and that her North Dakota kitchen was so cold, "I often put on overshoes and tied a scarf over my head before preparing breakfast." During her first winter on the plains, the treasured jars of fruit she had brought along froze, and "their precious contents were a total loss."[38] In the great blizzard of 1880, she had to bring chickens and pigs in to keep the animals from freezing. Straw and manure were piled around the foundations of prairie homes for winter insulation, and with doors and windows covered by black tar paper and sealed tight, the interior was dark and gloomy.

Yet to have a log cabin, as these women did, was something of a luxury. Many settlers lived in the dark earth itself. On the treeless plains west of the Mississippi they had no choice, for no other building materials were available. The first settlers lived in dugouts, which were cavelike homes dug into hillsides or creekbanks. After the creek land was taken, sod houses sprang up on the flat prairies. Made of blocks of soil that were interlaced with centuries of unplowed grass roots, these homes featured walls several feet thick, which kept them cool in summer and warm in winter—dark and ugly though they were.

Homes made of dirt and grass actually may have been more of a shock to Yankees than they were to Europeans, who were usually familiar with thatched roofs made of similar natural materials. When Kjersti Jonsson arrived with her husband and three children from Skove, Sweden, in 1869, for example, they lived in what they called a "gopher hut," which was a mixture of wood and grass. It was a ten by twelve by six room with "common lumber" for walls and roof. When the walls were insulated with "plowed sod"* and the roof thatched with slough grass, the structure clearly bore a Swedish imprint.[39]

Indeed, though New Englanders had lived in wooden homes since the Pilgrims, the Irish who settled in Massachusetts in the 1840s built hovels "strangely like the sod houses of the western plains later in the century."[40] Each was "a crude shelter, generally half board, half dug-out . . . without windows" and with dirt mounded about for insulation. Quickly and cheaply built, they were intended to be abandoned as soon as possible. With "inexpensive kindliness," those "families who moved to better quarters left these huts standing for their successors."[41]

Sometimes midwestern settlers did not make the erection of even such crude habitations their first priority, for they almost always arrived in spring and planting the summer's crop was the immediate need. Meanwhile, they lived camp style. Dutch Cornelia Schaddelee recalled the shock of her 1847 arrival:

> There we stood, on the shore of Lake Michigan, 4,500 miles away from the motherland, with no covering over our heads than the blue sky . . . All that was to be seen was a few booths, constructed of sticks driven into the ground, and branches of trees overhead, in which a few families lodged for the time being . . . [We] were obliged to make a similar booth . . . [and kept] a campfire going night and day, to serve as a beacon during the night for other immigrants who might arrive, and also to ward off wild beasts . . . Two stakes were driven in the ground . . . with a crosspiece, and kettle and pot . . . In this way, our parents managed the housekeeping.[42]

From a campfire, the next stage was often a cookhouse to shelter fuel and food from rain, and then a house would be built around the cookhouse. It was also fairly common for immigrants to move into the abandoned abode of earlier settlers—like

---

* When the author's Norwegian great-grandparents moved from a creekbank dugout to a wooden house, they insulated the walls with flax chaff.

Jette Bruns did already in 1836—for foreigners in the Midwest often followed restless Yankees who went still farther west.

One family spoke of moving into an abandoned house and linking it to their new cookhouse with a walkway, for even after their camping days were over, many Europeans viewed having a kitchen that was separate from their sleeping quarters as necessary in what they saw as the torrid heat of America. "It is out of the question," Elisabeth Koren wrote, to have the stove "inside the cabin during summer." But there were nonetheless problems: "It is raining so hard today that I do not know how I shall prepare dinner; my stove will no doubt be full of water."[43]

Many women would have considered it a pleasant problem to have, for the Korens' summer kitchen, after all, was attached to a three-room wooden home that they shared only with a maid. Most lived much longer in dugouts or sod houses—but Elisabeth Koren wrote that a dugout was "not as bad as one might think."[44] Others agreed that good housekeepers could make earthen homes surprisingly pleasant. Mrs. Brandt wrote of her friends who lived thus: "When floors were scrubbed, walls freshly whitewashed, and the broad window sills filled with blooming geraniums, such homes were by no means unattractive. She added, however, 'that such houses had their drawbacks. They were apt to become damp and in time would settle so that the roof and walls would become lopsided.'"[45]

Settling and dampness were not the only drawbacks. Snakes and burrowing animals thought this sod no different from any other; overcrowding was apt to be more severe, and livestock in the home more common; windows were scarce and wintertime depression was worst of all on the unprotected plains where the wind swept down from the polar north. Blizzards howled for days and snow swirled until it buried the little house. Indeed, midwesterners out walking with snowshoes or driving teams with sleighs were cautioned to keep an eye out for chimney pipes, so that they would not crash through the roof of prairie homes.

Still they survived. When spring came, women set about their housecleaning with fervor. Down came the tar paper and the manure insulation and up popped the flowers they had planted last fall. Linka Preus and Elisabeth Koren both wrote of long searches in the American woods for wildflowers similar to those they had known back home; Elise Waerenskjold, after forty years in Texas, was still writing back to Norway for plants she could not obtain here. They set up their woman-to-woman networks of exchanges, and as the years passed, Linka and her friends grew such difficult houseplants as callas, fuchsias, mums, and primroses. Indeed, when Linka's diary was finally printed in 1952, the editor revealed that her descendants grew plants "which, through a series of transplanting of slips, trace their ancestry back to her bay window."[46]

Moving Up the Housing Ladder

Life in a sod house was easier to bear because of the conviction that it was not permanent. One year would be the bonanza: the grain crop would be good and farm prices would stay high and their little hoard of savings would go over the top and the family would place their order for lumber and the railroad would bring their new home. This happened eventually for almost everyone on the plains. Likewise, the city immigrant tolerated her tenement because she too did not believe she would be there forever. This was not the promise of America.

The reasons for getting out of the ghetto were economic as well as aesthetic. It did not make sense to pay the rents that slumlords charged for these wretched hovels. With maintenance nil and rents high, the profits on this human misery averaged 40%, and examples were cited of returns on investments of more than 100% annually.[47] "The great majority" of Italian families in a 1908 New York City study spent over 25% of their income on rent, and some families paid more than 50%.[48] Two French women who arrived in New York said that they

> were horrified when we found that we must pay $2 a week for a miserable room . . . All the first week after our landing we lived on potatoes—that we roasted over the gas flame—and stale bread. The woman who kept the house walked about in the passage smelling the air and saying someone was cooking in one of the bedrooms, but she did not find us out. That was a horrible place. Most of the people in it seemed to be mad . . . The partition that separated our room from the one next door to it was thin and there was a hole in it, through which a man once peeped. He talked at us, but we nailed a piece of tin over the hole.[49]

It was only natural that with such conditions immigrants moved often in the hope of something better. It was usually women who on took on the challenge of finding a little more for a little less, and Rose Cohen explained: "We liked moving from one place to another. Everyone . . . moved often. It meant some hard work but we did not mind that because it meant change in scenery and surroundings. None of the places were pretty and most were dingy. But moving even from one dingy place to another is a change."[50]

Nor was it only turn-of-the-century "new immigrants" who moved often. Angelea and Nicklaus Heck, for example, moved more than a dozen times in their three decades of letter writing back to Germany, always within New York City and always in rented housing. Even when they finally crossed the East River to Williamsburg, they rented. There they lived in another German community, for in 1865 approximately 70% of the adult population was German born.[51] They had a choice of German newspapers, churches, and other amenities, for they lived among upwards of 20,000 self-segregated Germans.

Yet turn-of-the-century social critics asserted that "old immigrants" had assimilated rapidly, and they lamented the parochialism of newcomers—even when landlords refused to rent to these southern and eastern Europeans. Rent discrimination would remain real for many decades into the future, and immigrants naturally crowded into ghettos with each other. Government investigation just prior to World War I found numerous cases of entire buildings whose occupants all came from the

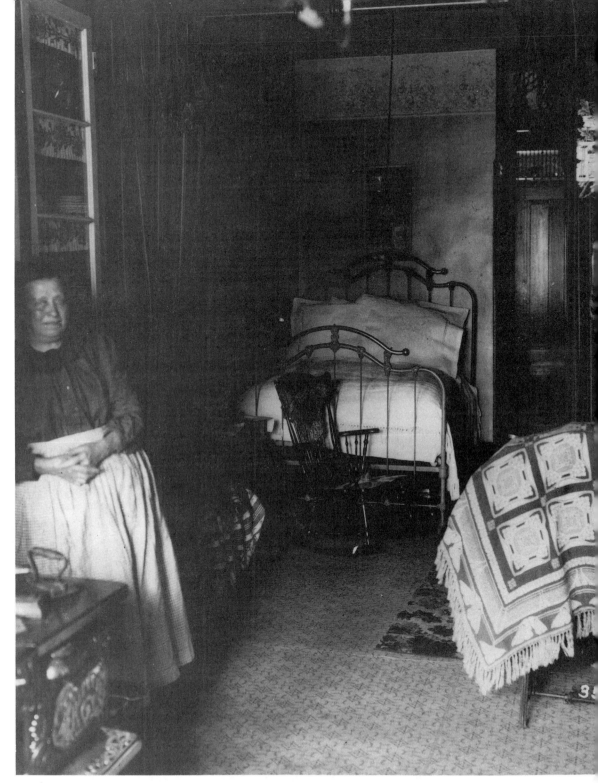

The well-kept home of a prospering urban woman. Note the careful needlework on the bed linens and the borders on the wall and china closet. The calendar reads "Time is Money." (LIBRARY OF CONGRESS)

same remote corner of Europe.[52] Even in the 1930s, as many as 85% of some Chicago neighborhoods were of the same ethnic group.[53]

Similarly, when the Greenwich House settlement project opened in 1902, Greenwich Village was not yet a haven for artists. Instead, "it was a region 80 per cent Catholic, deeply religious, antagonistic to 'outsiders.' Housing and other living conditions were so bad that the village's death rate was nearly twice that of the rest of the city . . . There were no public baths and few private ones; few streets were . . . paved; there were no playgrounds."[54]

Immigrant women found themselves the targets of complaints about the appearance of such neighborhoods—complaints by Americans who did not stop to reflect that both the public infrastructure and the buildings were controlled by other Americans. Exterior appearances indeed were shabby and interiors nearly impossible to restore to decency, and the wonder is that many women managed to do quite well. A Jewish East Sider remembered: "The surroundings were dilapidated. The streets were filthy. They used to throw garbage out of the windows of apartment buildings. . . . But my mother kept our apartment clean and kosher."[55] In fact, social workers consistently reported that many women, both Jewish and non-Jewish, made "efforts that are little short of heroic to keep their homes and their children clean and neat. That these women so often succeed in making their miserable flats into real homes is evidence of their courage and their almost inexhaustible patience."[56]

But they did get discouraged, for theirs were individual solutions to communal problems. What was needed was building codes, sewage systems, and control over landlords; what was lacking was political consciousness, economic power, and even the vote. A woman continued to be judged by the home she kept, and too often she was condemned as lazy and slovenly by Americans who had no comprehension of her powerlessness. The solution that seemed most viable to her was individual ownership.

Peasants who had been the chattel of a propertied aristocracy had one burning desire in America—to own for themselves. To own one's house was to be secure, to be at last free. This explains their frequent resentment of the efforts of well-intended reformers to ameliorate their lot. The tenement was temporary, and so they begrudged every cent that had to be put into it. They were content to live in a hovel if the rent was low and they could save. They recognized that "improvements" in the tenements would only raise the rent and prolong the time to their ultimate goal.

As soon as they could afford it, most bought a home, even though they might carry two and three mortgages for the rest of their lives. While nativists accused them of irresponsibility, immigrants in fact put down roots quickly. In Paterson, New Jersey, for example, where silk mills long attracted female immigrants, these weaving women put their paychecks into housing: even before World War I, twice as many foreign-born employees owned their homes compared with their native co-workers. The pattern held in Pennyslvania silk mill towns, where just 25% of natives owned their homes, while 54% of the foreign-born did.[57] Especially in smaller localities where buying a home was more conceivable than in the great cities, immigrants quickly made reality of their dreams.

Anna Maria Klinger's typical struggle for home ownership was recounted in letters back to Germany; she arrived in New York in 1847 and, after marriage a year or two later, continued to contribute to the family income with washing and sewing. By 1856, her husband wrote hopefully, "In the spring we may have bought a house, but the man wants eight hundred dollars in cash for it." Her own attitude was more worried, as she added, "You always live in such fear here, there are so many fires in the city . . . so we want to live in our own house all alone, then we want to take out fire insurance."[58] Later that year, the triumphant letter was written from Albany:

> We have bought a nice house, which cost us the sum of one thousand dollars, of which we paid five hundred dollars now and have to pay the other five hundred in five years . . . It isn't built like the houses in Germany . . . It is 22 feet wide and 30 long and with the garden 70 feet long, and in front of the house there's a small flower garden . . . it was built just one and a half years ago, we have 4 rooms and a small cellar, during the day we're in the two downstairs rooms, we sleep upstairs . . . our furniture and fixtures cost three hundred dollars, I'd just love to show it to you.[59]

This house proved a wonderful investment for her; when her husband died in 1860, she married again the following year—but that man too "fell ill right away and died . . . after 5 weeks." Paying the rising property taxes during the Civil War was difficult, but she managed, and in 1882 her brother wrote, "Marie is still a widow and is also well off."[60] The house was doubtless an important factor in her security; she owed no rent and probably grew a garden and rented rooms. Indeed, many immigrant women supported themselves as landladies.

Nevertheless, statistics on home ownership may prove misleading in terms of the comfort they brought. While many did buy and enjoy a single-family home, others bought a home and rented out most of it, continuing to live as poorly as before. The pattern appeared repeatedly in Chicago: A Slavic family, for example, owned an apartment house that brought in $1,000 a month in rent, while their payments were only $400—but they did not live in their own building and instead rented a cheaper apartment elsewhere. A family from Lithuania bought a house with four apartments and rented them all, while they occupied a tiny attic, which they shared with chickens. Still another home-owning Lithuanian family lived in the cellar, which was so low that a moderately tall person could not stand upright. This report concluded, "One schedule after another showed that it was not uncommon to find the owner occupying the least desirable apartment in his tenement."[61]

Women usually had considerable control over family financial matters, and it was almost always women who made the arrangements in the frequent moves and new rentals. Thus it seems that such self-privation, at least in many families, must have reflected the woman's idea of the proper route to family success. It is possible, too, that some were motivated by a desire to hide their rising affluence from the evil eye. Fatalistic peasants had no egalitarian notions about deserving better, and perhaps such women simply could not face the peril of moving so visibly beyond what they saw as their ordained station in life.

Those who lived in squalor despite a rising income were a minority. More often the drabness of a rented home changed when a woman had her own place and a bit of discretionary income. Often it was decorated with more zeal than taste, but the overall effect was one of color and cheer. Social workers among Slavic women observed of their decor:

> The floors are . . . scrubbed to an amazing whiteness. The walls are hung with gorgeous prints of many-hued saints, their gilt frames often hanging edge to edge so that they form a continuous frieze around the walls. The mantel is covered with lace paper and decorated with bright-colored plates and cups, and gorgeous bouquets of homemade paper flowers. . . . Gayly colored cotton curtains at the windows . . . and numerous canaries in cages—I have found as many as ten in a single kitchen—lend vivacity to the scene.[62]

Nor was this solely a characteristic of eastern Europeans; a student of Irish, English, and Germans in New York reported the same pattern, indicating that perhaps taste in home decoration was more a matter of class than of nationality. "Everybody," she wrote,

> had drawings of relatives done by itinerant artists who sold their portraits on the installment plan. Most homes also had copies of sentimental pictures and the Catholic ones inevitably had images and prints of saints. Pictures of Washington, Lincoln, and McKinley were common, many of them obtained with coupons. The most common attempts at original decoration were samplers done by the women and pictures drawn by children, one of which was done in chalk on the kitchen wall and was entitled, "The House My Aunt is Going to Live in When She Gets a Feller."[63]

Dreams such as this did come true, sometimes rather quickly. Though her first habitation was rude and though it seemed to take forever for her house to be built, Jette Bruns was able to say a decade after emigration: "We are as well situated, indeed better situated, as in Oelde; we have furniture, and even some luxuries, such as a carpet, a fine lamp, vases, etc."[64] The most prized of her possessions, though, was a set of portraits her family sent in 1846. "It touched tremendously to see you so vividly in front of me," she wrote, and concluded her lengthy thanks with, "the pictures are the dearest thing to me that you could have sent in all of the world."[65] It was, indeed, the happy remembrance of the old that made the new into a meaningful home.

11

CLEANING, CHILD CARE, AND CLOTHING

New Ways of Old Work

A curious language pattern was noted by social workers: while immigrant women "could discuss their factory work in English quite fluently," they "lacked a vocabulary relating to their home life."[1] This revealing comment speaks volumes about the isolation of housework, about the extent to which women are simply on their own in this area, and the loneliness inherent in this vocation that keeps women housebound while their men and children go out into the world.

They "lacked a vocabulary" because there was no one to teach them in the way that employers teach employees. Nor was what they knew from European homemaking experience totally adequate in America, as Gro Svendsen explained: "Life here is very different from life in our mountain valley. One must readjust oneself and learn everything all over again, even to the preparation of food. We are told that the women of America have much leisure time, but I haven't yet met any women who thought so!"[2]

Some aspects of this readjustment were pleasing. One Minnesota writer was thrilled by the ingeniousness of Yankee inventions:

> Our milk pails are so made that we can strain the milk as we pour it out of the pail. Churning butter is also very easy and seldom requires more than ten minutes . . .

Our washboards are also covered with zinc and designed to make washing very easy and quick . . . We heat [irons] by putting them on a stove lid, and they are much better for ironing than those we had in Norway.[3]

Emilie Koenig was fascinated by all aspects of Indiana housekeeping at midcentury. Though her original intention had been to "of course, live according to German custom," she rushed to elaborate on the wonders of the new:

You should see the cooking stove we selected . . . It is the cutest stove one can think of . . . With the stove one gets all the things one needs for cooking: pots, pans, teapot and coffeepot, a large kettle for boiling clothes, a roaster and all one needs for baking . . . And with all that, the stove only cost $21. It is the most expensive piece of furniture we have . . .

At twelve thirty sharp we have our dinner. Then Fredrich usually reads to me while I do the dishes . . . One washes and irons here every week. On Saturday one cooks also for Sundays, windows are cleaned, the rugs are sprinkled over with tea leaves and swept clean . . .

A great show is made of the beds here, for they frequently have them in their living rooms . . . They have a variety of covers, the best-liked being the quilts. But it takes much time to make them![4]

In housekeeping as in other aspects of life, Linka Preus was more reluctant to abandon Scandinavian ways. She was especially fretful about the failure of Americans to sweep their chimneys and sought a skilled chimney sweep in vain. But she also was insightful enough to notice her own assimilation and later wrote, "Perhaps I have become more Americanized—if that is the case it must be in this respect alone—never any more do I think of having the chimney swept."[5]

Dirty chimneys had the potential of danger, but there were other more significant hazards in the adaptation to new ways. Norwegian Mrs. Brandt, for example, ran her new gasoline stove for several hours heating the water for laundry, while her four children played. "I had never heard of such a thing as carbon monoxide," she wrote. "Suddenly I felt a little faint, and things seemed to grow dark before me. I looked through the open door into the living room, and saw all four of the children lying on the floor motionless!"[6] She barely got into the fresh air, revived herself, and brought her children to safety; they all could have died from the seemingly innocuous American machine to aid housewives.

Indeed, new housekeeping methods were not necessarily easily learned or appreciated. This was even more likely to be the case in cities, for rural immigrants were apt to own their homes, which gave women more control over their homemaking style. In rented housing in cities, however, landlords complained endlessly about ignorant peasant women who did not know how to care for their homes.

Immigrants were especially untutored in the functions of plumbing. There were many cases of bathtubs put to strange uses and toilets that clogged because users did not understand how they differed from outhouses. Similarly, the method of floor scrubbing that had worked fine in Europe—throwing water on the floor and then swabbing it with a broom—in America was "disastrous to the ceiling of the apartment below."[7]

Struggles between building owners and their occupants about the care of facilities occupied endless social worker time. One Passaic expert suggested as a solution

> *women* inspectors . . . [who] could work wonders in showing tenement people how to adjust themselves: let them explain the relation of landlords to tenants, and in telling them that the law compels landlords to provide light rooms and outside windows, it is an easy matter to add that tenants have duties and should not use their air-shafts as their dumping ground, or the bath-tubs, if they are fortunate enough to have them, as coal bins.
>
> A knowledge of their rights . . . would soon put an end to the fear of reporting necessary repairs . . . I have in mind a case where fourteen families were without running water for three weeks one winter because every one was afraid to report that the pipes had "bust."[8]

Those who arrived with the mass of immigration at the turn of the century also came at a time when Victorian standards of housekeeping had reached their epitome in the United States. Every middle-class housewife of the era had at least one maid, and some employed as many or more servants as there were members of the family. Books were written on the standards these servants were to meet as the field of home economics took root. Multicourse meals required long hours of cleanup; furniture, carpets, and drapes were heavy with dust-gathering ornamentation; fashion in decor required that almost every inch of space was covered with something to be cleaned.

The housekeeping standards of many immigrants, in contrast, were extremely simple. "We had no blinds and no curtains and the floors were all made of stone," a Sicilian woman recalled fondly. "You have no idea how simple life is over there. Here one must wash two or three times a week; over there once or twice a month."[9] A 1903 Italian writer pointed out that homes in Italy had only a half dozen pieces of furniture and that "the floor is usually the natural earth."

> So when it is asked why these people do not keep their houses cleaner, the answer is—they do not know how, and further, they not see the need for it. Besides, the Italian women who comes from Southern Italy is accustomed to nothing but work of the hardest kind, in the open field—her knowledge of housekeeping is limited to rearing children and the simplest kind of cooking. She has no idea of clean windows, spotless floor[s], and a glistening range, for the simple reason that none of these things have entered into her experience.[10]

Similarly, the Irish maids who made up the majority of the nation's domestic workers also came from simple European homes. "In Ireland, in 1841, almost one half of the total population, and fully 90 percent of the population of Connaught, lived in one-room, windowless cabins." Forty years later, 68% of Connaught residents still lived in such rude accommodations.[11]

The same was true for most eastern Europeans, including Jews, who despite kosher standards, were untutored in ways that Americans considered vital. The changed norms can be seen in the memories of Samuel Chotzinoff, who went beyond the ghetto to become a concert pianist. He wrote of a traumatic visit to his music teacher's home in suburban New York, when he inadvertently brought along a bedbug. The hostess screamed at him, "There's never been a bedbug in this house before!"[12]

"I could not believe she was telling the truth," he remembered. "I had never heard of a house that had no bedbugs." His mother's response to the desperate unhappiness of the boy was to call his hostess an "all-right-nick" who was putting on airs. "Yet," he added, "the incident was not without its effect on her. She engaged more frequently in housecleaning. I would find my underwear and socks removed after a single week's wear."[13]

But even after an understanding of American expectations was absorbed, to accept the necessary adjustment in housework was also to accept a commitment of much time and energy. So many jobs had to be done that are forgotten today: To do any cleaning at all, water had to be drawn, carried, heated, and emptied again; wood had to be chopped or coal brought in to create the fire to heat the water; the fire had to be laid and the ashes taken out (some frugal women cooled the ashes and then went through them looking for reburnable coal);[14] often soap had to be made from scratch; oil lamps had to be cleaned and trimmed to be able to see to do the work. The list goes on and on. Indeed, a factory life could seem a virtual escape from work.

Laundry was the job spoken of more frequently than any other aspect of housework. After the water was pumped, carried home, lifted onto the stove, and a fire built to heat it, each garment had to be scrubbed on the washboard—which was in itself a marvel of modernism to some. These garments had to be rinsed, starched (after the starch was cooked), wrung, and hung to dry. Finally it was taken down, sprinkled, and ironed with a heavy flat iron that also had to be heated on the stove.

Gro Svendsen explained the work necessary just to prepare for laundering in her hard-water area of Iowa, a task that was wholly unfamiliar to one from the pure mountain water of Norway: "First one must prepare the lye. This is poured into boiling water, and immediately the lye forms a white scum . . . The frothy scum must be skimmed off before one puts the clothes into the water. The lye is very strong and must be removed, so you can see there is a lot of extra work."[15]

Mrs. Brandt had the same problem and told of the result when she ignorantly used untreated water: "I used it once—and only once—for washing clothes. A dark, gummy substance" so seriously damaged her laundry that even after she spent long hours trying to undo the damage, "some of the garments were still so bad that they had to be discarded." In her North Dakota, there was no choice except to collect rainwater for laundry—which meant tubs of water that were "an unfailing source of attraction to our small daughter."[16]

Other women did not have this peculiar problem, but laundry remained a heavy and continual task, for as one observer noted, many immigrant families were so poor that "it is wash day all the week round, for a change of clothing is scarce."[17] Moreover, the air pollution in some industrial immigrant towns was so serious that clothing dirtied very quickly; one conscientious Italian in Massachusetts said that coal dust even indoors was such a severe problem that she laundered the bed linens every day.[18] Then, in tenements where pullied lines or porches were not available, women carried the waterlogged clothing to the roof, where they also had to keep a close eye on their children. After it was hung, they had to worry about the possibility of theft—and rain and snow and soot—while it dried.

A number of immigrant women made the interesting observation that it was easier for them to go out and do someone else's housework than to do their own. "I don't mind the work at Mrs. Van Hoozer's," said a woman who earned her living by cleaning. "Her family is small and things are convenient in the laundry. It's the washing here at home for him and the boys that breaks my back. Here I ain't even got a wringer."[19] Seeing these needs, one charity organization provided laundry facilities—but despite this experiment's popularity, the idea was little duplicated. Today's coin-operated laundromats did not yet exist, and the established commercial laundries, where newly invented machines were first introduced, were too expensive for most immigrants.

After clothes were washed and dried, the ironing was often avoided for the simple reason that few had closets or any storage space that would keep garments looking fresh. The solution adopted by many was to carefully launder Sunday's clothing on Monday—just as the Americans did—but then, instead of ironing on Tuesday as the era's work week commanded, they waited until Saturday or even Sunday morning to iron the things that were necessary to a proper appearance for church and Sunday outings.

A dearth of storage space was only one influence that overcrowding had on housework. Ironically, prosperity could actually increase the crowding and the demands of work, as in this case of a woman affluent enough to own a sewing machine and an organ who nonetheless lived in a two-room home that she shared with four men and two children. In a kitchen

> steaming with vapor from a big washtub on a chair in the middle of the room, the mother was trying to wash, and at the same time to keep the elder of her two babies from going into [another] tub full of boiling water . . . Asleep . . . in the second room were one boarder and the man of the house. The two other boarders were at work.[20*]

---

* Implicit in this commentary is the probability that "the man of the house" worked at night, while the woman slept in the little home with two male boarders.

Despite such difficult conditions, a remarkable number of women managed to do an excellent job of housekeeping. Many writers agreed with premier sociologist Edith Abbott, who called the housework efforts of Chicago's immigrant women "heroic," especially in view of their "dilapidated tenements."[21] A specialist on southern Italians wrote, "Mothers so inculcate orderliness and cleanliness into each Italian girl that American visitors are constantly filled with admiration at the neatness and attractiveness of their small apartments."[22] A third marveled that "when you find twenty-four families living in a twenty-four roomed shack . . . the wonder is that they can be even presentably clean."[23]

Social workers even deemed immigrant women who also held full-time jobs to be good housekeepers; one study reported that five of every six homes of working women were clean.[24] This report noted that English women who worked in textile mills abroad brought with them the habit of carefully balancing housework and jobs and that their homes were cleaner than those of nonworking women.

Similarly, a student of Slavs said succinctly of their homes, "everything is spotless,"[25] and a second agreed—until she reevaluated her data. "It is with something both of surprise and resentment," she wrote, "that one faces figures (albeit gathered by one's self) which assert that over thirty per cent of Polish homes and over forty per cent of Russian and Ruthenian homes vary from 'dirty' to 'very dirty.'"[26] Clearly, her positive impressions had been so striking that they had simply erased the negative ones. It was this unacknowledged managerial ability that surprised the careful observer. "After watching the busy lives and the problems of these women," wrote one thoughtful investigator of the housewives in Pennsylvania's steel area, "I came to believe that the women who can keep her home healthful and attractive on $15 or less a week has in her elements of genius."[27]

Housekeeping Variations

Scientific investigation into the question of who did what housework yielded varying results. A government study of women and girls in New England textile mills showed that 60% of them said they did no housework, a remarkably high number that doubtless is skewed because of the inclusion of "girls." This study also "ascertained that often the unemployed husband . . . had taken charge of the house," adding "the standard of housekeeping . . . among the foreign operatives . . . is very low."[28]

Another study of working mothers that included no girls had the opposite result. Of seven specific tasks listed, in all but one* the mother did more than half of the work alone: the full-time employee also did 77% of the mending, 72% of breakfast preparation, and so forth. When the column of figures for "mother with help" is added to her work alone, the result shows that it was extremely rare for working women not to do, at least partially, all of the tasks of homemaking.[29]

---

* The one exception was lunch preparation.

The clearest indicator of the amount of housework a woman was expected to do was not her employment status but rather her national origin. Bohemian women, for example, had worked outside the home in the Old World, and this tradition, plus the generally liberated attitudes of Bohemians, combined to make sex roles less rigid and the work load more equitable. A study of them said:

> The most noticeable effect of having the mother go to [the] factory is that the ordinary masculine aversion to doing women's work is greatly moderated. The boys run home from their play after school hours to start the kitchen fire, so that the water may be boiling when their mothers come home. They make beds and sweep and clean house. I have known a boy of 11 to acquire sufficient knowledge of housework so that, at this mother's death, he was able to do all the housework for a family of four. Several times I have come into a home and found the strong young husband washing, and not at all embarrassed to be caught at the washtub.[30]

Few other ethnic groups encouraged such candid helpfulness on the part of males, but some exhibited a middle course. Among Slavic families in the Pennsylvania coal country, for example, it was acceptable for a man to "turn the machine" when the first washing machines were invented.[*] Widowers and men whose wives were sick had to accept housework roles, however awkward they might feel about them. When Emilie Koenig was sick during the pregnancy that eventually caused her death, she explained to her family, "Fredrich nursed me and took care of the house. That is the custom in America that if the wife is ill the man takes care of the housework."[31]

Jette Bruns also spoke of her brother's assumption of housework during his wife's long struggle with tuberculosis: "I feel very sorry for Franz; he is quite patient and usually cares for her himself."[32] After her death, however, he seemed incapable of assuming household duties in the way women were expected to do; eight years after her sister-in-law's death, Jette still worried, "Franz cannot decide on anything . . . And then there are his children. What is he doing for them?"[33]

While men might attempt housework when there was no other choice, it was especially rare in Mediterranean cultures for a man to do any work in the home. One

---

[*] An interesting idea worthy of further attention is that when machines are introduced—and a job therefore becomes easier—it also becomes acceptable for men to do that job.

For example, women were hired for centuries as "cleaning ladies" to scrub the floors of public buildings on hands and knees, but when vacuum cleaners and power scrubbers were introduced, men were hired to run them. Similarly, as long as washing clothes was a backbreaking job done over a washboard until the knuckles bled, it was "women's work." But when the mechanical washers came along, it was not emasculating for these steelworkers to be seen "turning the machine."

Probably novelty is the key factor. After the particular machine has been around awhile and men are bored with it, the job again becomes "women's work"—for example, typewriters and telephones, which at first were exclusively operated by men.

Italian woman recalled bitterly: "Washing was woman's work. Cleaning was woman's work. Cooking was woman's work. Babies were woman's work. Everything was woman's work . . . The only thing that my husband did was the shopping and that was because he insisted on handling the money himself. Also, he could meet his cronies and talk and gossip for awhile."[34]

The difference between ethnic groups in willingness to ease housework burdens is clearly illustrated by the use of a laundry, for the chore was so tiresome that its elimination was one of the first signs of rising affluence. Almost all—86%—of the Bohemian women interviewed on this subject used laundries. More revealing is the fact that Jewish women used this service at the same rate, for they rarely worked outside the home after marriage if that could be avoided: Italians were similar to Jews in avoiding female employment after marriage—but only 12% of Italians used laundries, and that number did not rise as their incomes increased.[35]

It was not only women and female sociologists who noted the inequitable distribution of household tasks in most immigrant ghettos. An Americanized male observer wrote of the street scene in New York's Mulberry Bend:

> Down the street comes a file of women carrying enormous bundles of firewood on their heads, loads of decaying vegetables from the market wagons in their aprons, and each a baby at the breast supported by a sort of sling that prevents it from tumbling down. The women do all the carrying, all the work that one sees going on in "the Bend." The men sit or stand in the streets, on trucks, or in the open doors of the saloons smoking black clay pipes, talking and gesticulating.[36]

Still another housewife skill was involved in the purchase of the pushcart items that these women carried—the ability to haggle. It was an ability considered to be of real value, and women took pride in the bargains they drove. Their daughters soon learned, however, that this skill was unappreciated by Americans and that a lady didn't bicker over prices. One recalled her Italian grandmother:

> At the pushcarts, she would haggle and bargain with the peddlers and I hated to shop with her. I'd be embarrassed as she'd take a piece of fruit with some spots on it and say, "Look at this, it's gone bad, you don't want to sell this—no one would buy it—give it to this poor little kid here, her father doesn't make much money." And she'd push it to my mouth while the peddler yelled. Or she would complain that the vegetables were 2¢ cheaper on the next street and get her price reduced.[37]

Haggling was a necessity in her youth, and though this woman was now quite wealthy, she still wanted to demonstrate her ability—something that her Americanized offspring instead found humiliating. It was the only assertive behavior acceptable in the otherwise docile world of women in southern Europe, but, in the American marketplace, women were not supposed to drive bargains. Haggling became a lost art, for its use diminished, rather than enhanced, a woman's reputation.

There were other losses. The one spoken of most frequently was the way in which American housework was individualized, while European ways often offered communal work situations. Especially in southern Europe, a housewife's day was spent largely out of doors, and she often worked in the company of other women. Laundry was done in streams and dried on rocks or bushes; baking and even cooking was done in outdoor ovens and summer kitchens; sewing was done in sunlight rather than in the dim light of thick-walled homes.

The isolation of American homemaking was, of course, even more pronounced for rural immigrants, especially those who lived where winters were severe. Even in the mild climate of Missouri and despite living in a colony of other Germans, Jette Bruns spoke of the lonely confinement of housekeeping. Five years after emigration, she wrote, "Now our family is limited to [her brother] Bernhard and one [hired] girl, which pleases me immensely. Never before in America have I had such a small household . . . Now I would be satisfied if I were not so lonely."[38] She did not mention the four children she had at the time, so this "small household" actually had eight members—but loneliness is not necessarily dependent on the number of people around. She had written earlier, in a larger household that included other immigrants, "How lonely I am; there is not another congenial female being with whom I could exchange now and then my feelings when I need some relief . . . I rarely go out of the house. Business does not permit it; however, if the mill is finished, then I will have to catch up on my visits."[39]

"Business does not permit it" is a key phrase, for Jette—like all too many other unacknowledged women—was in fact a businesswoman as well as a homemaker. The mill she spoke of was intended to supplement her physician husband's income, and when he traveled to care for patients, it was she who supervised it, the brewery and other enterprises in which they engaged. Similarly, an Italian woman who had not been outdoors for three months was not confined solely by housework, but rather because she sewed to increase the family income.

Seldom did these thoughts occur to census takers or other collectors of economic data, however, and these women were almost invariably listed as "housewife." In America, it was understood, a woman's place was literally in the home.

Child Care and the "Placing Out" of Orphans

Almost always, that place in the home was reinforced by children, often in large numbers. Rearing children in America brought additional adjustments. In the Old World, they commonly joined their parents in the fields or in family occupations; Lithuanian Edna Vidravich, for example, began tending pigs at age six. While some urban families in America put their children to work at flower making or finishing sewing or other forms of home contract labor, this was not entirely comparable to European work systems, for it did not receive the community approbation that was the case in Europe.

Employment in America implied being away from one's children, while in the Old Country not only was there a good chance that children and parents worked together, but in addition, watchful villagers kept an eye on the young. In America, however, such extended families often did not exist, at least not in the early days of a group's immigration. Children instead were left unsupervised amid strangers. There were few playgrounds, and crowded city streets offered no swimming holes or fields for exploring. Recreational opportunities for girls were even more scarce than for boys.

But many girls had no chance to think of play, for they were already busy mothering at a tender age. The situation of Rosa Cavalleri's family is typical:

> I was all the time gone to work and my children were alone on the street. My Visella was 8 or 9 years old and she had to be the mother to the other children. And I had more trouble because the landlord was so mean. He was all the time beating the children. One day he kicked Visella and beat her terrible because they were playing house in the back alley and moved some boxes.[40]

Leaving children like Visella in charge of other children was not unusual. A study of working mothers found that the second most common "method" of child care was in fact for the children to be on their own.[41]

PROVISION FOR CHILD CARE OF WORKING MOTHERS
PHILADELPHIA, 1918

Total	1,430
Adult in household	742
No one	408
Nursery	165
Neighbor runs in	64
Neighbor in her own home	51

Nobody and everybody was in charge of the unattended children of immigrant ghettos. While some, like Rosa Cavalleri, resented those adults who took it upon themselves to discipline the children of strangers, others found communal child supervision to be a positive. A New England Italian, for example, wanted the entire community involved in raising her children:

> I was a widow at thirty-four with five small children . . . In our neighborhood the children were treated like children. They were expected to respect adults and they did, or else. And if you saw a neighbor's child doing something wrong, you treated him as though he were your own, and his parents were grateful for it. Looking back, I know I couldn't have survived those first years without my neighbors and friends. The neighborhoods were like great, big families.[42]

Similar neighborhood responsibility for care was reported by a turn-of-the-century government study of children whose mothers worked in New England textile mills. Most children casually "played about the streets or homes." Occasionally, "children were taken to the mills, where they either worked or were allowed to play." Women who did this, however, were in violation of "rules because of the fear that the children may be caught in the machinery."[43]

That these rules were "frequently overlooked by mill officials"[44] was due to the need for skilled female labor in such relatively isolated mill towns, but this was not at all a typical situation. Most women did not have bosses who were indulgent enough to allow children in the workplace. In fact, it was not unusual for women to work such long hours or at such distances from home that Sunday was the only day of the week when they saw their children awake. Disruption in child care, illness, or even death did not constitute sufficient excuse for missing work, and children went unattended by mothers who were more afraid of losing their jobs than of losing their children.

Social workers not infrequently found cases such as that of a Slavic woman who locked in her "two little children" with a "lunch of bread and coffee" while she worked.[45] A Polish widow left three children alone, all of them under six, and one was badly burned when he tried to start a fire to warm their cold home.[46] An Italian girl of just seven had to tend her little brother instead of playing with her friends; she was so resentful that she wished he would die, and when he did die at age three, she "thought she had caused his death by wishing it."[47]

It was the child-care problem that was almost always the motivating factor for women who worked at night. By working during the night, they could be available when the children were awake—though the mothers got no rest themselves. A 1926 New Jersey mother who worked as "carder in the Botany mill" spent her nights doing "the heaviest work imaginable":

All night she stands, from 7 o'clock in the evening until five the following morning. She then returns to her home where six children . . . await her care. In exhaustion, she "falls on the bed" until 6 o'clock when she must get up, prepare her husband's breakfast, get him off, and then get three children ready for school.

When they are gone, there are still three younger ones to look after.

For an hour or two she may try desperately to get a little rest with them at play in the same room with her . . . Presently she staggers to her feet, and sets about washing or cleaning or preparing something for the children to eat who come home at noon from school . . . Occasionally, she says, she . . . lets them play in the street below. "But how I know while I try to sleep, they not get kill from automobile?"[48]

Systematic, supervised child care was rare, and today's profit-making day-care center was simply unknown. Occasionally, a charity created a nursery and charged a nominal fee for its use—a dime a day was typical—but these remained philanthropies,

not businesses. The extensively documented budgets of immigrant families almost
never contain any expenditure for child care.

Moreover, many women were reluctant to use what nurseries did exist, opting
instead for even the haphazard services of relatives and neighbors. They viewed these
institutions with suspicion, a distrust that was grounded in the immigrant's experience
with almost any sort of institution in Europe. Their suspicion of the American

"Prayer Hour in the Nursery; Five Points House of Industry" was the title of this 1889 picture taken in
the Five Points section of New York City.
    *Women who placed children in such facilities were rarely allowed any input into their children's
lives. Because Protestant expressions of faith were mandatory in most, they were avoided by Catholic
and Jewish immigrants.*   (LIBRARY OF CONGRESS, PHOTOGRAPHY BY JACOB RIIS)

day-care centers also had some basis in fact, for much of this charity came with strings attached.

If she once placed her children in a nursery, a mother was made to feel that she had surrendered her control over them and had given social workers limitless rights to interfere with her life and her budget. Worse was the fact that she was often subjected to appalling pressure by social workers to consign some of her children to orphanages or foster homes after they had been taken by a nursery.

The extent to which the institution controlled its clients is shown by the pettiness of nursery rules. In one, for example, mothers were forbidden to bring their babies in carriages because the look-alike baby buggies had caused confusion—so after a long day of work, the tired woman had to carry her children home in her arms instead of letting them ride in the buggy she had bought for this purpose. Mothers were seldom consulted on anything, and their fears often were ignored or scorned. Immigrant women frequently worried about the baths given to their children, for instance, but nurseries seldom used such opportunities for parental education. One social worker, sympathetic to the mothers in this power struggle, summarized the situation well: "The attitude of the management too often shows the strain of autocracy with which we are prone to dilute our charity."[49]

But even more than petty rules and annoying attitudes, women feared the damage that nurseries might do to children's souls. To understand this, one must recall that until the influx of foreigners at the beginning of this era, the United States had been almost wholly Protestant, and entirely too many natives thought Protestantism and Americanism were synonymous. Rabid anti-Catholicism existed, and it sank to violence and deception in its efforts to "save souls." Difficult though it may be to believe today, many immigrant mothers felt they had reason to fear that if they left their children in the hands of Protestants, the children could be shipped off to the West by these agencies.

The fear had a basis in fact, for societies to aid neglected and orphaned children indeed did send them to foster homes in the country's interior, where their labor was valued on farms and ranches and where, presumably, they received a good (and Protestant) home. The report of one such organization in 1875, for example, clearly indicates that immigrant children—and especially those born in traditionally Catholic countries—dominated their activity: they sent off 2,124 foreign-born children, while only 1,509 American-born children were sufficiently neglected to merit this change. Moreover, almost half of the foreign-born were Irish and presumably Catholic.[50] While it is true that immigrants were likely to be among the poor who needed charity, these numbers are so disproportionate compared with the numbers of foreign-born children in the population as to indicate a genuine racism.[*]

---

[*] This is especially true when one considers that most women emigrated when they were young and relatively free of children; their offspring largely were born in this country and thus did not fall into the category of foreign-born children.

The following view of a priest, though it probably exaggerated the facts, none-theless exhibits the honest emotions of Catholic immigrants:

> I heard a distinguished philanthropist of Boston, and member of the City Govern-ment, say, that the only way to elevate the foreign population was to make Protestants of their children . . . To aid in the work of perversion, societies were formed to receive Catholic children, and provide for them, till a number should be collected sufficient to fill a [railroad] car; when they were swiftly steamed off to some Western state, and there sold, body and soul, to farmers and squatters. Missionaries, both male and female, were hired to prowl about certain quarters of the city, to talk with children . . . and urge them to leave their friends and homes, picturing to them vistas of food, clothing, and money.[51]

In another case, a priest reported that he had accidentally come across Catholic children who were to be shipped West that very day, despite the fact that many of their "poor mothers had paid their board in advance just to avert this catastrophe."[52] Whether or not these reports are valid, it is clear that such views from clergymen whom they respected would make immigrant women extremely wary of placing their children with an agency of any kind.

The New York Children's Aid Society, for example, began in 1853 with un-abashed bias. "Immigration," said its founder, "is pouring in its multitudes of poor foreigners, who leave these young outcasts everywhere in our midst." He called upon "Christian men" to deal with the problem, warning that "these boys and girls will soon form the lower class of our city [and will] poison society."[53] Aiming to "drain the city of this class," the Aid Society "placed out" some 150,000 poor children before dissolving in 1929. Yet the majority of those who rode these "orphan trains" to midwestern farm homes seem not to have been the children of recently arrived immigrants. Although parental origins were often unknown, estimates are that as many as 94% were either American born or of the "old immigration," while Jews and Italian Catholics probably accounted for fewer than 1% of the children, even during the decades when these groups were the most numerous newcomers.[54]

Rhetoric about "draining the cities" of immigrant children, however, struck fear into the heart of many a mother. Their anxieties were so profound that it was difficult to allay them, even when charities had the best of intentions. Benevolent women in Holyoke, Massachusetts, for example, opened a nursery in the 1880s, but it soon had to be abandoned; the working mothers, most of whom were Catholic, would not leave their children in the care of these Protestant natives. Holyoke's Catholic leadership, on the other hand, did nothing to meet the needs of working women, and a nursery run by nuns did not begin until 1916.[55]

While kidnapping plots were not as pervasive as feared, it certainly was true that the point of most social agencies was in fact the Americanization of immigrants. The era held little appreciation for any positive aspects of European ethnicities, and almost all Americans in a position to influence young minds unquestioningly imparted the view that the new ways were better than the old. The result was that when parents sometimes did voluntarily place children in the care of Americans, their offspring grew up in a culture so alien from their own that future healthy family relationships became impossible.

Anatasia Molarsky is an excellent example. In 1914, when she was three, her mother took her older sisters to seek husbands in their native Galicia, where they were caught by World War I. For complicated reasons, Mrs. Molarsky stayed abroad until 1926; meanwhile, Anatasia's aunt quickly "became tired of taking care of [the] very active and inquisitive child." Her father placed her in a Protestant orphanage, and she grew up there. When finally reunited with her family, she was a typical Ohio teenager who was accustomed to different standards in lifestyles and behavior. There was no way that she and her dominating Old World mother could ever live amicably together.[56]

Even though such a loss of family heritage would inevitably result in a clash of cultures for children placed even temporarily in orphanages, most charities routinely insisted that widows, widowers, and others in need of emergency child care use these institutions. The frequency of this use is seen in the assertion that, during the years prior to 1880, only about one-sixth of the children in these places were full orphans who had lost both of their parents.[57] Moreover, a great number of such institutions existed, and they were under the aegis of Protestants, Catholics, and Jews alike. An incomplete list of those in Baltimore in 1879, for instance, includes St. Mary's Female Orphan Asylum, St. Anthony's German Orphan Asylum, Kelso Home for Orphan Children, and the Hebrew Orphan Asylum.[58]

Mothers were forced to put children in these places to satisfy the budget standards of charitable agencies, and fathers often did the same because they lacked sufficient child-care skills. The case of a Polish family in New Jersey is revealing: the woman died when her baby was nine weeks old, leaving two other children under age four. Because "the baby cried too much," the landlady insisted that the father find another home for the infant. He "started out after supper to find a relative or friend in a position to care for it," but the support systems that he would have expected in Europe were no longer available. In late-night desperation, he found an American, a librarian who was sympathetic to immigrants, and she "telephoned two hospitals, a day nursery and an orphan asylum, only to find them all profuse in apologies." Finally, she found an immigrant widow "with four young children" who "made room for the little stranger."[59]

It was only after the institutional facilities rejected her, however, that this Americanization expert turned to less formal care. Her predilection was same as that of most of charity workers and social agencies: they placed children in institutions both because of their cost efficiency and because of their effectiveness at turning immigrant children into Americans. The routine prescription of an orphanage as the solution to child-care difficulties was especially likely for widows, and it makes the records of many agencies read almost as though they are battling against a client rather than aiding her. Again and again they show that a widow was urged to commit her children to an orphanage and that she refused.[60]

The way the records are written, of course, makes the widow sound obstinate, but she undoubtedly was trying to do what was right, not only because she did not want to be separated from her offspring but also because she understood that they would be better off in their own homes than in an impersonal institution. This was especially true after a father's death or other trauma had brought the family to neediness, but many social agencies missed that human point. They were quite ready to label a mother "unfit" if she did not cooperate with their ideas for her children.

To preserve her individualism and do what her conscience told her was right for her children took courage, for aid was often refused if clients did not submit to the charity's plan—which often included giving up the youngest of her children and putting the oldest to work. Having lost the argument and with it the financial assistance, a woman then had to make heroic efforts to support her family alone.

Rose Schneiderman's mother became a widow soon after the young family arrived from Russia. She kept the family together for a time by working and taking in lodgers, but still they "often went hungry to bed." After a year, her four-year-old son was committed to an orphanage run by the Hebrew Sheltering Guardian Society. The next summer Rose joined him as an inmate. "When I first saw him I could have wept, for he looked so woebegone wearing a dress." The place was not at all a happy home; the matrons, she said, "were very strict and even very cruel."[61]

Nor was it less cruel for her mother, for visits were not regularly allowed. When Rose was able to return home after a year, she and her mother went surreptitiously to see her brothers who remained. They obtained permission from a farmer whose property bordered on the institution, took a picnic lunch there, and the boys "would steal down the hill to where we would be waiting. We always had sweets and fruit for them, which we handed over the fence."[62]

When she contrasted this to the warmth of a European village where uncles, aunts, cousins, and friends looked after each other's offspring, a woman had to question the American way. Surely this was wrong; surely monetary values were again supplanting more important human values. This time there was no ambivalence; she knew she was right about the desire to be with her own children. The questions became instead what could be done about it, and was it worth it? Only the future could tell; only the child—too young to know now—would be able to say whether or not the heart-aching decisions the mother made were the right ones.

To Be American Is to Look American: Clothing

When Anatasia Molarsky and her mother clashed over the Americanized ways the girl had learned in the orphanage, nothing caused more arguments than clothing. Her dresses were her "dearest possessions," but the shabby home in which her parents lived offered not even a closet, and the precious clothes had to be "stuffed into a

The costume of this Hungarian woman, who arrived with her child in 1912, marks her as a "greenhorn." Especially the shawl and backpack were items scorned by those who wished to be seen as Americanized and fashionable. (COURTESY OF THE BOSTON PUBLIC LIBRARY, PRINT DEPARTMENT; FROM THE BOSTON *HERALD-TRAVELER*, FEBRUARY 16, 1912)

suitcase" for storage. The mother, who was "horrified" by her daughter's "extravagance in dress," refused to buy her anything more, and "Anatasia retaliated by borrowing clothes from the neighbors, saying she had nothing to wear."[63]

Apparel was still another thing that required accommodation to America. Nothing gave clearer clue of how recently one had arrived; nothing else was as conspicuous as unconventional clothing. When twenty-two-year-old Hilma Ulrika Maki arrived from Finland in 1901, her "Americanized" sister Helena, whom she had not seen for several years, greeted her in New York. "The first thing she did was to look me over—and then to make me over," said Hilma. "She told me I had to put my braid up, as no one would think of giving me a job looking so much like a child."[64]

While the newcomer took this advice, she held back on other adjustments Helena advocated. "My sister proved somewhat of a trial to me," Hilma wrote later, "as our ideas were quite different and our sense of values far apart. She was interested primarily in the new (to us) American stylish clothes and wanted me with my first pay to get myself all decked out in new clothes and to have my picture taken to send back home . . . I wanted to start to repay my uncle for the money he had advanced to me for my trip to America. Besides, I wanted to send my mother a little each month."[65]

Although Hilma's sense of responsibility was the value that societal moralists would deem superior, at the same time Helena's advice may well have been less giddy and more practical than it appears, for it was true that "no one would give her a job" unless she looked more like the American standard. Wearing what the Americans did was a vital sign of assimilation, and for women and girls, the best indication of this was what was worn on the head—hats for women and big bows for girls:

> The first visible sign we have that . . . American habits are beginning to take root [is] when you see the foreign child adorned with that ribbon which she has found a necessity . . . You can guess that one morning she made a stand against her family and refused to go to school until she was provided with this coveted badge of respectability, and probably after threats of what the law might do if she was not found in school, the poor parents succumbed . . . and one more bow was added to a class room.[66]

The adjustment in dress often began even before immigrants left Europe. Americans jeered at the curious clothing of new arrivals in the early days of any ethnic group's immigration, and, having felt themselves the objects of scorn, the earliest arrivals passed this message back to their sisters in Europe. By the height of the immigrant era one expert reported:

> Few of those who wear a peasant costume at home arrive in it at Ellis Island. They leave their beautiful embroidered garments behind, carefully instructed to do so by their friends in America. They know that such things would excite derision here,

and indeed they themselves are prone to despise them in comparison with the cheap, ready-made goods which they buy at the port where they embark.[67]

The elaborately embroidered garments that were left behind were handcrafted, sometimes completely back to shearing the wool from the sheep or growing the flax for the linen. Many garments had been part of a bridal trousseau and were associated with happy memories. Sometimes, too, these things were indicative of status in the Old World—a status that often was never regained in America, especially for older, married women. A Dutch woman who "had accumulated some worldly store," for example, was reluctant to emigrate, but at her husband's insistence, "she sold the precious things she knew would be of little value in America: Even the gold clasps on her Sunday mantle* had to be parted with. In Holland, a woman's station in life is determined by the fastenings on her cloak . . . Hers were gold set with garnets. She was very proud of them and it almost broke her heart to sell them, but even they had to go to get money for the new venture."[68]

Women sold their treasured things or gave them to loved ones whom they might never see again. Even if a garment was too cherished to part with, it remained stored in a trunk in America, for here the native costume was scorned, not valued. Shedding her old dress was symbolic of a woman's intention to become a new person.

"Once established here," they began to buy new things. "The process of expansion of wants is a rapid one . . . Nothing is too good for them, especially for their children and their young women."[69] During the first year after immigration, expenditures for dress were a serious problem because so many new items had to be bought—at the same time that one was also getting a job and establishing a home. Nor was it entirely a desire to be in style that motivated these purchases, for immigrants soon learned that Americans required conformity in clothing.

It was not unusual for a woman to be turned down for a job because of her dress; an expert on Pittsburgh industry reported that appearance was a hiring criterion even in dirty metal factories.[70] One candy manufacturer who hired many Italian women stated that he would not employ one who came to apply bareheaded or wearing a shawl, for he felt that if she had not adopted American hats, the woman was not sufficiently assimilated.[71] Dress thus became another factor limiting employability, for often a woman could not afford to ape American style in order to get these low-paid jobs. A hat could easily cost a week's wages.

But when they could afford to buy clothes, they did so, and—as was the case with spending money on physicians—they did not necessarily look for a bargain. An Irish shopkeeper in a Pennsylvania mining town said of the turn-of-the-century arrivals from eastern Europe: "They want the best goods and they want them up to date. If they do not know themselves what is the style, or if they do not speak English, they bring a friend with them who does."[72] A student of Italians agreed, saying that

---

* Mantle is an old-fashioned word for a cloak or cape.

they soon bought silk underwear for their girls and that competition in dressing children reached burdensome heights in some neighborhoods.[73]

Similar willingness to spend money on clothing, particularly for special occasions, appears early in the immigrant era, even among traditionally frugal Germans. Angela Heck wrote home to Prussia in 1869, "Our daughter Eva had her first Holy Communion . . . I wished you could have seen it. Her clothing cost us 25 talers without the candle. She had a white dress and a white veil that came down to the ground, a lovely wreath of rosemary around her head."[74] Since both of the Hecks sewed for a living, the cost of the garment is particularly striking; four years earlier, Angela had written optimistically of a combined income of twenty talers a week.

The Klinger family, siblings who emigrated by increments from the German province of Württemberg at midcentury, repeatedly recognized the importance of good clothing—even the men spent freely on it. Barbara Klinger's brother cared for her illegitimate, half-Jewish son with a tenderness exhibited through gifts of apparel; he wrote in 1854, "I sometimes take him out just on Sundays. His outfit consists of a little grey felt hat with a blue ribbon on it, baby clothes and jacket, shoes and socks with leggings on top and mittens, which cost four dollars."[75] Five years later, Rosina Klinger's brother-in-law advised her prior to emigration, "You can't walk around in America dressed like you are in Germany . . . Don't buy any clothes since you can't wear German clothes here."[76]

Rosina wrote home after arrival, "From Mari I got 2 dresses right away and a hat with red and white flowers and a green ribbon and from Katharina I got a pink-checked dress and a coat, a petticoat and a white skirt and from Gottlieb's wife I got some *Kelgo* [calico] for 2 aprons." Not to be outdone, sister Katharina added that Rosina "didn't recognize me, I looked too fine and was dressed too fancy. I also don't look much like the other brothers and sisters, they are all jealous of me."[77]

It was, in fact, young newcomers who were most likely to spend money on the visible demonstration of rising affluence that apparel provides. A turn-of-the-century ranking of the clothing expenditures of workers in New England textile mills also showed that the newly arrived groups spent the most—even though the governmental investigators had ignored their own data to make the sweeping (and false) statement that "the Portuguese, Polish and Italians spend less on their clothing" than the English, Irish, and French Canadian "old immigrants."[78] A careful analysis, however, shows that Polish and Italian families spent the most, while an English family came in last. The newcomers probably spent more because they had more needs, and they also may have understood that to overcome the prejudices against them, it was especially important to look as though they belonged.

Such bias about the "new immigration" was wrong, but one crucial distinction between the two time periods is important relative to clothing. In the "old immigrant" pre–Civil War period, "ready-made clothing for women was unheard of except for shoes, stockings and corsets, and the amount of sewing which women had to do is staggering."[79]

Jette Bruns arrived in frontier Missouri during this period, and her experience illustrates the complexity of clothing production at the time. When a neighbor went to Germany on business in 1841, she took the opportunity to obtain clothes:

> I have spoken with Bruns, who thought it would not be too inconvenient to have some dresses sent . . . I would like to have two cotton dresses and one of simple Merino; they are to be made to the measure of sister Johanna but about the width of three fingers wider around the waist . . .
>
> Then I also want a little petticoat with bodice for the two-year-old girl, quite warm . . . If everything works out, I hope that you . . . will write me in the first letter what the cost was, and Bruns will transfer it with the proper interest.[80]

Later, she added that she needed some "gray linen" for her brother and "a piece of strong muslin" to make things for her children and herself. "Furthermore, we need thick gray beaver cloth for two petticoats . . . [and] a pair of nicely knitted woolen stockings and some extra yarn for darning and two pairs of ordinary stockings."[81] She explained the following year, "There is neither printed muslin nor gingham to be had here, nor woolen cloth . . . In the future I will not need any woolen yarn, for I began to spin and dye myself last winter. I enjoy this very much."[82]

It was the invention of the sewing machine at midcentury that changed all this, as well as the growth of both textile and garment factories. By the time of massive immigration at the end of the nineteenth century, mass-produced clothing was readily available. For most immigrants, this was a new thing, for their native lands were generally still in the preindustrial stage. They understandably thought of American ready-made apparel as not only convenient but also the epitome of sophistication and style.

Thus it was not necessarily vain ambition to spend money on clothes, but instead a realistic acceptance of American values. As one astute observer of Italians summarized, "girls in particular realize that they are judged largely by appearance."[83] Cornelia Parker, a sociologist who masqueraded as a working-class woman, was shocked to find that no man offered her a subway seat when she was dressed as a worker and not as a lady. She had only discovered the truism that the seeming ingenues had grasped immediately: appearance did indeed make all the difference.

Nothing was more important in that image creation than the hat; prior to World War I, a hat was absolutely essential to a lady's ensemble. This nonutilitarian, much-decorated item was the symbol of similar characteristics in its owner, and a woman who wished to be treated like a lady never appeared in public without one. But for immigrant women, there was even greater symbolic importance attached to the hat.

In Europe, only women of social status wore hats—other women had to content themselves with shawls for headcoverings. Wearing a hat, then, meant to them "stepping out of the serving class, and out of the ranks of the peasants."[84] Barbara Klinger conveyed her amazement at the changed standard when she wrote back to Germany in 1851: "Here you don't go out of the house without a hat or a *Barnet* [bonnet] you don't go out on the *Striet* [street] with your head bare, they all look at you and you'd be laughed at. If I were to run into you, none of you would recognize me with my hat on."[85] It was a privilege too good to be true, and a mystery to those who remained in Europe. "Tell me," said one Slovak lady of her former servant, now in America, "it can't be true, can it? She writes that she wears a hat. Of course even in America that is impossible."[86]

Once a woman was socially free to dress in style, the remaining obstacle was economic. Some families allowed their daughters to spend little of their money on dress, but others encouraged this. Among young women themselves, there were occasional exceptions who preferred to spend their money for books or classes, but most saw stylish dress as the best road to advancement. Sadie Frowne, a sixteen-year-old Jewish orphan who supported herself by working in a garment factory, explained:

> Some of the women blame me very much because I spend so much money on clothes. They say that instead of a dollar a week I ought not to spend more than twenty-five cents a week on clothes, and that I should save the rest. But a girl must have clothes if she is to go into society at Ulmer Park or Coney Island or the theater. Those who blame me are the old country people who have old-fashioned notions, but the people who have been here a long time know better. A girl who does not dress well is stuck in a corner, even if she is pretty, and Aunt Fanny says that I do just right to put on plenty of style.[87]

It is important to note, however, that Sadie saved the same 25% of her income that she spent on apparel. Virtually all young immigrant women put savings for their family ahead of personal desires. Steamship passage, feeding the family, education for brothers, all of these came ahead of their new dresses. But when money for style was available, they saw this as a practical investment in the future.

Clothing, like food, took a relatively larger portion of one's budget than it does today. A writer on working Italian women reported that "when earnings were less than $7 a week the women apparently were unable to get more than the barest necessities of the cheapest grade. Shoes could not cost more than $2 a pair, suits $8 or $10."[88] But, if the "cheapest grade" of a suit cost $8 or $10, it was over a week's wages for most of these women.

Despite the high costs compared with women's wages, that these items were in fact of "the cheapest grade" is also clear; the budgets of frugal people show purchases for shoes three or four times a year. Women put cardboard over the holes in their soles and wore them as long as possible, but the shoe life was only a couple of months. Women knew that quality clothes would last longer, but then they had to pay the extra cost of buying on installments or somehow do without while they tried to save. One Italian did decide that a quality suit would be worth the cost and paid $22 for a suit—on an income of $6 a week.[89] Almost one-twelfth of her annual income would have been spent on this one garment.

Clothing expenditures for these women were nearly as much as their average for rent.[90] Another study of living costs showed the same pattern: even when women spent very little on clothing, the few purchases that they did make were extremely expensive compared with their low incomes. These budgets had many examples of women buying one suit for the year and it costing $12 or $14, which was two or three times their average weekly income.[91]

It was no wonder then that wardrobes of new arrivals were limited to a few garments and that they laundered nightly. While her mother was still in Russia, teenage Rose Cohen wrote, "I used to hang my dress on a string over Mrs. Feleberg's stove to dry overnight. In the morning I pulled it straight and put it right on."[92] It is ironic, too, that she, like so many other ill-clad women, was employed in the garment trade. The mass-produced, ready-to-wear clothes that they made were condemned as "cheap"—and were in fact quite cheap in durability—but they were still too expensive for those who sweated their lives away sewing them.

An unmarried woman might spend a considerable portion of her income on dress with community approval, but once a woman wed, appearance ranked very low in importance. Marriage was for life, and the practical investment she had made in fashion had paid off. She no longer had to be concerned with pleasing men by being stylish. Her major concern instead became to dress her children, especially the girls, in fashion, and to dress her husband warmly. A study of New York budgets showed that clothing for the mother was consistently the lowest family expenditure.[93] The frugality of older women was illustrated by one notation of the investigator: "One hat, bought long before she knew him"—and the subject had been married ten years.[94]

An Irish cook stated proudly, "The McNabbs are no wasteful folk. I've worn one dress nine year and it looked decent."[95] Similarly, a German woman had only two new "calico wrappers" during her five years of marriage.[96] And older women from almost all ethnic groups saved the money that their daughters would spend on the obligatory hat. From the south of Italy to the north of Norway, most peasants who emigrated as married women never developed the self-confidence to wear a hat.[97] Even a new shawl appeared only once in a decade or so.

Rosa Cavalleri illustrates well the unimportance of dress to married women; though she had been very attractive in her youth, she wore extremely sloppy clothes late in life. She laughingly acknowledged that she was so fat that when women where she worked gave her their old skirts, she had to sew two or three together to make one big enough. "Nearly always," she wore "a neckerchief pinned with a safety pin, for in her girlhood in Bugiarno to expose a naked neck was a sin."[98] For married women, modesty was the only dress requirement.

Like a number of immigrant women, Rosa had very limited sewing skills. She had worked in a factory, married and emigrated young, and never had the domestic knowledge that some consider innate in women. Her ignorance was something she—and her family—found embarrassing:

> I have to tell you about the two gray hoods I made my Maria and Visella from somebody's thrown-away underskirt. I found that old petticoat in the trash . . . but it was wool and warm. All the other children in the sisters' school were Irish. They

used to laugh at my two little girls and call them "spaghetti." When those children laughed at those hoods . . . Gionin, he couldn't stand to see those girls crying . . .

So one day—he said nothing to me so I wouldn't stop him—he walked downtown to the Boston Store and he came home with two little red-and-black knit caps. He said he got them very cheap. Those little girls were just crazy to have the really caps!

I had stitched up those two hoods any which way so the cloth stayed on their heads. But after Miss Chase started teaching me, I made nice little dresses—well, not *so* nice with all old cloth, but they were not so funny anyway.[99]

It was a class at the settlement house that taught her to sew, and the same was true for many others. Neither Europe nor America had any systematic method of teaching domestic arts, and especially those who emigrated as teenagers could not be expected to know the homemaking skills that Victorians thought essential to womanhood. Even among the millions of women who worked in the garment industry, there were many who did not know enough about sewing to make their own clothes. The industry was set up so that they repeated only one small part of the complex task of designing, cutting, and stitching a garment.

A study of working women found very little sewing other than mending; these women said they didn't have time and thought it cheaper to buy clothes from a pushcart.[100] Most Italian families in another study made some of their clothes, but only three of forty-eight made all. More than half used a dressmaker or tailor occasionally, but virtually all bought their everyday clothing from department stores or from the pushcarts and shops of Jews on the Lower East Side.[101]

Like Rosa, others who came into sufficiently close contact with more affluent people found their used clothing to be an important source of apparel. Occasionally, even a very poor woman could be seen in an expensively tailored garment—a discard from the lady for whom she cleaned. "Mrs. Reilly, walking out in a tailor-made suit which was worn last year by the well-to-do woman for whom she washed, would give no hint of the tea and bread diet on which she and the children might be subsisting—which was exactly what Mrs. Reilly wished."[102]

Ambivalence in Appearance

While they adopted American dress with alacrity, there was also nostalgia for the colorful native costumes worn at home, especially as time passed. Clothing there had its own unique style, which often displayed more individual expression than the mass-manufactured American garments of their era. Though most Americans mocked the unconventionality of foreign dress, more thoughtful observers appreciated its special qualities. An artist, for example, was amazed at the "brilliant but harmonious" choice of colors in the dress of Polish girls.[103]

There were other good things in Old World ways: Slovak women remembered with pride their accommodation to spring mud, when they wore short skirts and high-heeled boots, fitted to the leg and crafted of soft leather worked into artistic patterns.[104] Far superior this was, they thought, to long American dresses with hems encased in dirty slush. Sicilians recalled the daily visits a hairdresser had made to their homes, brushing and arranging the hair of the females while serving as a courier of local news.[105] A pleasant practice some Slavic women enjoyed that disappeared in America was for a betrothed man to outfit his intended with a new wardrobe. She spent the day trying on clothes, while he waited to pay the bills.[106]

Unquestioning acceptance of American ways was the usual pattern, but educated immigrants were more likely to question such losses and criticize the new styles. Gro Svendsen wrote frankly:

> Norwegian clothes . . . are better and much warmer. We can get nothing but cotton goods . . . One advantage, at least, they do have. They get new clothes more often than we did in Norway, simply because the clothes here don't last. Working people wear out their clothes in just a few weeks . . . Everything Norwegian is of better quality than what can be bought here.[107]

When Americans sneered at newcomers, little did they suspect that among the more sophisticated Europeans there were women scorning them. Gro thought those who shared her steamer on the Great Lakes were "the vainest women I've ever seen . . . No moderation, no taste . . . Such vulgar looking women!"[108] Linka Preus agreed. After going to a fair, she wrote of "Yankee ladies" with fans and parasols, puffing with the heat; at the same time many were made-up, pale as porcelain dolls—Excellent style indeed! You are welcome to it. Yankee fashion remains in poor taste."[109]

Jette Bruns had initially agreed, finding German attire much better than American when she emigrated in 1836. A half century later, however, she felt that things had reversed; on her second visit to Europe in 1882, she wrote of the "rough clothing" and "wooden shoes" of working people in Munster. After returning to Missouri, she wrote to her sister-in-law in Germany of contrasts between the two cultures that she had not noticed before, including some on clothing. "The cut of dresses" in America, she wrote, "is more graceful and not at all stiff. We are, I believe, ahead of you." Then, probably eager not to offend the reader, she quickly added, "Naturally, these are ladies of fashion."[110]

It was in fact the class distinction that was the key factor in views on clothing. Educated people, both immigrants and natives, were often critical of newcomers who quickly adopted what they saw as tasteless American dress. New Jersey immigrant advocate Jane Maud Campbell several times referred to the attire of young immigrant women as "tawdry"—but she understood the newcomers' desire for it and urged her middle-class American listeners to empathize: "They have the same feminine fondness for dress, even if their taste runs to over-abundance."[111]

Educated immigrants also understood what was meant by "over-abundance" and cautioned their compatriots against adopting ephemeral fashions. On the other hand, while such women truly wished to prevent their sisters from being seen as cheap, their commentary shows more than a little resentment and discomfort at seeing servant girls rise above their former state. The usually charitable Linka Preus, for instance, wrote, "I was displeased with the country girls—some of whom no longer wore their embroidered Norwegian costumes—to see them sitting with their fans."[112]

Others were even less kind. When the *Irish-American*, a New York newspaper of the 1850s, devoted space to chiding Irish domestics for not staying in their proper place, it was clothing that was uppermost in the editorial mind. Young women attired themselves "too expensively and showily for their calling" and were adopting "unbecoming airs."[113] Many men agreed with the Scandinavian who wrote home for an "unspoiled" woman to marry, saying that he would not have one of his community, who wore new dresses to church the second Sunday after their arrival and hats and parasols the third.[114]

And yet in their quick adoption of American ways, women did lose more than cantankerous prospective husbands. In their rush to become Americans, they threw out the good with the bad, exhibiting only their strong desire to belong to their adopted land. The nostalgia for the old, the ambivalence about accepting the cheap yet costly American garments, all of these points succumbed to the omnipresent practicality. To succeed in America, one simply had to look like an American.

Ultimately that would be the solution to all of the questions, all of the ambivalence. To some extent, the immigrant would shape America to resemble more closely her values and lifestyle. She would have a tremendously positive influence on American cuisine, for example, and immigrants must have helped humanize harsh American ideas on child care—but largely the ambivalence about the New World and its ways would simply fade with time. The need of conformity for success would overpower the remembrance of the old; sentimentality would step aside to practicality. A mother might question, but a daughter would accept—and a granddaughter would probably never even notice.

PART IV

THE
CONTRIBUTIONS
OF THESE
WOMEN

12

SUPPORTING FAMILIES

Some Stunning Statistics:
Unacknowledged Income Producers

Providing food, shelter, and clothing for her family and herself has ever been a woman's life work. These necessities—and how to acquire them—were central to the lives of immigrant women, for it was they who generally controlled the family budget and made the decisions of how to proportion the usually insufficient income. Occasionally an exceptionally controlling man insisted on handling all family funds, but usually this was considered an aspect of "women's work."

"The men are inclined to trust all financial matters to their wives," was the report from Slavic steel mill families in 1910. "It is the custom . . . for the workman to turn over his wages to his wife on pay day and to ask no questions as to what it goes for."[1] Greenwich Village families, half of whom were foreign, followed the same pattern: it was the wife who was "the financier of the family group. It is not an unattained ideal condition, but the regular standard of respectability that a good husband should turn over to his wife all his wages, receiving one or two dollars a week for his personal use."[2] A third observer agreed:

> She pays the rent [the receipt was made in her name]; she buys all his clothes as well as the children's; she decides whether cash is to be paid, and the curses of the small unpaid tradesman falls upon her; no one thinks of holding the man responsible. She gives him each morning his carfare and his lunch-money, if necessary. If he wants

ten cents for tobacco or five cents for a beer he gets it out of her if he can; if he can't, he goes without. It isn't a case of henpecking. The man thinks it is the only way to hold the home together. Women's economic position in the slums is high.[3]

In an 1882 discussion of family budgets in a German-language Chicago newspaper, Marie Reinhardt also argued that "a husband and father should bring home all his earnings," but she added perceptively, "it seems to me that the pocket money" for men "is more generously measured and spent" than any other household expediture. Indeed, these men kept their neighborhood saloons in business: most households spent more on beer than on books and newspapers, and Wilhelmine Bauer reported that her "husband spent at least $1.80 per week," at a time when that was a day's wages.[4]

Thus, woman's position as family financier was not really an enviable position, for even if all husbands lived up to the model of bringing home their pay, family needs usually exceeded the available funds. This was particularly a problem when the woman was new in America and unfamiliar with what goods were available and their comparative cost. Household management took real accounting ability, and these women have not been given sufficient credit for their effectiveness. In an era when both food and clothing were far more costly in relative terms than they are today, women managed well.

Even more noteworthy than their managerial skills, however, is the tremendous contribution that immigrant women made in earning family income. The image of a "typical" family in which the husband worked, the wife stayed home, and two or three children went to school was seldom accurate in an immigrant household. This was true from the earliest days of the era and of the "old immigrants" as well as the "new." A study of nineteenth-century English workmen in America, for example, concludes with this significant comment:

> Without exception these industrial workers expected their wives to work. They took it for granted that their wives would contribute to the family budget . . . also mentioned the contribution their wives made, and were expected to make to the family income . . . There is not a single expression of regret at this situation; nor is any hope recorded that one day it will not be necessary for their wives to work. At times women could get jobs more easily than male immigrants . . . If a woman did stay home to keep house, she earned something with her needle.[5]

The idyllic American picture of fathers as the sole support of families clashed against reality with a frequency that surprised the statisticians themselves. One, writing of survey data collected after World War I, summarized:

> A preliminary canvass of six industrial sections of Philadelphia revealed the fact that the majority of 11,073 families were not supported by the husband alone . . . Only six per cent of this entire group was of the conventional statistical type, husband, wife and three children, supported by the husband alone.[6]

An obviously skilled woman displays her "bobbin lace weaving" in the 1920s. Such homebound work added appreciable amounts to the income of immigrant families but was seldom acknowledged by economists. (ROCKEFELLER ARCHIVES CENTER)

Just 6% of households—fewer than one in ten—fit what was nonetheless called the "conventional type!" A study of artificial flower makers, most of whom were immigrants, again demonstrated the point: in 128 families, there were 807 members and 545 of them contributed to the family income.[7] In another study of 200 Greenwich Village families, "there were only 23 in which the earnings of the father were reported as the only source of income."[8] And if the figures lie in any way, it is probably in overestimating the fathers' contribution, for men sometimes saved their pride by reporting larger earnings than they had. A mason who gave his wages as $24 a week, for example, was found to have earned that only four weeks of the previous year, and for forty-four weeks he had not contributed one cent to the family budget.[9]

What is even more startling is the size of women's contributions. Since they were always paid less than men, women could work harder but their monetary contribution still would be less. Nevertheless, this study showed that the average Italian family received 48% of its income from male wage earners and 44% from female wage earners. When the 6% of average income obtained from home work and lodgers is added to the contributions of females—and it ought to be, since they did nearly all of this work—the contribution of women becomes slightly higher than that of the men.[10] This is especially significant because it is not percentage of contributors but percentage of *income*. Moreover, it is in Italian families where the stereotype of the nonworking woman is most fixed.

The above studies may be accused of bias because the investigators were women and because the studies were of families in which there were known to be employed women. It is therefore even more meaningful to find that male sociologists studying "typical" families agreed that the contributions of women were essential:

> It is a significant fact that, considering all the families together, the husbands contributed on the average . . . 54.4 per cent of the average family income . . . It was very difficult for most of our families to live upon the income which they derived from all sources. It would have been almost impossible for them to live upon the income from the husband alone.[11]

Another male investigator set out to study those families that he deemed "typical"—those having both parents present with no fewer than two and no more than four children under sixteen—passing by the doors of the numerous homes who did not fit into his preconceived mold. Women in these households would be least likely to work because of their young children, and yet even he had to admit that the fathers did not support the families alone. The only ethnic group in this study that received substantially more than half of its income from the father was the long-resident Irish.[12] Thus, even with this arbitrary standard of selecting families where the mother and children could *least* be expected to contribute to its support, they still accounted for more than half of its income!

Dutiful Daughters and Indigent Immigrants

The amount of money that women contributed to the families with whom they lived is clear from looking at those few women whose circumstances allowed them to support only themselves. It was an exceptional woman who lived outside a family unit; she was almost invariably attached as daughter, sister, or lodger to a home. In those rare cases where they lived alone, however, these women sometimes managed a better standard of living, low though their wages were. Sadie Frowne, a fifteen-year-old Jewish orphan, for example, described the frugal yet pleasant life that she and her roommate shared at the turn of the century:

> We had the room all to ourselves, paying $1.50 a week for it . . . We did our cooking on an oil stove, and lived well, as this list of expenses for one week will show:

ELLA AND SADIE FOR FOOD (ONE WEEK)

Tea	.06	Butter	.15
Cocoa	.10	Meat	.60
Bread and Rolls	.40	Fish	.15
Canned Vegetables	.20	Laundry	.25
Potatoes	.10	Total	2.42
Milk	.21	Add Rent	1.50
Fruit	.20	Grand Total	3.92[13]

Since their combined earnings totaled $9 weekly, they had a considerable surplus after food and lodging were paid for, and yet their diet was better than most. "Of course," Sadie acknowledged, "we could have lived cheaper, but we are both fond of good things and felt that we could afford them."[14] Examples of this kind of maturity are not uncommon among immigrant girls. At an early age they developed a strong sense of accounting and knew exactly how much it cost to live and how every penny could be spent to the best advantage. Nevertheless they were sometimes accused by social workers of being ignorant of budgeting, perhaps because they kept their accounts in their heads instead of on paper.

Even though they demonstrated their maturity, however, it was unusual for women as young as Ella and Sadie to live outside a family unit, and it was almost unheard of for a young woman to live alone. A few lived dormitory-style with other women; a New Jersey writer told of sixteen young Slovak women from the remote Tatra Mountains, who lived in a four-room tenement and worked in the Passaic mills:

> I never saw a more kindly lot of girls . . . caring, as a matter of course, for the newcomer who as an apprentice earned nothing at all. They had all come from the same village: sixteen families . . . had seen their young daughter . . . launch out for a strange country, and face unknown dangers, lured by the hope of earning from

$3.00 to $7.00 a week . . . They drew forth from a trunk—which also revealed clothing, boots, a large loaf of dark bread, cheese and bologna—a colored postcard of a tiny village . . . which they showed with evident pride as their home in the old country.[15]

Similarly, a YWCA social worker based in Akron in 1918 reported that in nearby Ravenna, Ohio, there were "some 500 or 600 Italians of whom there are some 300 girls in the woolen mills."[16] Doubtless most lived in lodgings with each other and sent their wages back to Italy. It was in fact this exportation of what otherwise might have been their savings that made living alone such a risk. While young women could live fairly well in good times, when industrial depression or sickness befell, then their youth and single state was a great disadvantage. Few had enough savings to carry them for very long, and even fewer had any health insurance. In those times a woman might starve. This fear, plus cultural taboos against women living alone, meant that most never separated themselves from the backing of some sort of family.

Katia Halperin, for example, paid more than Sadie Frowne for her board and yet lived much more unsatisfactorily. Like Sadie, she was a fifteen-year-old Jew, six months in America. She paid $3 of her $3.50 earnings to her aunt. Not having enough money for carfare, she walked forty minutes to work, put in a nine-and-a-half hour day, and made the long walk home, where she then had to help her aunt with the housework.[17] Like millions of immigrant teenagers, her family thought Katia was old enough for adult work but not old enough to handle the money she earned. Often it is difficult to decide whether such family attitudes were grounded in a desire to protect their daughters or to exploit them.

The protection of exploited workers was a high priority of activists in the Progressive Era, and, in order to agitate for a minimum wage, several states undertook to determine just what salary was needed for a decent lifestyle. The summary of one of these exhaustive studies was typical; it concluded that "in every item the estimates seem to have been pared down to the lowest possible figure"—but even then, most women did not earn enough to meet the standard. In Massachusetts, for example, the cost of living for female workers was estimated at $8.71 a week, yet a shocking 89% of women in a typical industry made less than $8.[18]

Further, these minimum standards included no provision for savings. To an immigrant woman, however, that was often the most important reason for a pay-check. Virtually all of them tried to save a large portion of their earnings to support a family overseas or to pay for passage of relatives. An Italian who made less than $7 weekly, for example, was committed to sending $8 monthly—or more than one week's wages—to her parents in Italy.[19] Similarly, Anna Klotin, a twenty-one-year-old Jew, sent $120 of her $480 annual income back to Russia. Fanny Wardoff, another Russia Jew, walked fifteen blocks from work to home so that she could save the carfare toward her brother's education.[20] These were wholly typical of millions of others who sacrificed and saved to achieve family goals.

The omission of any savings item in the living-standard estimates of immigrant women thus demonstrates a complete lack of understanding of their employment

Vendors in an open-air market under an elevated train at Hester and Norfolk Streets in New York. Older women who could not get factory jobs—or who had too many children to make such employment profitable—operated these kinds of informal businesses.   (LIBRARY OF CONGRESS, PHOTOGRAPHY BY G. G. BAIN)

goals. To the captains of industry—who surely put saving for the future at the head of their own priorities—a woman merited consideration only as long as she was working. They gave no thought to what happened to her when she became ill or suffered an accident or grew old or was laid off by the industry she sweated to serve. They surely did not understand that she might be supporting an entire family an ocean away.

These teenagers who supported families abroad were often lonely and overwhelmed by the difficulty of their aims. Yet having the family in America sometimes offered little respite. Social workers' records are replete with cases such as seventeen-year-old Louise Trentino, whose father was usually "idle" and whose $6 weekly income was the mainstay for him, her mother, herself, and a brood of younger children.[21] A Bohemian girl who went to work in an artificial tooth factory at age eleven was not highly unusual. Her father was a tailor, but the occupation was poorly paid and there were eight children, four of whom were sickly.[22] Among the saddest cases was that of an Irish girl who earned a pittance in a department store and tried to support a family of nine. Her sickly father finally went mad with worry over the family's debts and tried to murder the children.[23]

Other fathers didn't worry; the home situation of one such is far too typical:

> The family had an [annual] income of $907 with which to support a family of twelve. The father, a peddler of cheese, whose earnings were casual and spasmodic, preferred bullying every cent of their wages from his two young daughters, who were the chief support of the family, to going out himself in disagreeable weather to sell his wares. During twenty-eight weeks of the year he had made nothing, and his total earnings were somewhat less than a fifth of the entire income.[24]

This family had the dubious distinction of being chosen as having the lowest living standard of any in this study of Italian immigrant families. The one chosen as highest was headed by a widow. She had regular and well-paid employment and maintained her family of six pleasantly, even allowing the oldest to go to high school.[25] Having a man at the head of the household, even a healthy man, did not necessarily mean a better lifestyle. It could mean only additional expenses—especially for tobacco and alcohol—as well as interminable pregnancies.

Why some immigrant fathers did not do better at supporting their children is a complex question. In many cases, ill health prevented them; with some, the unemployment that also plagued women was a genuine cause; in other situations, they worked steadily but earned too little because they were unskilled or the skill they knew in Europe was not relevant; often there were simply too many stomachs to be filled.

The disruption of immigration and their unfamiliarity with the American economy often meant long periods of unemployment for a breadwinner—and while he searched for his niche, his wife was simply supposed to manage. Norwegian Barbro Ramseth, for example, wrote from Wisconsin in 1889, "Everything is filled up here in America too, with people looking for work. Well, he was gone nine whole weeks, without earning the least little bit, and you can imagine it wasn't easy for us at home, either."[26] Worse times might well be expected for this family of five children, for a few years later, during the Depression of 1893, immigrants truly learned the meaning of "everything filled up."

Barbro Ramseth's husband "wrote so seldom" during his nine weeks away, and other men showed similar indifference. Especially the records of urban social workers offer detailed evidence that many men did not try to feed the children they brought into the world. As a student of the German-Irish West Side said:

> In . . . the building trade there is always "slack time" or no work in the winter months. The men know about this beforehand, but they refuse to work at something else for lower wages. In several cases the husband was offered work in the wood yard and at street cleaning. He refused to take the job; it was "beneath him." The

men either sit at home and as one German woman said, "refuse to put on their shoes," or they go to the saloon and spend a day in loafing.[27]

Laziness, alcoholism, gambling, all played a part in leaving families destitute, but the particular experience of immigrant men probably was a strong factor. Many men had urged their wives to leave home with extravagant promises, and when they found that conditions were not what they had dreamed, the loss of pride was too much for them. Fear of failure may have become so strong that they could not risk trying. Old World patriarchal attitudes insisted that the father be given a position of at least outward respect, and rather than lose that position through having failed, he may have invented excuses for not trying—but Old World attitudes would still insist that his subordinates demonstrate their respect by earning for him.

Aagot Raaen's father was one whose sense of responsibility died with his emigration dreams. He had been an aide to the king of Norway, and the abject poverty of his North Dakota family was too much for his pride to bear. Aagot's memoirs are one long, sad record of the struggle made by her mother and the children:

> How hard everyone had worked . . . [Father] sold the grain as soon as the threshing was done, intending to pay the money on the mortgage. Instead he had gone away and had not returned until all the money was used up. Then he had sold three steers and two cows and used that money, too. The worst of all was when he took the cream checks. Kjersti shivered as she remembered how angry Aagot had been as she threatened: "After this I'll milk the cows onto the ground; I'll not carry those heavy milk pails up and down that steep hill for the saloon!" But Aagot had not carried out her threat.[28]

Of course it should be emphasized that most men were not of this sort. Most were hardworking, sober people who wanted the best for their families. Nevertheless, circumstances were such that very few could survive without the help of female wage earners, and occasionally men simply gave up and left the job to women. Their women went to work—no job was "beneath" a woman—but received little recognition for their efforts. Moreover, although these women were breadwinners, they did not exchange family roles with their husbands or fathers; instead they merely accepted a double burden of toil.

Nor did their hardworking lives become the stuff of family legend, for as immigrants realized just how far from the American ideal it was for women to earn most of the income, the role of their women was diminished in the telling of the family's story. Ashamed to acknowledge how they had lived, both men and women convinced themselves that the men of the family had always taken proper care of their women and children. Uncle Harry's struggles to rise in America would be enumerated and elaborated, but Aunt Sarah's would be overlooked, for the honor of the family would be in jeopardy if her part were told in full. Then it would be plain that the family had not been merely respectably poor but downright indigent. The pride of the family—the pride of the males—had to be salvaged, and so the women's story was not told.

Paving the Way to the American Dream:
Girls Supporting Families

The sacrificing attitude was inculcated early in girls, and throughout the immigrant era, there are examples of girls as young as three and four who helped earn the family's income. In the Panic of 1853, for instance, one-eighth of those assisted by the Children's Aid Society of New York were German; among them was "four-year-old Katrina K., who was found picking coal for her widowed mother."[29] Near the end of the era, an Italian mother insisted that the labor of her four preschoolers was essential: "[W]e must all work," she said, as the grubby little hands formed artificial flowers to pay for their existence.[30]

Moreover, as little girls grew into fully employed young women, they came to understand that more was expected of them than of their brothers. One investigator explained: "It was assumed as a matter of course that the girl's pay envelope should

A woman and her children shelling pecans on home contract, probably for a candy factory. Note that the man of the family, on the far left, does not join in this work. Except for cigar making, men rarely participated in such home industries.   (LIBRARY OF CONGRESS; 1911 PHOTOGRAPH BY UNDERWOOD & UNDERWOOD)

be turned over to her mother intact. 'It wouldn't look nice to pay board to the mother that raised you,' was the common view of the girls, while the question as to whether the brothers also contributed everything they made to the home received the answer, 'Oh, no, he's a boy.'"[31]

Even a government study agreed that girls did more for families than boys, though its bureaucratic language makes it easy to miss the point. "The contributions of the female children," summarized a Senate report, "form a larger percentage of total family income than do the contributions of the males of corresponding age." These economists went on to acknowledge that this was a noteworthy achievement in view of the unrelenting discrimination against women in the workplace: "The amounts contributed, moreover, are in a considerable number of cases greater, although the average earnings of the individual females would be somewhat less."[32]

The result of these family expectations was not only passive girls but also spoiled boys. In a typical Italian family, for instance, the girl gave her "pay envelope unopened to the mother," while no one even knew how much her brother made. It was not as though such families did not need additional income—this particular one was so poor that even the three- and four-year-old daughters had to help at flower making. Even though the son was on probation from the court, there apparently was no increase in discipline at home. "You know how it is with a boy," was the mother's explanation. "He wants things for himself."[33]

More was expected of sons in other nationalities, yet there were still inequities between siblings based on gender. Girls received less money for spending, and one study showed that while the employment rate for working children was higher than that of their fathers, boys were more likely to be unemployed than girls. In explanation the sociologist spoke of boys who "won't work" and added, "There are also girls on the West Side who 'won't work,' but they are rarer than the boys . . . The mention of a 'wild son' is not uncommon."[34]

Yet most sisters showed little resentment of the favoritism given their brothers, and many a girl made sacrifices so that his life could be better. One who had always worked while her brothers studied said that during the years one of them was in medical school, she had "brought home flowers from the shop at night and had worked sometimes until four or five o'clock in the morning. 'When he graduated,' she said, 'I cried all day and was as happy as though I had graduated myself. I often say to my mother that we treat my brother as if he were a king—but I can't help it.'"[35]

Such disparity between the treatment of sons and daughters was particularly ironic in view of the constant inequity in wages. Women were inevitably paid about half as much as men, so even if a woman worked all of her waking hours, she could not equal the wages her brother got. The hard reality is that a family might be poor only because their firstborn—who became the wage earners—were girls instead of boys. For the girl it was a double tragedy to be oldest, for not only did she work harder for less appreciation, but also she knew that if she had been born later, her life would have been much more pleasant.

Perhaps the one good aspect of the situation is that it took off some of the pressure European families had placed on their daughters to marry young. Of course for the young woman who wanted to marry, this was by no means a happy change in mores. Unless she could convince her prospective husband to take on the burden of supporting her family, she probably would have to give him up. Instead of pressure to marry, the opposite became true, for families would suffer a substantial cut in income if young working women married.

Petronila Cirsanchio, for instance, came to Tampa at age nine in about 1910; her mother left her with a married daughter, returned to Sicily, and never returned. Petronila was "immediately put to work in a cigar factory," where she remained for twenty years before she finally married—a decision that caused great strife. Her Italian family permanently "disowned" her for marrying a Cuban whom they considered "inferior," but an additional factor was that they did not want her to lose her income.[36]

Immigrant girls did in fact marry later than their mothers; and the most likely to remain single was also the group with the longest history of immigration—the Irish. The extent to which they ventured alone to seek their fortune is clear in the outbound statistics from Ireland: In 1885–90, 87% of female emigrants between fifteen and thirty five were single, and by 1908, that already high figure had risen to more than 90%. In some parts of the country, virtually all of the women departed without a man: during the period between 1901 and 1908, 98% of the 182,500 women who left Connaught were single.[37] Indeed, it would seem that a decision to marry was the same as a decision not to emigrate: couples simply did not go.

Unmarried women of other ethnicities also traveled alone, leading the way to America from the earliest years of the immigration era. German Marie Klinger, who emigrated in 1849, was one who came prior to any of the males in her family; like millions of others later, she worked, saved, and brought her siblings. "On the same day I arrived in New Jork," she wrote in her first letter home, "I went into service for a German family." In a month, she earned the equivalent of an annual wage for servants in Germany and self-assuredly insisted, "Only those who don't want to work don't like it here, since in America you must work if you want to amount to anything, you mustn't feel ashamed, that just how you amount to something."[38]

Even after she married, the goal of bringing her younger siblings remained her highest priority—and significantly, both she and her German husband, Franz Schano, thought it was wiser for women to come first and men to follow. Though her brother Daniel was older than the sisters, Marie and Franz wrote in 1850:

> We don't think it is a good idea for Daniel to come over first . . . Instead it would be better if the two girls came over first, because within a few days we could get more work for them than they'd want. For the girls earn a lot more than he does, and he can be sure that after the girls have been here for just one month, we can then take care of his passage . . . But if he doesn't want to wait so long, then he should take one of his girlfriends and bring her over here.[39]

Despite setting this precedent for her younger siblings, Marie was not the oldest in her family—and that seemingly unimportant circumstance is vital in a point too often ignored. While Marie set off to America, the oldest son in the family stayed home to inherit whatever property the family had. Though it is rarely acknowledged, the result of the European system of primogeniture was that women—who could not be the beneficiaries of inheritance if they had any male siblings—naturally had more motivation than their brothers to seek their own fortunes.

Just as gender was fundamental, so was age. While the oldest daughter was often pressured to stay single and earn, the youngest daughter also sometimes was pressured to stay single and care for elderly parents. With immigrants, this could mean remaining in Europe while the older siblings went to America. The five children of the Klinger family who came to America very much wanted their youngest sister, Rosina, to do this—even though their parents had two sons who planned to stay and inherit the family farm. Another brother offered the views of those on the American side of the ocean after the death of their mother, with words that were both patriarchal and self-contradictory:

> Rosina, too, will reap her reward for having served our dear mother to the end, but I don't think it quite fitting that she now wants to leave her old father and set off for America, but if father gives his permission and we've agreed to it here, then it won't be long . . . I also want to add that Katharina's husband wants you [Rosina] to come over here on your own before next spring, so you can start working for him, that is help with the sewing . . . All of us wish that you would stay clear of any liaisons, so you can be free and unhindered in coming over here, of course we don't want this to be an order, since we think you'll agree it's best.[40]

When Rosina finally received family permission to emigrate, it seemed clear that any "reward" she might actually reap for her long years of service to their elderly parents was of a heavenly sort, as she was put to work for her brother-in-law. Indeed, whether a woman emigrated or stayed, was employed or was not, married or remained single—in any of these cases and more, what she wanted was not so important as what her family wanted.

More often than is recognized, what those families wanted was for young women to be the primary wage earners. This was true even in those cultures where women were presumed not to be employed outside the home: Of 894 newly arrived Italian women interviewed by the YWCA in 1912–13, 164 had relatives abroad who were wholly dependent on these women for support, while 266 others were partially supporting a European family—a total of 430, or almost half of this "nonworking" group. All of them, of course, had to support themselves, too—at a time when the median wage of newly arrived women was $5.49, while $9 weekly was "generally accepted as the lowest wage on which a girl can live in New York City."[41]

Yet many European families, not only expected their teenage daughters to support themselves in the New World, but also to save enough to transport others.

"When Molly Davousta was thirteen," for example, "her mother and father, who had five younger children, had sent her abroad out of Russia, with the remarkable intention of having her prepare and provide a home for all of them in some other country."[45] Molly went first to London and had worked there four years when her father died. She came to New York in hope of better wages and at age seventeen earned $5 to $9 a week. Nevertheless she managed to send home nearly $100 that year, often going without lunch and breakfast to do so. With this money, her sister Bertha joined her, and together they supported the family in Russia until passage could be saved. By the end of her teenage years, Molly Davousta finally had her family with her—and then she could look forward to supporting them until she was too broken for a life of her own. Suffering from backaches and headaches, she was old before she was twenty.

Like Molly, Getta Bursova was self-supporting from age twelve. Born in Russia, she had worked six years in London and two in New York when interviewed at age twenty.[43] Sarah Silberman, an Austrian Jew, started work at nine. She had been entirely on her own since fourteen, having done machine sewing in Vienna, London, and New York.[44] There had been little reward for her effort, though; she lived with virtual strangers, sleeping in the kitchen, and was quite alone in the world in which she had traveled so far.

Nor were Jews the only ones to begin work so early. A thirteen-year-old Polish girl supported herself after her mother's death, though her father was alive; she married in her teens, but that made no economic improvement and she held the same low-paid job at eighteen that she had at thirteen.[45] Another began to earn her living as a nurse girl in Sweden when she was only ten and then did domestic work until she emigrated at twenty; she kept a boarding house for ten years after that and finally worked in a laundry.[46] Her record is an excellent example of the serious underestimate that traditional accounting makes of women's work, for only the last job would show up in occupational statistics—though she had worked since childhood.

Rose Cohen was one of those who made the voyage to America and began work as a child. Still growing, underfed, and working long hours, her strength was sapped before she really began to live. "During those days," she wrote, "I could not seem to get enough sleep."

> On coming into the room I would light the lamp and the kerosene oil stove and put on the soup to cook. Then I would sit down with my knees close to the soap box on which the stove stood, to keep myself warm. But before long my body relaxed, my head grew heavy . . . and I longed to lie down. I knew it was bad to go to sleep without supper . . . But it was no use. I could not eat then . . . The cot was so near . . . I would rise a little from the chair and all bent over as I was, I would tumble right in . . . It was on these nights that I began to forget to pray.[47]

13

WORK AND WAGES

The Oldest Employers:
Textile and Garment Industries

Decades before American observers began to take note of the phenomenon of working women, large numbers of women of every immigrant group were employed. As early as 1855, "two-thirds of the New York dressmakers, seamstresses, milliners, shirt and collar makers, embroiderers, . . . and artificial flower makers were foreign-born."[1] Women of the "new" immigration also worked; one expert asserted: "In my investigation of several thousand unmarried immigrant women and married immigrant women without children . . . fully 90 per cent were found at work or looking for work."[2]

Some industries were almost entirely composed of newcomers: garment manufacturing became overwhelmingly Jewish; New England textile mills were run by a motley mix of immigrants; foreigners made up over 75% of the employees of the silk-mill centers;[3] even in Pittsburgh cracker factories, seven of nine female workers were born across the sea.[4]

Yet most women had no consciousness of themselves as workers, no awareness of careers, no initiative to make changes that would improve their situation. Rosa Cavalleri, for example, had been a skilled silk maker in Italy, but she apparently thought so little in terms of careers that she never considered finding that work in America and spent the rest of her life in menial cooking and cleaning jobs. The immediate was more important; the family needed the $5 she could earn, and so, while a man might search for work in his field, a woman was expected to take the nearest job at hand.

The work that was available varied by locality, and often jobs that were considered too complex or laborious for women in one place would be allotted to them in another. While only 18 women, for instance, were employed as skilled spinners in 1919 in the silk mills of Paterson, New Jersey, the competing Pennsylvania mills hired 729.[5] Women also rose to be supervisors in the Pennsylvania mills, while that did not happen in New Jersey.[6] The explanation lies in the fact that in Pennsyl-

Thousands of immigrant women of all ethnicities worked in New England textile mills. So dependent were these mills on immigrant labor that it was not unusual for several dozen languages to be spoken by their employees. Skilled women who had done this work in Europe said that in America, they often were assigned more looms than they could tend without exhaustion. (LIBRARY OF CONGRESS)

vania, men worked in coal mines. Similarly, male Jewish tailors had the best jobs in New York's garment industry, whereas in Chicago women were discovered to be capable of these positions—because there men worked in industries such as meat-packing and left clothing to women.

Garment making and silk mills were, in fact, part of the giant industry of keeping America clothed, which employed more immigrant women over the decades than any other entity. As soon as the Irish arrived in the 1840s, they began to replace Yankee farm girls as laborers in the textile mills of New England. Experienced workers from Britain joined them, as did Germans and French Canadians. By the end of the century, these mills employed Poles, Italians, various Balkan peoples, Greeks, Syrians, and Armenians—in some, more than forty languages were spoken.

Literally thousands of small mills sprouted wherever waterfalls provided power and women within walking distance provided hands. The Philadelphia area alone developed some 800 textile mills[7]—and most of the industry was sited farther north. Because cloth manufacturing was traditionally feminine work in the home, women were early employed and long made up a majority of the workers. Decades prior to the immigrant era, American men wrote of the value of women in textile mills because of their "nimble fingers." Mills periodically tried to substitute male workers, but their results generally were disappointing. A Holyoke manufacturer summarized in 1869: "Over a period of sixty years Massachussets cotton or woolen manufacturers have experimented with training men to do women's jobs in order to keep machinery running after the women's day was ended. Men's fingers are not sufficiently dexterous to do the careful work."[8]

Some women were even recruited from Europe for the textile industry, particu-larly skilled women from England and Scotland. When, for example, the Amoskeag Mills of Manchester, New Hampshire, decided in 1868 to specialize in fancy gingham, an agent in Britain located some ninety female weavers willing to emigrate to this new employment opportunity.[9] The Pepperell Mills used similar methods; they even advanced a woman's ship passage, though they insisted on documentation of her ability to repay it. In 1881, the company did further recruitment, "hoping to get additional skilled help by sending for the husbands of women who had proved satisfactory."[10]

When these Scottish women proved "not sufficiently docile," an 1859 effort recruited forty-five French-speaking women from Quebec. The recruiter got $4 for every woman who traveled to the mills in a "great omnibus."[11] Much earlier, labor recruitment centered on even the unskilled Irish, with "handbills placarded" over a fifty-mile radius of Dublin, telling people "that laborers were so much wanted in America, that even women were employed to work at men's work."[12]

Moreover, this pattern of high levels of female employment continued through-out the immigrant era. The 1890 census revealed that "among English, Welsh, and Scottish immigrant workers . . . fully 48% of the men and 42% of the women were in industrial occupations."[13] Even as late as 1910, foreign-born women in the Lawrence mills had far more industrial experience than their male counterparts. In four of the town's five major immigrant groups, it was the women who had the greater skills based on longer work histories. Of the English women in the mills, for instance, 91% had done similar work prior to emigrating, while only 55% of the English men in the mills had such experience.[14]

PRIOR INDUSTRIAL EXPERIENCE AMONG IMMIGRANT WORKERS;
LAWRENCE, MASSACHUSETTS, 1910

	Experienced Women	Experienced Men
English	91%	55%
Irish	49%	16%
French Canadian	33%	9%
Italian	14%	2%
Polish	7%	8%

Philadelphia's textile mills, too, featured many Polish workers who "were not from peasant backgrounds but instead came from . . . Lodz, the center of cotton manufacturing."[15] The same was true in Paterson, New Jersey, where the "Italian population was quite distinct" from other such enclaves: like Rosa Cavalleri, they came from northern Italy, "where textile trades and indeed silk manufacture were . . . prominent."[16] Unlike Rosa, these Paterson women were able to stay with their trade and use their skills in America. For women, the point is vital: the key to success was tied to marital status. Had Rosa been anything other than chattel to be passed between her mother and her husband, she might have built on her skills and ended her life as a well-paid, unionized silk worker rather than as a charwoman.

But even many of the experienced women who came in response to recruitment were not entirely happy with their American employers. They considered them tyrannous in hours and pace of work and were especially upset that they had to manage more looms than in Europe. The English were shocked by publicly posted production charts on individuals, which encouraged unhealthy competition and lowered morale; they also said that cheaper raw cotton made their work more difficult. Employers became even more demanding as the century lengthened and new, more docile immigrants replaced those from northern Europe; by the 1870s, women tended six or eight looms instead of the two that had been standard in the 1830s.[17]

Textile mills also were notorious exploiters of children, and endless numbers of child labor investigators wrote of the presence of children in the mills. Mary, a Fall River weaver, typical of those who began their careers while still in girlhood: "My mother worked in the mills in England since she was nine years," Mary said. "I got a job [as a] "spool tender" when I was twelve—there wasn't the law then. I must of been about fourteen when I went to weavin' and I leart quick. My! but I was proud when I got them first four looms! I liked the mill better than working at home."[18]

By the end of her weaving career near the end of the century, however, Mary was assigned twelve looms; then, she said, "I didn't see that we could make out to live at all."[19] Moreover, though women like her were lifelong, skilled workers who were clearly valued by their employers, they were nevertheless paid unequally. Almost without exception, the era's standard rule was that the most skilled woman was paid no more than the least skilled man. Women in the Holyoke mills in 1871, for instance, averaged 75 cents to $1.60 a day, while men got $1 to $2.25.[20]

A Senate study added, "There are no promotions as far as female employees are concerned. Women never become section hands . . . or overseers." The government investigators approved of this discrimination on the ground that "under such a system an overseer can not offer girls higher pay or more desirable positions," thus tempting them into immorality.[21]

Mill work was a definite hazard to health. A study done in Lawrence in 1912 (when that city was 90% immigrant) painted an appalling picture: one-third of the spinners in the mills died before they had worked ten years. They died of respiratory diseases—pneumonia and tuberculosis—which were promoted by the lint and dust and machine fumes of the unventilated mills. That these deaths were from air pollution is clear from the fact that only 4% of the local farmers died from these diseases.[22]

Other peril came from the accident rate. The Pacific Mills had a thousand accidents in less than five years—or almost one every working day. In 788 of them, immigrants were the victims,[23] a figure that reflects both the large number of foreign born in textile work and the greater danger to those who did not understand warnings in English. The din of machinery also had serious effects, as Fall River Mary said: "At first the noise is fierce . . . but you get used to it. Lots of us is deaf . . . It's bad one way: when a girl gets hurt, you can't hear her shout."[24]

When at last the raw fibers had been woven into cloth, it generally headed south out of New England for the immigrants of New York and other cities to sew into garments. Until the Civil War era ready-made clothing, especially for women and children, was rare. In many communities in this still largely agricultural era, the only employment a woman could get other than domestic service was dressmaking.

New York seamstresses in 1845, many of whom were Irish, worked fourteen to sixteen hours a day to earn a pittance of $1.25 to $1.50 a week.[25] Even after the garment industry began, many factory tasks continued to be done on home contract. In the 1860s, German, Scandinavian, and Irish households began to take in this work. The cut clothes were brought home, and all members of the family worked at sewing. Most spent their days doing "finishing"—hemming, stitching buttonholes, attaching buttons, and such. The "sweatshop" had begun.

"A tailor is nothing," said a German man to an 1885 Senate investigating committee, "without a wife and very often a child."[26] Indeed—though the gender-based language meant that a woman would never be called a "tailor" no matter how adept she was—legions of women sewed for a living. In occupational statistics, however, millions of their hours of work would be allotted to men.

In the 1880s "revolutionary changes entered" the garment business. Electrically powered machines, national markets created by railroads, and legal restrictions on sweatshops played their parts, but "the greatest single factor" was immigration. "This is affirmed by manufacturers, who say that without the immigrants the industry could not have assumed its present proportions."[27] Most important among these immigrants were the Jews who brought not only armies of young women into garment making but also legions of male tailors. As usual, these men took over the best positions in what had been formerly considered "women's work." A government study concluded, "On the whole the changes of the period reshaped the industry in such a way as to assign a less important place to women."[28]

Instead of being known as "seamstresses," they became "operators"—those who ran the sewing machines, doing one small part of the complex task of making a garment.

Unless a woman was exceptionally fortunate, she instead would spend her days doing repetitive work that offered no future. It was a profound frustration to immigrant women who took pride in their needlework abilities; as Linda Bair, an expert embroiderer said, "In Italy it would take six months to do a pillow and here it must be done in three or four hours."[29] Another who had been a dressmaker in the Old World agreed, "They only do cheap work in this country. Everything must be done in a hurry."[30]

The harried pace that American employers expected increased the probability of eyestrain, which was a serious health hazard in this industry. Work on dark fabrics strained the eyes more than work on light ones, with the result that women in the men's clothing industry suffered more than those in ladies' garments. In fact, air pollution in Pittsburgh was so bad by 1910 that the garment industry there was limited to dark and heavy men's work clothes; pastels would have been ruined by simple exposure to the air.[31] Property had priority over personnel, so workers on quality goods were given enough light to do a proper job—but this did not happen where cheaper clothes were made for the blue-collar market. If women suffered headaches and went blind from straining to see tiny dark threads, management could be confident that others were crossing the sea to replace them.

Other Typical Jobs: Candy, Cigars, and Flowers

In the packing room of a candy factory where she worked, Cornelia Parker found "one Hungarian, two Germans, four Italians, two Spaniards, a Swede, an Englishwoman, and numerous colored folk,"[32] as well as two white Americans, both of whom claimed to have seen better days. A government study around 1910 said that two-thirds of the workers in this industry were foreign.[33]

The specific job that a person held in a candy factory made a great deal of difference. Most chocolates were hand dipped, and the "dippers" who made the swirls and other embellishments were recognized as artists. Packing chocolates also required considerable skill, for each of the dozens of pieces was assigned a specific spot in the box, and the boxes had to be packed with speed. Lowest on the scale were women who bagged children's candies and those who carried the heavy boxes and trays. Men did the cooking and were seldom seen by women.

Earning one's pay in this industry, like others, required a great deal of tedious toil: dippers were paid a cent and a half per pound in Pittsburgh in 1909; experts could do a hundred pounds a day, which gave these women, the acknowledged artists of their trade, a total of $9 for a six-day week. Those who packed "prize bags"—little sacks of a few peanuts, candies, and a trinket—were paid 4 cents a hundred. Fast workers could pack 3,000 a day (or 300 an hour or one every 12 seconds) to earn $7.20 a week. Women who spent their days putting sticks in suckers were worst paid. Each box in this factory contained 72 rows with 12 suckers to a row, and they were paid 3 cents a box—or 864 suckers for just 3 pennies![34]

Incognito sociologist Cornelia Parker stood packing candy from eight in the morning till six at night. At the end of her first day:

> When the bell does ring I am beyond feeling any emotion . . . During the summer I had played one match in a tennis tournament 7–5, 5–7, 13–11. I had thought I was ready to drop dead after that. It was mere knitting in the parlor compared to how I felt after standing at that table in that candy factory.[35]

Her ten-hour day was routine; the Christmas season brought thirteen-hour days at this factory. Pittsburgh women sometimes put in seventy-five and eighty hours a week packing candy before Christmas, working nearly all night.[36] When summer came, however, candy could not be handled because of the heat in this era before air-conditioning, so these women could expect no income then. The physical requirements of the candy also took precedence over that of the workers, as an Italian chocolate maker explained: "I must put nuts on the candy dripping with hot chocolate. The room must be so cold that . . . I wear two pairs of stockings and thick shoes, but my feet nearly freeze."[37]

A relatively large number of women reported that they dropped out of the candy industry because they could no longer take the cloyingly sweet odor; some said it took months to overcome the nausea it brought on.[38] The industry nonetheless was popular with immigrant women from many ethnic groups. Though they complained of standing for long hours and working in cold rooms, the pay generally was higher than most could expect in other employment.

Perhaps just as important, many women took pride in the bit of artistry that the work allowed and demonstrated this by staying with their jobs. Candy makers married an average of three or four years later than women in other employment, and the "percentage of change from this trade to others and within the trade itself" was "remarkably low." As one summarized, "Once a chocolate dipper, always a chocolate dipper."[39]

Like candy, cigar making was another industry that not only was a major employer of immigrant women—almost 80% were foreign born in 1910[40]—but it, too, gave women an exceptional opportunity for pride in their work. It also was stratified into three distinct levels: the skilled "rollers" or "makers"; the "bunchmakers," who arranged the tobacco into roughly the desired shape; and the "strippers," who deveined the leaves. Packing also was considered skilled in this industry.

Cigar making was a most unusual industry—at least for a time—because of the extraordinary position of a particular group of immigrant women:

> The customary method of Bohemian immigration was for the women to come first, leaving the men to work in the fields. Five or six wives would come over together, work at cigarmaking as they did in Bohemia, and send money back for their husbands' passage and the entire family would take up the manufacture of cigars, emulating the industry of the mother.[41]

Giving new meaning to "bohemian," these women began preceding their husbands and children to America in the late 1860s, and by the 1870s more than half of New York's cigar makers were female. One writer says of the Bohemian men, "Their wives taught them, after they came over, the relatively unskilled work of bunchmaking, while the women still did the more skilled and better paid rolling ... The women were considered by Americans to be more intelligent than the men."[42]

A Senate study of the industry confirmed this pattern of female leadership: "The first division of labor appears to have been introduced by the skilled Bohemian women who taught their husbands ... the art of 'bunchmaking,' they themselves doing the more difficult work of 'rolling.'"[43] A writer on Bohemians just before World War I not only verified this history but deplored it: "Bohemian families in New York send many of their wives and daughters to the tobacco factories," she said. "They learned their trade in Bohemia and are especially skillful in it, making more than the men of the family. This fact has a most demoralizing effect on the home life, as married women often prefer to work in the factory and hire a cheaper woman to help with the housework."[44]

But the halcyon days of female artisans were not to last. Molds were introduced for shaping the cigars, and the skilled met with competition from the unskilled. Though it was technology in the form of cigar molds that was to blame for displacing the craftsperson, many men were adamant in their belief that it was the entrance of immigrant women into the industry that had ruined it. They believed women lowered the wage standard and also created sweatshops, for understandably many Bohemian women had found it more profitable and convenient to work from home. At the same time that they made these charges, the men also kept women out of their union. A 1910 Senate investigation was surprisingly sympathetic to the women:

> As in all other skilled trades, women cigarmakers have been seriously handicapped by lack of training ... Where a trade union is powerful ... apprenticeship had been made a condition of employment in the trade and women have been practically shut out. The Bohemian women of the seventies were thoroughly trained in their own country. But since their day few women have acquired skill as cigarmakers, though

the occupation seems peculiarly adapted to them and one in which they should be able to acquire proficiency equal to that of the men.[45]

Famed writer Jacob Riis also took up the case of these unusual women:

> Often the wife is the original cigarmaker from the old home, the husband having adopted her trade here as a matter of necessity . . . As they state the cause of the bitter hostility of the trade unions, she was the primary bone of contention in the day of the early Bohemian immigration. The unions refused to admit the women, and, as the support of the family depended upon her to a large extent, such terms as were offered had to be accepted. The manufacturer has ever since industriously fanned the antagonism.[46]

Meanwhile—apparently unknown to writers focused on the industrial North—a more egalitarian cigar-making industry was developing in Florida. Although the number of immigrants who settled in the South was very small throughout the era, Tampa became an exception when cigar makers were recruited. Those who came to "Cigar City" were primarily Cubans of Spanish descent, with lesser numbers who emigrated directly from Spain, as well as a third group that came primarily from two towns in Sicily. Most had learned their skills in Havana or Key West, and women worked alongside men in dozens of cigar factories that flourished in Tampa at the turn of the century. They too were rollers and packers; they participated in unions and in several violent strikes; and, "prized for their nimble fingers and patience," they "earned impressive wages."[47]

Besides the wages, there were other advantages to this work. It was quiet, and skilled women in the early era were sufficiently valued that they were "allowed a good deal of latitude as to their hours."[48] Some came to work late and left early to accommodate the family's breakfast and dinner; others took breaks to breast-feed babies, for the industry was exceptional in the number of married women it employed.

As the field became less of a craft, unskilled workers found their way into it, but it remained a haven for married and foreign women. Even after World War I, only one female tobacco worker in every twenty-seven gave America as her birthplace.[49] Most were older women who considered themselves unassimilable; in a study of New York Italians, those in tobacco had "the largest proportion of women who could not speak English."[50] Inured to rough fieldwork in Europe during their youth, these women did not object to the smell or the stains on their hands.

Especially in the basements where the unskilled "stripping" was done, it was the newly arrived and docile immigrant woman who was hired. In Pittsburgh, it was Slavs, who with "their backs against a damp wall," worked by a "flaring gas jet. 'They would work all night,' a foreman said. 'We never have any trouble with them.'" By their era, the unionized men had won their war against women: that city's tobacco factories in 1909 gave only one skilled job in fifty to women, though they still outnumbered men by a ratio of three to one.[51]

The women who worked stripping tobacco leaves were at the bottom of that industry's hierarchy; those who rolled cigars—both women and men—were at the top. In this early-twentieth-century Tampa factory, a female cigar roller listens to a lectore, who read to cigar makers as they worked. Lectores were always male, and no one read in the rooms where women stripped tobacco. Note also the wide windows, which provided sunlight to see the gradations in tobacco color. (UNIVERSITY OF SOUTH FLORIDA SPECIAL COLLECTIONS)

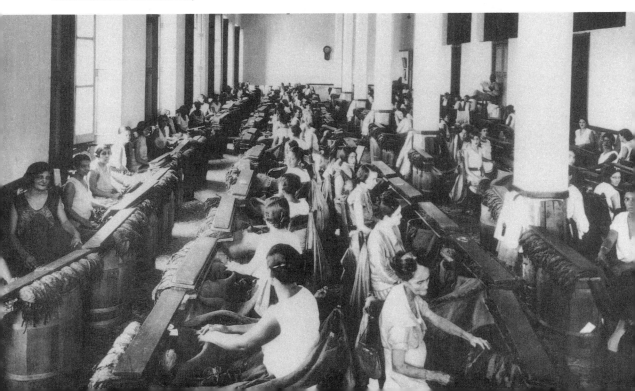

As the technology moved from hand-rolled cigars to molds and then to machines, flexible time disappeared and the demand for speed increased complaints of debilitating nervous tension. Throughout the era, rollers and packers strained their eyes, for tremendous importance was placed on matching the slight variations of tobacco color while wrapping a tight cigar. And, as some presciently noted, there were illnesses that were "the direct result of nicotine poisoning."[52] At the end of the immigrant era, a Labor Department writer poignantly summarized the plight of one:

> A young woman who had been working in a cigar factory since her arrival . . . pointed to her framed passport picture, which showed her to have been plump at that time. When her father met her three years later "he not know me, I so thin and skinny. Never sick before I came to America. Cigars not good to work."[53]

Though the epitome of masculinity, cigars provided employment to many immigrant women, and so too did flower making, an overwhelmingly feminine product. The era created a large demand, for artificial flowers were used in both home decoration and in the adornment of fashionably elaborate hats—and a hat was an obligatory part of every lady's apparel. "Flower shops" specialized in silk flowers for summer hats and feathers for winter ones, with the frequent addition of fruit, ribbon, and other embellishment. The trade was considered peculiarly suited to women; this was one thing men willingly said that women could do better. Men rarely helped their wives and children with flower making at home. The work was simply too effeminate.

For women, however, flower making offered an unusual opportunity for artistic expression—but while candy dippers and cigar rollers exhibited great pride in their crafts, flower makers seldom commented on this aspect of their work. Perhaps any sense of self-esteem disappeared in the world's judgment of value, for flower making was one of the worst paid of typical immigrant industries. More than half of those employed in flower shops in 1905 earned less than $6 weekly in the busy part of the year—and there were months with little or no work.[54] It may not be coincidental that this low value was in an industry in which both customer and crafter were women.

Early in the era, flower making was divided among various ethnic groups; one turn-of-the-century worker said her table of eight flower makers was made up of "Therese, who was a Neapolitan; Mamie, a Genoese; Amelia was born in Bohemia; the girl with the yellow hair was North German; and Nellie declared she was from County Killarney and mighty glad of it."[55] Between 1900 and 1910, however, the Italian population of New York more than doubled, and by the end of that decade Italians made up 72% of the trade.[56] Flower making appealed to them, for women could do traditionally feminine work with colleagues who were almost entirely female. The few men that the industry employed—some 1,200 of 8,500 New Yorkers in 1910[57]—worked as dyers, apart from the women who crafted the petals, stems, and leaves into flowers. In flower shops, even the foremen were forewomen.

Rose making was the pinnacle of the trade; one of the best used 175 petals in hers, and making five of them in a day was considered good.[58] "Branching" was also considered skilled, and women who did that earned about three times as much as the average flower worker. Most women, of course, did not have that level of employment; though artists could be found in the trade, the common opinion was that a child of three could—and did—make flowers. For most, the work was endless twisting of tiny wires that strained hands while tedious bits of glue wore out eyes.

But it was not tediousness or low wages and certainly not the entrance of Italians into the trade that ruined it, though some claimed all these circumstances. Instead, it was the whim of fashion. For most of the immigrant era, no respectable woman appeared in public without a hat, and the adornment of them employed tens of thousands—but in the 1920s, the flapper arrived. She flung away her hat, and with it her symbol of forced femininity, the artificial flower.

From Laundry to Foundry: More Women at Work

Women from all countries worked in laundries; half of the women in Chicago laundries around 1910 were foreigners. In a typical laundry, government investigators found three Irish women, seven Swedes, four Italians, three Germans, three Poles, one Jew, a Dane, and a Bohemian. Most began work as teenagers, some as early as ten or twelve, and many were widows or mothers whose husbands did not earn enough to support the family. Several were teenage orphans.[59]

Laundry was another job easily seen as "women's work," an extension of their assignments in the home and thus acceptable, even though work in commercial laundries was extremely heavy. Their most important product in that era was men's cuffs and collars that were starched to the point of rigidity. Getting limp cloth to resemble cardboard required a strenuous ironing process:

> The cuff is placed over the saddle-shaped padded head; pressure of a treadle raises the head against a steam chest, and pressure of another treadle causes the head to drop back as the cuff is finished. Only by violent exertion can hot metal and padded head be forced together . . . The whole body of the girl is shaken by the force . . . In one laundry the manager said, "No American can stand this. We have to use Hungarians or other foreigners. It seems to be unhealthful, but I don't know. The girls don't stay long enough for us to tell."[60]

This was only one of the perils of laundry life. Hands and hair could be caught in machinery; women told of co-workers who were permanently injured this way. No guards or stop mechanisms were standard when laundering machines were first introduced—though ironically, machines manufactured in America for export to England had these safety features.[61] Burns from irons, mangles, and scalding water were another constant danger.

Prior to electric fans, laundries were terrifically hot and humid. Windows had to be kept shut in some cities lest the surrounding soot dirty the clothes, and summer's temperature was routinely over a hundred degrees. Women spent a relatively large amount of their earnings to relieve thirst in this heat, and several laundry workers indicated that they frequently drank beer at work.[62] In winter, the contrast between indoor and outdoor temperatures brought colds; "most of the girls had colds most of the time."[63] On feet swollen from the heat, women often worked twelve- and fourteen-hour days. At the turn of the century, laundries frequently operated until nearly midnight on Saturday nights, getting out the white shirts that men wore on Sunday.

Conditions in this occupation were so poor that bright young women usually left quickly. The jobs remained for the newly arrived, the older women, the mentally mediocre. Most were aware that laundry was poor work. When asked her earnings, one Irish woman warned, "Now don't faint when I tell ye: I git *seven cents* an hour!"[64] Not only were wages low, but this industry was infamous for taking away from the toiler the mite she earned, as this collar starcher—who was at the height of her vocation—reveals:

> When I go to work . . . I am given a slip of paper marked on one side, "Received" and on the other "Returned." . . . When the collars are starched I turn them over to . . . boys . . . If for any reason at all the numbers do not tally . . . the starcher is docked . . . The boys are never docked, it being assumed, apparently, that they never make mistakes.[65]

Worse, starchers were docked *five dozen* collars if they dropped *one* collar, and absurdly, "the starcher is even held responsible after the collars leave her hands. If the bars on which the collars are dried happen to be dirty the starcher is fined, although the bars are supposed to be cleaned by other workers."[66] Gender discrimination was also clear with laundry sorters: this work was done entirely by men until a large Pittsburgh firm experimented successfully with women and others emulated them. "You can get two women where you got one man," management argued, "get twice as much done, and done just as well."[67] Yet though women did "just as well," in those firms that continued to employ both, women averaged $5 to $12 a week and men $12 to $20 for exactly the same work.[68]

Laundries existed in every city and town, for prior to the invention of home washers and dryers, most middle-class women sent their laundry out. Some did not use a commercial laundry, however, but rather employed a "day worker" as their washerwoman. These were almost always married women or widows with children who needed to be home. They—or their children—picked up and delivered the customer's laundry. Instead of using modern equipment and working in the company of other women, such women washed, starched, and ironed alone in their kitchens.

Most of them were older women who faced age as well as gender discrimination in the workplace and were thus forced to create their own small enterprises—which demanded both heavier physical labor and more risk, even as they aged. Among the laundresses in New York's nineteenth-century Kleindeutschland, for example, some

60% to 75% were over 40.[69] When her 1850 marriage ended Anna Maria Klinger's career as a live-in servant, she clearly felt defensive in explaining to her family in Germany that she was now a washerwoman. Trying to put the best face on this downward mobility, she wrote cheerfully of the superiority of the American system:

> You don't have to soak things in lye, soap is cheap, they don't carry the water on their heads here, either . . . The laundries are set up completely differently, you have a washboard . . . so one person can wash as much in one day as 2 washerwomen in Germany have to wash in 6 weeks. You probably never thought I would be a washerwoman, but in America you needn't be ashamed if you work.[70]

Instead of living on her husband's income, she worked to bring her younger siblings to America. Millions of immigrant women did similar homebound work but never entered the nation's statistical data base because the work they did was not in an organized industry. Census takers occasionally seemed to indicate their awareness of this problem: it is not unusual to see in their handwritten records, for instance, a question mark on the line for the wife that was directly beneath the husband's occupation—as though they were aware that she worked with the shoemaker, cigar maker, baker, confectioner, or saloonkeeper listed above, but they could not bring themselves to confer such titles on women.

Wards Eight and Nine in Baltimore were filled with such immigrant artisans in 1870. Perhaps the most unusual woman to appear in their census records was twenty-three-year-old Anne Nedwell, who had been born in Ireland. She had personal property worth $4,000 in the form of a variety store, which made her more wealthy than most native men. This young woman probably had been set up in business by her father, a sixty-year-old "house carpenter" who had a most uncommon $25,000 worth of property; he doubtless thought this daughter exceptionally competent, for she was the only one of four adult children living at home who was associated with the store.

The vast majority of immigrant women in these wards were listed as "Keeping House," with domestic servants—sometimes broken down into specialties such as cooks and governesses—running a distinct second. A city directory of the same era gives a more diverse view of women's lives, however, for in it, women defined themselves. In addition to advertisements for typically feminine areas such as nurses and laundresses, a sampling of women with German names includes two bakers and seven confectioners; seven dealers in "Bonnets, Ribbons, Silk and Straw Goods"; four dairy owners and three "Butter Dealers"; as well as six sellers of "Ladies Furnishings." Mrs. Carolina Boxbaum and Mrs. Johanna Kuhn were "Umbrella and Parasol Manufacturers and Repairers," while Mrs. Mary Wiltz was listed under "Cuppers and Leechers."[71]

Evidence of other immigrant women in business also appeared. The names under "Hair Dressers" were disproportionately French; the "Costumers" included Margaret Guidice and Mrs. P. Grossi; the corset makers featured four men along with Mrs. E.

Pohl, Mrs. Regina Seibert, and Mme. Marie Vaudens. A one-line list of dressmakers filled a single-spaced page that was generously sprinkled with German, Scottish, and French names, with the latter again disproportionate to their immigration rate. The grocers and others who owned property were likely to have German names, but it was Irish women who were most apt to list an occupation—including one who termed herself an "intelligence officer."[*72] (On the other hand, every one of the city's nine dancing academies was run by a man.)[73]

In other cities, women engaged in similar enterprises. Even urban women raised gardens and sometimes poultry to sell as produce; some developed specialties such as fancy cakes to sell. Multitudes were fruit and vegetable hawkers, pushcart sellers of dozens of products, operators of corner stores. Vestiges of the Old World remained with women who refurbished corn-stalk mattresses or concocted medicinal potions. When they could not manage their own small business, thousands worked in their homes on contract for factories; in addition to well-known work such as flower making and garment finishing, they did other odd jobs such as threading wires through tags or crocheting over curtain rings.[74]

Many created a living from sheer garbage—the era's "ragpickers" simply eked out an existence from other people's trash, like the old Slovak woman in Chicago who lived by "picking things up."[75] Railroad tracks were an especially great source of coal and wood for scavengers, who then sold these as fuel. Likewise, the 1890s "Industrial Branch" of the Association for Improving the Condition of the Poor was not truly industrial but rather "engaged poor women to make over and renovate second-hand clothing."[76]

There were other jobs not typically remembered. Immigrant women washed dirty railroad cars in cold Boston train yards seven days a week.[77] In the Midwest, women were among the "Russians, Bohemians, and South Slavs" who were "found following the crops."[78] Even greater numbers of European women worked on truck farms near northeastern cities; on Long Island, for example, Polish family farms hired extra women at harvest time, paying them around $10 a week and including "free house-rent."[79] Out west, some women mined: Swedish Mary Ann Larsen, for instance, headed a gold-mining operation in the Black Hills of South Dakota in the 1870s,[80] and a half century later, the census showed several hundred women, some of them foreign born, as miners.[81]

More common in mining camps—but still generally unusual—were women who worked as mobile cooks for crews of traveling men. Anna Ohlson, who immigrated in 1906, recalled:

> When I got to be about sixteen, I went away to work on a cook car. You go around with the threshing team and cook food for them as they go from farm to farm . . .

---

[*] This probably meant that she was in the business of linking domestic servants with employers, for "intelligence office" was a nineteenth-century term for an employment agency that specialized in servants. It is conceivable, however, that an independent Irish woman could have meant "intelligence" in the sense of covert information and was a detective.

Lots of work, but lots of fun. There's young boys, men, from all different countries
. . . One woman and I did all the cooking. We'd get up in morning before it was light
and start the stove up . . . We were busy. But, you know, it was fun. They'd help us
in the evening with the dishes . . . The cooks were paid the same as the men, but
there were two of us, so we had to divide it. We made more money than we would
with housework.[82]

Back east, another obscure occupational slot was the making of straw hats, which
required an uncanny talent; employers said only about one in every twenty women
who attempted it succeeded in learning the craft. Over a third of them were Italians,
who earned an exceptional $30 to $40 a week in the busy season.[83] Other fortunate
Italian women used their native background to sing in the choruses of professional
operas.[84] There were occasional women editors of immigrant publications, and some
worked as typesetters and bookbinders. Thousands were nurses, midwives, and
teachers, especially in parochial schools.

Occasionally unusual professional opportunities arose, especially for those who
emigrated young and grew up in America: Jette Brun's German daughter-in-law, for
example, used the contacts she made with legislators who boarded with Jette to
become a clerk for the Missouri Senate. Such professionals were likely to be found
among the better-educated immigrants from Scandinavia and Britain; among those
from the Continent, Bohemian women once again demonstrated their uniqueness:
the 1915 Chicago directory of Bohemians listed nineteen female and thirty-six male
physicians.[85]

The range of jobs that immigrant women found or created for themselves ran
the gamut from the uniquely womanly to the heaviest of traditionally masculine
labor. One exclusively feminine job was that of wet nurse; mothers with a sufficient
milk supply took on an additional baby to earn the money paid by orphanages. Nor
was this a rare thing; the Founding Asylum of the Sisters of Charity in New York
alone put out more than 1,100 such "pay babies" in 1889.[86] A quarter century later,
"even the death of a baby [was] an economic resource," for breast milk was worth
$10 to $12 a month for women to "bring home a nursing baby from the hospital."[87]

Wet-nursing was sufficiently common to warrant the attention of public health
authorities in 1908 concerned with venereal disease. A medical report on Italians
spoke of the "many mothers of the poor who take children from institutions to nurse
them" and thus were inadvertently exposed to disease via the newborn.[88] Much
earlier, German Barbara Klinger worked as a wet nurse after her 1853 illegitimate
pregnancy:

When he was five weeks old I got a job working for some Americans, they had a
ten-week-old baby, they promised me I would get ten dollars a month and I wet
nursed their baby for seven months; then I left and they didn't give me my money,
they kept putting it off from one month to the next. They didn't give me any more
than 27 dollars and still owe me 43 and I can't get it.[89]

On the other end of the occupational gender scale was rough manual labor in the metal industries. A 1909 government study found 4,500 immigrant women working at core making in foundries. "The work done by women," they reported, "is distinctly skilled," but it was also heavy—some of them lifted over sixty pounds. English speakers accounted for less than one-fifth of this group.[90] A similarly large number of women operated power-presses and riveters and did soldering and machine-tool work. Again, all but 13% were foreigners.[91] A third group was some 2,600 women—largely Polish, German, and Hungarian—who worked at nut and bolt making. The report summarized:

> Much of the work is singularly unpleasant in character . . . The action of the machine spatters oil or water over everything . . . including the operator and her clothing . . . A woman . . . turning out the maximum number of one-fourth inch nuts must press the treadle 50 times a minute—a rate which, in view of the fact that it is to be kept up for 60 minutes an hour and 10 hours a day, needs no comment.[92]

Since Pittsburgh men gravitated to the steel mills, leaving all other manufacturing jobs to women, it is rather amazing to find that in fact the metal industry there was the third largest employer of females, following only laundries and cigar making. Two-thirds of these women were Slavic—Hungarian, Polish, or Croatian:

> Fifty core makers work in the largest . . . room. All are women. Through the narrow entrance you can see them moving about among wreaths of coal smoke and black dust . . . They strike you as an incarnation of the activities of smoking ovens, boiling crucibles and iron soft with fierce heat. The dim light through windows encrusted with black dust . . . cannot dispel the impression of unreality.[93]

Slavic women also worked alongside men in the steel mills as "openers." Sheets of steel welded together came from the furnace; the openers' job was to take the sheet and "beat it on the ground to separate the parts; then with the lead piece in the glove, they make an opening. They forcibly tear apart the plates, holding part of the sheet down with one knee, while tearing the metal with the other. The violence of this work takes all the strength of even the earth-toughened peasant women . . . from Poland."[94] A midwestern manager of metalworks averred:

> We never use American women on assorting work . . . These Hunky women are strong. They come to work with their husbands in the morning. They don't mind working . . . where the men have to work "stripped." They can pull sheets of metal apart as well as any man can. No American woman would want this kind of work.[95]

There was other hefty toil outside of metal mills done by women. A study of working mothers in Philadelphia included "7 laborers employed by an oil refinery for heavy work, such as shoveling."[96] Women made up 47% of the employees of

Connecticut rubber plants in 1890.[97] In Pittsburgh, they did the cutting and soldering of tin cans in canneries, made cracker tins in cracker factories, and hammered caskets together—some worked alone lining coffins at night when a special order came in.[98] Women worked at tanning skins in Yonkers, while in Connecticut, they packed fuses in "imminent risk of explosion."[99]

Without question, immigrant women did "men's work." Obscurely and without recognition, they quietly toiled at hard labor, while Americans debated whether or not women should work outside the home in any job.

The Boardinghouse Boss

Perhaps the job that was most common to immigrant women and most likely to be overlooked by statisticians was that of the boardinghouse mistress. Nearly every immigrant had personal experience with the institution of boarding, either as a boarder or as a member of a family taking in boarders. A 1908 study of New York City Italians, for instance, found that 93% of the families also had at least one lodger: 33% housed one, 41% had two, and 19% had three or more. And these were in tiny homes—over half consisted of only one or two rooms.[100]

While most women who supplemented the family income this way accepted only a few paying guests, others ran boardinghouses that were genuine businesses. In the early days of any ethnic group's migration, the chances were that dozens of men had left their families behind, and they gravitated to the one or two available women of their ethnicity who spoke their language and could cook their food in the familiar way. A sociologist in the western Pennsylvania coal and steel area in 1910 found that, though Slavic homes were still crowded with boarders, conditions were much improved from a decade earlier: "From 50 to 100 of them used to live in one house, not a big one . . . Other people would not take them to board. If there was a man who had a wife, all flocked to him . . . Ten years ago they used to have plank shelves for bedding round the wall."[101]

A boardinghouse operator's day began before dawn, packing lunch pails and fixing breakfast. The night shift then arrived to occupy the beds during the day. More meals would have to be prepared, dozens of dishes and the laundry done. Clothes soiled by sweat and ingrained grime had to be rubbed on a scrub board, and the water needed to do this had to be drawn and heated. Doubtless a woman fell into bed so exhausted that she slept soundly, despite the fact that "the lodgers are given the best sleeping rooms while the rest of the family sleeps on the floor, the mother getting the most undesirable spot."[102]

In some communities, women cooked to individual tastes. Each man would place his personal order, and the woman would shop for and prepare a dozen different suppers, tagging each piece of meat with the name of its owner. Sometimes men did their own shopping and women prepared the food. In other cases, the men cooked, paying only for their laundry and the use of bed and kitchen. One especially curious method was found among Chicago Poles who paid $2 a month for lodging and bought their own food. The food, however, was cooked by the landlady, who was not paid for this service but was entitled to the leftovers, "and this is usually all that the family need."[103]

The earnings for this work varied, but it could be quite good. In western mining communities, a woman who boarded ten or fifteen men could earn $80 monthly circa 1910—as much as her husband made. Nevertheless, the woman who did the work did not get the credit; almost invariably, it was her husband who was known as the "boarding boss." Instead, she was, in the words of one Slavic woman, "a real slave."[104] She typically managed a place such as one serving Pennsylvania steelworkers that "consisted of two rooms, one above the other, each twelve by twenty feet."

> Along one side of the room was an oilcloth covered table with a plank bench on each side, and above a long row of handleless white cups . . . tin knives and forks. Near the up-to-date range, the only real piece of furniture in the room, hung the "buckets" in which all mill men carry their noon or midnight meal . . . In the room above, double iron bedsteads were set close together, and on them comfortables* were neatly laid. Here, besides the "boarding boss," his wife and two babies, lived twenty men.[105]

"When the children get to be 5 or 6 years old," according to a priest who ministered to them, "the parents leave the mining or factory settlement . . . By the time the eldest is six, there are enough little ones to keep the mother busy."[106] Immigrants saw this as a transitional stage that afforded them a rare chance for exceptional savings early in their lives, but American reformers decried the boarding institution as overcrowded, unsanitary, and dangerous to the nuclear family standard. They encouraged immigrants to decrease the numbers of strangers living in their homes, as in this case of a Protestant minister who reported:

> A man whose wife kept 18 boarders sleeping in two shifts came one day . . . and asked him if he thought it would do to take fewer boarders; his wife had no time to go to church. The minister naturally encouraged him to do so, and he cut the number down . . . to four men, trying to give his wife more time so that he could teach her to read. Finally he said that he wanted to live like the Americans, with no boarders and a parlor "where no one slept."[107]

A final factor in ending the practice was that, as one Slavic woman reported, "[t]he keeping of boarders has had a great tendency to break up homes and families."[108] The loss of privacy was harmful to a family, as was the close contact of a lone woman with males who lacked any other feminine companionship. One survey found that more households without husbands than with accepted lodgers,[109] and while it is plain that the husbandless woman would have greater need of income, the Victorian era saw this as dangerous to morals. Some welfare agencies cut off aid to

---

* An old-fashioned usage for the bed linens now called "comforters."

widows who took in boarders of the opposite sex, posing a great financial dilemma to these women—one study of 188 widows, for example, found that 117 of their 361 lodgers and boarders were unrelated men.[110]

Other immigrant women ran boardinghouses that were less an extension of their home and instead were definite, lifelong businesses. In the 1879 Baltimore City Directory, for instance, all but a handful of the 135 boardinghouses listed were run by women. About one-fourth of them seemed to have been run by immigrants; most were German, with lesser numbers of Scottish women and one Italian. In addition, several women were listed as proprietors of hotels.[111]

Baltimore also was home to an unusual boardinghouse that had a quasi-official standing as the local "Emigrants' Home." Located at the city's Locust Point port, the establishment was described as a saloon that also provided lodging. It was listed in the 1886 city directory as belonging to Augusta Marousek, widow of Bohemian John A. Marousek. Presumably she continued to operate this establishment until the turn of the century, with her identity buried beneath that of a second husband named Koether. In 1901, however, she again appears in sole possession, as Mrs. Augusta Koether.

Evidently Mrs. Koether did rather well in running this "immigrant station" during the busiest part of the immigration era, for she moved to a large house in a fashionable part of town in 1907. A decade later, however, she was back on Locust Point, perhaps returning to live in the poorer dock area when World War I brought immigration to a virtual halt. Augusta Jennie Koether, who was also the mother of two, had emigrated from Germany in 1869 and she died in Baltimore at age seventy seven; in all probability, she worked for decades to feed and house other American newcomers—but her contemporaries instead credited her two husbands for much of her enterprise.[112]

Occasionally an immigrant woman began catering to Americans and the Americanized. Elise Isely's Swiss aunt, for example, started a boardinghouse in St. Joseph, Missouri, which was a jumping-off place to the west. Because her cooking was good and the beds clean, men stayed for weeks. Grossinger's, the famous Catskills resort, had similar beginnings. Jennie Grossinger was born in Vienna, and her father became one of the myriads of Jewish tailors in New York. When his health collapsed, the family moved to a Catskills farm for fresh air, but neither the soil nor they were suited to farming. Jennie suggested that they take in boarders, Jewish workers like themselves who needed a fresh-air vacation and who would be subject to discrimination in other resorts. The idea worked, but not before Jennie and her family put in a lot of hard labor, as she recalled:

> We did all the work ourselves . . . Mama cooked and so did I. Harry, my husband, recruited guests in New York. Papa took care of the farming, marketing and meeting the guests at the railroad station. I remember we all put in 18-hour days until the midsummer of 1915 when we hired one chambermaid.[113]

Jette Bruns began in the boarding business almost accidentally, simply because the money was too good to pass up. When, after seventeen years in America, she moved with her family from rural Missouri to the capital of Jefferson City in 1853, she wrote: "Rent is terrifically high, and we have already rented several rooms. During the session of the legislature I rented a room to four gentlemen for several weeks for $16 a week."[114]

After her husband died, Jette continued in the business—but with considerable reluctance, for she felt diffident about having men in her house, even though she still had four children living at home. When the first legislative session occurred after her husband's death, her concern with respectability was clear: "On the advice of Hermann and because Bruns had always permitted it with some special friends," she wrote, "I have put up ten gentlemen during the session of the legislature. It is, to be sure, entirely against my inclination, but it is a way to earn something in a decent manner. Thus for a few months we really have to stir about . . ."[115]

Though she continued to write of her "reluctance to lodge strange gentlemen," it was clear that she had found a good source of income and also enjoyed her unusual clientele. In 1867, she "rented out the parlor along with the rooms, and that brings in $72 more per month . . ."[116]

Despite fretting over taxes and debts, she spent to maintain a good reputation: "To be sure, I have to keep a good table. This winter I again had gentlemen from the Senate and House, as I did last year, the same group, half German, half Americans; upstairs I had the lieutenant governor."[117]

In this and other indications of her political views, Jette revealed how Americanized she had become three decades after immigration. For most immigrant women, however, the status of boardinghouse mistress was temporary, a stage of life to be abandoned as soon as possible. Those who did this work did not consider themselves businesswomen but exceptionally overworked housewives. They were anxious to lay this burden down and obtain the American dream of living in a single family home. As a social worker summarized of the boardinghouse mistresses she had known: "With a house on the outskirts of town, and a garden about it, and a glimpse of the larger out-of-doors, they begin to feel that the dreams of their emigration have come true."[118]

14

WAYS OF WORK

Wages, Hours, and Other
Aspects of the Working World

Vastly lower pay rates for women were unquestioned through the immigrant era. Inferiority was so deeply ingrained in some that even when they were the victims of blatant inequality, they could not see the wrong. An Italian widow with five children, for instance, began work in a Providence bakery in the early twentieth century for $1 a week and finally worked her way up to $7: "Since business was good, he hired another baker, a man. We did the same work, the same hours. He was a widower with three children. His pay was $10.00 a week right from the start, which was just and fair, after all he was a man."[1]

In 1905, when the immigration wave was cresting, the Census of Manufacturers reported that three-quarters of male workers received more than $8 weekly, while over three-quarters of female workers received less than that. The disparity varied from industry to industry, but in no case did an average man earn less than an average women. The *highest*-paid female average was $7.60, and the *lowest* male was $7.71. The least disparity was in the country's oldest industry—cotton goods—where the weekly gap between the sexes was only $1.68.[2]

It was the skills of women weavers that was responsible for that relatively small gap, but never were women skilled enough to overcome the handicap of gender. The International Silver Company was typical in replying to a job inquiry from a skilled British woman: saying it would be delighted to employ her, the company unabashedly told her that skilled female help was paid 12 1/2 to 20 cents an hour, while unskilled male labor received 17 1/2 to 25 cents.[3] An industrial expert summarized, "Where skill and occupation are comparable, alike in skilled trades and in unskilled occupations, the man's wage is double the women's."[4]

In most industries, however, it was difficult to get such direct comparisons, for the corporate style was to separate workers by gender—and then, often, unthinkingly to label what men did as "skilled" while what women did was called "unskilled." Even female economists seldom questioned these labels, but a thoughtful examination raises doubts. In the garment industry, for example, the cutting of cloth was almost always done by men; even though they followed patterns in doing this, it was termed skilled work—while sewing, whether by machine or by hand, was deemed unskilled.

Pay rates were simply arbitrary. Further, what one was paid often depended on what one was successful in bargaining for, and women who lacked the courage or ability to demand raises never got them. One who started in a box factory at age eleven had worked there nineteen years and still earned the same $5.50 she made as a beginner.[5] In artificial-flower factories, women with ten years or more experience were found to be earning $6 or $7, while male workers who had been there just two or three years were getting $10 and $11.[6] Elizabeth Hasanovitz was a courageous woman who successfully insisted upon pay commensurate with her capability; after a trial week in a dressmaking shop:

> I asked the foreman for a price. He nearly fainted when I told him I wanted fourteen dollars a week. It was fortunate for me that two girls had left in the middle of the week, for the foreman, being very busy and having few skilled workers, was afraid to lose me, too. So after two hours' bargaining, I remained there for thirteen dollars a week, but was strongly forbidden to tell anybody in the shop of the "extravagant amount" I was getting. I was the highest paid worker.[7]

Few had the self-confidence to proclaim their worth for two hours as she did. There was in Lisa Hasanovitz's shop an interesting contrast to her: Sadie, also from Russia, also a talented and experienced dressmaker. She got only $10 and was a sycophant who stayed at this nonunion shop because the boss had vaguely promised to reward her some day, while exploiting her compatriots to please him. "Almost all the girls," Sadie said, "I brought here, as soon as they come over from Russia." The boss wanted her "to get him green girls for help. You know he does not like Americanized girls—they fuss too much . . . while green girls don't kick about the pay."[8] Sadie went on to say that the first three weeks her green girls worked for nothing and after that they earned $3 a week.

It was a common practice to take jobs without knowing what one was to be paid. The subservience of many newly arrived Italian women was seen by YWCA workers interviewing them who frequently found that the Italians did not know what their wages were, as the first pay day had not come yet.[9] One responded, "I'm not privileged to ask . . . It is what they give you."[10] Some had their own form of retaliation against this system; if after a week they found they were getting less than in their old place, they returned to their former jobs saying they had been sick.

Employers admitted that women could not live on the wages paid. Many purposely hired only girls with families "because the trade does not offer a living wage."[11] Others deceived the public—and occasionally even themselves—into believing their wages adequate, so that there often was a disparity between what firms said they paid and what workers said they earned. A study of Italian women circa 1912 found that 54% of them made less than $8 a week, but only 22% of the firms employing them reported their wages to be so low.[12]

One enthusiastic young executive, while escorting investigators through his factory, stated that the hundreds of women working there were paid $20 a week. A visitor doubted this, and he insisted that it was true. Finally he sent for the payroll records and discovered to his surprise that the women earned from $5 to $7. The forelady earned $20, but he had fixed that figure in his head for all of them and sincerely believed it to be so.[13]

In contrast to this would-be humanitarian were legions of employers who cheated their workers and attempted to prevent the payment of the little they earned. Legal Aid Societies cited many cases of "ridiculous pretexts to defraud" workers. One was

> a Lithuanian girl . . . employed as a scrub woman in an office building. During the influenza epidemic the other scrub women employed were unable to work. The janitor offered to pay this girl $16 per week if she would work double time and do their work . . . He gave her only $8, although she had worked not only her usual time from 8 to 11 but also from 11 to 3. When she demanded what he had promised he told her that he was only joking with her.[14]

Deliberately making mistakes in writing paychecks was another practice. "Sometimes the employer may have no funds in the bank . . . [and] promises to give another check . . . When he finally gets the check it may be for the original amount only, payment of the amount earned after that time being postponed."[15] Rose Cohen had the unfortunate experience of working for an employer who allowed wages to accumulate and then skipped town.

Danish Anna Walther had a worse experience. She decided to do millinery work out of New York for a season and went to Indiana (where she hoped to see Indians). After three weeks she was called to the manager's office and curtly informed that her model hats were not up to their standards. She knew this was not true because the hats were selling well, but since she had only a verbal contract and since the season was too far advanced to return to New York, she had to suffer a reduction in wages.[16]

Anna stoically accepted the situation, for she had no choice. The era's economy was harsh and few labor protections existed, especially for female workers. Moreover, many industrial managers believed in exercising discipline comparable to that of a schoolmaster. They saw themselves as authorities not to be questioned, while viewing their women workers as children in constant need of correction.

Stiff fines were imposed for minor infractions. Being five minutes late commonly cost an hour's pay, even when a woman may have stayed up until the wee hours with work she had taken home. Most outrageous was the practice of fining a pieceworker for being late, even when she had no work to do and would earn nothing—she actually could accumulate a deficit in wages during her first hours at work!

Many companies charged employees for necessary supplies. Some garment industry workers had to buy thread and needles, and they routinely supplied their own scissors, thimbles, and such. One Italian woman reported that she had 35 cents deducted from her paycheck to compensate for the electricity to run her machine.[17] Women sometimes even had to buy their sewing machines: Rose Schneiderman had just begun to pay for hers when the factory burned down. "This was very hard on the girls who had paid for their machines . . . The bosses got $500,000 insurance, so I heard, but they never gave the girls a cent to help them bear their losses."[18]

A moment of negligence could cost the worker money disproportionate to the harm done. One who make kid gloves had to pay for them if the machine stitched incorrectly. Two pairs were damaged one week and she had to pay $2.50 each: "It took nearly the whole week's pay."[19]

Similarly harsh attitudes appeared in the management of retail stores. One of the few New York stores that complied with the law requiring seats to be available for women workers then fined the women if they were caught using them. Department stores were infamous for low wages, long hours, and arbitrary rules. The irrationality of their unbending regulations was illustrated by the case of a girl who had worked at one for several years. When her father died and her consumptive mother was unable to work, they had to move farther out of town where the rent was low. But:

> I have to be at the store at eight o'clock. The train that leaves home at seven gets me to the store two minutes after eight, but though I've explained this to the manager he says I've got to be at the store at eight, and so, summer and winter, I have to take the train at half-past six and wait till the doors are open. It's the same way at night . . . The rules are that I must stop five minutes to help the girls cover up the goods, and that just hinders my getting the train till after seven, so that I am not home till eight . . . I told him that the girls at my counter would be glad to cover my goods, and if he would only let me go at six it would give me a little more time for mother.[20]

The investigator could scarcely credit this tale and so verified it with the management. She found it to be "true in every detail and also that she was a valuable assistant, one of the best among a hundred or so employed." Moreover, the young lady had offered to exchange her lunch hour for these seven minutes but had met only a stone wall of refusal; "she dared not speak again for fear of losing her place." The firm, ironically, gave "largely to charitable objects."[21]

Not many immigrants accepted these conditions. The language barrier also prevented the newly arrived from working in stores, but those who learned English, as well as English-speaking immigrants, stayed away. Store employees were largely

Americans who were willing to accept these poor working conditions because an American from a middle-class family lost status by working in a factory. The immigrants employed there usually were either young and inexperienced in the labor market or, less frequently, attempting to emulate the Americans. Instead, most immigrants saw all work as honorable, and the job that paid best was the one to choose.

For women, however, getting and keeping a job also meant dealing with demands for sexual favors. While many factories strictly segregated the sexes with only female bosses over women, in others, especially ghetto sweatshops, there was closer contact. Even children were not exempt. Rose Cohen was just twelve when she began work in a Jewish tailor shop that was all male except for herself and one other girl. Though her father worked there, he could not prevent the men from telling vulgar stories in her presence, and the other girl assured her, "What you hear in this shop is nothing compared with what you will hear in other shops."[22] Indeed, in another shop, teenage Rose experienced direct sexual harassment; her kindly-appearing boss invited her to his house to collect her wages and then made it plain on her arrival that he had something else in mind.

Elizabeth Hasanovitz lost two good jobs because her bosses could not control themselves. In the first, the boss's wife fired her because the old man kept hanging around her. In the second, she had gone to the office to collect her pay, when "he grasped me in his arms. I screamed, and with superhuman strength threw him from me and ran."[23]

Lisa pretended she had lost her pay rather than explain why she didn't have it. Most women were ashamed to tell anyone of these experiences and were tortured by the thought that somehow it was their fault. Rosa Cavalleri even experienced sexual harassment via her husband's job: she shyly reported that his boss "wanted me to be like a wife" during the 1893 depression. "So there my husband had that nice job in the hard times and he had to lose it," Rosa said. "He was good, no—to go away and lose that good job to save me from the boss?"[24]

A number of sociologists testified that when women asked for raises, employers encouraged them to sell their bodies instead. In the 1880s the Working Women's Society of New York commented, "It is a known fact that men's wages cannot fall below a limit upon which they can exist, but women's wages have no limit, since the paths of shame are always open to her."[25] Yet, as Jacob Riis commented, "To the everlasting credit of New York's working-girl let it be said that, rough though her road may be, all but hopeless her battle with life, only in the rarest instances does she go astray . . . New York's army of profligate women is not . . . recruited from her ranks."[26] If a job came with sexual strings attached, even women in dire need gave it up and searched for another.

Being married did not exempt a woman from sexual harassment, but the married state made getting a job much more difficult, for most employers were candid about their preference for single women. Several studies showed downward mobility after marriage; women simply could not get the work they had earlier. Many found themselves, for instance, scrubbing floors at night in the same kind of factory where they had once worked for far better pay. Discrimination against married women was so severe that a number said they had to resort to concealing their marriage to get work, and they wrote "Miss" on job applications. These women—most of whom were Irish and German—resented being forced to lie because they knew from their personal histories that they were better employees as mature women than they had been as romantic girls.

But not all jobs were a running battle. Laundries, for instance, employed married women as freely as single ones, and the one where Cornelia Parker worked was a sunny, cheerful place even if the work was hard. The women sang as they ironed, with the Italians offering bits of opera and all singing standard hymns. She also worked in a rural New York bleachery, which employed immigrants as well as Americans. "There was never the least 'factory atmosphere' about the place," she reported, and this company showed that contended attitudes increased production. There was always laughter:

> Nor was the laughter the giggling kind, indulged in when the forelady was not looking . . . Like as not the forelady was laughing with the rest . . . It is significant that with all the fun, the standard of efficiency and production in our bleachery was such that out of eighteen like industries in the country, we were one of the only two running full-time.[27]

Dorothy Richardson reported of a flower factory employing many foreign women that a child took each worker's grocery order, and when noon arrived:

> The pincers and tongs of the rose-makers, and the pressing molds of the leaf workers, were taken off the fires, and in their place . . . bacon and chops sputtered, steak sizzled; potatoes, beans, and corn stewed merrily . . . It was like a school girls' picnic . . . We ate our luncheon at leisure, and with the luxury of snowy-white tablecloths and napkins of tissue paper.[28]

The psychological environment of the workplace mattered a great deal. Immigrants were prone to suffer mental distress, for they often felt exclusion and alienation and were sometimes the direct object of insults. Strict segregation of ethnic groups was common. Situations were like that of a Pittsburgh hinge factory where the Slavic women were "kept sedulously apart from the Americans; they are paid at different times, and work in different parts of the room. Whether they are making less than the American girls or not they do not know."[29] Foreigners were almost invariably given the dirtiest, least-rewarding tasks. One sociologist testified:

> Although Italians, Russians, Irish, Polish, Germans, Americans and Swedes are employed in New York laundries, . . . the Irish receive the higher prices, the Italians the lower prices. The best-paid work, the hand starching . . . and hand ironing, is done by Irish women . . . The actual process of hand starching may be learned in

less than one hour . . . On the other hand, to learn the nicer processes of the ill-paid work of feeding at the mangle . . . requires from thirteen to fifteen days. The reason for the low wages listed for mangle work seems to lie only in nationality.[30]

Workers doing the superior tasks scorned those assigned to the more menial. When Cornelia Parker began laundry work, she sat down at the "wrong" table for lunch, and no one spoke to her the entire time. Foreladies, too, could make life hard for immigrants. Many of them fondly recalled the "good old days" when there was none of the riffraff that emigrated now from Europe. Miss Parker found that she was promised favorable treatment even before she began work simply because she was not "Eyetalian."

Immigrants could avoid some of this unpleasantness by staying in the ghetto sweatshops of their own nationality. Here there might be security among co-workers sharing a common background, but it certainly did not assure agreeable working conditions. The small shops of the newly arrived were more crowded, unsafe, ill lit; hours were apt to be longer and wages lower. Sadly often, the most exploitative employers were those who were cheating their own compatriots. Yet the comfort of being among one's own kind had great appeal, and many stayed in these places their entire working career. A study of the men's garment industry in Chicago in 1912 showed as many as 91% of Germans, 88% of Bohemian and 85% of Polish women worked in shops where the employer was of their nationality.[31] They evidently preferred working together to American industry where one ethnic group was often played against another.

Unemployment, Industrial Illness, and Death in the Workplace

Early in the morning and full of anticipation I made for the bindery . . . It must be where that crowd was on the sidewalk ahead, some thirty girls and as many men and boys . . . Rather too many wanted the same job, but there were no worries to speak of . . . Finally the prettiest and brightest of the lot peered in . . . "I see a bunch inside! Come on!"

    In we shoved our way, and there in the dismal basement-like first floor waited as many girls and men as on the sidewalk . . . We tore up the iron stairs . . . Up seven flights we puffed . . . Our group of nine surged in. There stood as many girls and men as were down on the first floor and out on the sidewalk. "My Gawd!" There was nothing else to say.[32]

Of this horde of job seekers, only two women—who had been promised jobs the previous week—were hired. Over a hundred women and an equal number of men had applied for just two jobs. Nor could one easily go on, for "it is something of a catastrophe if you do not land the first job you apply for Monday morning." By the time one reached a second prospect, those places were usually taken. "The third chance is slimmer still by far, and if you keep on until 10 or 11 it is mostly just plain useless. And if you do not land a job on Monday, that whole week is as good as lost."[33]

These fearful Monday mornings would be much worse for the unassimilated worker, who was usually unfamiliar with cities in general, to say nothing of the geography of this particular city; unfamiliar with the subway system; unable to read signs; unable to ask questions. All were excellent reasons for staying in the ghetto sweatshop run by a friend of friend from the Old World.

When they did venture out to seek new work, most immigrant women depended on rumor and pavement pounding. Rose Cohen had been in America for six years when, she said, "I learned to find a job it was not necessary to go from factory to factory. Instead you read the advertisements in the newspapers."[34] A Boston study of 266 newly arrived women at the turn of the century found that only two used advertisements to seek work.[35] In a YWCA study of over 600 Italian women, just three obtained their jobs through ads.[36]

Though unaware of newspapers, foreigners in the earliest days showed a willingness to use employment agencies where they existed. In 1850, the Boston Society for the Prevention of Pauperism reported that "their office . . . received, during the last five years, applications for employment from 15,697 females, of whom 14,044 or 90% were foreigners."[37]

But not all agencies were reputable. Sociologist Frances Kellor in 1903 did a detailed study with nine incognito investigators in several cities who found that the vast majority of these firms did not live up to minimal standards. In some, women applicants were assaulted when they resisted paying fees; in others, they were directed to brothels as potential employment. Most specialized in domestic servants, however, so their effect on the industrial scene was insignificant.[38]

Friends were by far the most important way to obtain employment. Over three-quarters of a large group of Italian women questioned on this had obtained their jobs through relatives or friends.[39] Rose Gorgoni, for instance, waited for the neighborhood network to come up with a job for her, taking no action herself "as she had no jobless friend to go around with and was 'ashamed' to go alone."[40] Responses to inquiries about job seeking show both a lack of system and persistence:

> "I was all over asking."
> "I went all over the places, nothings, nothings."
> "Walking and walking, I wore my feet out."
> "I walked all over, five or six weeks, and ask if she need a woman; I look, I look, came back and next day go again. They all say, 'too late,' 'call again,' 'will let you know.'"
> "When I first here I so foolish, I go out, I make chalk marks so I find my way home again; that how dumb I was. I was in the street and I saw a factory. I was coming in to ask for a job and they give me."[41]

No thought was given to aptitude. Often a woman ended up in the trade where friends secured her first employment and stayed there unhappily for years. Their fatalistic attitude can be summed up by the Sicilian who said bleakly, "I would like to be in another trade, but I never had any friend to take me into any other trade."[42]

Even when one had a niche in the labor market, seasonal unemployment plagued the best of workers. The era's industry was far more spasmodic than is the case today: because employers had to pay neither mandatory overtime nor unemployment compensation, there was little incentive for them to plan ahead and encourage the early orders that kept production constant. In candy factories, for example, women worked to exhaustion in the weeks before Christmas and then were forced into unemployment during summer. The same patterns existed with most other manufacturers, and even service industries such as laundries saw appreciable seasonal variation. In this era prior to air-conditioning, the affluent deserted the cities in droves for cooler country homes, and businesses lost their customer base for months on end.

Indeed, many working-class households functioned on the assumption that women would work in the winter, when the factories generally were humming, and that men would work in the summer, when construction jobs were available. In one study of working women, fewer than 5% had drawn full pay for an entire year, and almost half were jobless for eight weeks or more. Yet only 12% were unemployed because they quit their jobs, and only 17% took any vacation. And, as this investigator added, "It is a matter for comment that three-fourths of the women had lost no time on account of illness."[43]

Seasonal unemployment existed even in prosperous years, but when the economic cycle went on a downward trend, the continual scrambling for a job became even more futile. Rosa Cavalleri told how she and her children suffered during the Depression of 1893 when her husband had gone logging in Wisconsin and sent no money home. Pregnant Rosa tried to support the family alone:

> In that time I was scrubbing the saloon—all the floors . . . for 50 cents. But then I didn't get the 50 cents; the man he kept that for my rent . . . The city hall was giving food to the people . . . standing in line . . . Us poor women were frozen to death; we didn't have the warm clothes, and there was such a storm with the snow and the wind! Eight o'clock, when the door opened, all the people were pushing to get in. There came the police with their clubs and they were yelling like we were animals. Then one of those police hit the woman next to me on the head with his club . . . When I saw that, I said to myself, "Better I starve before I let that policeman hit me!" And I ran home from that line. And I never, never went there again.[44]

Rosa, like millions of others, went faithfully to work when jobs were available; these women wanted to work, but the economic system kept them idle and hungry. Elena and Gerda Nakov, for example, were beautiful and healthy when they came from Russia as teenagers. After thirteen years in America, "these young women's strength is simply worn out from years of overwork and strain and poor and scanty food," their doctor said, and, "they can never again be really well."[45]

Statistics on industrial health, however, can be deceptive, for most show that working women had fewer complaints than those not employed. Of over 700 employed mothers in one study, for example, 44% reported illness in the last year, but 63% of the housewives had been sick. The sociologist concluded that women who entered industry were stronger and that "they have less time to think about their health"[46]—but a more realistic explanation lies in the probability that the housewives were women who had in fact worked earlier in life. They may have well have literally given their best years to the industrial machine.

Some of them also may have suffered accidents at work that negatively affected their health for the rest of their lives, for safety regulations throughout most of the immigrant era were either nonexistent or ill enforced. Dangerous machinery was unguarded; floors were often wet or slippery; aisles were filled with obstructions to save space; haphazard buildings and unsanitary practices that allowed oil, rags, and lint to accumulate made these usually wooden structures into firetraps.

The dress code of that day also promoted accidents, as long skirts and uncut hair might brush against whirring machines. A Polish girl in a Lawrence mill let her hair get too close to her machine: "Seconds later, [she] lay writhing on the floor with part of her scalp torn off. After placing her scalp carefully in a paper bag, her friends carried her to a doctor, and . . . she survived."[47]

Too often the situation was like that of the manufacturer who considered his duty done when he posted a sign saying, "Girls must not work at any machine without board over shaft"—and that many machines were without them and had to be used was no concern of his.[48] Factories felt so little responsibility for safety, reported one sociologist, that elevators were "frequently decorated with the signs, 'You travel on this elevator at your own risk.'"[49]

Besides unsafe machines, the buildings that housed them were often inadequate. In the early part of the era, industrial engineering was still too new for architects to realize what safe standards were. The Pemberton Mill of Lawrence was a source of local pride in 1860, but it proved a deathtrap. The mill stood five stories high and had six-inch solid oak floors and wide windows. But the windows were too wide, the floors too heavy, and the supporting pillars too weak. The top floor collapsed, and within a minute, the entire building was on the ground. Townspeople worked for hours to free victims from the wreckage. Near midnight a fire broke out: "The moans of pain became screams of panic" as the trapped workers were burned alive. One hundred and sixteen people were seriously injured and eighty-eight perished.[50]

In this case the management was trying to do right but was simply uninformed or careless about engineering. Too frequently, the evidence is that management was deliberately callous in regard to safety. The unquestioned discipline of the era led to the policy of locking factory doors to prevent unnoticed late arrivals or the possibility that someone might slip out for a break. A Providence paper reported in 1866:

When the fire occurred, there were about two hundred operatives in the mill. From what we could learn last night, it appears that the doors were locked and the lower windows nailed down. As a consequence, a terrible panic prevailed among the operatives, very many of whom were females, and as the watchman refused to open the doors, they leaped from the second and third story windows to save themselves from death by flame or suffocation.[51]

In 1911 some factory doors were still being locked, and the resulting Triangle Fire was burned into the memories of immigrants who lived in Lower Manhattan. Triangle was a dress manufacturing company known for its shabby treatment of workers: They "always tried to get in newly arrived immigrants . . . who lived at the mercy of the bosses."[52] In the great garment strike of 1909, Triangle had been adamant in its refusal to improve conditions, and by 1911 the activists had left or been fired. Those remaining were mostly Italians and Jews willing to work in a nonunion shop.

It was late on a Saturday afternoon and the rest of the building was empty. Only the Triangle factory on the top floors worked on. Evidently one of the few male employees dropped a cigarette match into waste cloth near oil cans. The flammable fabric and sewing machine oil spread the fire quickly. Those who were not lucky enough to get to the elevators while they still functioned crowded about the windows, but the fire department's ladders stopped two stories short: "Five girls who stood together at a window close to the Green Street corner held their places while a fire ladder was worked toward them, but which stopped at its full length two stories lower down. They leaped together, clinging to each other, with fire streaming back from their hair and dresses."[53]

Survivors testified that many women had not jumped but were pushed out the windows by those behind them, the fire at their backs. After the first girl jumped and broke her body "into a thousand pieces," the crowd yelled, "Don't jump! but it was jump or be burned—the proof of which is found in the fact that fifty burned bodies were taken from the ninth floor alone. They jumped, they crashed through broken glass, they crushed themselves to death on the sidewalk . . . A heap of corpses lay on the sidewalk."[54]

Immediately after the fire, one of the owners rushed to deny that the doors were locked even before the charge was made. Labor leaders knew that Triangle's newly arrived immigrants would not be brave enough to challenge the owners publicly, so they published a list of persons to whom information could be secretly given. The next day, the district attorney had sufficient facts turned over to him to "show that doors . . . had been kept locked."[55] Moreover, two doors were intact after the fire, and they were locked: over fifty bodies were found piled behind them.

But the fire was in March, and by December, when the trial of owners Harris and Blanck was held, public outrage had dimmed. At one point the jury was evenly divided, but after two hours it issued an acquittal. The all-male jurors apparently agreed with one who said, "I think that the girls, who undoubtedly have not as much intelligence as others might have in other walks of life, were inclined to fly into a panic."[56]

Thus the deaths of 146 people went unavenged. "Most of them," reported the *Times*, "could barely speak English . . . Almost all were the main support of their hard-working families."[57] Many had emigrated alone and had no family here. While some mourners searched the morgue in a vain attempt to determine which of over fifty unrecognizably charred bodies was their loved one, other bodies went unclaimed. Quite probably their families were in Europe and long would be unaware of the calamity that had befallen their daughters.

The immigrant ghetto did not forget. The 25th of March was memorialized by garment workers. Within a few days of the fire, a factory safety committee received over a thousand reports of dangerous conditions similar to those at Triangle. By drawing attention to these abuses, the deaths were not in vain. Eventually safety standards were upgraded and laws enforced—though just days after the tragedy, Harris and Blanck shamelessly ran an advertisement for their new location. For them it was business as usual.

Unions, Strikes, and Solidarity

"I knew nothing about trade unions or strikes," said Rose Schneiderman as a $6 weekly cap maker, "and like other young people, I was likely to look upon strike-breakers as heroic figures because they wanted to work and were willing to risk everything for it."[58] But decades later, Rose Schneiderman would be a nationally known labor leader. Like thousands of the individualistic women who emigrated alone, she would see that the working conditions in America were not what she had envisioned and would come to understand that in union there is strength.

Not all immigrants were newcomers to unionism. British women especially were accustomed to working-class consciousness, and in 1859, German female shoemakers organized a union and affiliated themselves with the New York City General Labor Union.[59] The Bohemian female cigar makers were early unionists, much in advance of the Americans who broke their 1877 strike and the male-run unions that refused cooperation.[60] Later, most of the Jewish newcomers brought with them a leftist philosophy that included support of unions.

The immigrant was caught in the middle on the subject of labor disputes. If she did not strike, she was accused of lowering American wage standards. If she did, there were others ready to accuse her of being a foreign radical, an agitating Communist. The views of the women themselves were sometimes equally inconsistent; they held the same ambivalence on this that they had in many other areas.

Even those who had thought things through to the point of joining a union had periods of ambivalence when jobs were hard to get and a worker had to disavow her views. When one middle-aged woman cited her years of experience in a job interview, the employer immediately pounced on her: "You belong to the union, don't you?"

She admitted that she did but hurried to add, "That makes no difference. I'm perfectly willing to work with non-union girls."[61]

Cornelia Parker asked a co-worker if she had ever worked in a union shop and if it was any different, and the woman replied: "Different? You bet it's different. Boss wouldn't dare treat you the way you get treated here . . . They sure treat you like dogs here!" Despite the woman's vociferousness, Parker added, "The papers were full of a strike to be called next week throughout the city . . . It might as well have been in London. Not an echo of interest in it reached our factory."[62]

A leader was essential, but an avowed union member often found herself without a job. When she did get one, she often was punished for her beliefs by being given the least profitable piece work. Even in a well-organized shop, being a labor leader called for personal sacrifice, for the union representative had to attend to the complaints of others at her own loss. Elizabeth Hasanovitz, an elected chairlady in her shop, had 200 workers whose grievances had to be looked after:

> A complaint now came from an ironer who did not receive the scale [minimum wage], now a girl came late and she was sent away, now a girl was discharged for spoiling something unintentionally. I, as shop representative, had to take up every grievance with the boss . . . All of that required a great deal of time, and I was too often distracted from my machine. In the busiest weeks, when the workers were making more money, I was kept busy straightening out difficulties for them.[63]

These shop leaders, though insignificant to the public, were the backbone of trade unions. They endured the hatred and ridicule of their bosses. Anna Klotin, for example, was employed by a garment factory that was one of a handful not settling with the union in the 1909 garment strike. Her factory offered twenty of the more skilled women union terms but refused to do anything for the majority of their employees. Anna was one of the select group, but she refused to separate from her fellow strikers. Her solidarity could be measured in dollars, for after that Anna earned only $6 and $8 weekly instead of her pre-strike $12.[64]

A half century earlier, Irish newcomers had shown solidarity when the Holyoke mills vaguely promised to bring their pay up to that of nearby towns sometime in the future. They found, "instead of the grateful reception anticipated, nearly one hundred Irish girls demanded at once a flat rate of $16 a month, walked out at noon, and were joined the next day by others."[65] As the Massachusetts Irish became more assimilated, however, their identification with the working class lessened. In the 1850s the Irish were united as workers, but by the 1882 strike, they were to be found on both sides, and when the violent 1912 strike occurred, the Irish generally supported the owners.

Sometimes newcomers showed initiative in organizing even without support from existing unions. Scandinavian women in Chicago's clothing industry in 1897 asked the United Garment Workers to help them organize, but they were given no response. They proceeded independently and set up an effective union. A ten-hour day and closed shops were obtained, as well as wage increases that for some were

80%. The Swedish women insisted on the inclusion of the ill-paid Italians in their union, and they "lived well, maintained good homes and aspired to general education and culture."[66]

Indeed, the apathy and opposition of male unions to the addition of females to their ranks was one of the chief causes of the low wages that women received. Repeatedly men engaged in futile efforts to keep women out of the trades. Instead of demanding equal pay for women and thus maintaining a high pay rate, they vainly attempted to keep women from working at all. Such action only encouraged employers to hire women, who would work more dependably for less money.

The men in Rose Cohen's tailor shop joined a union but neither invited the women nor informed them of their action. The women found out only by observing their strange behavior—they did not start work until seven, they quit promptly at noon and did not start again until one, and left on the dot of seven. "We girls," Rose said, "watched them go enviously." As their discontent increased, the women acted without the encouragement of the men. Rose went to a garment workers' meeting and organized the others. Since she was only about thirteen at the time, she had a right to take pride in her achievement. "Now," she wrote, "our shop was a 'strictly union shop.' I'll always remember how proud I felt when the first evening at seven o'clock the presser blew the whistle and I with the other girls stood up with the men."[67]

Throughout the era, men preferred to promote the myth that women could not be unionized rather than to accept them as equals, but there were many cases in which women proved their willingness to organize and strike. In Fall River cotton mills, where 97% of the employees were of foreign birth or foreign parentage, it was the women who provided the strike leadership: "In 1874 the men weavers had met without the women and voted to accept a marked reduction of wages; but the women at a meeting of their own . . . decided to strike."[68]

The greatest strike by women began in 1909 in New York's garment industry. Natalya Urosova typified these workers; she and the women in her shop were unsure what to do, but at last they arose in fear and trepidation and left the shop. Arriving on the street, they were shown immediately the serious consequences of their decision. Policemen lined the sidewalk, and one greeted them, "If you don't behave, you'll get this on your head," shaking his club threateningly. "We hardly knew," said Natalya, "where to go—what to do next. But one of the American girls, who knew how to telephone, called up the Women's Trade Union League."[69]

The strike lasted from November to February and involved 30,000 to 40,000 workers, the majority of them immigrant women, mainly Jewish. Thousands of these women had emigrated alone and had no family or savings to support them. The strike meant weeks of hunger for them. It could also mean violence and imprisonment. Police were more than ready to arrest women, something that was proven by cases of mistaken arrests of women who happened to be in the area. One upper-class woman appeared at the offices of the *New York Times* to show them her coat, which had been ripped by attacking police. "While I am not a striker myself," she said, "I am deeply interested in the girl workers of the East Side." She continued:

Between twenty and thirty special policemen . . . hurled themselves upon us and threw us off the sidewalk onto the pavement . . .They shoved, elbowed and even kicked . . . I narrowly missed having my skull fractured . . . They called me the most vile and insulting names, and finally dragged me . . . I believe I should have been badly injured if a crowd had not gathered and shamed the men.[70]

Similarly, Mary Drier, "a women of large independent means, socially well-known throughout New York," was arrested when "she entered into a quiet conversation with one of the strike breakers." She was taken to the police station, but "when the sergeant recognized her . . . , he at once discharged her case, reprimanded the officer, and assured Miss Drier that she would never have been arrested if they had known who she was."[71]

Thousands gathered at the home of Maria and Pietro Botto during the 1913 strike of silk mill workers in Paterson, New Jersey. The Bottos, who also were silk workers before emigrating from Italy, built their dream home in 1908; today it houses a labor museum. (AMERICAN LABOR MUSEUM, BOTTO HOUSE NATIONAL LANDMARK, HALEDON, NEW JERSEY)

Poor and foreign strikers found that they were not allowed to inform anyone of their peremptory arrests; Natalya and her friend were arrested, tried, and carried to the Tombs in one day. The food in that notorious jail "smelled so bad it made you sick," and they had only iron springs for sleeping. Worse, though, was the attitude of their fellow prisoners. Prostitutes ridiculed Natalya and told her how much better off she was as a prisoner in America than free in Russia.

This 1909 strike was unusual in that upper-class women went to the support of their needy sisters, for the Women's Trade Union League included both working and nonworking women. Led by socialites such as Alva Vanderbilt Belmont, support of the working class became—briefly—quite the thing to do. The strikers, however, felt considerable ambivalence about these eminent capitalist helpers. Some appreciated the assistance, but others resented going before the wealthy women in the role of beggars instead of independently making their own way as they were accustomed. In return for humbling themselves they received sums that, in comparison with the wealth of these ladies, were minuscule. Labor leaders were also annoyed by the injection of the suffrage issue into the strike, for while most unionists believed in political equality, suffrage added another controversial element that was extraneous to their issues.

Nonetheless, the money donated was more than the strikers could hope for elsewhere, and it made a vital difference. More important was the influence of the society women, for employers apparently decided that they could not battle both their employees and their customers. To the credit of all of these women, the strike was largely successful.

Three years later there was another and more violent strike of immigrant women, though this time more men were involved. The textile workers of Lawrence, Massachusetts, walked out when their pay was reduced. This strike was extraordinary in view of the motley nature of that town in 1912: "No less than forty-five tongues are spoken by employees of Lawrence mills."[72] An Italian woman, Annie LoPezzi, was killed in this strike, and her death became a cause célèbre as the town's officials—without any reasonable justification—tried to convict the strike leaders of responsibility.[73]

Women also proved their loyalty to the cause by sending 300 children to be cared for by New York socialists when hunger began to be a factor. The city government accused them of using their children as pawns, but by sending their children to stay with strangers, these immigrant mothers demonstrated how seriously they took the strike. A reporter for a national magazine testified:

> I saw with my own eyes, under the gray light that precedes dawn . . . , a little group of twenty-five women shivering in the cold . . . I saw them pull their shawls over their heads as they laughed and chatted in low tones . . . This was "picketing," which even when peaceful, is unlawful in the Commonwealth.
> I saw them stamp their feet because they were cold.
> I saw a detail of men come down the street clad in police uniforms, with badges

gleaming as they passed under the arc light . . . I heard horses' hoofs upon the pavement . . . A detachment of cavalry was coming . . .

I saw the patrolmen surround the twenty-five women who had huddled and flattened like hens as the shadow of the hawk falls. I heard the voices of men, but no answer from the frightened women . . .

I saw the women at the command of the policemen move forward. I heard a rough voice call upon God to damn them. I saw the night sticks driven hard against the women's ribs. I heard their low cries as they hurried away.

I saw one who passed me.

"Listen," she called to a friend. "I go home, I nurse the little one. I be back yet."[74]

In the great Homestead steel strike of 1892, women as well as men rushed to the barricades. Women were machine-gunned to death in the 1914 Ludlow strike in Colorado. During a 1913 strike in Michigan copper mines, women were the employers of violence instead of the victims. An aide to the state's governor complained:

Women continually resort to rock throwing . . . At Trimountain the soldiers were rotten egged and were assaulted by women with brooms, which brooms had been dipped with human excrement . . . It is a very difficult thing to deal with women who resort to these tactics, and who are physically nearly the equal of an average man. Many of them profess to be unable to understand our tongue, and of course are excitable and impulsive, as is somewhat characteristic of the entire sex.[75]

Some women organized and used violence outside the usual realm of unionism. Jewish women in the West End of Boston, angered over high meat prices, managed to close down the kosher butcher shops. "Any person carrying a parcel bearing the slightest resemblance to meat was set upon by mobs of women, the bundle taken away and its contents broadcast," reported a newspaper. Women were completely in charge of the boycott, presiding over the meetings and doing picket duty: "Women were beaten with clubs by the police and seven arrests were made."[76]

Not everyone, however, was brave. While union leadership and male co-workers had to accept some of the blame, ultimately the disorganized state of female workers had to be the responsibility of the women themselves. A sociologist studying artificial flower makers found that these women, who were mostly Italian, were apathetic: "An attempt on the part of the Jewish girls to organize a trade union . . . failed so signally that not [for] . . . several months did we find any girls who had ever heard of such an effort."[77] Similarly, a study of 370 working mothers found only 4 union members.[78]

But statistics on union membership may not tell the whole story. Often when there was a point to be gained, women rallied, supported the union, and walked the picket lines. When they achieved their aim—or, sometimes, decided it was futile—they disbanded. A few leaders kept together a skeleton organization to have a base for the next struggle. Thoughtful labor leaders accepted this as necessary, given the circumstances

A mass meeting after six months of a 1920 strike in Tampa's cigar factories. After this strike, machinery was introduced that largely ended the power of tobacco worker unions.

Note how these workers, who were mostly Spanish, Sicilian, and Cuban—including black Cubans—segregated themselves more by gender than by race. (UNIVERSITY OF SOUTH FLORIDA SPECIAL COLLECTIONS)

of women's lives. They understood how difficult it was for a union to hold together when "the entire personnel of any given industry changes every five years."[79]

Not everyone was brave, but many were, and some were extraordinarily so. On the whole, immigrant women understood better than their American sisters the need for workers to unite.

"Are You Happy?": Attitudes Toward Work

One Friday Cornelia Parker asked her co-workers in a dress factory, most of whom were immigrants, if they weren't glad the next day was Saturday and they had the afternoon off. To her surprise, most of them were not glad at all, because they had to go home and clean house: "Gee, don't you hate work 'round the house?" and "Ever try workin' at home? Ain't it just awful?"[80] Several sociologists reported that many women—although they worked primarily because of need—also were glad to have the opportunity to be something other than housewives.

Some felt that work outside the home improved their mental health. Mrs. Pagano, for example, stayed home all her life, but when her son was killed, she discovered the therapeutic effect of joining her husband at his produce business and insisted over his objections that she be allowed to work there. Widows interviewed in one extensive study several times expressed the opinion that working eased their grief and anxiety. Cases were not unheard of in which widows gave up charity aid in order to work, rather than stay home as the philanthropists dictated.[81]

Lithuanian Edna Vidravich Balkus typifies the work ethic of many, especially those who were childless. Reflecting on more than thirty years in the Lowell mills as a weaver, she hid the pride that she took in her work under the cover of societally acceptable fatalism: "I have to [work] because I don't get children. What I got to do at home? My husband bring 7, 6 dollars for pay . . . I make more pay than he make . . . I used to like to work."[82]

While visiting Boston in 1910, an English philosopher, Graham Wallas, determined to inquire whether working women "were happy." The answers surprised him:

> I expected to hear those complaints about bad wages, hard conditions, and arbitrary discipline, which a body of men . . . would certainly have put forward. But it was obvious that the question, "Are you happy?" meant to the girls, "Are you happier than you would have been if you had stayed home instead of going to work?" And almost everyone answered "Yes."[83]

Yet a careful analysis of the women's comments indicates that many were not genuinely happy at all but rather viewed their work as an escape mechanism that allowed them to ignore fundamental depression. Some Irish laundresses, for example, "answered emphatically yes" when asked if they were happy, but they then went on say such things as work "leaves me no time to think" and "work 'took up her mind.'"[84] Their view of their working lives was not simplistically "happy" but rather fatalistically stoical. Twenty years later, similar questions brought the same type of responses:

> "I must like, I make a living."
> "My business to like it."

"Sure, I have to like it."
"So much baby, if I no work, I no eat."[85]

Their attitudes were characterized by an acceptance of fate, and optimism, when it appeared, was carefully shadowed so that it did not appear as hubris. Most immigrant women indeed worked because they had to, but even if they—like Edna Balkus—actually enjoyed their working lives, they cast this in ambivalent tones; they knew that women were not supposed to view themselves as careerists with a right to pride in their craft.

Nor did they believe that earning was solely a male obligation. They had been reared under a system in which the family was an economic unit and all members had a part in earning for it. The thinking of Americans that women should be supported by their husbands was foreign to many of them. Some clearly said they wanted to pay their own way, as the Irish girl who said that working "made her feel she was worth something."[86]

The earliest immigrants to America, the Puritans, thought women and children should work, believing that idleness promoted the devil's work. It was only later, at about the time of the Irish influx, when Americans became wealthier, that women were elevated to a nonworking pedestal. Even then, most women did more work than the public acknowledged, but the platitude became that respectable ladies should be supported by men.

Enforced leisure, like enforced labor, is a kind of slavery that only a rich society can afford, but the immigrants came from quite another background. Their values were closer to those of the Puritans, and productive work was seen as good no matter who did it. At the same time Americans began to look down on work—especially work done by women—as something suitable only for blacks, foreigners, and occasional poor whites. The immigrants kept for a while a different value system, but in time they aped that of the Americans. Then a woman's work was not recognized as valuable but as a source of shame. Her husband began pressuring her to stop being productive when he saw that in American eyes, he was inadequate in "allowing" her to work. Women who "hated workin' round the house" would be bound to their homes, as soon as their families could afford that luxury.

15

FOREIGN DOMESTICS

An American Tradition:
The Immigrant Household Worker

Housework, of course, was the most traditional occupation. If an immigrant woman was not so fortunate as to be mistress of her own home, then her proper place was often seen as a worker in someone else's home. From the beginning to the end of the era, millions of women assumed this role.

There were genuine advantages to domestic work, not the least of which was its constant availability. While factory women wore out their soles searching for a job, household positions continually went vacant. The advice of an 1869 correspondent was valid throughout the era: "America is an excellent country for capable and moral servant girls . . . People are constantly looking for . . . servant girls; and as they are treated very well, especially in Yankee families, there is no one whom I can so safely advise to emigrate."[1]

Women willing to work as domestics could find jobs even when men could not. Wisconsin in the 1850s was still inhabited by Indians, yet a Norwegian pastor asserted that those most likely to find work were servant women. An 1841 writer speaking of widespread unemployment added that this "applies to men. Women, especially young girls, will be able to do relatively better."[2] In the Far West, opportunities were always plentiful; when domestics in the East earned $9 or $10 a month, the West offered $20 to $25.[3]

A multitude of women took this advice. Though "the government excluded servants from its official definition of working women," one study reported in 1880 that 45% of the women in this work had foreign origins;* the Irish accounted for 39% of these, with Germans and Scandinavians following at 22% and 13%.[4] In some places, however, the numbers were much higher: an 1895 Boston study showed that 80% of that city's servants were foreign born.[5] In Chicago at the turn of the century, there were "many" employment agencies "entirely for foreign women," while New York City had "169 agencies run for the purpose of distributing immigrant house-workers, chiefly women."[6] And while it may be that they lacked the knowledge for any other response, a remarkable 84% of women entering the port of New York in 1905 gave domestic service as their intended occupation.[7]

The demand for domestics continued to exceed the supply. In the era between the Civil War and World War I, every aspiringly affluent household had at least one maid. Men did not feel that they could marry unless they could afford to provide their brides with this surrogate housekeeper, for the Victorian lady could not keep her social position in the community if she did her own housework. Indeed, it was not unusual for a newly married couple to live in a hotel rather than set up housekeeping without a maid.

The Irish filled this need from the 1840s on. Practically every middle-class home in the Northeast had its "Bridget," and one study reported that as late as 1920, the Irish accounted for 43% of all domestic servants.[8] The willingness of young Irish women to accept the most menial labor to help their families was lauded by many:

> The great ambition of the Irish girl is to send "something" to her people as soon as possible after she has landed in America . . . She will . . . risk the danger of insufficient clothing, or boots not proof against the rain or snow, rather than diminish the amount of the little hoard . . . To keep her place . . . , what will she not endure:— sneers at her nationality, mockery of her peculiarities, even ridicule of her faith . . . In populous cities the women send home more money than the men.[9]

Indeed, as this 1868 writer indicates, "ridicule" and other prejudice against Irish servants was real in the early era. Advertisements appeared such as: "None need apply without recommendation from their last place. IRISH PEOPLE need not apply" or "Woman wanted—To do general housework . . . English, Scotch, Welsh or German, or any country or color except Irish."[10] As late as 1870, Her Majesty's vice-consul in New York wrote, "Women household servants are always in demand, but in this, as in most cases, preference is given to all other nationalities before the Irish."[11]

Prejudice against the Irish was based in part on their religion. Some mistresses harbored hysterical fears that nursemaids would secretly baptize children into the

---

* The remaining 55% were almost equally divided between native whites and blacks. These women were more likely to live in smaller towns, in cities without ports, and in the South.

Women at an employment agency for domestic servants. Among the job categories legible on the wall signs are "Children's Nurses," "Scrubbers," "Chambermaids," and "Waitresses." The last probably did not mean waitresses in restaurants but rather women who worked between the kitchen and the dining room of an opulent home.

Note the two women at the center; the one with the hat and muff is doubtless an employer, while the woman wearing a shawl is the potential servant. (LIBRARY OF CONGRESS, FROM A WOOD ENGRAVING IN *FRANK LESLIE'S ILLUSTRATED NEWSPAPER*, MARCH 5, 1870.)

Catholic faith and that maids acted as spies for the Jesuits. Other negativism was based on Irish inexperience with American housework. One household advice writer tried to break through the bias:

> Do mop and broom in her hands do their task slightingly? . . . If you reflect that her floors at home were earthen ones, you will think it remarkable that she has learned to use such implements with half the skill she does . . . Does she nick the edges of your cut glass, and break more than the value of her wages? Perhaps if you yourself had done no more dainty work all your life that the farm-work of the fields . . . then china would slip through your fingers, too.[12]

To a large extent, Irish dominance of the field was by default—they got the jobs because few others would take them. Jewish and Italian females avoided domestic service almost entirely. What few Jews did do this work accepted employment only in Jewish homes, for to enter nonkosher kitchens was anathema to them. One historian of New York City reports that in his census searches, he found "no recognizably Jewish names among immigrant servants living in what seemed to be Christian homes."[13] Italian women avoided it because their cultural mores did not allow females to live outside the family circle. Married Italian women might sometimes do "day's work" as general houseworkers, but for an unmarried Italian woman to "live in," as most domestics did, was unacceptable.

FOREIGN-BORN WOMEN EMPLOYED AS SERVANTS BY NATIONALITY, 1900[14]

Ireland	132,662	Poland	6,292
Germany	58,716	Hungary	5,837
Sweden	35,075	Russia	4,850
England/Wales	13,620	Denmark	3,970
Norway	10,440	Italy	1,840
Austria	7,866		

The small island of Ireland provided almost 100 times as many workers for American households as the lowest-ranked Italians—and the Irish were not only English-speakers but also had been migrating in large numbers for six decades. Because getting inside an American home was one of the fastest ways to learn about the country, it is not surprising that there was a correlation between rapid acculturation and those groups in which women adopted this work. The Irish, German, and Scandinavians, whose women were often domestics, were quickly assimilated into the mainstream of American life, while those whose women did not go into domestic service—Italians and Jews—remained outside much longer.

Learning and Saving: The Job's Advantages

It was easy to pick up the language and the culture by working in an American home; a woman then married, taught her husband and children what she had learned, and ran her household according to the American example. A 1905 study reported that domestic workers learned English faster than either housewives or women employed in jobs outside the home.[15] Undoubtedly the nature of the work forced one to use a larger vocabulary than was required in factory labor, and some immigrants deliberately looked for this work for that reason. Writing in Russian, Marya Bazanoff complained to the Immigrants Protective League in 1914 about her job, "I could not stay there because I would never learn English . . . I would like to work for *American* people."[16]

Kyra Goritzina also testified to the language value of the work. An exiled Russian aristocrat, she did not know much about recipes in any language when she first began working as a cook in Park Avenue homes and certainly knew little about American foods and methods. "I had to bring down my English-Russian dictionary," she said, "and translate the whole recipe word for word, put it down in my notebook and then figure out the right way to follow it. For many months the dictionary was my inseparable and inestimable companion."[17]

Just as important as learning the language was acquiring skills. The diary of midwestern Kjersti Raaen shows her gratitude for this experience:

> It is a big house full of beautiful things. When I told Mor about the rugs and carpets on the floor she wouldn't believe me. The food is all different, too. I didn't think I could learn so many new things, but Mrs. Hoyt worked right with me the first three weeks. Yesterday I made a cake; it did not turn out right. When Mrs. Hoyt saw that I felt unhappy about it, she said, "You are clean, orderly and careful, and that is worth much more than being able to make cake." . . . I get two dollars a week; as soon as I can do everything alone she will pay me two dollars and a half . . . I wonder if I have done enough work for all this money![18]

During trips home, Kjersti made the first American-style pie and cookies her family tasted. She also bought a used coat from her employer, giving her mother a replacement for the plaid shawl she had worn all of her adult life. Kjersti's sister Aagot worked for an attorney's wife and there learned to make the first Christmas presents that these siblings, the children of an alcoholic father, ever received.

In addition to learning language and skills, the work could be broadening in other ways. Barbro Ramseth, for instance, wrote that her daughter Karen went to Chicago in 1888 to work for a "rich" Norwegian family who lived "completely like Americans . . . The cook is Irish and is Catholic . . . Karen says she makes the sign of the Cross in the evening when she goes to bed, and asks if Karen wants to do it too. But she is very kind and speaks only English."[19]

Women who had done domestic work on both sides of the ocean were unanimous in saying that it was vastly preferable in America. To the European mind, servants were only slightly above the level of serfs, and some masters exercised virtually complete control over their lives. Rosa Cavalleri's boyfriend, for example, who was employed by an Italian count, found it necessary to flee to France when he accidently broke some china. Because she held this view of service, Rosa was frightened when she knocked over a lamp while cleaning it:

> When I saw that beautiful pink glass lamp shade in a million pieces on the floor I fell over in a faint. I thought I would be put in jail! I thought I would be killed! Miss May and one other . . . they came running in to see what had happened. When they saw me there on the floor without my senses they woke me up and carried me into the kitchen and made me drink hot tea with sugar in it. "Rosa, Rosa," they said. "Where are you hurt? Where did it hit you?" And when they learned that I had only fainted from scare because I had broken the pink glass lamp they started to laugh . . . How can I *not* love America! In the old country I would have been killed for breaking a lamp like that![20]

A German girl who came to New York as a domestic thought her $14 monthly earnings a fantastic fortune, for in Berlin she had received $8.25 a *year*.[21] The reputation of America as an Eden for servants was early established, as letters reached Europe such as this one written in 1853 by pastor's wife Emilie Koenig:

> The servant girls in the church presented us with a beautiful rug ... You are probably wondering about such an expensive gift from servant girls. They really have it very good here in America. They earn very much money . . . and are treated almost like daughters in the house . . . They arrange the work the way they wish it, and they are never asked to do anything that the housewife herself thinks is beneath her ... They are dressed like the grandest ladies when they come to church.[22]

Indeed, servants in America expected and received democratic treatment. These expectations fundamentally changed women, giving them self-esteem and assertive ways of thought, in addition to their new knowledge of domestic arts. One student of immigration, speaking of people who returned to their native land, said:

> Most blessed are the girls who have been in service in American families. They have learned English well, and also the ways of the American household. They have tasted of the spirit of Democracy which permeates our serving class, and when such a one returns to her native village she unsettles the relations of servant and mistress. Therefore, her coming is dreaded by the "Housefrau" who has had one servant-girl through the years, paying her fifteen dollars a year and treating her like a beast. Shall I quote one of those mistresses? "What kind of country is that anyway, that America? These servant girls come back with gold teeth in their mouths, and with long dresses which sweep the streets, and with unbearable manners."[23]

Besides dependable employment and generally considerate treatment, another important advantage in domestic work was the opportunity to save. Since her room, board, and often clothing—sometimes uniforms and sometimes tailor-quality discards—came with the job, many women saved virtually all of their earnings. To immigrants who wanted to pay passages and fulfill family obligations, this was a tremendously important reason for choosing domestic work. Others were motivated by the fact that a home came with the job. The experiences of many are reflected in these statements from women who preferred domestic work:

> "I can make more. I have put $100 in the savings bank in a year and a half."
> "I came to a strange city and chose housework because it afforded me a home."
> "When I came . . . and saw the looks of the girls in the large stores and the familiarity of the young men, I preferred to go into a respectable family where I could have a home."
> "You can have better cooked food and a better room than most shopgirls."[24]

Life in a large, wealthy household could be idyllic in comparison with factory routine. Agnes was a German girl who had considerable ability as a milliner and dressmaker, but she resented the long hours required in that work. She decided to care for children: "These people had a fine place down on Long Island to which we all went in the summer, and there I had to ramble around with the children, boating, bathing, crabbing, fishing and playing all their games. It was good fun, and I grew healthy and strong."[25]

Similarly, Bridget Fitzgerald, who came from Ireland in 1921, found a job as a "useful girl" on a large estate where fifty people worked for one wealthy woman: "I had my own bedroom . . . a bathroom to each two girls. They'd give you a clean uniform every day . . . There were three cooks for the servants. The food was out of this world . . . There was a chauffeur to drive you to church if you wanted."[26]

Many domestics, in fact, worked in households where there were other servants and thus had the companionship of peers. A survey sent to alumnae of women's colleges and to members of "various women's clubs" found that one family in seven had as many or more servants as there were members of the family, "while in the average family one servant renders service to every two persons."[27] Although this sample had an upper-class bias, the work was not necessarily socially isolated. No factory worker, for example, could claim to have more fun than the German Agnes. She had an abundance of friends with whom she went to the beach, dances, or other amusements on her days off. Moreover, she could spend her money on recreation without worry, for food, clothing, and housing all came with her job.

It was these sorts of jobs that social workers and home economists had in mind when they consistently recommended domestic work to immigrant women. Most saw domestic work as ideal because of the preparation it gave young women for marriage. This attitude repeatedly appears: marriage was the chief goal and/or inevitable destiny of women, and so their premarital occupation should be designed to groom them for their "real job." Yet the evidence is that it was debatable whether or not domestic employment accomplished this purpose. One sociologist confessed that the facts did not coincide with the theory:

> To my surprise also I found that in some instances domestic service was . . . no . . . satisfactory preparation for housekeeping. I remember a kitchen where all was wretched, the children unwashed, the woman untidy, the room unswept. Though the man earned $3.20 a day, his wife, trained as a servant in a wealthy home, had learned extravagant ways, and realized helplessly that she could not "get caught up."[28]

A second writer, on the other hand, asserted that in "some families [where] the woman was a servant before her marriage, . . . the care these women take of their children's diet and health presents a striking illustration of the superiority of domestic service over factory training for developing intelligent homemakers."[29] It was, not surprisingly, this attitude that most Americans chose to adopt.

To immigrant women, however, arguments on domestic work as preparation for marriage were academic. Far more important to them was the excellent opportunity to save money that service afforded. Indeed: an extensive comparison between domestics and teachers in the 1880s showed that the servants could expect greater net worth. Bank clerks in small cities where the occupation of customers was generally known also bore out this impression. In one town of about 2,000 factory employees, a domestic had the biggest savings account among the women workers.[30]

In contrast to industrial workers, foreign-born domestics were better paid than natives. "This was found to be true in every class of occupations [cooks, parlor maids, chambermaids, etc.] in every geographic section, in the case of both men and women, and in the returns made by both employer and employees."[31] There are various explanations for this, including the lowering of the native average by blacks and the concentration of foreigners in cities where wages were higher. Other employers found social status in their exotic Swedish cook or French-speaking governess. For whatever reason, it is clear that many employers genuinely appreciated their servants and made it evident in the paycheck.

Nor was the pay the only benefit. Familylike situations in which problems were shared and consideration was real were far more common than in industry. It was understood that the housewife would pay the doctor should her maid fall ill, while that never happened in industry. Women could find employment in this area that took account of profound personal needs; both Barbara Klinger and Berta Kingestad, for instance, found helpful employers who accepted their illegitimate children into the household.

The Down Side of Servitude

While conditions for servants were better in America, there were, of course, cases of mistreatment and unscrupulous practices. It was not uncommon for domestics to be accused of theft or damage to household goods as a justification for withholding wages. An expert on the legal problems of immigrants reported:

> Many cases are brought to the legal aid societies, giving evidence of a deliberate plan on the part of the employer to let wages accumulate in his hands, and finally refuse to pay. This often happens in the case of domestic servants. The Educational Alliance of New York in a recent report on their legal aid work, asks, "Have you any idea of the number of immigrant young women employed as servants, who, when their wages became due, are thrown out bodily?"[32]

Anzia Yezierska had such an experience; her first job was in the home of an Americanized Russian Jewish family. She began work without a definite arrangement in regard to wages and expected payment at the end of the month. "Before dawn I rose. I shined up the house like a jewel box. I prepared breakfast and waited with my heart in my mouth for my lady and gentleman to rise." Breakfast passed. Lunch passed. Finally she could stand it no longer and burst out an inquiry about her wages. "'Wages? Money?' The four eyes turned into hard stone . . . 'Haven't you a comfortable bed to sleep in and three good meals a day? . . . You should be glad we keep you here. It's like a vacation for you.'"[33] Anzia left, never to return to domestic service.

Other employers were so suspicious of their servants that the home front became an unspoken war. Mistresses counted silver and linens, snooped in maids' rooms, and whenever something was lost, servants were accused of theft. Once in a great while their fears were justified. Fredrika "Marm" Mandelbaum, a German in New York in the Civil War era, "was a well-known dealer in stolen goods" who used information from dishonest servants on where and when to burglarize. There were other "notorious" German female criminals in New York in that era, including "Black Lena" Kleinschmidt, a blackmailer who made a great deal of money that she lavishly displayed.[34] The striking thing, however, is that millions of domestic servants were in a perfect position to blackmail and steal but rarely did.

More common was the "honest graft" that sometimes developed with highly placed servants in complex households. Cooks who ordered household groceries were in an especially good position to cheat employers, both by padding accounts and by getting rebates from merchants. A former cook casually said without guilt that "one could make a lot on the side" and that her sister, presently cooking, "made over $100 a month, counting what she got off tradespeople."[35]

While some had great latitude in making household purchases, other servants—especially those in smaller homes—enjoyed no such liberality. Likewise, even though immigrants almost always agreed that servants were fed better in America than in Europe, there were occasional employers who ate well while the serving members of their household were malnourished. A woman who worked for a family of four reported that when chops were on the menu, "the lady of the house ordered just four, which meant she who cooked the chops got none."[36] Rose Cohen did heavy domestic work when still a growing girl of fourteen and was constantly hungry. Her employer "always doled out the food on my plate. It was usually the tail of the fish, the feet and the gizzard of the chicken, the bun to which some mishap had occurred. And she would look through the whole bowl of apples to find for me a spotted one. She rarely failed to remark at meals, "'What an enormous appetite you have!'"[37]

Sadly, many of the most insensitive employers seem to have been of the same foreign origin as their servants. Like Jewish Rose Cohen and Anzia Yezierska, Norwegian Berta Kingestad worked for other Norwegians who "counted the crumbs" her son ate before she found a caring employer—who did not share her ethnicity. Many of these miserly employers remembered their own famine days and thus found it easy to rationalize mistreatment of their servants, convincing themselves that the servant "ought to be grateful for the chance." By European standards they were guilty of no particular wrong, and in this area, of course, they were reluctant to adopt the American norm.

The evidence sometimes appears in their own records. Elisabeth Koren, for example, wrote without self-examination of losing maids to American households. Linka Preus, too, had heard about "the problem of household help" even before she left Norway: "Not infrequently does it happen, when the house-mother asks her maid to do something, that she will answer, 'Do it yourself' . . . When I mentioned that I was thinking of taking a maid with me, Fru Dietricksen advised very strongly against it . . . 'The maids pay no attention to contracts.'"[38]

Even the usually generous Jette Bruns complained of the servant whose fare she had paid to America—along with that of the woman's illegitimate child. "Our Jenne," she wrote in 1839, "remains incorrigible . . . Whether she perhaps has more than a just claim here in America or whether her hopes of marriage have contributed in recent times, at any rate she can scarcely spend one minute without violent attacks against the children, against the dogs, against the cows, the cats, the chickens, or inanimate objects." Things came to a head when Jette was sick with her third pregnancy and Jenne refused to carry out work orders. "Now," Jette wrote in exasperation, "we employ as much consideration as possible in order to get through the winter at least, and then toward Easter she can marry if she can, or she can do whatever else she wants to do."[39]

The difference that was crucial here—and which went unexplained to newly arrived employers—was that in rural American households such as Jette's, class distinctions between employer and employee were deliberately obscured. Instead of "maids," these workers were "hired girls." Often the daughters of friends, they sat with the family at meals and did not serve the table as European housewives expected. Good household help was in fact difficult to obtain, for the hundreds of women who were available for such work in cities simply did not exist in farm country. A mask therefore was pulled over the usual employer/employee relationship, and the "help" tended to believe that they worked as something of a favor to the employer. This was reinforced by arrangements that were more time than task oriented—a hired girl helped through the harvest season or during a pregnancy and did not view herself as permanently a domestic worker.[40]

Even though, for instance, Berta Kingestad needed her housekeeping job to support her son, she became extremely independent while working for an Illinois farmer. Not only did she organize the work the way that she chose, giving herself most afternoons off, she also freely used a horse and buggy to go to town, where she bought flower seeds and other discretionary items. She clearly understood how different her situation was from what it would have been elsewhere, and she encouraged others to emulate her and leave their harsh European employers. "I really feel sorry for her having to work in that ugly barn . . . in big wooden shoes and shovel manure," she wrote of a sister in Norway. "She doesn't need to do that kind of heavy work here." Worlds away from that kind of serfdom, she was so self-assured about her occupation that, in 1890, Berta Serina Kingestad even bought "a little package of calling cards."[41]

Academic Attempts to Professionalize Housework

The chief complaints about domestic service were its long hours, isolation, and social status. Their hours were, in fact, much longer than those of overworked factory employees. In a 1919 YWCA study that was designed to encourage more young women to go into domestic work, for example, the statistician carefully worked the numbers to put the best possible face on service—but even with subtractions such as "time off for meals," the weeks were unreasonably long. The fewest net hours were put in by laundresses, but even they averaged 57 hours a week. Cooks averaged 66 1/2, chambermaids 75 1/2, and child nurses 82 hours weekly![42]

General domestics were expected to rise in the dark to fix the family fires, heat water, and prepare breakfast, and their day did not end until the fire had been put out at night. Kyra Goritzina said of one of her first jobs that she and her butler husband "never had enough rest . . . Having no friends among domestic workers we did not know about the general rule of regular days off for servants, and evidently our employer was taking advantage of our inexperience."[43]

Of course, Kyra had herself been an employer in Russia, and doubtless was among the European mistresses who treated her servants "like beasts"—otherwise, she would have understood that servants needed days off. It was her changed experience in America that brought these new notions of worker rights, but she seems not to have realized this shift from her earlier aristocratic self.

She also enjoyed the comforting companionship of her husband, but most domestic workers were single. Indeed, the social isolation of the work, especially in small households and for a young woman, was a genuine problem. It was difficult for her to meet people of her own age and class, to say nothing of nationality. Young women who wished to marry correctly viewed domestic work as a trap into spinsterhood.

These objections to the work motivated many women to leave it permanently, especially after World War I opened up new job opportunities. In response, women's clubs and other groups did extensive studies that put forth a number of proposals for the professionalization of domestic workers. One group, for example, recommended these changes for "home assistants":

Home assistants should live away from the place of employment.

All remuneration should be on a full cash basis with return if lodging and meals are provided.

A 48-hour week or 8-hour day should be considered the standard . . .

The minimum age should be 18 years . . .

A minimum wage of $12 per week should be paid inexperienced workers . . .[44]

Such ideas remained academic, however. The optimistic plans of upper-class women remained mostly words on paper and were seldom translated into genuine change. The young women whom they wished to turn into home service careerists were simply not responsive to such plans for their lives. "Scores of Young Women's Christian Associations and other organizations stand ready to conduct training schools," wrote one social planner in 1915, "but there are no young women to enter. Turn this way or that in our study, we run up against the fact that girls will not enter household employment."[45]

In fact, the percentage of women in domestic service continued to decline, dropping from 41% of employed women in 1890 to 32% in 1910,[46] and it plummeted further after World War I. Historian Ida Tarbell saw the trend for what it was and warned:

> The housewives of this country are seeing the great body of girls and women on whom they have always depended . . . accept employment in thousands of different kinds of shops and factories . . . This shift . . . is not local and sporadic. It is general and permanent.
>
> There are, of course, reasons . . . Most housewives have traditional notions of the factory as something cruel, dark, distressing. They are appalled that any woman should prefer to go to these places.[47]

That women preferred to work outside the home did not fit with Victorian notions, but it was the reality that America in fact encouraged with its values of freedom and individuality. Of the complaints that women had about domestic service, the most frequently expressed was the reduction in social status that it implied. A servant in the eyes of many was not a person but an automaton, as one sociologist wrote:

> The domestic employee receives and gives no word of recognition on the street except in meeting those of her own class; she is seldom introduced to the guests of the house, whom she may faithfully serve during a prolonged visit; she speaks only when addressed, obeys without murmur orders which her judgment tells her are absurd, is not expected to smile under any circumstances, and . . . obeys implicitly the commands of children.[48]

Even outside her "place" she was viewed as something less than a complete person because of her occupation. A maid had to have a note from her employer, for example, to obtain library books in some towns while other women, employed or not, could freely obtain them.[49] The customs of domestic service were such that the worker was constantly, subtly reminded of her inferiority. In fact it was this comparison with other kinds of work and the greater respect given those workers that drove women from domestic occupations.

Sociologists who made comparisons of the two general classifications of employment found that most women preferred work in industry. A YWCA Commission on

Household Employment, for example, interviewed over 100 young domestics and a similar number of factory workers on the relative merits of their jobs. Even though the questionnaire was loaded to solicit favorable responses for domestic employment, the commission found that most refused to agree. They were forced to conclude:

> Domestic workers themselves are not enthusiastic about advising other young women to enter their occupation, the advantages of health, wages, preparation for the future, not counterbalancing the present disadvantages of long hours, lack of place to entertain, dearth of social life and recreation, no opportunity for self-direction and self-development.[50]

In the end, as Ida Tarbell wrote, "There never was a clearer demonstration that money has less influence" than personal liberty. It was, she said, "a question of self-respect, a question of freedom, a question of opportunity to advance."[51] While the newly arrived may have gladly opted for the money and security of domestic work, the longer a woman stayed in America, the less likely she was to wish to live her life this way.

For some the choice was clear. Rose Cohen had tried both and she reasoned:

> Though in the shop I had been driven, at least there I had not been alone. I had been a worker among other workers who looked upon me as an equal . . . I was at home with my own people . . . while as a servant my home was a few hard chairs and two soiled quilts. My every hour was sold, night and day. I felt that being constantly with people who looked down upon me as an inferior, I was, or soon would be an inferior.[52]

The goal of aspiring young women was to work their way out of the serving class and into what they thought of as the "real America." Kate Bond, an English-woman who praised the Philadelphia "master" who employed her and her husband in 1870, later moved to a Kansas farm. She acknowledged that they had "very poor crops" but added, "it was still better than working for another."[53] This mental transition was key to Americanization. In time, independence simply became more important than security.

It was part of the change from European fatalism to American optimism. The European woman and her forebears had the notion of "place" bred into their bones—where one was born was where one stayed. Though they were not as physically comfortable as their masters, many peasants found a certain mental comfort, a sense of safety and security, in "knowing their place." Those Europeans who questioned the wisdom of this attitude took their first risk with emigration. In America, they would slowly develop more questions, take more risks, and so evolve from fatalism into the New World creeds of progress and faith in the future.

Those who looked to European immigration for the establishment of a permanent serving class were bound to be disappointed. American households would train the green immigrant and she would reward them with her dutiful service for a time, but always she hoped for something better. Even the privileged native males who wrote editorials for the *New York Times* could not miss the point that these anonymous women quietly made, and they wrote after World War I:

> The refusal of the domestic servant to return to her pre-war job is, perhaps, another phase of the emancipation of women . . .
>
> Why should she go back? She has discovered that the unskilled worker . . . can go out into the general labor market and in a few weeks learn to do, and to do well, with interest and enthusiasm, things that it was thought only men could do . . .
>
> The truth is many have had a lurking hope that somewhere there existed a strange sect or a hopeless caste, that would be without ambition and perfectly content to wait on our domestic wants . . . But there are no such creatures in America, and if any were brought here they would not remain in that condition. The American atmosphere does not foster them.
>
> We have come to the parting of the ways, and we must both reconstruct the job and reconstruct the home.[54]

16

HOMES ON THE RANGE

Frontier Fear: From Prairie Fire to Fatal Freeze

It must have seemed to the women who settled the Midwest that nature's behavior there expressed God's displeasure that they had left their homes. Never in Europe was there anything comparable to the power of midwestern thunderstorms; the capriciousness of locusts descending from heaven; the mysteriously started prairie fires that looked as if they had been sent from hell to destroy this fragile civilization. Gro Svendsen wrote of the enigmatic landscape:

> The thunderstorms are so violent that one might think it was the end of the world. The whole sky is aflame with lightening . . . Then there is the prairie fire . . . This is terrifying . . . It is a strange and terrible sight to see all the fields a sea of fire . . . No one dares to travel without carrying matches so that if there is a fire he can fight it by building another and in this way save his life.[1]

"Almost every evening there is a fire," wrote Elisabeth Koren in 1854. Like others, she watched the horizon and worried. Though they never fully comprehended how the grass seemingly set itself ablaze, settlers learned to cope. "One of the first things a farmer did," Swiss Elise Isely said of Kansas in the 1870s, "was to plow a fire guard." But when these safeguards failed, it was a woman's duty to meet unhesitatingly the enemies that appeared so suddenly. Norwegian Mrs. Brandt was alone one day in her North Dakota home when she noticed a fire advancing on their newly planted grove. "I immediately ran out," she said, "to see what I could do to save the trees. Slipping off my petticoat, I set to work to beat out the flames. A passer-by stopped to help me, and between us we saved the trees."[2]

Even stranger than these inexplicable fires were the swarms of locusts that came from nowhere. After having escaped frost and flood in spring, drought and disease in summer, people anticipating reward for their labor found in a moment their crops vanished. Elise Isely was chatting with a friend when:

> Suddenly to the west we saw what seemed to be a glistening white cloud . . . only it came faster than a thunderhead. Taking short leave of Mrs. Hatfield, I hurried for my own home, three quarters of a mile away. Soon I realized that I could not reach home before the storm struck, and I was worried about my baby whom I was carrying in my arms. Racing toward me, the cloud obscured the sun . . . I had not quite reached home when it suddenly descended to the earth . . . It fell about me . . . not a storm, but a plague such as ravaged Mosaic Egypt . . . millions of grasshoppers lit all around . . . In a few hours our prospects for a bountiful crop were gone . . . Trees stood under the August sun as naked as in the winter.[3]

Gro Svendsen wrote of year after year when she and her neighbors fought locusts with fire, hoping that miles of flame would destroy the eggs. Their method was not successful: "Last year," she wrote sadly, "the pests left enough so that we had our maintenance and seed for the following year. But this summer they consumed everything except a little corn and the potatoes. This was a hard blow for a family as large as ours."[4] Her future looked "hopelessly dark."

Despite plague and fire, European immigrants poured to the prairies. Abeline Pederson symbolizes them: in 1872, she left Nordfjordeid, Norway, with her husband, two children—and seed potatoes. They lugged this precious, heavy cargo down from the mountains of Norway, across the ocean, through North America, and then they planted it on virgin soil, where they also demonstrated their sophistication by taking advantage of a government tree claim.[5] Like her, millions of immigrant women settled, civilized, and contributed very directly to the growth of a nation.

Especially in the upper Midwest, they did this in very large numbers. In a 1984 list of Minnesota farms that have been in the same family for more than a century,[*] for instance, English names are a distinct minority. By far the majority of families were German or Scandinavian, with others—such as Wiskow and Huncha—reflecting origins that are farther east or south in Europe.[6] Though the ethnic groups are different from those on the coast—with few Jews, Italians, or Irish—the farming Midwest was a melting pot every bit as much as the urban Northeast. Indeed, it is an irony too seldom acknowledged that these immigrants, who lived on farms apart from each

---

[*] The oldest of these farms was homesteaded in 1857; in 1984, it belonged to "Miss Merle Standacher." More than 10% of the modern farms were owned by a woman alone.

other, assimilated faster than city groups who lived and worked in much closer proximity.

To some extent, this was because these immigrants came to stay, while many of the Mediterranean cultures on the East Coast had at least some expectation of returning to Europe. Moreover, the farming immigrants of the Midwest also showed a greater commitment to their land than did most Americans settlers. As an insightful 1898 writer observed, the "chief ambition" of many Yankees who moved west with the frontier "was to get and hold land and boom their locality till a million immigrants pushed them into opulence. They had to farm some to live, . . . but farming was only a time server and was not pushed very much."[7]

At the same time, much of the frontier remained lonely and isolated far into the immigrant era. Chippewa County, Minnesota, for instance, with its western boundary on the Minnesota River, was fine farmland, but growth was nevertheless slow. In 1880, four of its sixteen townships still had no reportable population, and the county's residents did not top 10,000 until 1895.[8] Likewise, the Michigan area where a Dutch family settled after World War I seemed more like 1718 than 1918. The remoteness worsened their suffering from the worldwide flu epidemic that year, as this Dutch woman remembered:

> My father, mother and myself had just arrived in America from the Netherlands, with little money.
>
> My father had to find work immediately, as well as a place for us to live. An acquaintance told him [of] . . . an old log cabin with a lean-to kitchen.
>
> . . . Wind blew through cracks between logs and around the windows. Mother stuffed rags in all the places where snowy winter winds came in . . .
>
> There was no doctor nearby. Even if there had been, we were snowed in . . . After weeks and weeks of illness, weakness and coughing, we miraculously recovered. We fared much better than others. One family in the little country church we attended lost five of their nine children.[9]

Winter in interior America was as awesomely threatening as the prairie fires of summer. Many immigrants from northern Europe expressed surprise at the depth of freezing cold on the prairies, for the lack of surrounding seas made summer hotter and winter colder than at home. Swedish Ida Lindgren wrote from Kansas in 1871, "It was so cold, so cold the week before Christmas that we never felt the like of it in Sweden . . . We sat around the fireplace, and still . . . Ida and Anna had frost on both their faces and hands."[10]

Elise Waerenskjold recorded sadly the damage done by unpredictable weather: "In the evening it was still so warm that it was uncomfortable to use a blanket; in the morning, cabbage, wheat, turnips, fruit trees and the like were frozen."[11] Such a capricious climate could mean the loss not only of crops but also of life. With no forecasts to guide them, unaware travelers were caught by blizzards. The husband of one Scandinavian woman had gone to town in the morning:

Two sod houses on the treeless prairie of southwest Minnesota offer interesting contrasts. The "half-timber" has a more conventional, but also more expensive and more dangerous, roof; the soil banked along its walls was for extra insulation from the cold. The roof of the other house is grass, in a more European style; note the thickness of its walls at the window. This photo is also unusual in having a woman at the forefront.   (PIPESTONE COUNTY [MINNESOTA] HISTORICAL SOCIETY)

In the afternoon the blizzard struck. Hours passed and no husband appeared. Finally Mrs. Jacobsen acted on a sudden impulse. Grabbing the dishpan and a mallet she went outside and banged away with all her might. The husband who had just passed the house and was headed for an unsettled stretch south of his home, heard the noise of the dishpan, turned his horse back and steered for the sound. He was saved. "It was God's finger," said Ole Jacobsen, "that moved my wife to act as she did that night."[12]

Mrs. Brandt one pleasant winter afternoon was watering the livestock with her husband. "When we finished and started up the incline toward the house we were suddenly met by . . . a wall of snow and wind. It almost carried us off our feet." Grandfather Brandt, unfortunately, had gone to the post office just earlier. Anxious about his safety, her husband determined that he must take his compass and go search. "It was a long night," she wrote. "I busied myself as much as possible. About midnight I had a nervous chill and began to tremble all over. But I took myself to task and told myself, 'We must do what is right, and leave the rest to the Lord.'"[13] Her husband had in fact made it safely to the store, as had the grandfather, and they and other men spent the night there, while their wives fearfully waited at home.

Maria Nilson, who came with her husband and four children from Dalsland, Sweden, in 1869 was not so fortunate. Her teenage son had gone to cut wood near a creek a few miles away (a necessity on treeless prairies) when a sudden, severe snowstorm developed. After the weather settled down, their native friends confidently helped the Swedes search, saying, "Indians find white man."[14] Despite their skills, however, the search was unsuccessful, and Axel Nilson's body was not recovered until nearly spring.

The emotional turmoil of such tragedies drove some to madness and suicide. Even lesser difficulties took their toll on personalities trying to adjust to so many new and sometimes vexing changes. Especially those who were accustomed to cultured European homes found the rudeness of frontier life trying, and they could not suppress all of their anxieties and revulsion at its untamed aspects. Iowa's Elisabeth Koren, for instance, wrote in disgust: "This is really too much! . . . A snake in the house!"[15]

Another Norwegian woman who had lived there longer "laughed heartily at our fright," for she saw grass snakes as "almost domestic animals."[16] But some snakes were not laughable; Elise Isely wrote that breaking prairie sod "really was dangerous because of rattlesnakes. Every acre held two or three nests of them and it angered them to be disturbed in the home which they and their kind had occupied since the Ice Age." Sympathetic though she was to the rattler's loss of a home, she agreed that, because their bite was "deadly poison," they had to be killed. "Their very combativeness undid them; for every time a pioneer plowed up a rattlesnake, he killed it."[17]

Nor were snakes the only wild things on the frontier. Elise Waerenskjold wrote from Texas:

To be sure, quite a few beasts of prey are found here, for there are panthers (a kind of tiger, the size of a dog but shaped like a cat), bears, wolves, foxes, oppossums, skunks, several kinds of snakes, and alligators in the lakes and rivers. But there is enough food for all these animals so they do not need to attack human beings . . . On my travels I myself usually sleep out . . . I have felt no more fear out in the woods or on the prairie, though at times a couple of days' journey from people, than I did at home in Norway behind well-locked doors.[18]

Native, Newcomer, and War

It was not terribly unusual for women to be alone when storm and fire struck, for frontier women spent a good deal of time by themselves while men cut wood or sawed ice or marketed cattle or did any number of other things. Sisters-in-law Frances and Barbara Pazdernik experienced months of frontier aloneness after emigrating from Pribram in Czechoslovakia in 1875: their husbands, who were brothers, found work on a boat going to Canada, and the women stayed on their homesteads, which were not particularly close together.

During this time, they said, "Indians were frequently seen along the river and would stop for food. A special opening was built high into the wall so that food could be passed out without opening the door."[19] The men continued to be away from the farm in winter for years, especially after Frances Pazdernik's house burned to the ground in 1881. To get cash to rebuild, her husband went to North Dakota, and once again, she ran the farm alone—without a farmhouse and while tending to six young children.

The precaution of giving food to natives from behind locked doors was sensible, for by the time the Pazderniks settled, the Midwest had seen major warfare in this clash of cultures. Earlier settlers were similarly wary, but a number of immigrant women found the natives less fearsome than they had been led to believe in Europe. Jette Bruns had been in Missouri less than a year when she wrote with more curiosity than fear, "Twice already Indians have been nearby. At first there was a group in Lisletown, where a Mr. Williams speaks their language . . . A little while ago again forty Indians with wives and children appeared in the Swedes' store on the Osage."[20]

Mrs. Assur Groth was similarly unafraid of the natives of her Iowa area, saying they "were friendly and did us no harm." Her family gave bread to nomadic bands, "which made them glad and thankful."[21] Similarly, Cornelia Slag Schaddelee, a Dutch woman who arrived in Michigan in 1847, recalled that "the Indians came nearly every day to buy something. They were . . . very honest . . . good-hearted people, and never molested any of us."[22]

But friendliness on both sides waned as whites insisted on plowing the prairie grass. Plains Indians were hunters, while Europeans and Americans were farmers; the two economies could not coexist, and war became inevitable. To most immigrant women, a hostile Indian was akin to a rattlesnake: both represented deadly poison and had to be eradicated. Gro Svendsen, for instance, who was so sentimental that she wept for dead birds, had not a mite of compassion for these humans. When the Sioux in 1862 tried to retake the homelands they had occupied for eons in southern Minnesota, Gro wrote from the relative safety of her Iowa home: "It isn't enough merely to subdue them. I think that not a single one who took part in the revolt should be permitted to live."[23]

Gro's fears were multiplied by the fact that this uprising took place during the Civil War, and her husband was one of those conscripted to fight. From the Native American point of view, of course, it was only reasonable to take advantage of the fact that troops were gone to attack this heart of immigrant settlement. But Gro, naturally, felt wildly angry and betrayed—she had came from peaceful Scandinavia to find herself with war on all sides. Her Ole and other immigrant men who wanted to be farmers, not soldiers, were faced with a draft in this nation that had earlier proclaimed its abhorrence of conscription and preached individual liberty. They were expected to fight in a war between Americans, while they still felt themselves to be foreigners.

Women were left alone to worry about husbands in battle; to try to care for the family and run a farm; to manage at the same time to defend themselves and their property from attacking warriors. To more than one writer it was an incredible irony that men should be taken to fight in one war, while their families were left unprotected in another. Worse, this sort of warfare was absolutely chilling to the hearts of German and Scandinavian settlers, as one wrote in the summer of 1862:

> They have already killed a great many people, and many are mutilated in the cruelest manner . . . Children . . . are usually burned alive or hanged in the trees . . . I believe that even if I described the horror in the strongest possible language, my description would fall short of reality . . . Every day larger numbers of settlers come into St. Peter to protect their lives . . . A few persons arrive almost naked, others wounded by bullets or other weapons, and some with their hands and feet burned off . . . I will relate one of the most gruesome incidents in detail. The Indians had captured about thirty women whom they used to herd cattle that they had seized. Immediately a small detachment of a few soldiers we have here was dispatched to their rescue. But as soon as the Indians found out that they were being pursued, they crowded the women into a house, set it on fire, and let them burn to death alive.[24]

Christine Zierke, "a very large and strongly built woman," saved her life and those of her five children, managing alone while her man escaped. Determinedly independent, she had left her husband, John Karl Schumacher, for Karl Zierke—an early pioneer from Mecklenburg known as "Dutch Charley"—about 1858. Perhaps to avoid community censure, they settled an isolated area in Cottonwood County, about fifty miles from the German town of New Ulm, Minnesota, and were on good terms with the natives when the 1862 uprising occurred. They started to New Ulm together, but Dutch Charley had gone "into the timber to get something to eat" when seven Sioux appeared. She spoke their language and convinced them not to kill her and the children. Instead, she went with them, driving her oxen "very fast" for five miles, until two scouts reported sighting soldiers.

Because they considered Christine Zierke to be a friend, the warriors "told her to go into an adjoining strip of timber and when the soldiers came, not to tell them that she had seen the Indians." There she sheltered the children for two nights before heading for New Ulm—but "when almost there, she smelled a great stench." Upon investigating, she found decaying carcasses of cattle and horses around burned-out farm buildings, and rather than venture farther into a war scene, "she determined to return to her former hiding place in the timber." From August 20 to their August 31 reunion, the locally famous Dutch Charley remained in the safety of New Ulm, while Christine Zierke—a true hero—successfully protected five children in the wilderness.[25]

Justina Kitzman Lehn Kreiger was another hardy German woman who survived when almost all about her perished. She had emigrated from Prussia as a married woman with three children, but her husband died soon after their arrival. In Wisconsin, she married again in 1857 and bore three more babies; with five stepchildren from her husband's first marriage, she had the care of eleven children at age twenty-eight. They moved to Minnesota in spring of 1862.

In sworn testimony delivered in German in 1863, Justina Kreiger reported that thirteen families headed for Fort Ridgley at the outbreak of warfare but paused in their flight when Sioux who were their friends caught up with them and told them that it was Chippewas on the warpath, not they. After the Germans stowed their guns and shared a meal, the Sioux turned on them: most of the men were immediately killed and the women were given a choice between capture and death. "Some were willing to go, others refused," Justina Kreiger said. "I told them I chose to die with my husband and children."[26] She not only was shot but also had a wagon driven over her—and survived by pretending to be dead. With tremendous self-control, she refused to scream even when she was knifed in the abdomen, which was "open to the intestines themselves." Nor did she cry out when she saw her niece, Wilhelmina Kitzman, dragged "up by the foot, her head downward, her clothes falling over her head . . . until the limb was entirely severed from the body, the child screaming frantically, "O God! O God!"[27]

Making a supreme effort, Justina Kreiger moved that night by the light of the aurora to a creek where she remained, "weak, sick, and faint from loss of blood, for three long days." Then she continued to move at night but saw only dead bodies and burned-out homes. Eating the tall prairie grass that hid her, she "thought to find Chippewa Indians, but I found none. I saw plenty of Sioux."[28] Thirteen days later, when "I felt sure I must die," soldiers rescued her—but the next morning, the cavalry was attacked. After a two-day battle, the only wagon left standing was the one in which the indomitable Justina Kreiger lay. Over 200 bullet holes were counted in this wagon when the Sioux retreated, but she said, "some five slight wounds was all the actual damage I sustained." The soldiers, she added, "seemed perfectly astonished on finding me alive."[29]

Fourteen-year-old Mary Schwandt saw her entire family atrociously killed, her pregnant sister having had the unborn baby ripped from her womb and nailed to a tree, where, witnesses said, "it struggled some time after the nails were driven through it."[30] Mary was taken captive and recalled some years later:

> I was sitting quietly and shrinkingly by a tepee, when [Little Crow] came along in full chief's costume and looking very grand. Suddenly he jerked his tomahawk from his belt and sprang toward me with the weapon uplifted . . . but I looked up at him, without any care or fear about my fate. He brandished his tomahawk over me a few times, then laughed, put it back in his belt and walked away, still laughing.[31]

In the same group of captives was Swedish Mary Anderson, who had a bullet lodged in her abdomen. "Waucouta tried to cut it out," Mary Schwandt reported, "but failed. Mary then took the knife from the hand of Waucouta, and removed it herself." Four days later, infection doubtless set in, and when "it rained very had . . . and water ran through the tepee," the feverish Mary Anderson died. "She was a good girl," her German friend Mary Schwandt summarized, "and before she died, she prayed in the Swedish tongue."[32]

These teenagers were clearly raped, too, though the 1864 editors found the "details too revolting for publication." Mary Schwandt is recorded as saying only: "One of them laid his hands forcibly upon me, . . . causing the blood to flow very freely. They then took me out by force, to an unoccupied tepee . . . and perpetrated the most horrible and nameless outrages upon my person. These outrages were repeated at different times during my captivity."[33] Ultimately, she "credited a friendly Indian woman, Snana," with her survival.[34]

So traumatic was the experience of fifty-one-year-old Guri Endresen that four years passed before she could bring herself to tell her relatives in Norway:

> I had to look on while they shot my precious husband dead, and in my sight my dear son Ole was shot . . . We also found my oldest son Endre shot dead, but I did not see the firing of this death shot. For two days and nights I hovered about here with my little daughter, between fear and hope and almost crazy before I found my wounded son and a couple of other persons, unhurt, who helped us to get away to a place of greater security. To be an eye-witness to these things and to see many others wounded and killed was almost too much for a poor woman, but God be thanked, I kept my life and my sanity.[35]

The facts, however, were different from what she wrote. Guri Endresen apparently could not permit herself to be a hero, and she understated her strength in meeting this horrifying fate. Her letter said that she found "a couple of other persons, unhurt, who helped us,"[36] but in fact she found two seriously wounded men. According to them, she dressed their wounds, obtained bedding and other supplies, and drove unbroken oxen thirty miles to safety, staying awake at night to guard her charges.

She apparently could not bring herself to tell her family across the sea of this courage and strength, presumably because she thought it unsuited to "a poor woman." The testimony that she gave to 1863 investigators was similarly reticent, though she did credit herself with "carrying my son-in-law out of the house on my back ... into the wagon."[37]

Justina Boelter, who emigrated alone from Prussia in 1854 at age twenty, married in Buffalo, New York, and came to Minnesota with her husband and three children in June of 1862. It may well have been the newness of the frontier to Justina Boelter that made her response to this crisis more fearfully traumatized than that of most immigrant women. On August 18, when news came of the outbreak, her husband went to secure their cattle, and she "never saw nor heard of" him again. Her young brother-in-law ran with the baby, while she and her two toddlers vainly attempted to keep up. After hearing German neighbors scream, she hid for several days before making her way, barefooted, to her in-laws. "I saw my mother-in-law dead on the floor, her head severed from her body."[38]

So traumatized was she that she again went into hiding on a creek bank, where, "at the end of five weeks, the elder of the two children died of starvation, and I had become too weak to get about, except with great difficulty." The younger child survived because, "the baby being taken from me, the next elder child, now over two years of age, had taken to the breast." But, she continued, "My milk failed me at the same time the eldest child died, and I now commenced feeding the one yet living on the grape-leaves" that grew wild. Finally, however, frost killed even this poor source of food, and carrying her daughter, Ottilie, she managed to stumble back to her "now desolate home."[39] Its larder had long since been looted, of course, and she was in the last stages of death from starvation when soldiers found her on October 27.

Far more fatalistic than most, she had spent more than eight weeks in hiding and had no plan for survival when she was found. On the other hand, since "the foraging party which brought in Mrs. Boelter buried forty-seven bodies," the opposite course of action was not necessarily better. "Doubtless hundreds ... will never be found," added the local newspaper, "as ... the prairie fires now ravaging the whole country will consume what may yet remain."[40]

It was another case of ambivalence, another instance of no clear answers, and to most, Justina Boelter's "trust in the arm of Him who is stronger than man" was the only truth. While they were unsure on many things, few immigrant women doubted this verity, and few doubted that what they were doing to native women and children was Right and Good and even sponsored by God. That they were God's agents and the Sioux were unworthy heathen was essential to their entire reason for being, their philosophy of life and death. They had to believe this, for without the belief that they were entitled to the land that they tilled, their decision to emigrate and all of their plans for the future would fall apart.

And thus Gro Svendsen—though "terrified" by prairie fires and "horribly afraid" of snakes and implacable in her hatred of the "savages"—never once expressed a desire to leave this land and return to her beloved Norway. Despite her anger at the government in taking her Ole to fight its war, she would not let her family in Europe think that the two of them regretted their decision to emigrate. Part of their mission in creating a new home was to civilize the wild, to build churches and schools where the tall grass had blown free, to make farms and fences where the buffalo had grazed. In the "struggle between man and nature," as Elise Waerenskjold termed it, nature was the foe. The purpose of civilization was to subdue the natural.

Subduing the Wild: The Female Farmer

"I have read in books," wrote Elise Isely, "that the people of the frontier kept moving ever westward to escape civilization":

> But if my experience counts for anything, such people were the exceptions. So eager were we to keep in touch with civilization that even when we could not afford a shotgun and ammunition to kill rabbits, we subscribed to newspapers and periodicals and bought books. I made it a rule, no matter how late at night it was or how tired I was, never to go to bed without reading a few minutes.[41]

But civilizing could not be done by reading alone. Women plowed, planted, and reaped; they cared for cattle and hogs; they cut wood and cleared land. They were farmers in every sense. Immigrant women sent home the details of crops and farming methods, and livestock receives more attention in most letters than children. Ann Whittaker, an Englishwoman in Illinois at midcentury, was but one of many such letter writers who proudly described their newly planted farms: "We have bought 80 acres of land . . . We have 2 cows, 4 calves, 2 horses, 24 pigs, 2 dogs and I cannot tell you the number of chickens . . . I still like the country."[42]

Conditions after the Civil War were less pleasant; railroad and industrial monopolies tightened their hold on farmers, while drought and blizzards complicated farmers' woes. Yet most immigrants, who could not easily return home, resolved to stick it out. Kate Bond, a Kansas Englishwoman writing during the calamitous 1880s, exemplifies their love-hate relationship with the land. "We have had two very bad years out here, but we have pulled through them and this year is better so far," she wrote with timid optimism, affirming clearly, "I like a Western life." But Kansas did not reward her faith, and a few years later as bad weather and low farm prices continued, Mrs. Bond was more discouraged. "We left to better ourselves, but sometimes I thinck [sic] we should have done as well if we had stayed. We have our own home and our children are all with us, but there is a lot of care."[43]

Fredricka Bremer wrote of the harsh disappointment of Wisconsin Swedes in the early 1850s. She knew of one sad woman who did the farm work alone after her husband broke his leg and who saw "her first-born little one frozen to death in its bed in the room, into which snow and rain found entrance." Like some other settlements of intellectuals, they had not understood what would be needed for survival:

> These Swedish gentry who thought of becoming here the cultivators and colonizers of the wilderness, had miscalculated their fitness and their powers of labor . . . The first year's harvest fell short. Then succeeded a severe winter, with snow and tempests, and the ill-built houses afforded but inadequate shelter; on this followed sickness, misfortune, want of labor, want of money, wants of all kinds.[44]

And yet, when the wilderness was tamed, it yielded bountiful rewards with only casual care. Letters went back to Europe expressing amazement that no manuring was necessary for luxuriant crops, that pasturage and hay were free for the taking on the prairie—for a decade or two. But the grass was soon overgrazed and the virgin soil eroded. Elise Waerenskjold wrote after fifteen years, "Texas has changed considerably . . . Much of the grass has yielded to all sorts of weeds that animals cannot eat . . . We could have been rich if conditions had continued as they were a decade ago."[45]

Elise, like most restless Americans, did not see that it was their fault that "Texas had changed." Instead of advising European methods of soil maintenance, her solution was to adopt the American way of moving on. Europeans built barns and tended their animals in winter; Elise had accepted the Texan method of allowing them to forage. She had, incidentally, a curious comment regarding these free-ranging animals: "Despite the fact that cattle, horses, and pigs run about in the woods without any supervision and at times may be away for days or even weeks and months, it is a peculiar thing that most of the animals here are more amiable than those in Norway. I have not seen a single mad bull here, while most of those I saw in Norway were very fierce."[46]

Jette Bruns, too, allowed her livestock to forage in frontier Missouri. She was amazed that "they have not been fed at all. The white oaks have much fruit, and the hogs begin feeding in the woods and continue through the winter." Of course, there were risks inherent in this free food, as she wrote in 1839, "Sixteen little pigs froze to death last winter."[47] But seventy hogs remained, and Jette showed no inclination to fence her livestock before neighbors made that necessary.

Mrs. Koren found these free-running animals less amiable. "These impudent hogs and cattle," she cried, "I wish I had Vige [a dog] here; he would certainly keep them from licking the window panes! They did great damage in the summer kitchen one night; they drank up all the water and chewed the oven door and the teakettle cover to pieces."[48]

Despite occasional impudence, the health and welfare of her animals formed a large part of the immigrant farmwife's letters. It was usually the woman who milked the cows, fed and watered them and the other stock, and it was invariably she who cared for the poultry—and slaughtered them, too. Though the animals provided food for the table, many women grew attached to them; they told their names in letters and wanted to know the names of animals back home. "Don't read this part of the letter to anyone who would chide me for being so childish," Gro Svendsen cautioned and then wrote a long paragraph on their animals.[49]

Likewise, Jette Brun's early letters were filled with such detail:

> And now we come to the geese . . . Last spring we had nineteen little ones, but we let them roam freely and . . . the little ones ate some poisonous weeds . . . And in addition a fox got one old one last year . . . The chickens, the young ones and the old ones, are around a hundred in number . . .
>
> And then I must not forget our deer . . . We own a young stag that is now a half-year old. For a long time he drank only milk and was quite impetuous when drinking, and now that he is finding the vegetables and corn very tasty, he also drinks water from the branch. He is getting fat, and . . . will soon furnish a beautiful roast. It also annoyed me that he always ate the sandwich for [two-year-old son] Max. He is already jumping over fences.[50]

Even when an occasional rural immigrant saw herself as too ladylike to be concerned with farm animals, she only revealed her own exceptionality: Elisabeth Koren, for instance, complained that whenever neighbors gathered together for visiting, the women always "went out and looked at the calves and livestock, which are among their chief interests and positively have to be inspected wherever we are."[51]

The labor of women indeed was essential in building a pioneer farm; men knew it, and none stayed single any longer than necessary. Single women were sought after and imported, and those with a reputation for hard work were those most highly recommended. Second to her own labor was the ability of a woman to provide children who would grow up to work on the farm. Loneliness was a third reason why marriage seemed essential to farmers. The winter was long; weeks could go by when one could not travel, and a congenial companion made life bearable. Some couples grew into inseparable partners through sharing all aspects of work. One Norwegian man whose wife was gone helping with their new grandchild found that "he just could not get used to not having her with him. He cannot even stack his hay unless he has Guri in the wagon treading down the hay."[52]

German Heinrich Moller, writing home in 1880, repeated the observation of many when he said, "Here in America the women are better off than the men, a woman only has to do her housework, no woman has to work in the fields."[53] And yet, while that was the American standard to which immigrants also came to aspire, women and girls in fact not only kept their husbands company while "treading down the hay," but they also did heavier labor when a household had insufficient males.

A Bohemian girl whose family settled in Nebraska just after the Civil War, for instance, plowed virgin prairie—work considered difficult even for men. An English-woman recalled her similar girlhood in frontier Michigan:

> The four oldest being girls, we had to take the place of boys . . . Father felled the large trees and then we would help him split them up into logs, and then we would

take the team to draw them up into large heaps to burn them . . . There were fences
to be built around the fields . . . Then the land had to be got ready for crops to be
planted, and then it had to be hoed and cared for, and there was the harvesting . . .[54]

As Victorianism rigidified divisions of labor by gender, however, immigrants
found themselves criticized when women were seen working beyond the barnyard.
As late as the 1920s, a YWCA official in South Dakota said, for example, "I think
many of the reports of excessive work are due to the fact that so many of the
German-Russian women share in the work of the fields, a thing which is so unusual
among native born Americans that . . . makes us point to them as mal-treated."
Americans thought these women from the Russian steppes were held in
archaic bondage, but a closer examination found their family farms to be an
egalitarian workplace. Moreover, the women had plenty of recreational opportunity after the fieldwork was done: "It was a matter of almost daily occurrence to
have some one ask us to 'Come over and bring the ice-cream freezer,'" reported
the YWCA investigator. Amazed that they stayed at barn dances until midnight
and rose at dawn for their chores, she went on to add that the foreigners'
reputation for miserliness also was not what it seemed: "Among a people who
spend money very sparingly, the home is still not the thing that is stinted. The
most modern conveniences are there for the women . . . And not merely conveniences, [but also] rare beauty."[55]
In and out of fields, and with or without the aid of men, immigrant women
worked as farmers. When Elise Waerenskjold's husband was murdered, the widow
went right on farming as before. She sheared the flock of 100 sheep herself, and with
her adolescent sons, she raised twenty-two acres of cotton, fourteen of corn, six of
rye, and seven of wheat, plus caring for 200 to 300 hogs, cattle, turkeys, and oxen.
Though Elise had worked in the past as a teacher and an editor, it was the weather,
crops, and farm prices that were the main topics of her correspondence.
Countless other widows took her path and continued to farm after their partners'
deaths. Gro Svendsen—who, like Elise, sheared sheep—several times mentioned
women who intended to farm emigrating without husbands, as though she found
nothing exceptional about this. Married and unmarried women alike filed for land
under the Homestead Act, which of course required residence on the land claimed.
In fact, though most women were reluctant to give themselves the title of farmer, a
surprisingly large number did appear: an analysis of the 1890 and 1900 censuses found
over 80,000. The vast majority of "agricultural laborers" were single (84.7%), while
most of those labeled "farmers and planters" were widows (66.3%).[56]
Even married women—even women whose husbands would not have been
officially listed as farmers—did genuine farm work. This was particularly true for
pioneer professionals, as is clear in records such as those of physician's wife Jette Bruns
and a number of diaries by ministers' wives. These men traveled circuits to visit
parishioners and patients, and they were gone more often than they were home. Linka
Preus, who was accustomed to servants in her home in Norway, found that now "with

Sina on my arm and Christian clinging to my skirts,"[57] she had to manage not only a parsonage but a farm as well.

Besides the routine work, sometimes there were unexpected crises. Linka was spinning wool one day when her chore boy rushed in to say a calf had slipped on the ice, knocked the well's cover off, and fallen in. She decided that she could not allow the calf to die and the well to be contaminated, and convinced the boy that she could safely lower him into the water and pull him and the calf out again. She did—but not without moments of gripping fear, which she controlled to meet this emergency. Her final comment was to hope that her absentee husband would now be serious about building the long-promised enclosure for the well.

Mary Sandoz, who emigrated to marry a stranger, found herself doing virtually all of the work, despite her husband's presence. He turned out to be both mentally and physically cruel, and it was Mary who rose before dawn while he slept until noon. It was she who corralled wild ponies, chopped wood, and tended both livestock and field crops, while he read, sued neighbors, and wrote complaining letters to newspapers. When her six children were old enough, they joined Mary in such exhausting enterprises as hunting cattle during blinding blizzards—and when as a petulant old man their father threatened to leave for South America, they told him to go. They and their mother could run the farm alone.

From Butter to Blueberries: Other Farming

The bit of recognition that a farm woman received for her hard labor was symbolized by the "butter and egg money." These areas were her domain, and if the husband was a decent sort, the proceeds were her own. She spent them on household needs, but there was here an acknowledged measurement of success. Elise Isely found that others appreciated her Swiss cheese-making abilities, and her product was regionally unrivaled. She also earned money selling butter:

> My butter was of extra quality, being firm and always sweet . . . There grew up a local demand for butter, and my product sold at a premium. I molded butter into pound rolls, being careful to give full measure or a little more. I finished the roll by imprinting on the top and sides a scroll of oak leaves. The mold with which I did this had been sent to me by relatives from Switzerland. This was my trademark, for nobody else had a print exactly like mine.[58]

Thus she became known by the Americans of her community. While the assumption is common that men had more opportunity for contact with Americans than women, her case shows that sometimes the opposite was true. A writer on a Czech colony isolated from the mainstream of immigration in Virginia agreed that the pattern appeared there: "The only contacts many Virginians in the city have with Bohemians are through these women peddlers."[59] A farmer there also acknowledged the importance of his wife—the mother of six—in raising and marketing this produce: "Me and my wife worked very hard. She helped me clear the land . . . Two times a week I hitched up the horse and my wife went to town to peddle. She took care of the cows and chickens and garden and kept the house that way. She always had steady customers."[60]

"She kept the house that way"—in other words, the woman earned most of the cash that supported this family, as well as caring for "the cows and chickens and garden" that directly fed them. She worked as both farmer and vendor, and her sales meant much more than pin money. Doubtless she learned work habits from childhood, for girls in this Czech community also did fieldwork. A twelve-year-old wrote that she stayed out of school two weeks each year to "shake peanuts and cut corn. I like to do all kinds of outdoors work," she continued, "but I like best to graze geese. I do that in the summer time and while they are grazing I study my lessons."[61]

Female farmers also worked beside male ones in the truck gardens of southern New Jersey and western Massachusetts, where Italians and Slavs produced food for New Yorkers and Bostonians:

> The women and girls . . . dress like men in overalls and without shoes or stockings. It is a familiar but picturesque sight, and one typically representative of their great patience, dogged perseverance and thrift, to see them, in blue jeans and huge straw hats, slowly crawling on their hands and knees up and down the long rows, astraddle the slender green onion tops, pulling out the tiny weeds . . . They do not stop to rest even on the hottest days, and at noon the women go back to the house, prepare the meal, and bring it out to the men.[62]

Vieno Raitanen grew up on one of these small farms in New Hampshire, where her family settled with other Finns at the turn of the century. Former mill workers, they saw the agricultural opportunities Americans had overlooked: "The Finnish people began to move into the farms discarded by the Americans. They took out mortgages on them and brought their children there, and the whole family worked in the fields—not only the men but the women and children, too."[63]

They specialized in blueberries, thus demonstrating an awareness of agronomy, for this native plant was suited to the soil and appreciated by the American Indians of that area—but not necessarily by New Englanders, who generally concentrated on the same European grains that grew better in the Midwest. The Finns used modern methods not only for this cash crop but also for their dairy herds. With a more scientific attitude than Americans, they encouraged a state program to eliminate tubercular cattle while local Americans refused to support it. The Finns also banded together to market their berries in an egalitarian way: "The meetings of the Cooperative are all held in the Finnish language," Vieno wrote, and "all the family attend—women and children as well as men—and all have a good time."[64]

That farming was good for family life was unquestioned; throughout the immigrant era, churches and other philanthropies developed plans to put more immigrants on farms, where they would be removed from the temptations of city life. The Italian settlement at Vineland, New Jersey, was one of the most successful of many such assisted emigration plans. The colony began in 1878, predating most Italian immigration, and in 1903, it had about 5,000 residents. A 1903 colony of "50 families from Alessandria" provided Memphis "with a large part of its fruit and vegetables."[65]

And in similar colonies of other ethnic groups, it was assumed that women would work the vineyards, fields, and dairies along with men. The class of European women most likely to emigrate was, in fact, peasantry accustomed to agricultural labor. As much as possible, these women lived the same type of working lives in America, concerning themselves with crops, animals, and weather, while their homes generally received less attention. Gro Svendsen, for example, wrote long letters detailing every aspect of farm life, but aside from once mentioning a new kitchen and some utensils, in fourteen years of letter writing she gave no idea what her house looked like.

They were not nearly so much housekeepers as farmers, yet if a census taker had asked one of these immigrant women for her occupation, she probably would have replied, "housewife." They did not question occupational stereotypes, nor did they completely break them, for the women who did farm work also did the housework. While women plowed and planted, men rarely sewed and cooked.

Indeed, although farming was assumed to promote family life, it may well have done so at the expense of women. Compared with the city immigrant, a farming woman was much less independent; though she worked from before dawn until after dark, she never really had a dime that she was legally entitled to call her own. The city woman worked long hours, too, but she was free from her job on Sunday and the pay envelope came with her name on it. A farm woman might keep her butter or egg money, but if she did, it was only through the largess of her husband, and always the majority of her prodigious labor went unpaid. She was dependent on her husband for any small thing she wished to buy, put in the position of a dependent, nonearning child, when in fact she worked hard all day, every day. Yet the money was legally his, and if she ever wished to leave him, what then? She had no savings and no skills that were salable enough to support her children. The garden, the animals, the farm that she poured herself into were not hers.

On the other hand, if the farm woman had a good relationship with her husband and children when they emigrated, she was more likely to keep it than her city counterpart. The farming husband was less likely to squander the family's income in drinking and gambling, simply because such entertainments were less readily available. Then, too, a farming mother didn't have to worry about her offspring as much as the woman in the city; she knew where they were and who they were with. Farm children were more likely to use the native language and less likely to look down upon their parents as ignorant greenhorns. Nor, in most cases, could children get jobs and be independent until parents were ready to give them land and set them up in farming; meanwhile, a mother's discipline over unruly sons was much more effective.

There were compensations for the isolation and hard work. While all members of the family were less free, they were more secure and more apt to have a close relationship than urban families where each went to his separate job and the tenement home was shared with many others. Yet for a woman, all of this was dependent to a large extent on the goodness of her man. If he was a scoundrel, the city woman could show him the door and get a job, but the farm woman often found no options available except insanity, suicide, or silent submission. Doubtless there were many who regretted that American-style farming placed neighbors widely apart, while in Europe, women enjoyed each other's company, for they had lived together in villages and went in groups to work the fields.

It was still another area of ambivalence, with good arguments on both sides of issues. But for most immigrants, regrets were ephemeral: more important was the fact that the family was rich in land, richer than they could ever have hoped to be in Europe. The family, the land, the farm—this was what mattered most. Land of this size and quality was beyond their most fervent hopes in Europe, and no sacrifice was too great to make those dreams come true. The lives and sanity of many—men and women, native and immigrant—were exhausted in building farms, but to these land-hungry people, the effort was worth the cost.

A woman would bury her sentimental longings and rejoice in the opportunity that America brought. And to make the most of that opportunity she, along with her sister immigrants in the city, would work. They poured themselves into the building of a country; they made their great unheralded contribution.

PART V

THE
COMPLEXITIES
OF IT ALL

17

TRAVAILS OF TRAVEL

When the Wind Blows: Early Emigration by Sail

Most of the millions of immigrants had never seen the sea before they crossed it, and that crossing could be a terrifying experience. Traveling on an 1855 sailing ship, Swiss Elise Isely described a storm that "turned our vessel over on its beam end so far that . . . those on the upper side clung to their bunks, fearful of being hurled down."[1] After a storm tossed her 1853 ship, Elisabeth Koren wrote that the beds were "thoroughly soaked" and the cabins "were a pitiful sight." Worse, "we had been served coffee . . . with a little of the precious milk in it, . . . but then all at once there was a lurch; the milk pitcher came sailing over Madam Zeplin and me."[2] The following year, German Angela Heck described a truly terrifying storm:

> The night of Easter Sunday . . . there was a noise on deck that was so loud that everyone awoke . . . We were now having such a terrible storm that we thought the ship would be torn apart . . . We all . . . prayed 17 rosaries . . . but things kept getting worse and worse . . .
>
> It was so loud . . . The ship started to crack, masts broke and their sails and ropes were ripped and torn to pieces. The ship sank down very deep . . . We repented our sins and we all prepared to die . . . We quickly put on our underskirts so we wouldn't be lying there naked when we died.[3]

The large steamers that replaced these sailing vessels later in the century would be safer, but nonetheless there would be seasickness. Like others, Rose Cohen thought she was dying. The first three days of her trip, "I was conscious . . . only part of the time . . . I heard voices screaming, entreating, praying. I thought we were drowning, but I did not care." On the fourth day she tried to get up to bring water, but the ship lurched and Rose fell. A man picked her up and carried her to the deck:

> I had heard that those who were very sick on the steamer and those who died were thrown into the ocean. There was no doubt in my mind, therefore, that that was where I was being carried . . . He went away, to fetch a rope, I thought. He returned in a few minutes. But instead of a rope there was half an orange in his hand . . . After a while Aunt Masha came creeping up the steps on all fours, hugging our little bag of zwieback. From that hour we improved quickly.[4]

Rose's fears of death were based on tales that made their way back to European villages, for conditions on early ships had been so bad, the voyage so long, the sanitation and medical inspections so indifferent that plagues of all sorts occurred. On some ships ravaged by epidemics, almost as many died as lived, and the "normal mortality" was about one person in every ten.[5] The most horrific year was 1847, during the Irish famine. Approximately 17,000 emigrants died at sea that year, with another 20,000 dying soon after arrival. During six monhs of that year, 8,691 people were admitted to a Quebec port hospital built for 200; of them, 3,228 died.[6]

For women, pregnancy could easily complicate illness. Whether or not Jette Bruns knew that she was pregnant at the beginning of their ocean voyage is debatable, but she almost certainly did not know when they made the decision to leave. Like most women, she ignored her pregnancy in writing of the voyage and made no mention of the additional burden of morning sickness with seasickness. Though she came from an inland area of Germany, she wrote of the trip like a veteran sailor:

> On the 6th of July 1836 we set sail. . . . We were thirty people and traveled second cabin but had all the privileges of the first, which didn't have any passengers. We were allowed to do our own cooking if we did not like the food for the steerage class. All in all it was a good group. We were cruising for three weeks in the North Sea, but then we succeeded in getting through the Channel.
> After 66 days we landed in Baltimore.[7]

In Baltimore, where she found the heat terribly oppressive, she wrote a more detailed letter. "The water was very bad, and the food was not very appetizing," she reported, adding that she greatly appreciated the Westphalian ham and wine they had brought. "We saw only a few fish," she said, but "once a dolphin was caught and provided us with beef steak for two days; at least it could hardly be differentiated from beef." When they arrived in Baltimore, "we immediately went and bought fruit and everything tasted magnificent."[8]

Her attention to the food on board is not unusual, for it was a topic of overwhelming concern, especially when trips were delayed or derouted by weather conditions and food ran short. Most passengers in the early days brought their own food. Some captains used this arrangement to make extra money: they deceived travelers on the length of the journey and then sold them provisions at a high price when they ran out.

"Eats were scant and not of the best," remembered one Swedish passenger. "After the passengers fell away through illness, then there was sometimes enough for all."[9] Some ships provided cooks, but on many early ships, the women cooked for their families, as Elise Isely reports:

> Eight sheds, called kitchens, were assigned to the steerage. These were on deck, sheltered from rain or snow by a roof, but otherwise open on all sides to the weather . . . Fire was laid by the seamen in the troughs, and . . . the passengers were summoned to cook. Woe to the passenger who did not respond immediately; for the coals died down, and there would be no more fire until the next meal! Woe to the passenger who spilled the water . . . for water was rationed, and he could get no more![10]

The 1855 ship on which her Swiss group traveled was captained by an Englishman who governed with extreme severity. They were bound for New Orleans—the quickest route to the interior in this prerailroad era—and were becalmed off Cuba. With no breeze, the tropical sun made these mountain people unbearably hot and thirsty, but the captain refused to increase their water ration. They then asked permission to send a rowboat ashore for water, but he refused that, too, saying their supply was ample. That night passengers sneaked to the water casks, found that there was indeed plenty, slyly bored a hole in one, and drank what they needed in secret during the rest of their long journey.

Anna Maria Klinger experienced one of the longest voyages on record: she was "at sea for one hundred and 5 days," and in addition, she said, "7 weeks we were docked at Blumuth [Plymouth] before our ship was done."[11] Anna Maria was the oldest daughter in a large German family; in 1849, at age twenty-seven, she set the precedent for five younger siblings who would follow her to America.

Despite traveling in only the second year of the wave of German immigration, she demonstrated good judgment. She reported to her parents, for example, "I met up with those girls who were also going from Stuttgart to America in Maintz, but . . . they started behaving so badly . . . couldn't stand such loose behavior."[12] By the time her younger sister Barbara followed, Anna Maria was married, and she and her husband—also a German—jointly wrote detailed directions:

> She should go . . . with this ticket here in this letter to Mannheim to Wilhelm to Deissman, and there she will get three *Tickets*, one she has to turn in at Mannheim when she gets on the steamship, the other when she goes from Rotterdam to Haver [LeHavre] and the third in Haver when she gets on the ship . . .
>
> And when she's asked at the depot if she has everything she's supposed to have,

then she should say yes and she should be sure not to take anything more than what we've written, and she shouldn't be scared if they say she can't leave or whatever else they might say . . .

   She doesn't need any papers except her certificate of citizenship from the mayor, since she won't be asked on the journey. And she ought to bring along a potato sack about two simmers* in size and then a straw sack and a pillow and anything else like that she needs . . . She should behave herself so she doesn't arrive here in a wretched state and become the laughingstock of everyone.[13]

All of this planning made for an easy journey, and Barbara made the crossing in just 26 days compared with Anna Maria's 105. Barbara added a note about her journey, saying that she had "one of the biggest ships that go between Havre and New Jork and even when the wind was strong it can't throw it around like the little ones . . . Such a big ship on the ocean is like a nutshell swimming in the lake at Korb." Like other passengers, she brought utensils and did her own cooking, and she described the accommodations for animals: "Two stalls, in one there are geese and in the other ducks and chickens and a pigsty and another stall for cows."[14]

   When the youngest sister emigrated in 1859—a decade after the first—she was bombarded with advice from the experienced travelers. Having learned from mistakes, they solicitously sought to ease every part of her passage: "When you get to Haver write a letter with the name of the ship you're coming on and the day it leaves Haver, we'll find it the next day in the newspaper, don't leave the building with anyone before we come and pick you up, if you arrive late in the afternoon, send a man to let us know, we'll pay for it."[15]

Steamships and Some Special Hazards for Women

The much quicker crossing provided by steamers later in the era greatly alleviated many immigration problems, for these ships could maintain regular schedules free of the whimsicalities of wind. The practice of bringing one's own food ended, and medical inspections and vaccinations were required. These improved conditions meant that steerage deaths, which had been common, became unlikely. Nonetheless, steerage sanitation still left much to be desired. The report of a female government investigator who disguised herself as a Bohemian peasant and made the crossing in 1911 told of the difficulties for women:

   The first morning out I took special care to inquire for the women's washroom. One of the crew directed me to a door bearing the sign, "Washroom for men." Within were both men and women. Thinking I had been misdirected, I proceeded to the

* There were four pecks in a German simmer, so two simmers amounts to about sixteen gallons.

other washroom. This bore no label and was likewise being used by both sexes . . .

The . . . same basin served as a dishpan for greasy tins, as a laundry tub for soiled handkerchiefs and clothing, and as a basin for shampoos and without receiving any special cleaning. It was the only receptacle to be found for use in case of seasickness . . .

Many . . . make heroic efforts to keep clean . . . It was forbidden to bring water for washing purposes into the sleeping compartments . . . On different occasions some of the women rose early, brought drinking water in their soup pails and thus tried to wash themselves effectively, but were driven out when detected by a steward . . .

The day of landing, when inspection was made by custom officials who came on board, the toilets were clean, the floors . . . were dry and the odor of disinfectant was not noticeable. All these were conditions that did not obtain during the voyage.[16]

A male passenger reported that on his 1906 ship there were seven lavatories to be shared by 2,200 steerage passengers—five for men and only two for women. If even a minimal 40% of the passengers were women and children, they would share their restroom with approximately 440 others. The five male facilities would average about 260—or about half as crowded as the women's rooms. Since the male lavatories were described as "exceedingly small and cramped, with the result that these places were simply packed, jammed to the doors, an hour before breakfast," the women's restrooms can easily be imagined to be an impossible situation.[17]

While steamers relieved passengers of the obligation of bringing sacks of food, there nonetheless were problems in this area, too. Differing national tastes were ignored, and the food in steerage often was served in an unappetizing manner, sometimes within sight and smell of the seasick passengers. The incognito investigator reported:

> The white bread, potatoes and soup, when hot, were the only foods that were good . . . The meats were generally old, tough, and bad smelling . . . The vegetables were often a queer, unanalyzable mixture, and therefore avoided. The butter was rarely edible . . . Breakfast cereals, a food foreign to most Europeans, were served in an abundance of water . . . During the twelve days only about six meals were fair and gave satisfaction. More than half of the food was always thrown into the sea . . . Many passengers made tea and lived on this and bread.[18]

Arriving twenty minutes after the bell meant no meal. Rose Cohen and her aunt, waiting in an embarkation station, discovered that "no sooner was the food put on the table than it was gone, and some of us were left with empty plates." Yet Rose wrote, "[G]oing hungry seemed easy in comparison with the shame we felt to put out our hands for the bread while there was such a struggle."[19] Immigrants soon were reduced to the base behavior that nativists loved to attribute to them.

"The steerage pays the ship" was a business adage of the era, and it probably was true. While steerage passengers were fed like animals at a trough, even third-class passengers ate at tables with cloth covers and napkins. A government investigator who traveled both steerage and third class said that though the fare differential was only $7.50, "the difference between accommodations is everything."[20] Between steerage and first class, of course, was an even greater gulf, but the difference in quality seems greater than the difference in price.

On the main passenger lines in 1906, steerage cost between $30 and $36, while first class was $75 to $90. A Sunday dinner in steerage was goulash or pasta (one only) with soup, potatoes, prunes, and bread—but the first-class menu offered flounder with shrimp sauce, lobster Newburg, turtle steaks, beef sirloin, lamb, corned beef, chicken, capon, roast beef, boiled ham, and roast turkey, plus assorted soups, vegetables, salads, and desserts. Moreover, the limited menu in steerage was not even wholesome; fat worms were found among the macaroni. On this ship there was again no provision for washing dishes; the harried steerage passenger "scraped with my fingernails" to clean his plate, while first-class passengers ate from tables set with china and linen.[21]

The behavior of the crew toward the differing classes of passengers also varied greatly, and the poorer women frequently testified to abuse they suffered at the hands of sailors. The common situation in steerage was that:

> From the time we boarded the steamer until we landed, no woman . . . had a moment's privacy. One steward was always on duty in our compartment and others of the crew came and went continually . . . The men who came may or may not have been sent there on some errand. This I could not ascertain, but I do know that regularly, during the hour or so preceding the breakfast bell and while we were rising and dressing, several men usually passed through and returned for no ostensible reasons.[22]

On Elise Isely's English sailing ship, one sailor was particularly mean and insulting to the women, and when they reached land, they retaliated: "Two or three score women, each of whom had suffered all sorts of indignities aboard ship, rushed upon him, striking him."[23] More than a half century later and despite government regulations on many aspects of transit, sailors' behavior remained the same: "Not one young woman in the steerage escaped attack," reported the incognito investigator, "and the writer herself was no exception." Women often had to stand on the lower berths to reach the upper, with their backs to the aisle, and "the crew in passing a women in this position never failed to deal her a blow—even the head steward. If a women were dressing, they always stopped to watch her, and frequently hit and handled her." Attractive women were "continually fleeing to escape," as there was "total disrespect for women."[24]

Women did not complain about these assaults partly because of the timidity that had been bred into their bones but also because it was in fact dangerous to resist too much before one had safely entered the United States. To incur the anger of a ship official was to risk admission, for he could easily lie in English about the woman's morality and thus keep her from entry at the port. For a week a steamship agent in Hamburg succeeded in forcing his attentions on Rose Cohen's aunt because she believed he had the power to send them back to Russia.

Not only sailors but also many male passengers also considered women traveling alone to be fair game. It was a fellow passenger who took advantage of Austrian Sylvia Bernstein during her 1914 passage, while a crew member responded with empathy to her innocent misstep. Like other young women, she was well warned before departure:

> The trip . . . I'll tell you. My mother was afraid, a girl alone. My mother said to me, "Don't talk to men, because if you talk to men you become pregnant . . ." So I came on the boat, and I can't speak English . . . There was a Russian from America, so I could talk to him a little. He says, "You want a cup of tea? There is the chef. Go over and ask him for a cup of tea." I says, "How do you ask in English?" He says, "Say to the chef, 'Give me a kiss.'" And I didn't know. I went over to the chef and I says, "Give me a kiss." He was an elderly man and the English are very polite and understanding. He looked at me and I looked at him, and I knew something was wrong.[25]

Even if a man did not succeed in forcing his attentions, he could cause serious trouble by lying about her rejection of him. Jette Bruns's ambivalence about the possibility of a younger sister joining her in Missouri in 1839 was based on an awareness of the probability of sexual harassment and baseless gossip. Her letter was full of hesitation and contradictory argumentation on whether or not this orphan could travel:

> What if Wilhelm could be Johanna's travel companion? No, no, he is too young, too inexperienced, and Johanna must not travel without a reasonable, reliable person who is an expert in the language . . . The reputation of a girl is never smudged more easily than aboard a seagoing ship where boredom and disgust invent many a fairy tale . . .
>
> Last year a young girl of sixteen, more to be called a child, came across the ocean with her brother-in-law; she slept in the same bunk with another women. A young prankster traveling with them later told many an evil thing and many unthinkable things about the young girl . . . The young man himself had courted her and . . . his efforts had been unsuccessful. This had driven him to revenge . . . But the great mass of people may perhaps condemn her as guilty in spite of everything; I only hope that her future will not be damaged by this![26]

Norwegian Berta Serina Kingestad, who was in the early stages of unwed pregnancy while at sea, was dismayed by the "depravity" of her fellow passengers. "There was gambling and dancing, card-playing and wretchedness," she reported to her parents in 1886, "and certainly no one thought about the fact that only a thin plank separated us from the deep grave." She added that she had been seasick during most of her thirteen-day journey, and when she was finally well enough to eat, it was "not of the food on board, for everyone found it almost inedible."[27]

Jewish Elizabeth Hasanovitz echoed her complaints: "The food in the immigration houses was not fit for animals," she raged, "but we were only immigrants." Worse than that, however, was the routine invasion of steerage privacy. All arriving with her ship in London had their baggage opened, and their clothes were "thrown carelessly together with those of other passengers to be disinfected by steam, then replaced in our trunks, all rolled up and wet. My things were so mussed that I had not even a clean shirt-waist fit to wear on the voyage."[28] Because she was an exceptionally skilled seamstress, appearance was important to her; her pride was wounded by the assumption that she had lice.

Jews indeed were singled out for bad treatment by many steamship authorities. They were commonly segregated from other immigrants, and while to some extent this action was justified by their need for kosher food, anti-Semitism was rife among crew members. Jewish baggage was disinfected while that of other groups was not.[29] Poor Rose Cohen worried over the money sewed into her underwaist, which the authorities insisted upon steaming. Luckily, the money came through unharmed, but her new shoes—the first good ones she had in her life—were ruined.

At the same time, steamship companies also recruited Jewish passengers by playing on the fears of their relatives in America. "There is a rumor of another pogrom," read a typical ad in a Chicago Yiddish newspaper. "Why let your dear ones languish and suffer in cruel Russia? Come to ———, friend of the Jews. He will let you have a ticket for which you need not pay until your dear one arrives."[30] Whether or not this promise could be trusted was debatable, but it was almost certain that the traveler would not be treated with the solicitousness that the advertising implied.

In debarkation stations all over Europe, emigrants complained that the personnel was rude and that they were often defrauded. A traveler reported of a German one:

> Sunday morning we tried to get either some coffee or tea. The canteen keeper was either still or again drunk . . . Finally after 9 o'clock, the wife of the canteen keeper appeared and she consented to get us some coffee. By ordering it immediately, we were able to have some dinner at noon . . . There was constant argument about overcharges, and watching the transactions there for some three hours I saw that the complaints were well-founded . . . It was practically impossible to get any food, while . . . liquor was the one thing with which a person could supply himself.[31]

Some ship officials displayed almost unbelievably inhumane attitudes toward their customers, such as an incident witnessed by Rosa Cavallari at Le Havre. A departing ship took on a French girl, but "when the mother and sister tried to follow, that *marinaro* at the gate said, 'No more! Come on the next boat!' And that poor family was screaming and crying. But the *marinaro* wouldn't let the girl off and wouldn't let the mother and sister on!"[32]

Lost and Alone: Ignorance, Indifference, and Fraud

Reaching land brought other kinds of dangers. Angela Heck wrote in 1854 of the scams that would welcome immigrants for decades into the future. "There was a young man," she said, "who was there to meet his countrymen, a real rascal. He led all of us who were in the ship to a German boardinghouse in New York." Though they stayed only one night, "everyone had to pay 7 francs . . . since they had put all the trunks in the cellar and no one could get them back before he paid . . . It was all very sad," she concluded. "Most of them didn't have enough money and couldn't go where they wanted."[33]

Much later, the Italian man who greeted Rosa Cavalleri and her companions followed exactly this pattern. His familiar tongue inspired confidence, so they believed him when he assured them that there was no train for Missouri, where Rosa was headed to join her iron miner husband, for three days. "He did put us on the train but he took all our money first, about $13 each one," said Rosa. "He left us not even a crust of bread for our journey. And we didn't even guess that he was fooling us."[34] She and her friends went from New York to Missouri without a bite, their leader being too proud to accept the charity offered by Americans, for they had learned to be wary of even seemingly generous strangers.

Two young Parisian dressmakers who had saved for years to emigrate were informed by a friendly Frenchman on their 1899 ship that they would need 100 francs in landing money instead of the 40 that they had. He offered, however, to lend each of them $50 if they would give him half of what they had as security. They agreed, and he did in fact lend them $100—in Confederate money. They were about to be deported, their years of effort gone, when other immigrants took pity on them and made a loan.[35]

How to tell the genuinely kind from the seemingly so was an unending dilemma, but as the era continued, governments began to intervene on behalf of the innocent. State governments that wanted to encourage immigration began publicity in Europe to give newcomers the information that they needed to make reasonable decisions. The Minnesota State Board of Immigration, for example, issued a publication titled "Cost of Coming to Minnesota," which clearly indicated a welcoming attitude on the part of the state and offered details to plan the trip.

Fares to St. Paul from twenty-eight European cities were listed, which included the total cost of both railroad and steamship lines, as well as a generous 100 pounds of luggage per passenger. Even heavy shoes and woolen clothing would not use up that weight allowance—with the result that women could take at least some household goods without extra cost. The lowest fare was from Antwerp, at $45.50, and the highest from Rome at $68.50. It is indicative of the most likely immigrant to Minnesota that the board added "Italy" to Rome, whereas most cities—including Trier, Cassel, and Stettin*—were listed without a country. The state also indicated its

---

* Trier is in extreme western Germany near the border of Luxembourg; Cassel, now Kassel, is in central Germany; Stettin, now Szczecin, is barely into modern Poland.

preference for farmers from the Continent to Irish ones: the fare from Ireland's busiest port, Queenstown (now Cobn), was $5 higher than that from Antwerp, even though Ireland is much closer than Belgium.[36]

While this progressive rural state attempted to create a safe and inexpensive voyage, scams in cities continued without appreciable abatement throughout the immigrant era. Sometimes the cheating began even before the trip, when bogus tickets were sold to the unsuspecting in America, who sent them to their dear ones in Europe. They in turn sold their goods, left their jobs, said their goodbyes—and when they arrived at the port city, found that their tickets were no good. One 1908 writer estimated that over a half a million dollars had been lost in New York alone through the sale of these worthless tickets.[37]

A young Jewish woman told the typical tale: she had paid ten dollars down and two dollars a week for a $45 ticket, which she sent to her sister in Russia. The sister traveled hundreds of miles to Antwerp, only to discover that the ticket would not be honored. While waiting there for the sister in America to earn the money for a replacement ticket, "she was arrested for begging . . . and nearly starved for eight months."[38]

Samuel Chotzinoff's Russian family found themselves stranded in London because of a ticket problem. His mother was the one to reason out a solution to their calamity:

> I heard my father and mother talking long and earnestly about our future. My father had little to suggest that was constructive. He spoke a good deal about "home" . . . But my mother, as usual, put her whole mind to . . . ameliorating our lot.
> . . . "Do we know anyone in London?" The query was obviously rhetorical . . . "Don't tell me *nobody*" she cried . . . "There must have been somebody who went— *not* to America!"
> . . . My father said hesitatingly: "I seem to remember—I'm not sure—Aunt Rivka's son-in-law's brother . . . He left Vitebsk about twenty-five years ago."
> "Did he go to London?" My father was not sure. "Well, did he go to America?" my mother persisted. On that point my father was certain . . . "Well, then," my mother cried triumphantly, "if he did not go to America, where else *could* he have gone to?"
> My father ventured a suggestion: "Africa, maybe?"
> . . . "Well," my mother went on, "there can be no doubt about it, Rivka's cousin, or whatever he was, *must* have gone to London. The question is how to find him. What was his name?"[39]

After much remembering, he finally decided the name was Horowitz, and she pushed him into a plan to search London's Jewish quarters. Every day during rush hours the family positioned themselves on street corners, stopping any likely candidate to inquire if he had ever lived in Russia and could his name be Horowitz. Six weeks later, this incredible venture paid off! Mrs. Chotzinoff stopped a man who replied affirmatively to inquiries about Russia and Vitebsk, but said his name was Harris. He had gone on when "suddenly he turned and came back to her. 'As a matter of fact,' he said slowly, 'it was Horowitz.' . . . Without a word my mother clutched him to her heart."[40] Mr. Harris, it turned out, had been successful in London, and he provided the family with a home and jobs until they were ready to go on.

Naïveté about geography was the usual case, and Mrs. Chotzinoff was not alone in a worldview limited to America and London. Often immigrants had little idea of where they themselves were from, let alone the details of their destination. Millions had never been more than a dozen miles from where they were born, and "the old country" was all that they knew of their origin. In America, many were absolutely dependent on others to get where they wanted to be. They wore their tickets on their shoulders and relied on ship and train officials to direct them, and naturally, there were mishaps.

An Italian woman traveling alone was carelessly ticketed to Carson, Iowa, instead of Carson, Louisiana, where she intended to join a colony of Italians. Fortunately, a railroad conductor who thought it strange for an Italian to be Iowa bound looked at her papers carefully and saved her from being stranded without money or friends a thousand miles from where she wanted to be. Train employees were less careful in the case of two women who boarded in Jersey City: "A Syrian woman destined to her husband in Memphis and a Finnish woman destined to her husband in Cincinnati" were routed oppositely, and "the Syrian was delivered to the Finn and the Finnish woman to the Syrian, to the general dissatisfaction of all four parties."[41]

Even with a valid ticket and even close to one's desired destination, it was still easy to run into serious problems. Berta Serina Kingestad wrote of her depression upon arriving in 1886 after a long sea voyage to Philadelphia, followed by a train trip to Chicago. She left her last traveling companion there and went on alone to her rural Illinois destination. "At eleven o'clock in the evening I arrived," she wrote. "There I stood, completely at a loss. There was not a single soul with whom I could speak a word."[42] Similarly, Anna Oleson was put on the wrong train and deposited at a small midwestern town, where she spent two nights and a day without sleep and very little to eat. In the words of her relatives, who filed a complaint against the railroad:

> When the trains came she went to the conductor with her ticket, but was not paid any attention to. At the station there were three young men who constantly kept an eye on her; one of them spoke broken Norwegian; they laid all kinds of plans to get her to go with them. The agent saw it but did not interfere. One of them took her handbag, and she had to follow them to a hotel, where she was taken into a room . . . In the handbag she had between $26 and $30 which they stole from her.[43]

Though everyone she met happened to be insensitive, at least Anna Oleson was a Norwegian in an area where many residents were from Norway. If one spoke a more obscure language, dilemmas could be much worse. Two Croatian teenagers bound for California had their tickets and most of their money stolen in a Buffalo

Two baskets that were presumably carried thousands of miles remain full, while women wait with their children in a receiving room at Ellis Island.

The federal government assumed responsibility for immigration from New York State with the opening of this facility in 1892, and 1907, the year in which this photo was taken, was the busiest of the entire immigrant era. Over a million newcomers arrived at Ellis Island in that one year. (LIBRARY OF CONGRESS)

Ellis Island as viewed from the air. The island housed a complex of buildings, and immigrants with legal or medical problems were sometimes detained there for weeks. (NATIONAL PARK SERVICE, THE STATUE OF LIBERTY MONUMENT)

train station. They found no one in Buffalo who could understand them, so they offered part of their remaining funds and were given tickets to Toledo. There they roamed the streets, vainly looking for someone who spoke Croatian. Finally, they spent the last of their money on tickets to Chicago, arriving there without a cent. A Traveler's Aid representative found them wandering in the station and brought them to a translator, and the California relatives were at last telegraphed for aid.[44]

Much earlier in the era, Gro Svendsen also found the inland portion of her journey more difficult than the crossing. Like others of the pre–Civil War era, she sailed through the Great Lakes to the interior. Despite traveling with husband and in-laws, Gro had problems with American sailors. "Adding to our discomfort," she wrote of the boat from Montreal to Minnesota, "were the sailors, most annoying and disgusting. I more than the others had to suffer unwelcome attentions. I understood very little of what they said, but their silly behavior was clear enough."[45] Others complained of these Great Lakes vessels, too. One traveler recorded:

> The poor immigrants suffer horribly on the journey, especially from Quebec [to Wisconsin] because the Americans in charge of them treat them worse than animals. A few weeks ago a family arrived, one of whose children died immediately. The three children in the family all contracted measles on the journey. To find a berth to put them in was too much to ask; so the parents had to carry them in their arms day

and night, exposed to wind and weather . . . When I comforted the mother at the
funeral, she answered, "If only the child had not suffered so much on the voyage."[46]

Much later, in 1910, a government report on inland steamers said, "There seems
to be no attention whatever paid to . . . care of immigrants on these ships." They
traveled with the freight, living as best they could. Outrageously, "passengers other
than aliens who pay the same price as the aliens have regular berths with mattresses
and pillows, and a dining room is provided."[47]

Nor were the early trains much better, in the view of Linka Preus. Her sea voyage
was pleasant, but the railroad ride was distasteful: "[T]he speed worried me a bit; I
was annoyed, too, when fiery cinders came through the windows and burned holes
in our clothes." An American inn at the end of the rail line was worse; the bed looked
"decidedly alive" with vermin.[48]

When Jette Bruns left Germany in July of 1836 to venture out to Missouri, not
even bad inns could be expected, and instead of railroad trains, she went by wagon
train. The route was less than direct, for they went north from their Baltimore landing
because "we had to go and get our cousin, Heinrich Niedieck, in New York." From
there, they returned south to Philadelphia and "continued on canal boats over the
Alleghenies." Despite being pregnant, Jette enjoyed the sights, "traveling beautiful
country in a free nation." In Wheeling, they waited a week for new wagons and then
continued a land-and-water route. From Pittsburgh, "we went down the Ohio, but
near Cincinnati we ran on a stump." The small boat that was substituted for the
damaged one was crowded and uncomfortable.

> My husband became sick and was very ill-humored. I was with the child in the ladies'
> cabin and could not always be with him. And the food was bad . . . For the first time
> I tried to express myself in English . . . I was able to persuade the black cook to take
> me to the meat storage room, where I looked for some meat for soup . . .
>
> Then we traveled on the Missouri up to Jefferson City . . . We went up the Osage
> River to the mouth of the Maries on flatboats . . . We disembarked at Mr. Henry
> Dixon's inn . . . until the new friends from Westphalia came to get us. I was shocked
> at their appearance, genuine backwoodsmen in rough clothing . . .
>
> Mr. John Shipley took us through thick and thin, often without any road . . . The
> next morning we were ferried across the river, and after a few hours we were at our
> new home. It was the second of November 1836.[49]

Jette's understanding of the geography of her trip was—like herself—unusually
sophisticated. More common were those immigrants, even in the twentieth century,
who had only the vaguest idea of where they were from and where they were headed.
Phrase books and maps were not part of the baggage of most, for nothing in their
European experience had told them even of the existence of these things, and many
adults were as naive as babes about the nature of the world. When Elizabeth
Hasanovitz left Russia, one of her neighbors delivered a sponge cake with the request

that it be taken to her daughter in New York. When Elizabeth replied that she was bound for Canada, not New York, the woman replied, "Oh, it's all right, my child. America is one world. You'll find her, you'll surely recognize her."[50]

Optimistic Expectations and Pleasant Journeys

While the horrors of steerage have been widely publicized, not everyone had a rough trip. The 1847 writing of Jannicke Saehle reads like the travelogue of any happy tourist. Though she was somewhat seasick, she mentioned none of the loathsome details that other passengers dwelled on; upon her arrival in New York, she rode around Central Park, visited a museum, and saw a play. The steamer to Buffalo was "very elegantly furnished," and after that leg of the journey, "things went merrily on the railroads."[51] Nor was Jannicke a giddy girl; she also recorded sensible information about crops and prices.

Expectations simply varied widely, and perhaps more important, so did attitudes and senses of humor. Though Angela Heck saw four children die on her ship, she managed to laugh off the pestilence that may have caused their deaths. "One other thing I want to tell you," she added in a postscript to her 1854 letter, "there were 300 of us when we went on board the ship. But when we left, our numbers had increased to the millions. And these countrymen were called lice. The ship was full of them."[52]

Even a young woman who traveled alone on an Irish ship just after the potato famine—when the worst of conditions were to be expected—had an optimistic attitude that made her memories not unpleasant:

> The ship was a sailin' vessel, the "Mary Jane." The passage was $12. You brought your own eating, your tea an' meal, an' most had flitch.* There was two big stoves that we cooked on. The steerage was a dirty place and we were eight weeks on the voyage—over time three weeks. The food ran scarce, I tell you, but the captain give some to us, and them that had plenty was kind to others. I've heard bad stories of things that went on in the steerage in them old times—smallpox and fevers and starvation and worse. But I saw nothing of them in my ship. The folks were decent and the captain was kind.[53]

Women with low expectations and cheerful attitudes could patiently endure even bad conditions. It was the behavior of traveling companions that seemed to be of ultimate importance, especially that of the captain and crew. If one could travel on a ship where the passengers and sailors were of the same ethnicity, where there was mutual understanding and respect, the chances of a pleasant voyage were much

---

* Flitch was salted and cured meat, akin to bacon.

greater. A Swiss woman who settled in Lancaster, Pennsylvania, in the 1820s wrote of this:

> I can also assure you that the friendship of the sailors, especially the cook and hands, is of more importance to a passenger than even that of the Captain. Even though a ship's crew is generally described as raw and wild, I must say on behalf of ours that here, too, there are exceptions. The Negroes, of whom there were ten on board, are a good-natured and grateful people. Their friendship provided us with many a measure of water and the best meat . . .[54]

Gro Svendsen traveled with a similarly friendly crew. The captain and mate, after expressing "astonishment" that she could write, encouraged her to browse among their books. "I have not had any of those unpleasant experiences that girls often have while traveling alone," she wrote. That she knew the reality of sexual harassment, however, is clear from her cryptic addition: "On this subject there is much to be said."[55]

The records of early, homogeneous travelers include many accounts of social activity, ranging from church services to dances under the stars. Weddings also were not uncommon:

> The bride wore a simple but pretty dress . . . The groom wore a black coat and pantaloons. All the passengers and the whole crew were dressed in their best clothes . . . In the evening there was dancing on board till midnight, and everybody had spent a very pleasant day.[56]

There were funerals as well as weddings, especially on the early ships with their longer, more harrowing voyages. Yet being in a smaller group in the company of one's compatriots could be a comfort. The captain of Gro Svendsen's ship was sensitive enough to even turn back after setting sail so that parents who had just lost an infant would have the consolation of laying their child to rest in the homeland. When a second baby died en route, the funeral was thoughtfully dignified: "The ship's carpenter made a little coffin and filled it half full of sand," so that it would sink instead of floating to the mother's distress. "We sang, 'Who Knows When My Last Hour Cometh,'" Gro wrote. "Next followed a prayer and the committal by the captain, and another song. Then the sailors lowered the little coffin. It was all strangely quiet and solemn. The waves hurried to cover the little coffin."[57]

Births of babies en route were also common events; Jette Bruns wrote of her husband delivering one, and many other ship diaries also mention newborns. Gro Svendsen's mother-in-law, being middle aged, risked her life to emigrate when pregnant. "She has been very ill," Gro wrote, "so for fourteen days we have had to take turns watching at her bedside . . . She has been ill largely because of the poor food. There is no fresh milk . . . There is not even good, nourishing beer."[58] Her baby was born prematurely and died after their arrival, but the family did not harbor any ill will for this against the ship or its crew, for they had done the best that they could.

People on Linka Preus's ship fished in calm weather, celebrated Norwegian holidays and passengers' birthdays, and enjoyed good food suited to their national taste. "We had fresh caraway sprouts with fried eggs!" Linka exclaimed. "Less than two hundred miles from New York and to be served such food . . . that ought to be recorded!"[59] On Ascension Day, 1851, she wrote of the worship service held on deck: "When we arrived, the congregation was already gathered, everyone in his Sunday best. Even the sailors were there and among them the cook, ordinarily all sooty, now clean as a whistle . . . The men [sat] on one side, the women on the other. From above, the sun in all its glory poured its cheering light."[60]

While Linka complained of the inland journey, Caroline Hjort, going to the Far West in the 1880s, felt her railroad trip to be an agreeable adventure:

> These sleepers are equipped in an unusually convenient and comfortable manner, better than I had expected of an emigrant car. The seats are not stuffed—just plain wooden benches—but even so, if one brings along a cover or two, one can have quite a good seat. These seats are made to be pulled out, so that two of them make up into a satisfactory bed. One must bring along one's own bedding, except for mattresses, which can be purchased on the train. For every two seats, too, there is a berth curtain, as on shipboard. At one end of the car is a cooking stove, on which the passengers themselves can make their coffee and tea; the rest of the necessary food is brought from home. Otherwise, one can go into the adjoining car, where meals are served as in a first-class hotel.[61]

Leaving Europe: Packing as the Least Vital Preparation

American trains were likely to be the last leg of the journey, the culmination of weeks or months of travel. The preparation for the journey is an aspect of emigration seldom considered and one that devolved mostly on women. After the decision to emigrate had been agonized over and made, all sorts of personal property had to be assessed for its value in the New World—and, in all probability, sold. At a heartrending auction or rummage sale, a woman sold her treasured wedding presents and cherished children's things. Her carefully sewn trousseau and national dress would be useless in America, and they too would go to another.

A Dutch woman remembered: "Rare pictures which had been in the family for years were auctioned off to the highest bidder, locks of my grandmother's heavy, dark hair were cut off and sold."[62] It had been the man of this family who pushed for emigration, but it seems to have been the woman who made the sacrifices. Especially in affluent European households and for middle-aged women, this was often the case.

And then there was the practical preparation. For those who emigrated on early ships, meat had to be slaughtered and salted down, cheese made and cured, vast quantities of bread baked, other food bought, utensils assembled. Warm clothing and bedding had to be readied; seeds and other essentials for beginning a house and garden in America had to be packed; even cages for animals had to be built. The legal necessities had to be attended to—and for some, this was a tremendous hurdle—and the good-byes said to loved ones who would never again be seen in this world.

In some respects the weeks and months of preparation were emotionally helpful. A woman had time to grow confident of her decision, to begin to adjust. Rose Cohen recalled that when her father sent her ticket, she suddenly became an important person in her village. The attention a potential emigrant received was both gratifying and pressuring. It made it difficult for her to change her mind and stay home; it was reassuring to know so many people cared, and yet that made it harder to leave them. Rose's feelings were typically ambivalent:

> I remember that when I convinced myself, by looking at the tickets often, that it was not a dream like many others I had had, that I would really start for America in a month or six weeks, I felt a great joy. Of course I was a little ashamed of this joy. I saw that mother was unhappy. And grandmother's sorrow, very awful in its calmness, was double now.[63]

Older women had even stronger roots in their native land, and Rose, still a child under the care of a young aunt, did not fully comprehend the mentally taxing complexities of the voyage. For women who traveled with children and without husbands—as millions did—the journey could be a real challenge. Men who were often essentially illiterate could not write letters sufficiently detailed for wives to benefit from their husbands' travel experience.

Even when literate, some seemed indifferent. A Norwegian man, for example, spent more space in his letter describing a Fourth of July celebration than advising his wife on the complex move. He offered only the sketchiest of information: "You should try to go either via Quebec or New York."[64] There was no word about disposing of their property in Norway, no advice on what goods to bring, no warnings of the difficulties she might expect, no estimation of the time it would take or how they would meet, no expression of hope for a safe journey. Apparently many women were similarly left very much alone with these problems.

Warnings from experienced emigrants could be very useful. When Rose Cohen's mother followed with the younger children, for example, she sold all their household goods except some precious linens and candlesticks. In Hamburg, however, she was told this luggage would not be allowed and sold them for far less than their value. The rumor, of course, was false, but no one had alerted her to con artists. Other women had much greater problems when families in America failed to inform them of what to expect: An Italian woman arriving in New York with three children thought that she had reached her final destination, even though her husband's address was in Houston.[65]

For some, the most important part of preparation was planning how to leave. Emigrants from many autocratic countries had government opposition to their departure, but for Russian Jews particularly, well-laid plans could be a matter of life or death. Rose Schneiderman's mother with her three young children left Russian-dominated Poland on a moonless 1890 night, paying a guide to show her the way around checkpoints. "It was pitch dark in the open fields," Rose recalled. "I walked holding on tight to one tail of Koppel's coat, while Harry held on to the other. The baby, of course, was carried in Mother's arms."[66] They walked most of the night, furtively crossing the border to Germany.

Mrs. Schneiderman's plan was astute in traveling alone, for a larger group could be fatally dangerous, as Rose Cohen shows:

> I noticed that Aunt Masha did not want to go into a wagon with small children. Nor did other women who had none of their own. At last, after much talking and swearing on the part of the drivers, . . . we were all placed. I was put flat on my face with ill-smelling hay. We were covered up with more of it, heads and all, then drove off, it seemed to me, each wagon in a different direction.
>
> We might have been driving for an hour, though it seemed much longer for I could hardly breathe, when I heard the driver's hoarse whisper, "Remember people, you are not to make a sound, nor move a limb for the next half hour."
>
> Soon after this I heard a rough voice in Russian, "Who is there?"
>
> "It is Mushka," our driver answered.
>
> "What have you in the wagon?" the Russian demanded.
>
> "Oh, just some bags of flour," Muska answered. I felt a heavy hand laid on my back . . . My heart began to thump so that I was sure he heard. And in my fear I began to pray. But I stopped at once, at a pinch from Aunt Masha and a nudge from her friend. Then I heard the clink of money. At last the rough voice called out loudly, "Flour? Go ahead."
>
> As we started off again I heard the crying of children in the distance, and shooting.[67]

Stealth had to be accompanied by bribery for government officials and fees for guides. Since so much hinged on their good-will, these men were in a position to extort whatever they wished, be that sexual or monetary. Guides sometimes insisted upon more than the agreed-upon price at the last minute, leaving women and children without sufficient money for the rest of their odyssey.

Even where bribes weren't necessary, unexpected expenditures depleted funds. A turn-of-the-century study of single women debarking in Boston found that 83 of 500 arrived without a cent and were detained until a relative or friend "called for them and guaranteed responsibility." The average amount these women had to begin life in America was $9.15, varying from $22.02 for Scots to $6.85 for Russian Hebrews.[68]

Nor did the end of the journey end one's difficulties. Mrs. Schneiderman, who slipped her children out of Russia at night, had to cope with measles en route. On ship this ill fortune turned into good, as they were quarantined in a stateroom and enjoyed unexpected luxury, but at New York it meant detention for the mother and two younger children. Rose was allowed to enter, but within a few days, the baby became very ill, was rushed to a hospital, and, with the mother, quarantined there for ten days. "Father and I didn't know to what hospital they had gone," Rose wrote, "and greenhorns that we were, we didn't know how to find out. But we knew Mother would come home as soon as she could." Little Rose stayed "alone all day in the apartment. I think it was the saddest, loneliest time of my life."

Her four-year-old brother was detained at the port and, having no visitors, felt truly abandoned. When Mrs. Schneiderman and her infant were at last released, "Mother had no idea where she lived . . . She took the baby and walked aimlessly for hours. At last she remembered the name of the travel agency where our passage tickets had been bought . . . and luckily, the agency was able to trace Father to the new address."[69]

The arrival of immigrants at their destination often seemed to depend on such luck. In the early days, when the arrival of ships could not be predicted, anxious families would check ports daily for news of their expected arrivals. Despite the detailed information provided to Barbara Klinger, for example, her sister and brother-in-law worried: "In the evening we heard that she was here and then until ten thirty at night we went around to all the inns and couldn't find her," they reported to the family in Germany, "and when we asked the people who were on the ship then one of them said she went to Philadelfia with some others, someone else said she already had a job somewhere else and so we had to go home again, and we hardly slept a wink."[70]

In the limited worldview of many immigrants, addresses no more specific than "South Chicago" seemed sufficient for their relatives to find them. The Immigrants Protective League of that city attempted to trace women who came alone to see that they had safely found their destination, but in the first eighteen months of that work, they received 734 addresses from ship manifests that were so inadequate they couldn't begin to locate them. Another 1,203 addresses seemed plausible, but no one there knew the immigrant.[71]

Sometimes friends or relatives moved after last writing to Europe, leaving no forwarding address. Frequently the address used was that of a steamship line or a neighborhood saloon, those places being more permanent than most of the roving foreign ghetto. Sometimes the newcomer was detained at port or had not left Europe or joined another relative instead, all of which caused confusion.

It was a confused process, and more depended on luck than should have. It was almost impossible for the average immigrant woman, given her limited knowledge of the world, to plan the journey with confidence. All that she could do was simply to put one foot in front of the other and keep going, dealing with the obstacles as best she could when they arose. Her most important intellectual baggage was her fatalism—her self-protective belief that what would be, would be.

18

STANDARDS AND
DOUBLE STANDARDS

Effects of Bureaucracy, War, and Quotas

Despite all of the obstacles, millions of women successfully traveled alone from the very beginning of the immigrant era. As the Victorian Age advanced, however, it became increasingly complex for women to move about freely—an ironic result of benevolent people worried about protection of female travelers.

While English women, for example, had left their textile mills for American ones from the earliest days of the industry, by 1910, the British Foreign Office took "special precautions in the case of women and young girls who desire to emigrate. Every application has to be personally supported by a responsible person, and all applications are the subject of very careful scrutiny . . . It is necessary to provide a certificate of the relatives living abroad or . . . a certificate of the employers." The Greek government after 1920 stated flatly: "[T]he emigration of women and minors of the female sex over 16 years of age is not allowed unless accompanied by a husband, father or mother, elder brother, uncle, son-in-law, brother-in-law or other near relation; or unless they are invited by such person or by their prospective husbands."[1]

Emigration became increasingly complex, and by the time of the Immigration Quota Acts of 1921 and 1924, it was a nightmare of red tape. Seldom did an immigrant woman have more than a few years of education and often she was totally illiterate, yet somehow she dealt with intricate paperwork problems. Moreover, early bureaucrats were commonly even more capricious and held even greater personal power. The grievance procedures and sensitivity training of today were inconceivable then, and the United States Immigration Commission struck fear in the heart of every alien: it was omnipotent, sometimes literally holding a life-or-death power. Especially for Jews escaping pogroms and for political dissidents, problems with its bureaucracy could be very serious.

But first, many potential emigrants had to battle their own governments over the right to leave. While nativists had nightmares of hordes of paupers shipped to the United States by European governments anxious to lighten their welfare rolls, this was only occasionally true, and when it was true, the offenders were most likely to be local governments of progressive nations such as Britain and Germany. The autocratic governments of the more benighted countries of eastern and southern Europe were anxious to keep their peasants home, paying the heavy taxes and serving in the army.

In the Austro-Hungarian Empire, priests were ordered to preach against emigration. Letters from America were opened by postal officials, and if they praised the new country, they were not delivered.[2] Border guards trumped up charges to arrest those attempting to go, especially Jews from Russia. Emigrants used all sorts of devices to leave for the Promised Land: they pretended to be going somewhere else; they disguised and hid themselves; they falsified documents, coded their letters with hidden meanings, and poured out their savings in bribes.

Besides government authority, potential emigrants—especially in the early era—also had to convince family authorities that traditionally held great power over individual lives. Jette Bruns, for example, was parentless, over twenty-one, married, and a mother, but her emigration was delayed while her uncles debated on the propriety of allowing her to go. She remained in Germany while her husband explored America because, as she said, "first I had to be declared of age and the guardians had to agree."[3] Her two younger brothers also had to get permission from the guardians of their parents' estate, who vetoed a younger sister's plan to accompany the group.

When Marie Klinger wanted to leave Württemberg in 1848, she had to ask local officials for permission. Her application stated that she had "100 guilders in cash and 100 guilders in clothing and the like" and that she was certifiably free of "defects" in the local police records.[4] Marie's request was granted in a month, but a decade later, the mother of her brother Daniel's illegitimate children, Friederike Kaiser, encountered much more difficulty with authorities who could not make up their contradictory minds. They were eager to be rid of this poor woman and her children, but on the other hand, they had never granted permission for Daniel and Friedrike to marry because he lacked sufficient assets. After the passage of legislation that disallowed admission to the "immoral," this family presumably would never have been able to unite in America.[5]

In the early era, the problems were more with emigration than immigration, but as the years passed, America's regulatory legislation increased and the standards for entry became more rigorous. Ultimately, the legal net was aimed at catching not only the "immoral" but also paupers, criminals, the sick, the insane or "feeble-minded,"

That these immigrants from Russia and Poland were among the earliest of their ethnic group is clear from the sail rigging of the ship. Some are resisting vaccination, which would have been frightening to those unfamiliar with the idea.   (LIBRARY OF CONGRESS, FROM AN 1881 ISSUE OF *FRANK LESLIE'S ILLUS-TRATED NEWSPAPER)* (By that year, incidentally, the Leslie publications were under the capable management of Miriam Leslie, who retained the use of her late husband's name.)

those "likely to become a public charge," those who had violated the Contract Labor Law, and even, in the end, the unlearned.

Individual cases are bewildering and sad. Take, for instance, the vague charge of feeble-mindedness, and look at the conflicting reports of social workers on the intelligence of one Katie Schultz, a "German-Hungarian" who had been in the United States for nearly a year when she came to the attention of some investigator who "became convinced that the girl was not moral and took her to Dr. X, of the Psychopathic Clinic, for an examination. He pronounced her feeble-minded to such a degree that she would be unable to protect herself; and as she is a pretty girl, it seems extremely dangerous for her to be at large."[6]

Katie was deported. Social workers in Budapest, however, had an entirely different view of her mental state: "She learns Hungarian so quickly that she will be able to speak it quite well in two or three months. She likes her work, is very diligent . . . His Excellency says that neither he nor anyone else could find why one would call her feebleminded; she is quite bright . . . She must have been shy and . . . did not speak sufficient English."[7]

Shyness and other emotional conditions could give a false impression to admittance officers whose "interviews" with potential immigrants were often only a few minutes. Rachel Rosenbaum, for example, was understandably upset at Ellis Island, for her husband died shortly after their arrival. Officials there interpreted her grief and anxiety as evidence of a weak mind. Although her prosperous family was well established in America, capable of and willing to support her and even had a congressman working in their behalf, she was deported. Since she had no family remaining in Europe, her life there would be lonely and sad.[8]

Indeed, eventually even a high-ranking immigration official acknowledged that the era's psychological methods were not capable of overcoming the variables of language and individual exigencies to deal fairly with these serious decisions. "A great deal of plain foolishness" was this Ellis Island official's judgment of intelligence testing, which was then in its infancy. He went on to cite a case of a teenage girl threatened with exclusion as "feeble-minded" because she could not tell time. It turned out merely that she "had lived under most unfavorable surroundings" and had never seen a clock.[9]

Even when legally justifiable, many exclusions appeared totally arbitrary. Complications arising from the Contract Labor Law probably were the most baffling. This law had been passed in 1885 at the urging of American labor unions to prevent employers from importing foreigners to serve as scab laborers in breaking strikes. It had, however, the paradoxical effect of putting immigrants in a hopeless dilemma: on the one hand, they had to prove that they would not become public charges; on the other hand, if they had contracted for a job in advance of arrival, they had violated the Contract Labor Law and were subject to deportation.

One Mrs. George Pearson of Nova Scotia, for example, wrote to a company in Connecticut and asked if work was available. When it replied in the affirmative, she and her family emigrated, but the government promptly produced a charge of violation of the Contract Labor Law.[10] Naturally immigrants wanted to know about

A woman undergoing the all-important eye examination. Trachoma, an eye disease prevalent in eastern and southern Europe, was one of the most frequent causes for rejection of potential immigrants. (NATIONAL ARCHIVES)

the availability of work before they risked their jobs and savings in moving. It must have seemed very strange that a government expecting them to prove they were self-supporting would also forbid them from making such inquiries.

It became simply an incredibly complicated venture. The unexceptional case of one Mrs. Kapolo serves as an example of hundreds of similar cases: like millions of others, her husband had preceded the family to America, leaving the woman to shepherd her brood of children halfway around the world alone. Eight-year-old daughter Mary had a severe case of measles en route that developed into nephritis, detaining them all at Ellis Island. If it became necessary for little Mary to be deported as failing the medical exam, the immigration officials insisted that her mother would also have to go back to Poland with the child.[11] Imagine then the predicament of that woman—herself and the sickly daughter in Poland, her husband and other children in Chicago, and years of hard-earned savings wasted on the trip, with no apparent hope of being reunited with her family. It took tremendous courage for women to deal alone with a process involving bonds, deposits, affidavits and appeals to boards and congressmen.

Katerina Kosice, a Slovak woman of twenty-one, exemplifies the red tape that could endanger one's trip. Katerina attempted three times to emigrate. On her first arrival at a port of debarkation, the steamship doctor sent her back for treatment of trachoma. She returned home and was under a doctor's care for four months. He pronounced her cured, and she traveled to Prague for a visa but found the Czecho-Slovak quota for immigrants filled. She was forced to return home again. The next year she finally got her visa, said her goodbyes once more, and made it to New York. The trachoma scars were detected at Ellis Island, the doctor decided she was subject to relapse, and Katerina was deported. "She feels so humiliated," her relatives in America wrote, "that she will not go home to live. Everybody knows that she has left three times already . . . Everybody will make fun of her."[12]

Like any bureaucratic procedure, the medical examinations were unpredictable. By the height of the immigrant era the newcomers were well aware of the chanciness of it all but considered it a risk worth taking. A young Italian girl who, like Katerina Kosice, emigrated alone found herself similarly detained by an eye infection. She got a room in Naples, saw a doctor for twelve days, and went back to reapply. This time the government doctor did not even examine her but merely waved her on. "All that time and money wasted!" she lamented.[13]

International political problems added to individual ones. In the crucial year of 1914, one Mrs. Arnoff arrived in Baltimore with her five youngest children, planning to join her husband and older children in Chicago. Kazia and Rachel had ringworm, however, and Mrs. Arnoff was to be returned to Russia with them, as "the mother is the natural guardian" and the hospitals of Baltimore were "disinclined to receive patients suffering from ringworm." After weeks of confusing communications and delay, Mrs. Arnoff was allowed to continue to Chicago with the healthy children, while the two girls returned to Russia under the care of an older brother. Three days out to sea, however, their ship returned when the war began. All passengers disembarked, except for the hapless children, who drifted in the harbor with only potatoes and tea for sustenance. The Immigrants Protective League finally received their desperate note: "I will wait until maybe a boat will pass not far away. I will wrap the letter with something heavy and will throw it into the boat."[14]

World War I was a cruel disruption to the migration of millions, and at a minimum, it meant additional years of separation, loneliness, and anxiety. However, even during peace, for a political or racial minority, exclusion from America could literally be a sentence of death. The friends of a Jewish widow wrote to the *Jewish Daily Forward*:

> This is about a family from Yekaterinaslav, Russia, who suffered greatly from the pogroms. The father and a child were murdered, the mother crippled, a twenty-year-old boy had his head split open . . . The survivors . . . came to America . . . The older boy, whose head had been split by the hoodlums, had a recurrence of the effects of the blow and was taken into government hospital . . . Then the authorities decided that he had to be sent back . . . His crippled mother intends to go with him, but she is desolate because she has to leave the other children behind.[15]

After World War I and the Russian Revolution there was even less chance for people to move about freely. The years of nativist fear of foreigners together with panic over the Communist revolution combined to bring xenophobia in America to its height. In the 1920s, immigration quotas for each ethnic group were set up. The quota system was biased to favor the countries of northwestern Europe—which sent relatively few immigrants in the twentieth century—and against those of southern and eastern Europe, where many still desired to join their compatriots in the United States.

The quota system made immigration a nightmare. Steamship companies were not to allow emigrating passengers in excess of the quota, but enforcement was difficult and companies would profit from women attempting to join their husbands. Just one of many possible examples was the Yugoslavian Reverez family: the husband spent $1,000 to pay passage and furnish a home in anticipation of the arrival of his wife and children, but they were immediately sent back because their national quota was full.[16] The steamship company had to bear the expense of return passage, but Mrs. Reverez would have to buy another set of tickets if they came again. Aside from the tremendous disappointment, women such as her now had to make their way from the port city back home, returning to a "home" where their property had been sold and their jobs abandoned—where they actually had no home at all.

Immigration officials said that they had a hundred appeals similar to the Reverez case from Yugoslavia alone. "The experience in the past," wrote one expert, "has been that the smaller quotas have usually been exhausted a few minutes after midnight on the first of each month." Yet the attraction of the magic name of America was so strong that people assigned these slim quotas made incredible efforts to figure a way around them. One group of sixteen Syrians—unrelated women, men, and children—traveled from Syria to India to Mexico to Cuba in various frustrated attempts to gain entrance into the United States, but their three-year odyssey was fruitless.

"White Slavery" and Protection versus Freedom

Even before the war and before the quota system, however, the evidence seems to be that women encountered more legal difficulties in entering the United States than men did. A man might have more trouble on the other side of the water, especially if he could not prove that he had fulfilled his military obligations, but in America, it was women who seemed to be the focus of investigators. The law provided for exclusion of the "immoral," so where a woman intended to live became a matter of vital concern. A man's abode could be anything from a park bench to a freight car—the officials did not bother to ask—but a woman's intended residence could be rigorously inspected, with dire consequences. A nineteen-year-old Russian woman, for example, who gave her uncle's address as her intended residence, was refused entrance largely because there were empty beer bottles in the apartment.[17] Eighteen-year-old Maryana Rosorzki was detained at port because the inspector in Chicago thought the house that she gave as her intended address was too crowded and unsanitary.[18]

It must have seemed strange indeed to the Maryanas of the world when immigration officials asserted that they were excluded for their own welfare, when they probably were accustomed to similar living conditions at home, when they had spent their entire fortune in getting here, and, most important, when they had little possibility of changing any of this without being allowed to try their wings in America. Moreover, millions of women had successfully done what they intended to do prior to the adoption of late Victorian rules.

There were, nonetheless, many such cases. A German girl coming to join an elderly male cousin was not allowed to enter because "[t]he Board think it strange that a young girl should permit a man . . . to support her." Yet they contradicted their own moral rectitude, officially excluding her as "a person likely to become a public charge"[19]—and the only conclusion that can be drawn is that a woman was damned if she let a man support her and damned if she did not. Rosa Markewicz, too, was sent back to Russia because officials did not approve of her joining an uncle, even though the man had worked for six years as a janitor for a congressman who vouched for his good character. The Immigrants Protective League also offered to find a domestic service job for this woman in a reputable home, but the bureaucrats—under the guise of protecting her chastity—shipped her out to face the world alone, disappointed, and penniless.

There is great irony in the fact that many of those most active in this movement to "protect" immigrant "girls" were themselves female and feminists. Their fear of incest and white slavery was vastly disproportionate to its genuine danger, and the effect of their protectionist efforts was to make women more dependent on men. One such woman such wrote proudly of the progress made in placing restraints on the free movement of others:

> Unprotected women and children are detained until their friends or family are telegraphed for. On no occasion is a woman or child allowed to enter New York alone . . . When a young woman comes to be married, if she is not chaperoned or cannot guarantee the observance of all the proprieties, she is married at Ellis Island. There is hardly a day without a wedding. In October there were forty-four.[20]

To a European woman who thought of her wedding as a wondrous once-in-a-lifetime occasion, a drab Ellis Island event in a language that she did not even understand was nothing but a sham. At other ports, too, such feigned ceremonies were common; in Philadelphia, "one part of the examination room was called the altar because under some conditions single women were prevented from landing, so that many harried unions were celebrated on the spot."[21] Nor could the American reformers see that their limitations on a woman's freedom might sometimes have the very effect they wished to avoid: the enforced slavery of a gullible woman to a devious man. A hapless young woman wrote to the *Jewish Daily Forward* of her government-imposed "wedding":

Dear Mr. Editor:

I have been in the country only two months, and I find myself in such terrible circumstances that I need your advice . . . My mother was married a second time to a man who had a son . . . When the son went to America my mother and stepfather decided I should marry him but didn't find it necessary to tell me about it.

Mother wrote to my stepbrother about the decision, and since he liked the idea, he sent me a steamship ticket. Still nothing was said to me about marriage . . . Before I left, Mother told me that when my stepbrother came to take me from the ship I should say he was my bridegroom, otherwise they would not let me into the country.

At the age of seventeen I left home, and when my stepbrother met me on my arrival in Castle Garden, I repeated what I had been told to say. Then they asked me and my stepbrother to hold up two fingers, a man said something, they told us to kiss each other, and they let me out.

. . . He took me to a room where he had his own belongings. I looked around in wonder and asked him, "Are you going to live here with me?" Then he answered that I was . . . his wife . . .

Two months have passed, and there hasn't been a day that we haven't had bitter fights. He shouts that he married me legally at Castle Garden. He's willing to go to the rabbi with me too, and threatens that he can have me arrested. It's impossible to live in the same room with him, because I have no more strength to fight him off.[22]

Paradoxically, while sometimes immigration agents insisted upon unwanted weddings, at other times they tried to prevent marriages that the people involved wanted. Throughout the immigrant era, women had come to enter into arranged marriages with partners whom they had not met, but in the post-World War I crackdown, immigration authorities attempted to put an end to this un-American practice. Rachel Badad was such a case: her parents arranged a marriage with the parents of David Solomon, an American-born man who had served his country in the Great War. Despite the consent of all involved, however, she was excluded as "a person likely to become a public charge"—a ridiculous conclusion in view of the fact that the Solomons owned their home and had savings of $12,000, and the potential groom was employed at $50 a week. Apparently their wealth was eventually persuasive, but even then, Rachel was not released to the Solomon family but rather to the custody of a great aunt who had to journey to New York for the purpose. Undoubtedly, a poorer couple trying to marry in accordance with their parents' wishes would have met with less success.

Though the frequent result of such protectionism was to make life more difficult for women, that, of course, was not the intention of the American women who busied themselves with this work. Instead, they saw a dangerous world and themselves as educated and affluent women capable of and willing to look after others who genuinely needed help. A letter from the National Board of the YWCA to the Immigration Commissioner at Ellis Island showed the special relationship these women had with government officials for meeting their 1911 goals. They aimed:

1. To search out the newly arrived immigrant young woman.
2. To make it possible for her to learn the English language.
3. To offer her technical classes that will enable her to raise her economic value; to offer practical and scientific instruction for those wishing it in domestic service.
4. To bring her into accurate understanding of American standards and American ideals; to place within her reach opportunities for wholesome recreation.
5. Accompanying all these practical agencies of benefit, we aim to aid and mould character . . .[23]

By 1917, there were "eighteen full-fledged branches" of this work, but the passage of immigration restrictions apparently caused questioning within the YWCA about its continuation. The female director of Social Service at Ellis Island encouraged them to carry on, saying that "both from the standpoint of the Government and the immigrant girl, such a service is greatly needed."[24] The work went on, and by 1929, the YWCA spoke of 684,000 women of thirty-one nationalities "who have come to the United States in the five years since July 1, 1924." Their representatives that year visited 9,527 new arrivals to help them "find work, English classes, and friends without delay."[25]

While citizenship classes aimed at men became commonplace late in the era, women were seldom routed to them. Even the protectionists—women with genera-tions-long American roots—were themselves nonvoting, second-class citizens in this era, and therefore it rarely occurred to them to encourage immigrant women to seek citizenship. Occasionally, though, this neglect had disastrous results, especially after the quota acts.

A Lithuanian widow, for example, returned in 1923 to show her childhood home to her teenage, American-born daughter. Before they were ready to return in 1924, the quota act was passed—and the mother, who had never obtained citizenship, was not admissible. Finally, she decided that she would "come as near to the United States as Cuba." There she remained, "alone in a strange land, not speaking the language and away from her daughter. The girl, returned to America, is without relatives here, is living alone to support herself and her mother in Cuba and waiting until she is 21 years of age that she may fill out form 633. Even then," the caseworker warned, "there is a long waiting list."[26]

Other women without citizenship found themselves deported even after very long residence. One who had been in the United States since childhood was ordered into exile after reaching adulthood because she had "become immoral."[27] In another case, a Mrs. Banir appeared to have been the object of constant surveillance by the authorities; her 1921 social worker's report read: "Charge immorality. Evidence against her is strong. Her house has been raided twice by police because of immoral conditions there. Inspector was very unfavorably impressed by her. "He said, 'She looked the part.'" Four days later, however, when the deportation hearing was held, the "strong evidence" had evaporated, and it was concluded that "there is really no evidence indicating immorality."[28]

While government officials focused on women if the charge was immorality, the one area in which men faced discrimination was the likelihood that they would be suspected of political radicalism. After the Russian Revolution, an irrational fear of foreigners and dissident ideas gripped the United States, and people were deported without the opportunity to defend themselves. Most of these deportees were male, but their departures caused serious suffering for wives left behind in America:

> Mrs. B——— read of her husband's arrest in the newspapers, and went to buy him some clothes. On Monday morning she called at the Barge Office at South Ferry, hoping to be allowed to take the clothes to him herself. The officials then told her that her husband had sailed on the *Buford* the day before. The official, she said, laughed at her. Angered by her own loss and his unconcern, she broke a window in the Barge Office. The act, committed in the presence of other wives, was distorted by the newspapers into a large-sized raid on the Barge Office. Mrs. B——— was arrested and spent five days in jail. There, she says, the other women prisoners—prostitutes, pickpockets, and so forth—jeered at her, calling her the wife of a "Bolshevik." She cried when she was telling this part of her story . . . "I can't express my feelings so good in English," said Mrs. B———, "but maybe it ain't necessary. You understand. Anybody would feel terrible to have a friend taken away without saying good-by, but I am his wife."[29]

Washington officials claimed that they had given orders "to prevent the separation of families, and the possible dependence and destitution of wives and children if the deportee was married," but "due to some unaccountable oversight," the directive was ignored.[30] There were several instances in which these men had money deposited in banks, but the distressed wife could not withdraw it because it was in his name.

The same immigration agents who were so suspicious of any radicalism on the part of men seemed incapable of believing that women could entertain a political thought. In a raid during a concert at the Ukrainian People's Home in Newark, forty agents blocked all the exits while detectives stopped the music and ordered the women to depart. "The women protested and did not want to leave their husbands, but were thrown out from the hall."[31] Despite the fact that females shared the same harsh working conditions that radicalized males—in fact, experienced even worse conditions—the police apparently believed that none of these women shared her husband's objections to capitalism. Women were seen as so wholly sexual beings that no official accused them of thinking.

The political deportations that victimized men occurred only for a few years at the end of the immigrant era. For most of the era, however, the double standard meant that women had more hurdles to jump. Women encountered greater difficulty because: (1) They were excluded if they were not properly married, were pregnant and unwed, had illegitimate children, or even if the admitting agent didn't like their looks. (2) Inspectors made it their business to approve a woman's intended abode, which never happened to men. (3) As "the natural guardian," mothers were apt to be excluded with "defective" children. (4) Women were more likely to be illiterate, girls having had less chance for education in most of Europe. (5) To immigration agents conditioned to think of a woman as economically dependent, she seemed more likely to become a public charge. (6) At the end of the era, the fact that women came later, following men, was a disadvantage, for they were more likely to encounter the post–World War I xenophobia.

Thus, for decades, women were subject to a double standard that inclined admission agents to wave a man on as presumably strong and able to take care of himself, while a woman was carefully checked. Emigration for her was a bigger gamble, a more complicated undertaking.

19

An Ocean Apart:
Separation and
Its Effects

Male Emigration:
Desertion, Bigamy, and Marital Strain

Rafaella Peppo was fourteen when she was wed to her twenty-four-year-old Italian husband. In 1898, after they had been married only a short while, he left for America. He stayed five years without sending a cent for Rafaella or their child. In 1903 he returned for a year and left again. This time he was gone ten years, while Rafaella had another child to support. At the end of this decade he sent word for her to join him in America: "However, he thoughtlessly failed to send money on which to come." Rafaella and her relatives managed to scrape together the fare: "After fifteen years of waiting, and by paying her own way across, Rafaella knew at last what it was to have at hand a husband and a father for her children."[1] But not for long. Michael found that having a family cramped his style, and he soon moved to Chicago. Rafaella dutifully followed, but he fled again, leaving a message that he would never be a part of their family again.

Millions of women lived through such geographical separations: A wife could live in a state of uncertainty for years, not knowing if her husband was dead or if he had deserted or if she would hear from him soon or if, indeed, he no longer was her husband. Solomon Maki, for instance, left Finland in the early 1880s, when his daughter Hilma, who was born in 1879, was so young that she had no memory of him. Hilma grew up knowing the excitement of an occasional letter from America, but over the years, the letters stopped coming.

Her mother did not know how to write and had to dictate her replies; moreover, her time was consumed in the hard work of making their little farm productive enough to support not only herself, two daughters, and a son but also her husband's aged parents. "I never found out how much money, if any, came from my father," Hilma wrote later. Successive freezes ruined the crops, and when she was thirteen, "my mother lost the farm. The animals and the gardening tools were auctioned . . . I hid behind a building and cried."[2] The family was split up, with the daughters going into service as dairy maids. From then until she emigrated at twenty-two—in futile search for her elusive father—Hilma worked at various aspects of tending cows, including shoveling manure. Her mother, meanwhile, lived an absolutely joyless life, never knowing if Solomon's last coal mining job had ended his life or if he had abandoned her or if, one happy day, another letter would finally arrive.

The memory of one's mate grew dim. While the woman usually had family, friends, and children whose presence prevented her from yielding to temptation, men footloose in America might well be attracted to others. "'Americanization,' in their cases meaning a taste for brighter lights, fancier clothing, more stirring amusements and less confined life, is not long in being acquired," said one sociologist. "Plain, hard-working Francisca or Gretchen in the Old Country cannot compare in style with their modernized counterparts in the cities of America."[3]

Bigamy was sometimes the result, for both his conscience and the legalities prevented an errant husband from getting a divorce. A woman in Europe continued to live in uncertainty while a woman in America was deceived, and both usually had children inadequately supported. A Jewish woman told of her separation:

> I was married six years ago in Russia . . . My husband] had no desire to serve Czar Nickolai and since I didn't want that either, I sold everything I could and sent him to . . . America . . . He couldn't send me anything to live on . . . I couldn't go to work because I was pregnant . . . Then his letters became fewer. Weeks and months passed without a word. In time I went to the rabbi of our town and begged him to have pity on a deserted wife. I asked him to write a New York rabbi to find out what had happened to my husband . . . I imagined perhaps he was sick, maybe even dead.
>
> A month later an answer came to the rabbi. They had found out where my husband was but didn't want to talk with him until I could come to America. My relatives from several towns collected enough money for my passage and I came to New York, to the rabbi. They tricked my husband into coming there, too. Till the day I die I'll never forget the expression on my husband's face when he unexpectedly saw me and the baby.[4]

The rabbi questioned the husband "sternly, like a judge," and the suspicions of bigamy proved true. The authorities saw that he was jailed, which of course made two families suffer instead of one. The newcomer adjusted remarkably well, however; instead of focusing on her loss, she got a job, went to lectures, and "began to read books I had never realized existed." Happy with her life in America, she forgave the desertion, even adding that she had sympathy for "his present wife, who certainly loves him, and her little boy living in dire need."[5]

Bigamy cases were sufficiently common that some immigrant parents took the trouble of checking out the backgrounds of their daughters' suitors, writing authorities back home to verify the man's unmarried state. Priests, too, gave thought to the matter. In one dramatic incident a foreigner was going to marry the daughter of a respected family. The banns had been published, an elaborate wedding prepared, and the guests were already assembled, when a priest rode up and informed the congregation that the intended groom had a wife in the Old World.[6]

While most men were conscious that what they were doing was illegal as well as immoral, bigamous practices were sufficiently common in some immigrant quarters that a simple man came to believe this was part of the Americanized lifestyle and did not try to hide his double marital status. One naive Slovak "brought his pregnant 'American wife' and two children to the . . . office of a charity . . . saying that the relatives in Europe of Anna, his first wife, had sent Anna to this country, and she was on the point of arriving. He added that, as manifestly it was not possible to support two families on his wages, he would like to provide for his second wife through 'the Charity.'"[7]

Second wives did suffer as much as the first, though theirs was likely to be a traumatic shock instead of years of doubt. A Bohemian woman had lived with a man for six years and bore three children by him when he suddenly decided to send back to the Old Country for his first wife "and turned her out."[8] Likewise, Polish Pauline Klimek came to America at age sixteen and was persuaded to live with a man. A year later, she discovered the reason for his reluctance to marry her—his wife returned from a visit to Poland and had both her mate and pregnant Pauline arrested for adultery.[9]

Perhaps the saddest case of bigamy was that of Mary Adamski, who suffered both rape and the loss of her children. She married in Poland in 1897 and was pregnant for the fourth time in 1903 when, "my husband decided to visit the U.S.A., much against my wishes." She bore the baby alone and after a year her husband returned, only to leave again two years later. "My husband hardly ever sent me money and it was a pretty tough proposition for us to live. Many days I went hungry for I hated to beg." Worse, Mary found herself the victim of a rape that was indirectly caused by her husband. The rapist, a family friend, explained after his act:

> You know I went to the U.S.A. before your husband and left my wife and children here. Your husband arrived in America sometime later and boasted of having intercourse with my wife . . . It broke me up considerably for sometime, until once I told him I would do the same thing and let him taste the same medicine.[10]

The rape resulted in pregnancy. Having to bear this unwanted child, having to support her other children alone, she wrote her husband and begged for help, but he coldly replied that he no longer wanted to hear from her. Three years went by and then he sent for the children. Mary did not wish to part from them, but family and financial pressures prevailed and "against my consent they were brought."

She followed to America and enlisted the support of Legal Aid to regain her children, who found that her husband was living with an extremely disreputable woman. Witnesses said of the couple, "They do things in front of the children so immoral that it is a pity that those children are kept . . . in such a house." Despite this appalling testimony, the judge awarded custody to the father, for he was earning $16 a week and "was able to look after the children better than their mother who could make only $7.50 a week." Mr. Adamski had no reason to doubt that his analysis of American justice was correct, for he had told a social worker that "he can have everything for money in this country."[11]

Cases of international bigamy became sufficiently frequent that some officials insisted a remedy must be had. A Scottish overseer of the poor, for instance, reported that during five years in his parish "340 families of emigrants . . . had applied to the parish for relief." His recommendation was to allow the emigration of married men without their families only under a system of probation whereby they would have to regularly report "to some constituted authority, with deportation on evidence of family desertion."[12]

A YWCA worker agreed, saying of men who had become citizens and abandoned their European families: "Unfortunately some judges have gone so far as to grant divorces to men without any investigation on the other side [of the ocean] of a man's charges against his wife, or with only a technical notification to the wife in Europe that divorce action has been taken against her." One Mrs. R., for example, struggled eighteen months to get to America in response to a notice from a judge:

> She finally obtained a place in the quota from her country, but arrived only to find that her husband had been many months divorced and that his accusation against her was that she was an immoral woman. Investigation on the other side has since discovered that she had for ten years ploughed and harrowed, cultivated and harvested the little farm and had supported his aged parents as well as her own three minor children without any aid from the husband.[13]

The detailed investigation necessary to determine such facts, involving an international bureaucracy as it would, was far too much to expect *laissez-faire* Americans to consider. Yet there was concern in this country, too. One sociologist recommended Congress legislate that "a foreign subject would be deported if . . . he . . . deserts his minor children and abandons his wife without supporting them according to their station of life and without due cause."[14] Uniform divorce laws in the states were also recommended to prevent women from unknowingly being divorced. Neither of these suggestions received any serious consideration from Congress.

Laws, however, could not readily cope with such domestic problems. Very often a woman could not even say with certainty whether or not she was deserted. Rose Schneiderman's mother probably did not think her husband had deserted her, for she had a happy marriage, but when he left Russian-dominated Poland for America, he did not tell her of his intentions. He simply went, hurrying off, witnessed by one of his children. Rose explained, "I suppose Father didn't tell Mother about his plan to leave so that if the police questioned us about his disappearance, we would truly know nothing of it."[15] He wrote when he was safely out of the country, and the family later followed in similar secrecy.

Even in cases where the marriage was less sound, however, desertion laws were difficult to enforce because for both women and men, their status and future was vague. The letters of Adam Strucinski are such a case. He was loving and full of promises for reunion, but they did not materialize. His wife had asked him to end his sojourn in America, and in 1911, he replied, "When the work goes worse, then it may be that I will come, but I will work as long as we have not a thousand roubles." A month later the work was indeed "going worse" and that became his reason for delay: "I cannot come because the work is going very weakly."

Another year passed, and Adam continued to excuse himself. He came close to revealing the truth when he told his wife that he did not want her and the children to come to America, for now "if something bad happens, I take a train and go ahead . . . but it is not so with a woman."[16] As time edged dangerously near to World War I, when he could not come back even if he so desired, Adam's letters continued to be filled with excuses and promises. Perhaps he had not deserted his family, but the attraction of America seemed stronger than the attraction of home.

A wife without children had even less claim. For almost two decades—from 1893 to 1912—Teofila Borkowska humbled herself in letters to her husband, asking him first to come home or for her to go to him, and finally reaching the point that she hoped only for occasional letters and money. Passages from her letters reveal Teofila's hardships and attitudes:

> April, 1894: . . . So, my dear, I beg you describe to me everything in detail, what I can take with me [to America] . . . I will take the image and the cross . . .
>
> December, 1896: . . . Don't be angry that I send registered letters, but you see you write so seldom I should think that my letter did not reach you . . .
>
> September, 1897: There are mostly days in my present situation when I have one small roll and a pot of tea for the whole day, and I must live so. And this has lasted almost 5 years since you left.
>
> August, 1904: For God's sake answer, what is going on with you. Perhaps our Lord God will make you free soon. I wish it myself, for I am also tired with worrying myself so in this world . . .
>
> August, 1910: I write you with great timidity, but despair obliges me . . . I tried to get from the Philanthropic Association at least a few tickets for a few pounds of bread and a few pints of gruel monthly, but they refused me, for they learned that

I have a husband. They say that it is for them all the same whether this husband is in Warsaw or in America . . . I begin to lose my eyes with sewing and crying . . .

July, 1912: They have taken everything for the rent . . . You won't let me die from hunger, for I know that you have a merciful and noble heart . . . Why, I have not much longer to live, for with such a hunger as I suffer now I shall not hold out long.[17]

Men did sometimes emigrate with the intention of shedding what they viewed as a bad marriage. Rosa Cavalleri said that it was gossiped of a querulous woman in her village that her husband "joined one of those gangs and went away to America just to get away from her scolding. And probably it was true, because he never sent back for her."[18] An Englishman wrote of his escape from his wife's family: "That infernal crew . . . wished me a thousand miles off, but I got four thousand miles from them."[19]

Even in cases of apparent desertion, however, there seems to have been relatively little infidelity on the part of women left behind in Europe. A Croatian schoolteacher made this assessment:

The women who are left alone here almost always remain faithful to their husbands. It is a rare case when now and then one forgets herself. But if it does occur the men show far more feeling and self-control than one might expect. A common peasant in such circumstances has often more strength and insight than an intelligent man from the better classes.[20]

According to another Slavic immigration expert, "Wives left alone at home sometimes misuse their freedom, and I have heard it said that infanticide has increased." She added that, "a curious story is quite widely rife in Croatia, and the returned emigrant seems to be responsible for it. It is reported, namely, that in America it is allowable to marry experimentally for a term of years." It was not clear how this misconception got started; it could have been "a *bona fide* impression made by American divorces . . . or possibly a convenient cover for American experiences of their own."[21]

Fear and suspicion on both sides of the Atlantic complicated separation. Nor could anxieties find the relief of articulation, for people of that era, particularly illiterate peasants, had difficulty verbalizing sexual feelings. Even communication about much simpler problems was hard, for European women were often unlettered and had to dictate their messages, making the expression of their emotions difficult. In a series of messages from an illiterate Polish woman to her husband, for instance, there are great differences depending on who was her secretary: her daughter attempted to express her thoughts exactly, while the missives written by her son were perfunctory and short.[22] Misunderstandings were to be expected.

Such letters reveal the tension that separation caused, and sometimes there were quarrelsome communications that must have left the recipient wondering whether he or she was indeed glad to get a letter. Scottish John Ronaldson, for instance, wrote angry words to his wife:

> You must [cease?] longwind stories . . . It wont [do to?] speak of dieing yet. Then you say your patience has been great. It dont look like it . . . You want a few explanations of my seeming coldness . . . You seem offended. I must say tis a pity . . . You conclude by saying that you are to resume your complaints, abuse and insinuations at another time. At any rate it means as much . . .[23]

Later John was apologetic and pleasant, saying, "Eliza, you mention about coming out and about wearying to see me. I believe you. Tis high time. This wont do long."[24] Separation caused strain, and the best of marriage partners could not help but question the activities of the other when they were parted so long. Nor were the complexities of human relationships the only source of dispute; women especially spent much of their letters reporting to their husbands on the details of family management, hoping that their decisions were correct and attempting to mollify criticism. Maryanna Lazowksa wrote typically: "Don't think I live here luxuriously with these children. I don't spend a single *grosz* in vain. It seems to you that you have sent me much money. But I have paid so many debts." When a daughter died and grief was added to the other frustrations, Maryanna wanted her husband so that she cried, "If it were by land, I would go afoot to America."[25]

When a woman was responsible for a farm or business, the chances were even greater that her husband would disagree with her judgment on some matter. Therefore, letters were filled with interminable details justifying her actions before they were questioned:

> Now you ask how much rye I have harvested. Well, I have harvested 5 *kopa* and 19 sheaves and of barley 2 *kopa* and 12 sheaves. I put it into the barn of Ignacy Pasek and I paid him 5 crowns, and the driving cost me 3 *gulden* . . . The vegetables cost 3 *renski* . . . I have sold that pig. God keep us from such pigs! . . . Will you allow me to sell the cow? For she is so bold that I cannot manage her . . . I have no firewood. I have burned all, and it is far to the forest, difficult to drive, and I have little money left.[26]

Husbands who had been gone for years became detached and gave glib, unthinking replies that were no help at all in dealing with the problems at hand. Another Polish woman—a midwife who could expect a higher standard of living than many— wrote in exasperation to her husband that she would live apart no longer:

> You have not even an idea how everything has stopped . . . If there were anything to steal, I would steal, but even this is impossible . . . You tell me to borrow, but I have already debts enough . . . So I write you the last letter and tell you, let it be once, either take the children or come yourself and suffer together with us. I write you decidedly, let it be so or so, for here I am neither upon ice nor upon water.[27]

Her firmness, however, had no effect, and six months later she was still alone, writing, "I have only wasted my young years in longing and grief, alone with these orphans, and I have no hope it will end soon."[28]

Some consolation could be found from women in the same condition, who might offer understanding and emotional support. A Croatian wrote of the feminine—and abandoned—nature of her community:

> Whoever has strength and youth is at work in America. At home are only the old men and women and the young wives with their children. Every wife has much to do for herself . . . The women help one another and live from day to day, dragging along waiting for letters and money. The money generally comes in autumn. Everything is bought on credit through the year; the dealer waits, for he knows that in the autumn it will all be paid.
>
> If not then, danger threatens the little house or at least the cow in the stall. At Christmas and Easter, too, and at mid-summer presents of a few dollars come to the fortunate ones. Others who have a hard lot wait months and years and never receive anything . . . Oh, how bitterly those at home feel this! They not only suffer; they are ashamed that they have been forgotten.[29]

Aside from the shame of abandonment, a woman who did not hear from her husband naturally worried about his safety and health. Despite the fervent prayers of their loved ones in Europe, husbands and fathers did die. Nor did America concern itself with those aliens whose family head may have laid down his life on the altars of national industry. Pennsylvania, home of the steel mills, had a law that barred workman's compensation to families of aliens if they were not in the United States, even if the accident was due to gross negligence on the part of the employer. U.S. Steel likewise gave death benefits only in the case of "married men living with their families."[30] This was rhetoric that seemed to promote families but in fact could have a devastatingly opposite effect. It also seemed to say to the male immigrant employee—a majority in the steel industry—that a family out of sight could be permissibly out of mind.

Moreover, even in those cases in which money was regularly sent, "the surprising fact," according to a male expert on Danes, was that the average amount was "relatively small." Money orders sent from the United States to Denmark averaged about 80 crowns—around $15—prior to 1886 and then dropped to "roughly 60 crowns" until World War I cut communications. In 1894, after the worst depression the American economy had known, Danes actually sent a larger amount to relatives in the United States.[31] Thus, a woman whose husband emigrated at the wrong time may have ended up subsidizing him instead of the expected reverse situation.

And yet, despite the genuine problems of those left behind and their true need for help, sometimes the reasonable reaction of a letter reader in America could be to rejoice that he (or she) was gone from Europe and out of family imbroglios. Particularly letters from siblings and parents, full of property quarrels and personal gossip, inspire this reaction. Swedish Kare Jons Dotter, for instance, wrote in 1846 to her offspring in America:

> You can well imagine the sorrow with which you burdened my weak shoulders . . .
> I wished to leave all this to you . . . [but] you did not regard it as a gift from God but
> rather as a poison that repelled you. This was the reward you gave me for all the
> unstinting efforts I made for your earthly future . . . Consider, dear children, how
> first of all you were the means of the early death of your little son.[32]

But not all letters were somber; there is humor and affection, too. Women seemed especially likely to express loving feelings by talking about those of their children and by quoting their comments: "Mamma, where is papa? . . . When shall we go to him? Perhaps tomorrow? Come, mamma, let us go!" and, from another, "When I ask her 'What will father buy you?' she says, 'Shoes.'"[33] Children were the primary link that bound the separated couple, and women probably thought that by talking of them they would encourage the father to hasten the reunion. "The children long awfully for you," reported a typical letter. "Joqus asks always where is father . . . Waldzio is already beginning to walk. Aniela had a good school certificate."[34]

Through Pogrom and War: Managing Alone

Aside from the routine problems of family and farm, occasionally there was drastic crisis when Europe erupted in one of its periodic outbursts of violence. This was particularly true for Jewish women, who never knew when a pogrom might appear. One Russian Jew whose husband and two teenagers had gone to America remained with five young children: "It was to be a time of sharp, close saving and poor living, until my husband could earn enough money . . . At length," she said, "I received . . . the tickets . . . I hastened to secure my passports. Everything was in readiness." She stayed on for Passover, to spend the holidays in her old home, when suddenly the rabbi warned people not to go out of their homes. "I . . . bolted the heavy door behind us . . . Even as I looked out . . . the flight of stones at the houses near became a bombardment."

She had neither food nor water in the house, "but to seek either was to tempt death. I set the ladder for the loft, bade my children ascend, followed them, and drew the ladder up after me." Flames could be seen and screams heard and even the little children understood there was danger. For a day and a night they went without food or water, while her two-year-old sobbed pitifully but quietly. "The massacres went on. And yet . . . the low wailing of little Molka, who was fast losing her strength, forced me to reconnoiter." Taking the ladder so the children could not follow, she looked in vain for aid. That night "the strain became too great for the . . . boys. They began to moan and cry aloud." Deciding that quick death in the streets was as acceptable as slow death from thirst, she ventured successfully out of the house. The family continued in hiding for the rest of the week, when it finally seemed safe. She hired a carriage for concealment and rushed to the railroad station, but even on the train menacing Russians followed the fleeing Jews:

> From station to station the horror that had been within my mind grew worse, for the Cossacks and the loafers told us that they were going to follows us to America. I think I became somewhat insane. I told the ladies . . . that they would do me a great favor if they would take my children to their grandmother when the train reached Radziwill. I, for my part, would jump into the river . . . Even after I . . . was safe on my way to America the fear of death and pursuit was on me . . . It was only when I felt my husband's heart beating against mine, in Philadelphia, in the United States, that I felt we were truly safe.[35]

The eruption of violence known first as the Great War and then as World War I had tremendously dire effects. The years just prior to the war had seen millions of immigrants pass the Statute of Liberty, and when the cannons boomed out across Europe in August of 1914, many were left stranded. If uncertainty had been a woman's lot before, with communications disrupted by war, it was doubly so. As Russian and German soldiers surrounded their town, a Polish family sent a desperate note to its breadwinner in America: "We send this letter through Japan, but whether it will reach you, we don't know. But a drowning man grasps even a razor."[36] Zofia Starkiewicz also felt the presence of war.

> [T]hrongs of soldiers are passing by us afoot and on horses; we see no end of them . . . Now nothing else but everybody prays and prepares himself for death . . . Rich people go to far Russia . . . Perhaps we shall no longer be alive when your letter comes . . . Few people are left, only women, for men have been taken, some to the war, others to digging trenches, others to transports; horses and carts are all taken.[37]

Because of the suddenness of the declaration of war, even people with valid claims on America were trapped in Europe. A Ruthenian woman exemplifies such complex problems—and how easily assumptions about women can be wrong. Almost anyone doing a global census in 1920, upon finding her in Galicia and her husband in America, would surmise that he had emigrated and left her behind, but instead it was she who was the traveler and the aggressive agent for her family. Ruthenians, the Molarskys had gone with their three daughters and a son to the steel mills of Ironton, Ohio, at the turn of the century. A final daughter was born in 1911, when Mrs. Molarsky was apparently into her forties. In 1914:

> After much discussion and correspondence with relatives in Europe, they finally decided to send their three older girls for a long visit to Eastern Galicia. Back in their minds was the hope that the girls would marry there . . .
>
> In the spring the three girls set off . . . The declaration of war in August . . . was

a great blow to them. Knowing something about the European situation, and a great deal about armies, they were terrified for the safety of their three daughters. Without hesitation they decided that the wife must go immediately, and bring them back with her . . .

Having arrived in Europe, the wife soon found herself caught in the full tide of the war . . . The Russian armies were sweeping over that country and this little group with their relatives had to flee. Nobody will ever know how they managed to exist during the five years [from] 1914 to 1919. The wife had neither the ability nor the desire to tell of their wandering in detail; the memories are too painful . . .

Eventually they were driven as far as . . . Odessa,* where they remained for some time, finding it easier to gain the means of livelihood in a seaport city. Along in 1919, the wife managed to get in touch with the husband again. He immediately sent some money . . . She felt she should remain in Europe for a while longer in an endeavor to secure the return of their little property in Kolomija; in addition, she secretly hoped that her daughters could marry and not return to America . . .

In both wishes she was satisfied. After a great deal of trouble she was able to prove her right and her husband's to the property . . . then her three daughters married . . . All this took time . . . so it was 1926 before she finally returned to America. She came with a feeling of satisfaction—a sense of having done rather well during twelve most trying years.[38]

When the war was over, Americans no longer extended their welcome to Europeans, and the flood of emigration was forced into a narrow trickle. Within a few years, immigration quotas would be imposed and separated families would suffer great hardship. These quotas "frankly" were intended to "insure a greater flow of Nordic stock," favoring emigrants from northern Europe and discriminating against those from the southern and eastern parts of the Continent. While Germany's quota was 51,000, for example, that for Greece was 100[39]—a particular irony in view of the fact that Americans had just finished fighting a war with Germany. The law imposed extreme hardships for women left behind, legally separating families for years and decades. The following case is extreme but illustrates well the complex individual situations that resulted from overly simplistic legislation.

In 1906, when Armenian Mrs. Demirjian was a three-month-old baby, her father left for America, intending to send the money for mother and child to follow. Like so many plans, his went astray, and the baby would not see her father until she was twenty-five years old. She and her mother lived alone "with barely enough food to keep us alive." The Turks massacred Armenians during this time ("I still have flashbacks from it—the dead bodies and the blood all over the ground"), and then

---

* As a Ruthenian, Mrs. Molarsky was from a province historically associated with Czechoslovakia; eastern Galicia, where her daughters went, was a province of Poland. Odessa is on the Black Sea in the Ukraine. She thus traveled at least 500 miles over the Carpathian Mountains, in an area that still lacks roads and services.

World War I prevented hope of emigration. The girl grew up and married, and when persecution broke out again, she, her husband, and her mother fled to Syria.

Her mother, at long last, went on to America as the wife of a citizen, but she and her husband could go only as far as France. Misfortune struck again; her husband died, leaving a penniless widow with two children. Her parents came to the rescue by arranging for marriage to an Armenian who was a U.S. citizen. He came to Marseilles and married her so that she could enter, and her daughter, who had been born in France, was allowed to enter under that country's quota. Her little seven-year-old son, however, had to be left behind until his mother became a citizen and thus could bring him.[40] The complications of the law and the whimsicalities of international events took no consideration of such human problems as a little boy whose mother was forced by law to leave him.

YWCA workers who were in Europe at the conclusion of World War I found their offices "filled with full-skirted peasants asking . . . how they could get back to the United States to join their son or their cousin."[41] The war—and even more, the restrictive legislation that followed—caused terrible headaches for social workers and great heartache to immigrants. Nor was it always the woman stranded in Europe and the man in America: in the case of one Italian family, for example, the man had gone home to see his dying father and then had become sick himself. When he attempted to reenter the United States, he "was informed at the Naturalization Office that he had broken continuous residence and must begin at the beginning." His wife in America bore their baby meanwhile, and the father had little "chance of seeing his son before he is five."[42]

The average separation in this wartime-restriction era was "ten to twelve years"[43]—an entire childhood. The result was a situation in which "we find desertion, non-support, divorce . . . and general deterioration as a result of long separation of the man from his wife and minor children." Moreover, these extreme hardships for women in Europe sometimes had only the slightest technical cause on the American side of the Atlantic. Among men who had lived in the United States for five years but were unable to obtain citizenship, one social worker cited several whose fundamental problem was merely an "inability to remember [the] name of [their] ship to verify legal entry."[44]

This and other aspects of the immigration process created a situation that was virtually designed to turn men into bad fathers. While women were forced to become more independent, men were encouraged by such policy to become more irresponsible toward their family obligations. The technicalities of quota law made a bad situation still worse with sexist assumptions not thoroughly thought out:

> There is . . . a quite unforeseen snag in the law, by which the wife or children of an alien resident . . . are perfectly free to make application for visas to come to America, but the wife or children of a citizen must wait for that citizen to take the initiative . . . This makes it entirely possible for a man who wishes to evade his family responsibility . . . to accomplish that."[45]

In other words, a family would stay forever in Europe unless a man—upon whom America had conferred citizenship—took the first step to bring them. The double standard went further in that "wives who are American citizens . . . cannot bring their husbands in excess of quota." One Mrs. G. was an example of this discrimination. She was born in America in 1906 of Polish parentage, and in 1923 she went to Poland for a visit. She married there, but, as a woman, the marriage did not confer citizenship or even a preferred quota for her man:

> She returned alone and immediately filed the form 633, asking for him to be given a place in the preferred quota, but was informed that it was of no value, because she was only 19 years of age. In time, her child was born here. She works to support it and herself, and is waiting for her 21st birthday so that she may again fill out form 633. Even then, her husband cannot come in excess of quota, as could the wife of a citizen husband."[46]

At nineteen, she was old enough to be eligible for a marriage license in any state in the union—old enough, in other words, to sign away her legal identity for life but not old enough to bring the father of her baby to this country. Such unexamined sexism in lawmaking had negative consequences for both individual lives and for the state of marriages and families. Couples naturally would drift apart during this enforced separation, and some fathers would be disinclined to take up the support of a child they had never known.

Then, too, the more common situation of separated couples, with the man in America and the woman in Europe, was especially prone to marital difficulties because this postwar era was one of tremendously rapid New World change, especially for women. When the twenties roared in, American women raised their skirts to historic heights, bobbed their traditionally uncut hair, began smoking cigarettes and driving cars. Husbands and wives who were an ocean apart lived very differently in these particular years, and they thus would encounter additional troubles upon finally reuniting. A European woman who managed to work her way through the quota maze arrived to find a situation and a husband much changed from what would have been the case a decade earlier.

> Frank K. had been in America ten years before he was able, under our present laws, to bring his wife to join him. In the meantime he had not only learned English and became a naturalized citizen, but, without realizing it, he had changed many of his ways and ideas. He had even learned to like American dishes and to admire the American clothes and short hair of the girls who worked where he did.
>
> Stasia arrived loaded with uncouth baggage, wearing many heavy skirts and with a kerchief over her tightly combed hair. She did not understand the American stove nor the laundry tubs. She wanted to bleach her linen on green grass, and she was homesick for her beloved white geese. She knew Frank was ashamed of her, and she was discontented and resentful.[47]

Seeing her marriage in jeopardy, however, Stasia took advantage of the assistance offered by a YWCA home visitor and "joined the English class, attended a club of women from her own land, bought an American hat and dress, and learned to make pies that a Yankee cook might envy. She now looks young and happy, and Frank," concluded the YWCA worker happily, "is never tired of bragging about his 'smart woman.'"[48]

Separation from family members other than husbands also occurred, the saddest being separation from young children. Kyra Goritzina, an aristocratic Russian exiled by the revolution, was forced to leave a daughter behind in Russia and a son in Belgium, with little hope of sharing their growing-up years. A Neapolitan woman likewise left her three-year-old son because his eye condition would jeopardize the entry of the rest of the family; five years passed before he could join them.[49] Similarly, the little daughters of a Greek man were not allowed, under the arbitrary quota law, to join their father in America until he was a citizen, even though their mother had died and they were alone.[50]

Separation before the quota law was particularly painful for older European women, for they usually had no realistic hope of ever seeing their children again. Except for letters, sending children to America was almost as permanent as sending them to their graves. After Rose Cohen's father had been arrested in Russia, but managed to escape and head for America, her grandmother commented philosophically:

> If I had been told a year ago that my only son would go away to the other end of the world, and that I would continue to live knowing that I would never see him again, I would not have believed it possible. And yet it has come to pass and I am ... contented that he should be away. Ah, how strange is life and its ways![51]

The Cohen family exactly fit the typical pattern of the father emigrating first, to be followed by earning-age children and then by the mother and younger children, while the grandparents were left behind forever. Most families that emigrated separately went about the process in that fashion, but there were exceptions to the rule of the wife staying behind while the husband emigrated. Appreciably more Irish women than men emigrated, and considerable numbers of Bohemian female cigar makers preceded their husbands to America. Occasional exceptions occur with other groups, too: a German woman on her way to Ohio with two small children was going there in 1905 to join her sisters—where all three women planned to work to earn the passage for husbands and teenage sons to join them.[52]

More surprising is that even some of the traditionally dependent Italian women came to prepare a home for their men. A 1912 YWCA study in New York noted twenty-one women who had left their children in Italy: "In every case the mother was to send money back for the support of the child, even though it had been left in the care of its father."[53] The mother of Sicilian Petronila Cirsanchio crossed the ocean twice, escorting daughters to the cigar factories of Ybor City in Florida; she was in Italy planning to make a third roundtrip when she was caught by World War I.[54]

Even when they did not go first, some women thought of themselves as the prime sponsor of the emigration process, as in the case of the young bride who "sold everything" to "send" her husband to America so that he could evade service to Czar Nickolai. In the case of betrothed couples, it was particularly common for the woman to come first, especially if her man had military obligations. Once in a while, too, a woman would fail to live up to her promises to one left behind: a young Polish man wrote with disappointment to his fiancée, "I expected that you would say something about the ship-ticket or that you would send me money for the journey, while you write me in a totally different way."[55]

Faithlessness happened, but despite temptations, the majority of men and women worked hard to reach their aim of reunion and longed for that day. Many made great sacrifices to bring the time closer. When the peddler came into Rose Cohen's tailor shop selling breakfast, everyone ate except Rose's father: he went hungry and saved the two cents towards his wife's voyage. The strong Slavs of Pennsylvania's steel mills may have seemed crude to the casual observer, but they too painfully missed their families. An expert on them relates a simple but touching little tale that shows the lonely pathos of separation:

> As I waited one day in one of the little railroad stations of Homestead, a Slav came in and sat down by a woman with a two year old child. He made shy advances to the baby, coaxing her in a voice of heart-breaking loneliness. She would not come and finally her mother took her away. The Slav turned to the rest of the company, and taking us all into his confidence said very simply, "Me wife, me babe, Hungar."[56]

They did miss each other and love each other, and most clung steadfastly to their belief that marriage was forever and that the family was the most important aspect of life. Yet often the care of that family for long periods of time was left entirely to the one who was its traditional center—the woman. She alone ran the farm, transacted the business, made the decisions. It was she who closed the home and sold the property and led the children halfway around the world. It was she who dealt with the brusque steamship officials and the powerful immigration authorities. She had never done anything like this in her life, and it was an important growing experience. She had handled tremendous complexities, and it was a first taste of success, of individualism, of budding freedom.

PART VI

THE TIES
THAT BIND

20

From Old and Male to Young and Female: Changes in Family Relations

Many Men, Fewer Women: Sex Ratios in Immigrant Culture

Managing alone in Europe and overcoming immigration obstacles gave new confidence to an immigrant woman, but another key factor in her improved American status was her relative scarcity. The ratio of women to men is a point often made in discussions of the American West: Women were treated with greater respect where they were scarce, and frontier states were much quicker to grant the right to vote and other civil rights. The same female/male ratio was a constant factor in immigrant cultures, for even as late as 1920, there remained a serious shortage of women in most immigrant groups.[1]

NUMBER OF MEN PER 100 WOMEN, 1920

Irish	74	German	108
English Canadian	87	Norwegian	120
Bohemian	98	Slovak	122
French Canadian	104	Polish	126
English, Scotch, Welsh	106	Italian	128
Swedish	107	Russian	129
Yiddish	107	Danish	148

The usual ratio of men to women had three exceptions: Irish women emigrated alone throughout the era; they found work and remained, to a larger extent than most immigrants, unmarried. English Canadian women were very similar; like the Irish, they had no language barrier and were attracted by jobs unavailable in their agricultural lands. Bohemian women established independent emigration patterns modeled on their cigar-making compatriots of the 1870s, when wives preceded husbands to America.

For all other immigrant groups, however, there was a relative scarcity of women. This situation gave women added status, for men became aware that if they did not treat a woman well, she could attract other men who would. A sociologist working incognito as a hotel kitchen maid, for instance, found that the foreign men employed there clamored for dates, saying how lonely they were. One was a shy Spanish man who wrote her notes and told her that though he had been in the United States two years, he had no friends and went nowhere on his time off because "it is no pleasure to go alone."[2]

The farther west a woman went, the more advantageous the ratio of the sexes became. While eastern cities sometimes had more immigrant women than men,* in Detroit in 1920 there were 141 men for every 100 women, in San Francisco 145, and in Seattle 146.[3] German men in pre–Civil War Milwaukee reported, "[Y]oung girls go here like lager beer."[4] It was not only women themselves that men missed but also feminine things culturally assigned to women. A Norwegian miner in California spoke touchingly of these scarcities in his world: "On Sunday," he said, "you often see the hardy miners on their way to the grocery store with bouquets of [wild] flowers . . . If there is a lady present, which is rarely the case, she is immediately chosen as judge of the flowers. But the prize for the finest bouquet is, it grieves me to report, whiskey."[5]

---

* This was especially true in Boston and New York, where Irish women predominated. More surprisingly, it seems to be also true for Baltimore as early as 1870.

An analysis of the census for that year showed women outnumbering men in the immigrant 9th Ward by a ratio of approximately three to two. Since Germans were the city's largest immigrant group, this would seem to indicate that more women emigrated from Germany outside family units than is generally thought.

These women presumably traveled alone several decades prior to the regularization of fast, low-cost steamships. Nor were they part of the exceptional migration of Bohemian women; the census lists the birthplaces of most as Hanover, Hesse, Bremen, Baden, and Saxony.

Swiss Elise Isely, who lived in western Missouri in the 1850s and worked in her aunt's boardinghouse, explained: "The frontier always has a preponderance of men, and St. Joseph was no exception. Most of the thirty men, perhaps all of them, who came to our table were bachelors. So great was the shortage of women in the West that many men of middle age were without wives. Girls of eighteen and twenty had their pick of suitors."[6]

The result was that women had far more opportunity to choose marital partners than in the Old World, and they could seek out husbands who offered superior financial and emotional support. Men lonely enough to walk around on Sunday mornings carrying hopeful flowers willingly entered into the competition for women, but despite loneliness, men generally sought women of their own ethnicity and did not marry until they could wed someone akin to themselves. Most rejected any notion of seeking American wives, for many saw American women as self-indulgent and lazy. The Scot who declared, "I would not have a Yankee; they only eat candy all day long"[7] spoke for Italian, German, and other men who expressed similar views.

Far from considering an American "a good catch" as nativists feared, immigrant women overwhelmingly preferred to marry men of their own nationality: even as late as 1920, some 700 to 800 of every 1,000 new mothers listed the fathers of their children as having been born in the same country as themselves. This phenomenon held true for Austrians, Hungarians, Italians, Poles, Russians, and even—despite eighty years of heavy emigration and no language barrier—the Irish.[8]

Moreover, when they did step out of their cultural group, the statistics showed that immigrants married either "Americans" or a nationality very close to their own. The Irish, for instance, married Scots, Welsh, or English; Hungarians chose Austrians most commonly; Poles chose Russians; and so forth. This tendency to marry within the cultural and religious group leads to the strong suspicion that when the statistics do show foreign-born women marrying American men, the men were in fact second-generation Americans who were very similar in language and culture and probably even were of the same nationality.[*]

Endogamous marriages prevailed, especially in the urban East. In the immigrant town of Lawrence, Massachusetts, for instance, marriages fell into three categories: those between persons in the same ethnic group, which accounted for 77% of all marriages; those between immigrants and Americans, at 19%; and those between immigrants of different backgrounds, which were only 4%.[9] Immigrant cities were

---

[*] Where statistics bewilder, a personal example may clarify. My paternal grandmother would go down in the records as a foreign-born woman marrying an American, but her lifestyle continued to be Norwegian; she was not "marrying an American" in the sense of joining the mainstream of American life. Likewise, my maternal grandfather, Emil Schultz, would be listed as a native marrying a native, yet he and his bride, Marie Otto, were German in their language, religion, and lifestyle. Moreover, his brother August would be statistically a foreigner, because he had been born a few years earlier in Germany; Emil and August in fact were completely alike in their background and culture—but nothing in the numbers would indicate that.

not the vast melting pots they superficially appeared to be, and in fact, endogamous marriages prevailed there longer than in rural areas. To this day, many Italians in the Northeast incur the displeasure of their families when they marry non-Italians, while on the prairies, Germans and Scandinavians were marrying each other and Americans during the first generation.

For both city and rural immigrants, however, the societal rule of endogamous marriages would eventually lessen. Women who in Europe were limited to husbands only from their own village and only in occupations similar to their fathers' would have much greater freedom of choice in America. Religion and ethnicity and finally even color began to become less important in choosing a mate than the merits of that individual. Again, the group lost power while the person gained; the family lost power, while its women gained.

Growing Egalitarianism:
New Husband/Wife Roles

Family structure saw other major changes because of immigration. People who had lived in large, extended families for as long as memory served left these units. Having once tasted greater freedom few would return to the family fold that was dominated by the old and the male. Even on American farms where large families were an asset, the usual situation was that one couple populated it with children, not that grandparents and uncles and cousins made up a household. It greatly strengthened the position of a wife, for there would be no contradictory aunt or mother-in-law. Moreover, couples lived apart in isolated homesteads, not in villages with relatives near as Europeans did.

The foundation of the nuclear family is the parents, and here too there was important change. European fathers, especially on the Continent, were regarded as unquestioned rulers of their families, but in America, women and children had more legal rights. Even more important than law, however, was the economic reality that forced immigrant fathers into sharing the breadwinner role. While wives and children had contributed to family incomes in Europe, too, usually they were not directly paid; in American cities, however, the pay envelope came with a name on it.

It is a testament to the great attraction of America that at least some males were aware that their superior status would be lessened, and yet they came. Italian men were forewarned in a 1911 advice book, "It is a crime severely punished in all states for a man to strike his wife . . . Treat women and children very kindly."[10] A sociologist traveling in remote Croatia found that "wives warn their husbands that in America things will be different, for women have more power there." One worried man inquired, "Is it true that when there is a lawsuit the woman goes to court and attends to it and the husband stays home?"[11] Though equality was not nearly so widespread as these women hoped, they saw the greater freedom of American females and wanted it for themselves. As a young Italian woman said to the Domestic Relations Court of her husband, "Now I am an American girl and I cannot stand for his treating me like a Dago."[12]

Even in cases of apparently arbitrary husbands and submissive wives, many women had a stronger voice in immigrant families than was easily seen from the outside. This was particularly likely to be true on farms, where a farmwife was absolutely essential to its success. Speaking of Czechoslovakian farmers, one writer explained:

> The father's role as head of the family is frequently misunderstood by outsiders, who are shocked at the way he "works" his wife and children and the mean circumstances in which he "forces" them to live . . . Upon closer examination, however, the relation of wife to husband does not prove to be one of submission on the one part and domination on the other. The wife is consulted in matters of general interest; she usually has a final voice in the buying and selling of land; she knows about the rotation of crops, and she knows which animals are to be sold and which retained. She is her husband's companion, intimately familiar with all details of managing the farm.[13]

While complaints were common that men insisted on having the final word on everything, the opposite situation also grew more likely in America. The trauma of immigration sometimes reduced male self-esteem, while the long separation of many couples made some men unwilling to assume traditional responsibilities. This was the case, of course, with deserters and drinkers who abdicated their duties without actually relinquishing their position as family head, but it could also be true of sober men, especially scholars and rabbis. These men sometimes left all financial worries to their wives and spent their days in the library or synagogue; Marie Syrkin, Elizabeth Stern, and Anzia Yezierska all wrote of marriages in which the woman assumed responsibility for virtually every aspect of temporal life.

Anzia Yezierska portrayed her mother as far less than happy to have this family "power"; she was instead so harried that she was woefully unhappy. When Anzia asked why she didn't have butter on her bread like a friend did, her mother shrieked, "Butter wills itself in you! Have you got a father a businessman, a butcher, or a grocer? . . . You got a father a scholar . . . He might as well hang the beggar's bag on his neck." When Anzia inquired what birthdays were and why she didn't have one, the reply was, "A birthday lays in your head? . . . You want to be glad that you were born into the world? . . . Wouldn't it be better if you was never born already?"[14] Perhaps life simply became too much for sensitive men like her father, and they fled to a spiritual realm where worldly pressures left them untouched. They were justified in their own eyes and in the eyes of the community as men whose lives had a higher purpose, but it caused suffering to their wives, who had to bear the practical burdens alone.

Even when men still viewed themselves as the unquestioned family head, in reality they often accepted modification of that position. In leaving Europe, couples naturally developed closer ties that resulted in more egalitarian marriages, especially when wives worked. The marriage of Mary and Martin Grubinsky was one such case. They cared deeply for each other, and even when they disagreed—as they did—they were careful of each other's feelings. They had gone from backwoods Hungary to Vienna, and then Martin had continued to America. Mary soon followed, leaving their children in the Old World.

> Mrs. Grubinsky cooked in a restaurant until her first "American" baby came . . . Three more "American" babies have been born. The children left in Hungary have begun to arrive . . . There has never been any question in Mary Grubinsky's mind as to whether she should work . . . She is enterprising and adaptable and takes the lead in Americanizing the family . . . .
>
> Two months ago she moved her family from a two room into a three room apartment . . . This was done in the face of Martin Grubinsky's flat command to the contrary . . . How should he know that an American family must have a sitting room besides a bedroom and kitchen, or that Tessie must have white shoes like the other girls?
>
> . . . Mrs. Grubinsky . . . would like to go to a moving picture show occasionally with the children, but Grubinsky will not hear of that, and so she doesn't go. But on the day of the woman suffrage parade, she ran nearly all the way to Fifth Avenue to see the women pass by . . . Sometimes Theresa brings home a story book in German . . . and her mother sits up late at night . . . and reads it . . . in her slow, unpracticed way . . . Martin Grubinsky cannot read and write. He once knew how, but has long since forgotten, which happens not uncommonly with working people.
>
> The Grubinskys have ideals and hopes. These center around the possession of a little farm in New Jersey . . . In the meantime, it is a sustaining hope equally for the husband and wife, and unites them through every other difference.[15]

Children and Parents, Sons and Daughters

In addition to the change from an extended to a nuclear family and the equalization of husband-wife roles, a third fundamental change in family structure was the relationship of parents and children. Women were particularly likely to be caught in the middle of this role changing. While a woman was apt to side with children in the diminution of patriarchal power, on the other had, she and her husband were united by challenges from their Americanized children. This change seemed the hardest of all, for often parents who had given up everything they knew and endured much suffering for their children's sake then found those children ungrateful and disrespectful, and themselves the objects of their offspring's scorn.

"Shut up talking about Bohemia," was the cruel comment of one boy to his mother, a thought all too common in many other homes. His observation that "we are going to live in America, not in Bohemia"[16] was true but not wise. A woman simply could not forget her homeland; moreover, the country beauty of her home compared with the ugliness of their Chicago stockyards district seemed an objective contrast worthy of comment. A mother also knew that her basic ideas on life had served her well and that a system of morality should not be subject to change merely because one had crossed an ocean. Children, however, could not be convinced of this; everything their parents believed was questionable in their minds, especially if those ideas were different from the prevalent American creed.

Immigrant mothers probably made this antagonism worse because of their European notions on the infallible status of elders. "I never heard a mother tell a child honestly that she herself did know about a thing,"[17] said one social worker. Ultimately, a mother undermined her authority this way, for chances were that her child would soon know more about American life than she, and her pretension to know things that she did not would damage her credibility in more important areas.

Nor was the change easy for the children. Rose Cohen, for example, was pained when she went against her parents' wishes, but she felt that she must leave them behind and adopt the ideas of the new country. She, like millions of other members of the second generation, did not truly fit anywhere. The children of immigrants straddled two worlds and were different from both their parents and their American peers. Activities that natives viewed as wholly innocent, for example, were wild by the standards of Italian parents; some put daughters in homes for wayward girls because they came in at ten at night or went to a dance.[18]

Respect for the father was so strong in some southern Italian homes that children and even wives used the formal "you" when addressing him rather than the familiar "thou."[19] Indeed, in many immigrant homes the strongest emotion children had for fathers was not love but fear. "The children fear Martin," reported a social worker of a tyrannical Irish father, "but mimic him in his absence. They do not ask God to bless him in their prayers."[20]

Elizabeth Stern suggested—and the conventional wisdom seems to agree—that there was a direct reversal in European and American views of fathers and mothers. She greatly respected and feared her father in the European tradition, while, she observed, her American boyfriend spoke of his mother with reverence and his father as more of a pal. Indeed, Americans have traditionally revered motherhood, whereas fathers are sometimes treated as a joke.

If the father ranked at the head of the immigrant family, the daughter ranked at the bottom. This was true even when daughters were adults and primary family-income earners. A Cleveland Hungarian named Jolan was typical of many such young women; she was the sole support of her family, for her father was unemployed, but he nonetheless was "very strict. He believes that girls should not stay out later than 8:30 PM . . . even if the girl is 20 years old and has a job." She added, "Mother sometimes tell him that girls need a few extra things, besides necessities, but she doesn't get very far with him, because he says, he is the boss."[21]

Another Hungarian echoed this experience, saying, "It burns me up to think that my kid brother does all these things and has more freedom that I have, just because he is a boy . . . My father thinks girls should not be out as much as boys, that girls should stay home, learn to cook, sew and clean the house." She saw the self-determination allowed to her brother as a direct reflection of her father's freedom, while her mother's life foreshadowed only dreary isolation. "I honestly wish my mother would get out a little more than she does," said this empathetic teenager, "but then none of her friends do."[22]

While a low status for daughters was true to some extent in all ethnicities, Italians illustrated the point in its baldest form. One sociologist commented:

> Here, as in Italy, the Italian girl is generally the least important member of the family. Her father and brothers, by the very fact of their sex, hold complete authority . . . while the mother has precedence . . . In one family that I know the 19 year old daughter is the sole support of a hard-drinking, idle parasite of a father, a sick mother and three shiftless younger brothers, yet she is not allowed to eat at the table and sleeps on a cot in the kitchen . . . I have known an Italian to drag his 13 year old daughter by the hair (its being unbobbed was another proof of his authority) before the little statue of the Virgin . . . and force her to remain on her knees before it for 3 hours, asking forgiveness for having helped herself before him at the table to the Sunday chicken . . . In fact, I have known an Italian to take the strap to his married daughter when he felt that her husband was handling her with too American a leniency.[23]

Some fathers were so wholly arbitrary that they expected their adult children to follow commands implicitly even in the most personal of areas. In one striking example, a Jewish father anglicized the family name, dropped all of his Jewish associations, and married his daughter to a Gentile. After encountering discrimination despite his disguise, the man became a fervent Zionist, readopted Hebrew customs, and insisted that the daughter could not visit the family until she divorced her husband and married a Jew.[24] Clearly, in such minds, a daughter had no right to a life outside her father's ideas.

Not surprisingly, a number of older women remembered their childhoods with resentment of their fathers and of what they came to see as exploitation by their families. A fifty-nine-year-old Italian recalled bitterly that in the Old Country, "girls never went to school, but were made to work." Another spoke with anger of the agricultural labor that she began at age seven: "I worked like a horse, not like a woman."[25] Even when such families became affluent enough in America to do without money from daughters, they still burdened leisure with restrictions. Girls who had left school but were not yet married were expected to spend their time indoors with their mothers, "practically prisoners at home."[26]

While immigrant daughters were subject to more severe family discipline than American girls, immigrant boys were virtually always less restrained than native sons. The primary reason for this was simply the superior status of the European male, but an additional factor may have been the clumsy intervention of American law into family strife. The traditional method of discipline in much of Europe was a severe beating, but in America, immigrants learned that was not allowed; the parent became the offender instead of the child. Their bewildered response to this sometimes resulted in no discipline at all, since they knew no method other than beating. The child, as he grew old enough to grasp the situation, was apt to take unfair advantage of the law.

The oldest Pagano son illustrated well the problems that families had with recalcitrant sons—and the divisions this could cause between husband and wife. The boy was in constant trouble with the school authorities. He "moved in and out of the house as he pleased" and went into professional boxing without his parents' knowledge. He gambled, chased women, got into fights, and was even stabbed. Finally the father got word of his boxing activities and exploded that his son should follow such a lowly profession and, worse, conceal it from his family. They had a row and the boy ran away. Mrs. Pagano was full of recrimination for the father and worry for her son; the following Christmas he turned up, in answer to his mother's prayers. The father ignored his presence, but the rest of the family welcomed him. To the younger children, he was a hero:

> It was almost as though he was boasting about his travels to irritate my father
> . . . For the first time in our memory my father had been pushed into the back-
> ground . . . And all of us shivered in secret delight. It was as though Lou were paying
> off the grievances which each of us . . . had accumulated against my father, and to
> which we had never, until now, had any recourse.[27]

Lou continued his dissolute habits, and the father maintained an icy silence as the son drove the wedge deeper between him and his wife. She was so grateful for her boy's return that she defended him blindly at first, but slowly she too grew disgusted with his behavior. One day she burst out in agitated Italian: "Always it is the same. First you do the bad thing to break your parent's hearts, and then you tell us to keep quiet. Keep quiet yourself! You are my son, and I am your mother."[28] Her admonition had no effect, and two weeks after this, Lou left again.

He turned up later in the army, fighting in World War I. Now the parental attitudes reversed. The father, carried away with wartime patriotism, was proud of his son, while the mother disapproved. She was fearful for his safety, but she also could not see that there was any logical difference between professional boxing and professional soldiering. And the gulf between them that this son caused grew deeper.

"My father wanted to have the [army] picture framed and put on the mantel. 'So that you can put out your chest and act proud? You, who acted like a mad dog when he was home!'"[29] It developed into the first serious fight they had in many years of marriage. She spat in his face and he left her. He saw to the family's support, but he refused to go home. She was equally stubborn and angrily refused relatives' appeals for compromise. This went on for months—until the news came that their son was dead. The father returned, and the grieving parents, whose child had caused them such tragedy, mourned him together. But the mistakes had been made when he was young, and they were typical of the mistakes immigrant parents made over and over again in giving their sons, especially the firstborn, more freedom than they could handle, while depriving their daughters of any.

The Immigrant Elderly, Stepchildren, and Surrogate Mothers

Old age was a major impediment to emigration, both because the aged were more reluctant to leave home and because they were less capable of surviving the rigors of travel and admission. The first-generation home, therefore, seldom had grandparents, who often had been present in Old World homes. For women, this meant the loss of live-in help with family chores; for children, it meant the loss of affection that grandparents give; for the aged, it meant loneliness at the end of life.

Rose Cohen's blind grandmother realized when her son fled to America that his family would soon follow and only her twenty-one-year-old unmarried daughter would be left. She understood that to burden this young woman with elderly parents and no dowry would ruin her chances in Russia, and so she bravely determined that her daughter should go to America, too, and the parents would remain in Russia to await their lonesome death. At last they were separated even from each other when no one was willing to board both of them. The sacrifices that such mothers made for their families were every bit as great as the sacrifices of younger mothers in America.

While the aged did not generally emigrate, within a decade or two immigrant homes had their own elderly, for the hard work of the industrial engine wore out bodies at an early age. The menial labor at which most toiled required youthful vigor, and both men and women had a hard time finding jobs past forty. Social workers commented that immigrants referred to themselves as old when they were still young by American standards. A forty-two-year-old Roman, for example, who earned only slightly more than his seventeen-year-old daughter, excused himself from any greater share in supporting his nine-member family because "it is hard for an old man to find work."[30]

These family members then sometimes became a burden, and resentment of the elderly began to appear. Despite rhetoric of veneration for the aged, there is evidence that younger family members on both sides of the Atlantic sometimes developed harshly opposite attitudes—especially in the case of men who had been brought up spoiled by mothers whom they did not learn to respect. Jette Bruns wrote of a German neighbor in Missouri whose mother meekly kept house for him: "She complained little," Jette said, "until she came to ask for some coffee. Anxiously, she paid in advance . . . It had to be secretly. Fortunately, she soon died."[31] Likewise, Anna Maria Klinger Schano wrote back to Germany in 1857: "I must admonish Eberhart and Jakob not to let our poor parents suffer want, for example when mother asks for some skim milk and you first ask for money. I am very sorry to hear that, aren't they your parents, too? Believe me the money we've sent them is hard-earned, too."[32]

It was money and work that was the center of such conflict, but neither Old World nor American mores condoned obvious mistreatment of the elderly. Neighborhood gossip would not permit their exclusion from the household, and the institutional nursing home did not exist for much of the immigrant era. And so the elderly—usually the widows of older men—stayed with their children, sometimes passed from home to home, knowing perhaps that they were unwanted. As an Italian woman succinctly explained, "My husband's mother lives with us. She makes me much work, but what can I do? We must keep her or lose face."[33] The reluctance of the Americanized to assume responsibility for elderly parents also is seen in this Jewish woman's missive:

> In Galicia, I was a respected housewife and my husband was a well-known businessman. God blessed us with three daughters and three sons and we raised them properly. When they grew up, one by one they left home, like birds leaving their nest . . . I was left all alone. I longed for the children and wrote to them that I wanted to come to America to be with them and the grandchildren. But from the first they wrote to me that America was not for me, that they do not keep kosher and that I would be better off staying at home.[34]

The young were not entirely selfish, for it was true that older immigrants would have special difficulty in adjusting. Most of them knew that, and they did not attempt to uproot themselves in the autumn of their lives. Nonetheless it is plain that grandparents, who were an unquestioned feature of Old World households, came to be viewed as a liability in many American homes.

While grandparents were less common in immigrants homes, stepchildren were more common. Immigrant parents often died young, leaving children motherless or fatherless, and because of their general distaste for the single state, stepchildren were part of many families. Justina Kreiger, for example, had eleven children when the Minnesota Sioux uprising occurred—some from her own first marriage, others from her husband's first marriage, and some whom they had had together. She used language indicating that she thought of all them as the same, however, saying in one case, "At the fort I found four of my children; all but one, children of my first husband." Only twenty-seven when her second husband was killed in August 1862, she married a third time in early November. Her groom was a "countryman of mine, who lost all his family," so this marriage brought no stepchildren—but given her age, they probably had more children together.

This kind of situation was sometimes a source of disruption in immigrant homes, as biological children and stepchildren battled each other and parents. The stereotype of the cruel stepmother had at least some basis in statistical fact: A study of delinquent Chicago children in 1912, for example, cited many examples of stepparents who were severe to the point of sadism, their cruelty leading to the delinquency of the child. One German-born woman was unabashed in her callousness toward her husband's children: "A person can barely care for her own children. How can she care for . . .

strange ones?" The probation officer added that she said "she hated the children and that her only interest in them was due to the fact that they could earn when they were fourteen years old."[35]

There were of course loving stepmothers, too. Jette Bruns made absolutely no distinction between her own children and the orphaned nephews and niece she took in after her brother died; indeed, there were times when she said complimentary things about those children in contrast to one of her own. She and her husband even assumed the financial obligations of educating the orphans when affluent family members in Germany refused to do so. Similarly, German Barbara Klinger's siblings lovingly cared for her half-Jewish little boy when she left him with them for years. At holidays, for instance, pride and joy were equal for the son and the nephew: "I also want to describe to you Wilhelm and Karl's Christmas presents, they've already got a drum, a flag, . . . and they're going to get a Christmas tree as well, you should just see how cheerful they are and they're always speaking English to each other."[36]

Rebekah Kohut, a Baltimore Jew, also had a loving stepmother—and she became one, despite the wishes of her own stepmother. While her stepmother had reared her and five siblings without apparent resentment, when Rebekah wanted to marry a widower with eight children, her stepmother was adamantly opposed. The wedding took place a year later, but Rebekah wrote, "My marriage seemed to her more like a funeral ceremony. As she told me later, the thought of my being immured within the walls of a home that was already filled with children seemed too terrible."[37] Indeed, many in the era seem to share this view of stepmothers as unfairly exploited by their foster children, and thus excused them when they were undeniably hard-hearted.*

There was another—and kindlier—surrogate mother in some immigrant homes. Older sisters were often forced into a motherhood role because their mothers were excessively burdened. Rosa Cavalleri's oldest daughter, when she was still under ten, cared for the other children while her mother worked; Rose Cohen's maternal attitude toward her siblings is seen in her continual references to them as "our children." Indeed, the position of oldest daughter became virtually institutionalized in immigrant families. The language used by a YWCA interviewer, in speaking of a thirty-two-year-old Slovene who worked as a trained nurse, reveals the acceptance of this concept of "little mother":

> Jean is the oldest in a family of eight . . . She has shouldered many home responsibilities since her earliest childhood and was a "little mother" in the home, making many personal sacrifices for the benefit of her younger siblings. She entered nurses'

---

* My own grandfather was put out to earn his living at age eleven by his German stepmother after his father died; she assumed responsibility for only her own baby and literally farmed out her late husband's four sons.

On the other hand, my Norwegian grandmother cared for her husband's orphaned nieces and nephews; these four children came to live in Minnesota after their Norwegian parents both died of tuberculosis in Chicago.

training quite late and only after considerable encouragement on the part of others who pointed out to her that there is no future for her in continuing to be the "little mother" at home. She had to overcome much passive opposition in her family in order to go into training . . .

She has . . . discovered the fact that she had always been a mediator between her parents and her younger siblings whenever they came in conflict over their opinions. This happens more frequently because they are less submissive than she was . . . Jean believes that she has smoothed the way for her sisters and brothers by being the first one to bring up questions of conflict.[38]

Sometimes, however, the sacrifices these girls made were unappreciated by the young, who instead resented the sister for assuming the authority of the mother. Even when siblings were older, the efforts of an oldest sister often went unappreciated. Theresa Malkiel wrote of her friend Clara, a big, clumsy girl whose work-roughened hands testified to her tender heart, for she had been in the factory since youth, working first to bring her siblings to America and then to educate them and provide them with luxuries she had never enjoyed. Their thanks was to scorn Clara's poor English and to be ashamed of her around their American friends.

Lotte Bauer, a German girl, was another sister who encountered all of the problems of mothers. Her father had been killed in one of Prussia's wars, and her grandfather held strict control over the family. He had resisted appeals to emigrate, but as one after another of his young sons were killed in the military, he went with his daughter-in-law and her children to America. At first things went well, but suddenly the mother sickened and died. Lotte had to redouble her efforts to replace this lost income, and then a younger child followed the mother to the grave. Unable to keep her fun-loving fourteen-year-old sister out of trouble, Lotte saw her run away to a brothel. The final calamity came when her grandfather was hit by a falling barrel while he worked as a stevedore and was left hopelessly paralyzed. For a year Lotte desperately tried to care for him and the younger children, while her longtime boyfriend abandoned her because she refused to institutionalize the children. She drove herself relentlessly, and it killed her. She suffered an apparent brain hemorrhage and died, quickly and young.[39]

Americanized Adults: Relationships between Siblings

Such families as Lotte's probably were broken up, and the children sent to foster homes or orphanages. It was something that happened with greater frequency to immigrant families, where death was more likely to claim parents before children were grown. The result was that children in many immigrant homes lived their adult lives without knowledge of their siblings. Oceanic separation and illiteracy of course increased the problem. An Irish woman said of her family:

> There were seven children of us. John and Matthew they went to Australia. Mother was layin' by for five year to get their passage money . . . We heard twice from thim and then no more. Not another word and this is forty year gone now—on account of thim not reading and writing . . . I suppose they're dead now—John would be 90 now—and in heaven.[40]

There was tremendous variation in the contact siblings kept with each other. Collections of immigrant letters show that some wrote home only every five or ten years, others wrote annually, and still others more often—and some never. What siblings had in common after many years of separation was a factor, too. Gro Svendsen, for example, kept in close contact with her family after years of separation. They were farmers as she was, and they even read the same publications, for Gro often made comments such as, "You already know from the newspapers . . ." Women who adopted new factory occupations and a city lifestyle unlike their European siblings, on the other hand, found they had fewer mutual interests and were more apt to give up communication with siblings who probably would never be seen again.

Even in America, there was variation among siblings in the contact they kept after emigration. Most of the German Klinger family stayed near each other in and around New York—and they seemed to resent their sister Barbara's illegitimate pregnancy less than her failure to keep in touch after going west. "I'm not counting on Babet," Katherina wrote harshly in 1858. "I haven't seen her for 5 years and not a word from her, if she'd rather be dead in the wilderness then you know she wouldn't be there."[41] But keeping in touch required a fondness for the written word, as well as fondness for letters' recipients. That, indeed, was the overriding factor for many who failed to write. Even if they were literate, many women simply could not find the time and mental resources to communicate unless there was an urgent need.

Jette Bruns was an amazing exception. Despite a busy life filled with eleven children, she cared enough about writing that she nurtured family ties through overseas mail from 1836 to 1898. In the early days, she sent New World curiosities such as panther pelts and tobacco seeds, and she went to a great deal of trouble to travel to a photographer for a picture of her young family to send home—in 1847, when one of the complications of the trip was a marauding bear. Her most faithful correspondent was her brother Heinrich ("My dear sisters distinguish themselves again through their silence"[42] was a comment repeated many times), but even after his death, she maintained the family connection. When she was past eighty and nearly blind, her daughter explained in a note, "Even if you cannot read the letters she writes, it nevertheless gives her a great deal of pleasure to write them."[43]

No matter how skilled the letter writer was, however, it was extremely difficult to convey the details of American life. After almost fifty years of writing, Jette added this revealing postscript: "Henriette forgot to add 'Missouri' to the address. This is absolutely necessary!"[44] She thus indicated that she believed her European relatives—none of whom ever visited her, though she visited there twice—still had no genuine conception of where she lived, and they had not truly grasped that states in America are as large as nations in Europe. Even a family as close as hers could not completely emphathize with emigrant kin.

Many of Jette's letters, especially the early ones, also were filled with financial detail—loans that had to be repaid, shares of estate money to be divided, reports on business enterprises. Other immigrants wrote similarly, for the ties between adult siblings often had a strong economic link. Like letter-writing habits, these monetary relationships also varied. Many Europeans—especially the Irish—brought relatives here without thought of repayment, but on the other hand, paying interest on loans even from close relatives was not at all unusual. Occasionally exorbitant rates were demanded; one young woman paid her brother-in-law 40% interest on a loan.[45]

Likewise, some families welcomed a newly arrived relative and were glad to board her without charge; others were grudging and charged more that the lodging was worth. The institution of boarding especially meant that siblings—or their spouses—often assumed a dictatorial role. A young Italian woman who lived with her sister, for example, found that her brother-in-law would not allow the women to drink the wine she had purchased for Christmas Eve. "He felt he could control my life the way he did hers," she said. "He resented the fact that I saved my money in a bank instead of handing it over to him to 'take care of it.'"[46]

Despite disapproving brothers-in-law, a sociologist who studied widowed and deserted mothers found that when these women went to a relative for help, they were far more likely to turn to sisters than brothers. "The brothers, no doubt," she concluded, "are making their contribution to the support of their wives' semi-dependent sisters."[47] It was an interestingly matriarchial arrangement whereby a man gave support to his wife's sister rather than his own. On the whole, however, both this study and others showed that family members took their financial debts very seriously and there was little generosity based on blood—even to impoverished widows.

Irish families, however, were an exception, for money seemed to matter less in their culture, while emotional bonds between adult siblings were particularly strong. Probably this was because they were more likely to remain single, and therefore devoted to siblings and parents rather than to husbands and children. The autobiography of an Irish cook fit exactly this pattern; she and her sister emigrated first and saved to bring their brothers and at last their parents. Her joy in accomplishing this goal is evident:

> We rented a little house in Kensington for them. There was a parlor in it and kitchen and two bedrooms and bathroom and marble door step, and a bell. That was in '66 and we paid $9 a month rent . . . It took all our savings to furnish it, but Mrs. Bent and Mrs. Carr [employers] gave us lots of things to go in. To think of mother having a parlor and marble steps and a bell! They . . . got here at night, and we had supper

for them and the house all lighted up. Well you ought to have seen mother's old face! I'll never forget that night if I live to be a hundred.[48]

All of the children in Mary Paul Hughes's Irish family remained single, with one dying young and another killed in the Civil War. Her mother, a widow with three sons and a daughter, had emigrated from Cahel County in 1830, and when she died in 1865, the daughter and her remaining brother became a nun and a priest.[49] A Fall River weaver showed considerable resentment against the one member of her family who did marry, saying, "If our family had all stuck together and joined a buildin' club, and Tom he hadn't gotten married, we could have owned a cottage by now."[50] Her father and a younger brother were shiftless drinkers while she and her sister provided the steadying influence in the family, but she resented their alcoholism less than what she saw as Tom's disloyalty in marrying.

Americans expected marriage and nuclear instead of extended families, however, and the law gave stronger status to an individual who could produce a marriage license than it did to a blood relative. This official disregard of ties between siblings came as a shock to some, especially to immigrants from Mediterranean cultures. A Syrian man who wanted to bring his sister in 1925, for example, ran up against the problem of a quota for Syria of just 100 new immigrants annually:

> Mr. O., a citizen, a soldier in the United States army for 1 1/2 years with over-seas service and honorable discharge, with great difficulty located his 17-year-old sister, his only living relative, who is living in an orphanage. He is unable to obtain a place for her in the small quota for years ahead. He too, found it impossible to believe that with his "credentials," he would be refused the right to bring his sister over for protection on this side. When he found that this was the case, he relinquished his citizenship and his army record and went back to the other side to make a home for her.[51]

He no doubt saw the law as both ironic and hypocritical—had he lied and said that his sister was his wife, or even his intended wife, the chances of her being allowed to join him would have greatly improved. His depth of caring was not considered, for despite rhetoric, national policy did not support family ties except in the case of marriages. It had the effect of encouraging individuals to separate from Old World families and to establish new, American-born families.

Leaving the group was thus almost an essential part of Americanization. For both women and men, that was the way to grow, to become independent, and those were the qualities that Americans most prized. Sometimes this gave a woman perspective on her family that she would not have obtained at closer range. Elizabeth Hasanovitz, for example, had almost no contact with her siblings in America and she had not seen her European parents in years, but it was this distance that allowed her to develop an understanding of her mother that was unusually empathetic for a young daughter. Writing of her parents, she said:

Of both of their lives, hers was the harder. From the time of her marriage she hardly had a carefree day—bearing children every two years, she fought with measles, scarlet fever, typhoid fever . . . she fed them; she clothed them. She gave her life to thirteen children, of whom she buried four . . . She never saw a bright day until her children grew up. And then—Her oldest boy was in the hated Russian army, another was in prison for carrying the message of Freedom, three children scattered in far-away America—this was the reward of her long years of struggle.[52]

It was, in fact, these memories that made Lisa Hasanovitz uninterested in marriage and suspicious of romance. Though she was over twenty, she had no thought of marriage and scorned those who saw it as a solution to problems. When World War I broke out, her family wrote of their suffering: "Your brother is being sent to the front. Nathan, who is such a youth, is being reserved. A fine was imposed on me for Sam . . . I fear we shall face starvation before long."[53]

Of course she was distraught. Yet if she had adopted the model of most immigrant women by putting family needs ahead of individual ones, she probably could have brought her loved ones out of Russia before the war. Being a skilled sample dressmaker, she earned high wages—but Elizabeth lost job after job when she protested on behalf of workers less fortunate than herself. Most women would have thought her devotion to this political ideal foolish; their ideal was the family, and they would have gladly made the money and paid the passage. She loved her family, but her career and her beliefs meant more to her.

America encouraged such individualism. Families changed from extended to nuclear; the male and the elderly lost their former power; the young had a right to assert themselves. The new nation emphasized the person, not the group, and this meant far greater freedom for the females of families.

21

WOMAN'S PLACE IN THE NEW WORLD

Later Marriage, Fewer Children:
Mother/Daughter Differences

In 1920, a mere 14% of foreign-born women over age fifteen were single—but 37% of second-generation women remained unwed.[1] In all sections of the United States and for different time periods, the pattern holds: immigrant women married frequently and young; women of native parentage had the second highest marriage rate; and those most likely to be unwed were women who had been born in the United States to foreign parents. Immigrant women clearly reared daughters in America whose life pattern was very dissimilar from their own.

Exactly why this was so is debatable. Certainly to some extent it was because young women saw the difficult lives of their mothers and saw that America offered alternatives. The case of Rachel Solomon and her sister-in-law is illustrative. The Solomons came from Syria and did well in the United States. After the death of the female head of the household, the family sought a surrogate housekeeper: "Mr. Solomon," a sociologist wrote, "has an unmarried daughter, but being an American-born girl she is not satisfied to stay at home to look after her father and three brothers but wishes to earn her own living. Bringing a Syrian girl from the Old Country to marry David and keep house was Mr. Solomon's solution of the difficulty."[2] Thus,

Rachel, the immigrant, married young, while her sister-in-law, the daughter of immigrants, did not.

She was typical of the daughters of immigrants, who did not necessarily view marriage as desirable and who firmly rejected arranged marriages. On the other hand, their later age at marriage was not always a result of choosing independence. Many young women found that instead of the traditional pressure to marry, they were pressured to remain single because their income was essential. When they finally did marry, the daughters of immigrants also rejected the large families their mothers had:[3]

PERCENTAGE OF WOMEN IN THE UNITED STATES AND MARRIED 10 TO 19 YEARS, BEARING MORE THAN 5 CHILDREN, 1900

Ethnicity	First Generation	Second Generation
Austrian	38.9%	19.1%
Bohemian	43.9	29.1
Danish	40.8	22.5
English	22.4	10.7
German	39.2	23.4
Irish	40.8	30.2
Norwegian	39.7	34.3
Polish	61.9	38.5
Scotch	23.2	11.6
Swedish	28.7	18.9*

* Note that the greatest drop in family size occurred among Poles, who were apt to live in cities; the least significant drop was among Norwegians, who were more likely to farm. Among native whites whose parents were natives, only 9.9% had more than five children.

Because they stayed single longer and had fewer children, it is to be expected that daughters of immigrants would be employed at higher rates, and that was indeed the case—more women of the second generation worked than either immigrants or natives.[4] Again, however, whether they worked from choice or because they were scrambling to support their parents' too-numerous offspring is debatable. There was, at least, some upward mobility in the jobs they found; one study of working mothers found that while 70% of them worked as domestics, over 90% of their daughters were in trade and manufacturing.[5] The daughters went to factories and even offices that their mothers saw only as cleaning women.

Daughters of immigrants held jobs more frequently than foreign-born women, but—in contrast to myths of hardworking young men—the sons of immigrants were less often employed than foreign-born men.[6] Upward mobility for women meant a factory job instead of domestic work, but for their brothers, it presumably meant higher education or increased leisure, while a larger share of family-support responsibilities fell to women.

When measured by the standards of the respective treatment of sons and daughters in a family, improvement in female status was thus admittedly slow, but compared with the status of women in much of Europe, the strides were tremendous. Such major attitudinal change had to begin with self-examination and discontent on the part of women themselves. It took courage to question the accepted ways, and breaking out of traditional molds was a painful process. America, however, made it easier by encouraging the ambitious. A Jewish woman who felt her husband's idea of her status was wrong, for example, wrote to a newspaper advice column in 1910 and to find support for her goals:

> Since I do not want my conscience to bother me, I ask you to decide whether a married woman has the right to go to school two evenings a week. My husband thinks I have no right to do this.
>
> I admit that I cannot be satisfied to be just a wife and mother . . . My children and my house are not neglected . . . My husband is not pleased and when I come home at night and ring the bell, he lets me stand outside a long time intentionally, and doesn't hurry to open the door . . . When I am alone with my thoughts, I feel I may not be right.[7]

Linka Preus began asking similar questions on gender roles much earlier, in the 1840s, while she was still unmarried and living in Norway. Saying that she was "glad that my parents sent me to a school where I learned a little of everything," she defiantly indulged in reading novels—something that was still considered somewhat risque on both sides of the Atlantic. "It may happen," Linka acknowledged, "that I pick up a novel even if my Bible is laying on the same table," and though she prefaced her thoughts with self-denigrating remarks, she went on with discontented musings about other limitations on women's lives: "Frequently I think of the many advantages a man has over a woman . . . Since I am convinced that Nature has equally endowed us, why then should we not without reproach develop our abilities? Certainly Nature has not given them to us just in order that we should season food and darn stockings."[8]

Linka's youthful ideas on expanded female roles were overwhelmed by the burdens of adult life, but other women grew more determined with age. This was especially likely for those who came from cultures where girls literally were beaten into subordination. Indeed, probably the most visible difference in the status of American women was the unacceptability of open physical abuse. A German man, for example, wrote in 1868 of a former friend, "He beat his wife for every little thing, and that's not done here, here a wife must be treated like a wife and not like a scrub rag . . . He who likes to beat his wife had better stay in Germany."[9] Another German, Christian Kirst, echoed this view in 1881: "As a man here things are the opposite from over there here the woman rules the roost, if a man comes home drunk and his wife reports him he gets put in *Prisong*, the first time for 5 days and then longer and longer if he does it again, . . . she doesn't need witnesses."[10]

Rosa Cavalleri had been beaten almost to death by both her mother and her husband in Italy, but after she freed herself of them in America, she grew very independent. Many times she spoke with contempt of the way that she and other Italian girls were easily frightened and with admiration of American females who were, in Rosa's view, beautifully self-reliant. Likewise, Mrs. Pagano began life in America as a half-starved waif essentially sold into marriage; as an adult, however, she became more and more assertive, taking the lead in pushing her family's upward mobility. The outwardly passive Italian wife who appeared to be dominated by her husband might in fact be assertive within her home.

Openly dominant women, however, were exceptional. More commonly men and women alike combined to keep gender roles well defined and to put defiers in their place. Even slight deviation from the traditional met with objection. Sister Blandina Segale's Cincinnati family, for example, hesitated about allowing her to become a nun. Even though they knew that this vocation should be a source of family and community pride, they nonetheless felt threatened by her independence from the family. Later, when she was assigned to travel alone to a mission in frontier Colorado, her parents—especially her father—tried to dissuade her from going. Even neighbors entered into the dispute, and "Mrs. Garibaldi threatened to take off my habit."[11]

Sister Blandina's belief that God had chosen her career gave her the strength to insist upon the right to live her own life, but many others lacked such courage. "I got married like everyone else. I did what was expected of me," said one Italian woman. "The only other possibility I had considered as a young girl was to become a nun, but my parents were against this. Even my grandparents, who were very kind and loving, told me to pray for a husband."[12] Her experience was that of millions of others, for girls were taught from birth not to have high expectations.

Many women even understood that they should expect less love, especially from fathers, whose pride in sons caused them to overlook daughters. The baldest cases of such came from eastern cultures. An Armenian woman who had two sons, for instance, said that when a daughter was born, "My husband was so disappointed because she was a girl that he refused to see her or name her."[13] A young Polish girl, writing to her father in America, likewise complained of disparate treatment of her and her brother: "I received one rouble from you, for which I thank you heartily. I am somewhat pained that you always make a difference between us two. . . . He always gets more than I do. . . . But nothing can be done. Dear father, if you love Romek more than me, what can I do?"[14]

In this case, the very fact that she dared to complain probably was based on her knowledge that she was loved as much or more, for her father himself wrote of his son, "he is very sentimental . . . while Hela has my iron nature."[15] But while he took pride in his daughter and was somewhat contemptuous of his son, the discrimination against her was automatic. Mothers joined fathers in discouraging daughters. One, who had "read in the paper what is going on in the world," would not allow her daughter to go out unaccompanied. When the girl argued that her brothers could do so, the stock reply came, "It is permitted to the boys, for they are boys . . . So, my dear husband," she continued, "admonish her always."[16]

A girl's goal was marriage, and all of her training was aimed at this end. If by some fluke she failed to marry, she could expect to be considered almost unnatural. A sociologist summarized her colleagues' experience with almost all ethnicities when she wrote, "Many a time has one of our investigators met with kindly and courteous, but pitying, comments of Italian men and women who have marveled at her cheerfulness though still unmarried after the ripe age of twenty-five."[17]

Social workers also noted that many women were so rigid in their wifely roles that they seemed incapable of anything else. Though some met hardships with resourcefulness, large numbers of others were willing to be totally dependent upon "the charity." The records of philanthropies are filled with cases of foreign-born women who preferred to put their children to work at an early age rather than seek jobs for themselves. While they admittedly faced many employment barriers, none was more important than their view of themselves as solely housewives.

Even when women who held such ideas on proper feminine roles did find employment, some found it hard to concede that they were stepping out of traditional roles. An enterprising Italian who had learned bookkeeping and typing, for example, could not wholly acknowledge this break with tradition: Her typing was "not fast like you have to do it here, but like a lady would know how to do it."[18] Being treated "like a lady" indeed became the goal of almost every immigrant girl, for they were quick to observe that the era's etiquette insisted that men display manners grounded in at least a semblance of respect for women.

Though Victorian manners indisputably limited female behavior, the code nonetheless also resulted in small courtesies that were new to immigrant women, and politeness sometimes required men to create genuine pleasures for women. Jette Bruns clearly welcomed both the greater freedom and increased leisure that she discovered in America's gender roles; her delight was clear when she wrote home in 1837: "Do you know that I also ride a horse? On the 4th of July I rode on a brand new side saddle to the Scheulens . . . There were several Americans and Germans there, and the noon meal took place in accordance with the American way. At first all ladies sat down, and several gentlemen served us."[19]

Jette also assertively laid claim to income from her husband's medical practice when she treated patients in his absence: "I have taken in the money for the medicine, and this money is mine," she wrote in 1844. "Good chairs have been put in the living room from this."[20] Yet her position was ambivalent, for, like other women in both Germany and America, she lacked the legal power to bring closure on any business matter, and the discussions of family finance that she carried on in letters always had to wait for her husband's final authority.

The business dealings of immigrant women were inherently more complex than those of American women because of their international nature. Even young women who simply sent their earnings home invariably dealt with exchange rates, postal systems, language usages, and even political impacts. It took considerable sophistication to understand such financial complexities, and women were further handicapped by inadequate educations and social taboos that kept them uninformed.

The problems of Jette Bruns's widowhood are illustrative, for they reveal the harm done by the common practice of great age disparity between husband and wife. Many men were like Dr. Bruns in dying in their sixties, while leaving children sired in their fifties for their widows to rear. She discovered only after his death that their assets were fewer and their debts greater than she had expected—and again like other widows, she was further victimized by men who assumed that they could take advantage of female ignorance. Those who tried to defraud Jette Bruns included, sadly, even her oldest son. The attitudes of most of her male associates almost seemed to assume that widowhood and poverty ought to be synonymous.

She even was threatened with losing guardianship of her orphaned nephews and nieces, and like a child had to report her every financial transaction to the probate court for almost a decade. A less intelligent woman would have given up and become dependent on her alcoholic oldest son, but she stood up to these problems. Not embittered by her experience with American capitalism and courts, she in fact acknowledged that widowhood would have been worse in Germany's patriarchal system: "I had a public sale, and . . . this means vacating as many rooms as possible in order to rent them out. Our bedroom was the first . . . In the beginning I was constantly shaking my head and did not know where to begin. Then I wanted to be strong . . . It is good, however, that one can help oneself better here than over there."[21]

Ordained by God and State: Definitions of Womanhood

The legal system, divisions of labor, and family training all taught female subservience, but perhaps the most serious of all pressures came from religious teachings. Linka Preus's youthful rebelliousness on gender roles was tempered largely because she believed that submission of women was divinely mandated; instead of exploring her thoughts on inequities, she often prayed that God "would crush my proud heart."[22] She suppressed her feminist yearnings and, to all outside observers, became a model pastor's wife.

Yet within her diary, she continued to make comments that reflected her disappointment on the intellectual limitations of the religious role assigned to women. "It would have been a real pleasure," she wrote when accompanying her husband to a minister's conference, "to have sat in a corner of the church, observing and listening." Spelling out her regret, she ended up with suspicions that wives were excluded because they might be tempted to laugh at the pomposity of their husbands: "Their dignity and earnestness would make old men of these ministers scarcely thirty . . . I probably should find it very easy to smile."[23] She doubtless could have shone in theological debate had she been allowed to speak, for Linka Preus often spent lonely evenings in her Wisconsin cabin reading such difficult philosophers as Kierkegaard.

Elise Waerenskjold similarly appeared to be a completely conventional Lutheran. She taught Sunday school, lent her home for church services, and worried endlessly over her community's inability to provide religious education to Norwegian youth. She would have served as a lay preacher had her gender allowed this—but her most telling argument for Lutheranism was that other religions treated women worse. In a secret "Confession of Faith," she indicated profound doubts on several doctrinal questions, but after surveying the world's major religions (an amazing accomplishment in itself, from frontier Texas), she rejected others because they "degraded half of the human race, namely the women."[24]

Indeed, virtually all religions taught that women were lesser beings whose inferior place was the intention of God, but this belief was more easily ignored in some creeds than in others. Probably those who agonized most over gender roles were Mormon women, for their faith differed dramatically from others in this area. Fanny Stenhouse, an English Mormon who also lived in France and Switzerland, wrote of her struggle between what she was supposed to believe and what she truly did believe:

> I now began to feel perfectly reckless, and even willing to . . . take "my chance of salvation," rather than submit to Polygamy; for I felt that the new doctrine was a degradation to womankind.
>
> . . . I would not have my readers think that I bore all my troubles meekly, like a saint. Indeed I did not . . . I was a sore trial to my husband. I was wicked and rebellious at times, and said very bitter things of the "Prophet of the Lord," and all his sex, my husband included . . .
>
> I was told by my husband, and the other elders . . . that it devolved on me to teach the hateful doctrine to the women of Switzerland. That was to be my mission, and I, poor, deluded thing that I was, believed it to be so. I concealed my feelings as best I could.[25]

After her emigration to Salt Lake City, Fannie Stenhouse wrote that young women were beginning to question the doctrine of polygamy, for it had "made such bad men of their fathers and such victims of their mothers. It is not our city girls who maintain so much the plural marriages, but it is chiefly the newly arrived English and country girls who supply the Patriarchs."[26]

Ironically, polygamous marriages often had the effect of making women more independent. Men with several families could not support them all, and women were enjoined to "eat their own bread." Sometimes a husband traveled a circuit between his various "homes," and a wife saw him only a few weeks of the year. Women farmed alone and supported themselves and their children. Though women supported the doctrines of the church into which they had been catechized, doubtless there was much quiet rejoicing when Congress made Utah's statehood contingent upon the outlawing of polygamy.

Congress failed to recognize that the relative independence of Mormon women had been recognized by Utah's government with legal rights, including the vote, that were superior to those elsewhere, but in ending polygamy, it aimed to uplift the status of women. Slow though progress might seem to be, the United States did in fact lead the world in organized efforts for women's rights during most of the immigrant era. The link between progressive politics and the suffrage movement was so strong, in fact, that some immigrants believed it was a part of political platforms: In 1881—four decades prior to final passage of women's enfranchisement—a German man wrote home, "The government is trying to give women the vote, whether that will go through is not yet certain."[27]

Immigrant men likewise became convinced of the superior status of American women through frequent female authority figures in their world. To them, no one was more vital and more powerful than the settlement worker, the visiting nurse, the immigration investigator. That many Americans were somewhat scornful of these women as "do-gooders" did not occur to them, and immigrants instead were deeply impressed by their abilities. When, for example, residents in Boston's North End discovered that services were threatened by 1921 budget cuts, a near riot broke out. An Italian man yelled at the Irish policeman who told him to "talk American":

> "How can we spikka da Americana when da book lady she leave? She give us da bed; she give us da stove; she tell us wash da bambinos; she talka da Americana to us. Every time anything happen, we go to da house, 11, 12, 1, 2, 3 o'clock in da morn we go. Always da lady she tell us what to do. She find da pipple who get lost. Who look after us when da book lady go?"[28]

Such capability in American women could not help but translate into an eventual higher status for Italian women, and doubtless many girls adopted "the book lady" as their role model. On the other hand, the rise of feminine status was unthinkingly delayed by female social workers themselves, for they also adopted the era's sex-based stereotypes. Their citizenship classes naturally were aimed at men, and caseworkers on immigration problems regularly demonstrated a predilection for working with the man of a family. Well-intended American women thus unconsciously conspired to keep the immigrant woman in her place. When a Passaic librarian, for example, spoke of things domestic, her references were female; when she spoke of things intellectual, her references were male:

> I was called to the desk one evening last winter to see if I could understand what a meant by an "rbcha" book. He was a Hungarian mason and had seen on the shelves a book of house-building designs . . .
>
> One of the surest ways to the heart of a foreigner is to ask him his native town and then show him that place on a big map . . . He will . . . come again and again bringing friends with him to get you to point out the dot on the map that means so much to him . . .

This flower-adorned woman, ready to depart from the Swedish island of Oland, was typical of millions of northern European women who emigrated alone. In some years at the end of the nineteenth century, women made up a majority of Swedish emigrants. (KALMAR LANS MUSEUM, KALMAR, SWEDEN)

> We have a room given over to boys and young men . . . They play checkers, chess, ping-pong . . . They have their own officers, hold business meetings in the most parliamentary way . . .
>
> Two evenings a week some ladies assist some [garment] factory girls with dressmaking . . . These girls . . . come in contact with ladies . . . and find that refinement means a quiet manner in dress and behavior, rather than loudness and tawdry finery . . .[29]

Note, too, that she used "girls" for employable-age women while the upper-class women she termed "ladies." A YWCA document was similarly revealing when, in the same sentence, it referred to "industrial girls" and "business and professional women."[30] These usages were in fact more a matter of class than of age. Unmarried, uneducated women as old as thirty-five were termed "girls" throughout the era—even though a younger female of higher class would be called a "lady" and a male of similar age would be called a man, not a boy. Many of these "girls" had worked for two decades and often were the primary support of their families, but even the language—even the language of kindly American women—conspired to keep them in their dependent, second-class place.

Government records, too, often demonstrate the era's unquestioned sexist assumptions. An 1875 census in southwestern Minnesota, where many immigrants settled virgin prairie land after the Civil War, showed some census takers so accustomed to thinking of women as inherently less important that they listed all of the boys in a family first, regardless of age, before listing any girls. The form used for citizenship petitions also assumed that the applicant would be male, and indeed, of almost 500 petitions in this area between 1884 and 1892, only five had recognizably female names. Not surprisingly, these women had exceptionally interesting backgrounds.

Maria Olson is the most unusual case. Born in Iceland in 1828, she would have been an uncommon fifty-four when she arrived late in 1882 and fifty-eight when she filed for citizenship in 1886; perhaps a widow starting life anew, she may have wanted citizenship as an extra protection for her property. The others were typically young. Two sisters from Belgium, Marie and Verene Lambert, had been born there in 1861 and 1864; they arrived in New York in 1884 and filed for naturalization in Minnesota in 1886. The other two applicants were more assimilated. Christine A. Olson had been born in Norway in 1869 and would have been just eight when she arrived in Quebec in 1877; she filed her papers in 1891 at age twenty-two. Finally, there was Louisa Flowers, born in England in 1861, who self-confidently filed for citizenship only six months after her 1877 arrival.

A third type of record, assessments of personal property in 1885, is again informative. Taxes were based not only on the expected items of farm machinery and livestock (including even dogs) but also on such feminine items as "sewing and knitting machines, watches and clocks, [and] household furniture." The use of this method, of course, resulted in records that demonstrate the presence of many more women. It also was graphic evidence of the argument of the era's suffragists that women—including immigrant women—were regularly taxed without the opportunity to vote on their taxers.[31]

Maiden Names and More:
Americanization and the Status of Women

Thus women's status again was ambivalently mixed, and the same was true of other areas of change for immigrant women. Generally, New World ways meant an improved condition for women, but there also were occasional regressions. One was the customary insistence in America that a woman take her husband's name, whereas in some European cultures a woman individualized her surname.

Polish and other Slavic women used their husband's names, but the feminine form differed—Wiktorya Osinska, for example, was the wife of Antoni Osinski. In

Latin cultures, including Spanish and Italian, babies sometimes were christened with newly created surnames that used part of both the maternal and paternal names. Czech women differentiated themselves by using their husbands' names with "ova" as a feminine suffix, and similar variations appear in other groups. Scandinavian women, including Danes, used a form of "daughter"—a woman, for example, was Pattersdotter while her brother would be Patterson.

Some Europeans did not adopt permanent surnames until the early twentieth century, and others found their names changed by immigration officials who either did not understand them or arbitrarily gave them more anglicized names. Unaccustomed to thinking in these terms, immigrant women sometimes used a variety of spellings and even widely differing names for themselves. Berta Serina Kingestad, for example, used both the original spelling and the Americanized Bertha for her first name, while for a last name she variously used Bjoravaag (her father's surname), Svendsen and Svendsdatter (variations of her father's first name), and Kjingestad, Kingestad, and Kingstad, all variants of a place-name, probably the name of her family's farm.

Most of the letters attributed to Gro Svendsen in fact were signed "Gro Nilsdatter." She once indicated her awareness of American names by writing "Svendsen" as "Swenson," but most of the time, if she signed her husband's name as well as her own, she wrote, "Ole Svendsen and Gro Nilsdot." After many years in America, she began writing "Gro and Ole Svendsen," but this form of signature was used only four times in the entire collection of letters—and even then she did not use it consistently. In the vast majority of letters, Gro called herself by her maiden name and obviously thought of that as her name. She may be objecting from the grave that Americans have recorded her as Svendsen instead of Nilsdatter—as the wife of a man, instead of as herself.

An even stronger indication of the relatively high status of Scandinavian women is that men sometimes took their wives' surnames at marriage. When Ole Olson married Martha Mentsdatter Tessum in Norway about 1811, for example, he took "Tessum" as his surname, for that was the name of the farm that, as an only child, she would inherit. Their son Mikel also took his wife's name when he married in 1837; while his brothers retained the Tessum surname, Mikel Tessum became Mikel Aas when he married Anne Bergitte Storkersen of Aas.[32]

Even the English-speaking women of Ireland were accustomed to using their own names prior to the twentieth century. The law and their usage simply differed: "Although legally they assumed their husbands' surname upon marriage, they did not go by that name but continued to use their maiden name." A commentator on the Irish in America at midcentury complained about this practice, saying that it made Irish women difficult to track down because no one knew them by the name that was recorded for them in British documents.[33]

Indeed, much of the loss of women's history can be attributed to the seemingly simple fact that it is much harder to trace women, especially in common cases of multiple name changes because of frequent widowhood. Justina Kreiger of the Sioux uprising, for example, had that name for only a relatively short portion of her life. In the Germanic tradition of changing surnames at marriage, she moved from Kitzman to Lehn to Kreiger to Meyer before disappearing from the historical record at twenty-eight. On the other hand, German usages honored women by conferring a title based on the husbands' profession, with the apparent assumption that a wife could not fail to absorb something of his learning. Jette Bruns was known as "Doctoress Bruns," even in widowhood. More than a decade after her husband's death, she wrote, "I continue to call myself, as do others, 'Frau Dr. Bruns.'"[34]

The practice was not an American one,* however, and in this, as in some other areas, immigrant women could expect a loss of status in America. Not only was a woman expected to adopt her husband's name, but even that was often ignored in the era's usage. Newspapers adopted the Victorian standard that a woman's name appeared only at birth, marriage, and death. A midwestern paper, reporting on an 1881 epidemic, was typical in its use of only masculine terms:

> Mr. Lucas' nine children were all down sick . . . Mr. Aaron Borene, who is a near neighbor to Mr. Lucas . . . has lost two children . . . T. Anderson of Milan has recently lost five of his children . . . The family of Edward Nelson of Tunsberg is indeed afflicted . . . In the family of Eric Ericson of Mandt . . . two children have recently died . . . Wednesday evening it was discovered that cases of Scarlet Fever existed in the family of Geo. Person.[35]

No woman's name was mentioned, nor were feminine pronouns used in any of the cases cited by the newspaper, but it is not rational to assume that all of these households were without mothers. The women were simply ignored. Nor was it only male American editors who defined female nonexistence in their pronoun usage; immigrant women themselves sometimes evinced a similar lowly status for themselves in the words they chose. Norwegian Guri Endresen, for example, who survived the 1862 Sioux attack on her Minnesota settlement, not only could not credit herself with rescuing wounded men, but in telling of the experience, her language revealed a nonegalitarian view of herself: "I went out and caught one of my husband's . . . oxen . . . and hitched them to a light sled belonging to my husband."[36]

Likewise, Ernestina Broburg, a sixteen-year-old Norwegian, used patriarchal terminology in testimony before the investigating committee on the Sioux uprising. "The Indians were at my father's,"[37] she said, when she meant that they were at her own home. Similar words used by German Justina Boelter deprived women of even that which would seem to be most likely to be defined in feminine terms, children: she spoke of "the dead bodies of the children of my brother-in-law."[38]

---

* American practice was so different that the records of such organizations as the American Birth Control League and the American Child Health Association contain several instances of female physicians who were referred to as "Miss," rather than "Dr." Instead of conferring a husband's degree on a wife, American usage denied this honor even to women who had earned the title.

Nor did the adoption of English change such predilections for masculine terminology. The Wisconsin Summer School for Workers in Industry, for example, had an all-female student body from its 1923 beginning until 1927, when two men were admitted—and pronoun usage immediately became masculine. Second-generationers Lydia Hiltunen and Marian Hoogebeem introduced the yearbook with language such as "education . . . for *him*" and "economics . . . makes *him* feel the importance of *his* work." A third writer, Wilma Beineman, was more thoughtful and adjusted by using plural terms, as in "workers . . . leave *their* work."*[39]

But important though language is, neither feminine nouns or pronouns nor maiden or individualized names necessarily denoted a firmly higher status for women. Irish women of this era used maiden names and lived independently of men in many ways, including emigrating alone in huge numbers—but the basic inequality of the sexes remained. One of the most shocking indicators of the lesser status of females lies between the lines of Ireland's sad mortality figures: During the "near famine of the late 1870s," for instance, "girls were given less food, and they suffered other physical deprivations." The result can be seen in the numbers: between 1881 and 1920, for every 100 boys between five and nine who died, 111 girls were fatally malnourished. The disparity rose higher for the next age group; as children grew into puberty, 133 girls between ten and fourteen died for each 100 boys.[40]

Slavic women also had names that differed from their husbands, but one writer who was sympathetic to Slavs could find no charitable words to say about the status of women in that part of Europe:

> [A]bhorrent even to the strongest "Slavophile" is the position occupied by women . . . To escape the charge of prejudice, I shall quote a few proverbs current among the Southern Slavs—a few out of many hundreds:
>
> "The man is the head, the woman is grass."
> "One man is worth more than ten women."
> "A man of straw is worth more than a woman of gold."
> "Let the dog bark, but let the woman keep silent."
>
> It would, of course, be unjust to charge every Slav with beating his wife, but unfortunately, it is the rule rather than the exception . . . That the Slavic woman possesses the qualities to make of herself a "new woman" can be plainly seen among the women of the higher class in Russia, where there is a second paradise for women; America, by common consent, being the first.[41]

Kyra Goritzina was one of those Russian women who enjoyed the "second paradise"; she too consistently spelled her name thus even after long residence in America, while calling her husband "Goritzin." Even more interesting is that she apparently believed in "a room of one's own." In most jobs that she and her husband took as cook-butler, they were given two rooms, and although they were very close

---

* Emphasis mine.

and she had great admiration and love for him, instead of using one room as a sitting room and the other as bedroom, they maintained separate rooms. This seemed to be important to her, for among her most happy writing is commentary on "my" room.

She had been one of the "women of the higher class" prior to immigration, one of those whose feminist behavior had developed because she had the advantages of privileged status. Class was indeed a more important factor than ethnicity in the status of women, for upper-class women had more in common with women halfway across Europe than they did with the manor slaves who served them—and lower-class women felt likewise. Though Americans like to think of themselves as classless, the era from the Civil War to World War I, when immigration was greatest, saw the most well-defined classes of national history, and immigrants were inherently lower class from an American point of view.

Sad cultural shock occurred among many immigrant women when they realized even if they achieved what they viewed as amazing good fortune, it would never be enough to rank with Americans. The factory worker could earn more than she ever dreamed in Europe, but she also came to understand that other factory workers scorned her as a greenhorn. The farm woman knew that the land she had in America would make her an aristocrat in the Old World, but she also knew that the American women in her farm town would never invite her to join their club.

Many suffered a loss in community status so severe that they could never again expect to recover. Jewish Mrs. Frowne, for example, was nothing in the new land but an important person in her old. Her daughter Sadie wrote that she had run a grocery store in her village: "That was in Poland, somewhere on the frontier, and mother had charge of a gate between the countries, so that everybody who came through had to show her a pass. . . . Her word was like law among them.[42]

That the poorly dressed woman who could scarcely make herself understood had once been an authority figure would seldom occur to Americans. They instead presumed her inferiority, and she, being treated this way so entirely, might come accept it. The inferiority that Americans imposed because of class and origin then would be reinforced at home because of gender. This varied depending on the power of individual personalities as well as on ethnic traditions, but throughout immigrant society, the fundamental inequality of the sexes was undebatable.

Most women as well as men accepted that this was the way life was and therefore ought to be. The fatalists were many and the rebels few. Linka Preus would not have found many receptive listeners had her musings been aloud, and knowing that, she tried to repress them. Sometimes, though, the truth would out, when she thought "of the many advantages a man has over a woman":

> It is not my opinion that he is more gifted than a woman, but that his mind has been better developed by many kinds of knowledge than has woman's. Her intellectual growth is regarded as of secondary importance, as something useless, bringing no benefit to the world. When these thoughts occupy my mind, I frequently become embittered, as it all seems so unjust.[43]

PART VII

CONTENT
AND
DISCONTENT

22

VIEWS OF THE
NEW WORLD

Variants in the Pace of Becoming an American

It was entirely possible to live for years and even decades in America without becoming Americanized. The stereotype of slow assimilation among older women in immigrant ghettos is especially well established, but even the young and bold could be trapped into patterns that put them in the new culture without being a part of it. Millions were like young Rose Cohen, who lived in America nearly five years after her immigration before she went beyond the East Side, and then only because her anemia demanded special hospitalization. For the first time, she met natives and saw another way of life:

> I had lived in practically the same environment which we brought from home. Of course there was a difference in our joys, in our hardships . . . but on the whole we were still in our village in Russia. A child . . . put into the shop remained in the old traditions, held back by illiteracy. Often it was years before he could stir away from it, sometimes it would take a lifetime.[1]

She found, after she was discharged from the hospital, that she could never "go home again." Instead, she felt "more and more disgusted" with life in the Jewish ghetto. Everything looked different to her; the family couch supported by a grocery box now appeared grotesque, and even her digestion had changed so much that she "craved substantial food" instead of the oatmeal gruel everyone else thought sufficient for a meal. She could never return to the person she had been, even though the change confused her, upset her family, and brought sorrow to them all.

And yet, though it was understandable that Rose felt her first five years in America were wasted, it was also true that both she and her family had made significant adjustments long before. Her description of an incident four years earlier shows that momentous changes could take place, and yet the long process of assimilation had only begun:

> Mother had been here only a short time when I noticed that she looked older and more old-fashioned than father . . . So I thought that if I could persuade her to leave off her kerchief she would look younger and more up to date. But remembering my own first shock, I decided to go slowly . . . So, one day, when . . . we two were alone in the house, I asked her playfully to take off her kerchief and let me do her hair, just to see how it would look.
>
> She consented reluctantly. She had never before in her married life had her hair uncovered before anyone . . . I was surprised how different she looked . . . I handed her our little mirror . . . She glanced at herself, admitted frankly that it looked well and began hastily to put on her kerchief . . .
>
> "Mamma," I coaxed, "please don't put the kerchief on again—ever!"
>
> At first she would not even listen to me . . . I . . . pointed out that wives often looked so much older . . . that the husbands were often ashamed to go out with them . . .
>
> I finally succeeded.
>
> When father came home that evening, he stopped and looked at her with astonishment. "What!" he cried, half earnestly, half jestingly, "Already you are becoming an American lady!" Mother looked abashed for a moment; in the next, to my surprise and delight, I heard her brazen it out in her quiet way.
>
> "As you see," she said, "I am not staying far behind."[2]

Another way in which Rose had begun to Americanize even before her mother arrived was in changing her name. She had gone from Rahel to Ruth to Rose, encouraged by her co-workers to have a New World name. This was standard procedure for many; Rose Schneiderman also was Rachel earlier, and her brothers Ezekial and Aaron became Charles and Harry. Their parents thought the new names "sounded nicer."[3] A Norwegian writer commented that "Aase, Birthe, Siri, at an incredible speed became changed to Aline, Betsy and Sarah,"[4]—but, on the other hand, there certainly were those who found such imitation distasteful and proudly clung to their native names of Linka and Gro.

The subject of names, said YWCA workers, was "one question that never fails to open a lively discussion . . . They were hurt at the lack of effort on the part of teachers and employers to pronounce their names," the report continued, "and many were asked by employers to have their names changed. They were unanimous in their feeling that it was definitely a handicap in employment."[5]

While some parents encouraged Americanized names, others were not willing to allow this surrender of identity—especially in the case of female family members, who would have a new surname with marriage in any case. A twenty-year-old

These children, who arrived at Ellis Island for Christmas, 1918, were given typically American toys. With the Stars and Stripes as a background for their somber, thoughtful faces, they represented the nation's future. (LIBRARY OF CONGRESS)

second-generation Hungarian was typical: when her paper-factory boss suggested that she change her "very foreign and too long" name, her father became "very angry." Even though he was unemployed and the family was suffering during the Great Depression, he vowed that she would give up her job before he would "permit her to change the family name. Jolan," added the YWCA worker, "seemed to have no opinion in the matter."[6]

Some young women ignored both parental wishes and the technicalities of law and simply began using a new name. Leah, an unusual case of a divorced immigrant woman who had managed to get secretarial training, "frequently uses a short English name when transacting business . . . because she feels that it is much more convenient . . . She has no compunctions about this."[7] The question of "compunctions," in fact, went beyond family defiance. A number of immigrants expressed fear that if they used a new name, people might assume that there was something in their past they were trying to hide. Still other foreigners had their names changed for them by immigration authorities who believed newcomers would benefit from a new name and arbitrarily changed it—and they fatalistically accepted whatever was imposed.

Adults often were sufficiently rooted in their personal identity that they could ignore such winds of change, but children had no such roots. They were apt to pressure parents to adopt all aspects of Americanization, without regard to financial or emotional cost. Rose Cohen's brother, for instance, was embarrassed by his sturdy Russian shoes. In desperation to be rid of this proof of his greenhorn status, he went to a strange neighborhood, climbed to the roof of a tenement, and flung the hated shoes in opposite directions into the dark. He knew he would incur the wrath of parents too poor to buy new shoes, but the punishment that he expected to endure was worth the new identity he would gain.

Swiss Elise Isely had more understanding adults around her, but the teasing of children was the same: "As I walked to school, I was taunted by 'Know-Nothing' children for being Dutch," she wrote of her childhood in the 1850s. "To them all foreigners were Dutch or Irish; and while they did not know my nationality, they knew I was not Irish."[8] Her experience was endlessly repeated, as even after immigrant groups became far more diverse in later decades, most Americans continued to refuse to grant newcomers the dignity of distinct ethnicity. Ukrainian Mary Ann Bodner also had schoolmates who "made fun of me and mocked me" and, worse, teachers who remained ignorantly unempathetic.

One teacher insisted that she play a Scottish girl in a school play; when the child preferred to portray her true origin, the teacher replied, "How can you be a 'Uralian' girl, when there isn't any such place?" Even in high school, the battle continued. Her essay, *Ukraine, the Land and Its People*, was returned with cruel commentary: "Where in the world did you ever get the ideas that you wrote in your essay? The entire thing is a product of your imagination."[9] She was threatened with expulsion for trying to explain.

The failure of Americans to learn the differences between the various Europeans not only was a constant irritation to newcomers but could also be extremely serious on another level. Kyra Goritzina, for instance, was a victim of the Russian Revolution, but she found that many American women refused to interview her for a cooking job when they discovered that she was Russian. Their knowledge of world affairs was too meager for them to understand that not all Russians were Bolsheviks.

Like others, she was caught by the common pattern of targeting the newest group for the greatest prejudice. Even immigrants themselves joined in discrimination against whatever group had arrived just after they did, and also brought their native prejudices along with their luggage: northern Italians looked down on southern Italians; Swedes scorned Norwegians; German Jews were embarrassed by Russian Jews.

Late in the immigrant era, YWCA workers tried to get young women to overcome these habits of thought. They found, for example, that even though a group of Polish women in Cleveland "stated they had no prejudice," these Poles not only exhibited bias against Greeks, Syrians, and Italians, but also held "definite prejudices within [their own] nationality, especially against the Galicians." The Polish women "wanted to be English because the English are *all* cultured, refined, and educated."[10]

Jette Bruns spoke several times of the reality of prejudice against even educated immigrants, and she considered those who should have been more urbane to be greater offenders than country bumpkins. She wrote, for instance, as Missouri recovered from the Civil War in 1868, "There is much building going on, and many strangers are settling here, Germans as well as people from the east. The latter are not as pleasant and are more inclined to bigotry."[11] Late in life, in responding to her brother's 1894 inquiry on the American Protection Association, she indicated her acceptance of prejudice against Catholics such as herself as routine—and, moreover, she was honest enough to admit to some bias of her own:

> To be sure, a secret alliance against foreigners, and particularly the Catholics, exists here . . . In St. Louis . . . there also are many . . . many bigoted bums. . . . In general, to this day the majority of immigrants have not left their home without some stain, and it is not amazing that we, the older immigrants, feel the same as the Americans and consider new immigrants with some disgust.[12]

Thus the cycle repeated itself, as even those victimized by prejudice admitted "disgust" with others. Only the passage of time would resolve the differences, as the alien became the alike. Other strangers would replace them as objects of scorn, and the process endlessly recycled.

While this adjustment took place, newcomers naturally had moments when they rued their decision and yearned for home. Historians generally have accepted the notion that women suffered from homesickness more than men, and that because it was more difficult for housebound women to become assimilated, they were more likely to insist upon returning to Europe.[13] The comment of a sociologist speaking of Slavs is typical:

I get the impression that women are more apt to be homesick than the men, and that in consequence wives often make their husbands return against their wishes . . . They miss, I think, the variety of work, the employment within doors alternating with field work . . . and most of all the familiar, sociable village life where . . . there are no uncomfortable superior Yankees to abash one, and where the children do not grow up to be alien and contemptuous. The men live more out in the world. They get more from America.[14]

Most immigrants in fact expressed homesickness in their first letters home; most, not surprisingly, felt like Anna Maria Klinger, who wrote in 1847 that she was "lonely and forlorn [with] no friends or relatives around."[15] She overcame the feeling to bring five siblings to America—and each initially felt homesick, even though they were welcomed by loved ones.

On the fourth anniversary of her arrival in America, Berta Serina Kingestad wrote that the "time has gone rather quickly," and yet she added a long paragraph on the reality of homesickness:

When I think back . . . I can still see Mother and Marta as they walked along the shore, and I surely never realized how precious Mother was . . . and it was the same when I parted with Anna and Father in Stavanger. Oh, that parting, how hard it was, and it is not erased by the first tears . . . I think about it more than ever before.[16]

Even immigrants who were personally happy nonetheless could remain home-sick for years. Gro Svendsen's letters were almost neurotic on this point: long after she emigrated, she tormented herself with attacks of conscience over the grief she had caused her parents in leaving them. Though she loved her husband and her new farm, she also pined for Norway's schools and books. The books, "such as they are, to be had here," she said, displayed the same "shoddy and careless workmanship" that distressed her in other aspects of American life. The result was that she "praised and defended Norway and things Norwegian so much that I have had heated arguments with some people who believe this land is paradise."[17]

Especially in the case of frontier women like Gro, homesickness was not exactly what troubled them; instead it was a yearning for the familiar, for the accoutrements and comforts of life unavailable in the new setting. What one missed, of course, depended on what one had been accustomed to. Just as some Slavic women in the steel towns missed farm life, so did a German writer at midcentury aver that his female compatriots in the Midwest missed German town life: "She has also renounced all the charming enjoyments of a more elegant household . . . and finds herself banished in a solitude which is only enlightened by pictures of the past which seem all the more dazzling from a distance."[18]

Many male observers took similar note of how forlorn and isolated the women were in new settlements—something that was certainly true, for compared with the freedom of men to travel and socialize, women were deprived. What these commentators failed to understand, though, is that women were more isolated in any social structure of that era. Women in both Europe and America, in both urban and rural settings, almost always lived in greater solitude than men, with an assigned lifestyle so restricted that some of it was literally known as "confinement." The male European who missed his daily pub visit, however, was less free to acknowledge his dependence on sociability and thus perhaps found it easier to attribute loneliness to women.

In homesickness, timing and personal situation were everything. Jette Bruns soon adamantly identified with the new land, but also wrote, "I tried again and again to overcome the melancholy feeling of homesickness, which was that much deeper since I tried to hide it from my husband and he was away so often."[19] Of course she was lonely—her husband was gone for days on end traveling his medical circuit, while she was heavily pregnant, with a toddler for company. Anyone would feel lonesome, even if she was at the same time hopefully building a new home. Homesickness, like everything else, was essentially ambivalent.

On one point of the process of adjustment, however, there was almost no ambivalence—at least among women—and that was the improved status of women in America. Yet though that involved change of real significance, occurring very quickly from a historian's point of view, to the individual woman, her longing for a brick oven might be more real than her daughter's not needing a dowry. The ambivalence remained, and the foreigner remained a marked stranger in the new land.

But at the same time that Americans were scorning these women as unassimilable, the women often thought themselves much changed by their transatlantic experience. Rosa Cavalleri's time of triumph came when she returned to Italy for a visit. She had been gone only a few years and to Americans was still unassimilated, for she knew very little English, but Rosa was already proud to be an American. When she went to the bank on business, she displayed a confidence that contrasted sharply with her former peers:

> All the time more men kept coming and the women had to wait and let the men go first. I stood there waiting and waiting and I got tired. There were some nice chairs there on the other side of a little railing—chairs for the high people . . . So finally I did it; I pushed open the little gate and went in and sat down.
>
> "Oh, Rosa!" gasped the other poor women in the line. "Come back! Come back! You'll get arrested. They'll put you in jail!"
>
> "The chairs are here and nobody is sitting in them," I said.
>
> Soon the janitor came. "*Che impertinenza!*" he said. "Who gave you the permission to sit down?"
>
> "Myself," I said and I smiled at him because I was no longer afraid. "The chairs belong to the bank, isn't that so? And the people who have money in the bank have the right to use them, no?"
>
> "You think you're smart because you come from America!"
>
> "Yes," I said, "In America the poor do get smart. We are not so stupid anymore."
>
> . . . At last all the men had finished their business . . . When it was my turn the

officer smiled and bowed and didn't say anything at all about my sitting in the chair.

"If you please," I said in English. "How do you do. Thank you. Goodbye." That Italian officer wouldn't know that the words didn't fit and I wanted to show him that I was learning to speak English. And there he was bowing and smiling so polite and the women were all looking and looking, with their mouths hanging open.[20]

Not for Everyone: Those Who Returned to Europe

A factor of overwhelming importance in assimilation was whether or not returning was feasible. To early immigrants from northern Europe, that option was remote; they departed with the knowledge that the decision was permanent. The Jews who came later also made a final decision, for they knew they would never go back to a land of pogroms. When oceanic crossing became easier, however, the slow assimilation of newcomers from southern and eastern Europe was a subject of frequent comment and criticism by Americans. Often illiterate and superstitious, the women trained to timidity, it was natural that their adjustment would take some time. Moreover, because even poor women like Rosa could readily travel back home, commitment to America understandably was lessened.

Those who returned home—either to visit or to stay—were little noticed. It is natural that Americans would choose to ignore that some returned, and that those who rejected the Promised Land would be dismissed as insignificant. Yet the truth is that from 1908, when the immigration authorities began keeping records on departures, until the end of the era, large numbers of immigrants left again. The statistics varied with business cycles and wars, but the surprising fact is that an average of three in every eight arrivals from 1908 to 1920 returned to their native land.[21]

The Great Depression of the 1930s would increase this phenomenon to the point that more people would leave America than would enter—and already during some years of the World War I era, "more foreign nationals left Boston to go home to Italy, Greece, Turkey and other countries than arrived."[22] A national sample from those years shows that returnees were common from all ports:[23]

IMMIGRANT ADMISSIONS AND DEPARTURES FROM U.S. PORTS

	Admissions	Departures
1908	782,870	395,073
1910	1,041,570	202,436
1912	838,172	333,262
1914	1,218,480	303,338
1916	298,826	129,765
1918	110,618	94,585
1920	430,001	288,315

The Immigration Commission studied these patterns at the turn of the century, and already by 1911, it had concluded that most of the departures from America were permanent and not the result of seasonal migratory labor. "At least one-third of all European immigrants who come to the United States eventually return to Europe," it summarized. Moreover, "a very large proportion of those who return to Europe do not come again to this country."[24] Significantly for women, these statistics do not validate those who thought of women as excessively homesick and likely to return. The Immigration Commission instead noted "a striking predominance of males in the movement from the United States to Europe, 82.7 percent of all departing aliens . . . being of that sex."[25] Those groups with the lowest rates of return—6 to 8 per 100 admissions during 1908–10—were Scottish, Irish, and Jewish, which were ethnicities with large numbers of female immigrants. On the other hand, the Immigration Commission found its highest return rates—69, 64, and 62 per 100—among Turks, Magyars and Italians, groups with many more male than female immigrants.[26]

Even more telling is a look at Irish and Swedish immigrants. In many of these years, women were a majority of the departees from those countries—especially from Ireland, where, as has been seen, significantly more women than men emigrated in the early twentieth century. Yet only 2% of Irish immigrants in this era returned![27] Clearly, these women suffered no irrepressible homesickness for the Emerald Isle.

Among the Swedes, women constituted an absolute majority in five of the years between 1899 and 1910, and they were close to that in the other years. Again, the return rate of 18% was small in comparison with countries with a higher number of male migrants.[28] That Swedish women returned more often than Irish was probably because Sweden was a more prosperous country with greater incentives for returnees and because the language adjustment was more difficult for them than for the Irish. In both cases, however, it is clear that the groups with the most women had the fewest immigrants who returned to the Old World. The numbers seem to indicate that women viewed the decision to emigrate as a permanent change, whereas males, both single and married, were more likely to view it as a fortune-seeking fling.

When women did return, it was duty to their European family that seems to have been their most likely reason. Few records were kept on motivations, but because aliens had to petition for permission to travel abroad during World War I, that era provided more complete insight into the decision to depart. The vast majority of these petitions again came from men—and in the case of married couples who intended to depart, the woman's existence was clear only on two lines of space alloted for that purpose. Belgian Margaret DeWinter, for instance, was departing with her husband Adolf; in an application of four legal-size pages, all that can be gleaned about her was that her maiden name was Sommerlinck and that she was born in Ghent of Belgian parents in 1884.[29]

Petitions from women planning to depart without a man, however, offer a glimpse into their lives in 1918, during the last year of the war. Emily Cocker, a Delaware resident since 1911, was "going to nurse dying brother and sick mother" in Lancashire. She planned to be gone "indefinitely" and was taking along her three young children.[30] Dorothy Hopkinson-Evans of New Jersey also was accompanied by her child; her marital arrangements, like her name, were unconventional: though she had been in the United States since 1904, she planned to "re-join" her husband in London and gave her father's address as her intended home.[31]

Edith Lily Manners was single and "undecided" about whether or not she intended to return to the United States. A "maid to a lady in delicate health," she had been living in an Atlantic City hotel since 1916. She intended to accompany her employer to Wales.[32] Emily Porter, on the other hand, had firm intentions of returning to the United States. Age twenty seven and married, she had arrived in Boston in 1913 and evidently was trapped by the war; she wanted to return to Nottingham because of "Death, and to bring my two Children back." Her husband would remain in Philadelphia, but why the children had not gone with her when she emigrated five years earlier was not clear.[33]

Christina Robertson of Harriman, Pennsylvania, also intended to return at some "indefinite" point, and she too was traveling because of duty to children: "To join my father and mother and also to take three motherless children to their grandparents in Renfrew Scotland." In addition to the three permanent returnees—all of them under ten and born in America—she had her own two-year-old daughter to care for on the trip.[34]

"I first came to this country on the 10th of November, 1902," wrote Belgian Helene Laurent, a single woman employed as a housekeeper. She had worked in Baltimore and Philadelphia, but as the warfare in her homeland ended late in 1918, she was clear about her intention to return there permanently: "I will stay in Brussels," she said firmly.[35] Belgian Pauline Janssens, born in Antwerp in 1883, also worked even though she was married. A dressmaker, she probably viewed herself as a war refugee. She left Belgium in October 1914, shortly after the war began and, during the next five years, had resided in Holland, England, France, England again, the United States, Canada, and the United States again. Now that the war was over, she intended to return permanently to her husband in Antwerp.[36]

These Belgians were native French-speakers, as was the case with Swiss Edmee Worsching, who had been born in Geneva in 1894. Worsching had arrived in November 1914, shortly after Europe became a battleground, and she had spent the war years working as a governess for three Pennsylvania and New Jersey households; she was going abroad in the employ of the last family for whom she worked.[37]

Her status as a governess contrasted sharply with an Italian woman born in 1862 who was probably illiterate; her application was apparently filled out by a civil servant so indifferent that her name was handwritten as "Rosa Maria Emilia," while the typed version had "Rosa Maria" in the blank for surname and "Emilia" as her first name—and the signature was still a third variation, appearing to be "Rosa Emilia Means," of which only "Rosa" seemed to be written by the woman herself. Whatever the name, her photograph showed a determined-looking woman wearing a decidedly masculine hat. A widow, she had been in Philadelphia only since 1916 and wanted to go to Genoa "for family affairs." She had no intention of returning to the United States.

Anna LoForte, born in Palermo in 1887, was traveling with her son, six-year-old "Mr." Salvatore Capoccia, to whom she had given birth in Philadelphia in 1912. She listed her husband's name also as "Capoccia," while clearly signing her own "LoForte." Presumably of a higher socio economic class than most immigrants, she had been back to Italy in 1915 and listed no occupation. She wanted permission to travel because "I have an aged mother, and she has sent for me, and I have many little affairs to straighten out, there." She was "undecided" about returning to the United States, and demonstrated her impatience with bureaucracy by responding to the query about departure plans: "It is impossible to give [the] name of steamer until I receive my permit."[38]

A similar higher-than-average status was shown by Mary A. Hayes, one of the relatively few Irish women with intentions of permanent return to the native land. Age sixty at the war's end, she had remained single and risen to the prestigious position of assistant superintendent of the University of Pennsylvania Hospital, which she also listed as her residence. Although her parents had died in Ireland and although she had been in America since 1896, she evidently intended to return home to live out her last years.[39]

Finally, Margaret Risk, an aptly named Irish woman, was akin to many other Irish in that she never married. Born in 1846—she did "not know the exact date"—she came to Philadelphia in 1881. After almost four decades toiling in an America that predated Social Security, she was leaving "to make a home with my brother, as I am no longer [able] to work to earn a living for myself." She planned only to "pass through England," however, for at age seventy-two, Miss Risk, as she termed herself, was headed around the world to her new home of Melbourne, Australia.[40]

In fact, many of those who left America permanently went because they were aged or ill and could no longer maintain their struggle for survival in the independent marketplace. A number of health authorities spoke of the frequency with which patients afflicted with incurable disease returned to die in their native lands. A physician wrote:

> The vast number of returning consumptives—both men and women—has taken such proportions of late that the Italian Government is considering special measures of quarantine both on board the ships and the point of debarkation. One little town in Sicily (Sciacca), whose inhabitants live in New York, all on Elizabeth street . . . has established a small sanatorium on the outskirts of the city to receive the returning consumptive emigrants, so as to protect the rest of the population . . . Those assisted with free passage from the Italian Benevolent Institute of New York in the five years, 1901–05, was 973 . . . Fully one-third of these were women.[41]

No one went to America intending to come home fatally ill, of course, but many did go with the intention of returning. These "birds of passage" who migrated between continents were usually male, but some women emigrated with a plan for taking advantage of American opportunity and then returning home to enjoy the fruits of their labors. Italian women were especially likely to say that came to earn a dowry. French women in the fashion business of dressmaking and millinery also averred that they had no intention of remaining in America but only wished to develop their skills and bank accounts before returning to Paris. Interviewers also wrote of a German candy maker who was saving for a farm back home;[42] a Portuguese family whose aim was to return to the Azores with a fortune;[43] an Austrian woman who was saving for the sad day when she would have to return to care for her blind father, who never could be admitted to the United States.[44]

Even when their initial aim was to earn money and return, however, often residence in America changed women's minds.

Many doubtless appreciated the superior status and independent income that America gave them and were reluctant to give that up. Their values changed, and while they still missed their homes, time dimmed the appeal of returning. A sociologist writing in the 1930s said of her clients:

> Generally speaking few Italians wish to return to Italy to live. Although this may not have been their original intention, immigrants usually stay. Despite early plans to save enough money to return to live in comfort in their old homes, children and the World War and other complications eventually made the prospects seem less alluring. "To visit Italy for a month or two, yes," commented a woman, "but not to stay. They always fight there; every ten years there is a war. The man he goes to fight and the woman she work like the jackass."[45]

Another Italian woman agreed with this consensus, commenting perceptively of her changed intentions: "I have never been back to the old country. When I had enough money, the war was on; when the war was over I couldn't afford it. Finally, when everything was right I just couldn't go back. Sometimes memories are better than reality."[46]

English Kate Bond had similar intentions to return that did not materialize. She lived in Connecticut in the 1870s and had definite plans to go back, but by 1898 she had moved west, and the long-postponed return was recognized as only a whim: "I would like to see you," she wrote, "but I shall never leave Kansas. This is my home as long as I am on this earth."[47]

Like her, others who were pleased with America nevertheless also spoke longingly of returning to see the homeland once again. Gro Svendsen was careful never to let her parents think that she regretted emigrating, but she several times expressed a desire to return for a visit. In 1874 she wrote, "When the railroad comes up through Hallingdal . . . then, I think, we shall have to make a short visit home."[48] Gro died young, her aim unaccomplished, but many others with longer lives got no further on their journey than expressing the wish. Elise Waerenskjold wrote in 1857, "If all goes well . . . it could happen that we might be able to visit."[49] She lived thirty-eight more years, but she never returned. She may have come to see, like the insightful Italian, that memories can be more readily cherished without a reality check.

Both Elisabeth Koren and Jette Bruns, on the other hand, showed that it was possible even in this early era for affluent immigrants to return merely to visit. In the 1870s the Korens and their seven children made a six-month trip to Norway, fulfilling her 1854 promise to herself: "To stay here forever—I cannot think of such a thing, nor can Vilhelm either . . . No matter if we were ever so . . . contented, I would still return. Never to gaze again on what I have left behind—that would be too heavy a burden."[50]

Jette Bruns began to dream of the possibility of a visit in 1848, after a newcomer to her community crossed the ocean in sixteen days. "Suddenly it occurred to me," she wrote, "that in four months we could be over to see you and back here again . . . It would really work." Her husband "agreed to fill the purse," and she was so excited that she could not sleep—but "a few days later I gave it all up . . . Don't say anything of this, for these are probably castles in the air!"[51] But someone did speak of her dreams, and she was ridiculed for them: "It seems as if people enjoy teasing me about this. And then the impossibility of it all! It is bitter."[52] In 1853, when she was thirty-nine, she was still arguing with herself: "Why do I imagine that my presence would be so pleasant for you? . . . You would be disappointed in me . . . There is none of the youthful freshness left, but instead a stiff, sad indifferent figure, without manners, without interest, with aged features, a mouth without teeth."[53]

A sound case, in fact, could be made for living apart secure in the knowledge that one remained eternally young in the memory of those left behind. But finally, after twenty years in America, Jette had no children who needed breast-feeding, and she and her husband returned. When they arrived in Bremen in 1856, she wrote, "Everything seems so strange to me and yet so familiar; it makes me sad. I would almost like to turn around and go back to Missouri."[54] In the end, however, they had a fine time visiting relatives on both sides of the family. Her second trip, a quarter century later, involved none of the internal argumentation, and she wrote as a widow in 1881:

> My new son-in-law Carl Hess wants to provide a sufficient sum for a trip to the old country for his wife and for me! This is a strange idea. At my age, and they are a young married couple! I said in confidence that I would be very happy if they would have an heir [instead]. Both of them consider it something so definite that they have ordered me there for the winter to prepare for the trip in the spring.[55]

As steamers replaced sailing vessels and fares dropped, more and more immigrants would be able to cross the Atlantic merely to visit. Women as well as men went home to do a bit of legal work or tend sick relatives or simply see old friends. A scholar traveling in Europe circa 1910 mentioned, for example, meeting "a simple peasant woman who had gone home on business" and who was so familiar with her route that she "knew every detail . . . , down to the right street car in Vienna."[56]

Working-class people developed international networks on job availability, and as transatlantic fares dropped, many immigrants returned to their homeland when the economy was better there. In a 1903 strike, "trade newspapers in the textile industry announced that freighters and passenger ships leaving Philadelphia were crammed with workers going to Britain, where they could work or visit kin during what promised to be a long and bitter battle here. Passage was cheap and the pace of work in Britain less enervating than in the United States." During the same period, a management publication reporting on a Fall River strike complained, "As if this were not unfortunate enough, the new factor has appeared in the movement . . . back to the old country. The fact is the textile industry in England was never in better condition than at present . . . thus probably it is explained that on one recent steamer bound for England, there were a thousand, mostly textile help, from many of the different American centers."[57]

Whether their trips were work related or not, a 1911 report on women in the cotton goods industry showed that many enjoyed trips home—over one in every three Scottish women saved enough to visit:[58]

PERCENTAGE OF WOMEN REPORTING ONE OR MORE VISITS ABROAD AFTER 10 YEARS IN THE UNITED STATES

Scotch	37	German	23
English	32	Polish	23
Portugese	32	Irish	21
Swedish	25	Italian	13

Edna Vidravich Balkus was one of these working-class women who returned to Europe merely to visit. More than thirty years of labor in the Lowell mills enabled her to afford two trips back home, even though she had no close family there. A keen observer, she noted improvements in Lithuania and was especially pleased that schoolchildren were taught in Lithuanian rather than in Russian as she had been—but her views of Europe remained negative. Her return trips served as confirmation that she had done the right thing in leaving.

Many others were like her; their motivation was not homesickness or even nostalgia. Rather, the return was a woman's way of proving to herself and to her peers that she had "made good." Because she had once visited Italy and enjoyed the respect given her, Rosa Cavalleri in her old age wished to go again. Then, although her Americanization was sufficient to impress the villagers, Rosa knew that she was still green—if she could go back again, her triumph would be complete:

> Only one wish more I have; I'd love to go to Italia again before I die. Now I speak English good like an American. I could go anywhere—where millionaires and high people go. I would look the high people in the face and ask them what questions I'd like to know . . . I'd be proud I come from America and speak English . . . They wouldn't dare hurt me now I come from America. Me, that's why I love America. That's what I learned in America: not to be afraid.[59]

Broken Dreams: The Disillusioned

As the debarkation figures indicate, there certainly were those who returned not just for a visit but permanently. Some came with high hopes, were disillusioned, and went back; others came with the expectation of returning. They were like the French seamstress who did not try to assimilate, candidly saying she came "on account of the money, as there is no country like France."[60] She and her partner had risen from beginning salaries of $6 a week—which they viewed as a huge improvement over Paris—to the truly munificent sum in early-century dollars of $40 weekly. But money was their object only in that it could be used to return: "To one born in England, Germany, Austria, Holland or Scandinavia this may appear fine, but not so to the French. There is but one France and only one Paris in all the world, and soon, very soon, Annette and I will be aboard some great ship that will bear us back there."[61]

Returning thus did not necessarily mean disappointment in one's American expectations. Often, too, discontent related less to America than to some separate factor of one's personal life. The Irish nursemaid whose little charge died at the same time that her boyfriend took her savings and disappeared, for instance, returned not because of any fault of the country but rather because her personal losses were more than she could bear. Danish milliner Anna Walther also was unhappy for her first several years, again not because she was particularly disillusioned with America but because of a frustrated love affair. The Scandinavian woman whose husband, parents, and son died soon after their arrival surely would have returned if she could have: "How hard and miserable it will be for me," she wrote home, "left behind with six small children, to settle on land that has not even been cleared . . . If I could talk to any of you, my . . . most fervent plea would be that you never think of America."[62]

Those most likely to be discontented were those with high expectations, especially educated Europeans who came to America with utopian ideas that they planned to impose on the new land. Westphalia, Missouri, where Jette Bruns immigrated in 1836, was planned by Catholics in Saxony for colonization of this far, foreign wilderness. The most prominent early settlers were a family named Hesse, who soon returned to Germany bitterly disillusioned. Though she was younger than they, Jette displayed far more maturity in her expectations: "Our first visit to Mr. Hesse's upset me very much. The lady . . . cried, and complained that she couldn't stand it here. They were the only refined family in the settlement . . . He had brought with him a teacher, a secretary, workmen, and a maid. He wanted to establish a distillery at a time when there weren't even fields there."

The Hesses departed less than a year later, and Jette commented in an 1837 letter, "A great deal of patience and perseverance are necessary in the beginning; otherwise I am afraid that Mrs. Hesse will find all kinds of women who will follow her back." Even the Hesses' return trip was tragic: a brother died in St. Louis; their only son died "on the train between Lancaster and Philadelphia"; and Mrs. Hesse "was twice at the edge of her grave."[63] All of this no doubt contributed to the negative view of America that Mr. Hesse displayed in an account that he published in Germany, to which Jette hotly responded in 1839:

> I have to tell you that I cannot take this book into my hand without annoyance . . . Mr. Hesse is really absolutely too unjust concerning this area . . . Even in his time it [Missouri] had not been like that for a long time, and how much less does his description correspond to the present condition of the area! Many Germans have arrived since Mr. Hesse departed . . . The church land has been occupied on both sides with several houses. The school abuts the church . . . I shall tell you more of the advantages of our town and of the area.[64]

She went on to describe the development of Westphalia with obvious pride. From the beginning, she had praised the natural environment; she noted with pleasure everything from the blossoms of wild dogwood and Judas trees in the spring to the abundance of nuts in the fall. Despite her firm words, however, letters from Germany told her of rumors there that she and her family were on the point of return—almost as though educated Germans could not accept the possibility that one of their own could be happy outside their setting. She came to expect these attitudes, and five years later, Jette forethoughtfully pointed out the negatives when she heard that a family similar to the Hesses planned to emigrate. She wrote in 1841:

> So there is probably no doubt anymore that Dr. Roer and his family will be coming over . . . I am always afraid when educated people come . . . She knows, I hope, that the wages for a servant girl amount to four dollars a month. Earlier it was hardly possible to get one . . . Many a person finds it difficult at first to eat cornbread and pork . . . It is also impossible to get seamstresses to come to one's house . . . If you find it appropriate, you can tell Mrs. Roer about this.[65]

Rosalie Roos, a woman of some wealth who spent four years in the antebellum South before deciding to return to Sweden, was akin to the Hesse family in growing disenchanted as soon as her American experience moved from the stage of traveling curiosity to daily reality. She was very pleased at first, writing upon arrival: "I felt as though I were in a dream . . . Wherever my eyes turned they came upon new, unusual, remarkable objects . . . It is a little paradise here." Yet soon afterward, she completely reversed herself: "I would not wish to advise anyone to come over who believes he is in a position to earn his bread in his homeland . . . May none of my brothers hit upon the idea of seeking their fortune in America!"[66]

Swedish Ida Lindgren never got over her initial disappointment, though she stayed in America over a decade. She returned to home in 1881, still remembering the unhappiness she felt upon arrival in 1870:

> What shall I say? Why has the Lord brought us here? Oh, I feel so oppressed, so unhappy! . . . We drove across endless, endless prairies . . . We were quartered here

in Albinson's attic . . . When I asked . . . to go up with the children and put them to bed, there was no table, no chair, no bed, *nothing*, and there we were to stay! I set the candle on the floor, sat down beside it, took the children in my lap and burst into tears.[67]

Going back, of course, meant not only admitting to one's peers in Europe that emigration had been a mistake, but especially in the early era, a return move was prohibitively expensive for most. Many clearly would have gone if the body could move as easily as the mind, for only poverty kept them from making the return voyage. A Jewish woman, who wanted "to mention that she came from a respectable family" and that her dowry had been six hundred roubles, described the trauma of her first years in the Promised Land:

When we came to America . . . we . . . went through a lot . . . Our two little children stretched out their bony little hands to us, begging for food . . . Because we owed the landlord six dollars for rent, he put us out on the street. I huddled with the two children near our few belongings . . . The neighbors and passers-by threw a few cents into a plate . . . But the clang of the coins falling into the plate tore at my heart and I wept bitter tears.[68]

The contrast between expectation and reality made it all so much harder to bear. Almost everyone in Europe believed that if American streets were not actually paved with gold, then some lesser version of that tale was indisputably true. They expected their virtue to be rewarded; they were sure that in a growing nation there would be work for willing hands. But unrestrained capitalism brought a great gulf between workers and owners late in the century, and many immigrants found that even when jobs were available, the pittance paid barely kept starvation from the door. An elderly German woman cried bitterly: "It is early that we begin . . . and all day we shall sew and sew. We eat no warm *essen* . . . No, we stand and eat as we must and sew more . . . My back have such pain that I fall on the bed to say, *Ach Gott!* is it living to work so in this rich, free America?"[69]

Maja Johnsson also saw no hope in the remainder of her days. When her husband died, she was displaced from their farm, and she wrote to her niece in Sweden: "Now I am alone in a foreign land, but I take comfort for His help. He is the same God here as at home . . . If you could send me a little money it would be good, for I am too old to do any work . . . Forget not one who is alone in a strange land."[70]

The disillusionment for youth also could be stunning, for the higher one's goals, the greater seemed the likelihood of disappointment. If a woman came merely to get a job or get married, that end could be fulfilled, but if her expectations were more lofty, she was apt to become bitter. Elizabeth Hasanovitz was one whose expectations were too high for the reality. Though her hopes were bright when she came, she attempted suicide a short time later. Sick from cold and hunger, she continued to be seriously discontented and depressed:

Two years in America! Two years in the golden country! What had I accomplished?—a weak stomach, headaches every other day, a pale face, inflamed eyes . . . I wanted a doctor and I could not afford one . . . I always got headaches travelling in the subways. In Russia no more passengers than seats are allowed. Here in free America the people are free to choke themselves with the suffocating subway air. They are thrown together like cattle and carried down to the industrial market . . . If I could forget all the humiliations and return to my old days, which, though very unhappy because of the Government's brutality . . . still after . . . American life, seemed the happiest.[71]

Nor did she ever get out of her bad situation through the traditionally proclaimed methods of hard work or good marriage. It was only the merest chance: an American man whom she knew through union activity decided that she would be an ideal person to write a book encapsulizing the struggles of workers. Her life changed overnight, and not because of anything that she did differently. Doubtless there were other Elizabeth Hasanovitzes who were not so lucky, whose suicide attempts did not fail.

But it was only that her mind was clouded by illness that caused Lisa Hasanovitz to say that she would be happier in czarist Russia. No rational Jew—certainly not an opinionated, freedom-loving one like herself—could say that in sane moments. Moreover, although they may have resented an economic system that they could neither understand nor manage, most immigrant women did not resent those who did control it. The Elizabeth Hasanovitzes were an anomaly. Most envied the rich only in the sense that they would ape them if they could. Rose Cohen was typical: working in a nineteenth-century dress shop, she heard a customer refer to a $64 hat as "a bargain" and was amazed but not resentful. Her attitude was that of the mass of workers, especially the young, who pored over the society pages and followed the activities of the Morgans and Belmonts with vicarious pleasure.

But it was only in fantasy that a woman compared her life to that of society ladies. The European background of most had instilled strong beliefs about the propriety of "keeping one's place." An immigrant woman hoped to rise in America, but it was only modest improvement that she expected—and that mostly for the sake of her family and not herself. Because she did not expect to be wealthy, it was easier to find contentment with her lot. Because she thought of the family first, it was easy to believe that even if life in America had not measured up to her hopes, her children would one day bless her for the decision to emigrate.

Thus, for almost everyone, the evaluation of America was mixed and the feelings ambivalent; there seldom was the quick acceptance of the new land and the complete renunciation of the old that Americans liked to believe of the "wretched, huddled masses." Americans also often ignored the fact that for many immigrants, the transition actually involved a reduction in social position and a loss of economic security that was not regained for a decade or even a generation. Cynthia Baas, a 1929 student at a Wisconsin summer labor school, wrote of the reduction in status that her grandmother felt after leaving Holland. Though emigration had been her husband's idea, it was her precious jewelry and artwork that was sold to finance the trip, and she never could expect to be the person of importance in America that she had been in Holland. Things in Michigan were not nearly as wonderful as her husband had expected; though they lived in a Dutch community, he could not find work and when he did, it was common labor. "They lived with friends . . . and then rented a small cottage, which was nothing like their old home in Holland."[72]

Time and place changed everything, and discontent could be felt on both sides of the Atlantic. Some of those who returned to Europe because they wanted to and planned to were then chagrined to find that home was not as they remembered it. Their experiences abroad had affected them so that they no longer were satisfied with Old World ways. Americanized attitudes made returnees less willing to show deference to officials and social superiors, made them more assertive and impatient. A traveler in Croatia, for instance, asked the villagers why they did not fix the tremendous hole in their road where vehicles broke down. The answer was, "No one told us to, sir."[73] Many who had lived away could no longer accept such docility and fatalism—but neither could they easily change the attitudes of those without their overseas experience.

Returnees thus could become strangers straddling two countries but belonging to neither, no longer happy in the Old World yet unwilling to accept the New. As Europe had appeared doubly attractive from afar, so memories of America might improve as time dimmed reality. The woman who had lived abroad generally was accorded special respect, and that could change her mind about the experience. "In a little village in Hungary," said one writer:

> I know a woman who in her youth had tasted . . . the freedom of life in Chicago. Now, although she has been married fifteen years and has lived away from America longer than that, she speaks with glowing eyes of the time when she lived on South Halstad Street, ate thin bread with thick jam on it, and the land was flowing with sausages, lager beer, and chewing gum.[74]

"A Good Country for Working People": A Finalization

Elise Waerenskjold, whose long life in Texas was filled with praise for her adopted land, nevertheless was candid enough to acknowledge that emigration was not for everyone. Demonstrating the overwhelming practicality of immigrant women, she advised:

> Anyone who is well situated in Norway ought, in my opinion, to remain. Provided he can lead an independent life there and has the means to hire others to work for him, he will not be better off here but probably worse, since he might not be able to hire help . . . For the poor and destitute, on the other hand, who have never enjoyed things . . . but from early childhood have been inured to drudgery and toil, there is little to lose and much to gain.[75]

The New World was for the poor, a land where people "inured to hardship and toil" could work and save and eventually build their fortune. Letters going back to Europe gave realistic encouragement to those who were willing to live by the sweat of their brow; they bore witness to the contentment of such writers. "Please to tell my Father," said English textile worker Jane Morris, "that . . . I am often uneasy when I think about him having so large a family to maintain in that country while there is a free and plentiful country so near . . . If sister Betty was here she could do very well . . . this would be the very place for brother William . . ."[76]

Three sisters in 1850 similarly implored their brother: "We all fear that after working so long on the farm in Norway you may eventually end up poor . . . Here you can work ahead to success and get to own a good deal of property, even though you did not have a penny to begin with."[77] Likewise, English Emily Tongate, writing from rural New York in 1874, was perplexed at why others did not follow her example: "John and I have talked quite a good deal about you all and wondered you did not try and come to America . . . You could have done well out here. This is a good country for working people."[78]

"We arrived here . . . in 1846 . . . without any means," Swedish Lisa Jonsdotter Hertman testified just four years after immigration. "Now we owe nobody, own a nice farm, have fenced our property . . . Those who move here can count on coming to the land of Canaan."[79] Maria Steffansson reported that while her husband "speaks a great deal of moving to Sweden, I don't favor it . . . I do not believe that I can leave this place until death takes me away . . . You will not regret coming here if you do not encounter misfortunes—and misfortunes are met with in every country."[80]

So many took the advice of women like her that both the Swedish and Norwegian governments became concerned about their "outwanderers," and during the early twentieth century, they undertook investigations into emigrants' motivations and their outcomes in America. Departing Norwegians between 1905 and 1916 were asked to fill out a questionnaire on their reason for leaving: Of five options offered in the first year, 64% of the 18,000 women surveyed cited "a lack of opportunity for well-paid work." The number of men leaving that year was smaller—approximately 13,000—and 85% of them gave the same reason.[81] The Swedish government also sought reports from those with experience in America. Many responded, including a North Dakota woman in 1907 who offered this information and creative advice:

I am a woman, born in Varmland and belonged to the poor class. I had to go out and earn my bread already at the age of eight . . . I got rotten herring and potatoes, served out in small amounts . . . But I was not allowed to neglect Sunday school, for they wanted to drill into us poor people certain Biblical passages, such as "Be godly and let us be contented."

. . . Would be best to get the Chinese to emigrate to Sweden. I remember when I was at missionary meetings in Sweden, how they cried and complained over the poor Chinese and his poor soul, and gave substantial contributions to improve his condition. Best to chase out your poor countrymen and take in the dear Chinese.[82]

"I had to work like a dog," said another anonymous respondent. "Go out and spread manure and dirt from the ditches during the summer, and on the snowiest days of winter I had to carry water . . . Here . . . I was ashamed to get paid for what little I did . . . Whoever wants to work can get ahead in America. It is a good country and has been a support to many poor people."[83]

Naturally there were also those—especially the young—who were charmed by the tinsel, the captivating playthings of this most modern of lands. There was the German girl who thought Coney Island to be "just like what I see when I dream of heaven,"[84] and the young Hungarian who thought "America is the best country" because she had "white bread and butter and candy, and I can chew gum to beat the band."[85] When Rose Cohen saw her first roller skater, she thought the boy must have lost his feet in an industrial accident: "That a boy could go . . . about in open daylight on a plain week day, amusing himself, would have never occurred to me."[86]

Roller skates, chewing gum, and many other little things went into building the attraction of the new land. The reasons for liking or disliking America were varied and complex, and they ranged from the trivial to the profound. They differed from woman to woman and within the same woman at different stages of acculturation, in different circumstances and moods. Jette Bruns had lived long enough in America to think like an American when she returned to Germany in 1882, and she wrote thoughtfully of the contrasts in many areas of life:

> In Munster . . . people are living together in such crowded conditions . . . They do not have as much and as fine fresh air as we have. I also see many people who are much poorer or who are doing rough work, and they are, of course, clothed much more poorly and wear wooden shoes and work much harder. Better society is just as it is with us, only they don't have anything to do with craftsmen and workmen, and those who have government positions are then really the masters, and they live with their ladies very comfortably.[87]

America was home now, and she was eager to be there again. When she got back, her observations continued to be sharp, and she wrote from Jefferson City with newly opened eyes: "I am very much amazed at the great luxury here. The people live in splendor. I did not notice it as much earlier. Now I make comparisons."[88] A trip away renewed her appreciation of the egalitarianism of the New World, and civic pride in the Missouri communities that she pioneered was always one of her strongest characteristics. Significantly, her very last letter, dictated when she was eighty-seven and blind, centered on the construction of a new bridge.

Indeed, whether or not one was contended may have as much to do with the nature of one's personality as it did with any objective reality. Jette, for example, had every reason to complain about a land in which she buried seven of her eleven children, her beloved husband, a young brother, and endless numbers of other loved ones. Her experience was indisputably harsh—but she did not allow that to poison her mind and was always open to the possibility of new wonders. In 1891, at age seventy-eight, she went out to Seattle to visit her sons and was enthralled: "If I were twenty years younger," she wrote, "I would not have objected to staying in Seattle. The youthful, strong striving, the healthy breeze of the sea air, all appealed to me very much."[89] At a train layover in Minneapolis, she wrote, "It is a magnificent city! The private residences look so friendly. All are individually surrounded by lawns. The streets with their posts are so clean and quiet. The public library, a very impressive building of red granite, caught my attention. . . ."[90]

Back home in Missouri, she compared Seattle with St. Louis: "Here everything is so regulated, so solidly rich, heavy and cold. There everything is easy and difficulties are quickly shoved aside. If it doesn't work going over the mountain, then one goes through it." The thought was highly revealing, for the same language easily could have been used to compare Germany and Missouri when she emigrated sixty years earlier. Indeed, the key to a successful immigrant experience lay in Jette's summarizing phase: "I am a pioneer by nature."[91] Another key to contentment she conveyed to her brother, who was increasingly crippled by rheumatism: "I hope that you keep on hoping."[92]

Hope and contentment are difficult to measure, and few scientific studies exist on whether or not immigrants were satisfied with the end result of their experience. One project in Boston at the turn of the century, however, asked that direct question in interviews with 500 women. The results showed an amazing willingness to express satisfaction: only about 10% "felt that their object in coming to this country had not been realized, or expressed a definite discontent or want."[93] Of those who were discontented, most were unhappy with their jobs and not specifically with America; only a few intended to return.

Another, less scientific study in a different time and place brought generally similar results. Swedish Fredricka Bremer, traveling in America in the 1850s, systematically "asked many, both men and women, whether they were contented." She found a difference between Norwegians and Swedes, with the Norwegians—who were usually poorer in Europe—being more apt to say, "Yes, we are better off here; we do not work so hard, and it is easier to gain a livelihood." The Swedes, however, were inclined to think that "if we were to work as hard in Sweden as we do here, we should be as well off there, and often better."[94]

There were few clear answers that rang unanimous for all. More often there was ambivalence; there were both advantages and disadvantages. Anna Walther serves as an excellent example, for her view was more objective and experience based than most. She had worked in Russia, Paris, several German cities, and even South Africa before coming first to New York and later to Indiana. An early careerist, she had consciously chosen to become a milliner because, with "her trade in her fingers," she would be free to follow her childhood ambition of traveling. She was critical of a number of aspects of America during her first years but also was astute enough to recognize that most of her unhappiness was due to her involvement with an unavailable man. Once she gave up on her lover, she was able to write: "America is my adopted country. Here I found happiness. Here my ambition for higher intellectual attainment is being realized."[95]

Indeed, although many college doors were still closed to women in this era, America opened more of them than any other nation at the time. Educational opportunity on the elementary and vocational levels was far more available to girls and women than was the case in most of Europe, and millions of single, working women took advantage of urban evening schools, libraries, settlement house classes, and other educational outlets that offered a range of learning virtually incomprehensible to women of their class in Europe. Even if the immigrant did not avail herself of these opportunities, almost all were keenly aware that their children would benefit from free schooling. "Children," summarized a group of Swedes interviewed in the 1850s, "have a better prospect here for their future than at home. They are admitted into schools for nothing; receive good education and easily have an opportunity of maintaining themselves."[96]

Millions joined the chorus, and millions more responded by packing their bags to come. It was "a good country for working people"; it was a place for the practical, the ambitious, the optimistic. Ultimately the best proof of their satisfaction is that they kept coming. They wrote back for their loved ones who streamed across the sea in ever increasing waves until finally America closed her gates. Even when a woman felt that she would never totally adjust, even when she judged her emigration to have been too costly in emotional terms, still she believed that the objective reality showed she had done what was best for her children.

Her offspring—if they stopped to think on it at all—would be plagued by no such questions. The individual born in this country who chose to emigrate to another would be extremely rare; future generations would validate their foremothers' decision by assuming that America, whatever its faults, was the best place to live. They would seldom stop to think of the sacrifice that had been made to give them this opportunity, and they never could completely understand the heartache and internal conflict that had been endured. An anonymous emigrant from Arendal, Norway, explains to us through the mists of time her ambivalence and her loneliness and her hope that the decision that was so painful for her in the present would prove right in the future:

> My dear sisters, it was a bitter cup for me to drink, to leave a dear mother and sisters and to part forever in this life, though living. Only the thought of the coming world was my consolation; there I shall see you all . . . Thanks be to the Lord who gave me the strength to carry out this step, which I hope will be for my own and my children's best in the future. So I hope that time will heal the wound, but up to the present I cannot deny that homesickness gnaws at me hard. When I think, however, that there will be a better livelihood for us here than in poor Norway, I reconcile myself to it and thank God, who protected me and mine over the ocean's waves and led us to a fruitful land.[97]

NOTES

Who, Where, and When

1. "Landed on Ellis Island; New Immigration Buildings Opened Yesterday," *New York Times*, January 2, 1892, p. 1. On the new heritage center at Cohn, see Valerie Tamis, "Harbor of Tears," *The Times*, January 16, 1994, p. 1E.
2. *Ibid.*
3. Janet A. Nolan, *Ourselves Alone: Women's Emigration from Ireland, 1895–1920* (Lexington: University of Kentucky Press, 1989), pp. 2, 100, 51.
4. 61st Congress, 3d Session, 1911, Senate Document 756, *Statistical Review of Immigration, 1820–1910* (Washington: Government Printing Office, 1911), p. 47.
5. Kristian Hvidt, *Flight to America: The Social Background of 300,000 Danish Emigrants* (New York: Academic Press, 1975), p. 88.
6. Joseph Logsdon, "Immigration through the Port of New Orleans," in M. Mark Stolarik, *Forgotten Doors: The Other Ports of Entry to the United States* (Philadelphia: Balch Institute Press, 1988), p. 108.
7. Russel L. Gerlach, *Immigrants in the Ozarks* (Columbia: University of Missouri Press, 1976), pp. 36–37.
8. *Ibid.*, p. 38.
9. Lawrence H. Fuchs, "Immigration through Boston," in Stolarik, *Forgotten Doors*, p. 18.
10. Fredric M. Miller, "Immigration through Philadelphia," in Stolarik, *Forgotten Doors*, p. 48.
11. Anne Stinson, "The Next Galatea," January 7, 1989, newspaper clipping in the Locust Point file, Maryland Historical Society, Baltimore.
12. Jane Maud Campbell, speech to the Daughters of the American Revolution, Schlesinger Library, Radcliffe College, box 1, folder 11 (hereafter cited as SCH).
13. Frederick C. Luebke, *Germans in the New World: Essays in the History of Immigration* (Urbana: University of Illinois Press, 1990), pp. 174–75.
14. Walter D. Kamphoefner, Wolfgang Helbich, and Ulrike Sommer, *News from the Land of Freedom: German Immigrants Write Home* (Ithaca N.Y.: Cornell University Press, 1991), p. 16.
15. John A. Hawgood, *The Tragedy of German-America* (New York: G. P. Putnam's Sons, 1940), p. 184.
16. Karen Johnson Freeze, "Czechs," in Thernstrom, *Harvard Encyclopedia of American Ethnic Groups* (Cambridge: Harvard University Press, 1980), p. 264.
17. This rounded-off number and those that follow are from Wesley M. Gewehr et al., *The United States: A History of a Democracy* (New York: McGraw-Hill, 1960), app. 8. Detailed statistics on immigration by ethnic group and era are available in a number of other sources, especially in annual reports of the U.S. Immigration and Naturalization Service and in U.S. Bureau of the Census, *Historical Statistics of the United States, Colonial Times to 1970* (Washington: Government Printing Office, 1975).
18. Roger Daniels, *Coming to America: A History of Immigration and Ethnicity in American Life* (New York: HarperCollins, 1990), p. 135.
19. Stanley Nadel, *Little Germany: Ethnicity, Religion, and Class in New York City, 1845–80* (Urbana: University of Illinois, 1990), p. 17.
20. Peter A. Munch, "Norwegians," in Thernstrom, *Harvard Encyclopedia of American Ethnic Groups*, p. 751.
21. Arnold H. Barton, *Letters from the Promised Land: Swedes in America, 1840–1914* (Minneapolis: University of Minnesota Press, 1975), p. 290.

CHAPTER 1—Fatalistic Conceptions

1. E. Estyn Evans, "Peasant Beliefs in Nineteenth Century Ireland," in Daniel J. Casey and Robert E. Rhodes, *Views of the Irish Peasantry, 1800–1916* (Hamden, Conn.: Archon Books, 1977), p. 42.

2. Phyllis H. Williams, *South Italian Folkways in Europe and America* (New York: Russell & Russell, 1938; reissued 1969), pp. 105–6.

3. Niles Carpenter, *Immigrants and Their Children, 1920: A Study Based on Census Statistics Relative to the Foreign Born and the Native White of Foreign or Mixed Parentage* (Washington: Government Printing Office, 1927; reissued by Arno Press and the *New York Times*, American Immigration Collection, 1969), p. 183.

4. *Ibid.*

5. 1870 U.S. Census, 9th Ward of Baltimore, in the Maryland State Archives, Annapolis; author's own analysis.

6. Nadel, *Little Germany*, p. 51.

7. Jette Bruns, *Hold Dear, as Always: Jette, a German Immigrant Life in Letters*, trans. and ed. Adolf E. Schroeder and Carla Schulz-Geisberg (Columbia: University of Missouri Press, 1988).

8. P. R. Eastman, "A Comparison of the Birth Rates of Native and of Foreign-Born White Women in the State of New York" (Albany: New York State Department of Health, 1916), p. 4; in the Russell Sage Foundation Collection, Cohen Library, City College of the City University of New York.

9. *Ibid.*, p. 2. Statistics were based on the federal census of 1910 and a state census in 1915.

10. "Hard Facts," *The Birth Control Review*, April 1919, p. 3, in the Mary Ware Dennett Collection, SCH, box 13, folder 234.

11. Antonio Stella, *The Effects of Urban Congestion on Italian Women and Children* (New York, 1908); reprinted in *Italians in the City: Health and Related Social Needs* (New York: Arno Press, 1975), p. 21.

12. Agnes de Lima, "Night Work by Mothers in Passaic," June 4, 1926, unidentified newspaper clipping in Mary Van Kleeck's papers, Sophia Smith Collection, Smith College, Northampton, Massachusetts (hereafter cited as SSC), box 96, folder 1521.

13. Mary Van Kleeck, *Artificial Flower Makers* (New York: Russell Sage Foundation, 1913), p. 95.

14. *Ibid.*, p. 96.

15. Gro Svendsen, *Frontier Mother: The Letters of Gro Svendsen*, trans. and ed. Theodore C. Blegen and Pauline Farseth (Northfield, Minn.: Norwegian-American Historical Association, 1950), p. 134. The letters were written between 1862 and 1878.

16. *Ibid.*, p. 137.

17. 61st Congress, 2d Session, Senate Document 282, *Reports of the Immigration Commission: Fecundity of Immigrant Women* (Washington: Government Printing Office, 1911), pp. 811–12.

18. Williams, *South Italian Folkways*, pp. 105–6.

19. Donald B. Cole, *Immigrant City: Lawrence, Massachusetts, 1845–1921* (Chapel Hill: University of North Carolina Press, 1963), p. 107.

20. Nadel, *Little Germany*, p. 52.

21. *Ibid.*, p. 187.

22. Nolan, *Ourselves Alone*, p. 28.

23. Elsa G. Herzfeld, *Family Monographs: The History of Twenty-four Families Living in the Middle West Side of New York City* (New York: James Kempster Printing Co., 1905), p. 19.

24. "Hard Facts," *Birth Control Review*, p. 3.

25. Elizabeth G. Stern, *I Am a Woman—and a Jew* (New York: J. H. Sears & Co., 1926; reissued by Arno Press and the *New York Times*, American Immigration Collection, 1969), p. 76.

26. Herzfeld, *Family Monographs*, p. 130.

27. Priscilla Long, Collection of Oral Histories, Lola Marot, "Oral Interview—Lola Anguini," p. 12, SCH.

28. Vice Commission of Chicago, *The Social Evil in Chicago* (Chicago: Gunthorp-Warren Printing Co., 1911; reissued by Arno Press and the *New York Times*, 1970), p. 224.

29. Williams, *South Italian Folkways*, pp. 105–6.

30. "For the Children's Sake: Excerpts from Letters from Mothers," *Birth Control Review*, undated, p. 6; in the Mary Ware Dennett Collection, SCH, box 13, folder 234.

31. Herzfeld, *Family Monographs*, p. 140.

32. "Hard Facts, *Birth Control Review*, p. 3.

33. Committee of One Hundred of the Voluntary Birth Control League, "The Birth Control Movement," 1917, p. 36, in the Mary Ware Dennett Collection, SCH box 14, folder 238.

34. Katharine Anthony, *Mothers Who Must Earn* (New York: Survey Associates and the Russell Sage Foundation, 1914), p. 154. In view of recent right-wing attempts to portray Susan Anthony as an anti-abortion activist, it may be noteworthy to point out that Katharine Anthony was Susan Anthony's niece.

35. "Hard Facts," *Birth Control Review*, p. 3.

36. Edward Shorter, "Female Emancipation, Birth Control, and Fertility in European History," *American Historical Review* 78, no. 3 (June 1973): 631.

37. "Study of Maternal Mortality under the Auspices of the New York Academy of Medicine in Cooperation with New York City Department of Health—Financed by the Commonwealth Fund," 1931, p. 2, Rockefeller Archive Center, North Tarrytown, New York (hereafter cited as RAC), Bureau of Social Hygiene Collection, series III, subseries 2, box 10, folder 202.

38. Committee of One Hundred of Voluntary Birth Control League, "The Birth Control Movement," 1917, p. 5; in the Mary Ware Dennett Collection, SCH, box 14, folder 238. According to the same source, p. 15, there were an estimated 8,000 abortions in New York in 1916.

   A 1925 intensive report on the sex habits of 1,000 women (most of whom probably were natives) showed an abortion rate of 11%. Even so, the physician reporting quickly added, "[B]ut it should not be forgotten that 20 percent of these women have never been pregnant," thus indicating his belief that the rate would have been higher had there been more pregnancies. Committee on Maternal Health, "Recent Studies in Normal Sex Life and the Relation of Sex Experiences," 1925, RAC, Bureau of Social Hygiene, series III, subseries 2, box 7, folder 172.

39. Vice Commission of Chicago, *Social Evil*, p. 225. For an extensive study, see James C. Mohr, *Abortion in America* (New York: Oxford University Press, 1978). Pages 91–93, 207, and 243 refer specifically to immigrants. In general, Mohr asserts that immigrant women were far less likely than natives to seek abortions during most of the nineteenth century. However, by the early twentieth century, when state legislatures had passed strongly restrictive antiabortion laws (largely because of lobbying efforts by organized medicine), a shifting of patterns seems to have occurred. Then, he states, "there is some evidence to indicate that a substantial proportion of the married women still having recourse to abortion by 1900 were lower-class and immigrant women."

40. Nadel, *Little Germany*, p. 52.

41. See Sarah Stage, *Female Complaints: Lydia Pinkham and the Business of Women's Medicine* (New York: W. W. Norton & Co., 1979), especially pp. 102 and 127.

42. Long, Oral Histories. Sarah Demirfian, "An Interview with My Mother," p. 5, SCH.

43. One of "hundreds of letters" collected by Mrs. Amos Pinchot, chairman, Committee of One Hundred of the Voluntary Birth Control League, undated document in the Mary Ware Dennett Collection, SCH, box 14, folder 238.

44. Elsa G. Herzfeld, "The Tenement House Family," *The Independent* 59, December 28, 1905, p. 1521.

45. Linka Preus, *Linka's Diary on Land and Sea, 1845–1864*, trans. and ed. Johan C. K. Preus and Diderikke Brandt Preus (Minneapolis: Augsburg Publishing House, 1952), p. 256.

46. Letter in the Mary Ware Dennett Collection, SCH, box 21, folder 371. This and the letters that follow were written in 1928 and 1929.

47. *Ibid.*, folder 372.

48. *Ibid.*, folder 373.

49. *Ibid.*

50. *Ibid.*, folder 371.

51. *Ibid.*

52. *Ibid.*

53. Mary Ware Dennett, "Statement Regarding Dr. Van Inghen's Criticism of the Voluntary Parenthood League," November, 1920, letter in the Mary Ware Dennett Collection, SCH, box 13, folder 229.

   Dennett's chart was neither alphabetized nor ranked in order; her data are used here to rank nations by birthrate, with the "baby death rate" as the secondary factor. The years studied were 1901–08. Dennett explained, "one has only to consult the charts of the British Registrar-General (who is considered the world authority on vital statistics) to see that the countries which have had a really *high* birth rate, are the countries which also have had the highest baby death rates . . . The rates are per 1000."

54. Correspondence between Mary Ware Dennett and Dr. Philip Van Ingen, 1920, in the Mary Ware Dennett Collection, SCH, box 13, folder 228.

55. Dennett, "Statement Regarding Dr. Van Inghen," citing Dr. Adolphus Knopf in the *American Journal of Public Health*, February, 1917. Knopf wrote a similar article for *The Survey*, November 18, 1916.

56. American Birth Control League, "A Message to Mothers," 1931, pp. 6–7, RAC, Bureau of Social Hygiene Collection, series III, subseries 2, box 7, folder 162.

CHAPTER 2—Those Uncontrolled Births

1. Williams, *South Italian Folkways*, pp. 87, 103.
2. Herzfeld, *Family Monographs*, pp. 19–20.
3. Michael M. Davis Jr., *Immigrant Health and the Community*, (New York: Harper & Bros., 1921), p. 192.
4. *Ibid.*
5. Williams, *South Italian Folkways*, p. 35.
6. *Ibid.*, p. 89.
7. Davis, *Immigrant Health*, p. 193.
8. *Ibid.*
9. Williams, *South Italian Folkways*, p. 156.
10. Herzfeld, *Family Monographs*, pp. 20–21, and "Tenement House Family," p. 1521.
11. Williams, *South Italian Folkways*, p. 35.
12. Marie Hall Ets, *Rosa: The Life of an Italian Immigrant* (Minneapolis: University of Minnesota Press, 1970), p. 178.
13. *Ibid.*, pp. 157–58.
14. *Ibid.*, p. 158.
15. *Ibid.*, p. 181.
16. de Lima, "Night Work," unpaged.
17. Elisabeth Koren, *The Diary of Elisabeth Koren, 1853–1855*, trans. and ed. David T. Nelson (Northfield, Minn.: Norwegian-American Historical Association, 1955), p. 351.
18. Kamphoefner, Helbich, and Sommer, *News From the Land of Freedom*, p. 561.
19. Bruns, *Hold Dear*, p. 93.
20. *Ibid.*, p. 99.
21. *Ibid.*, p. 106.
22. *Ibid.*, p. 117.
23. *Ibid.*, p. 137.
24. *Ibid.*, p. 143.
25. *Ibid.*, p. 145.
26. *Ibid.*, p. 165.
27. Emilie Lohmann Koenig, "Letters from America to a Family in Germany," trans. and ed. Mrs. Oscar P. Brauer, *Concordia Historical Quarterly* 29, no. 1 (spring 1956): 20.
28. *Ibid.*, pp. 22–23.
29. *Ibid.*, pp. 24–25.
30. Preus, *Linka's Diary*, p. 221.
31. *Ibid.*, p. 229.
32. *Ibid.*, p. 270.
33. *Ibid.*, p. 271.
34. *Ibid.*, p. 272.
35. *Ibid.*, p. 274.
36. Charlotte Erickson, *Invisible Immigrants* (Coral Gables, Fla.: University of Miami Press, 1972), pp. 175–78.
37. Committee of One Hundred of the Voluntary Birth Control League, "Birth Control Movement," 1917, p. 23, citing Dr. Grace Meigs of "the Government's Children's Bureau in Washington, D.C.," in the Mary Ware Dennett Collection, SCH, box 14, folder 238.
38. "Study of Maternal Mortality," p. 2, RAC.
39. "Hard Facts," *Birth Control Review*, p. 3.
40. 12th Census of the United States, 1900, vol. 3, *Vital Statistics*, p. ccxlviii.
41. Emily Balch, *Our Slavic Fellow Citizens* (Philadelphia: William F. Fell Co., 1910; reissued by Arno Press and the *New York Times*, American Immigration Collection, 1969), p. 376.
42. Davis, *Immigrant Health*, p. 188.
43. Herzfeld, "Tenement House Family," p. 1522.
44. *Ibid.*

45. See especially Davis, *Immigrant Health*, p. 190, citing Emma Duke, "Infant Mortality, Johnston, Pennsylvania," Department of Labor Children's Bureau, 1915, pp. 32–34, and Anthony, *Mothers Who Must Earn*, p. 78 ff.

46. Herzfeld, *Family Monographs*, p. 66.

47. Williams, *South Italian Folkways*, p. 89.

48. Evans, "Peasant Beliefs," pp. 42–43. Because this assertion almost strains credulity, it should be pointed out that Professor Evans was chairman of the Institute of Irish Studies at Queens University, Belfast.

49. Jo Pagano, *Golden Wedding* (New York: Random House, 1943), p. 60.

50. *Ibid.*, pp. 138–39.

51. Ets, *Rosa*, pp. 228–31.

52. Baltimore City Directory, 1879, in the library of the Maryland Historical Society, Baltimore.

53. Eastman, "Comparison of Birth Rates," p. 12.

54. Maternity Center Association annual report, 1927, pp. 8–9, RAC, Laura Spelman Rockefeller Memorial Collection, series III, subseries 1, box 3, folder 30. (This report contains a history of the organization, which explains why its date is more than a decade after the survey's date.)

55. Davis, *Immigrant Health*, p. 198.

56. One of "hundreds of letters" collected by Mrs. Amos Pinchot, Chairman, Committee of One Hundred of the Voluntary Birth Control League, undated document in the Mary Ware Dennett Collection, SCH, box 14, folder 238.

57. Davis, *Immigrant Health*, p. 201.

58. Anthony, *Mothers Who Must Earn*, p. 168.

59. Upton Sinclair, "Is *The Jungle* True?" *The Independent* 60, May 17, 1906, p. 1130.

60. Davis, *Immigrant Health*, p. 211.

61. *Ibid.*, pp. 212–13.

62. *Ibid.*, p. 214.

63. *Ibid.*, p. 215.

64. *Ibid.*, citing Dr. Abraham Jacobi, "The Best Means of Combating Infant Mortality," *Journal of the American Medical Association*, June 8, 1912, pp. 1740–44.

65. "Maternity Center Statistics," RAC, Laura Spelman Rockefeller Memorial Collection, series III, subseries 1, box 4, folder 34.

66. "Study of Maternal Mortality," p. 3, RAC.

67. *Ibid.*

68. Davis, *Immigrant Health*, p. 220.

69. Maternity Center Association annual report, pp. 8 and 7, RAC.

70. New York Milk Committee, "Are You in the Baby Saving Drive?" 1919, RAC, Laura Spelman Rockefeller Memorial Collection, series III, subseries 1, box 4, folder 46.

71. *Ibid.*

72. Maternity Center Association annual report, p. 12, RAC.

73. "Maternity Center Statistics," RAC, Laura Spelman Rockefeller Memorial Collection, series III, subseries 1, box 3, folder 30.

74. New York Milk Committee, "Baby Saving," RAC.

75. See the entry for Sheppard-Towner Act in Doris Weatherford, *American Women's History: An A to Z of People, Organizations, Issues, and Events* (New York: Prentice-Hall, 1994), pp. 315–16. A much longer discussion is in Sheila M. Rothman, *Woman's Proper Place* (New York: Basic Books, 1978).

76. Margaret Sanger, *Pivot of Civilization* (New York: Brentano's, 1922), p. 116.

77. Maternity Center Association annual report, pp. 8–9, RAC.

CHAPTER 3—In Sickness and in Health

1. Davis, *Immigrant Health*, p. 193.

2. Rose Cohen, *Out of the Shadow* (New York: George H. Doran Co., 1918), p. 233.

3. Williams, *South Italian Folkways*, p. 172.

4. 61st Congress, 2d Session, Senate Document 645, *Report on Condition of Woman and Child Wage-earners in the United States* (Washington: Government Printing Office, 1911–13), vol. 2, *Men's Ready-Made Clothing*, p. 312.

5.   Constance McLaughlin Green, *Holyoke, Massachusetts: A Case History of the Industrial Revolution in America* (New Haven: Yale University Press, 1939), p. 119.
6.   Cole, *Immigrant City,* p. 63.
7.   Ets, *Rosa,* p. 251.
8.   "Hard Facts," *Birth Control Review,* p. 3.
9.   Bessie Olga Pehotsky, *The Slavic Immigrant Woman* (Cincinnati: Powell & White, 1925), pp. 49–50.
10.   Herzfeld, *Family Monographs,* p. 27.
11.   "Women, Work and Ethnicity in Lowell," an oral history project by University of Lowell students, interview of Athena Theokas by Lewis Karobatsos, 1974, unpaged. In the Morgan Center for Lowell History, Lowell, Massachusetts (hereafter cited as MC). It is noteworthy that Theokas shared this information only late in the interview and was talking to another Greek.
12.   *Ibid.*
13.   Knut Gjerset and Ludvig Hektoen, "Health Conditions and the Practice of Medicine Among the Early Norwegian Settlers, 1825–1865," Norwegian-American Historical Society, *Studies and Records* 1 (1926): 33, citing Svein Nilsson, editor of *Illustrert billed-Magazin.*
14.   Williams, *South Italian Folkways,* p. 178.
15.   Davis, *Immigrant Health,* p. 123.
16.   Louise C. Odencrantz, *Italian Women in Industry* (New York: Russell Sage Foundation, 1919), p. 234. Although published in 1919, the data for this book were collected in 1912–13.
17.   Anthony, *Mothers Who Must Earn,* p. 159.
18.   Herzfeld, *Family Monographs,* p. 67.
19.   Evans, "Peasant Beliefs," p. 42.
20.   Davis, *Immigrant Health,* citing Peter Roberts, *The New Immigration* (New York: Macmillan, 1912), p. 134.
21.   Williams, *South Italian Folkways,* p. 9.
22.   Cornelia Stratton Parker, *Working with the Working Woman* (New York: Harper & Bros., 1922), p. 158.
23.   Antonio Mangano, *The Italian Colonies of New York City* (New York, 1903); reprinted in *Italians in the City: Health and Related Social Needs* (New York: Arno Press, 1975), p. 29.
24.   *Ibid,* p. 30.
25.   Ets, *Rosa,* p. 12.
26.   Koenig, "Letters from America," vol. 28, p. 177.
27.   Gjerset and Hektoen, "Health Conditions," p. 46.
28.   Marjorie Roberts, "Italian Girls on American Soil," *Mental Hygiene* 13 (October 1929): 766.
29.   Stella, *Urban Congestion,* pp. 27–28.
30.   Nolan, *Ourselves Alone,* p. 56.
31.   Stella, *Urban Congestion,* p. 32.
32.   *Ibid.,* p. 28.
33.   Bruns, *Hold Dear,* p. 139.
34.   Stern, *I Am a Woman,* p. 72.
35.   Karobatsos, interview of Athena Theokas, unpaged, MC.
36.   Jane Maud Campbell, handwritten note in the Jane Maud Campbell Collection, SCH, box 1, folder 13.
37.   Gjerset and Hektoen, "Health Conditions," p. 33.
38.   Craig Donald Jacobs, "Death, Disease, and Deliverance: Chippewa County in the Late Nineteenth Century," p. 9, part of a series, *Historical Essays on Rural Life,* Department of History, Southwest State University, Marshall, Minnesota, 1991.
39.   Herzfeld, *Family Monographs,* p. 27.
40.   Williams, *South Italian Folkways,* p. 168.
41.   Ets, *Rosa,* p. 43.
42.   Gjerset and Hektoen, "Health Conditions," p. 36.
43.   *Ibid.,* p. 37.
44.   Gwendolyn Salisbury Hughes, *Mothers in Industry: Wage-Earning by Mothers in Philadelphia* (New York: New Republic, 1925), p. 225. (Data were collected in 1918–19.)
45.   Williams, *South Italian Folkways,* p. 164.
46.   Herzfeld, *Family Monographs,* p. 129.
47.   12th Census, vol. 3, p. lxxxviii.
48.   Jacobs, "Death, Disease and Deliverance," pp. 12, 14.

49. Theodore C. Blegen, *Land of Their Choice: The Immigrants Write Home* (St. Paul: University of Minnesota Press, 1955), p. 77.

50. Elise Waerenskjold, *The Lady with the Pen: Elise Waerenskjold in Texas*, trans. and ed. C. A. Clausen (Northfield, Minn.: Norwegian-American Historical Association, 1961), pp. 61–62.

51. Bruns, *Hold Dear*, p. 171.

52. *Ibid.*, p. 131.

53. *Ibid.*, pp. 146–47.

54. Svendsen, *Frontier Mother*, p. 54.

55. Mrs. Realf Ottesen Brandt, "Social Aspects of Prairie Pioneering: The Reminiscences of a Pioneer Pastor's Wife," Norwegian-American Historical Association, *Studies and Records* 7 (1956): 6.

56. Gjerset and Hektoen, "Health Conditions," p. 11.

57. Bruns, *Hold Dear*, p. 89.

58. Blegen, *Land of Their Choice*, p. 265.

59. Bruns, *Hold Dear*, p. 89.

60. Jacobs, "Death, Disease and Deliverance," pp. 21–22.

61. Bruns, *Hold Dear*, p. 84.

62. Annie P. Dingman, "Report of Immigration and Foreign Community Secretary, Ohio and West Virginia, Nov. 1–30, 1918," in the YWCA files, SSC, box 32, folder 6.

63. Brooklyn Bureau of Charities advertising copy, in general budget files for 1920–28; RAC, Laura Spelman Rockefeller Memorial Collection, series III, subseries 1, box 1, folder 8.

64. New York City Department of Health, "Some Special Problems of Italians in New York City," 1934; reprinted in *Italians in the City: Health and Related Social Needs* (New York: Arno Press, 1975), pp. 3–9.

65. Association for the Improvement of the Conditions of the Poor, General Budget, RAC, Laura Spelman Rockefeller Memorial Collection, 1919–25, box 6, subseries 1.

CHAPTER 4—The Immigrant Way of Death

1. Cole, *Immigrant City*, pp. 64, 76.

2. *Ibid.*, p. 76.

3. Jacob Riis, *How the Other Half Lives* (New York: C. Scribner's Sons, 1890; reissued by New York: Sagamore Press, 1957), p. 27.

4. Anthony, *Mothers Who Must Earn*, p. 154.

5. Gjerset and Hektoen, "Health Conditions," p. 32.

6. Jacobs, "Death, Disease and Deliverance," p. 6. Jacobs does an excellent job of demonstrating his thesis that most childhood deaths then were caused by disease, while most now are caused by accidents.

7. Anthony, *Mothers Who Must Earn*, pp. 166–67, 180.

8. Committee of One Hundred, "Birth Control Movement," p. 22, citing a survey "of the families of 1,600 wage earners" by Dr. Alice Hamilton, *Bulletin of the American Academy of Medicine*, May 1910.

9. *Ibid.* See also Mary Ware Dennett, citing a survey done by the Children's Board of Johnstown, Pennsylvania, in "Statement Regarding Dr. Van Inghen."

10. Eastman, "Comparison of Birth Rates," p. 10.

11. New York Milk Committee, "Baby Saving," RAC. While most immigrant cities had infant mortality rates markedly higher than cities of similar size without a large immigrant population, there were enough exceptions to confirm the efficacy of public health progress: Brockton, Massachusetts, and Hoboken, New Jersey, for example, were immigrant towns that did well in comparison with other cities their size.

    See also a letter from Lillian Wald to John D. Rockefeller Jr., March 17, 1920, thanking him for funds that had enabled a 200% reduction of infant mortality; RAC, Laura Spelman Rockefeller Memorial Collection, series III, subseries 1, box 2, folder 14.

12. Stella, *Urban Congestion*, p. 2.

13. Eastman, "Comparison of Birth Rates," p. 2.

14. Senate Document 645, vol. 13, *Infant Mortality and Its Relation to the Employment of Mothers*, 1912, p. 143.

15. *Ibid.*, pp. 138–61.

16. Herzfeld, "Tenement House Family," p. 1522.

17. Anthony, *Mothers Who Must Earn*, p. 155.

18. *Ibid.*

19. Kamphoefner, Helbich, and Sommer, *News From the Land of Freedom*, p. 375.

20. Stern, *I Am a Woman*, pp. 57–58.
21. Koren, *Diary of Elisabeth Koren*, p. 159.
22. Preus, *Linka's Diary*, p. 239.
23. Waerenskjold, *Lady with the Pen*, pp. 64–65.
24. Herzfeld, *Family Monographs*, pp. 107–8.
25. Stella, *Urban Congestion*, p. 25.
26. Herzfeld, *Family Monographs*, p. 64.
27. *Ibid.*, pp. 69, 84.
28. Erickson, *Invisible Immigrants*, p. 221.
29. *Ibid.*, 222.
30. *Ibid.*, p. 223.
31. Svendsen, *Frontier Mother*, p. 130.
32. *Ibid.*, p. 134.
33. *Ibid.*
34. Bruns, *Hold Dear*, p. 111.
35. *Ibid.*, p. 112.
36. *Ibid.*, pp. 115–6.
37. *Ibid.*, p. 127.
38. *Ibid.*, p. 156.
39. *Ibid.*, p. 128.
40. Svendsen, *Frontier Mother*, pp. 145–47.
41. Solveig Zempel, *In Their Own Words: Letters from Norwegian Immigrants* (Minneapolis: University of Minnesota and the Norwegian American Historical Association, 1991), pp. 122, 125.
42. Erickson, *Invisible Immigrants*, p. 366.
43. Waerenskjold, *Lady with the Pen*, p. 48.
44. Kamphoefner, Helbich, and Sommer, *News from the Land of Freedom*, p. 79.
45. Jacobs, "Death, Disease and Deliverance," p. 19.
46. *Ibid.*, pp. 19–22.
47. Gerlach, *Immigrants in the Ozarks*, p. 35.
48. Stella, *Urban Congestion*, chart inserted between p. 24 and p. 25. On the relative frequency of accidental death by gender, see Senate Document 645, vol. XIV, *Causes of Death among Women and Child Cotton-Mill Operatives*, pp. 87–89, which shows "accident or violence" to be the second-ranked cause of male death, while for women, this factor was "next to the bottom of the list." Irish women died disproportionately from accidents/violence, perhaps because their rate of marriage (and thus maternal death) was lower.
49. Stella, *Urban Congestion*, p. 26.
50. *Ibid.*
51. Bruns, *Hold Dear*, pp. 174–75.
52. *Ibid.*
53. *Ibid.*, p. 187.
54. *Ibid.*, p. 189.
55. *Ibid.*, pp. 193–94.
56. *Ibid.*, p. 194.
57. *Ibid.*, p. 226.
58. Koenig, "Letters from America," vol. 29, p. 25.
59. Ets, *Rosa*, p. 252.
60. Riis, *How the Other Half Lives*, p. 196.
61. Louise B. More, *Wage-Earners' Budgets: A Study of Standards and Costs of Living in New York City* (New York: Henry Holt and Co., 1907), p. 145.
62. Mary E. Richmond and Fred S. Hall, *A Study of Nine Hundred and Eighty-Five Widows* (New York: Russell Sage Foundation, 1913), p. 15.
63. Herzfeld, *Family Monographs*, pp. 43–44.
64. Odencrantz, *Italian Women in Industry*, p. 201.
65. *Ibid.*, p. 200.
66. Kamphoefner, Helbich and Sommer, *News from the Land of Freedom*, p. 79.
67. Zempel, *In Their Own Words*, p. 114.
68. Koenig, "Letters from America," vol. 29, p. 26.
69. Theodore C. Blegen, *Grass Roots History* (Port Washington, N.Y.: Kennikat Press, 1947; reissued by Kennikat Press, 1969), pp. 93–94.

CHAPTER 5—Religion Here and Hereafter

1. Cohen, *Out of the Shadow*, pp. 78–79.
2. Koren, *Diary of Elisabeth Koren*, p. 281.
3. Svendsen, *Frontier Mother*, p. 33.
4. *Ibid.*
5. *Ibid.*, p. 42.
6. Elise Dubach Isely, as told to her son, Bliss Isely, *Sunbonnet Days* (Caldwell, Idaho: Caxton Printers, 1935), pp. 185–86.
7. Koren, *Diary of Elisabeth Koren*, p. 192.
8. Erickson, *Invisible Immigrants*, pp. 182–83.
9. Bruns, *Hold Dear*, pp. 68, 82.
10. Waerenskjold, *Lady with the Pen*, p. 40.
11. Koenig, "Letters from America," vol. 29, p. 11.
12. Blegen, *Land of Their Choice*, p. 324.
13. "St. John's Church Over a Century Old," *Pocahontas (Arkansas) Star Herald*, 1986.
14. Ruth Fritz Meyer, *Women on a Mission* (St. Louis: Concordia Publishing House, 1967). See also Ludwig Ernest Fuerbringer, *Persons and Events* (St. Louis: Concordia Publishing House, 1947) and same author and publisher, *Eighty Eventful Years* (1944).
15. Kenneth O. Bjork, *West of the Great Divide: Norwegian Migration to the Pacific Coast, 1847–1893* (Northfield, Minn.: Norwegian-American Historical Association, 1958), pp. 182, 191.
16. *Ibid.*, p. 200.
17. *Ibid.*, p. 204.
18. Interview by Steinitz, part of a Cleveland YWCA study of second-generation women, in the YWCA files, SSC, box 31, folder 5.
19. Interview by Livia Baciu of "Jolan," a twenty-year-old paper-factory worker, in the YWCA files, SSC, box 31, folder 5.
20. Bruns, *Hold Dear*, p. 109.
21. *Ibid.*, p. 137.
22. Cohen, *Out of the Shadow*, p. 86.
23. *Ibid.*, p. 104.
24. *Ibid.*, p. 105.
25. Hvidt, *Flight to America*, p. 154.
26. Fanny Stenhouse, *Expose of Polygamy in Utah: A Lady's Life among the Mormons* (New York: American News, 1872), p. 55.
27. *Ibid.*, pp. 65–66.
28. *Ibid.*, p. 13.
29. Herzfeld, *Family Monographs*, p. 140.
30. *Ibid.*, p. 24.
31. John Curtis Kennedy, *Wages and Family Budgets in the Chicago Stockyards District*, (Chicago: University of Chicago Press, 1914), p. 59.
32. More, *Wage-Earners' Budgets*, p. 150. Robert Coit Chapin, *Standard of Living among Workingmen's Families in New York City* (New York: Russell Sage Foundation, 1909), p. 207, showed wide disparity between two Catholic groups—seven-eighths of Irish households reported donations, while only a quarter of Italians did. Several explanations are possible. The Irish, with their longer residence and smaller families, could better afford to give. They also dominated the clergy in America and had a generally better relationship with the church in Europe. Finally, Irish women were more likely to be single and to work and thus could contribute more generously without needing husbands' approval.
33. Koenig, "Letters from America," vol. 29, pp. 14–15.
34. Herzfeld, *Family* p. 23.
35. Herzfeld, "Tenement House Family," p. 1521.
36. Odencrantz, *Italian Women in Industry*, p. 206.
37. Hamilton Holt, *The Life Stories of Undistinguished Americans as Told by Themselves* (New York: James Pott & Co., 1906), p. 88.
38. Williams, *South Italian Folkways*, p. 152.
39. Helen Campbell, *Prisoners of Poverty: Women Wage-Workers, Their Trades, and Their Lives* (Boston: Roberts Brothers, 1895), pp. 137–38.
40. Zempel, *In Their Own Words*, p. 118.

41. Thomas Capek, *The Cechs (Bohemians) in America* (Boston: Houghton Mifflin, 1920), p. 119.
42. Bruns, *Hold Dear*, p. 209.
43. Williams, *South Italian Folkways*, p. 102.
44. Cohen, *Out of the Shadow*, p. 162.
45. Cole, *Immigrant City*, p. 35.
46. See Pehotsky, *Slavic Immigrant Woman*.
47. "The Mesable and Vermillion Ore Ranges of Minnesota," a report from the Presbytery of Duluth, June 8, 1914, in the YWCA files, SSC, box 32, folder 6.
48. "The German-Russian People of South Dakota," 1920; in the YWCA files, SSC, box 32, folder 6.
49. Mary Ann Bodnar, "What It Means to Be a Second-Generation Girl: Talks Given at the Second-Generation Youth Dinner of the National Board of the Y.W.C.A." (New York: Womans Press, 1935), in the YWCA files, SSC, box 31, folder 4.
50. Bruns, *Hold Dear*, p. 139.
51. *Ibid.*, p. 155.

CHAPTER 6—Courting Customs

1. Balch, *Our Slavic Fellow Citizens*, p. 166.
2. Long, Oral Histories; Lola Marot, "Oral Interview," p. 6, SCH.
3. *Ibid.*, p. 7.
4. Roberts, "Italian Girls," p. 764.
5. Williams, *South Italian Folkways*, pp. 81–82.
6. Interview of Katherine Speronis by Judith Dunning, June 25, 1980, University of Lowell Oral History Project; in the Mogan Center for Lowell History, Lowell, Massachusetts, pp. 15–16, MC.
7. Roberts, "Italian Girls," p. 764.
8. Long, Oral Histories; Lola Marot, "Oral Interview," p. 7, SCH.
9. Cohen, *Out of the Shadow*, p. 201.
10. *Ibid.*, pp. 204–5.
11. Ets, *Rosa*, p. 124.
12. *Ibid.*, p. 157.
13. *Ibid.*, p. 205.
14. University of Wisconsin, "Summer School for Workers in Industry," 1929 yearbook, p. 25, Mariam Coffin Canaday Library, Bryn Mawr College, Bryn Mawr, Pennsylvania, box 11, folder 9 (hereafter cited as MCC).
15. Barton, *Letters from the Promised Land,* p. 266.
16. Kamphoefner, Helbich, and Sommer, *News from the Land of Freedom*, p. 361.
17. Mari Sandoz, *Old Jules* (Boston: Little, Brown & Co., 1935), pp. 164–65.
18. Edith Abbott, *Immigration: Select Documents and Case Records* (Chicago: University of Chicago, 1924; reissued by Arno Press and the *New York Times*, American Immigration Collection, 1969), pp. 783–84.
19. William I. Thomas and Florian Znaniecki, *The Polish Peasant in Europe and America* (Chicago: University of Chicago, 1918; reissued by Dover Publications, 1958), vol. 1, p. 592.
20. Balch, *Our Slavic Fellow Citizens*, p. 185, from the appended notebook of one Miss Gazvoda.
21. Kamphoefner, Helbich, and Sommer, *News from the Land of Freedom*, p. 431.
22. Koenig, "Letters from America," vol. 28, p. 168.
23. *Ibid.*
24. *Ibid.*, p. 177.
25. *Ibid.*, vol. 29, p. 5.
26. Issac Metzker, ed., *A Bintel Brief: Sixty Years of Letters from the Lower East Side to the Jewish Daily Forward* (Garden City, N.Y.: Doubleday & Co., 1971), pp. 69–70.
27. In addition to censuses, see, for example, Cole, *Immigrant City*, p. 104 ff, Brandt, *Deserters*, pp. 18–19, and Carpenter, *Immigrants and Their Children*, p. 235 ff.
28. Adelaide K. Zitello, "Evaluation of Interviews of Twenty-one Second Generation Girls," unpublished paper of the International Institute, YWCA of Cleveland, 1939, in the YWCA files, SSC, box 31, folder 5.
29. *Ibid.*
30. Interview by Livia Baciu with "Helen, a 19 year old WPA seamstress," in the YWCA files, SSC, box 31, folder 5.
31. Interview by Livia Baciu of "Irene," in the YWCA files, SSC, box 31, folder 5.

32. Holt, *Life Stories*, pp. 141–42.
33. Kamphoefner, Helbich, and Sommer, *News from the Land of Freedom*, pp. 72–73.
34. *Ibid.*
35. Bruns, *Hold Dear*, p. 107.
36. Theresa Wolfson, *The Woman Worker and the Trade Unions* (New York: International Publishers, 1926), p. 190.
37. Koenig, "Letters from America," vol. 29, pp. 8–9.
38. Bruns, *Hold Dear*, p. 209.
39. Abbott, *Immigration*, p. 356.
40. Blegen, *Land of Their Choice*, pp. 341–42.
41. *Ibid.*, p. 331.
42. Pagano, *Golden Wedding*, pp. 32–33.
43. Balch, *Our Slavic Fellow Citizens*, p. 366.
44. Pagano, *Golden Wedding*, p. 75, 81.
45. John Curtis Kennedy, *Wages and Family Budgets in the Chicago Stockyards District* (Chicago: University of Chicago Press, 1914), p. 75.
46. Margaret Byington, *Homestead: The Households of a Mill Town* (New York: Russell Sage Foundation, 1910), pp. 149–50.
47. Parker, *Working with the Working Woman*, pp. 166–67.
48. Williams, *South Italian Folkways*, pp. 79, 85.
49. Interview of Edna Vidravich Balkus by Martha Norkunas, August 1, 1983, p. 4, MC.
50. *Ibid.*, first page.
51. Metzker, *Bintel Brief*, pp. 103–4.
52. Cohen, *Out of the Shadow*, p 99.
53. Parker, *Working With the Working Woman*, p. 208.
54. Cohen, *Out of the Shadow*, pp. 302–3.
55. Bruns, *Hold Dear*, p. 116.
56. *Ibid.*, p. 118.
57. Williams, *South Italian Folkways*, p. 194.
58. Thomas and Znaniecki, *The Polish Peasant* vol. 1, pp. 582–84.

CHAPTER 7—Marriage, Divorce, and Desertion

1. Kate Claghorn, *The Immigrant's Day in Court* (New York: Harper & Bros., 1923; reissued by Arno Press and the *New York Times* as part of the American Immigration Collection, 1969), p. 82.
2. Herzfeld, *Family Monographs*, p. 104.
3. Letter in the Mary Ware Dennett Collection, SCH, box 21, folder 373.
4. Anthony, *Mothers Who Must Earn*, p. 20.
5. *Ibid.*, 22.
6. Erickson, *Invisible Immigrants*, pp. 480–81.
7. Parker, *Working with the Working Woman*, p. 210.
8. Anonymous, "A Collar Starcher's Story," *The Independent* 59, August 10, 1905, p. 306.
9. Anthony, *Mothers Who Must Earn*, p. 23.
10. Bruns, *Hold Dear*, p. 115.
11. Herzfeld, "Tenement House Family," p. 1522.
12. Parker, *Working with the Working Woman*, p. 53.
13. Preus, *Linka's Diary*, pp. 127–28.
14. Herzfeld, *Family Monographs*, p. 104.
15. Williams, *South Italian Folkways*, pp. 157–58.
16. Davis, *Immigrant Health*, p. 397.
17. Thomas and Znaniecki, *The Polish Peasant*, vol. 2, pp. 1708–9, from the records of the Chicago Legal Aid Society.
18. *Ibid.*, pp. 1722–23.
19. Hughes, *Mothers in Industry*, p. 75.
20. Senate Document 645, vol. 1, *Cotton Textile Industry*, p. 591.
21. U.S. Department of Commerce, *Statistical Abstract of the United States, 1930*, p. 26, and 12th Census, *Vital Statistics*, vol. 1, 1902, p. lxxix.

22. Abbott, *Immigration*, p. 799.
23. Thomas and Znaneicki, *Polish Peasant*, vol. 2, p. 1709.
24. Claghorn, *Immigrant's Day in Court*, pp. 80–81.
25. Kamphoefner, Helbich, and Sommer, *News from the Land of Freedom*, p. 564.
26. *Ibid.*, pp. 565–66.
27. Metzker, *Bintel Brief*, p. 121.
28. Joanna C. Colcord, *Broken Homes: A Study of Family Desertion* (New York: Russell Sage Foundation, 1919), pp. 101–2.
29. Thomas and Znaniecki, vol. 2, p. 1715.
30. Ets, *Rosa*, pp. 204–5.
31. *Ibid.*, p. 205.
32. *Ibid.*
33. Colcord, *Broken Homes*, p. 8.
34. Earle Edward Eubank, *Family Desertion*, p. 16.
35. Lilian Brandt, *Five Hundred and Seventy-Four Deserters and Their Families* (New York: The Charity Organization Society, 1905), p. 15 and 16.
36. Colcord, *Broken Homes*, p. 21 and Earle Edward Eubank, *Family Desertion*p. 20.
37. Brandt, *Deserters*, p. 39.
38. Eubank, *Family Desertion*, pp. 26–27.
39. Brandt, *Deserters*, pp. 26–27.
40. Hughes, *Mothers in Industry*, p. 80.
41. Colcord, *Broken Homes*, p. 50.
42. Metzker, *Bintel Brief*, pp. 108–9.
43. Claghorn, *Immigrant's Day in Court*, p. 209.
44. Eubank, *Family Desertion*, p. 49, citing *Report of the National Desertion Bureau*, 1912–15, p. 7.
45. Hughes, *Mothers in Industry*, pp. 69–70.
46. Metzker, *Bintel Brief*, pp. 83–84.
47. Thomas and Znaniecki, vol. 2, pp. 1727–28.
48. Eubank, *Family Desertion*, p. 47.
49. Metzker, *Bintel Brief*, pp. 111–12.
50. Eubank, *Family Desertion*, p. 45.
51. Colcord, *Broken Homes*, pp. 34–35.
52. Brandt, *Deserters*, p. 35.
53. Colcord, *Broken Homes*, p. 34.
54. Anthony, *Mothers Who Must Earn*, p. 181.
55. Brandt, *Deserters*, p. 53.
56. Eubank, *Family Desertion*, p. 42, citing Zilpha D. Smith, *Deserted Wives and Deserting Husbands*, p. 4.
57. Brandt, *Deserters*, p. 46.
58. Anthony, *Mothers Who Must Earn*, p. 183.
59. Claghorn, *Immigrant's Day in Court*, p. 88.

CHAPTER 8—Illicit Sex

1. Abbott, *Immigration*, pp. 377–82.
2. *Ibid.*, pp. 382–83. See also Balch, *Our Slavic Fellow Citizens*, p. 51.
3. Carpenter, *Immigrants and Their Children*, p. 245. Carpenter's work was based on the 1920 census and was published by the U.S. Government Printing Office in 1927.
4. Senate Document 645, vol. XV, *Relation Between Occupation and Criminality of Women*, pp. 84–87.
5. Nolan, *Ourselves Alone*, p. 28.
6. Hasia R. Diner, *Erin's Daughters in America* (Baltimore: Johns Hopkins University Press, 1983), p. 21.
7. Nolan, *Ourselves Alone*, p. 28.
8. Metzker, *Bintel Brief*, pp. 40–42.
9. Riis, *How the Other Half Lives*, p. 143.
10. Howard B. Woolstein, *Prostitution in the United States* (New York: Century Co., 1921; reissued by Appleton-Century, 1969), p. 18. Dr. Woolstein's work was heavily subsided by the Bureau of Social Hygiene, which operated with Rockefeller largess.
11. Senate Document 645, vol. 15, *Relation Between Occupation and Criminality*, p. 92.

12. Charles Booth, *Life and Labour of the People in London* (London: Macmillan and Co., 1902), 3d ser., vol. 1, p. 55.
13. Kamphoefner, Helbich, and Sommer, *News from the Land of Freedom*, pp. 533–34.
14. *Ibid.*, p. 535.
15. *Ibid.*, pp. 546–57.
16. Zempel, *In Their Own Words*, pp. 32–33.
17. *Ibid.*, p. 37.
18. *Ibid.*, pp. 39, 43.
19. Thomas and Znanecki, *Polish Peasant*, vol. 2, pp. 1721–22.
20. Claghorn, *Immigrant's Day in Court*, p. 78.
21. *Ibid.*
22. Metzker, *Bintel Brief*, p. 70.
23. Thomas and Znanecki, *Polish Peasant*, vol. 2, p. 1724.
24. *Ibid.*, p. 1717.
25. Svendsen, *Frontier Mother*, pp. 9, 10.
26. Claghorn, *Immigrant's Day in Court*, p. 71.
27. Zempel, *In Their Own Words*, p. 127.
28. Thomas and Znanecki, *Polish Peasant*, vol. 2, p. 1721.
29. Herzfeld, *Family Monographs*, p. 102.
30. Claghorn, *Immigrant's Day in Court*, p. 84.
31. Letter to Raymond B. Fosdick from the Committee of Fourteen, August 7, 1914, RAC, Bureau of Social Hygiene Collection, series III, subseries 2, box 9, folder 197.
32. "A Plan Concerning the Establishment of a Department Especially Designed for the Study and Treatment of Syphilis in Connection with the Out-Patient Service of the Johns Hopkins Hospital," 1915, RAC, Bureau of Social Hygiene Collection, series III, subseries 2, box 8, folder 182.
33. "Social Hygiene," 1932, p. 3, RAC, Bureau of Social Hygiene Collection, series III, subseries 2, box 10, folder 211.
34. "A Plan of . . . Johns Hopkins Hospital," folder 182.
35. "New York State Health Commission Report," 1931, pp. 8, 15, RAC, Bureau of Social Hygiene Collection, series III, subseries 2, box 10, folder 211.
36. "Proposed Division of Social Hygiene at the Boston Dispensary," 1929–30, RAC, Bureau of Social Hygiene Collection, series III, subseries 2, box 7, folder 168.
37. New York State Health Commission Report, folder 211.
38. See Chapter 2 in this Volume.
39. American Social Hygiene Association, meeting minutes, October 1931, pp. 2–3, RAC, Bureau of Social Hygiene Collection, series III, subseries 2, box 7, folder 164.
40. *Ibid.*
41. Williams, *South Italian Folkways*, p. 168.
42. NYC Department of Health, "Special Problems of Italians," pp. 2–3.
43. Stella, *Urban Congestion*, pp. 33–35.
44. Letter from Dr. George Walker to Dr. Abraham Flexner, January 13, 1916, RAC, Bureau of Social Hygiene Collection, series III, subseries 2, box 8, folder 182.
45. Elizabeth Beardsley Butler, *Women and the Trades* (New York: Charities Publication Committee and the Russell Sage Foundation, 1909; part of *The Pittsburgh Survey: Finding in Six Volumes*, ed. Paul H. Kellogg), p. 348.
46. Woolston, *Prostitution*, p. 275.
47. Women's Educational and Industrial Union, *Report of an Investigation of 500 Immigrant Women in Boston*, June 1907, SCH, p. 15.
48. Vice Commission of Chicago, *Social Evil*, pp. 43, 97.
49. Nadel, *Little Germany*, p. 104.
50. *Ibid.*, p. 78.
51. Marilyn Wood Hill, *Their Sisters' Keepers: Prostitution in New York City, 1830–1870* (Berkeley: University of California Press, 1993), p. 327.
52. Nadel, *Little Germany*, p. 89. The 6,000 figure was from William Sanger, *History of Prostitution*, 1858. Dr. Sanger was the chief medical resident of Blackwell Island and did an extensive study of prostitution in New York.
53. *Ibid.*, pp. 89–90.
54. *Ibid.*

55. Hill, *Their Sisters' Keepers*, p. 93, citing James D. McCabe, *New York by Sunlight and Gaslight* (Philadelphia: Hubbard Brothers, 1882).
56. Edward A. Steiner, *On the Trail of the Immigrant* (New York and London: Fleming H. Revell Co., 1906), pp. 316–17.
57. Diner, *Erin's Daughters*, pp. 116–17, citing E. A. Ross, "The Celtic Tide," *Century Magazine* 87, no. 6 (1914): 952.
58. Walter C. Reckless, *Vice in Chicago* (University of Chicago, 1933; reissued by Patterson Smith Publishing, 1969), p. 119.
59. Letter from Lt. Daniel E. Costigau, Police Department, City of New York to Hon. Arthur Woods, Secretary to His Honor, the Mayor, March 19, 1914, RAC, Bureau of Social Hygiene Collection, series III, subseries 2, box 9, folder 197.
60. *Ibid.*
61. "Study of Commercialized Prostitution in New York City," 1930, RAC, Bureau of Social Hygiene Collection, series III, subseries 2, box 7, folder 165.
    They did discover some scandalous behavior in dance halls, where women encouraged ejaculation during dances because this limited their risk of disease. There is, however, no evidence that these were immigrant women. This report is in the same series, folder 164, in a document labeled "PMK, Class E" and dated October 20, 1932.
62. *Ibid.*
63. 61st Congress, 3d Session, Senate Document 753, *Reports of the Immigration Commission: Importation and Harboring of Women for Immoral Purposes* (Washington: Government Printing Office, 1911), p. 62.
64. 61st Congress, 3d Session, Senate Document 750, *Reports of the Immigration Commission on Immigration and Crime* (Washington: Government Printing Office, 1911), p. 157. See also pp. 100–101 of this document for further confirmation of the disproportionate numbers of French in prostitution.
65. Senate Document 753, *Importation and Harboring*, pp. 62–64.
66. Vice Commission of Chicago, *Social Evil*, p. 227.
67. "Report of the League of Nations Traffic in Women and Children," 1932, RAC, Bureau of Social Hygiene Collection, series III, subseries 2, box 10, folder 203.
68. *Ibid.*
69. Woolston, *Prostitution*, p. 87.
70. *Ibid.*, p. 162.
71. Senate Document 753, *Importation and Harboring*, p. 82.
72. *Ibid.*, pp. 104–6.
73. Metzker, *Bintel Brief*, p. 104.
74. *Ibid.*
75. Blandina Segale, S.C., *At the End of the Santa Fe Trail* (Milwaukee: Bruce Publishing Company, 1948), p. 5, in an introduction by Sister Therese Martin.
76. Diner, *Erin's Daughters*, p. 136.
77. Senate Document 753, *Importation and Harboring*, p. 79.
78. Senate Document 645, vol. 15, *Relation between Occupation and Criminality*, p. 99. See also Thomas and Znaniecki, *The Polish Peasant*, vol. 2, pp. 1800–1827, on "Sexual Immorality of Girls," and George J. Kneeland, *Commercialized Prostitution in New York City* (New York: Century Co., 1913).

CHAPTER 9—The Fruit of the Land

1. Blegen, *Land of Their Choice*, pp. 262–63.
2. Koenig, "Letters from America," vol. 28, pp. 176–77.
3. Ets, *Rosa*, pp. 172, 175.
4. *Ibid.*, p. 191.
5. Blegen, *Land of Their Choice*, p. 268.
6. Williams, *South Italian Folkways*, p. 61.
7. *Ibid.*, p. 63.
8. Davis, *Immigrant Health*, p. 246.
9. "Appeal of the Association for Improving the Condition of the Poor," 1919, RAC, Laura Spelman Rockefeller Memorial Collection, series III, subseries 1, box 1, folder 6.
10. Davis, *Immigrant Health*, pp. 249–50.
11. *Ibid.*, p. 268.

12. Svendsen, *Frontier Mother*, p. 39.
13. *Ibid.*, p. 15.
14. Waerenskjold, *Lady with the Pen*, p. 93.
15. Chapin, *Standard of Living*, p. 132.
16. Ets, *Rosa*, p. 78.
17. Waerenskjold, *Lady with the Pen*, p. 135.
18. *Ibid.*, p. 41.
19. Koren, *Diary of Elisabeth Koren*, p. 156.
20. Blegen, *Land of Their Choice*, p. 108.
21. Koren, *Diary of Elisabeth Koren*, p. 231.
22. *Ibid.*, p. 231.
23. Ets, *Rosa*, p. 215.
24. Cohen, *Out of the Shadow*, pp. 156–57.
25. Bruns, *Hold Dear*, p. 288.
26. Senate Document 645, vol. 5, *Wage-Earning Women in Stores and Factories*, p. 149.
27. Cole, *Immigrant City*, p. 163.
28. Odencrantz, *Italian Women in Industry*, p. 227.
29. Campbell, *Prisoners of Poverty*, pp. 124–25.
30. Anzia Yezierska, *Children of Loneliness: Stories of Immigrant Life in America* (New York and London: Funk & Wagnalls, 1923), p. 18.
31. Green, *Holyoke*, p. 215, citing the *Holyoke Transcript*, August 1, 1868.
32. Nolan, *Ourselves Alone*, p. 30.
33. Erickson, *Invisible Immigrants*, p. 177.
34. Agnes de Lima, "Night Work," unpaged.
35. "Education That Changes Lives: The Story of Five Schools for Workers," 1933, MCC, box 1, folder 13, unpaged.
36. Williams, *South Italian Folkways*, pp. 65–66.
37. Balch, *Our Slavic Fellow Citizens*, pp. 363–64.
38. Kennedy, *Wages and Family Budgets*, pp. 68, 72–73.
39. Dorothee Schneider, "'For Whom Are All the Good Things in Life?': German-American Housewives Discuss Their Budgets," in Harmut Keil and John B. Jentz, ed., *German Workers in Industrial Chicago, 1850–1910: A Comparative Perspective* (DeKalb: Northern Illinois University Press, 1983), pp. 149, 151. Note that, despite the title of the book, this article analyzes New York City budgets.
40. *Ibid.*, p. 153.
41. *Ibid.*, p. 149, citing Massachusetts Bureau of Labor Statistics, *Fifteenth Annual Report*, July 1884, p. 465.
42. Odencrantz, *Italian Women in Industry*, pp. 198–99.
43. Williams, *South Italian Folkways*, p. 64.
44. Lucreatia Gregorio, "Paddy's Market," published by Bryn Mawr Summer School for Women Workers, 1927, in Mary Van Kleeck's papers, SSC, box 34, folder 609, p. 7.
45. More, *Wage-Earners' Budgets*, pp. 211–12.
46. Senate Document 645, vol. 16, *Family Budgets*, p. 177.
47. *Ibid.*, pp. 223, 220.
48. Koenig, "Letters from America," vol. 29, p. 11.
49. Erickson, *Invisible Immigrants*, p. 182.
50. Waerenskjold, *Lady with the Pen*, p. 29.
51. *Ibid.*, pp. 29, 37.
52. Svendsen, *Frontier Mother*, p. 71.
53. Bruns, *Hold Dear*, p. 106.
54. Koren, *Diary of Elisabeth Koren*, p. 300.
55. *Ibid.*, p. 309.
56. Bruns, *Hold Dear*, p. 85.
57. *Ibid.*, p. 89.
58. Blegen, *Land of Their Choice*, p. 29.
59. Fredricka Bremer, *America of the Fifties: Letters of Fredrika Bremer*, ed. Adolph B. Benson (New York: Scandinavian-American Foundation, 1924), p. 216.
60. Koren, *Diary of Elizabeth Koren*, p. 333.
61. Williams, *South Italian Folkways*, p. 122.
62. *Ibid.*

63. Bruns, *Hold Dear*, pp. 261, 262, 297.
64. Pagano, *Golden Wedding*, p. 269.
65. *Ibid.*, p. 276.

CHAPTER 10—Hovels, Homes, and Hopes

1. Cohen, *Out of the Shadow*, p. 304.
2. Jane Maud Campbell, "Immigrant Women," paper read at the New Jersey Conference of Charities and Corrections, April 3, 1911, p. 9, in the Jane Maud Campbell Collection, SCH, box 1, folder 13.
3. Cole, *Immigrant City*, pp. 70–71.
4. Julius Wilcox, "The Greatest Problem of Great Cities," *The Independent* 59, October 19, 1905, p. 906.
5. Elizabeth Hughes, "Chicago Housing Conditions," *American Journal of Sociology* 18 (November 1914): 306.
6. Dingman, "Report of the Immigration Secretary," SSC, unpaged.
7. Riis, *How the Other Half Lives*, p. 124.
8. *Ibid.*, p. 45.
9. Steiner, *Trail of the Immigrant*, p. 265.
10. Hughes, *Mothers in Industry*, p. 306.
11. Cole, *Immigrant City*, p. 66.
12. Riis, *How the Other Half Lives*, pp. 51, 8.
13. Mary Buell Sayles, "Housing and Social Conditions in a Slavic Neighborhood," *The Survey* 13, December 3, 1904, p. 260.
14. *Ibid.*, p. 261.
15. Senate Document 645, vol. 2, *Men's Ready-Made Clothing*, p. 262.
16. Edith Abbott, *The Tenements of Chicago, 1908–1935* (Chicago: University of Chicago, 1936), p. 23, citing Colbert and Chamberlin, *Chicago and the Great Conflagration*, 1871, pp. 273–75.
17. Riis, *How the Other Half Lives*, p. 8.
18. Senate Document 645, vol. 2, *Men's Ready-Made Clothing*, p. 263.
19. Stella, *Urban Congestion*, pp. 5–6.
20. Abbott, *Tenements of Chicago*, pp. 263, 346.
21. Ets, *Rosa*, p. 225.
22. Helen I. Wilson and Eunice W. Smith, "Chicago Housing Conditions among the Slovaks in the Twentieth Ward," *American Journal of Sociology* 20 (September 1914): 154.
23. Green, *Holyoke*, p. 116.
24. Barton, *Letters from the Promised Land*, p. 236.
25. Gjerset and Hektoen, "Health Conditions," p. 19.
26. Waerenskjold, *Lady with the Pen*, p. 83.
27. Koren, *Diary of Elisabeth Koren*, p. 330.
28. Koenig, "Letters from America," vol. 29, p. 6.
29. *Ibid.*, p. 8.
30. Bruns, *Hold Dear*, p. 74.
31. *Ibid.*, p. 80.
32. *Ibid.*, p. 81.
33. Preus, *Linka's Diary*, p. 194.
34. *Ibid.*, p. 213.
35. Koren, *Diary of Elisabeth Koren*, p. 168.
36. Waerenskjold, *Lady with the Pen*, p. 97.
37. Koren, *Diary of Elisabeth Koren*, pp. 282–83.
38. Brandt, "Social Aspects," p. 5.
39. Dorothy L. Wanless, *Century Farms of Minnesota: One Hundred Years of Changing Life Styles on the Farm* (Century Farm Heritage Committee, 1985), p. 15.
40. Cole, *Immigrant City*, p. 28.
41. Green, *Holyoke*, p. 112.
42. Cornelia Schaddlee, "Life During the Early Days of the Dutch Settlement," in Henry S. Lucas, *Dutch Immigrant Memoirs and Related Writings* (Assen, Netherlands: Van Gorcum & Co., 1955), pp. 407–8.
43. Koren, *Diary of Elisabeth Koren*, pp. 227, 241.
44. *Ibid.*, p. 222.
45. Brandt, "Social Aspects," p. 15.

46. Preus, *Linka's Diary*, p. 281.
47. Riis, *How the Other Half Lives*, pp. 4, 9.
48. Stella, *Urban Congestion*, p. 5.
49. Holt, *Life Stories*, pp. 110–11.
50. Cohen, *Out of the Shadow*, p. 186.
51. Kamphoefner, Helbich, and Sommer, *News from the Land of Freedom*, p. 369.
52. Senate Document 645, vol. 2, *Men's Ready-Made Clothing*, p. 286.
53. Abbott, *Tenements of Chicago*, p. 135.
54. "Mary Simkhovich Dead at Age of 84," *New York Times*, November 16, 1951, clipping in settlement file, SSC, box 4, folder 27. Simkhovich—who was not an immigrant but rather from a wealthy Boston family—headed Greenwich House. She married a Columbia University professor from Berlin.
55. Carole Blanck, "Oral History of My Mother," unpaged, Long Collection, SCH.
56. Abbott, *Tenements of Chicago*, p. 223.
57. Senate Document 645, vol. 4, *The Silk Industry*, pp. 310–11.
58. Kamphoefner, Helbich, and Sommer, *News from the Land of Freedom*, p. 549.
59. *Ibid.*, p. 551.
60. *Ibid.*, pp. 560, 565.
61. Abbott, *Tenements of Chicago*, pp. 378, 381, 382, 387, 388, 390.
62. Balch, *Our Slavic Fellow Citizens*, p. 373.
63. Herzfeld, *Family Monographs*, pp. 14–16.
64. Bruns, *Hold Dear*, p. 134.
65. *Ibid.*

CHAPTER 11—Cleaning, Child Care, and Clothing

1. Hughes, *Mothers in Industry*, p. 176.
2. Svendsen, *Frontier Mother*, p. 28.
3. Blegen, *Land of Their Choice*, p. 422.
4. Koenig, "Letters from America," vol. 28, pp. 6, 8, 12, 19.
5. Preus, *Linka's Diary*, p. 264.
6. Brandt, "Social Aspects," p. 37.
7. Cole, *Immigrant City*, 73.
8. Campbell, "Immigrant Women," p. 9, SCH.
9. Williams, *South Italian Folkways*, p. 49.
10. Antonio Mangano, *The Italian Colonies of New York City*, reprinted in *Italians in the City: Health and Related Social Needs* (New York: Arno Press, 1975), p. 28.
11. Nolan, *Ourselves Alone*, p. 21.
12. Samuel Chotzinoff, *A Lost Paradise* (New York: Knopf, 1958), p. 307.
13. *Ibid.*, pp. 308–9.
14. More, *Wage-Earners' Budgets*, p. 40.
15. Svendsen, *Frontier Mother*, p. 28.
16. Brandt, "Social Aspects," p. 14.
17. Riis, *How the Other Half Lives*, p. 35.
18. Long, Oral Histories, Elaine McGillvray, "Interview with Mrs. Lena Torresgrossa," SCH.
19. Anthony, *Mothers Who Must Earn*, p. 91.
20. Byington, "Mill Town Courts," p. 921.
21. Abbott, *Tenements of Chicago*, p. 223.
22. Williams, *South Italian Folkways*, p. 47.
23. Campbell, "Immigrant Women," p. 7, SCH.
24. Hughes, *Mothers in Industry*, p. 189, citing Edward Cadbury et al., *Women's Work and Wages*, p. 210.
25. Balch, *Our Slavic Fellow Citizens*, p. 372.
26. Sayles, "Housing and Social Conditions," p. 258.
27. Byington, *Homestead*, p. 79.
28. Senate Document 645, vol. 1, *Cotton Textile Industry*, pp. 540–41.
29. Hughes, *Mothers in Industry*, pp. 178–79.
30. Jane E. Robbins, "The Bohemian Women in New York," *Charities and the Commons* 13, December 12, 1904, pp. 195–6.

31. Koenig, "Letters from America," vol. 29, p. 17.
32. Bruns, *Hold Dear*, p. 139.
33. *Ibid.*, p. 164.
34. Long Oral Histories, Anonymous, "An Italian Immigrant Woman—1920," p. 6, SCH.
35. Chapin, *Standard of Living*, pp. 170–171, 181.
36. Riis, *How the Other Half Lives*, p. 45.
37. Long, Oral Histories, Lola Marot, "Oral Interview—Lola Anguini," pp. 3–4.
38. Bruns, *Hold Dear*, p. 110.
39. *Ibid.*, p. 105.
40. Ets, *Rosa*, p. 233.
41. Hughes, *Mothers in Industry*, p. 194.
42. Long, Oral Histories, Anonymous, "Italian Immigrant," p. 7, SCH.
43. Senate Document 645, vol. 1, *Cotton Textile Industry*, p. 541. See also Friedrich Kapp, *Immigration and the Commissioners of Emigration* (New York: D. Taylor, 1870), pp. 53–54, for information on nursing mothers whose children were brought to the mills to be fed.
44. *Ibid.*
45. Pehotsky, *Slavic Immigrant Woman*, p. 76.
46. Hughes, *Mothers in Industry*, p. 194.
47. Long, Oral Histories, Margaret Watkinson, "A Social History of My Family," p. 11, SCH.
48. de Lima, "Night Work," unpaged, SSC.
49. Anthony, *Mothers Who Must Earn*, p. 140.
50. Frances E. Lane, *American Charities and the Child of the Immigrant: A Study of Typical Child Caring Institutions in New York and Massachusetts Between the Years 1845 and 1880* (Washington: Catholic University of America, 1932), pp. 82–83.
51. *Ibid.*, p. 112, quoting Father G. F. Haskins, *Reports Historical, Statistical, and Financial of the House of the Angel Guardians* (Boston, 1864), p. 4.
52. *Ibid.*, p. 128.
53. Marilyn Irvin Holt, *The Orphan Trains: Placing Out in America* (Lincoln: University of Nebraska Press, 1992), pp. 46–47.
54. *Ibid.*, pp. 69–70.
55. Green, *Holyoke*, pp. 345, 362.
56. Department of Immigration and Foreign Communities of the YWCA, "Summary of a Case Record: Molarsky," undated, pp. 1–3, SSC, box 31, folder 5.
57. Lane, *American Charities*, p. 71.
58. Baltimore City Directory, 1879, in the archives of the Maryland Historical Society, Baltimore.
59. Campbell, "Immigrant Women," p. 5, SCH, box 1, folder 13.
60. For examples, see especially Richmond and Hall, *A Study of Nine Hundred and Eighty-Five Widows*, and Colcord, *Broken Homes*.
61. Rose Schneiderman, with Lucy Goldwaite, *All for One* (New York: Paul S. Eriksson, 1967), pp. 30, 32.
62. *Ibid.*, p. 33.
63. YWCA, "Molarsky," pp. 4–5, SSC.
64. Hilma Maki Minton, untitled and unpublished autobiography, written in 1971, privately held by the Minton family of Fairhaven, New Jersey, p. 24.
65. *Ibid.*, p. 25.
66. Jane Maud Campbell, speech to the West Boylston Library Commission, p. 2, in the Jane Maud Campbell Collection, SCH, box 1, folder 18.
67. Balch, *Our Slavic Fellow Citizens*, pp. 370–72.
68. University of Wisconsin, "Summer School for Workers, p. 15, MCC.
69. Balch, *Our Slavic Fellow Citizens*, p. 372.
70. Butler, *Women and the Trades*, p. 347.
71. Odencrantz, *Italian Women in Industry*, p. 64.
72. Balch, *Our Slavic Fellow Citizens*, p. 370.
73. Williams, *South Italian Folkways*, p. 71.
74. Kamphoefner, Helbich, and Sommer, *News from the Land of Freedom*, p. 380.
75. *Ibid.*, p. 548.
76. *Ibid.*, p. 556.
77. *Ibid.*, p. 557.
78. Senate Document 645, vol. 16, *Family Budgets*, pp. 178–80.

79. Green, *Holyoke*, p. 109.
80. Bruns, *Hold Dear*, p. 105.
81. *Ibid.*, p. 107.
82. *Ibid.*, p. 118.
83. Williams, *South Italian Folkways*, p. 71.
84. Balch, *Our Slavic Fellow Citizens*, p. 372.
85. Kamphoefner, Helbich, and Sommer, *News from the Land of Freedom*, p. 543.
86. Balch, *Our Slavic Fellow Citizens*, pp. 106–7.
87. Holt, *Life Stories*, p. 46. See also Sadie Frowne, "The Story of a Sweatshop Girl," *The Independent*, 54, September 25, 1902.
88. Odencrantz, *Italian Women in Industry*, p. 232.
89. *Ibid.*, p. 233.
90. Odencrantz, *Italian Women in Industry*, p. 201.
91. Sue Ainslie Clark and Edith Wyatt, *Making Both Ends Meet: The Income and Outlay of New York Working Girls* (New York: Macmillan Company, 1911).
92. Cohen, *Out of the Shadow*, p. 115.
93. Chapin, *Standard of Living*, p. 164.
94. *Ibid.*, p. 234.
95. Holt, *Life Stories*, p. 146.
96. Herzfeld, *Family Monographs*, p. 106.
97. Williams, *South Italian Folkways*, p. 71, speaks of the reluctance of older Sicilian women to wear hats, and photographs of the author's own Norwegian great-grandmother, who emigrated at thirty-one, show that she continued to wear a shawl while her adult daughters wore hats.
98. Ets, *Rosa*, p. 5.
99. *Ibid.*, p. 224.
100. Hughes, *Mothers in Industry*, p. 94.
101. Odencrantz, *Italian Women in Industry*, p. 202.
102. Anthony, *Mothers Who Must Earn*, p. 147.
103. Balch, *Our Slavic Fellow Citizens*, p. 371.
104. *Ibid.*, p. 92.
105. Williams, *South Italian Folkways*, p. 27.
106. Balch, *Our Slavic Fellow Citizens*, pp. 106–7.
107. Svendsen, *Frontier Mother*, p. 29.
108. *Ibid.*, p. 24.
109. Preus, *Linka's Diary*, p. 203.
110. Bruns, *Hold Dear*, p. 247.
111. Campbell, "Immigrant Women," p. 5, SCH.
112. Preus, *Linka's Diary*, pp. 187–88.
113. Robert Ernst, *Immigrant Life in New York City: 1825–1863* (Port Washington, N.Y.: Ira J. Friedman, 1949; reissued by same publisher, 1965), pp. 67–68.
114. Blegen, *Grass Roots History*, p. 107.

CHAPTER 12—Supporting Families

1. Byington, *Homestead*, p. 108.
2. More, *Wage-Earners' Budgets*, p. 136.
3. Anne Webster Noel, "On Twelve a Week," *The Independent* 59, October 26, 1905, p. 959.
4. Schneider, "For Whom Are All the Good Things?" p. 155.
5. Erickson, *Invisible Immigrants*, pp. 253–54.
6. Hughes, *Mothers in Industry*, p. 13.
7. Van Kleeck, *Artificial Flower Makers*, p. 74.
8. More, *Wage-Earners' Budgets*, p. 88.
9. Odencrantz, *Italian Women in Industry*, p. 172.
10. *Ibid.*, p. 187.
11. Kennedy, *Wages and Family Budgets*, p. 66.
12. Chapin, *Standard of Living*, p. 64. See also U.S. Department of Labor, Women's Bureau Bulletin #49, *Women Workers & Family Support*, A Study Made by Students in the Economics Course at the Bryn

Mawr Summer School Under the Direction of Prof. Amy Hewes (Washington: Government Printing Office, 1925).

13. Holt, *Life Stories*, pp. 38–39.

14. *Ibid.*, pp. 39–40.

15. Campbell, "Immigrant Women," pp. 7–8, SCH.

16. Dingman, "Report of Immigration Secretary," unpaged, SSC.

17. Clark and Wyatt, *Making Both Ends Meet*, p. 50.

18. Emilie Josephine Hutchinson, *Women's Wages* (New York: Columbia University Press, 1919; reissued by AMS Press, 1968), pp. 43–44.

19. Odencrantz, *Italian Women in Industry*, p. 238.

20. Clark and Wyatt, *Making Both Ends Meet*, p. 51.

21. Odencrantz, *Italian Women in Industry*, p. 100.

22. Senate Document 645, vol. 12, *Employment of Women in Laundries*, p. 81.

23. Riis, *How the Other Half Lives*, p. 128.

24. Odencrantz, *Italian Women in Industry*, p. 212.

25. *Ibid.*, pp. 214–15.

26. Zempel, *In Their Own Words*, p. 108.

27. Herzfeld, *Family Monographs*, p. 38.

28. Aagot Raaen, *Grass of the Earth*, (Northfield, Minn.: Norwegian-American Historical Association, 1950; reissued by Arno Press and the *New York Times*, 1979), p. 119.

29. Nadel, *Little Germany*, pp. 80–81.

30. Van Kleeck, *Artificial Flower Makers*, p. 95.

31. Odencrantz, *Italian Women in Industry*, p. 176.

32. Senate Document 645, vol. 2, *Men's Ready-Made Clothing*, pp. 366–67.

33. Van Kleeck, *Artificial Flower Makers*, pp. 229–35.

34. Anthony, *Mothers Who Must Earn*, p. 53.

35. Van Kleeck, *Artificial Flower Makers*, p. 86.

36. Aurora Thomas, "Family's Secret Revealed," *Tampa Tribune*, November 23, 1993, BayLife Section, pp. 4–5; author interview, December 6, 1993.

37. Nolan, *Ourselves Alone*, pp. 50–51.

38. Kamphoefner, Helbich, and Sommer, *News from the Land of Freedom*, pp. 536, 538.

39. *Ibid.*, pp. 540–41.

40. *Ibid.*, p. 556.

41. Odencrantz, *Italian Women in Industry*, pp. 307, 315, in a supplement by Henriette R. Walter.

42. Clark and Wyatt, *Making Both Ends Meet*, p. 104.

43. *Ibid.*, p. 58.

44. *Ibid.*, p. 100.

45. Senate Document 645, vol. 12, *Women in Laundries*, p. 99.

46. *Ibid.*, p. 118.

47. Cohen, *Out of the Shadow*, p. 115.

CHAPTER 13—Work and Wages

1. Ernst, *Immigrant Life*, p. 68.

2. Frances A. Kellor, "The Immigrant Woman," *Atlantic* 100 (September 1907): 401.

3. Senate Document 645, vol. 4, *The Silk Industry*, p. 15.

4. Butler, *Women and the Trades*, p. 62.

5. Senate Document 645, vol. 4, *The Silk Industry*, p. 194.

6. Hutchinson, *Women's Wages*, pp. 62–63.

7. Philip Scranton, "Immigration through the Port of Philadelphia: A Comment," in Stolarik, *Forgotten Doors*, p. 59.

8. Green, *Holyoke*, citing Lyman Mills papers, Bush to Davis, January 29, 1869.

9. Charlotte Erickson, *American Industry and the European Immigrant* (New York: Russell & Russell, 1957), p. 36. This work was published in cooperation with the Committee on Research in Economic History and was copyrighted in the name of the President and Fellows of Harvard College.

10. *Ibid.*, pp. 37–38.

11. Green, *Holyoke*, pp. 48, 69. See also Senate Document 645, vol. 4, *Beginnings of Child Labor Legislation in Certain States.*
12. *Niles Weekly Register*, August 26, 1837.
13. Rowland T. Berthoff, *British Immigrants in Industrial America* (Cambridge: Harvard University Press, 1953), p. 23, citing 11th Census of the U.S. (1890), vol. 2, pp. 484–88.
14. Cole, *Immigrant City*, p. 114, citing *Immigration Commission Reports*, vol. 10, 61st Congress, 2d Session (Washington, 1911), "Community A," pp. 755–56.
15. Scranton, "Immigration through Philadelphia," p. 57.
16. *Ibid.*
17. Senate Document 645, vol. 9, *History of Women in Industry in the U.S.*, pp. 108–9, quoting Harriet Robinson, *Loom and Spindle* (Boston: T. Y. Crowell & Co., 1898), pp. 71, 205. See also Berthoff, *British Immigrants*, pp. 34–35.
18. Gertrude Barnum, "The Story of a Fall River Mill Girl," *The Independent* 58, April 27, 1905, p. 242.
19. *Ibid.*, p. 243.
20. Cole, *Immigrant City*, pp. 118–20.
21. Senate Document 645, vol. 1, *Cotton Textile Industry*, p. 590.
22. Cole, *Immigrant City*, p. 76.
23. *Ibid.*, p. 75.
24. Barnum, "Fall River Mill Girl," p. 242.
25. Ernst, *Immigrant Life*, p. 68.
26. Abbott, *Women in Industry*, p. 223, citing *Report of Senate Committee on the Relations Between Labor and Capital*, 1885, i, p. 414.
27. Senate Document 645, vol. 2, *Men's Ready-Made Clothing*, p. 491.
28. *Ibid.*, p. 495.
29. *Ibid.*, p. 41.
30. *Ibid.* See also Mary Van Kleeck, *Working Girls in Evening Schools* (New York: Survey Associates for the Russell Sage Foundation, 1914), pp. 124–25.
31. Butler, *Women and the Trades*, p. 101.
32. Parker, *Working Woman*, p. 28.
33. Senate Document 645, Vol. XVIII, *Employment of Women and Children in Selected Industries*, p. 362.
34. Butler, *Women and the Trades*, p. 46.
35. Parker, *Working Woman*, p. 16.
36. See Butler, *Women and the Trades*, pp. 46–47, 50, and Odencrantz, *Italian Women in Industry*, pp. 84, 90.
37. Anthony, *Mothers Who Must Earn*, p. 83.
38. Senate Document 645, vol. 18, *Selected Industries*, pp. 53, 54, 80, 82.
39. Butler, *Women and the Trades*, p. 57.
40. Senate Document 645, vol. 18, *Selected Industries*, pp. 104, 106.
41. Abbott, *Women in Industry*, p. 199.
42. Balch, *Our Slavic Fellow Citizens*, pp. 357–58.
43. Senate Document 645, vol. 9, *History of Women in Industry in the U.S.*, p. 202.
44. Edith Fowler Chase, *The Bohemians: A Study of the "Land of the Cup and the Book,"* part of a series titled *Immigrants in the Making*, (New York: Fleming H. Revell Co., 1914), p. 62.
45. *Ibid.*, p. 205. See also p. 198 and citations from *American Workman*, September 30, 1871, and *3rd Annual Report of New York Bureau of Statistics of Labor*, 1885, p. 18.
46. Riis, *How the Other Half Lives*, p. 103.
47. Gary R. Mormino and Anthony P. Pizzo, *Tampa: The Treasure City* (Tulsa, Oklahoma: Continental Heritage Press, 1983), pp. 48–49. See also Mormino and George E. Pozzetta, *The Immigrant World of Ybor City: Italians and their Latin Neighbors in Tampa, 1885–1985* (Urbana: University of Illinois Press, 1987), and Doris Weatherford, *A History of Women in Tampa* (Tampa: Athena Society and Inkwood Books, 1991).
48. Robbins, "Bohemian Women," p. 195.
49. Odencrantz, *Italian Women in Industry*, p. 48.
50. *Ibid.*, p. 49.
51. Butler, *Women and the Trades*, p. 24. See also Hutchinson, *Women's Wages*, p. 55.
52. Campbell, *Prisoners of Poverty*, p. 205.
53. Caroline Manning, *The Immigrant Woman and Her Job*, U.S. Department of Labor, Bulletin of the Women's Bureau, No. 74 (Washington: Government Printing Office, 1930; reprinted by Arno Press and the *New York Times*, 1970), p. 129.

54. Van Kleeck, *Artificial Flower Makers*, p. 17.
55. Dorothy Richardson, *The Long Day: The Story of a New York Working Girl As Told by Herself* (New York: Century Co., 1905), p. 185.
56. Van Kleeck, *Artificial Flower Makers*, p. 29.
57. *Ibid.*, p. 5. See also U.S. Census Bulletin 93, *Earnings of Wage-Earners, Manufacturing*, 1905, pp. 82, 90, 98.
58. Richardson, *Long Day*, pp. 191–92.
59. Senate Document 645, vol. 12, *Women in Laundries*, p. 13 ff.
60. Butler, *Women and the Trades*, p. 182.
61. *Ibid.*, p. 171.
62. See especially Clark and Wyatt, *Making Both Ends Meet*, pp. 182–83, in a section by Carola Woerishofer.
63. Parker, *Working Woman*, p. 87.
64. Senate Document 645, vol. 12, *Women in Laundries*, p. 60.
65. Anonymous, "Collar Starcher," p. 307.
66. *Ibid.*
67. Butler, *Women and the Trades*, p. 191.
68. *Ibid.*, p. 190.
69. Nadel, *Little Germany*, p. 75.
70. Kamphoefner, Helbich, and Sommer, *News from the Land of Freedom*, pp. 541–42.
71. Baltimore City Directory, 1879, in the library of the Maryland Historical Society, Baltimore.
72. 1870 U.S. Census, 9th Ward of Baltimore, in the Maryland State Archives, Annapolis.
73. This analysis of the 1879 Baltimore City Directory was done in the library of the Maryland Historical Society in Baltimore; the 1870 census was reviewed at the Maryland State Archives in Annapolis.
74. Manning, *Immigrant Women*, pp. 151–52.
75. Helen I. Wilson and Eunice W. Smith, "Chicago Housing Conditions among the Slovaks in the Twentieth Ward," *American Journal of Sociology* 20 (September 1914), p. 127.
76. "Hartley House; An Industrial Settlement," settlement house, SSC, box 4, folder 23.
77. Abbott, *Immigration*, p. 527, citing *Report of the Massachusetts Commission on Immigration*, pp. 58–69.
78. Pehotsky, *Slavic Immigrant Woman*, p. 54.
79. William P. Shriver, *Immigrant Forces* (New York: Missionary Education Movement of the United States and Canada, 1913), p. 84.
80. Kenneth O. Bjork, *West of the Great Divide: Norwegian Migration to the Pacific Coast, 1847–1893* (Northfield, Minn.: Norwegian-American Historical Association, 1958) p. 376, citing Rev. C. L. Clausen, "Reise til Blackhills," *Folkebladet*, November 4 and November 11, 1880.
81. 14th Census, vol. 11, *Mines and Quarries, 1919* (Washington: Government Printing Office, 1922), pp. 32–33. See also the experiences of Danish Emily Romig, who went to Alaska in search of gold, in *A Pioneer Woman in Alaska* (Colorado Springs: privately printed, 1945).
82. Joan Morrison and Charlotte Fox Zabusky, *American Mosaic* (New York: E. P. Dutton, 1980), p. 16.
83. Odencrantz, *Italian Women in Industry*, p. 63.
84. See Anonymous, "The Experiences of a Chorus Girl," *The Independent*, July 12, 1906, p. 82.
85. Capek, *The Cechs*, p. 85.
86. Riis, *How the Other Half Lives*, p. 144.
87. Anthony, *Mothers Who Must Earn*, p. 160.
88. Stella, *Urban Congestion*, p. 35.
89. Kamphoefner, Helbich, and Sommer, *News from the Land of Freedom*, p. 548.
90. Senate Document 645, vol. 18, *Employment of Women*, p. 138.
91. *Ibid.*, pp. 180–94.
92. *Ibid.*, p. 234.
93. Butler, *Women and the Trades*, pp. 210, 228.
94. *Ibid.*, p. 227.
95. Wolfson, *Woman Worker and the Trade Unions* p. 36.
96. Hughes, *Mothers in Industry*, p. 131.
97. Senate Document 645, vol. 18, *Employment of Women*, pp. 277–83.
98. Butler, *Women and the Trades*, pp. 36, 43, 262–64.
99. Balch, *Our Slavic Fellow Citizens*, p. 355.
100. Stella, *Urban Congestion*, p. 5.
101. Balch, *Our Slavic Fellow Citizens*, p. 375.

102. Pehotsky, *Slavic Immigrant Woman*, p. 35.
103. Abbott, *Chicago*, p. 346. See also MacLean, "Life in the Pennsylvania Coal Fields," p. 332.
104. Pehotsky, *Slavic Immigrant Woman*, p. 47.
105. Byington, "Mill Town Courts," p. 919.
106. Balch, *Our Slavic Fellow Citizens*, p. 352.
107. *Ibid.*, p. 252.
108. Pehotsky, *Slavic Immigrant Woman*, p. 35.
109. Hughes, *Mothers in Industry*, p. 96.
110. Richmond and Hall, *A Study of Nine Hundred and Eighty-Five Widows*, pp. 29–30.
111. Baltimore City Directory, 1879, in the library of the Maryland Historical Society, Baltimore.
112. Dean R. Esslinger, "Immigration through the Port of Baltimore," in Stolarik, *Forgotten Doors*, p. 70, says: "In 1869, several of the steamship companies signed a contract with a Mrs. Koether to run a large boarding house at Pier 9 on Locust Point . . . Over the next half-century, Mrs. Koether . . . received as many as forty thousand per year at her boarding house."

 With this intriguing beginning point, the author and reference librarian Francis P. O'Neill undertook extensive searches at the Maryland Historical Society in Baltimore and the State Archives in Annapolis. Little confirmation was found, however. The 1910 federal census is clear on Koether's emigration date of 1869, which makes it improbable that she signed contracts with steamship companies in the same year.

 Though she probably operated for a shorter period and with less authority, it is nonetheless true that Augusta Marousek Koether headed Baltimore's "Emigrant House" during the late nineteenth and early twentieth centuries.
113. *New York Times*, Grossinger obituary, November 21, 1972.
114. Bruns, *Hold Dear*, p. 165.
115. *Ibid.*, p. 199.
116. *Ibid.*, p. 205.
117. *Ibid.*, p. 216.
118. Byington, "Mill Town Courts," p. 921.

CHAPTER 14—Ways of Work

1. Long, Anonymous, "Italian Immigrant Woman," p. 9, SCH.
2. Hutchinson, *Women's Wages*, p. 26, citing *Census of Manufacturers*, 1905, Bulletin No. 93, p. 11.
3. Abbott, *Immigration*, p. 269.
4. Butler, *Women and the Trades*, p. 340.
5. Anthony, *Mothers Who Must Earn*, p. 116.
6. Van Kleeck, *Artificial Flower Makers*, p. 66.
7. Elizabeth Hasanovitz, *One of Them: Chapters from a Passionate Autobiography* (Boston: Houghton Mifflin Company, 1918), pp. 115–16.
8. *Ibid.*, p. 115.
9. Odencrantz, *Italian Women in Industry*, in a supplement by Henriette R. Walter, p. 317.
10. Manning, *Immigrant Woman*, p. 117.
11. Butler, *Women and the Trades*, p. 261.
12. Odencrantz, *Italian Women in Industry*, p. 132.
13. Butler, *Women and the Trades*, p. 4, in a statement made by Paul U. Kellogg, in the editor's foreword.
14. Abbott, *Immigration*, p. 585, quoting from Massachusetts Board of Immigration, Second Annual Report, 1920, pp. 38–39.
15. Claghorn, *Immigrant's Day in Court*, pp. 17–18.
16. Anna Walther, *A Pilgrimage with a Milliner's Needle* (New York: Fredrick A. Stokes Company, 1917), p. 229.
17. Odencrantz, *Italian Women in Industry*, p. 157.
18. Rose Schneiderman, "A Cap Maker's Story," *The Independent* 58, April 27, 1905, p. 936.
19. Odencrantz, *Italian Women in Industry*, p. 159.
20. Campbell, *Prisoners of Poverty*, p. 177.
21. *Ibid.*, p. 178.
22. Cohen, *Out of the Shadow*, pp. 87–88.
23. Hasanovitz, *One of Them*, p. 109.

24. Ets, *Rosa*, p. 218.
25. Riis, *How The Other Half Lives*, p. 176.
26. *Ibid.*, p. 183.
27. Parker, *Working Woman*, pp. 153–54.
28. Richardson, *Long Day*, p. 188.
29. Butler, *Women and the Trades*, p. 224.
30. Clark and Wyatt, *Making Both Ends Meet*, p. 194.
31. Senate Document 645, vol. 2, *Men's Ready-Made Clothing*, p. 421.
32. Parker, *Working Woman*, pp. 111–12.
33. *Ibid.*, p. 110.
34. Cohen, *Out of the Shadow*, p. 287.
35. Women's Educational and Industrial Union, *500 Immigrant Women in Boston*, SCH, p. 16.
36. Odencrantz, *Italian Women in Industry*, p. 315, in a supplement by Henriette R. Walter.
37. Edith Abbott, *Historical Aspects of the Immigration Problem* (Chicago: University of Chicago Press, 1926; reissued by Arno Press and the *New York Times* as part of the American Immigration Collection, 1969), p. 597.
38. Frances A. Kellor, *Out of Work* (New York: G. P. Putnam's Sons, 1904). See also Grace Abbott, "The Chicago Employment Agency and the Immigrant Worker," *American Journal of Sociology* 14 (November 1908).
39. Odencrantz, *Italian Women in Industry*, pp. 272–73.
40. *Ibid.*, p. 275.
41. Manning, *Immigrant Woman*, pp. 103–5.
42. Odencrantz, *Italian Women in Industry*, p. 115.
43. *Ibid.*, pp. 121, 124, 283.
44. Ets, *Rosa*, p. 211.
45. Clark and Wyatt, *Making Both Ends Meet*, pp. 141–46.
46 Hughes, *Mothers in Industry*, p. 226.
47. Cole, *Immigrant City*, p. 75.
48. Butler, *Women and the Trades*, p. 108.
49. Odencrantz, *Italian Women in Industry*, p. 67.
50. Cole, *Immigrant City*, p. 32.
51. "Disastrous Fire in the Woonasquatucket Valley," *Providence Daily Journal*, February 3, 1866.
52. Hasanovitz, *One of Them*, p. 216.
53. *New York Times*, March 26, 1911.
54. *Ibid.*
55. *Ibid.*, March 27, 1911.
56. *Ibid.*, December 28, 1911.
57. *Ibid.*, March 26, 1911.
58. Schneiderman, *All for One*, p. 47.
59. Senate Document 645, vol. 10, *History of Women in Trade Unions*, p. 60.
60. *Ibid.*, pp. 93–94, citing *Cigarmaker's Journal*, May 10, 1878.
61. Holt, *Life Stories*, pp. 45–46.
62. Parker, *Working Woman*, pp. 113–14.
63. Hasanovitz, *One of Them*, pp. 252–53.
64. Clark and Wyatt, *Making Both Ends Meet*, p. 81.
65. Green, *Holyoke*, p. 57.
66. Senate Document 645, vol. 10, *History of Women in Trade Unions*, p. 164.
67. Cohen, *Out of the Shadow*, pp. 124–27.
68. Abbott, *Women in Industry*, p. 145.
69. Clark and Wyatt, *Making Both Ends Meet*, p. 62.
70. *New York Times*, December 9, 1909.
71. Clark and Wyatt, *Making Both Ends Meet*, p. 63. See also Theresa Serber Malkiel, *The Diary of a Shirtwaist Worker* (New York: Cooperative Press, 1910), and Andria Taylor Hourwich & Gladys L. Palmer, eds., *I Am a Woman Worker* (New York: Affiliated Schools for Workers, 1936; reprinted by Arno Press, 1974). Pages 109–52 deal especially with strikes.
72. *New York Times*, January 16, 1912, p. 1.
73. See especially *Evening Tribune*, Lawrence, Massachusetts, January 30, 1912.
74. Richard Child, "The Industrial Revolt at Lawrence," *Collier's* 48, March 9, 1912, p. 15.

75. Priscilla Long, *Mother Jones, Woman Organizer*, p. 18, citing letters from F. L. Abbey to Governor Ferris, September 3, October 4, and August 29, 1913, Michigan Historical Commission, Ann Arbor. Long's paper in Schlesinger Library gives several other examples of women's support of the United Mine Workers.
76. From unidentified, undated clippings in the scrapbook of Eva W. White, Schlesinger Library, Radcliffe College, Cambridge, Massachusetts.
77. Van Kleeck, *Artificial Flower Makers*, p. 36.
78. Anthony, *Mothers Who Must Earn*, p. 81.
79. Zoe Beckley, "Finds Hard Job Unionizing Girls Whose Aim Is to Wed," *New York Telegram & Sun*, June 18, 1922. See also Theresa Wolfson, "Where Are the Organized Women Workers," *American Federationist* (June 1925): 455, and other items in the files of Mary Van Kleeck.
80. Parker, *Working Woman*, p. 134.
81. Richmond, *Deserters*, p. 70.
82. Norkunas, Balkus interview, unpaged, MC.
83. Graham Wallas, *The Great Society: A Psychological Analysis* (New York: Macmillan Co., 1929), pp. 341–43.
84. *Ibid.*
85. Manning, *Immigrant Woman*, pp. 112–14.
86. Wallas, *Great Society*, p. 341. For additional information on general working conditions, see also Carroll D. Wright, *The Working Girls of Boston* (Boston: Wright & Potter Printing Co., 1889; reprinted by Arno Press and the *New York Times*, 1969), and *Working Girls of Cincinnati*, an Arno Press 1974 reprint of three studies done by the Cincinnati Consumers' League in 1918, 1927, and 1930.

   Further detail on a number of items in this chapter can be found in Doris Weatherford, *American Women's History: An A to Z of People, Issues, Organizations and Events*, which includes entries on Alva Vanderbilt Belmont, Mary Drier, Rose Schneiderman, the Women's Trade Union League, the Lawrence strike and others.

CHAPTER 15—Foreign Domestics

1. Blegen, *Land of Their Choice*, p. 436.
2. *Ibid.*, p. 76.
3. Bjork, *West of the Great Divide*, p. 160, citing a letter from Rev. Christian Hvistendahl in *Foedrelandet og emigranten*, May 18, 1871.
4. Daniel E. Sutherland, *Americans and Their Servants: Domestic Service in the United States from 1800 to 1920* (Baton Rouge: Louisiana State University Press, 1981), pp. 58, 179.
5. Women's Educational and Industrial Union, "Immigration as a Source of Supply for Domestic Workers," 1905, Schlesinger Library, Radcliffe College, Cambridge Mass., p. 1. See also Carroll D. Wright, *The Working Girls of Boston* (Boston: Wright & Potter Printing Co., 1889) and Robert Ernst, *Immigrant Life in New York City, 1825–1863* (Port Washington, N.Y.: Ira J. Friedman, Inc., 1949). Both contain statistics showing the overwhelming number of foreign-born women among domestics in these cities. (Wright was commissioner of the U.S. Department of Labor.)
6. Kellor, "The Immigrant Woman," p. 402. On employment agencies for domestics, see also Frances Kellor, *Out of Work*, as well as Kellor's "Immigration and Household Labor," *Charities* 12, February 6, 1904.
7. *Ibid.*
8. Carpenter, *Immigrants and Their Children*, pp. 288–89.
9. Abbott, *Historical Aspects*, pp. 522–24, citing John Francis Maguire, *The Irish in America* (London, 1868), pp. 313–32.
10. Ernst, *Immigrant Life*, p. 67.
11. Abbott, *Historical*, p. 385.
12. Harriet Prescott Spofford, *The Servant Girl Question* (Boston: Houghton Mifflin Co., 1881; reprinted by Arno Press and the *New York Times*, 1977), p. 44.
13. Ernst, *Immigrant Life*, p. 245.
14. 61st Congress, 2d Session, Senate Document 282, *Report of the Immigration Commission, Occupation of the First and Second Generation of Immigrants in the United States* (Washington, 1911), pp. 71–79. The report's failure to distinguish between place of birth (nationality) and true ethnicity makes it difficult

to determine how many of these may be Jewish; the most likely origins for any Jewish women, however, would have been Poland, Austria, and Hungary

15. Women's Educational and Industrial Union, *Immigrant Girls in Boston, 1905–06,* SCH.
16. Abbott, *Immigration,* pp. 378–79.
17. Kyra Goritzina, *Service Entrance: Memoirs of a Park Avenue Cook* (New York: Currick and Evans, 1939), p. 77.
18. Raaen, *Grass of the Earth,* p. 131.
19. Zempel, *In Their Own Words,* pp. 104–5.
20. Ets, *Rosa,* p. 221.
21. Anthony, *Mothers Who Must Earn,* pp. 115–16.
22. Koenig, *Letters from America,* vol. 29, p. 13.
23. Steiner, *On the Trail of the Immigrant,* p. 337.
24. Lucy Maynard Salmon, *Domestic Service,* 2d ed. (New York: Macmillan Co., 1901), pp. 132–36. An entry on Salmon and her research on domestic workers is included in Doris Weatherford, *American Women's History: An A to Z of People, Issues, Organizations, and Events.*
25. Holt, *Life Stories,* pp. 133–34. The Mary Van Kleeck files, SSC, detail training for domestic work; on child nursing, see especially "Training Schools for Infant Nurses and Nursery Maids in New York City," unpublished paper, box 60, folder 999.
26. Morrison and Zabusky, *American Mosaic,* pp. 42–43.
27. Salmon, *Domestic Service,* pp. 107–8.
28. Byington, *Homestead,* p. 79.
29. More, *Wage-Earners' Budgets,* p. 137.
30. Salmon, *Domestic Service,* pp. 98–101.
31. *Ibid.,* pp. 91–92.
32. Claghorn, *Immigrant's Day in Court,* pp. 14–15.
33. Yezierska, *Children of Loneliness,* pp. 41–42.
34. Nadel, *Little Germany,* p. 89.
35. Parker, *Working Woman,* p. 203.
36. *Ibid.,* p. 203.
37. Cohen, *Out of the Shadow,* p. 176.
38. Preus, *Linka's Diary,* p. 105.
49. Bruns, *Hold Dear,* p. 91.
40. The distinction between "hired help" and "domestic service" was outlined by Vasser historian Lucy Salmon in her classic work. It has since been detailed by others, especially David M. Katzman, *Seven Days a Week: Women and Domestic Service in Industrializing America* (New York: Oxford University Press, 1978), Daniel E. Sutherland, *Americans and Their Servants: Domestic Service in the United States from 1800 to 1920* (Baton Rouge: Louisiana State University Press, 1981), and Faye Dudden, *Serving Women: Household Service in Nineteenth-Century America* (Middletown, Conn.: Wesleyan University Press, 1983).
41. Zempel, *In Their Own Words,* pp. 40, 48.
42. "Household Employment—History," April 1919, in the YWCA files, SSC, box 45, folder 1.
43. Goritzina, *Service Entrance,* p. 76.
44. Louise C. Odencrantz, "Basis of Employment for Household Assistants," 1919, in the papers of Mary Van Kleeck, SSC, box 96, folder 1498.
45. "First Report of the Commission on Household Employment," presented to the YWCA national convention in Los Angeles, May, 1915, p. 5 in the YWCA files, SSC, box 43, folder 5.
46. *Ibid.*
47. Ida M. Tarbell, "What a Factory Can Teach a Housewife," reprinted from *The Association Monthly,* November, 1916; in the YWCA files, SSC, box 43, folder 5.
48. Salmon, *Domestic Service,* p. 158.
49. *Ibid.,* p. 154.
50. YWCA Commission, SSC, box 43, folder 5.
51. Tarbell, "What a Factory Can Teach."
52. Cohen, *Out of the Shadow,* pp. 180–81.
53. Erickson, *Invisible Immigrants,* pp. 312–13.
54. "The New Emancipation," *New York Tribune,* May 29, 1919, clipping in Mary Van Kleeck's papers, SSC, box 96, folder 1498.

CHAPTER 16—Homes on the Range

1. Svendsen, *Frontier Mother*, p. 40.
2. Koren, *Diary of Elisabeth Koren*, p. 196; Isely, *Sunbonnet Days*, p. 188; and Brandt, "Social Aspects," p. 35.
3. Isely, *Sunbonnet Days*, pp. 196–98.
4. Svendsen, *Frontier Mother*, pp. 124–30.
5. Wanless, *Century Farms*, p. 136.
6. *Ibid.*, pp. 57–58.
7. C. F. Case, "Historical Sketches . . . Written by One Who Was Here Part of the Time," *Lyon County (Minnesota) Reporter*, 1898, reprinted in *Prairieland Pioneer* (Marshall, Minnesota: Southwestern State University) 10, no. 2 (winter 1993): 41.
8. Jacobs, "Death, Disease, and Deliverance," p. 5.
9. Dena Wykstra, "Immigrants Struggled to Survive Outbreak," *Tampa Tribune*, February 1, 1994, BayLife Section, pp. 2–3.
10. Barton, *Letters from the Promised Land*, p. 147.
11. Waerenskjold, *Lady with the Pen*, p. 51.
12. Paul Knapland, *Moorings Old and New* (Madison: State Historical Society of Wisconsin, 1964), p. 215.
13. Brandt, "Social Aspects," pp. 26–28.
14. *Lincoln County History, 1873–1973*, p. 18, in the Southwest Minnesota State University History Center, Marshall, Minnesota.
15. Koren, *Dairy of Elisabeth Koren*, p. 258.
16. *Ibid.*
17. Isely, *Sunbonnet Days*, p. 174.
18. Waerenskjold, *Lady with the Pen*, pp. 29–30.
19. Wanless, *Century Farms*, p. 310.
20. Bruns, *Hold Dear*, p. 82.
21. Gjerset and Hektoen, "Health Conditions," p. 11.
22. Schaddelee, "Dutch Settlement," p. 409.
23. Svendsen, *Frontier Mother*, p. 32. See also Blegen, "Immigrant Women and the American Frontier," Norwegian-American Historical Association *Studies and Records* 5 (1930): 27.
24. Blegen, *Land of Their Choice*, p. 427.
25. Rev. H. O. Hendrickson, "Oldest Settlement in Cottonwood County," 1940, manuscript on file at the Southwest Minnesota History Center, Marshall, Minnesota, pp. 5, 11–12.
26. Charles S. Bryant and Abel B. Murch, *A History of the Great Massacre by the Sioux Indians in Minnesota* (Cincinnati: Rickey and Carroll, 1864; reprinted in Germany, 1973), p. 306.
27. *Ibid.*, p. 315.
28. *Ibid.*, p. 316.
29. *Ibid.*, pp. 318–21. I wish to thank my brother, Norman Barge, who tracked down the 1864 Kreiger narrative, as well as those of other women, at the Granite Falls, Minnesota, Public Library.
30. *Ibid.*, pp. 300–301.
31. Richard O'Connor, *The German-Americans* (Boston: Little, Brown & Company, 1968), p. 192, citing Evan Jones, *The Minnesota: Forgotten River*.
32. Bryant and Murch, *Great Massacre*, pp. 340–41.
33. *Ibid.*, pp. 339–40.
34. Kenneth Carley, *The Sioux Uprising of 1862* (St. Paul: Minnesota Historical Society, 1976), p. 22.
35. Blegen, *Land of Their Choice*, pp. 429–30.
36. *Ibid.* See also Blegen, *Grass Roots History*, pp. 67 and 78, citing Victor E. Lawson, Martin E. Twe, and J. Emil Nelson, *History of Kandiyohi County* (St. Paul: Pioneer Press, 1905), pp. 106–10.
37. Bryant and Murch, *Great Massacre*, p. 401. Her name is Anglicized in this account as Gure Anderson.
38. *Ibid.*, p. 328.
39. *Ibid.*, pp. 329–32.
40. *Ibid.*, pp. 334–35, citing the St. Peter, Minnesota *Tribune*, November 4, 1862.
41. Isely, *Sunbonnet Days*, p. 180.
42. Erickson, *Invisible Immigrants*, pp. 184–85.
43. *Ibid.*, pp. 219, 221.
44. Bremer, *America of the Fifties*, pp. 208–9.

45. Waerenskjold, *Lady with the Pen*, p. 60.
46. *Ibid.*, p. 30.
47. Bruns, *Hold Dear*, pp. 91–92.
48. Koren, *Diary of Elisabeth Koren*, p. 321.
49. Svendsen, *Frontier Mother*, p. 35.
50. Bruns, *Hold Dear*, pp. 91–92.
51. Koren, *Diary of Elisabeth Koren*, p. 201.
52. *Ibid.*, p. 280.
53. Kamphoefner, Helbich, and Sommer, *News from the Land of Freedom*, p. 217.
54. "A Michigan Farmer's Wife," letter to the editor entitled "Women on the Farm," *The Independent* 58, March 9, 1905, pp. 553–54.
55. "German-Russian People," YWCA, SSC.
56. Helen M. Waite, "An Investigation of Women Farmers from the Census," c. 1900, in the papers of Mary Van Kleeck, SSC, box 96, folder 1501.
57. Preus, *Linka's Diary*, p. 262.
58. Isely, *Sunbonnet Days*, pp. 171–72.
59. Nels Anderson, "Czecho-Slovaks in Virginia," in Edmund Brunner, *Immigrant Farmers and Their Children* (Garden City, NY: Doubleday, Doran, and Company, 1929), p. 194.
60. *Ibid.*, pp. 189–90.
61. *Ibid.*, pp. 200–1.
62. Balch, *Our Slavic Fellow Citizens*, p. 329.
63. Vieno Raitanen, "A Finnish Girl in New England," in "What It Means to Be a Second-Generation Girl: Talks Given at the Second-Generation Youth Dinner of the National Board of the Y.W.C.A." (New York: Woman's Press, 1935), p. 28, in the YWCA files, SSC, box 31, folder 4.
64. *Ibid.*, p. 32.
65. Mangano, *Italian Colonies*, pp. 56–57.

CHAPTER 17—Travails of Travel

1.   Isely, *Sunbonnet Days*, p. 40.
2.   Koren, *Diary of Elisabeth Koren*, p. 6.
3.   Kamphoefner, Helbich, and Sommer, *News from the Land of Freedom*, pp. 371–72.
4.   Cohen, *Out of the Shadow*, pp. 62–64.
5.   Oscar Handlin, *The Uprooted* (New York: Grosset & Dunlap, 1951), p. 51. This Pulitzer Prize–winning epic is, of course, basic to a beginning student of immigration, but its undocumented nature limits its value for researchers. His *Boston's Immigrants* (New York: Atheneum, 1968) and *Immigration as a Factor in American History* (New York: Prentice-Hall, 1959) are also classics; the latter, however, lacks an index, while the former has only seven entries for "women" in a 382-page book. (The contribution of Boston's Irish women is devalued, for example, on page 61: "There was room in the comfortable households of Boston's middle class for the Irish daughter or sister who wished to lighten her family's load by supporting herself and perhaps contributing a little something besides.") Nonetheless, Handlin is excellent at drawing a graphic picture of the crossing.
6.   Daniels, *Coming to America*, p. 135.
7.   Bruns, *Hold Dear*, p. 67.
8.   *Ibid.*
9.   Elizabeth Hampsten, *To All Inquiring Friends: Letters, Diaries, and Essays in North Dakota* (Grand Forks: University of North Dakota, 1979), p. 217.
10. Isely, *Sunbonnet Days*, p. 31.
11. Kamphoefner, Helbich, and Sommer, *News from the Land of Freedom*, p. 537.
12. *Ibid.*
13. *Ibid.*, pp. 541–42
14. *Ibid.*, pp. 542–43.
15. *Ibid.*, p. 556.
16. 61st Congress, 3d Session, Senate Document 753, *Reports of the Immigration Commission: Steerage Conditions* (Washington: Government Printing Office, 1911), p. 8.
17. Kellogg Durland, "Steerage Impositions," *The Independent* 61, August 30, 1906, pp. 499–504
18. Senate Document 753, *Steerage Conditions*, p. 19.

19. Cohen, *Out of the Shadow*, p. 60.
20. Senate Document 753, *Steerage Conditions*, p. 37.
21. Durland, "Steerage Impositions," pp. 499–504.
22. Abbott, *Immigration*, pp. 82–86.
23. Isely, *Sunbonnet Days*, p. 28.
24. Senate Document 753, *Steerage Conditions*, pp. 21–22.
25. Morrison and Zabusky, *American Mosaic*, p. 85.
26. Bruns, *Hold Dear*, p. 94.
27. Zempel, *In Their Own Words*, p. 28.
28. Hazanovitz, *One of Them*, p. 13.
29. Senate Document 753, *Steerage Conditions*, p. 27.
30. Viola Paradise, "The Jewish Immigrant Girl in Chicago," *The Survey* 30, September 6, 1913, p. 700.
31. Senate Document 753, *Steerage Conditions*, p. 30.
32. Ets, *Rosa*, p. 163.
33. Kamphoefner, Helbich, and Sommer, *News from the Land of Freedom*, p. 373.
34. *Ibid.*, p. 168.
35. Holt, *Life Stories*, pp. 109–10.
36. Minnesota State Board of Immigration "Cost of Coming to Minnesota," undated, in the files of the Southwest Minnesota State University Historical Center, Marshall, Minnesota.
37. Francis A. Kellor, "The Protection of Immigrant Women," *Atlantic* 101 (February 1908): 248.
38. *Ibid.*, p. 248.
39. 39. Chotzinoff, *Lost Paradise*, pp. 46–51
40. *Ibid.*, p. 51.
41. Victor Safford, *Immigration Problems: Personal Experiences of an Official* (New York: Dodd, Mead and Company, 1925), p. 93.
42. Zempel, *In Their Own Words*, p. 28.
43. Abbot, *Immigration*, p. 598, from the files of the Chicago Immigrants Protective League.
44. *Ibid.*
45. Svendson, *Frontier Mother.*, p. 23.
46. Blegen, *Land of Their Choice*, p. 383.
47. Senate Document 753, *Steerage Conditions*, p. 40.
48. Preus, *Linka's Diary*, p. 178.
49. Bruns, *Hold Dear*, pp. 67–70.
50. Hasanovitz, *One of Them*, p. 214.
51. Blegen, *Land of Their Choice*, p. 260.
52. Kamphoefner, Helbich, and Sommer, *News from the Land of Freedom*, p. 374.
53. Holt, *Life Stories*, p. 145.
54. Robert H. Billigmeier and Fred Altschuler Picard, *The Old Land and the New: The Journals of Two Swiss Families in America in the 1820s* (Minneapolis: University of Minnesota Press, 1965), p. 149.
55. Svendsen, *Frontier Mother*, pp. 6–7.
56. Blegen, *Land of Their Choice*, p. 97–98.
57. Svendsen, *Frontier Mother*, p. 14.
58. *Ibid.*, p. 6.
59. Preus, *Linka's Diary*, p. 170.
60. *Ibid.*, pp. 151–52.
61. Bjork, *Great Divide*, p. 412, quoting a letter from Caroline C. Hjort in the *Decorah (Iowa) Posten*, December 1, 1886.
62. University of Wisconsin, "Summer School for Workers, MCC.
63. Cohen, *Out of the Shadow*, p. 34.
64. Blegen, *Land of Their Choice*, p. 298.
65. Martha Reid Robinson, "Immigrants at the Port of New York," *World Events* (March 1905): 195.
66. Schneiderman, *All for One*, p. 25.
67. Cohen, *Out of the Shadow*, pp. 55–56.
68. Women's Educational and Indusrial Union, *Report*, p. 8, SCH.
69. Schneiderman, *All for One*, p. 25.
70. Kamphoefner, Helbich, and Sommer, *News from the Land of Freedom*, pp. 542–43.
71. Abbott, *Immigration*, p. 472.

CHAPTER 18—Standards and Double Standards

1. Abbott, *Immigration*, pp. 62–63, from International Labor Office, *Emigration and Immigration: Legislation and Treaties* (Geneva, 1922), pp. 13–24.
2. See especially Balch, *Our Slavic Fellow Citizens*, pp. 135–37.
3. Bruns, *Hold Dear*, p. 46.
4. Kamphoefner, Helbich, and Sommer, *News from the Land of Freedom*, p. 534.
5. *Ibid.*, p. 535.
6. Abbott, *Immigration*, p. 420.
7. *Ibid.*, p. 426.
8. *Ibid.*, p. 300.
9. Safford, *Immigration Problems*, p. 253.
10. Abbott, *Immigration*, pp. 268–69.
11. *Ibid.*, pp. 303–7.
12. *Ibid.*, p. 312.
13. Long, Oral Histories, SCH; Anonymous, "Italian Immigrant," p. 2.
14. Abbott, *Immigration*, pp. 319–332.
15. Metzker, *Bintel Brief*, p. 97.
16. Abbott, *Immigration*, pp. 392–95.
17. *Ibid.*, pp. 350–51.
18. *Ibid.*, p. 345.
19. *Ibid.*
20. Robinson, "Immigrants at the Port," p. 195.
21. Fredric M. Miller, "Immigration through the Port of Philadelphia," in Stolarik, *Forgotten Doors*, p. 47.
22. Metzker, *Bintel Brief*, pp. 62–63.
23. Edith Baldwin Terry, letter to the Honorable William Williams, Commissioner of Immigration, Ellis Island, May 2, 1911, in the YWCA files, SSC, box 33, folder 4.
24. Letter on stationery for the U.S. Department of Labor, Immigration Service, from Helen Russell Bastedo to Mrs. R. L. Dickinson, Chairman of Immigration Service Bureau, Y.W.C.A., April 5, 1921, in the YWCA files, SSC, box 33, folder 4.
25. "The First Six Months Are the Hardest," circa 1929, in the YWCA files, SSC, box 33, folder 1.
26. Ethel Bird, "Separated Families and the Immigration Law," undated (after 1924), p. 7, in the YWCA files, SSC, box 33A, folder 4.
27. Claghorn, *Immigrant's Day in Court*, p. 317.
28. *Ibid.*
29. *Ibid.*, pp. 437–48, citing *The Survey*, January 10, 1920.
30. *Ibid.*, p. 436.
31. *Ibid.*, p. 462.

CHAPTER 19—An Ocean Apart: Separation and Its Effects

1. Eubank, *Study of Family Desertion*, p. 40.
2. Minton, untitled autobiography, p. 11.
3. Eubank, *Study of Family Desertion*, p. 39.
4. Metzker, *Bintel Brief*, pp. 56–57.
5. *Ibid.*
6. Segale, *Santa Fe Trail*, pp. 193–94.
7. Colcord, *Broken Homes*, p. 100.
8. Senate Document 645, vol. 12, *Women in Laundries*, p. 107.
9. Thomas and Znaniecki, *Polish Peasant*, vol. 2, p. 1719.
10. *Ibid.*, p. 1712.
11. *Ibid.*, pp. 1713–14.
12. "Probation for All Emigrant Husbands," *The Survey* 30, no. 12, June 21, 1913, p. 385.
13. Bird, "Separated Families," p. 6.
14. Hugo Eugene Varga, "Desertion of Wives and Children by Emigrants to America," *Proceedings of the National Conference of Charities and Correction* (Fort Wayne, Indiana: Fort Wayne Printing Co., 1912), p. 260.

15. Schneiderman, *All for One*, pp. 18–19.
16. Thomas and Znaniecki, *The Polish Peasant*, vol. 1, pp. 863–68.
17. *Ibid.*, pp. 874–93.
18. Ets, *Rosa*, p. 140.
19. Erickson, *Invisible Immigrants*, p. 241.
20. Balch, *Our Slavic Fellow Citizens*, p. 188, from the notebook of Miss Gazvoda.
21. *Ibid.*, pp. 170–71.
22. Thomas and Znaniecki, *The Polish Peasant*, vol. 1, pp. 394–450, the Osinski series.
23. Erickson, *Invisible Immigrants*, pp. 372–77.
24. *Ibid.*
25. Thomas and Znaniecki, *The Polish Peasant*, vol. 1, pp. 837–38.
26. *Ibid.*, pp. 825–26.
27. *Ibid.*, p. 909.
28. *Ibid.*, p. 913.
29. Balch, *Our Slavic Fellow Citizens*, p. 186, from the notebook of Miss Gazvoda.
30. Byington, *Homestead*, p. 161.
31. Hvidt, *Flight to America*, pp. 187–90.
32. Barton, *Letters from the Promised Land*, p. 44.
33. Thomas and Znaniecki, *The Polish Peasant*, vol. 1, pp. 851, 592.
34. *Ibid.*, p. 825.
35. Tauba Leah Meyer Cohen Forman, "The Blood Thirst in Kishineff," *The Independent* 55, June 18, 1903, pp. 1430–33.
36. Thomas and Znaniecki, *The Polish Peasant*, vol. 1, p. 900.
37. *Ibid.*, pp. 850–52.
38. Department of Immigration and Foreign Communities of the YWCA, "Summary of a Case Record: Molarsky," SSC, box 31, folder 5.
39. Bird, "Separated Families," p. 4.
40. Long, Oral Histories, SCH, Sarah Demirfian, "Interview with My Mother," unpaged.
41. Department for Foreign-Born Women, "Report to the Federal Advisory Commission on Social Welfare Work for Immigrants," 1921, in the YWCA files, SSC, box 33A, folder 2.
42. Bird, "Separated Families," p. 5.
43. *Ibid.*
44. *Ibid.*
45. *Ibid.*
46. *Ibid.*
47. "The First Six Months Are the Hardest," circa 1929, in the YWCA files, SSC, box 33, folder 1.
48. *Ibid.*
49. Long Collection, Watkinson, "Social History of My Family," p. 2.
50. Bird, "Separated Families," p. 7.
51. Cohen, *Out of the Shadow*, p. 22.
52. Robinson, "Immigrants at the Port," p. 195.
53. Odencrantz, *Italian Women in Industry*, p. 309, in a supplement by Henriette R. Walter.
54. Thomas, "Family's Secret Revealed," p. 4.
55. Thomas and Znaniecki, *The Polish Peasant*, vol. 1, p. 973.
56. Byington, *Homestead*, p. 181.

CHAPTER 20—From Old and Male to Young and Female: Changes in Family Relations

1. Carpenter, *Immigrants and Their Children*, p. 169.
2. Parker, *Working Woman*, p. 205.
3. Carpenter, *Immigrants and Their Children*, p. 408.
4. Kathleen Neils Conzen, *Immigrant Milwaukee 1836-1860: Accomodation and Community in a Frontier City* (Cambridge: Harvard University Press, 1976), p. 54.
5. Blegen, *Land of Their Choice*, p. 317.
6. Isely, *Sunbonnet Days*, p. 107.
7. Koren, *Diary of Elisabeth Koren*, p. 94.

8. Carpenter, *Immigrants and Their Children* p. 235.

9. Cole, *Immigrant City*, p. 104.

10. John Foster Carr, *Guide for the Immigrant Italian*, published under the auspices of the Connecticut Daughters of the American Revolution (New York: Doubleday, 1911; reprinted as part of *Assimilation of the Italian Immigrant*, Arno Press, 1975), pp. 36–37.

11. Balch, *Our Slavic Fellow Citizens*, p. 377.

12. Claghorn, *Immigrant's Day in Court*, p. 98.

13. Brunner, *Immigrant Farmers*, p. 200.

14. Yezierska, *Children of Loneliness*, p. 20.

15. Anthony, *Mothers Who Must Earn*, pp. 186–90.

16. Mary E. McDowell, "The Struggle in Family Life," *Charities* 13, Dec. 3, 1904, p. 197.

17. Herzfeld, *Family Monographs*, p. 57.

18. Williams, *South Italian Folkways*, p. 96.

19. *Ibid.*, p. 77.

20. Herzfeld, *Family Monographs*, p. 94.

21. Interview by Livia Baciu of "Jolan," a twenty-year-old paper-factory worker, YWCA files, SSC, box 31, folder 5.

22. *Ibid.* Interview subject was "Elisabeth," an eighteen-year-old Hungarian currently unemployed.

23. Roberts, "Italian Girls," pp. 760–61.

24. Lawrence Guy Brown, *Immigration: Cultural Conflicts and Social Adjustments* (New York: Longman, Green & Co., 1933; reissued by Arno Press and the *New York Times*, 1969), pp. 255–56, citing Konrad Bercovici, "The Greatest Jewish City in the World," *The Nation*, September 12, 1923, p. 259.

25. Odencrantz, *Italian Women in Industry*, p. 28.

26. *Ibid.*, p. 204.

27. Pagano, *Golden Wedding*, pp. 67, 107.

28. *Ibid.*, p. 128.

29. *Ibid.*, p. 179.

30. Van Kleeck, *Artificial Flower Makers*, p. 235.

31. Bruns, *Hold Dear*, p. 72.

32. Kamphoefner, Helbich, and Sommer, *News from the Land of Freedom*, p. 553–54.

33. Williams, *South Italian Folkways*, p. 190.

34. Metzker, *Bintel Brief*, p. 128.

35. Sophonisba Breckinridge and Edith Abbott, *The Delinquent Child and the Home: A Study of the Delinquent Wards of the Juvenile Court of Chicago* (New York: Russell Sage Foundation, 1917), p. 285.

36. Kamphoefner, Helbich, and Sommer, *News from the Land of Freedom*, pp. 550–51.

37. Rebekah Kohut, *My Portion* (New York: Thomas Selzer, 1925), p. 118.

38. Interview by Steinitz, part of a Cleveland YWCA study of second-generation women, c. 1930, in the YWCA files, SSC, box 31, folder 5.

39. Campbell, *Prisoners of Poverty*, pp. 88–99.

40. Holt, *Life Stories*, pp. 143–44.

41. Kamphoefner, Helbich, and Sommer, *News from the Land of Freedom*, p. 556.

42. Bruns, *Hold Dear*, p. 289.

43. *Ibid.*, p. 297.

44. *Ibid.*, p. 248.

45. Paradise, "Jewish Immigrant Girl in Chicago," p. 703.

46. Long, Oral Histories, Anonymous, "An Italian Immigrant Woman," pp. 3–4.

47. Hughes, *Mothers in Industry*, p. 99.

48. Holt, *Life Stories*, p. 147.

49. Leona Murphy, S.C., "The Life Story of the Sisters of Charity of Cincinnati, Ohio," manuscript, 1941, Sisters of Charity Archives, College of Mount St. Joseph, Ohio, p. 246.

50. Barnum, "Fall River Mill Girl," p. 242.

51. Bird, "Separated Families," p. 7.

52. Hasanovitz, *One of Them*, p. 236.

53. *Ibid.*, p. 249.

CHAPTER 21—Woman's Place in the New World

1. Carpenter, *Immigrants and Their Children*, p. 220.
2. Abbott, *Immigration*, pp. 353–54.
3. Senate Document 282, *Fecundity of Immigrant Women*, pp. 811–12.
4. Carpenter, *Immigrants and Their Children*, p. 270.
5. Anthony, *Mothers Who Must Earn*, p. 61.
6. Carpenter, *Immigrants and Their Children*, p. 281.
7. Metzker, *Bintel Brief*, pp. 109–10.
8. Preus, *Linka's Diary*, pp. 198–99.
9. Kamphoefner, Helbich, and Sommer, *News from the Land of Freedom*, p. 139.
10. *Ibid.*, p. 473.
11. Segale, *Santa Fe Trail*, p. 15.
12. Long, Oral Histories, Marot, "Oral Interview," SCH, p. 11.
13. *Ibid.*, Demifiran, "Interview with My Mother," SCH, p. 2.
14. Thomas and Znaniecki, *Polish Peasant*, vol. 1, p. 923.
15. *Ibid.*, p. 930.
16. *Ibid.*, p. 952.
17. Van Kleeck, *Working Girls in Evening Schools*, p. 25.
18. Odencrantz, *Italian Women in Industry*, p. 28.
19. Bruns, *Hold Dear*, p. 81.
20. *Ibid.*, p. 125.
21. *Ibid.*, p. 202.
22. Preus, *Linka's Diary*, p. 210.
23. *Ibid.*
24. Waerenskjold, *Lady with the Pen*, p. 18.
25. Stenhouse, *Expose of Polygamy*, pp. 34–36.
26. *Ibid.*, p. 78.
27. Kamphoefner, Helbich, and Sommer, *News from the Land of Freedom*, p. 473.
28. Untitled speech by "E.K.J.," c. 1921, in the Jane Maud Campbell Collection, SCH, box 1, folder 10.
29. Jane Maud Campbell, speech to the Daughters of the American Revolution, SCH, box 1, folder 11.
30. Department for Foreign-Born Women, "Report to the Federal Advisory Commission," 1921, in the YWCA files, SSC, box 33A, folder 2.
31. All records are for Lyon and Lincoln Counties and were excerpted in *Prairieland Pioneer* (Marshall, Minnesota: Southwest State University) 10, no. 2 (winter 1993): 44–68.
32. Manny Aws, "Migration Saga for Sesquicentennial Year," *Minnesota Posten*, fredag mars 7, 1975, in the archives of the Southwest Minnesota History Center, Southwest State University, Marshall, Minnesota.
33. Diner, *Erin's Daughters*, p. 18, citing John Francis Maguire, *The Irish in America*, (New York: D. & J. Sadlier, 1868), p. 203. See also Nolan, *Ourselves Alone*, p. 29.
34. Bruns, *Hold Dear*, p. 236.
35. Jacobs, "Death, Disease, and Deliverance," p. 7, citing the *Montevideo (Minnesota) Leader*.
36. Bryant and Murch, *Great Massacre*, p. 400.
37. *Ibid.*, p. 402.
38. *Ibid.*, p. 328.
39. University of Wisconsin, "Summer School for Workers in Industry," 1929 yearbook, MCC, box 11, folder 9.
40. Nolan, *Ourselves Alone*, p. 56.
41. Steiner, *Trail of the Immigrant*, p. 187.
42. Frowne, "Sweatshop Girl," p. 2279.
43. Preus, *Linka's Diary*, p. 198.

CHAPTER 22—Views of the New World

1. Cohen, *Out of the Shadow*, p. 246.
2. *Ibid.*, p. 153.
3. Schneiderman, *All For One*, p. 27.

4. Blegen, *Land of Their Choice*, p. 307.
5. Untitled, undated report on interviews with members of Helen Modjoska Club in Cleveland, YWCA files, SSC, box 31, folder 5.
6. Baciu, "Jolan" interview, YWCA files, SSC, box 31, folder 5.
7. Steinitz interview, YWCA files, SSC, box 31, folder 5.
8. Isley, *Sunbonnet Days*, p. 62.
9. Bodnar, "Second-Generation Girl," pp. 16–17; YWCA files, SSC, box 31, folder 4.
10. Helen Modjoska Club interviews, YWCA files, SSC, box 31, folder 5.
11. Bruns, *Hold Dear*, p. 217.
12. *Ibid.*, p. 291.
13. See, for example, Wilbur Shepperson, *Emigration and Disenchantment* (Norman: University of Oklahoma Press, 1965), esp. p. 187.
14. Balch, *Our Slavic Fellow Citizens*, pp. 59–60.
15. Kamphoefner, Helbich, and Sommer, *News from the Land of Freedom*, p. 537.
16. Zempel, *In Their Own Words*, p. 39.
17. Svendsen, *Frontier Mother*, p. 129.
18. Abbott, *Historical*, p. 309, citing Karl Buchele, "The Educated German in America," *Land und Volk der Verington Staten von Nord Amerika* (Stuttgart, 1855), pp. 476–81.
19. Bruns, *Hold Dear*, p. 74.
20. Ets, *Rosa*, pp. 190–91.
21. 67st Congress, 1st Session, Dillingham Committee on Immigration, Report No. 17, April 28, 1921, p. 6.
22. Lawrence H. Fuchs, "Immigration through Boston," in Stolarik, *Forgotten Doors*, p. 23.
23. 67st Congress, Report No. 17, pp. 3–8.
24. 61st Congress, 3d Session, Senate Document 748, *Reports of the Immigration Commission: Emigration Conditions in Europe*, 1911, p. 41.
25. *Ibid.*, p. 45.
26. *Ibid.*, p. 41.
27. Nolan, *Ourselves Alone*, p. 71, citing *Reports of the Immigration Commission*, p. 359.
28. *Ibid.*, pp. 114–15, citing Lars Ljungmark, *Swedish Exodus*, trans. Kermit B. Westerberg (Carbondale: Southern Illinois University Press, 1979), p. 141.
    Hvidt, *Flight to America*, p. 181, gives figures from Scandinavian archives that are even lower—a 12% return rate for Swedes and 8.6% for Danes. Of Norwegians, he adds, "Women especially showed a tendency to return relatively soon"—but the chart illustrating the point shows only small variations between the behavior of men and women.
    Slightly more of the women who returned did so after living in America less than a decade (76.9% vs. 71.9%). Men showed a greater tendency to return after stays of ten and twenty years (27.3% vs. 21.4%).
29. Department of State, Alien's Application for Permission to Depart from the United States, Permit No. 1003, in the National Archives, Philadelphia Branch.
30. *Ibid.*, Permit No. 1091.
31. *Ibid.*, Permit No. 1135.
32. *Ibid.*, Permit No. 912.
33. *Ibid.*, Permit No. 1005.
34. *Ibid.*, Permit No. 1053.
35. *Ibid.*, Permit No. 1130.
36. *Ibid.*, Permit No. 1393.
37. *Ibid.*, Permit No. 1008.
38. *Ibid.*, Permit No. 1144.
39. *Ibid.*, Permit No. 1006.
40. *Ibid.*, Permit No. 1148.
41. Stella, *Urban Congestion*, p. 26. See also Davis, *Immigrant Health*, p. 55.
42. Parker, *Working Woman*, p. 25.
43. Senate Document 645, *Family Budgets*, pp. 212–14.
44. Clark, *Making Both Ends Meet*, pp. 91–92.
45. Williams, *South Italian Folkways*, p. 17.
46. Long, Oral Histories, Anonymous, "An Italian Immigrant Woman," SCH, p. 10.
47. Erickson, *Invisible Immigrants*, p. 225.

48. Svendsen, *Frontier Mother*, p. 125.
49. Waerenskjold, *Lady with the Pen*, p. 45.
50. Koren, *Diary of Elisabeth Koren*, p. 244.
51. Bruns, *Hold Dear*, p. 145.
52. *Ibid.*, p. 157.
53. *Ibid.*, p. 157.
54. *Ibid.*, p. 167.
55. *Ibid.*, p. 242.
56. Balch, *Our Slavic Fellow Citizens*, p. 119.
57. Scranton, "Immigration through Philadelphia," in Stolarik, *Forgotten Doors*, p. 59.
58. 61st Congress, 2d Session, Senate Document 633, *Immigrants in Industries*, "Cotton Goods Manufacturing in the North Atlantic States," 1911. vol. 72, p. 166.
59. Ets, *Rosa*, p. 254.
60. Holt, *Life Stories*, pp. 108–9.
61. *Ibid.*, p. 124.
62. Blegen, *Land of Their Choice*, p. 187.
63. Bruns, *Hold Dear*, pp. 71, 80.
64. *Ibid.*, p. 95.
65. *Ibid.*, p. 107.
66. Rosalie Roos, *Travels in America, 1851–55* (Carbondale: Southern Illinois University Press, 1982), pp. 24, 43.
67. Barton, *Letters from the Promised Land*, p. 143.
68. Metzker, *Bintel Brief*, p. 106.
69. Campbell, *Prisoners of Poverty*, p. 106.
70. Barton, *Letters from the Promised Land*, p. 224.
71. Hasanovitz, *One of Them*, pp. 193–94, 199, 308–9.
72. University of Wisconsin, "Summer School for Workers," 1929 yearbook, p. 15, MCC, box 11, folder 9.
73. Balch, *Our Slavic Fellow Citizens*, p. 61.
74. Steiner, *On the Trail of the Immigrant*, p. 337.
75. Waerenskjold, *Lady with the Pen*, p. 36.
76. Erickson, *Invisible Immigrants*, p. 153.
77. Blegen, *Land of Their Choice*, pp. 268–69.
78. Erickson, *Invisible Immigrants*, p. 207.
79. Erik Wiken, "Olof Back and the Hertman Family," *Swedish American Genealogist* 4 (March 1984): 16–17.
80. Barton, *Letters from the Promised Land*, pp. 100, 120, 136.
81. Hvidt, *Flight to America*, pp. 197–98.
82. Barton, *Letters from the Promised Land*, pp. 290–92.
83. *Ibid.*, pp. 285–86.
84. Holt, *Life Stories*, p. 140.
85. Steiner, *Trail of the Immigrant*, p. 336.
86. Cohen, *Out of the Shadow*, pp. 72–73.
87. Bruns, *Hold Dear*, p. 245.
88. *Ibid.*, p. 247.
89. *Ibid.*, p. 273.
90. *Ibid.*, p. 274.
91. *Ibid.*, p. 277–78.
92. *Ibid.*, p. 284.
93. Women's Educational and Industrial Union, *Immigrant Women and Girls in Boston*, SCH.
94. Bremer, *America of the Fifties*, pp. 224, 218–19. Although it does not necessarily signify a difference between men and women, it is interesting to note here that Theodore Blegen's important collection of Scandinavian letters, *Land of Their Choice: The Immigrants Write Home*, includes relatively few letters by women—but the only section that has a preponderance of female writers is titled "Cheerful Voices."
95. Walther, *Pilgrimage*, p. 250.
96. Bremer, *America of the Fifties*, pp. 218–19.
97. Blegen, *Land of Their Choice*, p. 265.

SELECTED BIBLIOGRAPHY

BOOKS AND ARTICLES

Abbott, Edith. *Historical Aspects of the Immigration Problem.* Chicago: University of Chicago Press, 1926; reissued by Arno Press and the *New York Times* as part of the American Immigration Collection, 1969.

————. *Immigration: Select Documents and Case Records. Chicago*: University of Chicago, 1924; reissued by Arno Press and the *New York Times*, American Immigration Collection, 1969.

————. *The Tenements of Chicago, 1908-1935.* Chicago: University of Chicago, 1936.

————. *Women in Industry.* New York: Appleton & Co., 1909.

Abbott, Grace. "The Chicago Employment Agency and the Immigrant Worker." American Journal of Sociology 14 (November 1908).

Anderson, Nels. "Czecho-Slovaks in Virginia." In Edmund Brunner, *Immigrant Farmers and Their Children.* Garden City, N.Y.: Doubleday, Doran, and Company, 1929.

Anonymous. "A Collar Starcher's Story." *The Independent,* August 10, 1905.

————. "The Experiences of a Chorus Girl." *The Independent,* July 12, 1906.

————. "Women on the Farm." *The Independent,* March 9, 1905.

Anthony, Katharine. *Mothers Who Must Earn.* New York: Survey Associates and the Russell Sage Foundation, 1914.

Balch, Emily. *Our Slavic Fellow Citizens.* Philadelphia: William F. Fell Co., 1910; reissued by Arno Press and the *New York Times,* American Immigration Collection, 1969.

Barnum, Gertrude. "The Story of a Fall River Mill Girl." *The Independent,* April 27, 1905.

Barton, Arnold H. *Letters from the Promised Land: Swedes in America, 1840–1914.* Minneapolis: University of Minnesota Press, 1975.

Beckley, Zoe. "Finds Hard Job Unionizing Girls Whose Aim Is to Wed." *New York Telegram & Sun,* June 18, 1922.

Berthoff, Rowland T. *British Immigrants in Industrial America.* Cambridge: Harvard University Press, 1953.

Billigmeier, Robert H., and Fred Altschuler Picard. *The Old Land and the New: The Journals of Two Swiss Families in America in the 1820s.* Minneapolis: University of Minnesota Press, 1965.

Bjork, Kenneth O. *West of the Great Divide: Norwegian Migration to the Pacific Coast, 1847–1893.* Northfield, Minn.: Norwegian-American Historical Association, 1958.

Blegen, Theodore C. *Grass Roots History.* Port Washington, N.Y.: Kennikat Press, 1947; reissued by Kennikat Press, 1969.

————. "Immigrant Women and the American Frontier." Norwegian-American Historical Association *Studies and Records* 5 (1930).

————. *Land of Their Choice: The Immigrants Write Home.* St. Paul: University of Minnesota Press, 1955.

Booth, Charles. *Life and Labour of the People in London.* 7 vol. London: Macmillan, 1902.

Brandt, Lilian. *Five Hundred and Seventy-Four Deserters and Their Families.* New York: Charity Organization Society, 1905.

Brandt, Mrs. Realf Ottesen. "Social Aspects of Prairie Pioneering: The Reminiscences of a Pioneer Pastor's Wife." Norwegian-American Historical Association *Studies and Records* 7 (1956).

Breckinridge, Sophonisba, and Edith Abbott. *The Delinquent Child and the Home: A Study of the Delinquent Wards of the Juvenile Court of Chicago.* New York: Russell Sage Foundation, 1917.

Bremer, Fredrika. *America of the Fifties: Letters of Fredrika Bremer.* Edited by Adolph B. Benson. New York: Scandinavian-American Foundation, 1924.

Brown, Lawrence Guy. *Immigration: Cultural Conflicts and Social Adjustments.* New York: Longmans, Green & Co., 1933; reissued by Arno Press and the *New York Times,* 1969.

Brunner, Edmund. *Immigrant Farmers and Their Children.* Garden City, N.Y.: Doubleday, Doran, and Company, 1929.

Bruns, Jette: *Hold Dear, As Always: Jette, a German Immigrant Life in Letters.* Translated and edited by Adolf E. Schroeder and Carla Schulz-Geisberg. Columbia: University of Missouri Press, 1988.

Bryant, Charles S., and Abel B. Murch. *A History of the Great Massacre by the Sioux Indians in Minnesota.* Cincinnati: Rickey and Carroll, 1864; reprinted in Germany, 1973.

Butler, Elizabeth Beardsley. *Women and the Trades,* part of Paul H. Kellogg, ed., *The Pittsburgh Survey: Findings in Six Volumes.* New York: Charities Publication Committee and the Russell Sage Foundation, 1909.

Byington, Margaret. *Homestead: The Households of a Mill Town.* New York: Russell Sage Foundation, 1910.

————. "The Mill Town Courts and Their Lodgers." *Charities and the Commons* 21, February 6, 1909.

Campbell, Helen. *Prisoners of Poverty: Women Wage-Workers, Their Trades and Their Lives.* Boston: Roberts Brothers, 1895.

Capek, Thomas. *The Cechs (Bohemians) in America.* Boston: Houghton Mifflin, 1920.

Carley, Kenneth. *The Sioux Uprising of 1862.* St. Paul: Minnesota Historical Society, 1976.

Carpenter, Niles. *Immigrants and Their Children, 1920: A Study Based on Census Statistics Relative to the Foreign Born and the Native White of Foreign or Mixed Parentage.* Washington: U.S. Government Printing Office, 1927; reissued by Arno Press and the *New York Times,* American Immigration Collection, 1969.

Carr, John Foster. *Guide for the Immigrant Italian.* New York: Doubleday, 1911; reprinted as part of *Assimilation of the Italian Immigrant,* Arno Press, 1975.

Cartwright, Otho G. *The Middle West Side.* New York: Russell Sage Foundation, 1914.

Case, C. F. "Historical Sketches . . . Written by One Who Was Here Part of the Time." *Lyon County [Minnesota] Reporter,* 1898; reprinted in *Prairieland Pioneer,* Southwestern State University, Marshall, Minn., 10, no. 2 (Winter 1993).

Chase, Edith Fowler. *The Bohemians: A Study of the "Land of the Cup and the Book."* Part of a series titled *Immigrants in the Making.* New York: Fleming H. Revell Co., 1914.

Child, Richard. "The Industrial Revolt at Lawrence." *Collier's,* March 9, 1912.

Chotzinoff, Samuel. *A Lost Paradise.* New York: Knopf, 1958.

Claghorn, Kate. *The Immigrant's Day in Court.* New York: Harper & Bros., 1923; reissued by Arno Press and the *New York Times,* American Immigration Collection, 1969.

Clark, Sue Ainslie, and Edith Wyatt. *Making Both Ends Meet: The Income and Outlay of New York Working Girls.* New York: Macmillan, 1911.

Cohen, Rose. *Out of the Shadow.* New York: George H. Doran Co., 1918.

Colcord, Joanna C. *Broken Homes: A Study of Family Desertion.* New York: Russell Sage Foundation, 1919.

Cole, Donald B. *Immigrant City: Lawrence, Massachusetts, 1845–1921.* Chapel Hill: University of North Carolina Press, 1963.

Commonwealth of Massachusetts: State Department of Health. *The Food of Working Women in Boston.* Boston: Wright & Potter Printing Co., 1917.

Conzen, Kathleen Neils. *Immigrant Milwaukee, 1836–1860: Accommodation and Community in a Frontier City.* Cambridge: Harvard University Press, 1976.

Corsi, Edward. *In the Shadow of Liberty: The Chronicle of Ellis Island.* New York: Macmillan, 1935.

Daniels, Roger. *Coming to America: A History of Immigration and Ethnicity in American Life.* New York: HarperCollins, 1990.

Davis, Michael M., Jr. *Immigrant Health and the Community.* New York: Harper & Bros., 1921.

Diner, Hasia R. *Erin's Daughters in America.* Baltimore: Johns Hopkins University Press, 1983.

Durland, Kellogg. "Steerage Impositions." *The Independent,* August 30, 1906.

Eastman, P. R. "A Comparison of the Birth Rates of Native and of Foreign-Born White Women in the State of New York." Albany: New York State Department of Health, 1916.

Erickson, Charlotte. *American Industry and the European Immigrant.* New York: Russell & Russell, 1957.

———. *Invisible Immigrants.* Coral Gables, Fla.: University of Miami Press, 1972.

Ernst, Robert. *Immigrant Life in New York City: 1825–1863.* Port Washington, N.Y.: Ira J. Friedman, 1949; reissued by same publisher 1965.

Esslinger, Dean R. "Immigration through the Port of Baltimore." In M. Mark Stolarik, *Forgotten Doors: The Other Ports of Entry to the United States.* Philadelphia: Balch Institute Press, 1988.

Ets, Marie Hall. *Rosa: The Life of an Italian Immigrant.* Minneapolis: University of Minnesota Press, 1970.

Eubank, Earle Edward. *A Study of Family Desertion.* Chicago: University of Chicago Press and City of Chicago Department of Public Welfare, 1916.

Evans, E. Estyn. "Peasant Beliefs in Nineteenth Century Ireland." In Daniel J. Casey and Robert E. Rhodes, *Views of the Irish Peasantry, 1800–1916.* Hamden, Conn.: Archon Books, 1977.

Forman, Tauba Leah Meyer Cohen. "The Blood Thirst in Kishineff." *The Independent,* June 18, 1903.

Frowne, Sadie. "The Story of a Sweatshop Girl." *The Independent,* September 25, 1902.

Fuchs, Lawrence H. "Immigration through Boston." In M. Mark Stolarik, *Forgotten Doors: The Other Ports of Entry to the United States.* Philadelphia: Balch Institute Press, 1988.

Gerlach, Russel L. *Immigrants in the Ozarks.* Columbia: University of Missouri Press, 1976.

Gjerset, Knut, and Ludvig Hektoen. "Health Conditions and the Practice of Medicine among the Early Norwegian Settlers, 1825–1865." Norwegian-American Historical Society *Studies and Records*(1 1926).

Goritzina, Kyra. *Service Entrance: Memoirs of a Park Avenue Cook.* New York: Currick and Evans, 1939.

Green, Constance McLaughlin. *Holyoke, Massachusetts: A Case History of the Industrial Revolution in America.* New Haven: Yale University Press, 1939.

Hampsten, Elizabeth. *To All Inquiring Friends: Letters, Diaries and Essays in North Dakota.* Grand Forks: University of North Dakota, 1979.

Hasanovitz, Elizabeth. *One of Them: Chapters from a Passionate Autobiography.* Boston: Houghton Mifflin, 1918.

Hawgood, John A. *The Tragedy of German-America.* New York: G. P. Putnam's Sons, 1940.

Herzfeld, Elsa G. *Family Monographs: The History of Twenty-four Families Living in the Middle West Side of New York City.* New York: James Kempster Printing Co., 1905.

———. "The Tenement House Family." *The Independent,* December 28, 1905.

Hill, Marilyn Wood. *Their Sisters' Keepers: Prostitution in New York City, 1830–1870.* Berkeley: University of California Press, 1993.

Holt, Hamilton. *The Life Stories of Undistinguished Americans as Told by Themselves.* New York: James Pott & Co., 1906.

Hourwich, Andria Taylor and Gladys L. Palmer, eds. *I Am a Woman Worker*. New York Affiliated Schools for Workers, 1936.

Hughes, Elizabeth. "Chicago Housing Conditions." *American Journal of Sociology* 18 (November 1914).

Hughes, Gwendolyn Salisbury. *Mothers in Industry: Wage-Earning by Mothers in Philadelphia*. New York: New Republic, 1925.

Hutchinson, Edward P. *Immigrants and Their Children, 1850–1950*. New York: Wiley, 1956.

Hutchinson, Emilie Josephine. *Women's Wages*. New York: Columbia University Press, 1919; reissued by AMS Press, 1968.

Hvidt, Kristian. *Flight to America: The Social Background of 300,000 Danish Emigrants*. New York: Academic Press, 1975.

Isely, Elise Dubach, as told to her son, Bliss Isely. *Sunbonnet Days*. Caldwell, Idaho: Caxton Printers, 1935.

Jacobi, Abraham. "The Best Means of Combating Infant Mortality." *Journal of the American Medical Association*, June 8, 1912.

Jacobs, Craig Donald. "Death, Disease, and Deliverance: Chippewa County in the Late Nineteenth Century." Part of a series, *Historical Essays on Rural Life*. Marshall, Minn.: Southwest State University, 1991.

Kamphoefner, Walter D., Wolfgang Helbich and Ulrike Sommer. *News from the Land of Freedom: German Immigrants Write Home*. Ithaca, N.Y.: Cornell University Press, 1991.

Kapp, Friedrich. *Immigration and the Commissioners of Emigration*. New York: D. Taylor, 1870.

Kellor, Frances A. "The Immigrant Woman." *Atlantic* 100 (September 1907).

———. "Immigration and Household Labor." *Charities*, February 6, 1904.

———. *Out of Work*. New York: G. P. Putnam's Sons, 1904.

———. "The Protection of Immigrant Women." *Atlantic* 101 (February 1908).

Kennedy, John Curtis. *Wages and Family Budgets in the Chicago Stockyards District*. Chicago: University of Chicago Press, 1914.

Knapland, Paul. *Moorings Old and New*. Madison: State Historical Society of Wisconsin, 1964.

Kneeland, George J. *Commercialized Prostitution in New York City*. New York: Century Co., 1913.

Koenig, Emilie Lohmann. "Letters from America to a Family in Germany." Translated and edited by Mrs. Oscar P. Brauer. *Concordia Historical Quarterly* 28, no. 4 (Winter 1955), and 29, no. 1 (Spring 1956).

Kohut, Rebekah. *My Portion*. New York: Thomas Selzer, 1925.

Koren, Elisabeth. *The Diary of Elisabeth Koren, 1853–1855*. Translated and edited by David T. Nelson. Northfield, Minn.: Norwegian-American Historical Association, 1955.

Lane, Frances E. *American Charities and the Child of the Immigrant: A Study of Typical Child Caring Institutions in New York and Massachusetts between the Years 1845 and 1880*. Washington: Catholic University of America, 1932.

Logsdon, Joseph. "Immigration through the Port of New Orleans." In M. Mark Stolarik, *Forgotten Doors: The Other Ports of Entry to the United States*. Philadelphia: Balch Institute Press, 1988.

Luebke, Frederick C. *Germans in the New World: Essays in the History of Immigration*. Urbana: University of Illinois Press, 1990.

MacLean, Annie M., "Life in the Pennsylvania Coal Fields, with Particular Reference to Women." *American Journal of Sociology* 14 (November 1908).

Malkiel, Theresa Serber. *The Diary of a Shirtwaist Worker*. New York: Cooperative Press, 1910.

Mangano, Antonio. *The Italian Colonies of New York City*. New York, 1903; reprinted in *Italians in the City: Health and Related Social Needs*. New York: Arno Press, 1975.

Manning, Caroline. *The Immigrant Woman and Her Job*. Bulletin of the Women's Bureau, no. 74. Washington: U.S. Government Printing Office, 1930.

Masaryk, Alice G. "The Bohemians in Chicago," *Charities*, December 3, 1904.

McDowell, Mary E. "The Struggle in Family Life." *Charities*, December 3, 1904.

Metzker, Issac, ed. *A Bintel Brief: Sixty Years of Letters from the Lower East Side to the Jewish Daily Forward.* Garden City, N.Y.: Doubleday & Co., 1971.

Miller, Fredric M. "Immigration through the Port of Philadelphia." In M. Mark Stolarik, *Forgotten Doors: The Other Parts of Entry to the United States.* Philadelphia: Balch Institute Press, 1988.

Miller, Randall M. "Immigration through the Port of New Orleans: A Comment." In M. Mark Stolarik, *Forgotten Doors: The Other Ports of Entry to the United States.* Philadelphia: Balch Institute Press, 1988.

Mohr, James C. *Abortion in America.* New York: Oxford University Press, 1978.

More, Louise B. *Wage-Earners' Budgets: A Study of Standards and Costs of Living in New York City.* New York: Henry Holt and Co., 1907.

Mormino, Gary R., and Anthony P. Pizzo. *Tampa: The Treasure City.* Tulsa, Okla.: Continental Heritage Press, 1983.

———, and George E. Pozzetta. *The Immigrant World of Ybor City: Italians and their Latin Neighbors in Tampa, 1885–1985.* Urbana: University of Illinois Press, 1987.

Morrison, Joan, and Charlotte Fox Zabusky. *American Mosaic.* New York: E. P. Dutton, 1980.

Murphy, Leona, S.C. "The Life Story of the Sisters of Charity of Cincinnati, Ohio." Manuscript, 1941, Sisters of Charity Archives, College of Mount St. Joseph, Cincinnati, Ohio.

Nadel, Stanley. *Little Germany: Ethnicity, Religion, and Class in New York City, 1845–80.* Urbana: University of Illinois Press, 1990.

New York City Department of Health. "Some Special Problems of Italians in New York City." 1934; reprinted in *Italians in the City: Health and Related Social Needs.* New York: Arno Press, 1975.

Noel, Anne Webster. "On Twelve a Week." *The Independent*, October 26, 1905.

Nolan, Janet A. *Ourselves Alone: Women's Emigration from Ireland, 1885–1920.* Lexington: University of Kentucky Press, 1989.

Norton, Grace P. "Chicago Housing Conditions: Two Italian Districts." *American Journal of Sociology* 18 (January 1913).

O'Connor, Richard. *The German-Americans.* Boston: Little, Brown & Co., 1968.

Odencrantz, Louise C. *Italian Women in Industry.* New York: Russell Sage Foundation, 1919.

Pagano, Jo. *Golden Wedding.* New York: Random House, 1943.

Paradise, Viola. "The Jewish Immigrant Girl in Chicago." *Survey*, September 6, 1913.

Parker, Cornelia Stratton. *Working with the Working Woman.* New York: Harper & Bros., 1922.

Pehotsky, Bessie Olga. *The Slavic Immigrant Woman.* Cincinnati: Powell & White, 1925.

Pitkin, Thomas M. *Keepers of the Gate: A History of Ellis Island.* New York: New York University Press, 1975.

Preus, Linka. *Linka's Diary on Land and Sea, 1845–1864.* Translated and edited by Johan C. K. Preus and Diderikke Brandt Preus. Minneapolis: Augsburg Publishing House, 1952.

"Probation for All Emigrant Husbands." *Survey*, June 21, 1913.

Raaen, Aagot. *Grass of the Earth.* Northfield, Minn.: Norwegian-American Historical Association, 1950; reissued by Arno Press and the *New York Times*, 1979.

Reckless, Walter C. *Vice in Chicago.* University of Chicago, 1933; reissued by Patterson Smith Publishing, 1969.

Richardson, Dorothy. *The Long Day: The Story of a New York Working Girl As Told by Herself.* New York: Century Co., 1905.

Richmond, Mary E., and Fred S. Hall. *A Study of Nine Hundred and Eighty-Five Widows.* New York: Russell Sage Foundation, 1913.

Riis, Jacob. *How the Other Half Lives.* New York: C. Scribner's Sons, 1890; reissued by Sagamore Press, 1957.

Robbins, Jane E. "The Bohemian Women in New York." *Charities and the Commons*, December 12, 1904.

Roberts, Marjorie. "Italian Girls on American Soil." *Mental Hygiene* 13 (October 1929).

Robinson, Martha Reid. "Immigrants at the Port of New York." *World Events* (March 1905).

Roos, Rosalie. *Travels in America, 1851–55.* Carbondale: Southern Illinois University Press, 1982.

Ross, Edward Alsworth. *The Old World in the New.* New York: Century Co., 1914.

Safford, Victor. *Immigration Problems: Personal Experiences of an Official.* New York: Dodd, Mead and Co., 1925.

Salmon, Lucy Maynard. *Domestic Service.* 2d ed. New York: Macmillan, 1901.

Sandoz, Mari. *Old Jules.* Boston: Little, Brown & Co., 1935.

Sanger, William. *The History of Prostitution.* New York: Harper and Brothers, 1858; reprinted by AMS Press, 1974.

Sayles, Mary Buell. "Housing and Social Conditions in a Slavic Neighborhood." *Survey*, December 3, 1904.

Schaddlee, Cornelia Slag. "Life during the Early Days of the Dutch Settlement." In Henry S. Lucas, *Dutch Immigrant Memoirs and Related Writings.* Assen, Netherlands: Van Gorcum & Co., 1955.

Schneider, Dorothee. "'For Whom Are All the Good Things in Life?': German-American Housewives Discuss Their Budgets." In Harmut Keil and John B. Jentz, ed., *German Workers in Industrial Chicago, 1850–1910: A Comparative Perspective.* DeKalb, Ill.: Northern Illinois University Press, 1983.

Schneiderman, Rose. "A Cap Maker's Story." *The Independent*, April 27, 1905.

———, with Lucy Goldwaite. *All for One.* New York: Paul S. Eriksson, 1967.

Scranton, Philip. "Immigration through the Port of Philadelphia: A Comment." In M. Mark Stolarik, *Forgotten Doors: The Other Ports of Entry to the United States.* Philadelphia: Balch Institute Press, 1988.

Segale, Blandina, S.C. *At the End of the Santa Fe Trail.* Milwaukee: Bruce Publishing Company, 1948.

Shorter, Edward. "Female Emancipation, Birth Control, and Fertility in European History." *American Historical Review* 78, no. 3 (June 1973).

Shriver, William P. *Immigrant Forces.* New York: Missionary Education Movement of the United States and Canada, 1913.

Sinclair, Upton. "Is *The Jungle* True?" *The Independent*, May 17, 1906.

Spofford, Harriet Prescott. *The Servant Girl Question.* Boston: Houghton Mifflin., 1881; reprinted by Arno Press and the *New York Times*, 1977.

Steiner, Edward A. *On the Trail of the Immigrant.* New York: Fleming H. Revell Co., 1906.

Stella, Antonio. *The Effects of Urban Congestion on Italian Women and Children.* New York, 1908; reprinted in *Italians in the City: Health and Related Social Needs.* New York: Arno Press, 1975.

Stenhouse, Fanny. *Exposé of Polygamy in Utah: A Lady's Life among the Mormons.* New York: American News Company, 1872.

Stern, Elizabeth G. *I Am a Woman—and a Jew.* New York: J. H. Sears & Co., 1926; reissued by Arno Press and the *New York Times*, American Immigration Collection, 1969.

Stolarik, M. Mark, ed. *Forgotten Doors: The Other Ports of Entry to the United States.* Philadelphia: Balch Institute Press, 1988.

Svendsen, Gro. *Frontier Mother: The Letters of Gro Svendsen.* Translated and edited by Theodore C. Blegen and Pauline Farseth. Northfield, Minn.: Norwegian-American Historical Association, 1950.

Syrkin, Marie. "In New York." In *Autobiographies of American Jews*, selected by Harold U. Ribalow; reprinted from *Nachman Syrkin: Socialist Zionist, a Biographical Memoir.* New York: Herzl Press and Sharon Books, 1961.

Thernstrom, Stephan, ed. *Harvard Encyclopedia of American Ethnic Groups.* Cambridge: Harvard University Press, 1980.

Thomas, William I., and Florian Znaniecki. *The Polish Peasant in Europe and America.* 5 vols. Chicago: University of Chicago, 1918; reissued by Dover Publications, 1958.

Tifft, Wilton and Thomas Dunne. *Ellis Island.* New York: Norton 1971.

Van Kleeck, Mary. *Artificial Flower Makers.* New York: Russell Sage Foundation, 1913.

———. *Working Girls in Evening Schools.* New York: Survey Associates for the Russell Sage Foundation, 1914.

Varga, Hugo Eugene. "Desertion of Wives and Children by Emigrants to America." *Proceedings of the National Conference of Charities and Correction.* Fort Wayne, Ind.: Fort Wayne Printing Co., 1912.

Waerenskjold, Elise. *The Lady with the Pen: Elise Waerenskjold in Texas.* Translated and edited by C. A. Clausen. Northfield, Minn.: Norwegian-American Historical Association, 1961.

Wallas, Graham. *The Great Society: A Psychological Analysis.* New York: Macmillan, 1929.

Walther, Anna. *A Pilgrimage with a Milliner's Needle.* New York: Fredrick A. Stokes Company, 1917.

Wanless, Dorothy L. *Century Farms of Minnesota: One Hundred Years of Changing Life Styles on the Farm.* Century Farm Heritage Committee, 1985.

Wilcox, Julius. "The Greatest Problem of Great Cities." *The Independent,* October 19, 1905.

Williams, Phyllis H. *South Italian Folkways in Europe and America.* New York: Russell & Russell, 1938; reissued 1969.

Wilson, Helen I., and Eunice W. Smith. "Chicago Housing Conditions among the Slovaks in the Twentieth Ward." *American Journal of Sociology* 20 (September 1914).

Wolfson, Theresa. "Where Are the Organized Women Workers." *American Federationist* (June, 1925).

———. *The Woman Worker and the Trade Unions.* New York: International Publishers, 1926.

Woolstein, Howard B. *Prostitution in the United States.* New York: Century Co., 1921; reissued by Appleton-Century, 1969.

Wright, Carroll D. *The Working Girls of Boston.* Boston: Wright & Potter Printing Co., 1889; reprinted by Arno Press and the *New York Times,* 1969.

Yezierska, Anzia. *Children of Loneliness: Stories of Immigrant Life in America.* New York: Funk & Wagnalls, 1923.

Zempel, Solveig. *In Their Own Words: Letters from Norwegian Immigrants.* Minneapolis: University of Minnessota and the Norwegian-American Historical Association, 1991.

ARCHIVAL DOCUMENTS

MIRIAM COFFIN CANADAY LIBRARY, BRYN MAWR COLLEGE, BRYN MAWR, PENNSYLVANIA (MCC)

"Affiliated Summer Schools for Women Workers in Industry." Undated.

"Barnard Record: Summer School for Women Workers in Industry." 1927 yearbook.

"Bryn Mawr Summer School for Women Workers in Industry." c. 1930.

Coit, Eleanor. "Six Little Schools at Bryn Mawr." *The American Teacher.* Undated.

"Education That Changes Lives: The Story of Five Schools for Workers." 1933.

McGarry, William A. "Highbrows of Our Mills and Factories." *Dearborn Independent,* August 19, 1922.

"New Gateways to Education." C. 1927.

"Schools for Women Workers." *Bryn Mawr Alumnae Bulletin,* December 1929.

"Some Results of the Bryn Mawr Summer School." 1928, 1929, and 1930.

University of Wisconsin. "Summer School for Workers in Industry." 1929 yearbook.

"Will You Help Us?" The Bryn Mawr Summer School for Women Workers in Industry. c. 1930.

MARYLAND HISTORICAL SOCIETY, BALTIMORE
City Directories for Baltimore
Locust Point file

MARYLAND STATE ARCHIVES, ANNAPOLIS
U.S. Census for Baltimore

MOGAN CENTER FOR LOWELL HISTORY, LOWELL, MASSACHUSETTS (MC)

University of Lowell. "Women, Work and Ethnicity in Lowell." Oral history project
Dunning, Judith. Interview of Katherine Speronis, 1980.
Karobatsos, Lewis. Interview of Athena Theokas, 1974.
Norkunas, Martha. Interview of Edna Vidravich Balkus and Soutana Pappaconstantinou, both 1983.

⚹ROCKEFELLER ARCHIVE CENTER, NORTH TARRYTOWN, NEW YORK (RAC)

Bureau of Social Hygiene Collection:
American Birth Control League. "A Message to Mothers." 1931.
American Social Hygiene Association. Meeting minutes. October 1931.
"New York State Health Commission Report." 1931.
"Plan Concerning the Establishment of a Department Especially Designed for the Study and Treatment of Syphilis in Connection with the Out-Patient Service of the Johns Hopkins Hospital." 1915.
"Proposed Division of Social Hygiene at the Boston Dispensary." 1929–30.
"Report of the League of Nations Traffic in Women and Children." 1932.
"Social Hygiene." 1932.
"Study of Commercialized Prostitution in New York City." 1930.
"Study of Maternal Mortality under the Auspices of the New York Academy of Medicine in Cooperation with New York City Department of Health and the Commonwealth Fund." 1931.

Laura Spelman Rockefeller Memorial Collection:
"Appeal of the Association for Improving the Condition of the Poor." 1919.
"Association for the Improvement of the Conditions of the Poor, General Budget." 1919–25.
Maternity Center Association Annual Report. 1927.
New York Milk Committee. "Are You in the Baby Saving Drive?" 1919.

Rockefeller Family Archives, Welfare—General:
Records of the
American Female Guardian Society, 1894–1919.
Henry Street Settlement, 1913–44.
Hull House Association, 1928–40.
Jacob Riis Settlement, 1904–40.

SCHLESINGER LIBRARY, RADCLIFFE COLLEGE, CAMBRIDGE, MASSACHUSETTS (SCH)

Jane Maud Campbell Collection:
Campbell, Jane Maud. "Immigrant Women." 1911.
Speeches by Campbell to the Daughters of the American Revolution, Kenilworth Club, League of Library Commissions and others, c. 1900–21.

Mary Ware Dennett Collection:
Documents by Dennett:
"The Case for Birth Control." *The Arbitrator*, August 1918.
"For the Children's Sake: Excerpts from Letters from Mothers." *Birth Control Review*. Undated.
"Hard Facts." *Birth Control Review*, April 1919.
"Statement Regarding Dr. Van Inghen's Criticism of the Voluntary Parenthood League." November 1920.
"The Stupidity of Us Humans." *Birth Control Review*, January 1919.

Many letters to Dennett inquiring about birth control; some replies

Documents by others:
Committee of One Hundred. *The Birth Control Movement*. 1917.
Irwin, Rev. Mabel. "The True Birth Control." *The Arbitrator*, August 1918.

Priscilla Long Collection of Oral Histories:
Anonymous. "An Italian Immigrant Woman — 1920."
Carole Blanck. "Oral History of My Mother."
Demirfian, Sarah. "An Interview with My Mother."
Long, Priscilla. *Mother Jones, Woman Organizer*.
Marot, Lola. "Oral Interview — Lola Anguini."
McGillvray, Elaine. "Interview with Mrs. Lena Torresgrossa."
Watkinson, Margaret. "A Social History of My Family."

Women's Educational and Industrial Union:
"Immigration as a Source of Supply for Domestic Workers." 1905.
"Immigrant Women and Girls in Boston." 1905–6.
"Report of an Investigation of 500 Immigrant Women in Boston." 1907.

SOPHIA SMITH COLLECTION, SMITH COLLEGE, NORTHHAMPTON, MASSACHUSETTS (SSC)

Mary Van Kleeck Collection:
de Lima, Agnes. "Night Work by Mothers in Passaic." 1926.
Gregorio, Lucreatia. "Paddy's Market." 1927.
MacAlpine, Jean Douglas. "Study of the Underwear Industry with Special Reference to Opportunities for Subnormal Girls." 1922.
"The New Emancipation." *New York Tribune*, May 29, 1919.
Odencrantz, Louise C. "Basis of Employment for Household Assistant." 1919.
"Speakers for and against Women Night Work Clash in Debate." *Passaic Daily News*, February 11, 1922.
Van Kleeck, Mary. "Training Schools for Infant Nurses and Nursery Maids in New York City." Undated.
Vineyard Shore Workers' School. "The Seekers." 1927.
Waite, Helen M. "An Investigation of Women Farmers from the Census." c. 1900.
"Women in Industry Set New Standard." *Christian Science Monitor*, June 3, 1922.
"Women Work Despite Law." *New York Times*, January 4, 1925.
"Women's Union Decides That Men Must Conduct Their Affairs." *New York World*, January 22, 1922.
"Why You Should Work for the 8 Hour Day and 48 Hour Week for Women." Unnamed source, c. 1919.

Settlement House Collection:
College Settlements Association. "List of Subscribers." 1895.

"College Settlement of Philadelphia Commemorates Fifty Years of Service." 1942.

"Dorothea Dix House." 1898.

"Fourth Annual Report of the St. Mary Street College Settlement of Philadelphia." 1895.

Gavit, John Palmer. "Bibliography of College, Social and University Settlements." 1897.

"Hartley House: An Industrial Settlement." c. 1897.

"Mary Simkhovitch Dead at Age of 84." *New York Times*, November 16, 1951.

"The Subjective Value of a Social Settlement." *The Forum*, 1892.

"What Does the College Settlement Association Mean to This Little Mother and to YOU?" Undated.

YWCA Collection:

Baciu, Livia. Untitled series of interviews with Hungarian women in Cleveland. 1930s.

Bird, Ethel. "Separated Families and the Immigration Law." c. 1924.

Bodnar, Mary Ann. "What It Means to Be a Second-Generation Girl: Talks Given at the Second-Generation Youth Dinner of the National Board of the Y.W.C.A.." New York: Woman's Press, 1935.

Bremer, Edith Terry. "American Foreign-Language Service Bureaus." 1917.

———. "Our International Communities and the War." 1918.

Department for Foreign Born Women. "Report to the Federal Advisory Commission on Social Welfare Work for Immigrants." 1921.

Department of Immigration and Foreign Communities. "Summary of a Case Record: Molarsky." c. 1927.

Dingman, Annie P. "Report of Immigration and Foreign Community Secretary, Ohio and West Virginia." November 1–30, 1918.

"First Report of the Commission on Household Employment." 1915.

"The First Six Months Are the Hardest." c. 1929.

"German-Russian People of South Dakota." 1920.

"Household Employment—History." 1919.

Mantopoulos, Mrs. George (Barbara Riter Mantopoulos). "An Appeal to Americans." October 10, 1947.

Newman, Minnie M. "The Teaching of English and the Foreign Born Woman." New York: Woman's Press, 1920.

Presbytery of Duluth. "Mesable and Vermillion Ore Ranges of Minnesota." Mission report. June 8, 1914.

Raitanen, Vieno. "A Finnish Girl in New England." In "What It Means to Be a Second-Generation Girl: Talks Given at the Second-Generation Youth Dinner of the National Board of the Y.W.C.A." New York: Woman's Press, 1935.

Roelofs, Henrietta. "The Road to Trained Service in the Household." 1915.

Steinitz, no first name. Untitled series of interviews with Slavic women in Cleveland. 1930s.

Tarbell, Ida M. "What a Factory Can Teach a Housewife." Reprinted from the *Association Monthly*, November 1916.

War Work Council of the Y.W.C.A. "For 'United America.'" 1918.

Zitello, Adelaide K. "Evaluation of Interviews of Twenty-one Second Generation Girls." Cleveland, 1939.

SOUTHWEST MINNESOTA STATE UNIVERSITY HISTORICAL CENTER, MARSHALL, MINNESOTA

Aws, Manny. "Migration Saga for Sesquicentennial Year." *Minnesota Posten*, fredag mars 7, 1975.

Daniels, Beverly ed. *Lincoln County History, 1873–1973*. Lake Benton, Minnesota: Journal Printing Co., 1973.

Hendrickson, Rev. H. O. "Oldest Settlement in Cottonwood County." 1940.

Jacobs, Craig Donald. "Death, Disease and Deliverance: Chippewa County in the Late Nineteenth Century." 1991.

Minnesota State Board of Immigration. "Cost of Coming to Minnesota." Undated.
Prairieland Pioneer 10, no. 2 (Winter 1993), property records for Lincoln and Lyon Counties.

MAJOR GOVERNMENT DOCUMENTS

61st Congress, 2d Session. *Report of the Immigration Commission.* Washington: Government Printing Office, 1911:
  Senate Document 282: *Occupation of the First and Second Generation of Immigrants in the United States*
  Senate Document 633: *Immigrants in Industries*

61st Congress, 2d Session, Senate Document 645: *Report on Condition of Woman and Child Wage-earners in the United States.* Washington Government Printing Office, 1911–13:
Vol. 1 *Cotton Textile Industry*
Vol. 2 *Men's Ready-Made Clothing*
Vol. 4 *The Silk Industry*
Vol. 5 *Wage-Earning Women in Stores and Factories*
Vol. 9 *History of Women in Industry in the U.S.*
Vol. 10 *History of Women in Trade Unions*
Vol. 12 *Employment of Women in Laundries*
Vol. 13 *Infant Mortality and Its Relation to the Employment of Mothers*
Vol. 14 *Causes of Death among Women and Child Cotton-Mill Operatives*
Vol. 15 *Relation between Occupation and Criminality of Women*
Vol. 16 *Family Budgets*
Vol. 18 *Employment of Women and Children in Selected Industries*
Vol. 20 *Statistical Review of Immigration*

61st Congress, 3d Session. *Reports of the Immigration Commission.* Washington: Government Printing Office, 1911:
Senate Document 282: *Fecundity of Immigrant Women*
Senate Document 748: *Emigration Conditions in Europe*
Senate Document 750: *Immigration and Crime*
Senate Document 753: *Importation and Harboring of Women for Immoral Purposes*
Senate Document 753: *Steerage Conditions*
Senate Document 756: *Statistical Review of Immigration, 1820–1910*

U.S. Department of Commerce:
12th Census of the United States, 1900. *Vital Statistics.* Vols. 1 and 3.
Historical Statistics of the United States, Colonial Times to 1970. Washington: Government Printing Office, 1975.
Statistical Abstract of the United States, 1930.

U.S. Department of Labor:
Manning, Caroline. *The Immigrant Woman and Her Job.* Bulletin of the Women's Bureau, No. 74. Washington: Government Printing Office, 1930.
Women's Bureau Bulletin #49. *Women Workers and Family Support.* A Study Made by Students in the Economics Course at the Bryn Mawr Summer School under the Direction of Prof. Amy Hewes. Washington: Government Printing Office, 1925.

Vice Commission of Chicago. *The Social Evil in Chicago.* Chicago: Gunthorp-Warren Printing Co., 1911; reissued by Arno Press and the *New York Times*, 1970.

INDEX

Entries are filed letter by letter. *Italic* page references indicate illustrations and captions. Page references followed by *t* indicate tables. Page references followed by *n* indicate footnotes.